WATERFOWL

An identification guide to the ducks, geese and swans of the world

WATERFOWL

An identification guide to the ducks, geese and swans of the world

Steve Madge and Hilary Burn

Houghton Mifflin Company
Boston   New York

For information about permission to reproduce selections from
this book, write to Permissions, Houghton Mifflin Company,
215 Park Avenue South, New York, New York 10003.

For information about this and other Houghton Mifflin
trade and reference books and multimedia products, visit
The Bookstore at Houghton Mifflin on the World Wide Web at
http://www.hmco.com/trade/

Library of Congress Cataloging-in-Publication Data

Madge, Steve
  Waterfowl: an indentification guide to the ducks,
geese, and swans of the world.
    Bibliography: p.
    Includes index.
    1. Waterfowl-identification.   2. Birds-identification.
I. Burn, Hilary.   II. American Birding
Association.   III. Title
QL696.A52M33   1987   598.4'1   87-26186
ISBN 0-395-46727-6
ISBN 0-395-46726-8 (pbk.)

VB 10 9 8 7 6 5 4

Printed in Singapore

For Penny and Bryony

CONTENTS

Systematic section

FOREWORD

Waterfowl have always held a special fascination for us. They are the most frequently depicted birds in ancient art, have always been hunted, and several species have thrived under domestication for many centuries.

Despite increasing awareness of the need for conservation a number of species are declining, some dramatically. The key to their future lies with the preservation of extensive suitable habitats, and these may be as varied as the variety of species themselves. Pressures on world waterfowl have probably never been greater than they are today. Wetlands have been drained on a huge scale, and forest destruction increases the risks of flash-flooding destroying not only the nests of waterbirds but also eroding their fragile habitats. Hydro-electric schemes, changes in agricultural methods, water pollution and the introduction of alien predators and competitors have all had serious effects on the populations of many species.

Collections of captive waterfowl have been created in various parts of the world. These not only educate the general public to appreciate the variety and beauty of these very special birds, but in many cases also help provide breeding stocks of the most vulnerable populations to restock dwindling numbers in the wild. Sadly, we have already lost too many species; even within living memory such strange birds as the Pink-headed Duck and Crested Shelduck have almost certainly gone, and unless we act doubtless there will be others.

The awareness of the special requirements of individual species can be appreciated only by studying the birds in the field. Waterfowl have been the subject of much research in recent decades, but the more we learn about them, the more we realize just how little we really understand. The basic need for any concerned field observer is a good identification manual that goes beyond a regional basis. Although several works on the waterfowl of the world have appeared over the years, none has filled the niche of being a handy, thorough identification guide that can be easily carried around.

Hilary Burn and Steve Madge have filled such a niche with the book you now have in your hand, which concisely summarizes a wealth of information on all 154 species of ducks, geese and swans of the world in one compact volume. Both artist and author are to be congratulated on producing such a wealth of concise information in a format that is both easy to use and contains a minimum of scientific terminology.

Hilary Burn is one of the finest young artists in Britain today and her beautiful artwork speaks for itself. She has skilfully depicted all major plumages of each species and her work reflects the affection, luckily shared by many, that she so obviously has for this beautiful group of waterbirds.

Steve Madge has expertly given a clear insight into the lives of the birds themselves, drawing from his own fieldwork undertaken in many parts of the world and sifting the literature of often weighty scientific papers that have appeared in many journals worldwide. The text not only clarifies identification techniques but fully discusses problematic plumages in detail, as well as providing a summary on world distribution and status complemented by clear distribution maps.

Waterfowl is a book not only for the world traveller or visitor to waterfowl collections, but will be found indispensable when trying to sort out that strange-looking duck on the local reservoir. Even those with primarily an armchair interest will delight in dipping into the book and learning about the lives of both the familiar and the curious waterfowl that paddle about our globe.

Roger Tory Peterson

INTRODUCTION

Wildfowl (ducks, geese and swans), which belong to the order Anseriformes, are among the most popular of all birds. The beautiful plumages of many of them appeal both to visitors to wildfowl collections and to watchers of wild birds alike. Yet there are also plenty of dull-coloured plumages and difficult groups to stimulate the enthusiasm of the discerning telescope-toting field birdwatcher.

This group of birds provides an insight into the study of avian evolution. Throughout the 160 or so species in this order can be found all manner of links between relatively different genera, while other genera have puzzled experts for generations as to their closest affinities. The evolution of the various island forms is a study in itself. The order Anseriformes also includes the screamers, an aberrant gamebird-like family (Anhimidae); these are not considered relevant to the identification of wildfowl, and are therefore not included in this book.

Ducks, geese and swans have fascinated mankind from the time of early history, whether as a food source, or because of the mysteries of their migration, or by their sheer beauty which inspired much early art. Probably wildfowl have been studied more than almost any other group of birds. From such magnificent books as Phillips' four-volume monumental work on the ducks (Phillips 1922-26) to the present, a mass of papers and books has been published on almost all aspects of wildfowl study. Despite this, there are many questions that need answering: for example, wild nests of such relatively widespread species as Hartlaub's Duck have never been described.

Wildfowl is an identification guide to all world species, and describes and illustrates in colour, for the first time in a single easily-carried volume, all major plumages and races. Its aims as an easy-to-use, yet thorough, work of reference have somewhat limited the amount of 'non-relevant' information provided on each species. Although wildfowl behaviour and breeding biology have received considerable study, albeit mostly in captivity for the majority of species, these subjects have comparatively little relevance to identification as such and space does not permit even a brief summary of the various complex displays exhibited by the ducks and their allies. Johnsgard (1965) should be consulted by those wishing to study this further. Excellent and very readable accounts of all of the various aspects of the lives of wildfowl are given in Kear (1985) and Todd (1979).

Wildfowl are basically birds of wetlands, from the marshes of the Arctic tundra to tropical-rainforest swamps, and they may be found from the open sea to high mountain lakes. Wherever they occur wildfowl are subject to pressures from man's influence, whether through over-hunting or through the alteration or destruction of their habitats. With this in mind, every one of us should support some of the national and international conservation bodies that seek to save such delicate habitats. Wildfowl in particular may be helped by joining The Wildfowl Trust, Slimbridge, Gloucester, GL2 7BT, England.

With such a wealth of papers published in a variety of journals, certain information may well have been overlooked while researching this book. The author would be extremely grateful to hear of any omissions or errors that may have crept in, for correction in future editions. Please address any correspondence through the publishers.

HOW TO USE THIS BOOK

This book has been designed to be used in the field. Many conventional field guides are constructed on the principle of having text, plates and maps together on facing pages. Such a format, however, imposes considerable constraints when discussing identification criteria and severely limits the amount of information that can be provided.

The book is basically in two major parts: the plates with facing pages of distribution maps and short texts which highlight points to concentrate upon or features not apparent from the illustrations; and the main species accounts, which describe each species and summarise aspects of their life histories which may be useful for field identification.

Some explanation may be necessary to help guide the user through the formalities followed in the layout of the book.

The Plates

All major plumages and extremes of racial variation have been illustrated, as well as flight figures to show upperwing and underwing patterns. Groups of similar-looking species from each geographical region have been depicted together for ease of reference, but this has not always been possible and some strange mixtures are together on a few plates which contain odd-looking or aberrant species. Figures are to scale within each genus or group of genera. Each figure has been numbered, allowing easy reference to the caption page or to the main body of the text. To overcome the difficulties of not having full texts facing the plates, short caption texts have been provided opposite them which draw attention to useful points to concentrate upon when consulting the illustrations.

The Maps

All species have distribution maps which show main breeding and non-breeding ranges. Migratory birds will occur outside these coloured ranges, and it may generally be taken that in unmarked areas between the colours the particular species could be expected on passage. Note that the maps are only a guideline, and that within a given range a species may be sparsely distributed or abundant depending on habitat availability and/or population numbers or density. Consultation of the main text will give a better idea of the ranges, status and vagrancy patterns of all species.

Key to map conventions

Yellow: Regular breeding areas. Where a species' range has contracted in recent decades, the current known range is shown. Consultation of the text will provide information on former range in such cases.

Green: Areas where the species may be expected throughout the year.

Blue: Areas where the species occurs outside the breeding season, either in winter or during seasonal dispersal. Note that areas where migrants can be expected to occur only on passage or as vagrants are not included.

The Species Accounts

These follow a specific format, the conventions of which are summarised below.

Species sequence

Sequence and naming of genera follow the format suggested in the recent review by Livezey (1986), with the exception that Salvadori's Duck is given a monotypic genus; owing to lack of study material, Livezey was unable to reach a conclusion over this species and somewhat tentatively included it within *Anas*. Sequence of species within genera follows that of Johnsgard (1978). Opinions on the evolutionary sequence of wildfowl have differed considerably among various authorities and it is hoped that Livezey's review will be a standard reference for many years to come. In a work of this nature it is impossible to show clearly the various evolutionary branches that are considered to have taken place, and Livezey's paper should be consulted by those who wish to delve further into the subject. A very readable account of wildfowl evolution is summarised in Lack (1974). Certain well-marked races and those races which could well be considered as full species have been given separate sub-accounts following the main species account: for example, Puna Teal is treated separately after Silver Teal.

Species number

Each species has been given a number purely for reference convenience when using the text and plates. The number has no taxonomic significance.

Vernacular name

Names are always something of a problem, with vernacular names differing in various parts of the English-speaking world. For example, there are birds known as 'Black Duck' in North America, Africa and Australia; all three are very different species and none is really black. Vernacular names of basically Palaearctic species follow Voous (1977) and Sharrock (1984), those of North American species follow the American Ornithologists' Union Checklist (1983) and those of South American wildfowl de Schauensee (1966). Australian species are named according to the style used in the RAOU's (1984) *Atlas of Australian Birds*, while Brown *et al.* (1982) was consulted for names of African species. In the past many races have received separate vernacular or common names, which has added to the confusion; these names are generally combined under the main species, except in the case of certain well-marked races with long-accepted common names such as Bewick's Swan and Mexican Duck.

A major problem arises with names such as Shelduck, Pintail and Shoveler. The addition of such ungainly prefixes as 'Eurasian' and 'Northern' has been avoided where possible, unless such an addition is widely used in a region where the species is a widespread breeding bird. Thus there is a Northern Pintail, a Northern Shoveler and an American Black Duck as these are 'official' names in the AOU Checklist, but Wigeon and Shelduck of the Old World have been kept as just that since any confusion arising would be purely academic.

Alternative vernacular names used in recent field guides and other works are given after the main heading. Wildfowl, being popular targets for hunting, have received a mass of local names, but these have not been listed; alternative names have been mentioned only to facilitate reference to other books.

Field identification

The species' total length is given in centimetres and in inches; wingspan is not included, since it is considered that this is of limited use (and possibly also misleading) in the field. This section summarises the major features of each species to enable a rapid identification in the field. Ageing and sexing criteria are not mentioned here unless relevant to distinguishing a species from other similar ones. In the case of very distinctive species this section may be brief, but it is considerably expanded when discussing difficult groups. This section is divided into 'At rest' and 'In flight' sub-sections for ease of reference.

Voice

The major vocalisations are summarised. Most species have a wider vocabulary than is indicated here, but many calls may be heard only at times of display or at the nest. The typical calls heard from flushed or flying birds are covered in this section.

Description

A relatively detailed plumage description of each major plumage stage is given in this section. The descriptions are not necessarily feather-by-feather, which would become too unwieldy to be of much use in the field, but rather summarise the basic patterns and colours of each plumage, thus allowing an expansion of the specific highlights given under Field Identification. Ageing and sexing features are discussed here. The terms used in the plumage descriptions are shown on pages 19-20. The terminology of plumage stages and moults varies, the British system being followed in this work. For ease of reference a comparison of the American (Humphrey and Parkes 1959) and the British (British Birds 1985) systems is outlined below.

British	American
Juvenile	Juvenal
First winter	First basic
First summer	First alternate
Adult breeding	Definitive alternate
Adult non-breeding (or eclipse)	Definitive basic

Bare parts

This section describes the coloration of the bill, legs, feet and iris of each species.

Measurements

Measurements may often be useful when comparing basically similar birds in the field; such subtleties as relative leg and bill lengths may be judged by comparing measurements. All measurements in this section are given in millimetres. Wing length is measured from the carpal joint to the tip of the longest primary on the folded wing; for tarsus it is the straight length of the leg from the centre of the 'knee' to the base of the middle toe; the bill length is that of the exposed culmen from forehead feathering to tip. Weights are also summarised and are given in grams; wherever possible an average weight only is given for each species, as wildfowl weights can vary tremendously according to season. Weights are possibly of little use in a book of this nature, but average weights can give an idea of the bulk of a bird in comparison with another similar species. It should be remembered that all measurements and weights refer to adult birds; juveniles and even first-winter birds are often smaller and less bulky than adults. All measurements and weights have been taken from other literature, principally Delacour (1954-64) and Johnsgard (1978).

Geographical variation

A number of species vary over their wide distribution. Some of these differences are constant and in many cases allow a species to be separated into recognisable subspecies or races. A summary of these differences is given in this section. Many differences are quite marginal and involve subtle coloration or mensural features, while others are so marked as to make the race clearly separable in the field. In the latter cases, some of the forms may prove to be full species in their own right; if this is so, this fact has been mentioned and the most strikingly different races have been given separate treatments following the main species account. The term 'nominate race' is used for the first-named of a group of races: for example, the nominate race of Brent Goose is *Branta bernicla bernicla*, the last part of the name being the subspecies or racial name and the same as the species name; other races were described later than the nominate race, so that the race *hrota* would be fully termed *Branta bernicla hrota*.

Habits

In a work of this nature, space does not allow a full discussion of the habits of each species. At an early stage it was decided not to include details of breeding biology, foods or display behaviour since these are only indirectly relevant to field identification. Aspects summarised here include flocking tendency, feeding behaviour, times of pair-formation and breeding season, nest sites and migrational tendencies, all of which are likely to be of use when identifying a particular species.

Habitat

The type of habitat in which the bird is likely to be

encountered is summarised. Odd birds can, however, turn up in the most unlikely places, especially at migration times; a sea-duck on an inland reservoir is no less likely than a dabbling duck on the open sea. This section should therefore be used only as a basic guideline to the favoured haunts of a particular species.

Distribution

This section expands and discusses the ranges shown on the maps and summarises the patterns of occurrence of vagrant individuals, which can turn up well away from their normal ranges, especially during migration periods.

Population

This section describes the overall abundance of each species. Where possible, estimates of regional numbers and even of the entire world population are given. The decline of and pressures on the rarer species are also summarised here.

References

The most useful literature sources used when writing the species accounts are cited. These may be found worthy of reference by anyone wishing to undertake further reading on a particular species. Details of the references will be found in the bibliography on page 292.

FIELD OBSERVATION

The skills of field birdwatching can develop only through familiarity with the commoner species. By regularly visiting local waters and recognising wildfowl at varying distances by their shapes and behaviour as well as by their plumage patterns and colours, these skills may quickly be cultivated. It is important to understand the seasonal changes that may take place in the plumages of many ducks. A mid-summer or autumn visit to a large inland lake can be quite bewildering when one is confronted by large mixed flocks of drab ducks, with females, juveniles and eclipse males in a variety of brown plumages. At such times, the importance of knowing the birds by their general proportions and shapes is soon apparent.

For the beginner, a good way of getting to know the various species is to visit likely waters from mid-winter onwards, by which time most males will be in full plumage and often in the company of females. The flocks will also be augmented by visitors from farther afield, and there is always a chance of discovering more unusual individuals among the flocks.

Visits to wildfowl collections are an ideal way to learn the subtle differences between many difficult species, although once again the best time to visit is during the winter months when males are in full plumage. It is also worth remembering that seeing birds in captivity is no substitute for observing them under wild conditions, and that at very close quarters birds may not show their subtle differences in shape so well as they do at longer distances. Even the keenest field birdwatcher can, however, learn a great deal from visiting such collections.

Because of the nature of the habitats used by wildfowl and their wary nature, a mounted telescope is essential if an observer intends to get the most out of watching them. Binoculars alone will allow scrutiny of only the closest birds and the frustration of having more-distant and therefore unrecognisable flocks will soon be realised. It is also important to remember not to disturb the birds unduly: by flushing flocks from feeding and roosting sites you may not only be disrupting their routine but may also be moving them on to other waters where they may be shot; any birdwatchers following your visit will also not be pleased to find that the birds have been moved on by such thoughtless behaviour. Using a telescope therefore reduces the disturbance factor, as you need not attempt to get so close to the birds as you would with binoculars. When observing flocks of ducks or geese, try to keep relatively hidden by using any available cover such as bushes and embankments to conceal yourself from the birds. It is better for both the birdwatcher and the birds if there is minimal disturbance.

To enable the reader to get the most out of using this book and for identifying wildfowl in general, a few problem areas and general points which need explanation are outlined below.

Wildfowl Topography

When consulting the descriptions, a number of ornithological terms will be encountered. These have been kept to a basic minimum and generally follow the system adopted and recommended by the journal *British Birds*. The drawings on pages 19 and 20 define the areas of the feather tracts and show the structural features mentioned in the text.

Plumage Sequences

Understanding the basic significances of plumage sequences is often a key to correct identification. Basically, all wildfowl species emerge from the egg as downy chicks and over a relatively short period of time develop their first feathers and acquire a *juvenile* plumage. The juvenile stage usually remains for a few weeks only. In some species it may appear little different from that of adult plumage, but in most it is either markedly different or resembles female plumage. Juveniles next acquire a *first-winter* plumage, which involves a moult of the head and body feathers in the first autumn, generally keeping at least some, and usually the majority, of their juvenile wing feathers until the following summer. Young males usually acquire their sexual plumage characters during their first winter. During their *first summer* many species undergo a full moult, after which they may be indistinguishable from adults. Fully *adult* plumage may sometimes not be attained until their *second winter* or *second summer*.

Adults of the majority of species undergo a full moult in summer, after breeding. The major flight feathers (primaries and secondaries) are shedded simultaneously and the birds become flightless for a few weeks. They are particularly vulnerable to predators at this time and most species gather together to moult in flocks on 'safe' waters, sometimes undertaking a considerable 'moult migration' to reach such waters. Many species of ducks then acquire an *adult non-breeding* plumage; in males this stage is often called an *eclipse* plumage, as most male ducks become drab and resemble females in plumage. Males may then be sexed by wing features, for their wing feathers will remain throughout the following year. A body moult in autumn and early winter then allows the true colours of *adult breeding* to show; by mid-winter the majority of males are in full colour, and display and pair-formation begin prior to the spring breeding season.

These are of course brief generalisations which may not apply to all species of wildfowl. The terminology of plumage and moult sequences followed in this book differs somewhat from the American system; the two systems are compared on page 16.

Unusual Plumages

From time to time wildfowl may be encountered

Topography of a typical duck: body and head

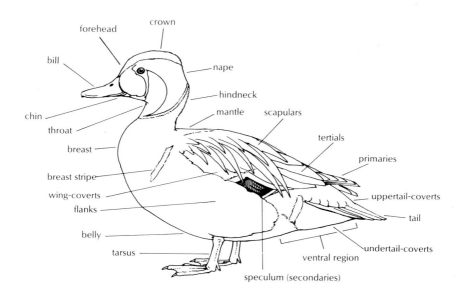

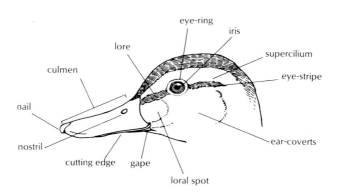

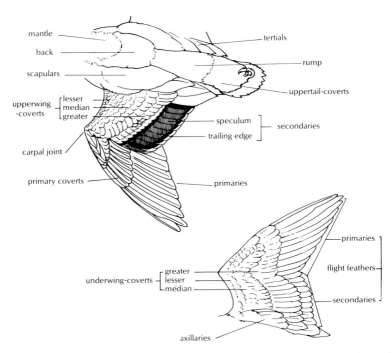

which do not seem to fit any species in the book. Birds with heavy feather wear, and at times of moult with markedly patchy plumage patterning, can appear distinctly peculiar. With such birds, the all-important size and structural features compared with other nearby individuals should provide the correct answer. Others, however, may prove to be individuals with some form of plumage aberration. Extensive areas of white in the plumage would indicate partial *albinism*; a true albino is extremely rare and can be deemed as such only if it is completely white, with pinkish bare parts. Others may show extensively blackish plumage (*melanism*) or have their entire plumage coloration pale and diluted, giving a washed-out appearance (*leucism*). Leucistic birds are perhaps the most frequent aberrations of wild wildfowl.

Among the dabbling ducks, feral Mallards often have an influence on wild populations, and oddly-plumaged individuals are not uncommon in Mallard flocks, even far from the influence of parks and suburban areas. They may be all white, black with white breasts, all buff or a mixture of these colours, and they may be markedly small or distinctly large and heavy. All, however, appear typically Mallard-like in general shape, particularly of the bill and head, and males usually show the curled central tail feathers. Feral Muscovy Ducks also often wander from habitation, but are less likely to be encountered among wild flocks of other species.

Plumage-staining may also produce remarkable appearances, especially on basically white or white-headed birds. The most frequent result of staining is the rusty appearance found on the heads, necks and underparts of swans and geese and stems from their feeding in ferrous waters of peaty regions.

Hybrids

Wild hybrids are rare, but are sometimes encountered. Males may show relatively obvious features of their parents, but not necessarily so. Some hybrids may show features not apparent in either parent, which provides an interesting insight into wildfowl evolution. Hybrids between Wigeon and Chiloe Wigeon appear remarkably like American Wigeons, and those between Mallard and Teal produce a striking facial pattern which closely resembles that of a male Baikal Teal. It is dangerous to attempt an assessment of the parentage of such hybrids, unless it is obvious — as with Mallard × Northern Pintail hybrids, which show obvious features of the parent species. Hybrids also vary according to the respective sex of each of their parents: for example, a hybrid male Tufted Duck × female Pochard may be quite different from that produced by a male Pochard × female Tufted Duck.

Hybrids are much more common in captivity, and some collections have a bewildering selection of intergeneric hybrids which are absolutely bizarre. Most hybrids encountered are likely to be escapes from captivity, and this possibility should be borne in mind when the observer is faced with a peculiar duck. Female hybrids are especially difficult to diagnose and are, hardly surprisingly, more easily overlooked.

Escapes

The majority of wildfowl species are kept somewhere in captivity, where many of them breed relatively readily. Wildfowl collections are a wonderful way of educating the general public into appreciating wildfowl and the survival pressures that many species are under. Captive breeding has produced excellent results with restocking and re-introducing rare species back into their former haunts. A number of wildfowl collections have free-flying birds which may wander considerable distances. This creates a headache for the wildfowl-watcher when something unusual is discovered, and for the authorities who judge records of rare-bird sightings. Many records of vagrant wildfowl in Europe, North America and elsewhere are suspected of being referable to escapes rather than to genuine vagrants, and it is difficult to prove either way. Escaped birds are not necessarily tame, or ringed, and may behave as truly wild birds. They may adapt to living normal lives and migrate with flocks of other species, even turning up in relatively remote situations. On the other hand many species are highly migratory, with histories of presumed vagrancy which fit into defined patterns. Such vagrants are the spice of life to many duck-watching enthusiasts. Obvious escapes — non-migratory species which are popular in captivity and way out of range, or exceptionally tame — may also be encountered.

Sifting Through the Flocks

Most wildfowl species are gregarious outside the breeding season, often forming somewhat mixed gatherings on estuaries, lakes and coastal bays. Searching through large flocks looking for something a little different requires not only patience but tests the observer's knowledge of the plumage variations of the commoner species. Frequently, flocks may need to be repeatedly and carefully examined before a bird worthy of closer scrutiny is located, and more often than not the birds will either all be asleep or else repeatedly diving. Occasionally your patience will be rewarded. Even among basically similar species there are subtle differences in shape, plumage tones and behaviour which may attract attention. It

Most diving ducks keep their wings tightly closed beneath the water, but others 'fly' underwater; the latter typically open their wings partially as they submerge

Dabbling and up-ending postures of surface-feeding ducks

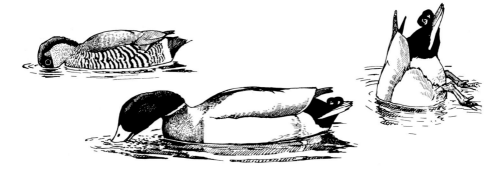

The position and extent of white on the upperwing is a useful identification aid: three typical patterns are shown. a: white forewing; b: white greater-covert bar and trailing edge to speculum; and c: white secondaries and inner primaries

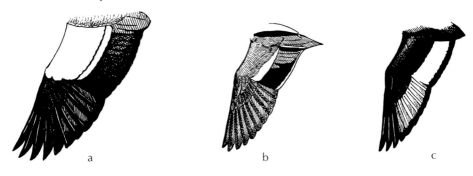

a　　　　　　　　　　　b　　　　　　　　　　　c

The position and extent of white on the underwing is important; three typical types of pattern are shown. a: white underwing-coverts; b: white central band and axillaries; and c: white secondaries

a　　　　　　　　　　　b　　　　　　　　　　　c

Most surface-feeding ducks rise suddenly and steeply when taking wing; most diving ducks patter for a short distance before becoming airborne

is impossible to summarise individual characters which are useful pointers, but as general guidelines the following features are worth checking while flock-scanning.

Birds on water: Prominence of tail, relative body length, flank pattern, pattern of ventral region, head and bill shape and colour. Does it dive or dabble? If diving, does it dive with wings closed or partially open?

Loafing birds on shore: Extent of white on belly or breast, pattern of flanks and ventral region, leg colour and relative length, head and bill shape.

Flying birds: Pattern and colour of both upperwing and underwing. Is belly uniform with or whiter than rest of underparts? Did bird rise steeply from water or patter across surface? Voice.

Goose flocks: Odd individuals of other species often accompany flocks of commoner species. They may be picked out by concentrating on the following: contrast between head and neck and breast; bill colour; leg colour; general tone of plumage; relative length of neck; and general size and shape of head and bill.

Constructive Wildfowl-watching

Anyone can contribute to our knowledge of world wildfowl by keeping accurate notes, even if merely of counts of birds at a local lake. Most regions and counties have an organised system of wildfowl-counting and would be pleased to have some assistance at local level. In Britain, the local organiser may be contacted through the National Organiser of Wildfowl Counts, The Wildfowl Trust, Slimbridge, Gloucester, GL2 7BT. Counts on a worldwide scale are organised by the International Waterfowl Research Bureau (IWRB). Many parts of the world receive inadequate coverage or none at all, and offers of help would be most appreciated; the IWRB may be contacted via The Wildfowl Trust at Slimbridge.

ACKNOWLEDGEMENTS

Firstly, we should like to acknowledge the great debt that we owe to people from all parts of the world who have gathered data on wildfowl over the years. The mass of publications that has resulted has been summarised in earlier works on world wildfowl of a more scientific nature, notably in the monumental treatises by Phillips (1922-26), Delacour (1954-64) and Johnsgard (1965, 1978). A glance at the bibliography of the present volume gives an idea of the variety of more recent research that has been carried out on ducks, geese and swans.

We should like particularly to thank The Wildfowl Trust in England, who have helped not only by allowing us to study a tremendous variety of species in life when we wished to check up on various points, but also allowed unlimited access to their skin collection during the production of the plates; we should like to offer our special thanks to Martin Brown for arranging this, and to Janet Kear who kindly read and commented on the text. Peter Colston at the British Museum (Natural History), Tring, England, also checked the plates, and we are grateful for his helpful comments.

The staff at Christopher Helm Publishers Limited receive our gratitude for their patience and encouragement, with special thanks to Christopher Helm and Jo Hemmings and to the production team: Melanie Crook, Ann Doolan, Joe Kenneway and Robert Kirk. Thanks also go to Mark Beaman for initially suggesting the project, and to David Christie for copy-editing and much helpful advice.

Many others helped us over sticky areas: special thanks to Alex Randall for Russian translations and cheery good humour; to Tim Inskipp, who unearthed rather obscure reference material; to the late Laurel Tucker for many useful discussions on wildfowl identification; to Mark Brazil for comments from the Far East; and to Drs Phil Humphrey and Brad Livezey of the Kansas Museum of Natural History, who advised on steamer ducks.

Thanks are also due to Klaas J Eigenhuis, John Engbring of the US Fish and Wildlife Service in Honolulu, Daniel W Moulton of Texas Parks and Wildlife, Eugeniusz Nowak and Iain Robertson for helping us with our enquiries.

The author wishes to thank Penny and Bryony for having lost a husband and father for endless months while he was either abroad or locked away in a world of wildfowl, and realises what an exceptionally understanding family he is fortunate to have. Special thanks to Penny not only for keeping the world at bay during the final stages of the book, but also for the exacting task of compiling the index.

PLATES 1-47

The text follows a recent classification review.
To ease cross-reference,
the text has been kept in numerical sequence,
but in some cases texts and maps
are not directly opposite the species illustrations.
When referring to caption,
check the species name and number.

2 Spotted Whistling Duck *Dendrocygna guttata*   **Text page 124**

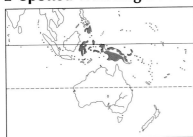

East Indies and New Guinea. Local by swamps and lakes. Often found in mixed parties with 5. Very dark, with whitish spotting on underparts. Smaller than 8, with pinkish tones to bill and legs, dusky eye-patch, and more uniform upperwing in flight; distribution quite different. Plumages similar.
a ADULT
b JUVENILE: Duller; markings on sides of breast more streaked.

3 Plumed Whistling Duck *Dendrocygna eytoni*   **Text page 125**

Northern and eastern Australia. Tropical grasslands. Pale, elegant whistling duck with elongated, pointed flank plumes. Plumages similar.
a ADULT
b JUVENILE: Plainer fore-flanks, shorter flank plumes.

5 Wandering Whistling Duck *Dendrocygna arcuata*   **Text page 127**

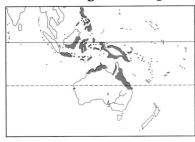

East Indies and northern and eastern Australia. Marshes and lakes. Range overlaps with similar 6, but larger with prominent flank markings, dark of crown reaches eye, dark scaling on breast and creamy sides to uppertail-coverts. Plumages similar. Three races, all similar in plumage; nominate race shown.
a ADULT
b JUVENILE: Duller; upperwing-coverts less chestnut, belly centre paler.

8 Black-billed Whistling Duck *Dendrocygna arborea*   **Text page 130**

West Indies. Wooded swamps. Largest of genus, habitually perches on palms. Most active at dusk. Very dark, recalling 2, but ranges well separated. Larger than 2, with blacker bill and legs, distinctly paler and greyer upperwing. Plumages similar.
a ADULT
b JUVENILE: Duller; spotting below more streaked.

2a

2a

2b

3a

3a

3b

5b

5a

5a

8a

8a

8b

Hilary Burn.

4 **Fulvous Whistling Duck** *Dendrocygna bicolor*   **Text page 126**

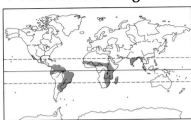

Extremely extensive world range: tropical Americas, Africa and Indian region. Open wetlands and marshes. Overlaps with 6 in Asia. Distinguished by larger size, whitish uppertail-coverts, darker lower hindneck, paler crown and richer underpart coloration. Plumages similar.

a ADULT
b JUVENILE: Duller, especially flank pattern; uppertail-coverts less conspicuous.

6 **Lesser Whistling Duck** *Dendrocygna javanica*   **Text page 128**

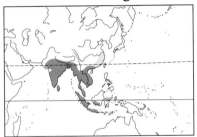

Tropical Asia and East Indies. Marshes, lakes and rivers. Range overlaps with 4 in India, with 5 in East Indies. From 4 by smaller size, darker crown centre and chestnut uppertail-coverts. From 5 by chestnut uppertail, dark of crown not reaching eye, lack of breast mottling, and more diffuse flank pattern. Plumages similar.

a ADULT
b JUVENILE: Paler and duller.

7 **White-faced Whistling Duck** *Dendrocygna viduata*   **Text page 129**

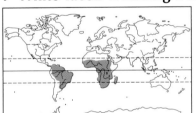

Widespread in tropical America and Africa. Lakes and rivers. Very dark, with contrasting white head. Plumages similar, juvenile drabber.

a ADULT
b JUVENILE: Duller, with pale greyish-buff 'face' and browner neck.

9 **Black-bellied Whistling Duck** *Dendrocygna autumnalis*   **Text page 131**

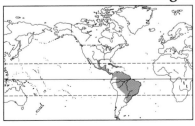

Widespread in tropical America. Sparsely-wooded country with lakes and marshes. Black underparts contrast with paler head and neck; whitish upperwing obvious in flight. Adults with red bill and pink legs. Two races; nominate race shown.

a ADULT
b JUVENILE: Duller and browner below, with blue-grey bill and legs.

Hilary Burn

1 Magpie Goose *Anseranas semipalmata* **Text page 123**

Northern Australia and southern New Guinea. Rivers, lakesides and open country, in large flocks. Unmistakable large black and white goose-like bird. Juvenile and female smaller than male.

a ADULT MALE

b IMMATURE: Juvenile with black areas of plumage greyer-brown.

11 Cape Barren Goose *Cereopsis novaehollandiae* **Text page 133**

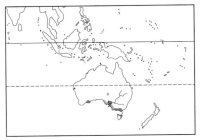

Southern Australia. Coastal grasslands and islands. Bulky grey goose, with spotting on upperparts; peculiar black bill, with extensive greenish cere covering all but tip. All plumages similar. Two similar races; adult nominate race shown.

36 Spur-winged Goose *Plectropterus gambensis* **Text page 160**

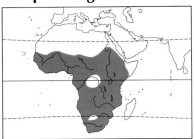

Tropical Africa. Rivers and lakesides. Large black and white goose, with black and white flanks and pale face. Reddish-pink bill and legs. Male larger than female. Plumages similar and somewhat variable, the races intergrading. Two races, both illustrated.

a ADULT MALE (nominate race): Most of Africa, except south.

b ADULT MALE (race *niger*): Southern Africa.

c JUVENILE FEMALE (race *niger*)

1a

1b

1a

36c

36a

36a

36b

11

11

Hilary Burn

12 Swan Goose *Anser cygnoides*

Text page 134

Eastern Asia. Rare. Steppe lakes and marshes. Long, heavy black bill and strongly-patterned head and neck distinctive. Male larger, but plumages all similar. Ancestor of domestic forms.
a ADULT
b JUVENILE: Duller, with browner crown and hindneck.

13 Bean Goose *Anser fabalis*

Text page 135

Europe and Asia. Breeds by marshes in tundra and taiga, wintering in open farmland. Darker and larger than 14, with orange legs and bill-band. Five races, intergrading, varying in overall size, shape, and bill pattern and shape. See text for ranges. Plumages all similar.
a ADULT (nominate race)
b JUVENILE (nominate race): Duller, with more scaled upperpart pattern.
c ADULT (race *rossicus*): Small, with short bill.
d ADULT (race *middendorffii*): Largest race.

14 Pink-footed Goose *Anser brachyrhynchus*

Text page 136

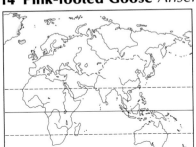

Breeds western sub-Arctic tundra and cliffs, winters lowland farmland of northwest Europe. Sometimes considered a race of 13, but smaller, greyer and with pink legs and bill-band.
a ADULT
b JUVENILE: Duller and browner; upperpart pattern more scaled.

12a

12a

12b

13a

13a

13b

13d

13c

14a

14a

14b

Hilary Burn

15 White-fronted Goose *Anser albifrons*

Text page 137

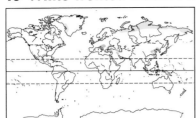

Northern hemisphere. Breeds taiga and tundra, winters farmland. Larger than 16, but very similar (see text). Adult with white frontal patch, blackish belly patches, orange legs and pink or orange bill. Four or five races, varying in intensity of overall coloration and bill colour; three shown. See text for ranges.

a ADULT (nominate race): Western Palaearctic.
b JUVENILE (nominate race): Lacks frontal patch and belly patches.
c ADULT (race *flavirostris*): Dark, with mostly orange bill. Breeds Greenland, winters western British Isles.
d ADULT (race *gambelli*): Large and dark. Breeds Alaska and northwest Canada, winters southern USA.

16 Lesser White-fronted Goose *Anser erythropus*

Text page 139

Range chiefly Asiatic. Breeds taiga, winters farmland and steppe, overlapping with 15 in winter. Very similar to 15, but smaller, with tiny pink bill; adult smaller, with yellow eye-ring and smaller belly patches, but identification difficult (see text). No races.

a ADULT
b JUVENILE: Lacks frontal patch and belly patches.

17 Greylag Goose *Anser anser*

Text page 140

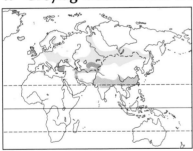

Most southerly-breeding 'grey' goose, apart from 18. Widespread in Europe and Asia, wintering south to North Africa. Lowland marshes and farmland. Large and heavily built, with relatively light head and neck, pale blue-grey forewing, pink legs and pink or orange bill. Two races. Juvenile similar to adult. Adults shown.

a Nominate race: Europe.
b Race *rubrirostris*: Asia. Paler, with bright pink bill.

15a

15a

15c

15b

15b

15d

16a

16a

16b

16b

16b

17a

17a

17b

Hilary Burn

19 Snow Goose *Anser caerulescens*

Text page 142

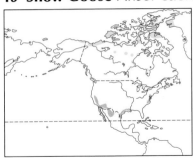

North America. Breeds Arctic tundra, winters farmland and lakes. Two colour phases. Similar to 20, but larger, with stouter bill and 'grinning patch' along cutting edge of bill. Juvenile with more extensive grey-brown above. Two races: nominate race, with blue phase common in certain areas; blue phase almost non-existent in race *atlanticus*. In captivity, compare 27 (plate 9). See text.

a ADULT SNOW PHASE (race *atlanticus*: Greater Snow Goose): Eastern North America. Larger than nominate race.

b ADULT BLUE PHASE (nominate race: Lesser Snow Goose): Remainder of range, including southeast USA in winter.

c ADULT SNOW PHASE (nominate race)

d JUVENILE BLUE PHASE (nominate race)

e JUVENILE SNOW PHASE (nominate race)

20 Ross's Goose *Anser rossii*

Text page 143

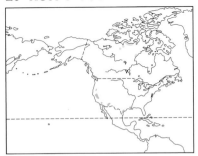

Breeds tundra of central Arctic Canada, winters chiefly farmland of western USA. Overlaps with 19. Very similar to 19, but smaller, with shorter neck, and smaller bill which lacks 'grinning patch'. Blue phase is very rare. See text.

a ADULT SNOW PHASE

b ADULT BLUE PHASE: Very rare.

c JUVENILE SNOW PHASE: Much whiter than 19e.

21 Emperor Goose *Anser canagicus*

Text page 144

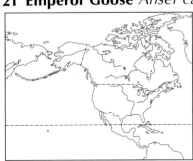

Resident Alaska and northeastern Siberia. Seashore and islands. Very stocky. Adult has dark, scaly plumage with white head and tail, head usually stained rusty. Juvenile sooty. Blue phase 19 very rare in range of 21.

a ADULT

b JUVENILE: Much stockier than 19d.

21a

21a

21b

20a

20b

20a

20c

19a

19c

19b

19d

19d

19e

Hilary Burn

PLATE 7: Bar-headed, Hawaiian and Canada Geese

18 Bar-headed Goose *Anser indicus*

Text page 141

Breeds by high-altitude lakes in southern Asia, wintering chiefly in wetlands of India. Adult head pattern diagnostic. Grey plumage of juvenile distinctive within range.
a ADULT
b JUVENILE

22 Hawaiian Goose *Branta sandvicensis*

Text page 145

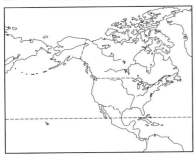

Endemic to volcanic slopes on some Hawaiian islands, where it is the only goose, although 15, 21, 23 and 25 have occurred as vagrants to the archipelago. All plumages similar. Adult shown.

23 Canada Goose *Branta canadensis*

Text page 146

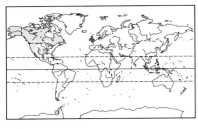

Widespread over North America and introduced into western Europe and New Zealand. Open country, lakes and rivers. Twelve races, varying in size and overall body coloration; extreme examples are shown. Most races intergrade, and relationships complex. All have black head and neck, with white facial patch and brown body. Juveniles resemble adults. Adults shown. See text for ranges and discussion.
a Race *maxima*: Largest; colour typical of eastern races.
b Race *occidentalis*: Darkest; colour typical of western races.
c Race *minima*: One of the smallest; size typical of Arctic races.

18a

18a

18b

18b

23a

23a

23c

23c

23b

22

22

Hilary Burn

24 **Barnacle Goose** *Branta leucopsis*

Text page 148

Breeds chiefly European Arctic tundra and islands, winters in coastal grasslands of northwest Europe. Small size and black neck and breast distinctive, contrasting with pale grey body and white head. Plumages similar.
a ADULT
b JUVENILE: White of head with dusky freckles; upperparts tinged brownish, with buffish feather edges.

25 **Brent Goose** *Branta bernicla*

Text page 148

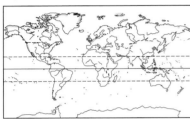

Breeds across Arctic tundra, winters on estuaries and coastal grassland. Small, very dark goose, with contrasting white rear body. Juvenile attains neck patch during mid-winter. Three races, all shown. Juvenile harder to separate racially than adult.
a ADULT (nominate race: Dark-bellied Brent Goose): Western Siberia and Europe.
b JUVENILE (nominate race): Lacks neck patch, has prominent bars on wings.
c ADULT (race *hrota*: Pale-bellied Brent Goose): Canada to Svalbard, wintering Atlantic North America and western Europe. Whitish flanks.
d ADULT (race *nigricans*: Black Brant): Eastern Siberia and western Canada, wintering Pacific coast. Flanks two-toned, with blackish belly; neck patches meet on foreneck.

26 **Red-breasted Goose** *Branta ruficollis*

Text page 150

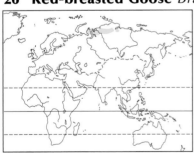

Breeds tundra rivers and cliffs of few areas of Arctic Siberia, winters chiefly farmland and steppe of southeast Europe. Small and beautifully marked, appearing black and white at long range. Plumages similar.
a ADULT
b JUVENILE: Slightly duller; paler sides of head, several fine bars on wing.

27 Coscoroba Swan *Coscoroba coscoroba*   **Text page 151**

Southern South America and Falkland Islands. Lakes and marshes. Almost a goose-like swan, adult having a waxy-red duck-like bill, pink legs and small black wing-tips. Range overlaps only with 34, which always has all-dark head and neck. In captivity, compare 19 (plate 6).
a ADULT
b JUVENILE

32 Mute Swan *Cygnus olor*   **Text page 157**

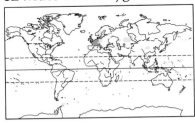

Familiar swan of suburban and urban lakes of Europe, native on freshwater marshes and lakes over much of central Asia; introduced elsewhere. Orange bill with black basal knob diagnostic of adult. Juvenile has blackish base to bill and pointed tail, which separates it from other northern swans (plate 10).
a ADULT
b JUVENILE

33 Black Swan *Cygnus atratus*   **Text page 158**

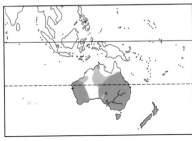

Lakes of Australia and New Zealand. Often in huge numbers. Appears all blackish, with white primaries obvious only in flight. Unmistakable.
a ADULT
b JUVENILE

34 Black-necked Swan *Cygnus melanocoryphus*   **Text page 158**

Southern South America and Falkland Islands. Lakes and marshes. Unmistakable, the only white swan with black head and neck.
a ADULT
b JUVENILE

33a

33a

33b

34a

34b

34a

32b

32a

32a

27a

27b

27a

Hilary Burn

28 Trumpeter Swan *Olor buccinator* — Text page 152

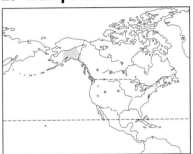

Western North America. Lakes, rivers and wet fields. Larger, longer-bodied and longer-necked than 30, with which it overlaps; also, forehead flatter and bill profile less concave and longer. See text.

a ADULT: From 30 by bill shape, lack of yellow patch before eye and more obvious reddish cutting edge.

b JUVENILE: Darker than 30b, with extensive blackish patches around bill-base. Unlike 30, retains brownish plumage into first spring.

29 Whooper Swan *Olor cygnus* — Text page 153

Europe and Asia. Lakes, rivers and wet fields. Larger than 31, with which it overlaps in winter, with longer neck and body, longer and deeper-based bill and larger head. See text.

a ADULT: Bill pattern less variable than 31, appearing bright yellow with a black tip, whereas bill of 31 appears more evenly black and yellow. Yellow extends in long point towards tip (yellow area more rounded on 31).

b JUVENILE: Similar in plumage and bill colour to 31b, but by first spring bill pattern recalls adult though lacks yellow.

30 Whistling Swan *Olor columbianus* — Text page 154

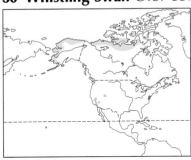

North America. Lakes, rivers and wet fields. Regarded as conspecific with 31 as 'Tundra Swan'. Smaller version of 28; distant or lone individuals problematic. Typically, shorter-necked and shorter-billed than 28, with slightly concave, less straight, profile to bill. See text.

a ADULT: Black bill, with variably obvious (sometimes absent) small yellow patch in front of eye. Red line along cutting edge less extensive than on 28.

b JUVENILE: Paler than 28b, becoming whiter during mid-winter, (unlike 28b, which remains brownish into first spring). Lacks blackish patches over base of bill of 28b, but bill pattern close to 31b.

31 Bewick's Swan *Olor columbianus bewickii* — Text page 155

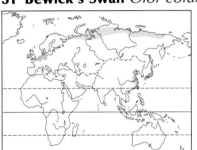

Europe and Asia. Lakes, rivers and wet fields. Now regarded as conspecific with 30 under the name 'Tundra Swan'. Smaller and relatively smaller-headed, shorter-necked and shorter-billed than 29, with which it overlaps in winter. See text.

a ADULT: Bill black with variable yellow basal half, yellow less extensive and more rounded than on 29.

b JUVENILE: Slightly paler and greyer than 29b, but size and structure best distinguishing features.

31a

31b

31a

30b

30a

29a

29a

29b

28a

28a

28b

Hilary Burn

38 Ruddy Shelduck *Tadorna ferruginea*

Text page 163

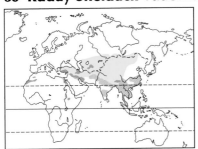

Europe, Asia and North Africa. Only rusty-orange shelduck in the northern hemisphere. Lakes and rivers in open country. In captivity, note that resembles 39 but lacks contrasting buff breast and ventral region and has pale buff to orange-buff head. Compare also 41b (plate 12). Sexing and ageing often difficult (see text).

a ADULT MALE BREEDING: In eclipse lacks collar.
b ADULT FEMALE: As a, but buffer head with white 'face' patch, lacks collar.
c JUVENILE: Duller than b and washed greyish-brown.

39 Cape Shelduck *Tadorna cana*

Text page 164

Southern Africa, where it is the only rusty shelduck. Lakes and rivers in open country. In captivity, compared with 38, has breast and ventral region usually paler and buffer and head greyer (head dark grey and white on female).

a ADULT MALE BREEDING
b ADULT FEMALE
c JUVENILE: Paler and duller than a.

43 Shelduck *Tadorna tadorna*

Text page 167

Europe, Asia and North Africa. Saline lakes and estuaries. Black and white plumage with rusty breast-band diagnostic, although latter lacking on drabber juvenile.

a ADULT MALE BREEDING: Bill-knob reduced after breeding. See also c.
b ADULT FEMALE: Duller than a, with whitish frontal area and diffuse breast-band. See also c.
c JUVENILE: Lacks breast-band; most of plumage washed greyish-brown. Eclipse adults also resemble juvenile (see text).

38a

38b

38a

38c

39a

39a

39b

39c

43a

43b

43a

43c

43c

Hilary Burn

PLATE 12: Australasian shelducks

40 Australian Shelduck *Tadorna tadornoides*   **Text page 164**

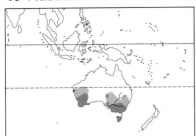

Southern Australia. Lakes and rivers in open country. Blackish male with narrow white collar, white forewing and chestnut breast distinctive, female additionally having white around eye. Owing to individual variation, sexing in the field can be problematic (see text). In captivity, compare 41d.

a ADULT MALE
b ADULT FEMALE
c JUVENILE FEMALE: Lacks collar and is duller; some white marks on sides of head (lacking on juvenile male).

41 Paradise Shelduck *Tadorna variegata*   **Text page 165**

New Zealand. Lakes, rivers and coastal shores. The only shelduck of New Zealand. Male blackish, with conspicuous white forewing. Female deep chestnut, with white head and forewing. Compare b with 38 and 39 (plate 11) in captivity.

a ADULT MALE: Similar throughout the year.
b ADULT FEMALE BREEDING
c ADULT FEMALE ECLIPSE
d JUVENILE FEMALE: Bird showing rusty colour appearing on breast and whitish on sides of head, recalling female of 40.

44 Radjah Shelduck *Tadorna radjah*   **Text page 168**

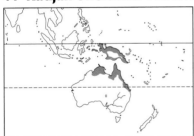

Northern Australia and the East Indies. Coastal swamps and rivers. Dark upperparts and dark breast-band contrast with white head and underparts. Plumages all similar. Two races, both shown.

a ADULT MALE (race *rufitergum*): Northern Australia. Browner upperparts.
b ADULT MALE (nominate race): East Indies and New Guinea. Blacker upperparts.
c JUVENILE (race *rufitergum*): Duller than adult.

41a

41b

41d

41a

41c

41b

40a

40b

40a

40c

44a

44c

44b

44a

Hilary Burn.

42 Crested Shelduck *Tadorna cristata*   **Text page 166**

Formerly northeast Asia. Almost certainly extinct, last sighting 1971. Probably bred in wooded river valleys and wintered in coastal regions. Male blackish, with pale sides of head and neck and white forewing. Female lighter and greyer, with bridled 'face' pattern. Bill and legs red. Unmistakable. Any sightings should be reported (see text).
a ADULT MALE
b ADULT FEMALE

46 Egyptian Goose *Alopochen aegyptiacus*   **Text page 170**

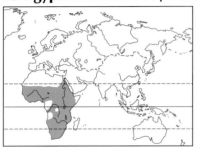

Tropical Africa, feral in Britain. Rivers, lakes and farmland. Bulky, brownish-buff sheldgoose with pinkish bill and legs, white forewing and dark eye-patch. Adults variable, some greyer than others.
a ADULT (FEMALE): Grey type.
b ADULT (MALE): Brown type.
c JUVENILE: Dusky crown and hindneck, drabber overall. Compare juvenile of 43 (plate 11).

47 Orinoco Goose *Neochen jubata*   **Text page 171**

South America. Tropical forest rivers. Pale head and breast, chestnut flanks and dark upperparts, including blackish wings above and below. Unmistakable. Plumages all similar.
a ADULT
b JUVENILE: Duller than a, with paler bill and legs.

42a

42a

42b

47a

47a

47b

46b

46a

46c

46b

Hilary Burn

49 Magellan Goose *Chloephaga picta*   Text page 172

Southern South America and Falkland Islands. Open country and farmland. Often in very large flocks. Males white, with black primaries and central wing-band; variably barred below, some almost all barred apart from head and neck, others barred only on upperparts and flanks. Females have wing pattern as male, but rufous-brown body, finely barred except for plain head and neck, resembling 51 and 52 (plate 15). Variation complex. It is possible that white-phase birds of both races form one species, and more restricted barred-phase adult males another (see text).

a ADULT MALE WHITE PHASE (nominate race: Lesser Magellan Goose): Mainland South America.

b JUVENILE MALE WHITE PHASE (nominate race): Adult male of barred phase is very similar.

c ADULT FEMALE (nominate race): Unlike male, shows no colour variation. Black underpart barring whiter than rufous bars; dark ventral region.

d JUVENILE FEMALE (nominate race): Duller, less clearly barred than c.

e ADULT MALE (race *leucoptera*: Greater Magellan Goose): Falkland Islands. All adult males similar. Juvenile males barred as on b.

f ADULT FEMALE (race *leucoptera*): Larger, with black underpart barring narrower than rufous bars, and ventral region whiter than on c.

g JUVENILE FEMALE (race *leucoptera*): Duller than f.

50 Kelp Goose *Chloephaga hybrida*   Text page 174

Southern South America and Falkland Islands. Rocky shorelines, confined to coast. Unmistakable. Male totally white, with black bill and yellow legs. Sooty female has contrasting white tail and rear body and white barring on underparts. Female wing pattern recalls 49. Two similar races, nominate shown.

a ADULT MALE

b ADULT FEMALE

c IMMATURE MALE: Developing male plumage features, compare male 49.

d JUVENILE: As b, but body barring broken, dusky mottles in ventral region.

50a

50b

50a

50b

50c

50d

49a

49a

49b

49c

49c

49d

49e

49f

49g

Hilary Burn

48 Andean Goose *Chloephaga melanoptera*   **Text page 172**

Western South America. High Andean lakeshores and plateaux. Very heavily-built white 'goose', with blackish wings and very small bill. Strongly patterned black and white in flight. All plumage similar, female considerably smaller than male. Unmistakable.
a ADULT (MALE)
b JUVENILE (FEMALE): Duller than adults.

51 Ashy-headed Goose *Chloephaga poliocephala*   **Text page 175**

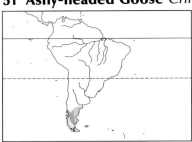

Southern South America. Open, often sparsely-wooded country with lakes and marshes. Recalls female of 49 (plate 14), but smaller, with grey head and neck contrasting with rufous breast; whitish belly and flanks barred black and white. All plumages similar.
a ADULT MALE: Breast may be barred or unbarred.
b ADULT FEMALE: Smaller than a, with barred breast.
c JUVENILE: Duller; head washed pale brown.

52 Ruddy-headed Goose *Chloephaga rubidiceps*   **Text page 175**

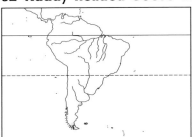

Southern South America (now very rare) and Falkland Islands (still numerous). Open country, especially coastal grasslands. Recalls female of 49 (plate 14), but smaller and paler, not so rufous, with very finely-barred body plumage. All plumages similar.
a ADULT
b JUVENILE: Slightly duller.

53 Blue-winged Goose *Cyanochen cyanopterus*   **Text page 176**

Ethiopia. Mountain lakes and rivers. Plump greyish-brown 'goose' with black bill and legs. In flight, shows pale blue wing-coverts. Normally carries head back on 'shoulders', with breast pouted. All plumages similar. Adult male shown. Rather drab, but unmistakable.

52a
52b
52a
51a
51b
51a
51c
53
53
48a
48a
48b

Hilary Burn

35 Freckled Duck *Stictonetta naevosa* Text page 159

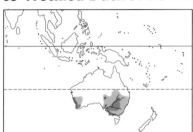

Australia, chiefly southeast and southwest, but somewhat nomadic. Freshwater marshes. Peculiar dark dabbling duck, with slender, high-based bill and slightly-tufted rear of head. Reddish on bill of male seasonally variable. All plumages similar.
a ADULT MALE: Red on bill seasonally absent.
b FEMALE: Browner and buffer than a, but similar.

54 Blue Duck *Hymenolaimus malacorhynchos* Text page 177

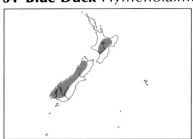

New Zealand. Fast-flowing mountain rivers in wooded regions. Heavily-built dark grey duck, with strikingly pale bill and iris. Peculiar bill flaps obvious only at close range, but bill looks square-ended in field. Swims and dives in rapids. Often stands on mid-stream boulders. All plumages similar.
a ADULT
b JUVENILE: Black stripe on culmen; browner plumage, especially wings.

55 Torrent Duck *Merganetta armata* Text page 178

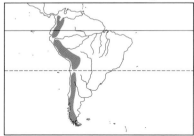

Western South America. Fast-flowing rivers, along almost whole chain of Andes. Male has striking black and white head and neck, but in Peruvian race *leucogenis* body plumage variable (see text). Female grey above and rufous below, similar in all races. Stands on mid-stream boulders. Swims and dives in rapids. Three races, two shown.
a ADULT MALE (nominate race: Chilean Torrent Duck): Northern Chile southwards.
b ADULT FEMALE (nominate race): Similar in all races.
c JUVENILE (nominate race): Similar in all races.
d ADULT MALE (race *colombiana*: Colombian Torrent Duck): Northern Ecuador northwards.

155 Musk Duck *Biziura lobata* Text page 289

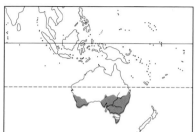

Australia, southern and western regions. Lakes and swamps, sometimes estuaries. Peculiar large diving duck, all dark with large stiff tail. Male with enormous lobe of skin under bill. Unmistakable. (Other stiff-tails shown on plates 46 and 47.)
a ADULT MALE: Largest size and largest lobe acquired after several years (see text).
b ADULT FEMALE: Immature male similar.

55a

55b

55a

55c

55b

55d

54a

54b

54a

35a

35a

35b

155b

155b

155a

Hilary Burn

NOTE: Field identification extremely difficult. The three flightless species are best separated by distribution; 56 overlaps with all three and can be very hard to distinguish. Many plumage sequences inadequately known. See text for fuller discussion.

56 Flying Steamer Duck *Tachyeres patachonicus*   Text page 180

Southern South America and Falkland Islands. Breeds by freshwater lakes inland, locally on coast; winters on coastal lagoons and shores. Slightly smaller and with less heavy head and bill than the flightless species, and wings reach further back towards tail. Often flies high and well, occurring well inland. Many individuals tend not to fly, and some populations not even capable of flight. Plumage variation complex; some shown, but see text.

a ADULT MALE (BREEDING): Pale-headed type.
b ADULT FEMALE
c JUVENILE
d ADULT MALE (NON-BREEDING)

57 Magellanic Flightless Steamer Duck *Tachyeres pteneres*   Text page 181

Southern South America. Only on coast. Overlaps with 56, but more massive, with heavier head and bill. Plumage and bill colour similar in both sexes, bill being bright orange (in 56, only male has orange bill). Head pattern plainer in both sexes, but can be quite pale grey on male in breeding season. Flightless, but see text.

a ADULT MALE (BREEDING)
b ADULT FEMALE
c JUVENILE

58 White-headed Flightless Steamer Duck
Tachyeres leucocephalus   Text page 182

Confined to coast of Chubut, Argentina. Overlaps with 56 only marginally in winter. Male pale-headed through most of year; female has broader white band behind eye than 56. Any pale-headed steamer duck on coast here will be male of this species. Juvenile all dark, but a little paler on sides of neck than other species. Flightless, but see text.

a ADULT MALE (BREEDING): Paler-headed than other steamer ducks for most of year.
b ADULT FEMALE

59 Falkland Flightless Steamer Duck
Tachyeres brachypterus   Text page 183

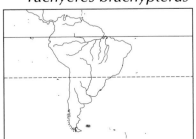

Confined to Falkland Islands. Only on coast, but walks to lagoons up to 1 km inland. Overlaps with 56. Larger and more massively built than 56, but plumage almost identical. Flightless, but see text.

a ADULT MALE (BREEDING)
b ADULT FEMALE
c JUVENILE

57a

57b

57c

59a

59b

59c

58b

58a

56d

56b

56a

56c

Hilary Burn

37 Comb Duck *Sarkidiornis melanotos* **Text page 161**

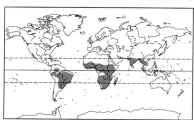

Extensive range: tropical South America, Africa and southern Asia. Lakes and marshes in sparsely-wooded open country. Pale head, neck and underparts and blackish upperparts, including both wing surfaces, and large size make this a distinctive duck. Two races, both shown; could be separate species (see text).

a ADULT MALE (nominate race): Africa and Asia. Small 'comb' in winter.

b ADULT FEMALE (nominate race): Smaller than a, lacks 'comb', has duller flanks.

c JUVENILE (FEMALE): Buff and brown, recalling female of 109 (plate 19).

d ADULT MALE (race *sylvicola*): Central and South America. Black flanks.

e ADULT FEMALE (race *sylvicola*): Smaller than d, lacks 'comb'.

61 Muscovy Duck *Cairina moschata* **Text page 184**

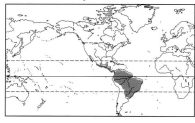

Central and South America. Tropical forest lakes and marshes. Ancestor of domestic forms. Large, bulky blackish duck, with striking white forewing when adult. Unmistakable.

a ADULT MALE

b ADULT FEMALE: Smaller and duller than a, lacks bill-knob.

c JUVENILE: Duller than b, usually lacks white in wings.

62 White-winged Wood Duck *Cairina scutulata* **Text page 185**

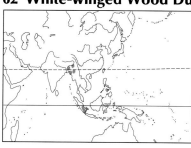

Southeastern Asia. Tropical forest lakes and pools. Rare and endangered, formerly more widespread, present known range shown on map. Chiefly nocturnal, easily overlooked. Large dark duck with striking white forewing and whitish head and neck. All plumages similar, but some birds show incidence of partial albinism (c).

a ADULT MALE

b ADULT FEMALE: Similar to a, but duller. Juvenile similar.

c ADULT MALE: Variant with extensive white fore parts; formerly thought to be Sumatran population only, but also recorded Assam.

Hilary Burn

63 **Wood Duck** *Aix sponsa*

Text page 186

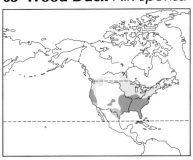

North America. Wooded lakes and marshes. Male a distinctive, beautifully-patterned duck. Female resembles 64, but native ranges do not overlap; both, however, occur widely as escapes from captivity. See text for further discussion.

a ADULT MALE BREEDING
b ADULT MALE ECLIPSE: Like c, but vestiges of male throat pattern, brighter bill.
c ADULT FEMALE: Like 64c, but eye-patch broader, wing-coverts glossed blue, speculum blue, head darker, nail on bill black, lacks facial striations. Resembles d in summer.
d JUVENILE: Like c, but browner, more streaked below, mottled belly and indistinct supercilium.

64 **Mandarin** *Aix galericulata*

Text page 188

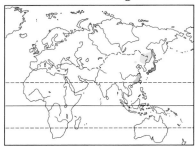

Eastern Asia, ferally established in Britain. Wooded rivers and lakes. Male unmistakable. Female resembles female of 63. See above and text for discussion.

a ADULT MALE BREEDING
b ADULT MALE ECLIPSE: Like c, but bill reddish-pink.
c ADULT FEMALE: Like 63c, but lighter on head and upperparts, narrower eye-patch, dull wing-coverts, greenish speculum, has facial striations and whitish nail on bill. Resembles d in summer.
d JUVENILE: Like c, but underparts more streaked, belly mottled, eye-patch very narrow, often just a narrow ring, no white around bill-base.

109 **Maned Duck** *Chenonetta jubata*

Text page 237

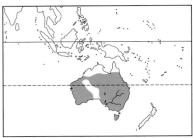

Australia, chiefly east and west. Wooded swamps and lakes. Male greyish, with dark head and mottled breast; female shows facial stripes and mottled underparts. In flight, has conspicuous white secondaries. Unlikely to be confused (but see 37c on plate 18).

a ADULT MALE
b ADULT FEMALE: Juvenile similar, but lighter.

109a

109b

109b

109a

109a

64a

64b

64a

64c

64d

64c

63a

63a

63c

63d

63c

Hilary Burn

63b

66 Green Pygmy Goose *Nettapus pulchellus*   **Text page 190**

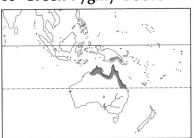

Northern Australia and southern New Guinea. Tropical lakes and pools. Tiny dark duck with white cheeks and pale greyish, finely-barred underparts. Male has dark foreneck. Distant female confusable with female of 67 in Australia: in flight wing pattern different, with white only on secondaries.

a ADULT MALE BREEDING
b ADULT MALE ECLIPSE: Like c, but darker neck sides.
c ADULT FEMALE
d JUVENILE: Like c, but 'face' and foreneck heavily mottled brown.

67 Cotton Pygmy Goose *Nettapus coromandelianus*   **Text page 191**

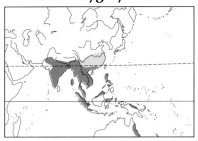

Tropical Asia south to northern Australia, where it overlaps with 66. Tropical lakes, marshes and swamps. Head, neck and underparts of male very white. Female browner, with dark eye-line. Distant female confusable with female of 66. Wing pattern quite different from 66: male with huge white band across full length of wing, female with brown wing and narrow white trailing edge. Two races, nominate shown; Australian race *albipennis* similar, but a little larger.

a ADULT MALE BREEDING
b ADULT MALE ECLIPSE: Like c, but whiter head and neck; retains breeding wing pattern.
c ADULT FEMALE
d JUVENILE: Like c, but duller, with broader eye-line.

68 African Pygmy Goose *Nettapus auritus*   **Text page 192**

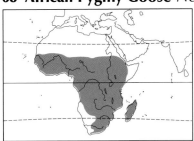

Tropical Africa; local, but commoner in south. Tropical lakes and pools. Tiny size, rufous underparts and whitish 'face' of male distinctive. Female duller, but rufous underparts still conspicuous. In flight, blackish wings show conspicuous white patch.

a ADULT MALE BREEDING: In eclipse is like b, but bill brighter.
b ADULT FEMALE: Juvenile very similar.

68a

68a

68b

68b

67a

67a

67c

67b

67d

67c

66a

66a

66c

66b

66c

66d

Hilary Burn

60 Hartlaub's Duck *Pteronetta hartlaubi*   **Text page 184**

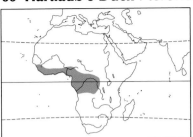

Tropical West Africa. Forest pools and rivers. Chestnut, with black head and neck, but often appears all dark in field, with white head patches of male conspicuous. Note blue-grey forewing in flight.
a ADULT MALE BREEDING
b ADULT FEMALE: Duller, lacks white on head; some pinkish on bill.
c JUVENILE: Duller than b, with buff tips to underpart feathers.
d ADULT MALE: Variant showing incidence of partial albinism, most frequent in Zaire.

70 African Black Duck *Anas sparsa*   **Text page 194**

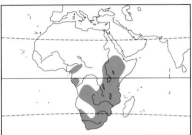

Southern and eastern Africa. Wooded streams and rivers in hilly country. Blackish, with prominent whitish or pale buff barring on upperparts and tail. Two, possibly three races, two shown.
a ADULT (nominate race): Southern Africa. Sexes similar.
b JUVENILE (nominate race): Duller, with narrower barring than a.
c ADULT (race *leucostigma*): Eastern Africa. Upperpart barring buffer, bill pinker than on a.

90 Yellow-billed Duck *Anas undulata*   **Text page 218**

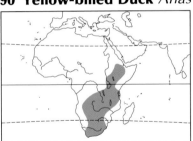

Southern and eastern Africa. Freshwater wetlands in open country. Dark plumage with yellow on bill diagnostic within range, lacks pale barring on upperparts of 70. Two races, both shown.
a ADULT (nominate race): Southern Africa. Sexes similar.
b JUVENILE (nominate race): Duller and browner than a.
c ADULT (race *ruppellii*): Northeastern Africa. Darker, with narrow feather fringes and deeper yellow bill than on a.

90a

90a

90b

90c

70b

70a

70a

70c

60a

60d

60b

60a

60c

Hilary Burn.

65 Crested Duck *Lophonetta specularioides*   **Text page 189**

Southern South America and Falkland Islands. Mountain lakes and coastal bays. Long-bodied buffish-brown duck with dark eye-patch and dark, pointed tail. Two races, nominate shown. Andean race *alticola* is less spotted below and has yellow, not orange-red, iris. In captivity, compare 111 (plate 34). All plumages similar.

a ADULT (nominate race): Southern South America and Falkland Islands.

b JUVENILE (nominate race): Lacks mane on rear of head. Duller, dark mask less conspicuous than on a.

94 Bronze-winged Duck *Anas specularis*   **Text page 221**

Southern South America. Flowing rivers in open or wooded country. White facial pattern and dark wings with large bronze speculum diagnostic.

a ADULT

b JUVENILE: Duller, with smaller facial patch than a.

110 Brazilian Duck *Amazonetta brasiliensis*   **Text page 238**

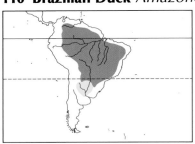

South America. Tropical forest rivers and lakes. Dull brown, with waxy-red bill and legs and pale facial patches of adult male diagnostic; female has bluish bill. Juvenile resembles female. Two phases, pale and dark. Two races, both shown. Compare 108 (plate 34).

a ADULT MALE (nominate race: Lesser Brazilian Duck): Most of range, except south. Dark phase.

b ADULT MALE (nominate race): Pale phase.

c ADULT FEMALE (nominate race): Pale phase.

d ADULT MALE (race *ipecutiri*: Greater Brazilian Duck): Southern portion of range. Larger than a, typically dark phase.

65a

65a

65b

94a

94b

94a

110a

110c

110d

110b

110d

Hilary Burn

71 Wigeon *Anas penelope*

Text page 195

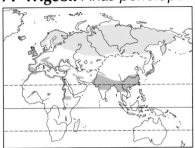

Europe and Asia, wintering south to Africa. Open wetlands, including estuaries. Black and white ventral region, grey body, pink breast and chestnut head diagnostic of male. Female plain and unmottled, with very white belly; very similar to female of 72 (see text), but underwing grey. Juvenile resembles female.
a ADULT MALE BREEDING
b ADULT MALE ECLIPSE: More chestnut than female; retains white forewing.
c ADULT FEMALE: Rufous type. Intermediates between the two types occur, some recalling those of 72.
d ADULT FEMALE: Grey type.

72 American Wigeon *Anas americana*

Text page 197

North and Central America. Open wetlands. Black and white ventral region, pinkish-grey body and whitish head with dark sides diagnostic of male. Female resembles that of 71, but head and neck paler, contrasting with more rufous flanks, underwing whiter (see text). Juvenile resembles female.
a ADULT MALE BREEDING
b ADULT MALE ECLIPSE: More chestnut than c; retains white forewing.
c ADULT FEMALE

73 Chiloe Wigeon *Anas sibilatrix*

Text page 198

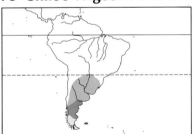

Southern South America and Falkland Islands. Open wetlands. Dark head with whitish patches contrasts with scaled breast and rufous flanks. Plumages similar.
a ADULT MALE
b ADULT FEMALE: Duller than a, but both sexes vary in brightness.
c JUVENILE: Drabber than adults, with obscure cheek patches. Variable.

71a

71a

71c

71c

71b

71d

72a

72b

72c

72c

72a

73a

73b

73a

73b

73c

Hilary Burn

74 Falcated Duck *Anas falcata*   **Text page 199**

Eastern Asia. Open wetlands. Male with large glossy dark head and maned crest, grey body, white throat and long, curved tertials hanging over black and white ventral region. Female recalls that of 75, but bill all dark, legs dark, head and neck plain, flanks weakly scalloped and has buffish line along sides of uppertail-coverts. Juvenile resembles female. See text.

a ADULT MALE BREEDING
b ADULT MALE ECLIPSE: Darker than c, with greyer forewing.
c ADULT FEMALE

75 Gadwall *Anas strepera*   **Text page 200**

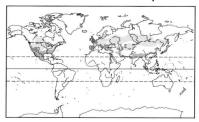

Throughout northern hemisphere. Open wetlands. Male appears grey with blackish rear end; white speculum often shows when on water. Female and juvenile resemble those of 84, but smaller, bill dark with orange sides, belly whiter and speculum absent or partly white. See text.

a ADULT MALE BREEDING
b ADULT MALE ECLIPSE: Greyer and darker than c, with upperwing pattern as a.
c ADULT FEMALE
d JUVENILE: Less marked than b, with warmer underparts and buffer head and neck.

76 Baikal Teal *Anas formosa*   **Text page 202**

Eastern Asia. Open wetlands. Male unmistakable, with stunning head pattern. Female larger than that of 77, more rufous, with strong white loral spot and broken supercilium. Wing pattern differs from those of 101-103 (plate 29), but see text.

a ADULT MALE BREEDING: Head pattern dulled in early winter.
b ADULT MALE ECLIPSE: Often retains some scapulars from breeding plumage.
c ADULT FEMALE
d JUVENILE: Drabber, less rufous, than c.

74a

74c

74b

74a

74c

75b

75a

75c

75a

75c

75d

76a

76c

76b

76a

76c

76d

Hilary Burn

84 Mallard *Anas platyrhynchos*   **Text page 211**

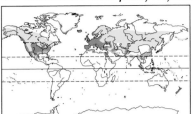

Throughout northern hemisphere; also introduced elsewhere. Open wetlands. Male, with grey body, dark green head, purple-brown breast, unmistakable. Female, with orange and black bill, resembles female of 75 (plate 24), but is larger, with different wing pattern. Often variable (see text) where influenced by feral populations. Wing pattern sometimes essential to separate darkest birds from 87 or 88. Hybridises with 88 and 91. Four races, three illustrated (see also plate 27). See text.
a ADULT MALE BREEDING (nominate race): Most of world range.
b ADULT MALE ECLIPSE (nominate race): Breast rustier than on c, bill uniform.
c ADULT FEMALE (nominate race)
d JUVENILE (nominate race): Underparts more spotted, less scalloped than on c, bill reddish-brown.
e ADULT MALE (race *diazi*: Mexican Duck): Mexico and southern USA. Resembles c, but darker, with dark tail and yellower bill.
f ADULT FEMALE (race *diazi*): Drabber than d, with dingier bill.

87 Mottled Duck *Anas fulvigula*   **Text page 215**

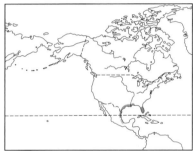

Florida to Texas. Coastal marshes. Resembles female of 84, but darker, with darker tail, yellower bill and virtually no white borders to speculum. Confusable with 88, but not so dark and speculum bluer. Two similar races, one shown. Identification rather complex, see text. Plumages similar.
a ADULT MALE (nominate race: Florida Duck): Florida.
b ADULT FEMALE (nominate race): Duller than a, especially bill.

88 American Black Duck *Anas rubripes*   **Text page 216**

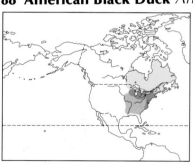

Eastern North America. Open wetlands, especially coastal marshes and estuaries. Resembles very dark females of 84 and 87, but much sootier, with contrasting pale sides of head and neck; lacks any pale in tail or edges to purple speculum. White underwing very striking in flight. Identification and ageing complex, see text. Hybridises with 84.
a ADULT MALE BREEDING
b ADULT FEMALE
c JUVENILE

84a

84b

84c

84a

84c

84d

84e

84e

84f

87a

87b

87a

88a

88a

88c

88b

Hilary Burn.

85 Hawaiian Duck *Anas wyvilliana*   **Text page 213**

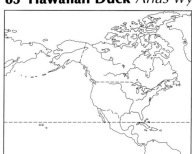

Hawaiian islands of Kauai and Oahu. Resembles small 84 (plate 25), but males never achieve full plumage. May be only a small race of 84.
a ADULT MALE: Brighter type.
b ADULT MALE: Dull type.
c ADULT FEMALE

86 Laysan Duck *Anas laysanensis*   **Text page 214**

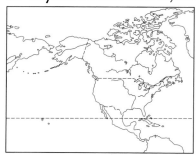

Endemic to Laysan Island (outer Hawaiian Islands). Smaller even than 85, with whitish eye-patches. May be only a small race of 84 (plate 25).
a ADULT MALE
b ADULT FEMALE

89 Meller's Duck *Anas melleri*   **Text page 217**

Endemic to Madagascar (Malagasy), also on Mauritius. Resembles female of 84 (plate 25), but with longer dark grey bill and plainer head; ranges do not overlap. All plumages similar.

93 Philippine Duck *Anas luzonica*   **Text page 221**

Endemic to several of Philippine Islands. Grey body and rufous head diagnostic. All plumages similar.

85a

85a

85b

85c

86a

86a

86b

93

93

89

89

Hilary Burn

84 Mariana Mallard *Anas platyrhynchos oustaleti*   **Text page 213**

Probably extinct, last record 1979. Endemic to Mariana Islands of western Pacific. Apparently a somewhat variable hybrid population of 84 (plate 25) and 91, but most birds closer to 91. Neither 84 nor 91 recorded from the islands. Currently regarded as race of 84, but position debatable. See text.
g ADULT MALE: Dull type
h ADULT FEMALE

91 Pacific Black Duck *Anas superciliosa*   **Text page 218**

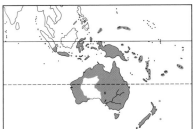

Australasia and western Pacific. Open wetlands. Buff-and-black-striped head pattern contrasts with dark body and bill. All plumages similar. Three races, all similar. Hybridises with introduced 84 (plate 25) in Australasia. Compare 92d.
a ADULT MALE (race *rogersi*): Australia.
b ADULT FEMALE (race *rogersi*): Duller.

92 Spotbill *Anas poecilorhyncha*   **Text page 219**

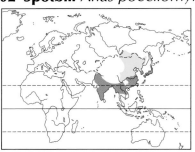

Tropical and eastern Asia. Freshwater lakes, marshes and rivers. Bright yellow bill-tip diagnostic of all races. Whitish sides of head and neck contrast with blackish lower body. White tertials conspicuous, except on d. Three races, two shown; race *haringtoni*, Burmese Spotbill, somewhat intermediate, but closer to nominate; d resembles 91, but bill-tip yellow.
a ADULT MALE (nominate race: Indian Spotbill): Indian subcontinent.
b ADULT FEMALE (nominate race): Smaller, duller; red spots at bill-base small and inconspicuous.
c JUVENILE (nominate race): Duller and browner than b, lacks red spots at bill-base.
d ADULT MALE (race *zonorhyncha*: Chinese Spotbill): Eastern Asia. Browner, lacks red spots on bill, very little white on tertials, and has short, dusky lower cheek-bar (recalling 91).

92a

92b

92a

92c

92d

92d

91a

91a

91b

84g

84g

84h

Hilary Burn.

80 Madagascar Teal *Anas bernieri*

Text page 207

Endemic to western Madagascar (Malagasy). Brackish lagoons and swampy lakes. Rare. Uniform mottled reddish-brown coloration unlike that of any other ducks of the island. All plumages similar. See text.
a ADULT (MALE)
b JUVENILE: Duller.

81 Grey Teal *Anas gibberifrons*

Text page 207

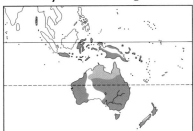

Australasia and East Indies. Open wetlands. Overlaps with 82 and 83. Dull grey-brown teal, with whiter throat and foreneck and very rounded forehead. Very dark wings in flight contrast with white central bar. All plumages similar. Four races, one extinct, two shown, all similar.
a ADULT (race *gracilis*): Australasia.
b JUVENILE (race *gracilis*): Paler, especially on head and neck.
c ADULT (race *albogularis* : Andaman Teal): Andaman Islands.
d ADULT (race *albogularis*): Extreme variant, with much white on head and neck.

82 Chestnut Teal *Anas castanea*

Text page 208

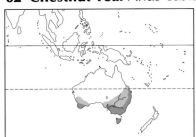

Southern Australia. Open wetlands, chiefly coastal. Male distinctive, with dark green head, chestnut body and black and white ventral region. Female resembles 81, but warmer brown, with buff face and throat (not contrastingly whiter as on 81).
a ADULT MALE BREEDING: In eclipse resembles b, but flanks rustier.
b ADULT FEMALE

83 Brown Teal *Anas aucklandica*

Text page 209

New Zealand. Coastal wetlands and island shores. All forms rare and endangered. Much darker than 81, with head uniformly dark, whitish eye-ring; body plumage varies with races. Three races, two shown, other confined to Campbell Island (race *nesiotis*, not shown on map). Nominate and race *nesiotis* both flightless. See text.
a ADULT MALE BREEDING (race *chlorotis*: New Zealand Teal): Main islands. In eclipse resembles b, but shows weak ventral patch.
b ADULT FEMALE (race *chlorotis*): Duller, lacks green on head and whitish ventral patch.
c JUVENILE (race *chlorotis*): As b, but darker markings below.
d ADULT MALE (nominate race: Auckland Islands Teal): Auckland Islands. Very dark and flightless.
e ADULT FEMALE (nominate race): Duller, flanks less barred, eye-ring narrower.

80a

80a

80b

81a

81a

81c

81b

81d

82b

82b

82a

82a

83a

83b

83e

83b

83c

83a

83d

Hilary Burn

77 Teal or Green-winged Teal *Anas crecca* **Text page 203**

Northern hemisphere. Open wetlands. Very small. Male distinctive, with grey body, chestnut and dark green head, and buff and black undertail-coverts. Female resembles others on plate, but head pattern plain, bill small, lacks blue or pale forewing and has green speculum. See also 76 (plate 24). Three races, two shown, other (race *nimia* of Aleutian Islands) similar to nominate.

a ADULT MALE BREEDING (nominate race: Teal): Europe and Asia, wintering south to Africa.
b ADULT MALE ECLIPSE: As c, but darker and duller; weaker eye-stripe.
c ADULT FEMALE
d JUVENILE: As c, but darker, with spotted belly centre.
e ADULT MALE BREEDING (race *carolinensis*: Green-winged Teal): North America. As a, but has white breast stripe, finer buff lines on head, and lacks white stripe along scapulars.

101 Garganey *Anas querquedula* **Text page 228**

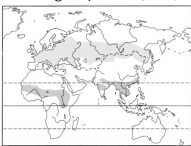

Europe and Asia, wintering mostly in northern tropics. Freshwater wetlands. Overlaps with 77. Male with white head stripe, brown head and breast, and pale grey flanks; in flight, upperwing very pale grey, including primary coverts. Female has strong head pattern, very white belly (mottled on juvenile), and pale grey-brown upperwing with dull speculum and white trailing edge. See text.

a ADULT MALE BREEDING
b ADULT MALE ECLIPSE: Like c, but upperwing as a.
c ADULT FEMALE
d JUVENILE: Like c, but belly mottled.

102 Blue-winged Teal *Anas discors* **Text page 229**

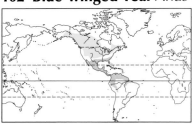

Americas. Freshwater wetlands. Overlaps with 103. Male has dark grey head, white facial crescent, spotted underparts and black and white ventral region. Female resembles 101, but head much duller with whitish loral spot, belly mottled, and has blue forewing with dark primary coverts and secondaries. See text.

a ADULT MALE BREEDING
b ADULT MALE ECLIPSE: Like c, but broader greater-covert bar on upperwing.
c ADULT FEMALE
d JUVENILE: Like c, but legs greyer.

103 Cinnamon Teal *Anas cyanoptera* **Text page 231**

Americas. Freshwater wetlands. Overlaps with 102. Bright rusty male unmistakable. Other plumages very close to 102, but head plainer and body colour warmer brown; wings similar. See text for discussion. Five races, all similar; northern race *septentrionalium* shown, see text for others.

a ADULT MALE BREEDING
b ADULT MALE ECLIPSE: Like c, but broader greater-covert bar and rustier body plumage.
c ADULT FEMALE
d JUVENILE: Like c, but legs greyer.

77a
77c
77a
77c
77d
77e
77b

101c
101a
101a
101c
101d
101b

102c
102a
102c
102a
102d
102b

103c
103a
103c
103d
103a
103b

Hilary Burn

78 Speckled Teal *Anas flavirostris*   **Text page 204**

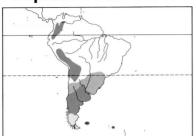

South America. Open wetlands and Andean lakes. Two groups of races, one with yellow bill sides ('Yellow-billed Teal'), the other with blue-grey bill sides ('Andean Teal'), perhaps two species. Only small dark-headed teal with plain flanks in South America. Compare with larger, longer and more mottled 96 (plate 31). Four races, three shown. See text.

a ADULT MALE (race *oxyptera*: Sharp-winged Teal): Andean lakes, from Peru to northern Argentina.
b ADULT FEMALE (race *oxyptera*): Duller than a.
c ADULT MALE (nominate race: Chilean Teal): Lowlands of southern South America, Falkland Islands and South Georgia. Duller and greyer-flanked than a.
d ADULT MALE (race *andium*: Andean Teal): Ecuador and Colombia. Drabber and greyer than a or c, with blue-grey bill sides.
e ADULT FEMALE (race *andium*): As d, but duller.

97 White-cheeked Pintail *Anas bahamensis*   **Text page 224**

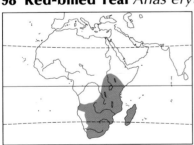

West Indies, Galapagos Islands and South America. Open wetlands, chiefly coastal. White sides of head and neck, buffish pointed tail and red bill-base diagnostic. Compare 98 in captivity. Three races, nominate shown. All similar, but Galapagos race *galapagensis* duller. All plumages similar. See text for racial distribution.

a ADULT MALE
b ADULT FEMALE: Smaller and duller, with slightly shorter tail.
c LEUCISTIC: Common aberration in captivity, frequently escapes.

98 Red-billed Teal *Anas erythrorhyncha*   **Text page 225**

Southern and eastern Africa. Open wetlands. Pale sides of head and neck, dark crown and nape and red bill diagnostic within range. In captivity compare 97, which has red only at bill-base, longer tail, and is brighter overall. All plumages similar.

a ADULT
b JUVENILE: Duller and buffer, with dingy bill.

78a

78a

78b

78c

78d

78d

78e

97a

97b

97a

97c

98b

98a

98a

Hilary Burn

95 Northern Pintail *Anas acuta* **Text page 222**

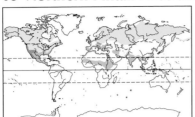

Northern hemisphere, with isolated island races in southern Indian Ocean. Open wetlands. Male has white breast, dark brown head, grey body, pale buff and black ventral region and long tail. Female more elegant than other northern *Anas*, with plain head and neck, pointed tail, grey legs and slender bill. In flight, underwing marbled grey and neck long. Three races, two shown. Southern island races perhaps full species, 'Eaton's Pintail'. See text.

a ADULT MALE BREEDING (nominate race): Most of world range.
b ADULT MALE ECLIPSE (nominate race): Greyer above than c, with male wing and scapulars. Variable.
c ADULT FEMALE (nominate race)
d JUVENILE (nominate race): As c, but broader dark feather centres on flanks and darker upperparts.
e ADULT MALE BREEDING (race *eatoni*: Kerguelen Pintail): Kerguelen Islands, introduced Amsterdam and St Paul Islands. Smaller and darker than c, does not attain full breeding male plumage. Crozet Island race *drygalskyi* similar.
f ADULT MALE BREEDING (race *eatoni*): Very bright individual.
g ADULT FEMALE (race *eatoni*): Smaller and darker than c.

96 Yellow-billed Pintail *Anas georgica* **Text page 223**

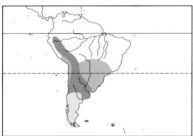

South America, Falkland Islands and South Georgia. Open wetlands. Apart from some races of 78 (plate 30), only yellow-billed duck in South America. Differs from 78 in being larger, longer and more elegant, more uniformly brown, with mottled flanks and long pointed tail. All plumages similar. Three races, one extinct, others shown. See text.

a ADULT MALE (race *spinicauda*: Chilean or Brown Pintail): South America and Falkland Islands. Large race.
b ADULT FEMALE (race *spinicauda*): Duller, with shorter tail than a.
c ADULT MALE (nominate race: South Georgia Teal or Pintail): South Georgia. Smaller, shorter-bodied and darker than a.

95a

95a

95c

95d

95c

95b

95e

95g

95f

96a

96a

96c

96b

Hilary Burn

79 Cape Teal *Anas capensis*

Text page 206

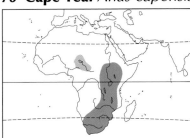

Sub-Saharan Africa. Open wetlands. Very pale, with plain head, spotted flanks and red bill-base. Unmistakable. All plumages similar.
a ADULT
b JUVENILE: Body markings more diffuse than on a.

99 Silver Teal *Anas versicolor*

Text page 226

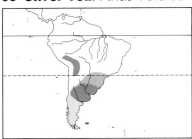

South America. Open wetlands and mountain lakes. Blue sides to bill, blackish crown and very pale sides of head and neck diagnostic within range, but compare 100 in captivity. All plumages similar. Three races, two shown. Race *puna* probably a separate species (see text).
a ADULT MALE (nominate race: Silver Teal): Lowland South America south to central Chile and Argentina.
b ADULT FEMALE (nominate race): Duller, with less yellow at bill-base and shorter tertials than a.
c JUVENILE (nominate race): Duller than b, crown browner, tertials short.
d ADULT MALE (race *puna*: Puna Teal): Andean lakes, from northern Chile to Peru and Bolivia. Large, lacks yellow on bill; flank bars narrower than on a.
e ADULT FEMALE (race *puna*): Duller and browner below than d, with wider brown flank barring.

100 Hottentot Teal *Anas hottentota*

Text page 227

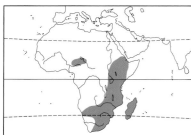
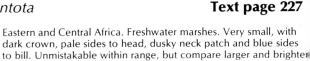

Eastern and Central Africa. Freshwater marshes. Very small, with dark crown, pale sides to head, dusky neck patch and blue sides to bill. Unmistakable within range, but compare larger and brighter 99 in captivity. All plumages similar.
a ADULT MALE: Female is duller, especially on bill, with speculum less extensive.
b JUVENILE: As female, but duller, especially speculum.

79a

79a

79b

100a

100b

100a

99a

99a

99b

99c

99d

99d

99e

Hilary Burn

Freshwater dabbling ducks with enormous bills. The four species are similar in size and structure, and identification of other than breeding males can be tricky, although ranges do not normally overlap. In all species juvenile similar to female, but speculum dull, forewing drabber grey and greater-covert bar narrower. See texts.

104 Red Shoveler *Anas platalea*   **Text page 232**

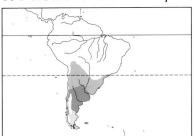

Southern South America, where the only shoveler. Longer-tailed and more slender than other shovelers. Male has plain head, intensely-spotted underparts and white sides to pointed tail. Female more clearly marked than others, with very dark bill and pointed tail. Compare eclipse male of 103 (plate 29), which has similar wing pattern.
a ADULT MALE
b ADULT FEMALE

105 Cape Shoveler *Anas smithii*   **Text page 233**

Southern Africa, where 107 occurs as vagrant. Stockier than 107b, with darker body, bill and tail and with yellower legs.
a ADULT MALE
b ADULT FEMALE

106 Australasian Shoveler *Anas rhynchotis*   **Text page 234**

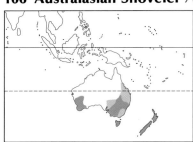

Australia and New Zealand, where only shoveler, but 107 recorded as vagrant to Australia. Compare also 45 (plate 34). Male close to 107c (see text). Female darker than 107b, and with duller legs. Two races, both shown.
a ADULT MALE BREEDING (race *rhynchotis*: Australian Shoveler): Australia.
b ADULT FEMALE
c ADULT MALE ECLIPSE: More rufous on flanks and bluer forewing than b.
d ADULT MALE BREEDING (race *variegata*: New Zealand Shoveler): New Zealand. Brighter than a, with whiter breast, clearer facial crescent and less mottled flanks.

107 Northern Shoveler *Anas clypeata*   **Text page 235**

Northern hemisphere, where the only shoveler. Recorded as a vagrant within ranges of 105 and 106. Male has white breast, chestnut flanks, dark head and huge bill. Latter easily distinguishes female from that of larger 84 (plate 25). Fleshy-orange gape and pale sides to tail useful distinction from other female shovelers.
a ADULT MALE BREEDING: Eclipse male differs from b in having forewing brighter and bluer.
b ADULT FEMALE
c ADULT MALE SUB-ECLIPSE: Autumn plumage stage attained between female-like eclipse and breeding; remarkable resemblance to 106a and 106d.

107a

107b

107c

107a

107b

106a

106b

106d

106c

106a

106b

104a

104b

104b

104a

105a

105a

105b

105b

Hilary Burn

45 Pink-eared Duck *Malacorhynchus membranaceus*   **Text page 169**

Australia. Shallow fresh water. Unmistakable. Large bill recalls 106 (plate 33), but smaller size, barred flanks and black facial patches diagnostic. Underside appears pale in flight. All plumages similar.
a ADULT
b JUVENILE: Slightly duller.

69 Salvadori's Duck *Salvadorina waigiuensis*   **Text page 193**

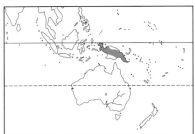

New Guinea. Mountain rivers and lakes. Long-bodied, barred greyish-brown with darker head, and yellow bill (adults). Often perches on river boulders. All plumages similar.
a ADULT
b JUVENILE: Duller, with dingy bill.

108 Ringed Teal *Callonetta leucophrys*   **Text page 237**

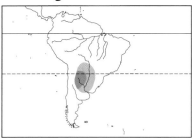

South America. Forest lakes and pools. Small. Male has pale head and underparts, spotted pink breast, dark crown and nape centre, and black and white vent. Female brown, darker above, with white face patches and weakly-barred flanks. All plumages with blackish wings showing white central patch on upperside. Compare female of 110 (plate 22).
a ADULT MALE
b ADULT FEMALE: Juvenile resembles female, but face pattern duller, flanks less barred.
c IMMATURE MALE

111 Marbled Duck *Marmaronetta angustirostris*   **Text page 239**

Mediterranean and western Asia. Lakes. Pale sandy-brown, with dusky mask and bill. In flight, pale and plain-winged. All plumages similar. In captivity, compare larger, dark-tailed 65 (plate 22).
a ADULT (MALE)
b JUVENILE: Duller, with less spotted flanks; lacks loose mane on nape.

45a

45a

45b

111a

111b

111a

69a

69a

69b

108a

108b

108c

108a

108b

Hilary Burn

113 Red-crested Pochard *Netta rufina*

Text page 241

Europe and Asia. Freshwater lakes. Male with red bill, rusty-orange head, black breast and ventral region, dark brown upperparts and white flanks. Female with pale sides of head and neck, dark brown crown and nape. Compare female of 134 (plate 42). All plumages with extensive white in wings.

a ADULT MALE BREEDING
b ADULT MALE ECLIPSE: Like c, but bill red.
c ADULT FEMALE: Juvenile is similar, but bill duller.

114 Southern Pochard *Netta erythrophthalma*

Text page 242

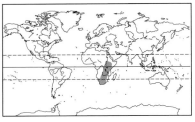

Africa and South America (where very rare). Lakes. Male very dark, with broad white wing-band, relatively long, pale grey bill, and slight peak at rear crown. Female recalls that of 115, but darker, with strong white facial pattern and dark underwing. Two races, both similar. African race *brunnea* shown.

a ADULT MALE
b ADULT FEMALE
c JUVENILE: Less white on face than b, lighter brown.

115 Rosybill *Netta peposaca*

Text page 243

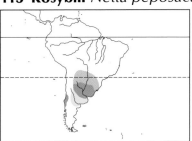

South America. Freshwater marshes and lakes. Male unmistakable with red bill, blackish plumage, grey flanks and white undertail-coverts. Female recalls that of 114, but lighter brown, with whiter underwing and undertail-coverts, head usually plainer.

a ADULT MALE
b ADULT FEMALE: Often lacks whitish on head. Juvenile is similar.
c IMMATURE MALE

113a

113a

113c

113c

113b

114a

114a

114b

114b

114c

115a

115a

115b

115c

115b

Hilary Burn -

116 Canvasback *Aythya valisineria*

Text page 245

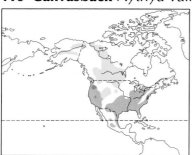

North America. Open wetlands. Range overlaps with that of 118, but larger, with all-dark longer bill and sloping head profile. Male like those of 117 and 118, but larger, with much whiter body, blacker front of head, different head-and-bill shape, and blackish bill. Other plumages resemble 117 and 118; size and shape of head and bill most useful differences, but body typically paler. Ageing difficult (see text).

a ADULT MALE BREEDING
b ADULT MALE ECLIPSE
c ADULT FEMALE
d JUVENILE

117 Pochard *Aythya ferina*

Text page 246

Europe and Asia. Open wetlands, chiefly fresh water. Head-and-bill shape intermediate between 116 and 118, but ranges do not overlap. Male smaller and slightly greyer on body than 116, with two-toned bill and all-red head. See also 118. Female darker than that of 116, with less remarkable head shape; bill usually shows pale band but often all dark, body typically darker. Ageing difficult (see text). Compare also female of 119 (plate 38).

a ADULT MALE BREEDING
b ADULT MALE ECLIPSE
c ADULT FEMALE
d JUVENILE

118 Redhead *Aythya americana*

Text page 248

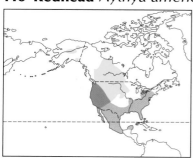

North America. Open wetlands. Overlaps in range with 116, but smaller, with rounded forehead and two-toned bill. Compared with 116 and 117, male darker grey, with yellow (not red) iris; head all red as on 117. Female more uniform and warmer brown than females of both 116 and 117. Ageing difficult (see text). Compare also female of 119 (plate 38).

a ADULT MALE BREEDING
b ADULT MALE ECLIPSE
c ADULT FEMALE
d JUVENILE

117a
117b
117a
117c
117c
117d

116a
116a
116b
116c
116c
116d

118a
118b
118a
118c
118c
118d

Hilary Burn

White-eyes include four species of freshwater pochards (with 120 of plate 38). Males are reddish or chestnut-brown, have white undertail-coverts, prominent white upperwing-stripes and white irides. Females and juveniles are duller, with dark eyes, recalling similar plumages of 125 (plate 39), differing in head shape and prominence of white undertail-coverts (see text). Ranges of white-eyes do not overlap (except occasionally 121 and 122).

121 Baer's Pochard *Aythya baeri*   Text page 251

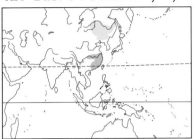

Eastern Asia. Freshwater lakes and rivers. Range marginally overlaps with that of 122 in winter. Larger, with white belly showing above water line (only on fore-flanks when swimming lower in water than depicted). Head less peaked and bill heavier than on 122, male with dark green head when breeding. Compare 125 (plate 39). See text.
a ADULT MALE BREEDING
b ADULT MALE ECLIPSE: Head reddish as on c, but iris white.
c ADULT FEMALE: Light brown loral spot, lacking on 122c.
d JUVENILE: Duller and less uniform than c.

122 Ferruginous Duck *Aythya nyroca*   Text page 252

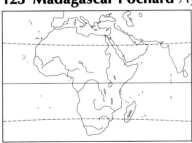

Southern Europe and Asia, winters south to North Africa. Freshwater marshes and lakes. Marginal overlap with 121. Smaller and richer chestnut than 121, with taller crown and more slender bill. White belly normally below water line; if visible, does not reach peak on fore-flanks. Female and juvenile recall those of 125 (plate 39), but head shape differs and bill lacks prominent pale subterminal line. See text.
a ADULT MALE BREEDING
b ADULT MALE ECLIPSE: Duller, but retains white iris.
c ADULT FEMALE: Lacks loral spot of 121.
d JUVENILE: Duller and browner than c; slightly mottled on flanks and head.

123 Madagascar Pochard *Aythya innotata*   Text page 253

Central Madagascar (Malagasy). Plateau lakes. Perhaps extinct, last report 1970. Larger and darker than 122; the only pochard of Madagascar, so confusion unlikely. None in captivity.
a ADULT MALE BREEDING
b ADULT MALE ECLIPSE
c ADULT FEMALE
d JUVENILE

121a

121a

121b

121c

121d

122a

122c

122a

122d

122b

123a

123a

123c

123b

123d

Hilary Burn

119 Ring-necked Duck *Aythya collaris*   **Text page 249**

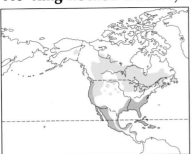

North America. Open wetlands, chiefly fresh water. Prominent bil bands and high peak to rear crown distinctive in all plumages. Male recalls partial-eclipse 125 (plate 39), with which it overlaps a a vagrant, but head shape and bill pattern differ. Female recalls dark females of 117 and 118 (plate 36), but note head and bill differences. See text for discussion on ageing. In flight, lacks white wing-band of 125.

a ADULT MALE BREEDING
b ADULT MALE ECLIPSE
c ADULT FEMALE
d JUVENILE
e FIRST-WINTER MALE

120 Hardhead *Aythya australis*   **Text page 250**

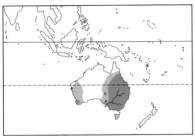

Australia. Freshwater wetlands. Occasional irruptions take it to outlying regions (see text). Only member of genus in Australia. Longer-bodied and longer-necked than other white-eyes (see plate 37), with broad pale subterminal bill-band, most prominent on males. See text.

a ADULT MALE
b ADULT FEMALE: Duller and browner than a; iris dark, bill-band narrower.
c JUVENILE: As b, but paler; belly mottled.

124 New Zealand Scaup *Aythya novaeseelandiae*   **Text page 254**

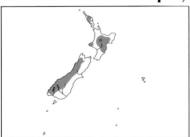

New Zealand. Upland lakes and coastal lagoons. Both sexes very dark, with steeply-rounded forehead. Female with white frontal band recalls 126 and 127, but ranges do not overlap. In captivity, distinguished by darker body and more black at bill-tip than on 126 and 127.

a ADULT MALE
b ADULT FEMALE
c JUVENILE: Lacks frontal patch, belly paler than on b.

120a

120c

120b

120a

124a

124c

124b

124a

119a

119d

119c

119e

119c

119b

119a

Hilary Burn

125 **Tufted Duck** *Aythya fuligula*

Text page 255

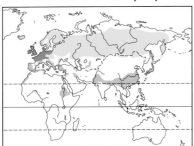

Europe and Asia, winters south to Africa. Open fresh water. Male distinctive: black, with white flanks, and long drooping crest on nape. Other plumages confusable with several others of genus. Head-and-bill shape important, showing steeply-rounded forehead, flat crown centre, and ruffled appearance to rear crown. Compare head shapes of 122 (plate 37) and 119 (plate 38). Female and juvenile variable, often showing whitish undertail-coverts of 122 or frontal patches of 126 and 127. See text for discussion.

a ADULT MALE BREEDING
b ADULT MALE ECLIPSE
c ADULT FEMALE: Variant with whitish face.
d ADULT FEMALE: Variant with white undertail-coverts.
e JUVENILE: Tuft indistinct; buffish-brown areas on lores and flanks.

126 **Greater Scaup** *Aythya marila*

Text page 256

Northern hemisphere. Lakes and coastal waters. Very similar to 127, but more marine outside breeding season. See 127 for differences. Male with pale grey upperparts, white flanks and black head and breast. Female and juvenile recall those of 125, but larger, with larger bill which has less black at tip, rounded head shape, lacking tuft, and often pale 'ear' patch; body plumage with grey 'frosting'. Two similar races, nominate shown. See text for ageing and full discussion.

a ADULT MALE BREEDING
b ADULT MALE ECLIPSE
c ADULT FEMALE: Fresh plumage, 'ear' patch obscured.
d ADULT FEMALE: 'Ear' patch shows with wear.
e JUVENILE

127 **Lesser Scaup** *Aythya affinis*

Text page 258

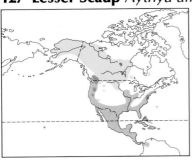

North America. Open wetlands. Very similar to 126, but smaller, with small tuft on rear crown, smaller bill with more concave culmen. Male has darker vermiculations above; head usually glossed purple (rarely, green as on 126). Other plumages similar; shape easiest distinction. Female often shows weak 'ear' patch like 126. In flight, white confined to secondaries, not extending to inner primaries as on 126. See text for full discussion and ageing. Beware hybrid 117 × 125 in Europe.

a ADULT MALE BREEDING
b ADULT MALE ECLIPSE: Darker than 126b.
c ADULT FEMALE: Shows weak 'ear' patch when plumage worn, like 126d.
d JUVENILE

125a

125d

125e

125c

125b

125d

125a

126a

126c

126d

126e

126c

126b

126a

127a

127d

127c

127c

127b

127a

Hilary Burn

Large sea-ducks of northern coastal waters. Adult males distinctive, but other plumages similar; immatures take two or more years to reach maturity, males having confusing variety of piebald plumages. Head-and-bill shape important, especially extent of feathering onto bill-base.

129 Common Eider *Somateria mollissima*   Text page 260

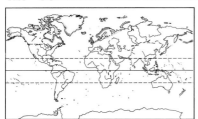

Northern hemisphere. Coastal waters. Male with black crown and underparts, white breast and upperparts. Female and other plumages like those of 130 and 131. Partial-plumage males often with white on scapulars (not on 130) or breast (not on 131). Female barred on flanks (like 131, but flank marks angled on 130), with feathering reaching nostrils in point and line of gape straight and inconspicuous (compare 130). See text for discussion, including ageing and races. Six races, three shown.

a ADULT MALE BREEDING (nominate race): Europe.
b ADULT MALE ECLIPSE (nominate race): Only partial eclipse shown.
c ADULT FEMALE (nominate race): General tone of colour varies racially from dull greyish-brown to rufous-brown.
d JUVENILE (nominate race)
e IMMATURE MALE (nominate race)
f ADULT MALE BREEDING (race *borealis*): Canada to Svalbard. Bill orange, even in eclipse (compare 130b). Eastern populations greyer-billed.
g ADULT MALE BREEDING (race *dresseri*): Northeastern North America. Broad strip of facial skin to eye, narrower in other races.

130 King Eider *Somateria spectabilis*   Text page 262

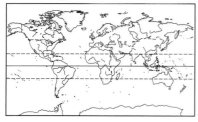

Northern hemisphere. Arctic coasts. Male with black upperparts and underparts, white breast, light blue head, swollen orange forehead and red bill. Female with angled flank markings (compare 129 and 131), shorter head than 129, with rounded feather extension at bill sides falling short of nostrils; gape line curves up and crosses small pale spot at gape. In flight, underwing whiter than on female 129 or 131, but see smaller 128 (plate 41). See text for discussion.

a ADULT MALE BREEDING
b ADULT MALE ECLIPSE: Compare 129f.
c ADULT FEMALE
d JUVENILE
e IMMATURE MALE

131 Spectacled Eider *Somateria fischeri*   Text page 263

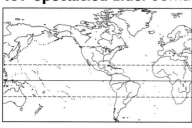

Alaska and eastern Siberia. Arctic coasts. Bill cloaked by feathering and 'goggles' apparent in all plumages. Male slaty-black and creamy-white, with black breast and greenish crown. Female more rufous-buff than other eiders, and dark brown forehead contrasts with pale 'goggles'. In flight, underwing darker than on others. See text.

a ADULT MALE BREEDING
b ADULT MALE ECLIPSE
c ADULT FEMALE
d JUVENILE

129a

129c

129f

129a

129g

129c

129b

129d

129e

130a

130a

130c

130c

130b

130e

130d

131a

131c

131b

131a

131d

131c

Hilary Burn

131c

128 Steller's Eider *Polysticta stelleri*   **Text page 259**

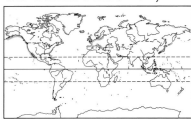

Eastern Siberia and Alaska. Arctic coasts. Smallest eider, with conventional bill shape and feathering. Male with rufous-buff underparts, contrasting with black and white upperparts, black ventral region, and whitish head with black collar. Female uniform dark rusty-brown, less obviously marked than larger eiders. Immature males show more mottled transitional plumage than others. See text.

a ADULT MALE BREEDING
b ADULT MALE ECLIPSE
c ADULT FEMALE
d JUVENILE
e IMMATURE MALE

132 Harlequin Duck *Histrionicus histrionicus*   **Text page 264**

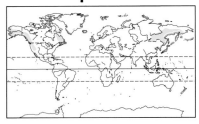

Eastern Asia, North America to Iceland. Coastal waters and mountain rivers. Male distinctive, but appears dark at long range with white stripes and facial crescent. Female and juvenile similar, very dark with white face spots; approached by darkest juvenile 137, but underparts dark, not whitish (although belly centre slightly lighter).

a ADULT MALE BREEDING
b ADULT MALE ECLIPSE
c ADULT FEMALE

137 Long-tailed Duck or Oldsquaw *Clangula hyemalis*   **Text page 270**

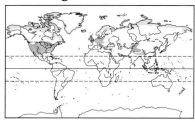

Northern hemisphere. Lakes and coastal waters. Small sea-duck, with rounded head and short bill. Plumage variation and moults complex, ageing difficult (see text). Adult male unmistakable; others variable, typically with dark upperparts and breast and white flanks, belly and eye-patches. Most likely confusion is of darkest birds with 132, but flanks and belly always whitish.

a ADULT MALE SUMMER
b ADULT MALE WINTER
c ADULT FEMALE SUMMER
d ADULT FEMALE WINTER
e JUVENILE
f IMMATURE MALE

128a

128a

128c

128b

128c

128e

128d

132a

132c

132a

132c

132b

132a

137a

137b

137a

137b

137c

137e

137d

137c

137b

137d

137f

Hilary Burn

134 **Common or Black Scoter** *Melanitta nigra*   **Text page 266**

Northern hemisphere. Coastal waters, occasionally lakes. Male all black, with yellow on bill; lacks white in wings of 136 or on head of 135. Female dark brown, with very pale sides of head and neck; recalls female of 113 (plate 35), but shape differs, and latter a freshwater duck with much white in wing (hidden when on water). Juvenile resembles female, but paler, with whiter belly. Two races, which may be separate species; only males separable in the field.

a ADULT MALE (nominate race: Common Scoter): Europe and western Asia.
b ADULT FEMALE
c IMMATURE MALE (nominate race): With pale cheeks obscured by adult male feathers, head pattern recalls that of female and juveniles of 135 and 136.
d ADULT MALE (race *americana*: Black Scoter): Eastern Asia and North America. Bill chiefly yellow, with black tip.

135 **Surf Scoter** *Melanitta perspicillata*   **Text page 267**

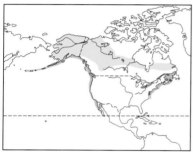

North America. Coastal waters, occasionally lakes. Heavy head-and-bill shape recalls that of 129 (plate 40). Male with brightly-coloured bill and large white head patches, otherwise all black. Female and juvenile with pale cheek spots like those of 136, but lack white in wing and are stockier, especially head and bill. Beware 134c.

a ADULT MALE
b ADULT FEMALE: Usually pale nape patch and dusky belly.
c JUVENILE: Browner than b, with whiter belly and dark nape.
d IMMATURE MALE: Less white on head than a.

136 **Velvet or White-winged Scoter** *Melanitta fusca*   **Text page 268**

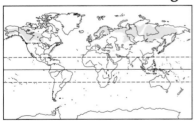

Northern hemisphere. Coastal waters and lakes. Largest scoter, differing from other two in having white secondaries (hidden on water). Head shape recalls 129 (plate 40), but less bulky than 135. Male black, with pale bill and black basal knob. Female dark brown with pale cheek spots, recalling female of 135 and immature male of 134, but larger, longer-bodied and with white in wings. Three races, two shown, which may be two species (see text).

a ADULT MALE (nominate race: Velvet Scoter): Europe and western Asia.
b ADULT FEMALE: Cheek spots obscured in fresh plumage. Juvenile is similar, but lighter brown.
c IMMATURE MALE (nominate race): Duller than a, lacks eye-patch.
d ADULT MALE (race *stejnegeri*: White-winged Scoter): Eastern Asia. Taller knob on bill than a, with more black at base. American race *deglandi* has intermediate bill and browner flanks.

134a

134b

134b

134a

134d

134c

136a

136a

136b

136b

136c

136d

135a

135b

135a

135c

135b

135d

Hilary Burn

138 Bufflehead *Bucephala albeola*

Text page 271

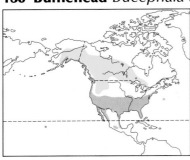

North America. Lakes and coastal waters. Small. Male distinctive, with enormous black and white head; bill stubbier than on 142 (plate 44) and flanks whiter, lacking breast stripes. Female and juvenile grey-brown, with darker head and white flash behind eye Wing pattern recalls 140.

a ADULT MALE BREEDING
b ADULT MALE ECLIPSE: More white on head and wing than c.
c ADULT FEMALE: Juvenile is similar, but paler brown.
d IMMATURE MALE: Larger head patch than female by late first winter, but full male plumage not gained until second winter.

139 Barrow's Goldeneye *Bucephala islandica*

Text page 272

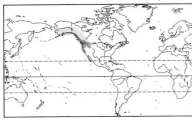

North America and Iceland. Lakes and coastal waters. Larger than 140, with more bulging forehead in all plumages. Male with blacker upperparts and white facial crescent. Female and juvenile similar to those of 140, head shape and larger size most useful feature; western females have all-yellow bill, very rarely so in 140. See text for discussion.

a ADULT MALE BREEDING
b ADULT MALE ECLIPSE: Partial shown. Full eclipse like c, but bill black and wing as breeding.
c ADULT FEMALE: Western type, with yellow bill.
d ADULT FEMALE: Eastern type, with bill like 140c.
e JUVENILE: Duller than c/d, with dark bill and greyer breast.
f IMMATURE MALE: Late first winter, with male features developing.

140 Common Goldeneye *Bucephala clangula*

Text page 273

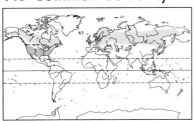

Northern hemisphere. Lakes and coastal waters. Smaller than 139, with more sloping forehead giving triangular head shape. Male with less black above than 139 and small round loral spot. Female and juvenile differ from 139 chiefly in size and head shape; bill very rarely all yellow. See text for discussion. Two races, similar, nominate shown.

a ADULT MALE BREEDING
b ADULT MALE ECLIPSE: Partial shown. Full eclipse like c, but wing-coverts white as breeding.
c ADULT FEMALE
d JUVENILE: Duller than c, with dark bill and grey breast.
e IMMATURE MALE: Late first winter, with male features developing.

138c

138a

138c

138b

138a

138c

138d

140d

140c

140a

140b

140a

140e

140a

140c

139d

139a

139a

139b

139c

139e

139d Hilary Burn

139f

PLATE 44: Small sawbills and Brazilian Merganser

141 Smew *Mergellus albellus* Text page 274

Europe and Asia. Lakes and coastal waters. Small diving duck. At longer distances, male almost white, with black face patch; unmistakable. Female and juvenile grey-brown, with chestnut head and white throat and lower cheek; juvenile much as female, but lores browner, not blackish. Sometimes hybridises with 140 (see text).

a ADULT MALE BREEDING
b ADULT MALE ECLIPSE: Like c, but more white on wing-coverts.
c ADULT FEMALE
d IMMATURE MALE: Late first winter; resembles adult breeding by second winter.

142 Hooded Merganser *Lophodytes cucullatus* Text page 276

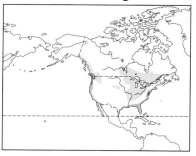

North America. Lakes and slow rivers. Small, with bushy crest and slender bill in all plumages. Male recalls 138 (plate 43), but flanks vermiculated dull rufous, bill slender, and has black and white breast stripes. Female and juvenile like small, short 144 (plate 45), but crest more bushy. Very little white in upperwing in flight. Cocks tail well up when resting on water, recalling 150 (plate 47).

a ADULT MALE BREEDING: Crest may be elevated into broad fan, or depressed when white shows as broad strip; crest shown partially elevated.
b ADULT MALE ECLIPSE: Like c, but iris pale and bill blacker.
c ADULT FEMALE: Juvenile is similar, but crest slightly shorter.
d IMMATURE MALE: Mid first winter; as adult by second winter.

143 Brazilian Merganser *Mergus octosetaceus* Text page 277

Eastern South America. Tropical forest rivers. Rare. Long-bodied, slender, greyish diving duck of rushing waters; spiky crest and long bill unlike any other species in its range. Unlikely to be confused. All plumages similar (see text). Compare 110 (plate 22) in flight.

a ADULT MALE
b ADULT FEMALE: Much as a, but bill and crest shorter.

143a

143b

143a

142a

142c

142a

142b

142a

142d

142c

141c

141a

141b

141a

141d

141c

141c

Hilary Burn

144 Red-breasted Merganser *Mergus serrator*   Text page 277

Northern hemisphere. Lakes, rivers and coastal waters. Overlaps i range with 145 and 146. Long-bodied, slender-necked diving duck, with spiky crest and thin bill. Male has dark head and upperparts, white collar, patterned breast sides, grey flanks, and shows extensive white in wing. Female and juvenile dull grey-brown, with whiter breast and warmer brown head and neck, ragged crest and slender bill; head and neck pattern diffuse and drabber than on larger and bulkier 146. See also 145.

a ADULT MALE BREEDING: In eclipse is like b, but has blacker mantle and retains white wing-coverts.

b ADULT FEMALE

c JUVENILE: Like b, but drabber, with shorter crest and greyer breast and central underparts.

d IMMATURE MALE: Late first winter, showing developing male features.

145 Chinese Merganser *Mergus squamatus*   Text page 279

Eastern Asia. Forested rivers and lakes. Rare. Overlaps in range with both 144 and 146, even on same rivers. Slender, more like 144 than 146 in proportions, with very long spiky crest. Male lack dark breast of 144, but has flanks finely scaled. Female differs from 144 in being brighter, with scaled flanks. Juvenile (and possibly summer female) very similar to 144, lacking scaling of breeding female, but nostrils midway along bill (close to bill-base on 144). See text.

a ADULT MALE BREEDING: In eclipse is like b, but retains male wing pattern and has blacker mantle.

b ADULT FEMALE: Juvenile is similar, but lacks underpart scaling. Summer females also possibly lack scaling (see text).

c IMMATURE MALE: Mostly juvenile (little scaling). See text and above.

146 Goosander or Common Merganser *Mergus merganser*   Text page 280

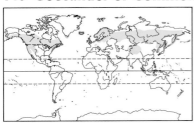

Northern hemisphere. Freshwater lakes and rivers. Larger and bulkier than 144 and 145, with which it overlaps, and has maned rear to head (not spiky). Male with dark head and central upperparts and pinkish or creamy-white breast and underparts. Female and juvenile with darker head and neck than 144 or 145, cleanly demarcated from white breast and throat; upperparts purer grey. Three similar races, nominate shown. See text.

a ADULT MALE BREEDING: In eclipse is like b, but retains male wing pattern and has whiter underparts.

b ADULT FEMALE

c JUVENILE: Duller than b, with lighter brown head and less pure grey upperparts; also has pale loral streak.

d IMMATURE MALE: Develops adult male plumage during first winter, but retains juvenile wing pattern to first-summer moult.

144a

144b

144a

144c

144d

144b

146b

146a

146c

146a

146d

146b

145a

145b

145a

145c

145b

Hilary Burn

10 White-backed Duck *Thalassornis leuconotus*   Text page 132

Africa. Freshwater swampy lakes. Peculiar grebe-like diving duck; swims very low in water, with tail-less appearance and bulky head and bill on slim neck. Plumage barred buff and brown, with darker head and prominent whitish loral patch. All plumages similar. Two races, nominate shown.
a ADULT
b JUVENILE: Duller, with more freckled sides of head and less distinct loral patch than a.

151 White-headed Duck *Oxyura leucocephala*   Text page 285

Mediterranean and western Asia. Freshwater lakes. Only stiff-tail of the region, but vagrants overlap (rarely) with feral 150 (plate 47). Enormous swollen-based blue bill and mostly white (to above eye) head of male diagnostic. Plumages complex (see text).
a ADULT MALE BREEDING
b ADULT MALE ECLIPSE: Body less rufous and has a little more dusky on head than a.
c IMMATURE MALE BREEDING: First-spring males attain extensive blackish mottling on head, in extreme cases head appears all black; otherwise plumage as a.
d ADULT FEMALE: Bill more swollen at base and cheek-bar broader than on most other stiff-tails. Facial bands curve down to bill.
e JUVENILE: Duller than d, with tips of tail feathers spiked.

152 Maccoa Duck *Oxyura maccoa*   Text page 287

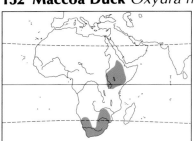

Africa. Freshwater lakes. Only stiff-tail of the region. Distinctive within range, but in captivity male resembles 150f, 153 and 154. Bill larger and broader and with broader and whiter nail than others, but shorter than long-billed 150f. Foreneck chestnut (unlike 153 and 154), rump mottled brown and tail rather shorter than 153. See text for discussion.
a ADULT MALE BREEDING
b ADULT MALE ECLIPSE: Resembles c, but head blacker.
c ADULT FEMALE: Resembles 151d, but bill less swollen at base and upperparts with narrow buff barring, less peppered.
d JUVENILE: Resembles c, but duller and tail tips spiked.

154 Blue-billed Duck *Oxyura australis*   Text page 288

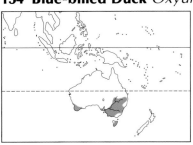

Australia. Only stiff-tail of the region. Distinctive within range, but in captivity male resembles 150f (plate 47), 152 and 153. Wholly black neck distinguishes it from 152 and 150f, and smaller bill and shorter tail from 153. See text. See also 155 (plate 16).
a ADULT MALE BREEDING
b ADULT MALE ECLIPSE: As c, but head and neck blacker, bill brighter.
c ADULT FEMALE: Very plain-headed, lacking strong facial pattern.
d JUVENILE: As c, but paler and with dull greenish-grey bill.

10a

10a

10b

151a

151a

151d

151d

151c

151b

151e

152c

152a

152c

152d

152a

152b

154a

154a

154c

154c

154d

154b

Hilary Burn

148 Black-headed Duck *Heteronetta atricapilla*   **Text page 282**

South America. Swampy freshwater lakes and pools. Distinctive shape, with rather long body, short tail and wings, long bill and fla[ ] crown. Male dull dark brown, with blackish head, blue-grey bill (red at base when breeding) and slightly-vermiculated or peppere[ ] flanks. Female dusky-brown, slightly vermiculated below, with indistinct lighter supercilium and throat. Best identified by shape.

a ADULT MALE BREEDING: Bill is all grey when not breeding.
b ADULT FEMALE: Bill-base becomes yellowish or pink when breeding. Juvenile inseparable.

149 Masked Duck *Nomonyx dominica*   **Text page 282**

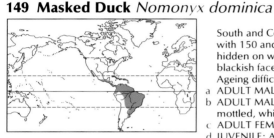

South and Central America. Freshwater marshes. Overlaps in rang[ ] with 150 and 153. At all ages white wing patches distinctive, but hidden on water. Male has stout blue bill with black tip, and blackish face contrasts with rufous, mottled, body plumage. Ageing difficult.

a ADULT MALE BREEDING
b ADULT MALE ECLIPSE: As c, but head buffer, flanks more strongly mottled, white wing patch larger.
c ADULT FEMALE: Two black stripes across side of head.
d JUVENILE: As c, but tail spiked at tip and a little duller.

150 Ruddy Duck *Oxyura jamaicensis*   **Text page 283**

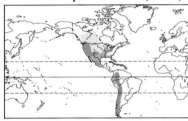

North and South America, ferally in Europe. Range overlaps with 149, 151 (very rarely) and 153. Large black-headed Andean race (f) confusable with 153. In captivity, see also 152 and 154 (plate 46). See text for discussion. Three races, all shown, perhaps f and g separate species but e intermediate.

a ADULT MALE BREEDING (nominate race): North America and Europe.
b ADULT MALE ECLIPSE (nominate race)
c ADULT FEMALE (nominate race)
d JUVENILE (nominate race): As c, but duller; cheek-bar more diffuse and tail-tip spiked.
e ADULT MALE BREEDING (race *andina*: Colombian Ruddy Duck): Colombia. Variable cheek pattern (see text).
f ADULT MALE BREEDING (race *ferruginea*: Peruvian Ruddy Duck): Southern Colombia southwards. Large, long-billed, with black head. Compare 153a.
g ADULT FEMALE (race *ferruginea*): Large and very dark, with weak head pattern. Compare 153c.

153 Argentine Blue-bill *Oxyura vittata*   **Text page 287**

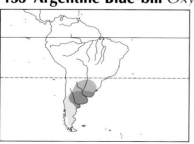

Southern South America. Lowland freshwater lakes. Overlaps locally in range with southernmost 150f and 150g. 153 is smaller, shorter-billed and longer-tailed; male has black (not chestnut) foreneck and female has stronger facial pattern. In captivity, compare 152 and 154. See text.

a ADULT MALE BREEDING
b ADULT MALE ECLIPSE: As c, but body often more rufous.
c ADULT FEMALE: Like 150c, but darker, especially flanks.
d JUVENILE: As c, but lighter, with buffer feather fringes and spiked tail-tip.

148a

148b

148a

149a

149c

149d

149a

149c

149b

150a

150a

150c

150b

150c

150e

150d

150f

150g

153a

153c

153b

153a

153d

153c

Hilary Burn

SYSTEMATIC
SECTION

FAMILY ANSERANATIDAE (MAGPIE GOOSE)

A unique 'goose', although superficially recalling Spur-winged Goose (36) of Africa, the Magpie Goose exhibits many features linking the true wildfowl with the terrestrial screamers (Anhimidae) of South America, the latter resembling gamebirds rather than waterfowl. The long hind toe, slightly-webbed feet, gradual moult progression (thus lacking a flightless period), greatly-elongated trachea (in both sexes) and family trios (one male, two females) are all features that isolate this strange bird.

1 MAGPIE GOOSE   Plate 3
Anseranas semipalmata

Alternative names: Pied Goose, Semipalmated Goose

A peculiar 'goose', the most aberrant of all waterfowl, being the link between the more coventional geese and ducks and their gamebird-like relations, the screamers.

FIELD IDENTIFICATION Length 75-85 cm (30-34 in). **At rest:** Unmistakable. Goose-like size and shape coupled with black and white plumage should prevent confusion with all other Australian wildfowl. Head, neck, most of wings, tail and 'thighs' black (duller and sootier in juveniles), remainder of plumage white. There is no seasonal plumage variation, but during the dry season, when water levels are low, the plumage tends to become stained reddish-brown from stagnant water. **In flight:** Flight action rather slow and ponderous on broad, round-tipped, but well-fingered, wings. From below, shows white underwing-coverts and body, contrasting with black primaries and secondaries, head, neck and tail; from above, the wings are chiefly black and the pied appearance is enhanced by the contrast between the white mantle, uppertail-coverts and lesser wing-coverts and the black wings, rump, tail, head and neck.
VOICE Both sexes quite vocal, uttering a loud and resonant honk, louder and higher in pitch from the male. Calls may be given in flight or on the ground, a call from a male being answered typically by one or more females. On ground, calls may be uttered deliberately with head uplifted, or more rapidly, in the latter case usually triggering similar responses from other birds.
DESCRIPTION Sexes similar in plumage, but male considerably larger than female, with more pronounced cranial knob, although latter develops with age and younger males may be difficult to sex accurately in the field. **Adult:** Head, neck, upper breast, most of wings, rump, tail and tibia black. Underparts, mantle, underwing-coverts, lesser upperwing-coverts and uppertail-coverts white. **Juvenile:** Resembles adult, but black parts of plumage dull and sooty greyish-black, with white areas of plumage sullied with greyish-brown.
BARE PARTS Adult: Bill relatively long and straight with well-developed nail, fleshy-yellow to reddish-flesh with dusky subterminal area and greyish nail; bare facial skin back to eye, dull fleshy, or reddish

in breeding season. Legs relatively long and toes only very slightly webbed, dull yellowish. **Juvenile:** Bill dusky, cranial knob lacking, and leg colour more fleshy, less yellow.
MEASUREMENTS Males considerably larger than females. **Male:** Wing 368-450, tarsus 90-105, bill 72-92, mean weight 2766. **Female:** Wing 356-418, tarsus 80-92, bill 63-82, mean weight 2071.
GEOGRAPHICAL VARIATION None.
HABITS Highly gregarious throughout the year. Found in family parties that gather into enormous concentrations in favoured areas. Feeds on land and on water, by wading, swimming and up-ending. Swims with rear end held high. Perches quite easily, but rarely needs to do so in the wild. Breeding begins with the first rains of the wet season (October/November), some males taking on two females which lay in the same nest; the bond, however, is considered to be for life. Breeds colonially, but breeding density varies according to location and annual conditions of suitability.
HABITAT Wet and dry floodplains of tropical rivers, swamps and damp grasslands, usually within 80 km of the coast.
DISTRIBUTION Breeds over much of northern Australia and southern New Guinea. Reasonably sedentary; local movements occur when locating suitable wetlands during the dry season, but quite extensive movements may be involved in some districts, e.g. some north Australian birds move to New Guinea, where numbers increase greatly from time to time owing to immigration. During exceptionally dry conditions considerable displacement may occur, with birds turning up throughout Australia, some reaching South Australia; vagrants have even been recorded in Tasmania, but today many such birds suspected to be of feral origin. Recent re-introduction attempts have been made in Victoria, but with only limited success as yet.
POPULATION Locally abundant in northern Australia, where it can be legally hunted in the Northern Territory. Elsewhere in Australia it is protected, but breeding areas in southern Australia have long been destroyed by over-hunting. Drainage and intensification of agriculture are possible future threats to favoured sites. An estimate of 350,000 birds was made during 1955-58 in the floodplains between Darwin and Arnhem Land, but no total population estimates seem to have been made.
REFERENCES Frith (1967), Tulloch and McKean (1983).

FAMILY ANATIDAE (TRUE WATERFOWL)
SUBFAMILY DENDROCYGNINAE (WHISTLING DUCKS)

A group of tropical waterfowl, formerly often referred to as 'tree ducks', though many species do not perch and some go nowhere near trees. Generally they are relatively long-legged, long-necked and short-bodied ducks, many species being equally at home walking on dry land as they are on the water. Most species are highly gregarious by nature, gathering in close flocks both at feeding grounds and at their roosts, flighting to and from roost around dawn and dusk. Pair-bond of whistling ducks is considered to be for life. Their peculiar shape renders them relatively easy to identify in flight as whistling ducks, having a slightly hump-backed, long-necked appearance, broad wings (with blackish undersurface and shallow beats) and long legs, which allow the feet to project beyond the end of their short tails. Most species have shrill whistling calls, given freely in flight. The plumages are similar within each species, with hardly any sexual or seasonal variation, although a distinctly drab juvenile plumage is exhibited for a few weeks; immatures soon attain adult-like plumage.

2 SPOTTED WHISTLING DUCK   Plate 1
Dendrocygna guttata
Alternative name: Spotted Tree Duck

Relatively little-known whistling duck of the East Indies and New Guinea. Despite its superficial similarity to Black-billed Whistling Duck (8), it is probably most closely related to the Plumed Whistling Duck (3) of Australia.

FIELD IDENTIFICATION Length 43-50 cm (17-19 in). **At rest:** A dark, medium-sized whistling duck superficially resembling Black-billed Whistling Duck of the West Indies, but distinguished by smaller size, indistinct reddish tones to bill and legs, dusky lores and spotted breast and flanks. Range overlaps with Wandering Whistling Duck (5), which is much paler and buffer on head, neck and breast, has tawny-rufous belly and flanks (latter with clear whitish-buff stripes) and solidly blackish bill and legs. Both species sometimes occur together in mixed flocks. Note that Plumed Whistling Duck has occurred as a vagrant in New Guinea. **In flight:** Typical whistling duck shape. A very dark whistling duck, quite uniform in overall coloration, although rather lighter sides of head and paler belly centre contrast with darker, white-spotted flanks and breast (spotting may not be apparent unless birds at close range). Wandering Whistling Duck shows obviously very pale head and neck, contrasting with uniform tawny-rufous belly and flanks, but note that juvenile Wandering also has pale belly centre. A useful pointer is that Wandering shows a clear whitish uppertail-covert patch, most apparent when birds rising from water ahead of observer; uppertail-coverts appear dusky on Spotted in flight, although they are in fact mottled.
VOICE Generally less obviously vocal than most other whistling ducks, but in flight the wings produce a strong whirring sound. Pairs converse with repeated low whistling sounds, at least in captivity. Calls include a whistled 'whee-ow', a more repeated 'whe-a-whew-whew' and a few low, harsh notes.
DESCRIPTION Sexes similar. **Adult:** Crown, hindneck, collar, eye-patch and lores dusky. Sides of head and neck, supercilium and throat dingy greyish-white. Breast and flanks rufous-brown, profusely marked with white spots which are bordered blackish, largest and most obvious on flanks which appear blackish with white spots, the markings extending to uppertail- and undertail-coverts. Centre of belly to vent dull whitish. Upperparts, including tail, dark brown, with rufous feather edges, most intense on mantle and back which appear basically warm brown with darker feather centres. **Juvenile:** Similar to adult but duller, less warm brown, lacking breast spotting; flank pattern less obvious, as feathers whitish with dark borders, giving a weakly white-streaked rather than spotted appearance.
BARE PARTS All plumages: Bill dark grey, profusely mottled fleshy-pink towards base and along cutting edge. Legs and feet dark grey, with fleshy-pink tones, particularly on tarsus and toes; webs solidly dark grey. Iris dark brown.
MEASUREMENTS Sexes similar. Wing 212-223, tarsus 47-51, bill 41-46, mean weight ca. 800.
GEOGRAPHICAL VARIATION None.
HABITS Despite reasonably extensive range, this species has been little studied in the field. It is generally to be found in pairs or small parties, perched on partially-submerged branches and trees by shallow-water lakes in lowland areas. Larger concentrations, sometimes reaching several hundred birds, gather to roost, flighting in small parties until well after dusk to perch at the tops of tall dead trees. In areas where particularly numerous, daytime feeding concentrations also occur, mixing freely with numbers of Wandering Whistling Ducks in New Guinea. The breeding season seems to be variable, or at least rather prolonged, as in southern New Guinea there are records of broods having been seen in March, a female with a well-formed egg was collected in April, and nesting is on record in September. Almost certainly the main breeding season occurs at the start of the wet season, from September onwards. Nests are placed in hollow trees, but little is documented about the breeding habits in the wild.
HABITAT Lowland marshes and lakes with extensive grassy margins and trees.
DISTRIBUTION Local but often quite common resident, fairly widespread on larger islands in the East

Indies. Recorded from the Philippines (Mindanao and Basilan), Indonesia (Sulawesi, Buru, Seram, Ambon, Tanimbar, Aru and Kai Islands) and New Guinea (including Bismarck Archipelago).

POPULATION Very little documentation on present status, but no doubt under pressure from intensification of agriculture on some islands; certainly common and widespread in lowland New Guinea in mid 1960s, however, and doubtless this species is under no immediate threat.

REFERENCES Delacour (1954-64), Johnsgard (1978).

3 PLUMED WHISTLING DUCK   Plate 1
Dendrocygna eytoni

Alternative names: Plumed Tree Duck, Eyton's Whistling or Tree Duck, Grass Whistling Duck

An elegant whistling duck of the tropical grasslands of northern and eastern Australia, its overall pale appearance and elongated flank plumes being a unique combination of features.

FIELD IDENTIFICATION Length 40-45 cm (16-18 in). **At rest:** Long-legged, delicate whistling duck usually encountered loafing in large flocks by shores of lakes in open country. General coloration pale, with darker greyish-brown upperparts, buffish head, neck and underparts and pink legs. Perhaps the most obvious plumage feature is the elongated straw-coloured flank feathers which curve prominently upwards, usually projecting well above body line; these are highlighted somewhat by rufous, narrowly black-barred flanks. Range overlaps only with that of Wandering Whistling Duck (5), which is less erect in posture both on ground and on water, lacks conspicuously-elongated flank feathers, has black (not pink) legs and has richer, almost uniform tawny-rufous, underparts. At long range, however, differences between the two species may not always be apparent, especially when on water, although Plumed tends to swim more buoyantly with fully erect neck than rather darker Wandering, which swims low in water, with head lower, showing pale flank stripes close to water line. **In flight:** Typical whistling duck shape, but wings longer and more pointed than those of Wandering. Compared with Wandering, Plumed is almost uniformly pale on underbody and has pale brownish underwing, whereas Wandering has darker body, contrasting strongly with pale head and neck, and much darker underwing; on birds rising from water, the whitish band across uppertail-coverts is more conspicuous on Wandering.

VOICE Flocks are noisy both at rest and in flight, giving a continuous twittering interspersed with whistles. Typical call is a shrill, high, whistled 'wa-chew', repeated to become a whistling twitter. Wings produce a whistling sound in flight.

DESCRIPTION Sexes similar, although within known pairs males tend to have rather longer flank plumes. **Adult:** Crown, hindneck and breast sandy-brown, lighter on breast. Sides of head and neck paler, whitish-grey. Flanks rufous-brown with vertical black barring; rear flank feathers greatly elongated and pointed, pale buffish-yellow with narrow

black border. Lower belly and undertail-coverts creamy-white. Uppertail-coverts buff, with dark mottling. Rump and tail dark brown. Upperparts greyish olive-brown, darker on wings. Underwing-coverts pale brown. **Juvenile:** Duller than adult, with broader black margins to less obviously elongated flank feathers and unmarked dull fore-flanks.

BARE PARTS All plumages: Bill fleshy-pink, freckled with dark spotting. Legs and feet fleshy-pink. Iris pale yellow or pale flesh.

MEASUREMENTS Sexes similar. Wing 215-245, tarsus 53-56, bill 37-49, mean weight ca. 790.

GEOGRAPHICAL VARIATION None.

HABITS A whistling duck of open treeless country. Gregarious by nature, it is usually encountered in enormous flocks, although it may also be found in smaller parties and individuals may become mixed with flocks of Wandering Whistling Ducks. Being a nocturnal feeder, it spends most of the day asleep in closely-packed concentrations by the shores of open waterbodies, flighting to feeding grounds from late afternoon onwards until after dark; feeding grounds may be over 30 km from the daytime roost site, the birds returning at dawn. Feeds over dry grassy plains, on land by the edges of lagoons and in open meadows. It spends little time on the water except in breeding season and generally is a rather reluctant swimmer; frequently dabbles when on water, but never dives. The concentrations break up at the onset of the wet season, many birds dispersing over considerable distances to the extent that the species is somewhat nomadic in its appearance in many areas. The nest is a mere scrape under a small bush or in long grass, usually not far from water in the, now, wetter and lusher grasslands. The breeding season in northern Australia begins in February and March, but in the more localised populations of southern Australia seems to be in September and October. The season depends partly on the extent of the rains; in very dry years it may be later or only part of the population may breed.

HABITAT Open grasslands with scattered pools and lakes, edges of swamps and lagoons in estuarine floodplains, and man-made tanks.

DISTRIBUTION Widespread over northern and northeastern Australia, with range extending over parts of eastern Australia in recent years; the majority breed from northeastern Western Australia across the plains of Northern Territory and Queensland to northeastern New South Wales. There is some seasonal movement within the range, indicating species' somewhat nomadic behaviour; in years of high rainfall, birds may move temporarily into regions where normally absent and sporadic breeding can occur (such a situation happened in the mid 1950s when a population arrived by the Murray River in the extreme southeast of the country, where it has now established itself). During periods of drought in tropical Australia, numbers move southwards and take up temporary residence in areas where normally virtually absent, but breeding seldom occurs. Such wanderings have resulted in occasional individuals occurring far from normal range: following periods of severe drought in Northern Australia, a number of birds were collected in southern New Guinea in 1959 and 1961. Vagrants have also occurred in Tasmania, and even New Zealand (one record).

POPULATION No total population estimates have been made and certainly over the main breeding range there is no threat, as human population is relatively low and shooting has little effect on numbers. It is protected in the southern part of its range, but some birds are shot by hunters; such relict populations may, however, be only of a relatively temporary nature and disappearance of some of these is more likely to be due to natural factors.

REFERENCES Frith (1967).

4 FULVOUS WHISTLING DUCK   Plate 2
Dendrocygna bicolor

Alternative names: Fulvous Tree Duck, Large Whistling Teal

The extraordinary distribution of this duck includes no fewer than four continents, a range comparable with that of the Comb Duck (37).

FIELD IDENTIFICATION Length 45-53 cm (18-21 in). **At rest:** Resembles large version of the Lesser Whistling Duck (6), but latter overlaps only in Asiatic range of Fulvous. Fulvous has a warm brown crown, only a little darker than rufous-buff of rest of head, and a dark band down centre of hindneck; Lesser has a clear dark crown centre forming a narrow cap, and hindneck only a little darker than neck sides, not blackish. The sides of the neck on Fulvous are paler, with fine dark streaking (not a very noticeable feature), whereas on Lesser the sides of neck and head are uniform buffish. Closer inspection of the rear end may reveal the whitish uppertail-coverts of Fulvous (these are chestnut on Lesser). Fulvous is also much larger and lankier, and certainly in India forms smaller flocks, than the very gregarious Lesser, although odd Fulvous do become mixed with flocks of Lessers. Juveniles of both species are duller than adults. Juvenile Fulvous may lack white uppertail-coverts, and the brown rather than blackish crown is a useful guide, but such birds would usually be accompanied by adults when in this plumage. Confusion also possible with juvenile Comb Duck, which has a perching habit, but is bulkier in the body and has dark cap and eye-stripe and dingier coloration to head and under-parts. Beware also juvenile White-faced Whistling Duck (7) in South America and Africa, which has black crown, extensively-barred flanks, chestnut breast and black uppertail-coverts. **In flight:** Typical whistling duck shape. From below, the uniform rufous-buff head and underparts contrast with the blackish underwing. The upperside is fairly uniformly dark, with the only obvious feature being a distinctive white horseshoe on the uppertail-coverts, immediately distinguishing it from Lesser Whistling Duck which has maroon-chestnut upper-tail-coverts and leading wing-coverts, latter indistinctly rufous on Fulvous.

VOICE Very vocal, both when feeding and on the wing. Typical flight call a wader-like thin whistle, 'k-weeoo', usually repeated. Also a harsh 'kee' repeated several times during disputes. Both calls heard from feeding and loafing flocks. Wings produce a dull muffled sound in flight.

DESCRIPTION Sexes similar. **Adult:** Has crown and upper nape rich rufous-brown, becoming blackish down centre of hindneck. Sides of head, neck and almost entire underparts rich rufous-buff, with centre and sides of neck paler, almost whitish, with fine dark striations. Somewhat elongated flank feathers creamy-buff, with black outer webs forming weakly-streaked appearance. Undertail-coverts and ventral region creamy-white. Entire upperparts dark brown with rufous feather fringes, darkest on wings and rump. Underwing blackish. Tail blackish, contrasting with creamy-white uppertail-coverts. **Juvenile:** Similar to adult but markedly duller and greyer, less fulvous or rufous, with flank pattern much reduced; uppertail-coverts initially greyish, not white.

BARE PARTS All plumages: Bill, legs and feet dark grey. Iris dark brown.

MEASUREMENTS Males average slightly larger than females. Wing 203-225, tarsus 55-61, bill 44-48, mean weight ca. 680.

GEOGRAPHICAL VARIATION Despite wide range in three faunal regions, no subspecies are recognised.

HABITS Gregarious, although normally forms much smaller flocks than Lesser Whistling Duck, but associates freely with other species. Usually found in small parties, but large concentrations occur where particularly numerous. Feeds chiefly at night, in shallow freshwater lakes and pools with extensive fringe vegetation, in some areas particularly attracted to ricefields. When feeding, spends most of time in water, up-ending and dabbling; also dives surprisingly well, flocks often doing so in unison. Rarely perches, but walks well, and daytime roosts contain loafing flocks on ground or water not far from feeding areas. Generally shy and wary. With such a wide distribution, it is not surprising that the breeding season varies according to location, but in India it is chiefly in the monsoon season in July and August. In southern Africa the wet season again is favoured, whereas north of the Zambezi the drier months are preferred; a selection of African breeding periods includes July-September in Ghana and Nigeria, May-June in Uganda and December-March in South Africa, but the African situation is very complex. In the Americas, it has been found breeding between November and February in Argentina, January and February in Colombia and from April to September in southern USA. It is something of a colonial breeder, nests being placed in relatively close proximity in fringe vegetation of freshwater bodies; in India, however, it is said to be primarily a tree-nesting species, utilising hollow trees and even taking over disused stick nests of large birds such as kites and crows.

HABITAT Variety of lowland freshwater habitats in open country, avoiding well-wooded areas, locally also by upland lakes and marshes. Favours areas with extensive fringe and emergent vegetation, but also locally in ricefields (as in southern USA).

DISTRIBUTION Local resident, with some quite extensive seasonal movements, over the Americas, Africa and the Indian subcontinent. In the Americas, it breeds over suitable country in the lowlands of northern and eastern South America south to northern Argentina in the east and Colombia in the west, the range extending northwards through Central America to southern USA; it has relatively recently extended its range northwards to colonise new regions in the lowlands of southern USA, although to many of these it is primarily a summer visitor. Wandering individuals, sometimes in small parties, have occurred north to British Columbia and New York and west to Hawaii (has bred). The range expansion has also taken it to the West Indies (Cuba and the Greater Antilles). In Africa, it has a similarly wide distribution south of the Sahara, from Senegal across the sub-Saharan belt to Ethiopia and southwards down the entire eastern half of the continent to South Africa and Madagascar, although everywhere its distribution is somewhat local and discontinuous, subject to seasonal fluctuations and movements. Vagrants have been recorded very rarely north of tropical Africa, presumably originating in West Africa; there are records from southern Spain and southern France (both in September) and in 1977 a small flock arrived in Morocco, where breeding possibly took place. The Indian population is everywhere local, possibly somewhat nomadic, and subject to the intensity of the wet season; the main concentration is in the northeast and Bangladesh, but it is recorded throughout the subcontinent, including Burma and Pakistan, and vagrants have occurred south to Sri Lanka and north to Nepal.

POPULATION Everywhere somewhat local in its appearance, but its widespread distribution and local abundance indicate that nowhere, except possibly in parts of the Indian subcontinent, is there any major threat to its numbers. The increasing aridity of the sub-Saharan zone after years of drought must have dramatically affected the population; a survey of major wetlands in West Africa, east to Chad, in January 1984, however, revealed a total of some 70,000 birds.

REFERENCES Ali and Ripley (1968), Brown et al. (1982), Jepson and Baker (1984), Roux and Jarry (1984).

5 WANDERING WHISTLING DUCK
Dendrocygna arcuata   **Plate 1**

Alternative names: Wandering Tree Duck, Water Whistling Duck, Diving Whistling Duck

An abundant aquatic whistling duck of northern Australia and the East Indies, its combination of features includes those of both Lesser (6) and Fulvous (4) Whistling Ducks, but its range overlaps only with that of the former.

FIELD IDENTIFICATION Length 40-45 cm (16-18 in). **At rest:** A highly gregarious whistling duck, overlapping chiefly with Plumed Whistling Duck (3) in Australia. Unlike Plumed, Wandering spends most of its time on the water, swimming with body lower and head held less erect than Plumed, and diving freely. It is stockier than Plumed, with less erect carriage and relatively shorter neck and legs when on land. It lacks strongly-elongated flank plumes,

showing merely a pale band along the upper flanks which contrasts well with the tawny-rufous underparts. The dark crown and hindneck and pale sides of head and neck give a much more patterned appearance compared with the almost uniformly pale plumage of Plumed Whistling Duck, and the bill and legs are blackish, not fleshy-pink. Superficially it is closer to Lesser Whistling Duck, with which it overlaps on some East Indian islands, but Lesser lacks the dark hindneck of Wandering and has only the centre of the crown dark, the cap not reaching the eye. Lesser's flank pattern is diffuse and it lacks the indistinct dark scaling on the breast of Wandering. Inspection of the rear end of the bird should reveal chestnut uppertail-coverts on Lesser, creamy-white on Wandering. See also Spotted Whistling Duck (2). **In flight:** Typical whistling duck shape. Wandering shows contrasting underside pattern, with pale sides of head and neck, tawny-rufous body and blackish crown, hindneck and underwing. From above, the clear whitish outer uppertail-coverts contrast with the dark rump and tail and in good light chestnut leading edge of wing may be apparent. Plumed is relatively longer-winged and more uniform overall, especially from below, and the underwing is browner, although it appears distinctly dark in shadow. Lesser shows similar underside pattern to Wandering but, from above, the uppertail-coverts are rich chestnut. See also Spotted Whistling Duck.

VOICE Flocks are very vocal both on water and in flight, although the whistling call is a little weaker than that of Plumed Whistling Duck but basically similar. It may be uttered singly or repeated to become a shrill twittering. In flight, the wings produce a whistling sound.

DESCRIPTION Sexes similar. **Adult:** Crown and hindneck blackish-brown, the dusky cap reaching eye. Sides of head, neck and breast pale dull buffish, with dark scaling on breast and lower foreneck. Flanks and belly tawny-rufous. Slightly-elongated flank feathers, creamy-buff with black outer webs. Ventral region, undertail- and outer uppertail-coverts creamy-white. Tail, rump and central uppertail-coverts blackish. Upperparts and upperwing dark brown, with rufous-chestnut feather fringes to mantle and scapulars and chestnut lesser coverts. Underwing blackish. **Juvenile:** Duller than adult, with less obvious flank pattern, less intensely rufous underparts, and paler belly which separates darker flanks.

BARE PARTS All plumages: Bill, legs and feet greyish-black. Iris brown.

MEASUREMENTS Sexes similar. Race *australis*: Wing 196-231, tarsus 44-48, bill 39-52, mean weight ca. 735. Nominate *arcuata*: Wing 180-203, tarsus 43-45, bill 42-48. Race *pygmaea*: Wing 173-183, bill 41-44.

GEOGRAPHICAL VARIATION Relatively slight. Three subspecies recognised on size differences, measurements given above. Largest is *australis* of Australia and southern New Guinea; nominate race of the East Indies is a little smaller, whereas isolated and endangered *pygmaea* of New Britain and formerly Fiji is the smallest. Populations of some of the more southern East Indian islands approach *australis*, being on average a little larger than those of more northerly islands.

HABITS Gregarious whistling duck of lakes, marshes and riverine lagoons in open country. Often encountered in very large concentrations by waterside. Unlike Plumed Whistling Duck, with which it often associates, this is an aquatic bird, feeding in relatively deep water by dabbling and diving, flocks often doing so in unison. It is primarily a daytime feeder, feeding flocks constantly on the move with much nervous activity, small groups moving from the rear to the head of the flock so that the whole mass is continually moving forward. During the heat of the day it retires to the shallows or the banks, loafing in dense packs. Generally shy and wary. The large concentrations break up at the onset of the rainy season, and move off to suitable breeding habitats as the surrounding areas become waterlogged. Intensity of breeding activity is related to water depth, a factor which influences the extent of seasonal movements to breed in areas where normally absent. Like many other Australian species, it is somewhat nomadic. The nest is a mere scrape in grassland, usually not far from the waterside. The breeding season varies with the intensity of the rains, and during very wet seasons it can be far more prolonged than in drier years. The breeding season in southern New Guinea and northern Australia is generally from December to May, and in the Philippines from January to May.

HABITAT Lagoons, lakes and swamps with relatively deep water and emergent vegetation. Seasonally, also in flooded grasslands.

DISTRIBUTION Locally abundant resident and seasonal migrant, the isolated race *pygmaea* being resident on New Britain. The nominate form is a resident and partial migrant in the East Indies, including the Philippines, southern Borneo and Indonesia (Java, Bali, Sulawesi, Sumba, Ambon, Timor and Roti). Northern New Guinea birds are somewhat intermediate between the nominate form and the race *australis* of northern Australia and southern New Guinea. In Australia, it is basically resident by permanent water in the tropical lowlands from Kimberley in the west to central coastal Queensland in the south and east; further south it is erratic in its appearance, usually associated with drought conditions in the north, but it occasionally appears as far south as the Murray River in the southeast. In New Guinea it was formerly considered to be a winter visitor, but it is now known to be a widespread resident in southern regions. Movements between the New Guinea and Australian populations are, however, known to take place, probably primarily at night, over the Torres Strait.

POPULATION No total estimates have been made. The Fiji population of *pygmaea* has possibly already been exterminated by the introduction of the mongoose, although it was rediscovered in 1959. Information concerning its present status there and on New Britain is required; this is almost certainly a seriously-endangered form. Little information exists from many of the islands where the nominate form occurs, although it is still known to be abundant on some of the Philippines. The New Caledonian birds are thought to be extinct. In parts of New Guinea

and Australia it is locally abundant, although the range in Australia is considered to have contracted a little on the eastern side of the continent since the last century. Estimates made of two of the largest dry-season concentrations in the north in 1964 were of 30,000 on the Mary River and 40,000 on the Daly River (Northern Territory); there were known to be several other not quite so large concentrations elsewhere in the north at that time.

REFERENCES Frith (1967), RAOU (1984).

6 LESSER WHISTLING DUCK   Plate 2
Dendrocygna javanica

Alternative names: Lesser Tree Duck, Lesser Whistling Teal, Indian Whistling Duck, Javan Whistling Duck

An abundant little whistling duck, the only species over much of southeastern Asia.

FIELD IDENTIFICATION Length 38-40 cm (15-16 in). **At rest:** Small, very sociable aquatic whistling duck of tropical Asia, with range overlapping with that of superficially similar Fulvous (4) and Wandering (5) Whistling Ducks. Obviously smaller and dumpier than Fulvous, it generally occurs in larger flocks. Is best distinguished from Fulvous by its chestnut, not white, uppertail-coverts, dark grey-brown crown centre and upper hindneck, diffusing into pale grey-brown lower hindneck and sides of neck (blackish lower hindneck of Fulvous becomes merely pale brown on upper hindneck and crown), duller and greyer body coloration (when on water), and lack of whitish, finely-streaked collar. Wandering has more extensive dark crown which reaches down to eye, dark scaling on breast, clearer pale flank stripes and whitish uppertail-coverts. **In flight:** Typical whistling duck shape. Dark chestnut forewing and uppertail-coverts rule out Fulvous, but chestnut forewing shared by Wandering, which, however, has clear whitish sides to dark-centred uppertail-coverts, a feature that should be apparent on rising birds. Flight action relatively weak; when flushed, flocks generally do not fly far, but circle area waiting for intruder to depart to allow them to settle again rather than, as most other waterfowl, flying directly away.

VOICE Rather noisy, especially on wing, when flock incessantly utters a clear, low, whistled 'whi-whee' as it circles overhead. A subdued quacking call may also be heard. Wings produce a whistling sound in flight.

DESCRIPTION Sexes similar. **Adult:** Centre of crown, including forehead, dusky grey-brown. Rest of head, including supercilium, and neck and breast pale dull greyish-buff, becoming almost whitish on throat and darkening on neck sides and upper hindneck. Flanks and belly tawny-rufous, with ill-defined creamy streaks along upper flank line. Undertail-coverts and ventral region whitish. Upperparts dark brown with rufous feather fringes, lesser wingcoverts chestnut. Rump blackish. Uppertail-coverts rich chestnut. Tail dark brown. Underwing blackish. **Juvenile:** Duller, with paler fringes to upperparts; underparts paler and duller, less rufous, and crown often paler grey-brown than adult.

BARE PARTS All plumages: Bill blackish-grey. Legs and feet dark blue-grey. Iris dark brown, with narrow pale yellow eye-ring.
MEASUREMENTS Sexes similar. Wing 170–204, tarsus 40-50, bill 38-42, weight 450-600.
GEOGRAPHICAL VARIATION None.
HABITS Sociable little whistling duck of tropical freshwater pools and lakes, feeding in small packs among dense emergent vegetation. Unless seen in flight, often first spotted as a mass of erect necks peering at observer from among vegetation. Usually feeds by dabbling on surface, but often dives; sometimes grazes on land, though in close proximity to water. Depending on degree of human disturbance feeds by day or night, roosting in trees or on partially-submerged branches and islands close to feeding sites. Locally, also resorts to roost in sheltered coastal bays or lagoons, returning at dusk to feed among ricefields. Feeding in rice-paddy is a somewhat local habit, but in some areas this species has been deemed a pest and is hunted; although said to be partial to rice, it also eats quantities of insects to counteract the problem. Usually met with in parties of some 20-50 birds, but flocks may number 1,000 or more in areas where species is particularly numerous. Flocks break up for breeding at onset of rains: this is generally during July-August in India and Burma, but timing varies according to the intensity of the rains and breeding has been reported from June to October in India; in the Malay Peninsula it is more extended, from August to January or February, while breeding has also been reported in Sri Lanka from December to January, as well as in July and August. Nest site varies: often a platform of sticks, leaves and grasses among waterside vegetation, sometimes in a tree hole, but more frequently is constructed in a tree fork, or an old nest of large birds such as kites or crows may be taken over; it is rarely more than 5 m above ground, but occasionally at a considerable distance from water.
HABITAT Lowland freshwater pools, lakes and swamps with extensive emergent vegetation, partially-submerged trees and fringe cover. Avoids wide rivers and lakes with little vegetation, but locally feeds in ricefields; in areas where feeding grounds disturbed, may even roost in coastal lagoons and sheltered coastal bays.
DISTRIBUTION Abundant resident in tropical Asia, from Pakistan in the west to tropical eastern China (north to the lower Yangtze in summer). Southwards the range extends through southeast Asia to as far as western Borneo, Sumatra and Java, and in the Indian Ocean includes the Andaman and Nicobar Islands. Although resident over most of this range, it is only a summer visitor (March to May) to the northern limits in China, including Hainan and Taiwan. Local movements occur, depending on the amount of water available; in very dry years, considerable dispersal may take place as birds search for suitable habitat.
POPULATION No total estimates have been made, although certainly in India numbers today do not seem to reach the vast concentrations reported in the last century. Generally, however, this is an abundant species which does not seem to be under

any other than local threats to its numbers. Some island populations could disappear if persecuted, especially those at the limits of the range, where recolonisation from elsewhere is less likely; the species seems now to have disappeared from both Okinawa and the Ryukyu Islands (Japan). Although not hunted for food to any great extent, it is shot in places as a pest of ricefields.
REFERENCES Ali and Ripley (1968).

7 WHITE-FACED WHISTLING DUCK
Dendrocygna viduata **Plate 2**
Alternative name: White-faced Tree Duck

This distinctive whistling duck is perhaps most closely related to the Black-bellied Whistling Duck (9), although it is widespread in the Afrotropical as well as the Neotropical region.

FIELD IDENTIFICATION Length 43-48 cm (17-19 in).
At rest: The general dark plumage contrasting with chiefly white head makes this perhaps the easiest of the genus to identify. Range overlaps with those of Fulvous (4) and Black-bellied Whistling Ducks, but it is hardly likely to be confused with either, although caution may be needed with juveniles. The white fore part of the head and throat contrasts sharply with black rear of head and upper neck. Breast, lower neck and back chestnut, with sides of body closely barred buffish-white and blackish-brown. Belly and tail blackish. The rest of the upperparts are tawny-brown, with slightly darker feather centres. Duller juvenile may be distinguished from juvenile Fulvous by black, not greyish or whitish, uppertail-coverts, blackish, not brownish, crown, more prominently barred flanks and dull chestnut breast. Juvenile Black-bellied has extensive white in the wing. **In flight:** Typical whistling duck shape. Appears wholly dark with contrasting white head; underwing completely dark and upperwing only a little paler, the latter showing chestnut coverts in good light and contrasting a little with paler back. Black-bellied shows extensive white in upperwing, while Fulvous is pale on neck and underparts, shows white on both uppertail- and undertail-coverts and lacks black belly.
VOICE Quite vocal, the usual call being a clear three-note whistle, 'tsri-tsri-trseeo'. Anxiety call (from breeding birds) a single 'whee'.
DESCRIPTION Sexes similar. **Adult:** Front half of head backwards to beyond eye, and chin and upper throat white; rear half of head, upper hind-neck and often-incomplete band across upper throat black. Foreneck, lower hindneck and upper breast rich chestnut. Central underparts from lower breast to include ventral region, and uppertail- and undertail-coverts, tail and rump black. Sides of breast and flanks finely barred blackish and buffish. Mantle, back and scapulars pale brown, latter with darker feather centres. Upperside of wing very dark, with chestnut lesser coverts. Underside of wing blackish. **Juvenile:** Duller than adult, with greyish replacing white of head and chin; rear of head blackish-grey. Chestnut of breast duller and less extensive than on adult, initially pale greyish with paler belly. Full adult colour not attained until about

four months, but shows very dark colours on head, neck and belly within a few weeks.

BARE PARTS All plumages: Bill black, with pale grey subterminal band. Legs and feet greyish-black. Iris brown.

MEASUREMENTS Males tend to be slightly smaller than females. Wing 216-240, tarsus 48-55, bill 45-49, mean weight ca. 670.

GEOGRAPHICAL VARIATION Despite its extensive range in two faunal regions, no differences between the populations are recognised.

HABITS Aquatic and terrestrial by nature, this species spends much of the daytime in large dense flocks by almo‑* any form of open water. Flocks mix freely with Fulvous Whistling Ducks. Unlike some members of the genus, it very rarely perches, but is a good swimmer, walker and even diver. It feeds by various methods: by dabbling in the shallows while wading, by swimming and up-ending, and to a certain extent even by diving. Although flocks usually fly to feeding grounds at night, a certain amount of daytime feeding is undertaken, especially during the winter months. Swimming posture quite buoyant, with head held high. Breeding season varies according to location, but the appropriate wet season is preferred. Most-detailed known information is on African populations: in southern Africa, the season extends from October to March, whereas in northern parts of the African range it is in July and August; September and October breeding is reported from Senegal. In Madagascar, the species is said to breed from September to November and again in January and February. The nest is usually located on ground in long grass, but sites vary, with nest sometimes in reedbeds and even occasionally in the fork of a low waterside tree; in South America there are even reports of nests in hollow trees.

HABITAT Freshwater lakes, reservoirs, marshes, swamps, large rivers, floodplains and river deltas, often with some emergent vegetation, but prefers open waterbodies, even if quite small.

DISTRIBUTION Widespread over both Africa and South America. In Africa, it is common in the tropical lowlands from Senegal across the sub-Saharan belt to East Africa, southwards down entire eastern half of the continent, including Madagascar and the Comoro Islands, to South Africa; it is generally absent from the western part of the continent from Zaire to the Cape except as a sporadic visitor. According to season, quite extensive movements may occur depending on water levels and food availability, but distances not normally over 500 km; since this species has been reported as a vagrant to Spain, however, occasional individuals possibly do wander northwards from the Seychelles and tropical Africa (as does Fulvous Whistling Duck), though such records are difficult to judge owing to its popularity in captivity. In South America it is widespread, but somewhat patchily distributed, from Costa Rica southwards through Central America, including Trinidad, over the lowland tropics to Argentina, Paraguay and Uruguay in the east, and to the Amazonian lowlands of Colombia, more rarely as far as Peru, in the west; vagrants have been reported from several West Indian islands.

POPULATION Locally abundant, its adaptation to man-made waterbodies indicates that there is no major threat to the populations of this species. It has disappeared from Panama, where it was formerly quite numerous.

REFERENCES Brown *et al.* (1982).

8 BLACK-BILLED WHISTLING DUCK
Dendrocygna arborea **Plate 1**

Alternative names: Cuban Whistling Duck, West Indian Tree Duck

Confined to the West Indies. Unlike many of the genus, lives up to its alternative name by habitually perching in trees.

FIELD IDENTIFICATION Length 48-58 cm (19-23 in). **At rest:** Largest and bulkiest of the whistling ducks, its restricted range making confusion with others unlikely as only Black-bellied (9) and Fulvous (4) Whistling Ducks are regular on some islands. The rather dark general coloration is relieved only by extensive black and white spotting along the flanks and by pale face and foreneck. Superficially resembles Spotted Whistling Duck (2) (though owing to widely-separated ranges confusion possible only in captivity), but larger Black-billed lacks pinkish tones to bill and legs and defined eye-patch of Spotted. Confusion of very young juvenile with Fulvous Whistling Duck is possible, but Black-billed is bulkier and has some spotting on flanks, blacker crown and upperparts and black uppertail-coverts. Its arboreal habits are most apparent at night, when it resorts to feeding on palm fruits. **In flight:** Typical whistling duck shape. Altogether a very dark whistling duck, both above and below. In good light the spotted underparts should be visible from below, and from above the paler and greyer upperwing-coverts offer some contrast, though not enough to suggest the gleaming white upperwing patches of Black-bellied.

VOICE Considered to be relatively less vocal than most other whistling ducks. The call is similar to that of Black-bellied, a shrill, but rather harsh, whistled 'visisee'.

DESCRIPTION Sexes similar. **Adult:** Crown and nape blackish; sides of head and neck buffish-white, whitest on throat, with somewhat variable area of ill-defined dusky smudging on sides of head, and fine black streaking at sides of neck, most prominent on lower neck where forms dusky collar. Breast rufous-brown with darker feather centres, breaking up into black and white spotting from lower breast downwards, the spots being largest and their effect most striped along upper rear flanks. Lower belly whitish, becoming marked with black on undertail-coverts. Rump, uppertail-coverts and tail blackish. Upperparts and upperwing blackish-brown with rufous-brown feather fringes, latter most extensive on back, mantle and scapulars. Upperwing-coverts paler and greyer. Underwing blackish. **Juvenile:** Paler and less streaked on head and neck, lacking dusky facial smudges and browner forecrown and sides of head; general plumage duller brown, less rufous-brown, with black markings of underparts less developed (the black markings may even

be absent on very young juveniles).
BARE PARTS All plumages: Bill, legs and feet blackish. Iris dark brown.
MEASUREMENTS Sexes similar. Wing 230-270, tarsus 62-75, bill 45-53, mean weight ca. 1150.
GEOGRAPHICAL VARIATION None.
HABITS Little studied in the wild. Spends little time on the water. Much of the daytime is spent hidden in swampy areas, loafing in small parties on waterside banks or perched among partially-submerged trees and branches. Feeds mostly at night, flighting at dusk to feed on fruits of tall Royal Palm trees, where it perches in the treetops; is adept at perching, unlike many of its congeners. There is evidence to suggest that it grazes in agricultural land; indeed, in some areas it has been deemed an agricultural pest. Is said not to be particularly shy or wary, but its nocturnal feeding habits render it rather inconspicuous. The breeding season seems to be from June to October, but may vary according to location as on Puerto Rico this species is said to breed from October to December. Nests have been reported in tree holes, among branches of palm trees and clumps of bromeliads, generally quite high above the ground though nests have also been found on the ground among roots of fallen trees and in bushy cover, but normally not far from water.
HABITAT Wooded swamps, including coastal mangroves.
DISTRIBUTION Locally numerous over several islands of the West Indies, where it is basically resident, although a vagrant has been recorded from Bermuda. It is known from the Bahamas, Cuba, Cayman Islands, Jamaica, Hispaniola, Puerto Rico, Virgin Islands, Leeward Islands and Martinique.
POPULATION No total estimates have been made, although this species must be classed as endangered on many islands as a result of hunting, habitat destruction and predation by the introduced mongoose. Despite official protection on the Bahamas, Cuba, Jamaica, Puerto Rico and the Virgin Islands, persecution through shooting and the collection of eggs for food continues on several of these islands. It is said to be still common, but declining, on Cuba and Hispaniola, reasonably common on the Cayman Islands and some of the Bahamas, and there have been recent reports of its continued presence on Puerto Rico and Jamaica.
REFERENCES Bond (1985), Johnsgard (1978), Kear (1978, 1979).

9 BLACK-BELLIED WHISTLING DUCK
Dendrocygna autumnalis   **Plate 2**

Alternative names: Black-billed Tree Duck, Red-billed Whistling or Tree Duck

A distinctive white-winged whistling duck of the tropical Americas.

FIELD IDENTIFICATION Length 48-53 cm (19-21 in).
At rest: Gregarious and often terrestrial whistling duck, the combination of bright reddish bill and legs, large white wing patch, black underparts and greyish head renders it unmistakable. The tail and lower underparts are black, contrasting with the extensive whitish area visible in the folded wing.

Duller juvenile, with greyish bill and legs, differs from juvenile White-faced Whistling Duck (7) in having paler bill and obvious pale wing patch, even when on the ground. **In flight:** Typical whistling duck shape. Appears dark overall, with conspicuous, broad whitish band along full length of centre of upperwing, broadest across bases of primaries and becoming browner along median coverts, contrasting with blackish of remainder of flight feathers. Even from below, when the whole of the underside of the wing and body appear dark, the white is visible, flashing with each downbeat of the wing.
VOICE A noisy bird, especially on the wing, uttering a loud, whistling 'pa-chew' or 'wa-chew-we-we-whew'.
DESCRIPTION Sexes similar. Nominate race described. **Adult:** Crown, nape, lower neck and breast chestnut-brown, richest on the lower neck and breast. Remainder of underparts from lower breast downwards solidly black, becoming mottled with white on ventral region. Sides of head and upper neck pale buffish-grey. Eye-ring whitish and conspicuous. Mantle, back and scapulars chestnut-brown, becoming darker, duller brown on tertials. Inner upperwing-coverts chestnut-brown, outer upperwing-coverts and bases of flight feathers white or whitish; rest of flight feathers blackish. Rump, uppertail-coverts, tail and underwing blackish. **Juvenile:** Considerably duller than adult, with whole plumage, especially underparts, much greyer; on very young birds, the belly is quite pale with indistinct cross-barring.
BARE PARTS Adult: Bill bright waxy reddish-pink, often yellower at very base. Legs and feet bright pink. Iris dark brown. **Juvenile:** Bill, legs and feet yellowish-grey to bluish-grey.
MEASUREMENTS Both sexes and races similar. Wing 229-248, tarsus 51-65, bill 49-56, mean weight ca. 830.
GEOGRAPHICAL VARIATION Two subspecies recognised: the nominate form described above, from Central America, north to southern Texas, south to Panama; and a southern race, *discolor*, from eastern Panama southwards. The latter is slightly smaller on average than the nominate form, with varying amounts of grey in plumage of lower breast and upper back. The two forms intergrade somewhat in eastern Panama.
HABITS A relatively large and long-necked whistling duck, adept at perching and grazing and less of a water bird than many of the genus. Very much nocturnal by nature, it is perhaps most easily seen when flighting between roosting and feeding grounds in noisy, often large, flocks. During the day, it roosts on sandbanks, mudflats and even in waterside trees, perching on low branches overhanging a safe stretch of water. Flocks feed in cultivation, habitually seeking out ricefields and even cornfields, where perching abilities allow them to perch on the stalks to get at the grain. Flocks numbering several thousand may be formed in some areas. Breeding season varies according to location, being June-July in Texas, July and August and perhaps later in Surinam, July and September in Brazil, but the data are inadequate over most of South America. Nests

can be found both in hollow trees and, less frequently, on the ground, normally quite close to water.

HABITAT The vicinity of tropical and subtropical lagoons, in low-lying and lightly-wooded but well-cultivated regions. Near inland lakes and cattle ponds, swamps and marshes, but avoids deepwater lakes unless with extensive shallow margins.

DISTRIBUTION Differences in distribution between the two subspecies are summarised under Geographical Variation above. The species is widespread in the lowlands of the tropical Americas, from southern Texas south to northern Argentina on the eastern side and to Ecuador on the western side, occasionally south to coastal and Amazonian lowland Peru. Its seasonal movements within this extensive range are not clearly understood, but extreme northern populations certainly move southwards into Central America in winter. It regularly turns up in the West Indies at almost any time of the year, and vagrants have wandered north to California.

POPULATION Locally abundant, its extensive range and adaptation to man-made habitats such as cultivation indicates no threat to the species, though in some areas the resulting crop damage means that control measures are taken, as in Mexico. The colonisation of extreme southern parts of the United States is considered to be due to the increasing number of stock ponds being provided by cattlemen.

REFERENCES Johnsgard (1975).

SUBFAMILY THALASSORNINAE (WHITE-BACKED DUCK)

Monotypic subfamily created for an African diving duck formerly considered to be related to the stiff-tails (Oxyurini), but now generally accepted to be most closely related to the whistling ducks. Its affiliation to the latter is based on internal anatomic features rather than on external appearance.

10 WHITE-BACKED DUCK   Plate 46
Thalassornis leuconotus

An aberrant, almost grebe-like African diving duck. Its systematic position has been the subject of much speculation, but it is now generally agreed to be most closely related to the whistling ducks.

FIELD IDENTIFICATION Length 38-40 cm (15-16 in). **At rest:** Unlikely to be confused with any other duck, its low sloping back, often erect neck, and brownish coloration suggesting a large Little Grebe rather than a duck. Its dull brown general appearance is relieved by a conspicuous white patch at the base of the bill, contrasting with a dusky head, clearer tawny neck and prominently-banded black and tawny flanks. Its tropical African distribution overlaps only with that of vaguely similar female Maccoa Duck (152), which, however, often shows its long tail held cocked above water line, lacks white face patch and has fatter, more swollen bill and body. **In flight:** Rarely observed in flight, but, when seen, its virtually tail-less appearance gives a striking shape, with prominent feet and relatively short wings, and it appears uniformly dark with conspicuous white back. Patters over surface for some distance when taking off, wingbeats deep and high when well underway. Most flights for relatively short distance and at no great height.

VOICE Calls both when on water and in flight; typical call not unlike that of a whistling duck, a clear whistled double note that has been rendered 'tit-weet'.

DESCRIPTION Sexes similar. **Adult:** Crown and hindneck blackish, freckled warm buff; sides of head intensely freckled black and buff, with clear whitish oval patch between eye and bill. Front and sides of neck clear, unmarked tawny-buff. Breast and entire underparts tawny-buff, barred blackish; finest on breast and broadest along flanks; lower belly and ventral region duskier. Upperparts tawny-buff, barred blackish. Upper back, rump and uppertail-coverts blackish, narrowly barred white. Lower back white. Wing-coverts and scapulars dark brown, barred and spotted buff and white. Primaries and secondaries pale brown, paler on inner webs of primaries and with narrow whitish trailing edge to secondaries. Underwing buffish-brown. Tail vestigial. **Juvenile:** Very similar to adult but less clearly marked, a little duller, with facial patch smaller and duller and sides of neck freckled.

BARE PARTS All plumages: Bill relatively large, with prominent strong nail, blackish, mottled fleshy or greenish-yellow at sides. Legs and feet greenish-grey. Iris dark brown.

MEASUREMENTS Sexes similar, though males tend to be a little larger than females. Nominate *leuconotus*: Wing 150-180, tarsus 35-41, bill 35-45, weight 625-790. Race *insularis*: Wing 135-150, bill 32-37.

GEOGRAPHICAL VARIATION Two subspecies recognised: the nominate form of mainland Africa and *insularis* of Madagascar. The two forms are similar in plumage, although Madagascar birds are more strongly marked, with head darker and body barring blacker against a lighter buff ground colour; Madagascar form is also a little smaller (see Measurements).

HABITS Peculiar diving duck of freshwater lakes and pools. Entirely adapted to an aquatic existence, it is almost useless on land, with feet placed far to rear of body. Generally met with in small parties, but larger concentrations of 100 or more gather on favoured lakes. Spends most of day dozing among emergent vegetation; most active around dawn and dusk, but not strictly nocturnal. Feeds almost entirely by diving, but takes some food from surface of water. When disturbed, prefers to lower body into water and swim away with neck erect, flying only as a last resort. Probably pairs for life. Breeding season varied and prolonged; over most of range breeding takes place at almost any time of the year, depending primarily on local water levels. Nest is placed close to water's edge; sometimes uses old nests of grebes or coots, or anchors floating platform to emergent vegetation. The large glossy brown eggs are unique among waterfowl.

HABITAT Shallow freshwater lakes and pools with emergent vegetation, backwaters and quiet bays of lakes, floodplains with scattered large pools, and marshes and swamps.

DISTRIBUTION Widespread throughout most of tropical Africa, including Madagascar. Everywhere somewhat local and nowhere abundant. Occurs in narrow belt in western and central Africa, from Senegal and Nigeria to Chad, and in eastern Africa from Ethiopia to South Africa, avoiding equatorial rainforest zone. Seasonal movements poorly understood, but disperses during rainy season to take advantage of newly-formed shallow waters.

POPULATION Little information available on numbers, but concentrations of 500 reported from Kenya and Zambia. It is locally common over most of its range and cannot be considered to be under any kind of direct threat. It makes poor eating and is therefore rarely hunted. The Madagascar subspecies, with its restricted distribution, could be more vulnerable, but there is no recent information on its status.

REFERENCES Brown et al. (1982), Wintle (1981).

SUBFAMILY ANSERINAE (GEESE AND SWANS)

Tribe ANSERINI (GEESE)

Large, long-necked waterfowl, easily recognisable as geese by their long necks, honking calls and sociable nature. Plumage shows little sexual, and often only minor age, variations. Most species feed primarily by grazing, but are good swimmers. All *Anser* and *Branta* species are highly gregarious and most are highly migratory, breeding in open upland situations and wintering in lowland farmland and marshes. Pair-bonds may be formed in winter quarters, and during the autumn and winter individuals keep together in family parties within the flocks. Non-breeders form moulting flocks in summer, when they become flightless, and are joined by breeders a few weeks later. Some species perform short, or even fairly extensive movements to safe moulting waters (moult migration). Winter behaviour of many species is basically similar: gathering in large concentrations in open country and making evening and early-morning flights to and from feeding grounds. During migration, which generally follows set routes known as fly-ways, flocks come down to feed at favoured stop-over points, often remaining for several weeks, some species not arriving at limits of winter range until forced to do so by weather conditions. Arrival on nesting grounds of northern-breeding forms depends on weather conditions, with birds waiting at stop-over points until breeding grounds relatively snow-free. Flocks fly high, moving in chevrons (V-formation) when well underway.

11 CAPE BARREN GOOSE   Plate 3
Cereopsis novaehollandiae

Alternative name: Cereopsis

A primitive Australian goose, formerly considered an aberrant sheldcuck and sometimes given its own monotypic tribe, Cereopsini, close to the swans.

FIELD IDENTIFICATION Length 75-100 cm (30-39 in). **At rest:** Unmistakable, the only goose-like bird within its range. A large, plump, stumpy-billed, uniform medium-grey goose with extensive pale green cere which almost totally obscures bill. At closer ranges, well-spaced black spots visible on wings. Grazes in open country in small flocks or family parties, spending little time on water. **In flight:** Typical goose shape, with bulky body and relatively broad wings. General appearance uniform grey but, from both above and below, shows some contrast with black tail and black trailing edge to primaries and secondaries. Flight action powerful, with shallow but rapid wingbeats. Flies in straggling lines or loose groups.

VOICE Noisy when alarmed or displaying. Males utter very loud and harsh trumpeting honks, 'ark, ark-ark, ark-ark'. Females have a pig-like, low-pitched grunt. Juveniles keep in contact with the family by reedy whistling cries.

DESCRIPTION All plumages similar. **Adult:** Almost entire plumage ashy-grey, with centre of crown paler, almost white. Scapulars and wing-covert feathers have a dusky subterminal spot. Tips of secondaries and primaries, and tail and uppertail-coverts, black. **Juvenile:** Resembles adult, but spotting on wings and scapulars heavier and general coloration a little paler grey.

BARE PARTS Adult: Bill black, but almost completely obscured by greatly-enlarged greenish-yellow cere. Legs pale flesh to dark reddish, with blackish lower tarsus, toes and webs. Iris reddish-brown. **Juvenile:** Much as adult, but legs initially greenish or blackish; iris dull brown.

MEASUREMENTS Males average a little larger than females. Wing 450-490; tarsus 100-110; bill, including cere, 48-53; mean weight of male 5290, of female 3770.

GEOGRAPHICAL VARIATION Two populations recognised. Recently-described western subspecies *grisea*, from the Recherche Archipelago of Western Australia, is a little stockier and has more extensive white area on crown than nominate form of rest of the species' range.

HABITS A goose of the southern Australian coast and islands. Sociable, but generally found in smaller concentrations than northern geese, flocks only rarely reaching 300 birds in size. During the breeding season (April-October) it resorts to small islands with tussock grassland, building its nest chiefly on or close to the ground, but occasionally in bushes and low trees. Although it breeds colonially, the nests are well spaced and the site is vigorously defended by the occupants. After fledging, the younger birds gather into small flocks which move to adjoining islands and even to the Australian mainland. Shy and wary by nature. Primarily a grazing bird, the eastern populations spending much time grazing on pasture, where they seem to have become something of a local problem for stock-farming. Despite its close association with the coast, it rarely swims, taking to the water only when danger threatens a brood of goslings. It is thought to pair for life, and, like most other wildfowl, has a flightless period when moulting.

HABITAT In the breeding season, offshore islands with tussocky grass and areas of short pasture, with some foraging along the seashore. After breeding, many move to low-lying coastal pasture and fringes of brackish and freshwater lakes in open country.

DISTRIBUTION Confined to southern Australia, where there are four breeding areas: the Furneaux group of islands in the Bass Strait; islands off Wilson's Promontory in Victoria; islands of Spencer Gulf and adjacent areas of South Australia; and the Recherche Archipelago of Western Australia, whose population is now recognised as subspecifically distinct. There is movement to adjacent larger islands and mainland areas outside the breeding season, but much of this involves flocks of immatures which are joined by adults after the post-breeding moult, although at least some adults probably remain about the breeding islands throughout the year. Long-distance movements are occasionally recorded and may be more frequent than is generally realised, with one ringing recovery at a distance of 800 km.

POPULATION Population now at its height, with eastern birds benefiting from adaptation to feeding on agricultural pasture, although this has raised some complaint from stock-farmers. It is partly protected, an experimental short shooting season now being permitted in Tasmania to alleviate farmers' complaints; experiments are, however, underway to attract grazing summer flocks to areas where they are welcome. Although the population was considered as low as 5,300 individuals in 1967, it is now known to be considerably higher, with current estimates being in the region of 15,000 birds. Recent population estimates are of 10,000 in South Australia; 500 in southeastern Australia; 5,000 in Tasmania; and 1,000 (of subspecies *grisea*) in Western Australia.

REFERENCES Dorward *et al.* (1980), Frith (1967), RAOU (1984).

12 SWAN GOOSE Plate 4
Anser cygnoides

Alternative name: Chinese Goose

Although familiar in its domesticated form, the original wild ancestor is poorly known and probably endangered.

FIELD IDENTIFICATION Length 81-94 cm (32-37 in). **At rest:** A distinctive 'grey' goose, with its long, deep, blackish bill, relatively small head and slender neck giving a slightly top-heavy appearance. The pattern of head and neck is also diagnostic, having crown and hindneck dark brown and contrasting with very pale brown throat, sides of head and fore-

neck, although much of the rest of the plumage is unremarkable and similar to that of many others of the genus. At closer ranges, the narrow whitish band around the base of the bill is visible, being highlighted by the heavy blackish bill, but this band is absent on juveniles. Legs orange. Domesticated forms may recall the wild bird in coloration, but are much fatter, lacking the slender appearance of the true bird, and have a well-developed frontal knob at the base of the bill. **In flight:** Typical 'grey' goose, with wing pattern close to that of White-fronted Goose (15). Under reasonable viewing conditions, however, the long and heavy blackish bill on markedly slender and pale neck is distinctive, although it should be noted that males appear heavier-headed than females. Because of rarity, unlikely to be encountered in very large concentrations today, but lone birds or family parties likely to become mixed with others, e.g. Bean Goose (13).

VOICE Has honking and cackling calls, given chiefly in flight. The voice of the wild bird is close to that of the more familiar domesticated forms, although perhaps not quite so loud or clamorous. Typical sound is a prolonged, resounding honk ending at a higher pitch, but the alarm is a harsh, short note repeated two or three times.

DESCRIPTION Sexes similar, although males larger and longer and heavier-billed than females, with longer neck. **Adult:** Crown and hindneck dark chestnut-brown, contrasting with pale buffish-brown throat, sides of head and front and sides of neck, whitest on upper neck. Narrow whitish band of varying intensity around base of bill. Flanks and upperparts dark ashy-brown, with almost whitish feather margins and broad whitish border to upper flank. Breast medium-brown or pale brown, darker than foreneck but paler than flanks. Ventral region and uppertail-coverts white. Rump dark grey. Tail dark grey, with whitish sides and extreme tip. Upperwing-coverts grey-brown, paler on lesser coverts and primary coverts, darkest on median and greater coverts; secondaries blackish, primaries dark grey, paler on inner webs. Underwing medium-grey. **Juvenile:** Resembles adult, but lacks whitish band around base of bill; crown and hindneck duller dark brown and fringes to feathers of upperparts and flanks more scaled until first winter, as in other 'grey' geese.

BARE PARTS All plumages: Bill, black; long and deep-based. Legs and feet deep orange. Iris reddish-brown, duller brown on juveniles.

MEASUREMENTS Males considerably larger than females. **Male:** Wing 450-460, tarsus 80-82, bill 87-98, weight ca. 3500. **Female:** Wing 375-440, bill 75-85, weight ca. 3000.

GEOGRAPHICAL VARIATION None.

HABITS Although known in domestication as the Chinese Goose for many centuries, perhaps as much as 3,000 years, as a wild bird this is one of the least-known of all Palaearctic waterfowl. On the breeding grounds it is a bird of steppe and mountain-valley lakes. It arrives in small flocks during April, taking up territory in waterside meadows and marshes; although not a colonial breeder, several pairs may be located in favoured areas. The nest is placed on dry ground, such as a low hillock, among dense vegetation, but normally not far from water; egg-laying commences from late April onwards. Flocks form for post-breeding moult, and the breeding grounds are forsaken from mid August to mid September. Even in the days when more numerous, no large concentrations seem to have been recorded, with flocks rarely exceeding 100 birds. Outside the breeding season sometimes encountered in open steppe far from water, but normally a bird of waterside marshes, where it grazes primarily on sedges, although little specific information is available. Generally shy and wary, owing to persecution both on breeding and on wintering grounds. Rarely swims, except when forced to do so by an intruder during moult period or when breeding.

HABITAT Breeding haunts are steppe and forested steppe marshes and lakesides. Precise habitat varies according to location, but includes river deltas, wide river valleys with meadows, and margins of brackish and freshwater lakes; in mountainous areas, even in relatively narrow valleys by fast-flowing rivers. In winter, frequents lowland lakeside marshes and wet cultivation, such as ricefields.

DISTRIBUTION Former breeding range extended from the southern regions of the Altai mountains, through Mongolia to Sakhalin and coastal northern China, taking in a broad sweep of steppe and forest-steppe/taiga country, but range probably much more fragmented today (see Population). In winter formerly in Japan, Korea and over large area of eastern China, but today almost certainly regular only in eastern China. As a vagrant, it has occurred on Taiwan and also west to Uzbekistan SSR.

POPULATION No total estimates have been made, although the species has clearly declined in numbers this century. The Soviet population is considered to be no more than 300-400 pairs. Certainly western populations have been severely decimated through hunting and destruction of breeding habitat, and it may well be that the major headquarters of the Swan Goose remain in Mongolia, where 1,000 were estimated at a summer concentration by a lake in the north-central steppe region in 1977. Although winter numbers in parts of eastern and southern China are still reasonable, its decline is reflected by its status in Korea and Japan, where it has become only an occasional winter straggler. Because of its scattered breeding and wintering ranges, overall protection would be difficult to enforce, but clearly steps need to be taken to protect this goose.

REFERENCES Dementiev and Gladkov (1952), Kear (1978), Kitson (1978).

13 BEAN GOOSE   Plate 4
Anser fabalis

A complexity of races of this goose breeds right across the northern Palaearctic: it is almost the Palaearctic equivalent of the Canada Goose (23).

FIELD IDENTIFICATION Length 66-84 cm (26-33 in). **At rest:** There is considerable individual and racial variation in overall size and in bill pattern and structure (see Geographical Variation). Basically a large, long-necked, long-billed, dark-headed 'grey' goose, with orange legs and orange and black bill, the extent of black on the bill varying from small patches to almost entirely dusky. Juvenile White-fronted (15) often has dark nail and indistinct dusky shades on bill, but Bean has darker head, contrasting more with paler breast, and a longer bill (except race *rossicus*) with clear blackish patches. Confusion most likely with Pink-footed (14), especially small Beans of race *rossicus* which may have similar bill shape, but Pink-footed is smaller, with more rounded head, greyer upperparts, and has deep fleshy-pink legs and band on bill. Exceptionally, Bean has dull fleshy legs, and it should be borne in mind that under some lighting conditions it may be difficult to decide whether leg colour is dull orange or dull pink, this being especially true of duller juveniles. Some Beans have a very narrow whitish line around base of bill, but never enough to suggest White-fronted. **In flight:** A large, very dark 'grey' goose with relatively longer neck than other species, although beware *rossicus*, which is smaller and stockier. The wing pattern is darker than on other 'grey' geese, showing little contrast between the coverts and the flight feathers, although not unlike pattern of White-fronted. Both upperwing and underwing lack the distinctive pale grey tones of Pink-footed or Greylag (17).

VOICE Less noisy than other 'grey' geese, even when in winter flocks. Cackling cries of the genus are all basically similar, although with experience a few key call notes among the honking and cackling help identify the various species. Bean Geese are vocally quite close to Pink-footed and their vocabulary includes a similar double 'wink-wink' phrase, although in the Bean it is considerably deeper in tone, more of a 'hank-hank'.

DESCRIPTION Sexes similar. Nominate race described. **Adult:** Head and neck dark brown, darkest on head; often narrow whitish line around base of bill. Breast and underparts medium-brown, flank feathers dark-centred and pale-edged with narrow white line at upper border of flanks. Mantle, scapulars and tertials dark brown, with pale fringes to feathers forming obvious pattern. Back, rump and tail dark brown. Uppertail-coverts, tail border and ventral region white. Upperwing-coverts dark ashy, palest on lesser and primary coverts. Primaries and secondaries blackish. Underwing dark ashy-grey. **Juvenile:** Resembles adult, but head and neck dull brown, not so dark as on adult. Pattern of upperparts and flanks more scaled than on adult, and pale fringes browner, less whitish. Lacks white at base of bill. Generally resembles adult by mid-winter, but tail and rump often appear darker.

BARE PARTS All races, both sexes. **Adult:** Bill variably patterned orange-yellow and black (see Geographical Variation). Legs and feet deep orange or orange-yellow. Iris dark brown. An uncommon colour variant has orange of bill and legs replaced by pink, thus recalling Pink-footed Goose; it has been given the vernacular name of 'Sushkin's Goose'. **Juvenile:** Similar to adult, but legs and bill duller orange, becoming brighter as first winter progresses.

MEASUREMENTS Males average larger than

females. Nominate *fabalis*: Wing 434-520 (mean: male 481, female 460); tarsus 73-90; bill 55-70 (mean: male 64, female 60); mean weight of male 3198, of female 2843. Race *johanseni*: Wing 425-520 (mean: male 479, female 451); bill 58-72 (mean: male 67, female 62). Race *middendorffii*: Wing 440-558 (mean: male 492, female 488); bill 64-81 (mean: both sexes 73). Race *rossicus*: Wing 405-478 (mean: male 454, female 433); bill 49-63 (mean: male 58, female 55); mean weight of male 2668, of female 2374. Race *serrirostris*: Wing 420-524 (mean: male 474, female 449); bill 58-72 (mean: male 66, female 63).

GEOGRAPHICAL VARIATION Owing to individual variation both in size and in bill pattern, it is not possible accurately to diagnose subspecies in the field except by locality of observation. Basically, the species falls into two major groups of races, tundra-breeding forms and taiga-breeding forms, although intergradation complicates the issue. The nominate race, which breeds in the taiga from Scandinavia east to the Urals, is large, long-billed and long-necked; its bill is basically orange, with black over distal portion and patches over culmen and towards bill base, most individuals having equal amounts of black and orange, or more orange than black. In the region of the Urals this race intergrades with the similar but slightly larger and darker-billed *johanseni*, which breeds in the taiga and forested tundra from the Urals east to the region of Baikal, where it intergrades with the next form; *johanseni* is somewhat intermediate between nominate *fabalis* and the eastern taiga form *middendorffii*, which is the largest of all, with long and deep-based black bill with orange restricted to a subterminal band; this last form breeds over the taiga of eastern Asia. The tundra populations breed to the north of the taiga races, although the two groups intergrade in the forested tundra zone: the smaller western *rossicus*, breeding from Kanin to the Taymyr Peninsula, is smaller and shorter-necked than nominate *fabalis* and has a shorter and deeper bill, which in shape and structure recalls Pink-footed Goose but is almost all blackish, with an orange subterminal band; towards the south of its range *rossicus* intergrades with nominate *fabalis*, and towards the east with the larger and very stout-billed *serrirostris* of the tundra from the Lena delta to Anadyr.

HABITS Breeding season varies a little according to location, with nesting territories occupied from mid to late May, although arrival may be delayed during migration if weather unfavourable. Nest sited on low, dry hummocks. After post-breeding moult, departs breeding areas in first half of September, arriving in winter quarters from late September to well into October. Highly gregarious in winter, although does not form huge, dense concentrations of many other 'grey' geese. Feeds primarily on lowland farmland in winter, family parties mixing freely with other goose species. Spends little time on water. Shy and wary, typically seen with neck fully erect, being easily alarmed by possible intruders. Roosting flights less extensive than those of most other geese, roosting close to feeding areas.

HABITAT Breeding habitat varies according to subspecies, the more northern tundra forms nesting in open damp tundra, coastal regions and on Arctic islands. The taiga forms breed mostly in sub-Arctic regions, favouring scrubby birch forest and even relatively dense coniferous-forest zones with boggy clearings. The two forms overlap widely, however, in the forest-tundra regions, where such distinctions do not hold true. Winters in open areas, favouring damp steppe and open agricultural land, but almost always in very open country.

DISTRIBUTION Breeds in scattered pockets across northern Europe and Asia, the breeding ranges of the five races having been outlined under Geographical Variation. There are two major wintering areas: the temperate lowlands of Europe, and the corresponding region of eastern Asia. To a certain extent races intermingle in winter, with European birds belonging to nominate *fabalis* and *rossicus*, although some *johanseni* have been identified in central Europe. Main winter centre of *johanseni* is in western China, where *rossicus* also reported, although intergrading of subspecies has caused much confusion over the years. Eastern Asian winter populations otherwise belong to *serrirostris* and *middendorffii*, but recent information sparse. Formerly regular in western USSR, especially by Black Sea in winter, but these populations believed to have now shifted winter quarters farther westwards in Europe. In Britain, where formerly wintered in good numbers, now very scarce. Majority of wintering flocks in Europe occur in areas centred around the southern shores of the North Sea and the Baltic, and in central Europe (Austria, Hungary and Yugoslavia). Vagrants have occurred south to North Africa, Nigeria, northern India and Burma; west to Iceland, the Azores and Madeira; and east to Alaska and Iowa.

POPULATION A widespread bird, with no general threats to any populations, decreases in certain winter populations in recent decades, e.g. Britain and Black Sea, suggesting shift of wintering grounds elsewhere owing to changes in agricultural methods. Forest clearance and human persecution no doubt cause of local declines on breeding grounds of some populations, e.g. Norway and Sweden. Estimate of wintering numbers in Europe, races *fabalis* and *rossicus*: some 4,000 in Spain, 40,000 in Baltic-North Sea region and 100,000-150,000 in central Europe. Eastern Asian winter populations less well known, but some 5,000, chiefly *serrirostris*, in Japan, where species has increased markedly since early 1970s.

REFERENCES Cramp and Simmons (1977), Ogilvie (1978).

14 PINK-FOOTED GOOSE Plate 4
Anser brachyrhynchus

Often considered merely a race of Bean Goose (13), this attractive goose winters primarily in Britain.

FIELD IDENTIFICATION Length 60-75 cm (24-29 in). **At rest:** A dark-headed, dark-billed 'grey' goose with deep rose-pink legs and bill-band. Smaller, shorter-necked and with rounder head and stubbier bill than closely-related Bean, but often matched in structure by some Beans of race *rossicus*. Deep pink legs and band on bill distinctive, although beware occasional Beans with similar bare-part colour (so-called 'Sushkin's Goose') when considering individuals outside normal distributional range. General body coloration paler than Bean, with more contrasting dark head and flanks. Under good lighting conditions, upperparts washed almost silvery-grey on scapulars and tertials, although this most obvious on fresh adults. Some individuals show narrow white line around base of bill, as on Bean. Duller juveniles less distinct, with browner upperparts and duller, sometimes almost fleshy-yellow, legs: can be problematic unless accompanied by adults (but in flight note pale upperwing). Confusion with other 'grey' geese unlikely, except at long range. **In flight:** Distinguished from other 'grey' geese by markedly light grey forewing, although this not so strikingly pale as on Greylag (17). Neck relatively shorter than on most other species, giving slightly 'waisted' look to rounded head. Distinguished from Greylag by shorter neck, darker head, darker underwing and flanks and by voice.

VOICE Highly vocal, with incessant cackling when in flight. All calls higher-pitched and shriller than larger species, with distinctive double or treble 'wink-wink' phrase and high-pitched 'ahng-ahng-ahng' included.

DESCRIPTION Sexes similar. **Adult:** Dark brown head and darker rear flanks. Rear flanks dark, with around base of bill. Lower neck, breast and fore-flanks light brown, contrasting markedly with dark head and darker rear flanks. Rear flanks dark, with pale feather fringes and narrow white upper border. Upperparts medium-brown, washed pinkish-grey, becoming almost silvery-grey on scapulars and tertials in fresh plumage, feathers with narrow whitish fringes. Back and rump dark grey. Tail dark grey with white border. Uppertail-coverts and ventral region white. Medium-grey lesser and median upperwing-coverts, contrast a little with rather darker greater coverts and strongly with blackish flight feathers. Underwing medium ashy-grey, appearing dark in field. **Juvenile:** Similar to adult, but plumage duller and browner, lacking grey tones to upperparts. Upperparts with more scale-like pale feather fringes, lacking strongly-barred appearance of adult. Underparts often show weak spotting on breast and belly. Becomes more as adult during first winter.

BARE PARTS Adult: Bill variably patterned, black with bright pink subterminal band and other patches along sides of upper mandible. Legs deep pink, very rarely orange; male often has deeper pink legs than female. Iris dark brown. **Juvenile:** Similar to adult but duller; legs and feet dull pale greyish-flesh, sometimes yellowish-grey, but becoming pinker during first winter.

MEASUREMENTS Males average larger than females. Wing 405-460 (mean: male 443, female 420); tarsus 65-80; bill 40-52 (mean: male 47, female 43); mean weight of male 2620, of female 2352.

GEOGRAPHICAL VARIATION None. Often considered a race of Bean Goose, to which it is obviously closely related. Occasional pink-legged Bean and orange-legged Pink-footed reinforce the close relationship, and small race *rossicus* of Bean is quite close in structure.

HABITS Highly gregarious goose, breeding in northern tundra. Arrives on breeding grounds from mid May to early June. Nests constructed on low hummocks in snow-free areas in open tundra, locally also on cliff ledges and tops of rocky pinnacles (as in Iceland). Breeds as territorial pairs, which may form loose colonies. Some non-breeding Icelandic birds move to Greenland to moult. Following post-breeding moult, flocks form to leave for winter quarters from late August to mid September. Arrives on winter grounds from mid September onwards, with main arrival through October. Winters chiefly on lowland farmland, feeding on stubbles, potato fields and winter cereals. Forms large concentrations in winter. Flies some distance to favoured daytime roost sites, which include estuarine mudflats, lochs and reservoirs. Shy and wary. Swims well and quite freely. Tends not to form mixed flocks with other geese, except for isolated individuals or family parties which may attach themselves temporarily.

HABITAT Breeds in open tundra, often in mountainous areas with deep rocky ravines and gorges. Winters in lowland farmland and by wide estuaries, feeding both in fields and on extensive areas of saltmarsh.

DISTRIBUTION Three breeding areas: eastern Greenland, Iceland and Svalbard. Collected Franz Josef Land in June 1914, but no evidence of breeding there. Greenland birds move to Iceland after breeding and both populations then move south together to winter in Britain, primarily in Scotland and northern and eastern England. Svalbard population moves southwards over western Scandinavia to winter in coastal lowlands from western Denmark through West Germany and the Netherlands to Belgium. Occasionally reported farther east along Baltic lowlands, and in southern Britain and Ireland in very small numbers. Vagrants have occurred east to Finland and western USSR; south to Romania, Italy, Spain, the Canary Islands, Madeira and the Azores; and west to Newfoundland and northeastern USA.

POPULATION Comparatively well known. Current estimates indicate some 100,000 wintering in Britain (originating from Greenland and Iceland) with numbers fluctuating between 70,000 and 85,000 in most recent winters. Svalbard population estimated at 25,000-28,500 from counts made during migration in Denmark. Breeding estimates of the Greenland and Icelandic populations indicate some 1,000 pairs in Greenland and 10,000 in Iceland. From monitoring winter counts it is evident that both populations are increasing markedly, although changes in agricultural practices in recent decades have shifted some of the wintering grounds, as in West Germany where fewer than 1,000 now winter.

REFERENCES Cramp and Simmons (1977), Madsen (1984), Ogilvie (1978).

15 WHITE-FRONTED GOOSE   Plate 5
Anser albifrons

Alternative name: Greater White-fronted Goose

Several races of this well-marked goose breed across the tundra of almost the whole of the northern hemisphere.

FIELD IDENTIFICATION Length 66-86 cm (26-34 in). See also very similar Lesser White-fronted Goose (16). **At rest:** Compared with other 'grey' geese, this relatively stocky and orange-legged species is easily distinguished when adult by its combination of extensive white patch surrounding base of bill and large black belly patches. The white 'face' is most apparent when bird is facing observer, and is individually variable in extent, as are the belly patches. Juveniles lack white 'face' and belly patches and in addition bill often shows dusky nail and dark shades, offering possible confusion with Bean (13), but White-fronted is chunkier in shape, with shorter neck, relatively more square head shape, and shorter bill which lacks clear-cut black patches of Bean. Greylag (17) is larger, bulkier, with longer neck and more massive bill, pink legs and distinctly pale grey wing-coverts (often hidden when on ground), but note that legs of White-fronted can sometimes appear distinctly fleshy in colour under certain conditions. Bill colour and general plumage contrasts vary according to subspecies. **In flight:** Relatively heavily-built 'grey' goose, with fairly dark upperwing pattern, although under good viewing conditions upperwing-coverts paler than flight feathers, with primary coverts palest. However, upperwing obviously darker than on either Pink-footed (14) or Greylag, but not so dark as on Bean. Large black belly patches of adult obvious when overhead, but lacking on juvenile. Flight silhouette shows a heavier head and neck than Pink-footed, lacking 'waisted' appearance. See also Lesser White-fronted, which is hardly separable in flight.

VOICE Noisy, with typical goose cackling. Characteristic flight sound includes repeated, musical 'lyo-lyok' of varying pitch. Calls all higher in pitch than those of Bean or Greylag, but less shrill than Pink-footed.

DESCRIPTION Sexes similar. Nominate race described. **Adult:** Fairly extensive white surround to base of bill. Head and neck medium dull brown, darker immediately behind white 'face'. Lower foreneck and underparts paler buffish-brown, with series of irregular black patches across lower breast and upper belly. Flanks dull brown, with darker centres and narrow pale fringes to rear flank feathers. Narrow white border line to upper flanks. Upperparts, including mantle, scapulars and tertials, medium grey-brown, with pale feather fringes forming transverse barring. Back, rump and tail dark grey. Uppertail-coverts, tail border and ventral region white. Upperwing-coverts ashy, lighter on primary coverts and contrasting with blackish primaries and secondaries. Underwing dark grey. **Juvenile:** Lacks adult's white 'face' and belly patches, which are gradually acquired from late winter into first summer. Upperparts lack clear transverse barring of adult, barring being less distinct and more scaly as in others of genus, but upperparts become more like those of adult during first winter.

BARE PARTS See also Geographical Variation. Nominate race described. **Adult:** Bill fleshy-pink, becoming more yellow towards base, nail white. Legs and feet orange or yellowish-orange. Iris dark brown. Some males have inconspicuous narrow yellow eye-ring. **Juvenile:** Bill duller than adult, with dusky nail and occasionally with greyish shade along sides, becoming more as adult during first winter. Legs and feet duller, often greyish-yellow or even fleshy-yellow.

MEASUREMENTS Males normally larger than females in most races, except *flavirostris*. Nominate *albifrons*: Wing 393-444 (mean: male 428, female 404); tarsus 63-80; bill 39-50 (mean: male 46, female 43); mean weight of male 2290, of female 2042. Race *flavirostris*: Wing 389-463 (mean: male 426, female 423); tarsus 63-84; bill 44-60 (mean: male 53, female 52); mean weight of male 2543, of female 2526. Race *frontalis*: Wing 389-445; bill 45-57. Race *gambelli*: Wing 403-474; bill 52-63.

GEOGRAPHICAL VARIATION Four, possibly five, races recognised. Nominate race (described above) breeds across Arctic Siberia from Kanin Peninsula to Kolyma River. Rather larger *frontalis*, with longer bill and darker head and upperparts, breeds in northeast Siberia from the Kolyma River eastwards across tundra of Arctic Canada to Queen Maud Gulf. Birds from western Greenland, race *flavirostris*, are larger and darker on head and upperparts than the nominate form and have bill chiefly orange-yellow, becoming slightly pinker towards tip. Isolated *gambelli*, which breeds in the taiga of the Mackenzie Basin region of Canada, is larger and darker than *frontalis*, with relatively longer bill. Recently-described *elgasi*, found breeding near Anchorage, Alaska, is larger and darker still than *gambelli* and has a tendency to show a yellow eye-ring, but the validity of this form has been questioned.

HABITS Very much as others of the genus. Arrival on breeding grounds depends much on location, but in Arctic Siberia from mid May to early June. Nests are widely scattered, although loose colonies may be formed in some areas. Nest site is a low hummock on dry ground, just about at level of thawing snow. After post-breeding moult, assembles to move south to winter quarters. Leaves breeding grounds from late August through September, arriving in winter quarters quite late in autumn via several stop-over sites. Outside breeding season highly gregarious, forming large concentrations in winter quarters. Shy and wary, perhaps more so than others of genus.

HABITAT Breeds on lowland tundra, often by lakes and rivers. In winter quarters a bird of open steppe and farmland, improved grassland, stubble fields, wide estuarine saltmarsh, and locally upland bogs (race *flavirostris*).

DISTRIBUTION See Geographical Variation for breeding ranges of the various races. Nominate race winters primarily in Europe and the Middle East, in Europe including England and Wales, the Netherlands and Belgium, moving south to Atlantic France in cold winters. Large numbers also winter in the steppes of Turkey, western lowlands of the Black Sea and in parts of southeast Europe, halting on the plains of Austria and Hungary in early and late winter; in cold winters, small numbers move south to Nile delta. A further population winters along southern shores of Caspian Sea, moving south into Iraq. Greenland race *flavirostris* migrates to Iceland and continues on to winter in Ireland and western Scotland, with small numbers still in west Wales, and is occasional on eastern seaboard of North America. Pacific race *frontalis* winters in China, Japan and western and southern USA south to northern Mexico. Race *gambelli* winters in coastal lowlands of Texas and Louisiana south into Mexico. Tule race *elgasi* winters in central California. Vagrants have occurred south to Spain, Portugal, Madeira, the Azores, most North African countries, Oman, Afghanistan, northern India, Burma and Hawaii, although to some of these countries species is a scarce rather than an accidental visitor.

POPULATION Population figures for the various forms indicated by winter estimates. Nominate race: 100,000-130,000 wintering in northern Europe, although in recent years much scarcer in France and western England; 65,000-100,000 in southeastern Europe, with lower numbers in Italy than formerly; 100,000 in western Black Sea region, but up to 500,000 in exceptional years, no doubt including many birds from southeast Europe and perhaps Turkey; 100,000 in Turkey and 10,000-40,000 in Caspian Sea region. Race *flavirostris*: 12,000 in Britain and Ireland. Race *frontalis*: 200,000 in North America, 3,500 in Japan, plus unknown numbers in eastern China. Race *gambelli*: at least 2,000 in Gulf coast of USA and Mexico. Race *elgasi*: 5,000 in central California.

REFERENCES Cramp and Simmons (1977), Johnsgard (1975), Ogilvie (1978), Wege (1984).

16 LESSER WHITE-FRONTED GOOSE
Anser erythropus   Plate 5

Relatively little-known goose, very similar to White-fronted (15), with which it often associates in winter.

FIELD IDENTIFICATION Length 53-66 cm (26-34 in). See also very similar White-fronted Goose. **At rest:** At all ages very difficult to separate from White-fronted, especially when mixed with flocks of that species. Typically, smaller and daintier than nominate White-fronted, although there is a certain amount of overlap between small White-fronted and large Lesser White-fronted. Compared with nominate and *frontalis* White-fronted, it has a smaller, shorter and brighter pink bill, more rounded head, rather shorter body and neck, slightly shorter legs, and longer wings which project a little farther beyond tip of tail (on White-fronted, wings reach tail-tip, only occasionally projecting beyond). At reasonably close ranges the bright yellow eye-ring may be visible; although this is shown by occasional White-fronted, it is never so clear as on Lesser. Adult has white 'face' patch usually extending a little farther up onto forecrown and ending in more of a point than on White-fronted, but this is difficult to judge on feeding bird unless it stops momentarily to hold head up. The belly patches are often smaller than on nominate White-fronted, but again this feature is individually variable in both species. Lesser is a generally darker, brighter-looking bird with relatively darker head and neck and brighter white flank line than White-fronted. Juvenile is still more difficult, differing from adult in much the same way as in White-fronted, and, like some juvenile White-fronted, often shows dusky nail and shading on the bill; it is best distinguished from White-fronted by structure and darker general coloration. Lesser also has a quicker feeding action and walk than White-fronted, which can help to locate individuals among White-fronted flocks. Many of the above features are difficult to discern in the field, but may be digested during prolonged observation once a possible Lesser is located. Locating individual Lesser White-fronted among numbers of White-fronted can be very difficult owing to the variations in size, frontal patch and postures, but Lesser can appear markedly different once pinned down. As with White-fronted, legs can at times appear to be distinctly fleshy. **In flight:** Wing pattern close to White-fronted, but can sometimes be picked out if flying among small group of White-fronted by smaller size, shorter neck, smaller body and bill, relatively longer wings, slightly faster wingbeats and higher call note.

VOICE Some calls are relatively loud, particularly on breeding grounds, where alarm is an almost grating 'queue-oop'. Flight calls notably squeakier, quicker and higher in pitch than those of White-fronted; typically include repeated 'kyu-yu-yu', which is slightly lower in pitch from female.

DESCRIPTION See also Field Identification. Sexes similar. **Adult:** Very much as nominate White-fronted, but whole plumage darker brown, especially head, neck and upperparts. White frontal patch usually extends farther up onto forehead in more of a point. Black belly patches usually smaller. **Juvenile:** Similar to that of nominate White-fronted, but overall darker brown, acquiring adult features during late first winter and first summer.

BARE PARTS All plumages: As nominate White-fronted, but bill brighter pink, lacking yellow basal tinge. Eye-ring conspicuously swollen, bright yellow.

MEASUREMENTS Males usually larger than females. Wing 361-388 (mean: male 378, female 373); tarsus 57-68; bill 29-37 (mean: male 37, female 31); weight of male 1950-2300, of female 1400-2150 (few data).

GEOGRAPHICAL VARIATION None recognised, but there is possibly a cline towards slightly larger birds in east of range.

HABITS Relatively poorly known compared with larger relative, no doubt owing to difficulties of identification. Arrives on breeding grounds in May, where pairs select isolated territories and nest on low hummocks, often among scrub and usually not far from water. After post-breeding moult, flocks leave breeding areas during late August and early September, arriving in winter quarters from mid October (a few) to mid December, having had prolonged stop-overs en route. Sociable outside breeding season, odd individuals often located among flocks of other geese, usually Bean (13) or White-fronted. Winter roosts formed on large lakes and rivers. More agile than White-fronted, both on wing and when walking, often running short distances. Occasional mixed pairs with White-fronted have been recorded in the wild, but no wild hybrids proven, although occasionally suspected.

HABITAT Breeds on tundra, by coasts and islands, and among scrubby tundra and fringes of the taiga farther south in its range, tending to be south of main breeding populations of White-fronted and less in open tunda; locally, also up into mountain foothills and lakes. Winters in salt steppe, arable farmland and meadows, tending to prefer more semi-arid country than White-fronted.

DISTRIBUTION Breeds across the whole of Arctic Europe and Asia, from declining populations of northern Scandinavia eastwards to northeastern Siberia. Winters primarily in south Caspian lowlands, with declining numbers in southeastern Europe, the lower Euphrates (Iraq/Iran), Kazakhstan SSR and in lowland eastern and southern China. Odd individuals regular in western Europe, particularly Britain, mixed with flocks of White-fronted, and occasional in winter in central Europe, Turkey, Egypt, Pakistan, northern India and Japan. Vagrants have also occurred in Novaya Zemlya and Spain. Occasional North American records most likely to be of escapes.

POPULATION Has certainly declined considerably at both western and eastern limits of range, although no precise or recent data available for many regions. The world population was estimated at some 100,000 individuals in 1965, but there is reason to believe that the species has declined since then. The Scandinavian breeding population has now almost disappeared. Formerly an abundant winter visitor to Japan, this species is now no more than a rare visitor there, and the same can be said of its former haunts around the western lowlands of the Black Sea, while data from China, although sparse, indicate a considerable decline in winter numbers. The southern Caspian lowlands are now thought to be its major winter stronghold, but in Caspian Iran current numbers are considerably lower than in mid 1950s.

REFERENCES Cramp and Simmons (1977), Dementiev and Gladkov (1952), Jonsson (1978).

17 GREYLAG GOOSE   Plate 5
Anser anser

The most southerly breeding 'grey' goose, this is the wild ancestor of many breeds of domestic geese.

FIELD IDENTIFICATION Length 75-90 cm (30-35 in). **At rest:** Largest and bulkiest 'grey' goose, with heavy head and bill, bulky body and relatively thick, although long, neck. Legs and feet pink, bill orange or pink depending on race. General plumage coloration rather uniform greyish-brown, with head and neck not markedly darker, unlike other 'grey' geese, in which at least head is typically darker. All plumages are similar. Pink legs shared only by Pink-footed (14), which has mostly dark bill, smaller darker head, shorter neck and is smaller overall. Juvenile White-fronted (15) and Lesser White-fronted (16) lack white 'face' of adults of those species, but have orange legs and darker head and

neck than Greylag. Confusion with others less likely. In some regions (e.g. Britain), has been reintroduced and occurs alongside Canada Goose (23), with which it sometimes hybridises under feral conditions. Greylag is the most likely 'grey' goose to be seen in southwest Europe or North Africa and the only one likely in Europe south of the Arctic region in summer, although injured 'grey' geese of other species, not capable of sustained flight, may oversummer on winter grounds. **In flight:** Perhaps the easiest 'grey' goose to identify in flight, with its strikingly pale grey forewing and light grey underwing-coverts, which can appear almost whitish in bright light. This pattern is approached by Pink-footed, but latter is nowhere near so pale, especially on underwing, and additionally has a shorter neck, small bill and darker head, and different voice. Typically, Greylag shows a long, thick neck, with chunky head and massive bill, neither markedly darker than the brown of body plumage, and lacks obvious belly marks of adults of the two white-fronted species.

VOICE Familiar to all as the voice of the farmyard goose. Typical flight calls consist of a loud, clanging, honking series of notes, including repeated deep 'aahng-ahng-ung', deeper and more clanging than other 'grey' geese. Has several other, more conversational notes.

DESCRIPTION Sexes similar. Nominate race described. **Adult:** Head, neck, breast, flanks and upperparts greyish-brown, rather uniform in tone, but breast a shade paler and rear flanks with darker feather centres. Often a narrow and indistinct white line surrounding base of bill. Distinct white line bordering upper flanks. Variable dark spotting on belly, rarely obvious. Pale feather fringes to upperparts form indistinct transverse barring. Back, rump and tail grey. Uppertail-coverts, tail border and ventral region white. Upperwing-coverts pale bluish-grey, contrasting markedly with darker flight feathers. Underwing-coverts pale grey, similarly contrasting with darker flight feathers. **Juvenile:** Similar to adult, but lacks spots on belly and upperpart pattern more scaly as on other 'grey' geese. Becomes more as adult during first winter, but does not acquire belly spots until second winter.

BARE PARTS See also Geographical Variation. Nominate race described. **Adult:** Bill orange, with fleshy-pink subterminal area behind whitish nail. Legs and feet fleshy-pink. Iris dark brown. Eye-ring narrow, pinkish or yellowish. **Juvenile:** Bill and legs duller, often tinged greyish. Eye-ring whitish. Becomes brighter during first winter.

MEASUREMENTS Males usually larger than females. Nominate *anser*: Wing 412-480 (mean: male 465, female 442); tarsus 71-93 (mean: male 85, female 79); bill 58-74 (mean: male 67, female 62); mean weight of male 3612, of female 3138. Race *rubrirostris*: Wing 395-515 (mean: male 468, female 448); bill 47-78 (mean: male 69, female 64); mean weight of male 3455, of female 2921.

GEOGRAPHICAL VARIATION Two subspecies recognised which intergrade in eastern Europe and western USSR. Nominate race is European breeding form, although certain introduced populations (e.g. in Belgium) are *rubrirostris*-type birds. Race *rubri-*

rostris of pure stock breeds over Asiatic part of species' range, west to western USSR and Turkey; compared with nominate *anser*, it is an overall distinctly paler bird with a wholly bright pink bill, although juveniles tend to have a yellowish tone to bill-base, which is soon lost, and a pink eye-ring. Birds from Iceland, Scotland and Norway tend to have rather shorter bills and have been separated as *sylvestris*, but this form is not generally recognised.

HABITS Very much as other 'grey' geese, being typically grazing birds in open country. Generally a little less wary than other species. Introduced feral populations in Europe (chiefly Britain) often in farmland, tolerating close proximity of towns and villages and breeding by man-made lakes and reservoirs. Nests in isolated pairs, but locally colonially, with site close to water, often hidden in reeds or other waterside vegetation, sometimes even in low trees. Outside breeding season highly gregarious, flocks frequenting lakes and surrounding farmland. Take-off more clumsy than that of other 'grey' geese, with some pattering over ground before rising into air. Swims readily and perhaps more habitually than many other geese.

HABITAT Variety of habitats in open country with extensive wetland areas, from southern fringes of the tundra in the far north to steppe lakes of central USSR and eastern Europe. Winters in lowland farmland, by estuaries, reservoirs and lakes in open country.

DISTRIBUTION Both breeding and wintering ranges tend to be more southerly than those of other 'grey' geese. Breeds across Europe and Asia, from Iceland, Britain, Scandinavia and eastern Europe across central and southern USSR, south into Mongolia and northern China. Icelandic birds winter in Britain, joining the resident British population. Scandinavian birds move southwest over Europe to winter chiefly in France and the Iberian Peninsula, while central and southern European populations winter around Mediterranean basin, including parts of North Africa. Breeding birds of western USSR winter around Black and Caspian Seas and filter into Iraq and Iran; many of these are doubtless *rubrirostris*. Farther east, major wintering areas lie across northern India to Burma and the lowlands of southern China; to a lesser extent also Soviet Central Asia. Has been successfully re-introduced into parts of Britain and Belgium and elsewhere in northern Europe. Vagrants have occurred north to Svalbard and Jan Mayen; south to Kuwait, Israel, Sri Lanka, Madeira, Azores, Canary Islands; and east to Japan.

POPULATION Over much of range has been, and still is, extensively hunted. In the past, further human persecution facilitated by the accessibility of nesting sites and flightless moulting flocks contributed to locally extensive declines. Drainage of wetlands has further sealed the fate of many populations. Re-introduction attempts into Britain and elsewhere have proved to be locally successful. Although the eastern European populations are somewhat fragmented and relatively small, increases are reported from several countries. North European numbers are growing quite dramatically, as echoed by the Icelandic population which has increased from 3,500 pairs in 1960 to some 18,500

by 1973. The same cannot be said for the eastern race *rubrirostris*, which is considered to have declined in numbers quite strikingly; although there are no figures available, its range is no doubt far more fragmented than the distribution map shows.

REFERENCES Cramp and Simmons (1977), Ogilvie (1978).

18 BAR-HEADED GOOSE   Plate 7
Anser indicus

One of the most attractive of all geese, and a colonial breeder of the high plateaux of central Asia.

FIELD IDENTIFICATION Length 71-76 cm (28-30 in). **At rest:** Adult is unmistakable, having a white head and white stripe down side of full length of neck contrasting with black hindneck and double crown-bands and grey body plumage, latter darker on foreneck and flanks. Juvenile is only a little less striking, but lacks crown-bands, the dusky hindneck extending up onto rear crown. Confusion of adult with other geese unlikely; juvenile, however, recalls young Snow Goose (19), but is easily separated by its yellowish bill and legs and light grey underparts. **In flight:** Differs from other 'grey' geese in having light grey body plumage, contrasting little with wing-coverts, although flight feathers are markedly darker. The light grey underwing-coverts are matched only by Greylag (17), with which it winters in India, but the dark foreneck contrasting with white head and lack of brown tones in plumage are obvious on birds overhead.

VOICE Typical goose honking calls in flight, but perhaps less strongly vocal than several other species, each note being relatively slowly uttered, rather low and distinctly nasal in tone.

DESCRIPTION Sexes similar. **Adult:** Head, throat, and stripe down full length of side of neck white. Two black bands on rear crown, the larger upper band stretching from eye to eye across rear crown. Hindneck blackish. Foreneck dark grey. Breast, flanks and entire upperparts medium-grey, darkest on rear flanks. Scapulars with indistinct pale transverse barring. Ventral region, uppertail-coverts and narrow tail border white. Tail otherwise grey. Upperwing- and underwing-coverts medium-grey to light grey, contrasting with dark grey flight feathers. **Juvenile:** Similar to adult, but crown and hindneck brownish-grey, lacking bands, forehead whitish with dusky line between eye and bill. Attains adult plumage during first winter, but not fully until second winter.

BARE PARTS Adult: Bill deep yellow, almost orange-yellow, with pinkish tones towards black nail. Legs and feet yellowish-orange. Iris dark brown. **Juvenile:** Bill and legs duller yellow, attaining brighter coloration by first winter.

MEASUREMENTS Males usually larger than females. Wing 406-482 (mean: male 454, female 424); tarsus 63-80; bill 47-63; weight 2000-3200.

GEOGRAPHICAL VARIATION None.

HABITS A remarkable goose, breeding on the high plateaux of central Asia and wintering in the lowland marshes of northern India. Highly gregarious, both when breeding and in winter quarters. Arrives on breeding grounds from late March to mid April, breeding in densely-packed colonies by lakeshores, nests being as close as pecking distance of neighbour will allow (although the really large colonies seem to be in Tibet rather than farther north). Occasionally, nests on cliffs and in low trees. An association with nesting pairs of Upland Buzzards is reported, which affords some protection from ground predators. After post-breeding moult, flocks start to leave breeding areas from late August through September. Arrives on Indian winter grounds from mid October onwards, having migrated over the high Himalayas; indeed, one migratory flock was recorded flying at 9375 m over Mount Everest. Winters in cultivation and swampy country, feeding in dense packs. Roosts on riverine sandbanks and lakes, flighting to and from feeding grounds at dusk and dawn. Shy and wary in winter, more approachable on breeding grounds. Swims well. Looks remarkably stocky when feeding, keeping slender neck tucked well into body in curve. Stocky body gives short-legged appearance, enhanced by very rolling gait.

HABITAT Breeds by high-altitude (up to 5000 m), often saline, lakes, frequenting boggy ground in open country. Winters by marshes, lakes and rivers.

DISTRIBUTION Formerly bred over extensive area of central Asia, from the Tien Shan in the west, north to Mongolia, east to northwestern Heilongjiang (Manchuria), Ningxia and Qinghai, and south across Tibetan plateau to Ladakh and Wakhan (northeastern Afghanistan). Although some birds reported to remain in winter in parts of southwestern China, the bulk of the population crosses the Himalayas to winter across the northern half of the Indian subcontinent, west to Pakistan and east to northern Burma. Migrates over and through Nepal and Assam. Vagrant to southern India. Popular in captivity, frequently escapes and is regularly reported at large in western Europe and North America; at one time a small feral population became established in southern Sweden for a number of years.

POPULATION Now much reduced, this reflected in lack of recent winter reports from either Pakistan or Burma. Soviet breeding population recently estimated at 1,500-1,600 individuals, mostly in Uzbekistan, Kirghizia and Tadzhikistan SSR. In Mongolia considered to be still present in good numbers, but few data from China. Flooding of breeding sites, persecution by shooting and egg-collecting (for food), and heavy natural predation are factors associated with the decline. Present world population estimated at somewhat over 10,000 individuals.

REFERENCES Dementiev and Gladkov (1952), Gole (1982), Kitson (1978), Ogilvie (1978), Ouweneel (1984).

19 SNOW GOOSE   Plate 6
Anser caerulescens

Alternative name: Blue Goose

A beautiful Arctic goose, popular in collections and occurring in two colour-forms.

FIELD IDENTIFICATION Length 65-84 cm (26-33 in). See also Ross's Goose (20) for separation of these two very similar species. Occurs in two distinct colour-phases, a white or snow phase and a dark or blue phase (formerly called 'Blue Goose'), plus intermediate individuals. **At rest, snow phase:** Adult totally white, except for black primaries, which are partially concealed at rest by elongated tertials. Rusty staining is common on head and neck. Bill and legs pink. Apart from very similar Ross's, unlikely to be confused with any other goose. Occasional albino 'grey' geese occur, but these do not show neat black primaries or elongated, pointed tertials of Snow. See also Coscoroba Swan (27). Juvenile has pale greyish-brown upperparts, crown and nape, with paler 'face', sides and front of neck and underparts, and shows some contrast between greyish upperparts and black primaries; bill and legs dusky. Confusable only with juvenile Ross's, but beware occasional leucistic 'grey geese', which differ in same way as from adults. See also juvenile Bar-headed (18). **At rest, blue phase:** Adult has white head and neck contrasting with dark grey of much of remainder of plumage, some individuals darker than others, but darkest on body, often with whitish undertail-coverts. Wing-coverts paler grey. Bill and legs pink. Emperor Goose (21) is much stockier, has yellow legs, pure white tail and cleaner, neatly-barred plumage. See also blue-phase Ross's Goose, which is very rare. Juvenile at first almost completely sooty-brown, with dusky bill and legs; gradually attains adult plumage during first autumn and winter. Juvenile Emperor is similar, but stockier, has sootier head and neck and upperparts lightly scaled. **In flight:** Snow phase almost unmistakable, adult having pure white plumage contrasting with black primaries; juvenile similar, although washed grey-brown on upperparts and wing-coverts. Only Ross's presents real identification problem. Blue phase dark, with contrasting paler grey wing-coverts and pale rump and tail; adult also has white head. Emperor has less obviously-pale coverts, is bulkier and with contrasting pure white tail.

VOICE As with all geese, very vocal, flying birds calling almost constantly, with a hard cackling, rather nasal and high-pitched 'la-luk', at distance not dissimilar to barking of a small dog.

DESCRIPTION Sexes similar. **Adult snow phase:** Completely white, except for grey primary coverts and black primaries. **Adult blue phase:** Head and upper neck white. Lower neck and entire underparts very dark grey, often paler or even white in ventral region. Mantle and scapulars very dark grey. Back and rump paler grey. Uppertail-coverts whitish-grey. Tail variable, dark grey with whitish feather fringes, often more or less all whitish. Elongated tertials blackish-grey with whitish fringes. Upperwing-coverts paler grey, contrasting with black primaries and secondaries. Underwing-coverts pale grey, sometimes dark grey. **Juvenile snow phase:** Crown, rear and sides of neck, mantle and scapulars greyish-brown. Foreneck, sides of head and entire underparts whitish, indistinctly mottled pale grey-brown. Back, rump and uppertail-coverts whitish, mottled grey-brown. Tail grey-brown, fringed whitish. Elongated tertials dark grey with whitish fringes. Upperwing-coverts greyish-brown, fringed and marbled whitish. Underwing whitish. Primaries black. Gradually attains adult plumage during first winter and summer. **Juvenile blue phase:** Totally dark slaty-brown, becoming browner on upperparts and often paler on ventral region. Begins to attain whitish mottling on head early in first winter, and resembles adult by late winter or first summer. **Intermediate:** Relatively common between the two phases. Closer to blue phase in general appearance, but with extensive areas of white on underparts, often merely showing dark upperparts and breast-band.

BARE PARTS All phases. **Adult:** Bill reddish-pink, with black cutting edges and white nail. Legs and feet reddish-pink. Iris dark brown. **Juvenile:** Bill, legs and feet dark grey.

MEASUREMENTS Males usually larger than females. Nominate *caerulescens*: Wing 380-460 (mean: male 430, female 420); tarsus 75-91; bill 50-62 (mean: male 58, female 56); mean weight of male 2744, of female 2517. Race *atlanticus*: Wing 425-485 (mean: male 450, female 445); tarsus 80-97; bill 57-73 (mean: male 67, female 62); mean weight of male 3626, of female 3065.

GEOGRAPHICAL VARIATION Two subspecies recognised, differing chiefly in size (see Measurements). Nominate race, known as 'Lesser Snow Goose', breeds over most of species' range, from Wrangel Island (USSR) across Arctic North America to Baffin Island; its blue phase was formerly in minority but is now abundant, having increased among the population in recent decades. Larger race *atlanticus*, sometimes called 'Greater Snow Goose', has heavier bill; it breeds on islands in north Baffin Bay and northwest Greenland, and its blue phase is very rare.

HABITS Highly gregarious throughout the year, breeding in closely-packed colonies on the Arctic tundra. Arrives on breeding grounds as soon as snow melts, with egg-laying in June. Breeding adults tend to mate with their own colour-phase by preference, but when mixed pairing occurs blue-phase young predominate; certain populations have therefore become mostly blue, as choice of mate becomes more difficult for snow phase. Following post-breeding moult, breeding grounds are vacated at onset of colder weather, in late August and September. Has well-defined migration routes to and from winter quarters. Arrival in winter quarters varies with each population, some having quite long stop-overs en route, whereas others move quickly onwards; generally, however, northward spring migration is slower than the autumn one. Winter flocks often attain tens of thousands in coastal farmland. Roosts on water, swimming freely, but feeds by grazing, usually pulling out plants by roots, rather than by grazing off tops. Mixes freely with other geese on winter grounds, although main portions of flocks keep separate. Even on breeding grounds, other Arctic geese may nest in fairly close proximity and occasional wild hybrids have been recorded with such species as Ross's, White-fronted (15) and Canada (23) Geese.

HABITAT Breeds by low tundra, usually within 10 km of water, but race *atlanticus* chooses sites in rockier ground or on wet tundra in lee of mountains. On winter grounds resorts to cultivation; fields of sprouting corn, pasture and stubble fields in lowland coastal zones are favoured.

DISTRIBUTION Breeds across Arctic North America, with an isolated outpost on Wrangel Island off the coast of northeast Siberia. Breeding ranges of the two races are given under Geographical Variation. The nominate race winters chiefly along the Gulf coast of USA in Louisiana and Texas, but more western populations (in which blue phase is absent or rare, but has even been recorded west to Wrangel Island) winter in central California, north-central Mexico and adjacent regions of southern USA. Race *atlanticus* winters along Atlantic coast between Maryland and North Carolina. Occasional in winter in Hawaii, eastern China and Japan, where now much rarer than formerly following decline of Soviet population. Very popular in collections; most vagrants in Europe considered escapes, but wild individuals certainly occur, especially in Iceland and Ireland, sometimes mixed with parties of White-fronted Geese from Greenland. Recorded occasionally from most European countries, south to the Azores and east to Finland and East Germany. Many reports of stragglers away from recognised areas in Asia have proven to be albino 'grey' geese of various species.

POPULATION Abundant. Nominate form considered to number about 2 million individuals in USA in winter. On Wrangel Island, the only remaining Soviet population was considered to contain 87,000 birds in 1976, but only 6,000 nests were estimated. Although dense, this latter population is declining after human settlement on the island, damage to colony by herds of introduced reindeer, and increasing population of Arctic foxes feeding on the waste from reindeer-farming; hunting of this population on its winter grounds in Pacific United States has now been controlled to help the situation. The *atlanticus* population is increasing, being estimated at 400,000 in 1984, whereas in 1969 it was only 90,000; this dramatic increase is considered to be due to more-restricted hunting and the setting up of refuges.

REFERENCES Bousfield and Syroechkovskiy (1985), Ogilvie (1978, 1985).

20 ROSS'S GOOSE   Plate 6
Anser rossii

A diminutive version of Snow Goose (19) in all respects, but with more restricted breeding and wintering ranges.

FIELD IDENTIFICATION Length 53-66 cm (21-26 in). **At rest:** Very similar to snow phase of Snow Goose, though considerably smaller, with tiny, deep bill lacking Snow's 'grinning patch' along cutting edge of mandibles, but has indistinct bluish warty protuberances over base of bill, most obvious on old males. Has smaller, more rounded head, shorter and thicker neck and relatively shorter, dumpier body than Snow. Flocks of the two species normally keep separate, but individuals and family parties often mix with Snow, especially on Gulf coast of USA, where separating the odd Ross's from a huge, varied flock of Snow Geese is very difficult. Very occasional blue-phase individuals are reported from time to time (see Habits). Ross's is less inclined to become stained with rusty colour on the head than Snow Goose. Juvenile differs from that of Snow Goose in being much whiter, having only a weak greyish wash to hindneck and scapulars. **In flight:** Not easy to distinguish from Snow, owing to similar plumage pattern, but may be separated by combination of smaller size, relatively shorter neck, smaller head and bill and rather quicker wingbeats. Differences most noticeable when lone Ross's flying with small party of Snow.

VOICE All calls much higher in pitch than those of Snow Goose. Flight calls include a short grunt, 'kug', and a weak cackling 'kek, ke-gak'.

DESCRIPTION Sexes similar. **Adult:** Basically as snow phase of Snow Goose in plumage pattern and coloration. **Adult blue phase:** Very rare. Similar to that of Snow Goose, but apparently always with extensive white belly. **Juvenile:** Much as juvenile snow phase of Snow Goose, but brownish-grey areas of plumage paler and less extensive, being merely washed pale greyish-brown on rear crown, nape and scapulars.

BARE PARTS Adult: Bill deep reddish-pink, with paler nail and variably extensive bluish warty area over basal portion of bill, most extensive on older males and almost lacking on females and younger males. Legs and feet reddish-pink. Iris dark brown. **Juvenile:** Bill and legs greenish-grey, becoming pinker during first winter.

MEASUREMENTS Males typically larger than females. **Male:** Wing 360-380, tarsus 61-70, bill 40-46, mean weight 1315. **Female:** Wing 345-360, bill 37-40, mean weight 1224.

GEOGRAPHICAL VARIATION None.

HABITS This attractive little goose is closely related to Snow Goose and shares similar behaviour patterns. The warty protuberances on the bill are considered to be a useful isolation character that prevents extensive hybridisation where the two species breed alongside each other, although, like other geese, Ross's arrive on the breeding grounds already paired. A number of hybrids and mixed pairs have been reported, however, and the occasional blue-phase individual may indicate the presence of some blood of the larger species, although specimens examined support the view that such birds are true Ross's on measurements and structure. Highly gregarious on both breeding and winter grounds. Arrives on breeding grounds mid to late May, soon settling down to breed. Nests are often closely packed on lowland tundra and islands, usually situated among scrubby cover or in lee of rocks. After post-breeding moult, flocks start to leave breeding grounds in September, and majority arrive in winter quarters by mid October. Despite fairly rapid autumn migration, spring migration is slower, with longer stop-overs; birds start to leave winter quarters in early March. Breeding range overlaps to limited extent with that of Snow Goose and in winter flocks do not generally mix, although individuals and family parties become mixed with Snow Goose concentrations and are very easy to overlook.

HABITAT Breeds along lowland tundra shores, preferring large islands. Winters in lowland cultivation and grassland, also ricefields and stubble fields during autumn migration.

DISTRIBUTION Breeds almost entirely in the Perry River region of the North-West Territories of Canada, with occasional breeding reported elsewhere in Arctic Canada, notably Banks and Southampton Islands and along McConnell River. Formerly wintered exclusively in Sacramento valley of California, but now known to be more widespread, or winter habits possibly changing with agricultural methods. During migration, passes through Oregon, northwest Montana and Alberta/Saskatchewan border. In winter small numbers reach south to New Mexico and even northern Mexico, and regular now in small numbers along Gulf coast of Louisiana and Texas among vast numbers of Snow Geese, these birds having probably migrated down Mississippi fly-way with Snow Geese. Occasionally reported as a straggler elsewhere in USA, down west coast and occasionally to Atlantic coast. Individuals occasionally reported in northwest Europe, chiefly Britain but also Netherlands and Iceland, almost certainly escapes; two which nested in Iceland and returned to Britain with Pink-footed Geese were known to have escaped from a British collection.

POPULATION Quite well known owing to rather limited range. Breeding population estimated at some 77,300 individuals in 1976. Seems to be increasing, despite still being hunted, but biggest threat may result from limited range and close-flocking behaviour, which would make the species particularly vulnerable if a disease were to break out.

REFERENCES McLandress (1979, 1983), Melinchuk and Ryder (1980), Ryder (1967).

21 EMPEROR GOOSE   Plate 6
Anser canagicus

An attractive, tubby relation of the Snow Goose (19) from western Alaska and northeastern Siberia.

FIELD IDENTIFICATION Length 66-89 cm (26-30 in). **At rest:** A white-headed dark grey goose of Arctic coastal regions of the northern Pacific. The general blue-grey plumage, at reasonable ranges seen to be scaled black, contrasts with white head, neck and tail and blackish foreneck. Legs deep yellow. This stocky, relatively small-billed and short-necked goose is unlikely to be confused with anything other than blue Snow Goose, which it recalls in plumage coloration. Blue-phase Snow Goose, however, is almost unknown in western populations, has larger bill, longer neck, reddish-pink legs, white foreneck and often whitish ventral region and dusky hindneck. Like many other white-headed Arctic birds, Emperor Goose often shows rusty staining on head and neck. The all-dusky juvenile also recalls juvenile blue Snow Goose and is perhaps best distinguished by structure, although at close range it appears indistinctly barred (less obviously so than adult); it lacks juvenile blue Snow's whitish chin and has relatively blacker head and neck. Adult-like plumage is attained quite early in first winter. **In flight:** Bulky body, with relatively short neck and broad wings, and dark grey general coloration with white head, hindneck and tail are obvious features in flight. The wingbeats are quite shallow and, unlike other geese, this species flies relatively low.

VOICE Flight call is a distinctive, high-pitched but hoarse, repeated 'kla-ha, kla-ha', but when flying shorter distances a shrill, pleasing 'yang-yang'. Other conversational calls are uttered, but generally not so vocal as many other species.

DESCRIPTION Sexes similar. **Adult:** Head and neck white, although in the wild usually heavily stained rusty-orange. Chin and foreneck black. Entire body plumage, including ventral region and uppertail-coverts, scapulars and wing-coverts, blue-grey, profusely scaled, with blacker subterminal band and whitish terminal fringe to feathers. Tail white. Flight feathers greyish-black. Underwing grey. **Juvenile:** Entire plumage sooty-grey, duller and browner than adult, with head and neck finely mottled dark grey, blackest on foreneck, and with indistinct white flecking on head. Body plumage less clearly scaled than adult, with scaling narrower. Tail pale. Resembles adult quite early in first winter, but first-winter individuals show dark freckles on white head and neck until first summer.

BARE PARTS Adult: Bill pink, with black nostril, cutting edge and underside; pale blue tinge around basal portion. Legs and feet deep orange-yellow. Iris brown. **Juvenile:** Bill blackish. Legs and feet dull olive-brown to yellowish-grey, attaining adult coloration during first winter, but distinctly greyer until at least first spring.

MEASUREMENTS Males usually larger than females. **Male:** Wing 380-400, tarsus 66-72, bill 40-49, mean weight 2812. **Female:** Wing 350-385, bill 35-40, mean weight 2766.

GEOGRAPHICAL VARIATION None.

HABITS A maritime species, breeding about coastal tundra and wintering along rocky seashores and islands. Less gregarious than other geese, feeding in family parties among seaweed-beds and estuarine mudflats, but in summer feeds on wet tundra. Forms larger concentrations in winter and to moult. Arrives on breeding grounds in second half of May, nesting in scattered loose colonies by tundra pools not far from waterside. After breeding, adults moult fairly close to breeding grounds. Non-breeders, however, which seem to make up a large percentage of the population, gather to moult in large numbers at key locations. Alaskan non-breeders gather on St Lawrence Island, whereas less abundant Soviet populations gather at several locations along northern side of Chukotsky Peninsula. After breeding, undergoes relatively short migration to winter quarters, primarily in Aleutian Islands. Because of mostly coastal habit, does not mix much with other geese, but vagrant individuals and family parties have occasionally become mixed with other geese.

HABITAT Breeds by coastal tundra lakes and lagoons, locally inland on tundra with scattered pools. Winters along rocky seashores with extensive seaweed-beds and estuarine mudflats.

DISTRIBUTION Breeds in small numbers along coast of northeastern Siberia, with bulk of population in coastal Alaska. Non-breeders flock to St Lawrence Island, but migrates south to winter along chain of Aleutian Islands and Gulf of Alaska, some birds wintering south to Kamchatka. Vagrants occur in winter down western seaboard of Canada and USA, south to California, some even turning up inland with other geese. Vagrants have also occurred on Wrangel Island (USSR) and even Hawaii and Japan.

POPULATION Soviet population never abundant, but considered to be declining; formerly occurred west to Kolyma River, but now known only from coast of Anadyr Gulf and Chukotsky Peninsula, where population is at least 12,000 individuals. Alaskan population estimated at 150,000 in 1976, but considered to have declined since.

REFERENCES Dementiev and Gladkov (1952), Kistchinski (1971), Petersen and Gill (1982).

22 HAWAIIAN GOOSE   Plate 7
Branta sandvicensis
Alternative name: Néné

One of conservation's success stories: at one time on the brink of extinction, Hawaii's only goose is now established back in the wild following a captive-breeding programme.

FIELD IDENTIFICATION Length 56-71 cm (22-28 in). **At rest:** Unmistakable. Endemic to the Hawaiian Islands, where it is normally the only goose, although vagrants of several other species have been very rarely recorded from the islands. A brownish goose, with buffish sides of head and neck and blackish crown, face and hindneck. The neck feathering is distinctly grooved, producing the effect of weak striping in the field. Highly unlikely to be confused with any other species, even in captivity. **In flight:** General plumage pattern in flight recalls Canada Goose (23), but foreneck is buffish, not black.

VOICE Not so highly vocal as most other geese. The typical call is a low moaning note, typified by its native name, 'Néné'. During courtship it becomes more vocal and raucous.

DESCRIPTION Sexes similar. **Adult:** Chin, sides of head back to eye, and crown and hindneck brownish-black. Sides of head and front and sides of neck buff, with distinct lines of feather grooves. Narrow dark ring at base of neck. Upperparts, breast and flanks medium-brown; flanks and scapulars have darker feather centres and pale buff terminal fringes, producing transverse barring on upperparts. Rump and tail black. Ventral region and uppertail-coverts white. Wing-coverts brown with darker feather centres, flight feathers darker. Underwing brown. **Juvenile:** Much as adult, but duller, with browner black on head and neck and weakly-scaled rather than transversely-barred body plumage. Much as adult after first moult.

BARE PARTS All plumages: Bill, legs and feet black. Iris dark brown. The toes are only partially webbed.

MEASUREMENTS Males slightly larger than females. **Male:** Wing 351-404, tarsus 76-90, bill 36-43, mean weight 2165. **Female:** Wing 347-368, tarsus 74-83, bill 32-40, mean weight 1930.

GEOGRAPHICAL VARIATION None.

HABITS A rare bird of the volcanic uplands and mountain slopes of some of the Hawaiian Islands. Formerly quite abundant, it was reduced to the verge of extinction, but after extensive releases of captive-bred birds to supplement the tiny wild population it seems to have recovered (see Population). Unlike most other wildfowl, it has little webbing between its strong toes, an adaptation to living on land and feeding among the scant vegetation of the lava flows. Spends part of the year in family groups, although during the period June-September the families flock together for the 'winter'. Flocks break up by September as pairs settle down to breed. Unlike other geese, except Cape Barren Goose (11), copulation takes place on land. The nests are situated among vegetation by lava flows. During the fledging period, the adults become flightless and flocks form for the post-breeding moult. Non-migratory.

HABITAT Barren volcanic slopes with sparse vegetation between 1525 m and 2440 m.

DISTRIBUTION Endemic to the Hawaiian Islands, where it is found on Hawaii (slopes of Mauna Loa, Hualalai and Mauna Kea) and tenuously on Maui (Haleakala Crater).

POPULATION Formerly abundant, with about 25,000 estimated at end of eighteenth century. Through hunting pressures, and because of predation on nests and during flightless period by introduced mongooses, cats, pigs and dogs, the numbers had dwindled away until only some 30 remained by 1952. Extensive captive-breeding programme began in 1949, with first releases into the wild in 1960; over 1,000 now released on Hawaii and 400 on Maui, with some success on Hawaii but little evidence of a good breeding population yet being established on Maui. In 1976, there were considered to be about 650 in the wild on Hawaii and 100 on Maui. The programme continues, linked with the control of feral predators. Luckily, the species responds well to captive breeding and there are good numbers breeding in captivity, notably at Slimbridge (England) and in Hawaii, to perpetuate the species. Fully protected by law.

REFERENCES Kear and Berger (1980), King (1981).

23 CANADA GOOSE Plate 7
Branta canadensis

Alternative names: see Geographical Variation

The racial extremes of this goose are unique: largest birds may be as much as seven times heavier than the smallest.

FIELD IDENTIFICATION Length 55-110 cm (22-43 in). The size variations between the various populations of this goose are more extreme than those of any other bird. Smallest individuals may be only the size of Mallard (84), the largest at least twice that and considerably different in structure. See Geographical Variation. **At rest:** Despite the size variation, all populations may be easily identified as Canada Geese by their combination of brown body plumage, black head and neck and extensive white facial patch. The brown of the body varies from dark reddish-brown to dull greyish-brown, and the breast may be either paler than flanks or darkly uniform with them. Barnacle Goose (24) has black neck and white face, but also has black breast, grey body and the white of face so extensive as to appear almost white-headed at long range. **In flight:** Combination of brown body plumage, black head and neck and white face distinctive. Dark-breasted races can appear markedly dark, with contrasting white ventral region and uppertail-coverts.

VOICE Varies somewhat among the races. All forms are very vocal, especially in flight. Larger races have a deep, almost musical, rolling honking 'ah-hank', repeated at varying pitches as the bird takes to the air. Smaller races have a distinctly different high-pitched yelping or cackling, 'yelk, yelk, a-lick, a-lick'.

DESCRIPTION See also Geographical Variation. Sexes similar. Nominate race described. **Adult:** Head and entire neck black. Broad white cheek-band, running from throat to rear of eye, sometimes partially divided by dark throat centre. Breast very pale, almost whitish, merging into darker buffish-brown flanks. Upperparts medium-brown with paler feather fringes, most marked on scapulars and forming weak transverse barring. Back, rump and tail black. Ventral region and uppertail-coverts white. Wing-coverts brown with pale fringes, flight feathers darker. Underwing brown. **Juvenile:** Very similar to adult, but upperparts more irregularly and less distinctly pale-barred, cheek patch washed light brown, head and neck a browner black. Even closer to adult by first winter. Not easy to age, except by fresher plumage in early summer, i.e. before post-breeding moult.

BARE PARTS All races, all plumages: Bill, legs and feet black. Iris dark brown.

MEASUREMENTS Males usually larger than females. See Geographical Variation.

GEOGRAPHICAL VARIATION Differences between the various races are not so clear-cut as may be indicated by the summary below, since many areas are intergrade zones between one or more races. Generally, there is a cline of increasing colour saturation towards the west and an increase in size towards the south: smallest forms are therefore in the high Arctic and paler-breasted populations in the east. Basically, the dark birds are reddish-brown with similarly-coloured breast, whereas the paler greyer or lighter brown birds have breast noticeably paler than flanks. Smaller individuals have markedly shorter neck, more rounded head and shorter, smaller bill than larger forms. The following races are recognised:

Nominate *canadensis*: Described above. Wing 450-550; tarsus 78-95; bill 48-65; mean weight of male 4880, of female 4390. Breeds southeast Canada and northeast USA, winters Atlantic coast USA. USA winter population ca. 36,000. European feral populations also chiefly of this form, but somewhat of a racial mixture, many being closer to *maxima*.

Race *interior*: Slightly smaller than nominate form and a little darker, with narrower feather fringes to upperparts. Wing 410-549, tarsus 75-91, bill 43-64, mean weight 3859. Breeds in region south and east of Hudson Bay, winters southeastern USA. Population ca. 1,250,000.

Giant Canada Goose, race *maxima*: Largest race, with longer neck and bill than but similar in colour to nominate form, although slightly paler. Wing 480-550, tarsus 90-106, bill 60-68, mean weight 5200. Chiefly resident in Great Plains region of northern USA. Population ca. 27,000.

Race *moffitti*: Much as *maxima*, but with rather plumper, shorter body and relatively shorter bill and legs. Wing 455-520, tarsus 82-101, bill 48-59, mean weight 4086. Breeds Great Basin region of northeast USA and southwest Canada, east of Rockies, winters western USA. Population ca. 115,000.

Lesser Canada Goose, race *parvipes*: Similar to *moffitti*, but considerably smaller. Wing 410-442, tarsus 73-88, bill 36-49, mean weight 2730. Breeds Arctic Canada west to eastern Alaska, winters southern USA, chiefly interior California but east to Gulf coast and south into Mexico.

Richardson's Goose, race *hutchinsii*: Smallest of the pale forms, with very pale breast and small bill. Wing 350-408, tarsus 65-75, bill 31-39, mean weight 2270. Breeds Arctic Canada (Melville Peninsula, Southampton, Ellesmere and Baffin Islands), winters Gulf coast of Texas and Mexico.

Race *fulva*: Large, uniformly dark rufous form. Wing 432-513, tarsus 84-100, bill 45-60, mean weight ca. 4200. Chiefly resident coastal British Columbia north to southern Alaska, winters south to northern California. Population 80,000.

Dusky Canada Goose, race *occidentalis*: Darker and smaller than *fulva*, with shorter and deeper bill; usually lacks neck-ring. Wing 395-460, tarsus 70-84, bill 41-48, mean weight 3800. Breeds coastal southern Alaska, winters Vancouver and Oregon. Population 20,000.

Aleutian Canada Goose, race *leucopareia*: Very small form, with tiny deep-based bill; slightly paler than other western forms, with fairly prominent white neck-ring. Wing 358-405, tarsus 66-81, bill 31-36, mean weight 2270. Breeds some Aleutian islands, winters central California. Population 1,600; endangered.

Cackling Goose, race *minima*: Darkest of the small forms and smallest of all, with tiny bill and short neck; thin white neck-ring may be present. Wing 330-370, tarsus 60-70, bill 26-32, mean weight 1590. Breeds coastal western Alaska, winters chiefly interior California south to northern Mexico. Population 150,000.

Some taxonomists have suggested that the species could be split into up to four species, and it is true that the small tundra-breeding high-Arctic forms not only appear quite different, but also sound different. The presence of intergrading zones between a number of races, however, lends much weight against these proposals. In some cases, as in the form 'tavenneri', there is an intergrading link between small and dark *minima*, large and dark *occidentalis* and pale *parvipes*.

HABITS Highly gregarious goose, with close attachments to natal areas and lifelong pair-bonds, which no doubt are the reasons why so many races have evolved in a variety of different breeding habitats. Northern forms breed by open tundra, whereas southern forms breed by lakes and rivers in open country and forested areas. Breeding season varies somewhat according to location, larger southern forms nesting earlier. Nests on dry ground close to waterside; fairly solitary, but loose colonies formed in some regions. For post-breeding moult, has extensive migration, which is as much as 1500 km in race *maxima*. Many southern populations partially resident, whereas others highly migratory. Swims freely, but spends most of time feeding by grazing. Flights to roost on water, moving to and from feeding grounds at dawn and dusk. Mixes freely with other goose species in winter. Where introduced, e.g. Europe, has become very much a bird of farmland and even lakes and reservoirs close to large towns. Wild hybrids reported rarely with blue Snow (19) and in Europe with feral Greylag Geese (17).

HABITAT Breeds by variety of lowland habitats, from the tundra to wetlands of the Great Plains and farmland with lakes, reservoirs and gravel-pits. In USA, winters primarily in stubble fields and by both inland and coastal marshes.

DISTRIBUTION Breeds across the whole of northern North America from the Aleutian Islands and Alaska east to the Atlantic coast. Winters across whole of southern North America, north on Pacific coast to British Columbia and south to Mexico. Casual western Greenland (where *hutchinsii* has bred). Vagrant to Jamaica, Bahamas, Hawaii, northeastern Siberia and Japan. Introduced populations in Britain and Ireland, Norway, Sweden and Finland and New Zealand basically resident, but Swedish birds move south in winter, some as far as Germany and the Netherlands. Vagrants reported from many European countries, probably coming from feral stock; some occurring in western Britain, Ireland and Iceland, often mixed with White-fronted (15) and Pink-footed Goose (14) flocks from Greenland, believed to be genuine transatlantic vagrants, including birds of smaller races, but possibility of escaped birds confuses the issue.

POPULATION Abundant as a species. Aleutian Islands form *leucopareia* endangered, presently known as a wild breeding bird on only two tiny islands, Buldir and Chagulak, but has been reintroduced onto Aggatu, where 1,630 birds wintered in central California, where 1,630 birds counted in 1977. This race was once widespread across Aleutians and adjacent Komandorski and Kurile Islands off Siberia, latter population considered to be the one that formerly wintered in Japan, where it is now only a very rare vagrant. Population estimates for most other races are given under Geographical Variation.

REFERENCES Bailey and Trapp (1984), Delacour

(1954-64), Johnsgard (1975), Kear (1979), Lack (1974), Terres (1980).

24 BARNACLE GOOSE   Plate 8
Branta leucopsis

Common name derived from the crude similarity of the head-and-neck pattern to the stalk and shell of the goose barnacle. An ancient theory produced long before the birds breeding grounds were discovered held that these barnacles, which attach themselves to flotsam and drift along the ocean currents, were in fact young Barnacle Geese.

FIELD IDENTIFICATION Length 58-71 cm (23-28 in). **At rest:** Distinctive little goose, which winters almost exclusively in northwest Europe; popular in captivity. The black neck and breast, mostly-white head, barred grey upperparts and very pale underparts render it unmistakable. Only Canada Goose (23) shares black neck and white face, but Canada has pale or brown (never black) breast, narrow white cheek-band, and brown body plumage. **In flight:** Black neck and breast, mostly-white head and pale underparts distinctive, even at quite long range. The rear pattern of the upperparts is similar to that of Canada Goose, with black rump and tail and white 'U' on uppertail-coverts.

VOICE Flocks are noisy. A high-pitched chattering 'hogog, hogog', interspersed with the occasional louder note, is uttered almost constantly by grazing flocks. In flight the noise continues, being a rapidly-repeated short, high barking note; at distance, flock sound recalls a pack of yelping dogs.

DESCRIPTION Sexes similar. **Adult:** Throat, sides of head and forehead white or creamy. Lores black, of varying intensity; some individuals also have black forehead. Crown, neck and breast black. Flanks whitish, with grey feather centres. Ventral region and uppertail-coverts white. Scapulars blackish, with grey bases and pale fringes to feathers forming transverse barring. Mantle, back and rump blackish, with weak grey feather fringes. Tail black. Upperwing-coverts grey, with blackish subterminal bands to feathers of greater and median coverts. Flight feathers darker, almost blackish. Underwing pale grey, with darker flight feathers. **Juvenile:** Similar to adult, but duller, with black of head and neck sullied with brown or grey, whitish head has dark freckling, upperparts tinged brownish, with duller pattern than on adult, flanks washed buffish, lacking distinct whitish feather fringes. Early in first winter becomes more as adult, but retains some juvenile feathering on upperparts until first summer. **BARE PARTS All plumages:** Bill, legs and feet black. Iris dark brown.

MEASUREMENTS Males tend to be larger than females. Wing 376-429 (mean: male 410, female 392); tarsus 64-80; bill 27-33 (mean 29); mean weight of male 1827, of female 1619.

GEOGRAPHICAL VARIATION None.

HABITS Highly gregarious little goose, feeding in dense concentrations on coastal grassland in winter and breeding in small, but often closely-packed, colonies. Arrives on breeding grounds from mid to late May. Nest site often among rocky crags or on steep cliff, but may also be on ground on small islands, even among seabird colonies. On Novaya Zemlya sometimes nests in close proximity to breeding sites of Gyrfalcons; this would afford some protection from ground predators, which may be driven away by falcons. Following post-breeding moult, flocks start to leave breeding areas from late August to mid September, arriving in winter quarters late September to late October, having regular stop-overs en route. Swims readily, but spends most of time grazing on coastal pasture. Rather less wary than most other geese, possibly owing to protection afforded it by most countries. Compared with other geese, seems to spend more time flying about in winter quarters, flocks constantly rising, circling and dropping in to feed again. Roosts on water, including lakes, rivers and estuarine sandbanks.

HABITAT Breeds in high-Arctic coastal regions, including small islands. Winters on coastal pasture and grassy islands.

DISTRIBUTION Three breeding populations: eastern Greenland, Svalbard, and Novaya Zemlya (also adjacent Vaygach Island, sporadic on nearby Yugorskiy Peninsula). Greenland population migrates to Iceland and continues south to winter in western Scotland (Hebrides) and Ireland. Svalbard population migrates to coastal Norway and crosses North Sea to winter on the Solway Firth (southwest Scotland and northwest England). Novaya Zemlya birds migrate over White Sea and the Baltic to Denmark, to winter primarily in the Netherlands. Occasional elsewhere in Baltic region and along coasts of English Channel to northern France. Any individuals outside main areas likely to be escapes from captivity, as very popular in collections. Vagrants reported most European countries, Morocco, Egypt, the Azores and Bear Island, but many of these suspected of being escapes; indeed, even a bird which nested in Iceland considered to be of captive origin. Occasional birds reported from northeastern North America also perhaps of captive origin, but doubtless some are wild birds.

POPULATION Despite rather limited range, the total population is stable and even increasing. Estimates of the populations have been made from counts of geese in their winter quarters. Greenland population 8,000 in 1959, growing to a peak of 33,800 in 1978 and dropping to 25,000 by 1983; Svalbard population 3,000 in 1970, increasing to 10,400 by 1985; and Novaya Zemlya population reached 50,000 in early 1980s.

REFERENCES Cramp and Simmons (1977), Ebbinge et al. (1986), Mehlum and Ogilvie (1984), Ogilvie (1983), Ryff (1984).

25 BRENT GOOSE   Plate 8
Branta bernicla

Alternative name: Brant (North America)

Small, very dark high-Arctic goose that resorts to estuarine flats in winter.

FIELD IDENTIFICATION Length 55-66 cm (22-26 in). **At rest:** An exceedingly dark small goose which winters on estuaries and coastal pastures. The black head, neck and breast contrast only a little with the dull, dark brown upperparts, and in the nominate race the overall dark plumage is relieved only by the striking white ventral region. At close range, a small white patch on the sides of the upper neck is visible, although this is lacking on juveniles until mid-winter. The three races may be separated by underpart coloration when adult, although juvenile and first-winter individuals are less easy and even some adults may be difficult. Dark-bellied nominate race has relatively dark, dull brownish flanks; Pale-bellied race *hrota* has almost whitish flanks; and Black Brant race *nigricans* has whitish upper flanks, contrasting with blackish belly, and very extensive white neck patches which meet on foreneck. Pattern of race *nigricans* less obvious when swimming as dark belly hidden, but striking when on land. **In flight:** Very dark, small, short-necked goose with conspicuous white rear end, the black tail being almost hidden by white uppertail-coverts. Pale flanks of Pale-bellied race usually obvious in flight, contrasting with very dark underwing.

VOICE Typical call a low, rolling 'raunk, raunk', uttered both in flight and from feeding flocks.

DESCRIPTION Sexes similar. Nominate race described. **Adult:** Head, neck and breast black. Irregular white patch at sides of upper neck. Flanks and belly dark greyish-brown, with variably paler feather fringes to rear and upper flanks, rarely extensive enough as to suggest other races. Mantle, back, rump, scapulars and upperwing-coverts dark slaty-brown, with very narrow and indistinctly lighter fringes. Flight feathers black. Uppertail-coverts and ventral region white. Underwing dark brown. **Juvenile:** Similar to adult, but head, neck and breast duller, sullied brown, and lacks white neck patches. Flanks more uniform, but not so dark as on adult. Upperparts browner than adult and not quite so dark, with more conspicuous paler feather fringes forming transverse barring. Attains neck patches during first winter, but retains light barring above until at least first summer.

BARE PARTS All plumages: Bill, legs and feet black. Iris dark brown.

MEASUREMENTS All races. Males usually larger than females. Wing 317-353 (mean: male 340, female 324), tarsus 56-67, bill 29-38, mean weight 1464.

GEOGRAPHICAL VARIATION Three well-defined races. Nominate form breeds over Arctic Siberia east to Taymyr Peninsula, where it intergrades with race *nigricans* which breeds across Arctic eastern Siberia, Alaska and Canada east to Perry River region; *nigricans* is typically darker than nominate, with very dark belly and fore-flanks, rear and upper flanks have broad white feather borders which contrast very strongly with dark belly, giving a white-flanked field appearance, and white neck patches are more extensive, usually meeting on foreneck to form white collar. Race *hrota* breeds over remainder of Arctic Canada, Greenland, Svalbard and Franz Josef Land, apparently intergrading with *nigricans* in central Arctic Canada: neck pattern as nominate race, but flanks and belly whitish with broader whitish feather fringes obscuring brown feather bases, although latter may be visible on rear flanks, but juveniles have brownish belly and flanks and are close to some nominate *bernicla*; upper-

parts more constantly different in all plumages, having buff fringes to feathers, particularly mantle, and browner cast to whole of upperparts.

HABITS Breeds on high-Arctic tundra, birds arriving on breeding grounds in early June and nesting in small, loose colonies on coastal tundra, often on small islands. After post-breeding moult, flocks leave breeding grounds in early September, some arriving in winter quarters as early as mid September, whereas others have stop-overs en route. In winter, feeds in huge gatherings on tidal mudflats, associating freely with Wigeon. Specialises in feeding on eel-grass *Zostera*, a plant which forms extensive beds over muddy estuaries. Species' dependence on *Zostera* brought about drastic reduction in its numbers in the 1930s, when a widespread disease destroyed the plant. Surviving geese turned to feeding on maritime pastures, which have become an increasingly favoured food source. Now favours feeding in pasture in many parts of its winter range. More approachable than many other geese, owing to protection afforded it in some countries; it is often remarkably confiding, particularly isolated individuals and family parties. Unlike many other goose species, flocks often move about in packs or in oblique lines (but also sometimes in shallow V-formation), and migrating flocks often keep quite low over the sea. Roosting may take place either in sheltered coastal waters or in tidal bays at high tide, flocks flighting to favoured feeding areas as tide recedes. Does not mix much with other geese. Leaves winter quarters from mid March to mid April.

HABITAT Breeds by low coastal tundra, with pools and small inlets and islands. Winters on tidal mud and sandflats, estuarine and coastal grassland. Rarely occurs on fresh water, except sometimes on passage.

DISTRIBUTION Breeds across high-Arctic tundra (see Geographical Variation). Birds from eastern Siberia and western North America (*nigricans*) winter primarily on Pacific coast of North America from British Columbia south to Baja California, with some straggling inland and occurring as vagrants on Atlantic coast and in Texas (some of these may have moved south with *hrota*). Vagrant *nigricans* also now annual in western Europe (Iceland, Ireland, England, Netherlands, Germany, Sweden, Finland) with flocks of both *hrota* (Ireland) and nominate race. On Asiatic side of Pacific, smaller numbers winter around shores of Yellow Sea and in southern Japan, and vagrants have occurred on Hawaii and in Shansi (inland north China). Canadian *hrota* winter chiefly in northeastern North America from Cape Cod to North Carolina, with vagrants south to Barbados, whereas some join Greenland birds which winter in Ireland; Svalbard and Franz Josef Land population winters in Denmark and northeast England, some moving a little further south as far as northwest France and Florida, and a straggler has been recorded from the Azores. Nominate race winters in northwest Europe in Netherlands, England and western France, with smaller numbers remaining in Denmark and coastal Germany. Vagrants have occurred south to central and southeastern Europe and North Africa east to Egypt.

POPULATION Population estimates have been

based entirely on winter counts. Race *nigricans* wintering along Pacific USA, 140,000; Asiatic winter population low, but no figures, only scarce winter visitor China, and in Japan winter counts of up to 340 in early 1970s. Nominate race increased dramatically after decline in 1930s (*Zostera* beds destroyed by disease): 16,500 in mid 1950s increased to 30,500 in mid 1960s, 110,000 in mid 1970s and 150,000 in the early 1980s. Pale-bellied *hrota* populations from Greenland estimated at 24,000 in mid 1980s, Svalbard and Franz Josef Land population 4,000 Denmark and England), and in North America some 100,000 in 1981. In all populations, numbers fluctuate considerably according to annual breeding success; in some years few young are reared.

REFERENCES Cramp and Simmons (1977), Mehlum and Ogilvie (1984), van den Berg *et al.* (1984).

26 RED-BREASTED GOOSE   Plate 8
Branta ruficollis

The most beautiful of all geese, breeding in central Arctic Siberia and wintering chiefly in the lowlands by the Black Sea.

FIELD IDENTIFICATION Length 53-55 cm (21-22 in). **At rest:** Unmistakable little goose, with rounded head and tiny bill. Gaudy plumage pattern can be surprisingly inconspicuous at long ranges, when goose basically appears very black with contrasting white ventral region and upper flank stripe. When seen feeding head-on, the white vertical breast-band appears almost to encircle body. The head-and-neck pattern is particularly inconspicuous at long range, but closer views reveal the chestnut foreneck, breast and sides of head, finely bordered in white. Vagrants to western Europe usually encountered among flocks of White-fronted (15) and Dark-bellied Brent (25) Geese. **In flight:** Small size, relatively short neck, and very black plumage which contrasts with white ventral region and flank stripe are the most obvious features. The colour and pattern of the head and neck are almost impossible to discern in flight. Confusion possible with Brent, especially race *nigricans* which also has contrasting white flanks with blackish belly, but Red-breasted is blacker, with narrower flank stripe, white rear belly, and shows more extensive black on tail (tail almost hidden by white tail-coverts on Brent).

VOICE Typical flight call a jerky, squeaky, staccato, repeated 'kik-yoik, kik-yik'.

DESCRIPTION Sexes similar. **Adult:** Face, throat, crown and hindneck black, with oval white patch on lores. Large deep chestnut patch on sides of head, bordered with white band. Foreneck and breast deep chestnut, with white band separating chestnut and black of neck, narrower towards base of neck. White band completely encircles fore body, crossing lower breast and mantle. Upper belly and flanks black, with broad white band along upper flanks, coming down towards legs, where black feather bases show through to break up white. Ventral region and uppertail-coverts white. Upperparts, including mantle, back, rump, tail, scapulars, wing-coverts and flight feathers, black.

Two white bars on upperwing formed by white tips to greater and median coverts. Underwing black. **Juvenile:** Similar to adult but a little duller, with black of plumage slightly sullied brown, chestnut a little duller, white bordering lines on head and neck less clear-cut, and chestnut patch at side of head smaller, sometimes almost whitish (forming extensive whitish patch). Pale tips to wing-coverts narrower, but forming several fine lines rather than two conspicuous bands of adult. Tail with narrow whitish tip. Becomes much as adult during first winter.

BARE PARTS All plumages: Bill, legs and feet black. Iris dark brown.

MEASUREMENTS Males usually larger than females. Wing of male 355-379 (mean 367), of female 332-352 (mean 343); tarsus 54-65; bill 22-27; mean weight of male 1375, of female 1094.

GEOGRAPHICAL VARIATION None.

HABITS This beautiful little goose breeds on the tundra of the Taymyr Peninsula. It arrives on the breeding grounds in early June and settles down to nest in small colonies of about five pairs, with nest site usually being on a steep bank or low cliffs with scrubby cover. Nests in close proximity to nest sites of Peregrine, Rough-legged Buzzard or large gull. Derives protection from these aggressive birds, which drive nest predators from the vicinity of their own breeding sites, thus indirectly protecting the Red-breasted Geese; the geese may nest as close as 5-10 m to a Peregrine eyrie. After post-breeding moult, flocks start to leave breeding areas in first half of September, moving in narrow belt southwest to current primary winter grounds by Black Sea. Arrives in winter quarters during November, having had stop-overs en route. In winter highly gregarious, with flocks associating with White-fronted Geese in rolling steppe stubble fields. Odd individuals become mixed with other goose species and turn up as annual vagrants to western Europe. Flies in small closely-packed groups rather than in defined V-formation. Feeding flocks noisy, constantly uttering squeaky calls; all movement rather quick, feeding with rapid, jerky head movements. Swims readily, although feeds almost entirely by grazing. Roosts on both lagoons and freshwater lakes. Leaves winter quarters during March.

HABITAT Breeds by tundra, or scrubby 'wooded' tundra, in close proximity to rivers and gulleys. Winters in open steppe and open rolling lowland hills, feeding among pasture, stubble and crop fields.

DISTRIBUTION Breeds in central Arctic Siberia, almost entirely within Taymyr Peninsula. Migration routes follow valleys of Tas and Ob towards north Caspian, then westwards to north of Caucasus, to winter primarily in lowlands bordering north and western shores of Black Sea. Until recently also wintered in good numbers in Aral and Caspian Sea lowlands, with some moving down into Iraq, but now rare in these regions. Very small numbers spill over into southeast Europe and Turkey. Vagrants reported over most of central and western Europe south to Italy and Spain, all Scandinavian countries, and Cyprus, Israel and Egypt (also depicted on ancient Egyptian friezes, indicating that it was formerly a regular visitor). Farther east, occasional vagrants have been recorded east to Irkutsk and Chukotsk Peninsula in Siberia, in Hupeh (China) and in northern India, but these are all old records, indicating its decline in recent decades. Being attractive, this little goose is popular in captivity, some vagrants probably being referable to escapes.

POPULATION Sadly declining, at least until the 1960s, but now considered to be stable. In the 1950s the population was estimated at over 40,000 birds, but by 1963 it had fallen to 25,000. Disturbance and human persecution on its breeding grounds, with both eggs and moulting birds being collected for food, have contributed to the decline. Following the excessive use of pesticides in the 1950s, the Peregrine population also severely declined, and this has no doubt affected the protection needed by the geese during the breeding season. Hunting of wintering birds was high during the Second World War, but was banned in 1959. Soon after this, the geese shifted their wintering grounds from the Caspian/Iraq region to the Black Sea. Recent counts in Romania indicate a winter population of some 6,000 birds, but 15,000 were counted during autumn 1975 on migration between Black and Caspian Seas; other winter counts include 16,000 in Bulgaria in 1980 and 2,000 in Greece in 1985. An estimate of 7,500 breeding pairs was made during 1972 and 1973 on the breeding grounds, among a total population of 25,000 including young birds and non-breeders. Although frequent in European collections, this species does not breed readily at temperate latitudes; an effective captive-breeding programme needs to be formulated.

REFERENCES Cramp and Simmons (1977), Kear (1979).

Tribe CYGNINI (SWANS)

An easily recognisable group of waterfowl, with long necks and (except Black (33) and Black-necked (34) Swans) white adult plumage. Swans spend a great part of their time swimming, although most species also feed by grazing. They feed by submerging head and long neck and freely up-end in deeper water, but normally never dive unless pursued when wounded. All species are migratory to a varying extent, often forming goose-like V-formations when well underway. They rise heavily from the water surface, pattering for some distance before becoming airborne. Swans pair for life and keep in family parties until onset of following breeding season, migrating as family units within the flocks. Adult plumage is attained by second winter and sexes are alike in plumage; although juveniles are distinctly different, there is no seasonal variation in plumage. Northern species are generally difficult to separate in flight unless at reasonably close range. The classification recommended by Livezey (1986) is followed here, with recognition of *Cygnus* and *Olor* as valid genera (usually *Olor* has been absorbed into *Cygnus*).

27 COSCOROBA SWAN   Plate 9
Coscoroba coscoroba

An aberrant South American swan with much-discussed relationships. Some authorities have even suggested that it might be related to the whistling ducks (2-9), but there is general agreement that it is a true swan, with some affinities with the geese (11-26).

FIELD IDENTIFICATION Length 90-115 cm (35-45 in). **At rest:** Unmistakable, the only all-white swan in the Neotropics, with range overlapping only with Black-necked Swan (34). Rather smaller and a little shorter-necked than other swans, adult at rest appears totally white with a brilliant waxy-red bill which is feathered to the base and lacks any basal knob; legs and feet bright pink. Juvenile is whitish, but has patches of greyish-brown on crown, back and wings and grey bill and legs. **In flight:** All-white plumage, swan-like shape and small black wing-tips are obvious in flight and present a unique combination in South America. Juvenile differs from young Black-necked Swan in lacking dusky head and neck, although young Black-necked has dusky tips to primaries, but not so extensive as on Coscoroba. **VOICE** Has loud toy-trumpet-like call, 'cos-cor-oo', the first syllable being longer and higher in pitch. Female's calls are higher in pitch than those of the male. The species' name is derived from the call. **DESCRIPTION** Sexes similar. **Adult:** Completely white, except for black terminal third of outer six primaries. **Juvenile:** Duller than adult, with greyish-brown patches on crown, nape and upperparts. Becomes whiter during first winter, but some patches remain until adult plumage fully attained by second autumn.

BARE PARTS Adult: Bill duck-like, bright waxy-red, with paler nail. Legs and feet bright pink. Iris yellowish to reddish-orange (sexing by iris colour not reliable). **Juvenile:** Bill blue-grey, with whiter nail and cutting edges. Legs and feet blue-grey. Iris dark brown. Adult bare-part coloration attained by first summer.

MEASUREMENTS Males typically larger than females. Wing 427-480; tarsus 88-98; bill 63-70; mean weight of male 4600, of female 3800.

GEOGRAPHICAL VARIATION None.

HABITS Sociable to a limited extent; flocks rarely exceed 100 birds, even in areas where numerous. Isolated pairs, rarely small loose colonies, build their bulky nests by tall fringe vegetation or on small islands by shallow water. The breeding season varies somewhat according to location, but is reputed to be from October to December in Chile and June to November in parts of Argentina. Unlike swans of genus *Cygnus*, does not carry young on back. Post-breeding moulting flocks gather on favoured waters, where numbers may perhaps reach a couple of hundred individuals. It performs little-understood migrations, confused by varying breeding seasons, dispersing northwards after the moult. It feeds either by dabbling or by wading in the shallows, sometimes by grazing on waterside pasture, walking easily with its relatively long legs. Its longer legs no doubt help it take to the air with greater ease than other swans, as it does not patter during take-off. Generally shy and wary.

HABITAT Freshwater lakes and lagoons, with fringe vegetation.

DISTRIBUTION Breeds over southern South America from Cape Horn to approximately 45° S. Somewhat patchily distributed and rather local, with centre of population in southern Chile. Disperses northwards after breeding, reaching as far as central Chile, northern Argentina, Paraguay, Uruguay and southeastern Brazil. An increasingly frequent visitor to the Falkland Islands, where breeding possible but remains unproven.

POPULATION Throughout its range this is quite a local bird, but its non-gregarious habits and the relative inaccessibility of much of its breeding range make it a difficult species to assess. Concern has, however, recently been expressed by the Chilean government, which estimated that fewer than 1,000 remained in Chile in the late 1970s, and that these were confined to the extreme south of the country. As Chile is considered to be the main headquarters for this unique species, clearly there is urgent need for overall censusing throughout the bird's range.

REFERENCES Kear (1979), Scott and the Wildfowl Trust (1972), Todd (1979).

28 TRUMPETER SWAN   Plate 10
Olor buccinator

The largest and rarest of the swans, the American counterpart of the Whooper Swan (29).

FIELD IDENTIFICATION Length 150-180 cm (60-72 in). **At rest:** Very large, straight-necked swan of northwestern North America. Very similar to the more abundant Whistling Swan (30), from which it is best distinguished by comparative size and structure. Breeding and winter ranges only marginally overlap with Whistling Swan. Larger, longer-bodied and longer-necked than Whistling, with longer and thicker bill. Bill all black, with reddish cutting edge visible towards base in close views; Whistling rarely shows this line, though it is present and may be quite visible when close, but does normally show variable small yellow patch in front of eye, though this is frequently absent. The profile of the bill is straight along the culmen, whereas on Whistling it is slightly concave, giving a retroussé look to the bill-tip, although this appearance is more noticeable at longer ranges than on birds that are very close. The feathering on the forehead of adult extends into the bare facial skin in a broad point, whereas on adult Whistling it is straighter or rounded; immature Whistling can, however, retain some feathering extending into centre of facial skin at forehead, so this feature should be used with caution. The nostrils are centrally positioned between the eye and the bill-tip (on Whistling, the nostrils are a little nearer to bill-tip than to eye), and where the bare facial skin meets the eye it is broader in Trumpeter, Whistling having eye almost isolated from skin,

which meets eye in narrow point. Head rather shorter and crown more rounded on Whistling. These differences are subtle, but are important when distinguishing Trumpeter from those Whistling that lack small yellow patch on face. When at ease, Trumpeter carries base of neck well back on 'shoulders', the neck rising vertically from back, giving pout-breasted appearance when swimming; Whistling carries shorter neck more upright from base, showing little breast pout. Juvenile is darker than juvenile Whistling and has blackish patches towards base of bill; unlike Whistling, which becomes progressively paler during the first winter, young Trumpeter retains brownish plumage into first spring. All-black bill easily separates adult from Whooper Swan, which is a rare visitor to Alaska, while juvenile Whooper is paler and has black only at tip of bill. Head and neck often stained rusty. Voice also distinctly different from Whistling Swan (see Voice). **In flight:** Typical swan. A very large, white swan with all-black bill. Lone individuals usually difficult to distinguish from Whistling in flight, but if together Trumpeter is larger, with longer neck and body and different voice (see below).

VOICE Typical call deeper and more resonant than that of Whistling Swan, a single or double bugling 'ko-hoh', likened to that of a crane, whereas call of Whistling is higher-pitched and more goose-like, almost barking.

DESCRIPTION Sexes similar. **Adult:** Completely white, although head and neck often stained rusty from feeding in ferrous waters. **Juvenile:** Overall greyish-brown, slightly darker on crown and hind-neck; underparts paler grey, flight feathers and tail whiter. Adult plumage attained by second winter, birds being paler during first summer but with some greyish-brown on head, neck and wings.

BARE PARTS Adult: Bill and bare facial skin black, occasionally with very small, ill-defined pale spot in front of eye; narrow red line at cutting edges of mandibles. Legs and feet black. Iris dark brown. **Juvenile:** Bill fleshy-pink, with black nail, nostril and variably extensive black patches around bill-base and facial skin. Legs and feet greyish-flesh. Adult coloration attained by second winter.

MEASUREMENTS Males usually larger than females. **Male:** Wing 605-680, tarsus 120-140, bill 107-120, mean weight 11900. **Female:** Wing 604-636, tarsus 110-125, bill 105-118, mean weight 9400.

GEOGRAPHICAL VARIATION None recognised although Alaskan population averages larger. Sometimes considered to be conspecific with Whooper Swan. Owing to the close relationships between Trumpeter, Whooper, Whistling and Bewick's (31) Swans, some authorities advocate lumping them all into one species, 'Northern Swan'.

HABITS Breeding territories may be established as early as February, but the migratory Alaskan population does not arrive on the breeding grounds until late March or April. A solitary breeder, needing a large territory. Nests are situated close to the water, either on the shore or on small islands and even on muskrat houses and beaver lodges. Egg-laying commences in late April, a month later in Alaska. Adults moult during and before the incubation period. Alaskan birds leave breeding grounds in October, once cygnets are fully fledged. Outside breeding season forms small flocks, but population not high enough to permit large concentrations. Feeds chiefly while swimming, submerging head and neck below surface and up-ending in deeper water.

HABITAT Riverine wetlands, by lakes, ponds and marshes, even in open wooded regions and prairies and, in winter, on tidal estuaries.

DISTRIBUTION Formerly widespread across northern North America from Alaska to central Canada, south to Idaho and Illinois. Much persecuted during last century, to verge of extinction. Now two major population types remain: a migratory section in Alaska which winters from southeastern Alaska along the coastal regions of British Columbia south to the mouth of the Columbia River; and a series of small relict groups which are chiefly resident across the Great Basin region in Alberta, Washington, Oregon, Nevada, Montana, Wyoming, South Dakota and Minnesota. Some of the latter, e.g. those in Alberta, are somewhat migratory. Most of these populations have evolved from successful re-introductions to former breeding areas. In recent years, occasional vagrants have been recorded south to California.

POPULATION Formerly abundant, but settlers in North America killed them in large numbers for food and feathers, the latter being used for hat-making and the down in powder-puffs. By 1930s only 66 known to remain, these in Yellowstone Park area. Transportation of birds to other areas has resulted in a spectacular comeback, aided by the discovery of the Alaskan population. Total population estimated at 6,000 birds in 1975, 4,500 of these in Alaska. Totally protected throughout its range.

REFERENCES Banko (1960), Hansen (1973), Terres (1980).

29 WHOOPER SWAN Plate 10
Olor cygnus

Despite similarity of bill colour to Bewick's Swan (31), this is the Palaearctic cousin of the Trumpeter Swan (28).

FIELD IDENTIFICATION Length 140-165 cm (55-65 in). **At rest:** Closely resembles Bewick's Swan, but is larger, with longer body and neck, and has more angular head shape, exaggerated by longer bill which gives a 'roman nose' shape to front of head. Adult has a striking black-and-yellow bill pattern, shared only by Bewick's, but the precise pattern is normally quite different from latter's. On Whooper the bill appears yellow with a black tip, whereas on Bewick's it appears to be black with a yellow base, or at least shows equal amounts of black and yellow. The yellow on a Whooper bill covers the basal half and extends in a long projection along the sides towards the tip. Bill pattern of Bewick's is individually variable and some can approach Whooper (see p. 156). Eastern Bewick's populations tend to be larger and stouter-billed than western birds, but the bill pattern tends to show more extensive black than on western birds. Although eastern Whooper bill patterns tend to show rather more extensive yellow

than on western, the general pattern is individually less variable than on Bewick's. Juvenile is similar to juvenile Bewick's and best distinguished by structure, but tends to be a little darker in first autumn, although by latter part of first winter plumage is paler and more blotched with white than on young Bewick's, with bill pattern recalling adult although yellow at first represented by whitish coloration. First-winter Bewick's remains greyish-brown until first spring, when begins to attain extensive black on bill. Juveniles of both species paler, more cinnamon-grey than young Mute Swan (32), with brighter pink bill which lacks black at very base, and have rounded, not pointed, tail. Both Bewick's and Whooper spend much of their time grazing in winter, more so than Mute, and tend to hold their neck more stiffly erect when swimming. **In flight:** Typical swan shape. Along with Bewick's, distinguished by two-toned bill and rounded tail, with feet reaching tail-tip. Lone individuals difficult to identify but, if species flying together, Whooper is clearly larger, with longer neck and body, heavier head and bill, and has slightly slower wingbeats. Less agile at take-off and landing than Bewick's, coming on to water at shallower angle and with more skating over surface, taking off with more pattering. Wingbeats silent, or with quiet swishing at close range, unlike deep throbbing produced by Mute. Flying birds usually very vocal (see below).

VOICE Has a variety of honking and trumpeting calls, deeper and stronger than those of Bewick's. Typical flight call is a deep, resonant 'hoop-hoop', with second syllable higher.

DESCRIPTION Sexes similar. **Adult:** Completely white, although head and neck often stained rusty from feeding in ferrous water. **Juvenile:** Almost completely greyish-brown, a little darker on head and neck and whiter on underparts, tail and flight feathers. Becomes paler during latter part of first winter and whiter during first summer, attaining full adult coloration before second winter.

BARE PARTS Adult: Bill bright pale yellow, with black cutting edges, tip and distal portion of culmen, occasionally culmen black almost to base. Legs and feet black. Iris dark brown, occasionally bluish. **Juvenile:** Bill pink, paler at base, with dark brownish tip and cutting edges which blacken early in first winter. Legs and feet fleshy-grey. During latter part of first winter and first spring acquires adult bill pattern, but with white replacing yellow, full colour being attained during first summer.

MEASUREMENTS Males usually larger than females. Wing 562-635 (mean: male 610, female 583); tarsus 104-130; bill 92-116 (mean: male 106, female 102); mean weight of male 10800, of female 8100.

GEOGRAPHICAL VARIATION No races recognised. Now-extinct Greenland population was smaller and Icelandic birds somewhat intermediate in size, but more work needs to be done on these to see if their separation as race *islandicus* is valid. Eastern populations tend to have rather more extensive yellow on bill than western birds. Whooper and Trumpeter Swans are sometimes considered to be conspecific.

HABITS Highly sociable outside breeding period. Arrives on breeding grounds in second half of May, taking up well-spaced territories. Nest site close to water at edge of pool or on small island. Moults after breeding in mid-summer, finally leaving breeding grounds in small flocks or family parties during latter half of September. Migrating parties form lines and even V-formation when flying high, keeping in contact with frequent bursts of calling. Arrives in winter quarters during October and November. Wintering birds congregate into small concentrations of up to 300; although generally wintering in slightly different areas from Bewick's Swans, family parties often mix with them in areas of marginal overlap. Feeds primarily by grazing in arable fields and sprouting winter cereals, walking with greater ease than Mute Swan. Also feeds quite readily on water. Roosts on areas of open water, adjacent to feeding areas. Shy and wary, unlike Mute Swan, with which it may sometimes loosely associate. Arriving individuals joining flock on water are invariably greeted with much excited calling. Leaves winter grounds between mid March and early May, departing in small groups or family parties.

HABITAT Breeds by variety of open shallow water, from steppe lakes to pools in the northern taiga, also locally by coastal inlets, estuaries and rivers, but generally avoiding tundra zone, which is inhabited by Bewick's Swan. Winters in lowland open farmland, usually in coastal regions and inland in floodplains. Occasionally on passage in sheltered coastal bays and inlets.

DISTRIBUTION Breeds across entire breadth of northern Palaearctic from Iceland to northeastern Siberia, south in Europe to southern Sweden and Poland and in Asia to Aral Sea and Mongolia. Has nested sporadically in Scotland and formerly bred in Greenland. Winters in coastal lowlands of Europe and eastern Asia. Some Icelandic birds remain in winter, merely moving to coastal regions or to geothermal waters, but majority winter in northern Britain and Ireland. Scandinavian and western USSR population winters coastal Baltic and Norway and southern coasts of North Sea, with smaller numbers moving south into central Europe. Another major wintering area is the coastal lowlands of the Black and Caspian Seas, with smaller numbers south to southeast Europe and Turkey and east to the Aral Sea. More easterly breeders winter in coastal regions of eastern Asia, from Japan and Korea south along coastal China, with small numbers in the Aleutian Islands. Vagrants have occurred in USA (Alaska, where it has possibly even nested, California and New England), Svalbard, Jan Mayen and Bear Islands, most of southern Europe, Algeria, Tunisia, Egypt, Cyprus, Afghanistan, Pakistan, India and Nepal.

POPULATION Enormous breeding range makes estimates difficult, but local decreases have occurred through drainage of wetlands and hunting; Asiatic breeding range therefore no doubt more fragmented than is indicated on the map. Greenland birds exterminated by killing of both adults and young during flightless period. Icelandic population now some 16,700 individuals, with other winter counts in Europe indicating 14,000 in North Sea/Baltic region and some 25,000 in Caspian/Black Sea region. In Japan some 11,000 winter, but data from elsewhere in Asia are lacking. A world estimate of around 100,000 is probably reasonable.

REFERENCES Brazil (1981), Cramp and Simmons (1977), Scott and the Wildfowl Trust (1972).

30 WHISTLING SWAN   Plate 10
Olor columbianus

Alternative name: Tundra Swan (with Bewick's Swan)

North American counterpart of Bewick's Swan (31), with which it is now generally regarded as conspecific under the name Tundra Swan. For field purposes, however, the two are clearly separable.

FIELD IDENTIFICATION Length 120-150 cm (48-58 in). **At rest:** Range overlaps only with superficially similar Trumpeter Swan (28), distinctions being fully discussed under that species. Whistling is distinctly smaller, shorter-bodied and shorter-necked than Trumpeter, with rather shorter bill which is slightly concave along the culmen in profile. Adult has bill and facial skin all black, with indistinct reddish gape (less obvious than on Trumpeter) and usually a small yellow spot or patch at base of bill, but this is often minute or absent (see p. 156) or invisible at longer ranges. Juvenile is paler than juvenile Trumpeter, especially by late first winter, and lacks black patches around bill-base. Adults of both Whooper (29) and Bewick's Swans, which occur as vagrants in Alaska and western USA, are easily distinguished by their extensive yellow on bill (see p. 156), but juveniles are tricky; juvenile Whooper is larger, with more angular head shape, longer bill with straighter culmen, and longer neck and body, but juvenile Bewick's is not safely separable. See also Mute Swan (32), which has been introduced into parts of North America. **In flight:** Typical swan shape. Black bill shared only by Trumpeter Swan, but flight distinctions tricky, although Whistling is shorter-necked, shorter-bodied and has quicker wingbeats. Calls are different (see below).

VOICE Does not whistle, despite its name. Has variety of honking and clanging calls, all higher in pitch than those of Trumpeter Swan, recalling Canada Goose (23) rather than bugling of cranes. Typical flight phrase, similar to Trumpeter but higher-pitched and yelping, a more trisyllabic, soft, musical 'wow-wow-wow'.

DESCRIPTION Sexes similar. **Adult:** Completely white, although head and neck sometimes stained rusty. **Juvenile:** Overall greyish-brown, a little darker on head and neck and lighter on underparts, flight feathers and tail. Becomes paler and whiter during latter part of first winter and first spring. As adult by second winter.

BARE PARTS Adult: Bill and facial skin black, with variably extensive small yellow patch on facial skin below and in front of eye (sometimes lacking); reddish cutting edge apparent at gape, but less obvious than on Trumpeter Swan. Legs and feet black. Iris dark brown. **Juvenile:** Bill pink, paler towards base, with blackish cutting edge, nostril and tip, becoming blacker by first spring and as adult by second winter. Legs and feet fleshy-grey.

MEASUREMENTS Males usually larger than females.

Wing 501-569; tarsus 95-115; bill 92-107; mean weight of male 7100, of female 6200.

GEOGRAPHICAL VARIATION None as such, although generally regarded as conspecific with Bewick's Swan, the two together being called Tundra Swan.

HABITS Highly sociable outside breeding season. Arrives on breeding grounds in latter half of May to take up territory in coastal tundra regions. Nest site close to water by banks of pools and lakes, sometimes on small islands. Following post-breeding moult, birds start to leave breeding grounds from early to late October, arriving in winter quarters in November and December. Migrating birds follow specific routes to and from breeding grounds (see Distribution), using certain stop-over points en route; at Niagara Falls they sometimes become caught up in the strong currents and are swept to their deaths over the falls before they can rise from the water. On winter grounds feeds primarily in shallow water, but in recent years in some districts has taken to grazing in crop fields and winter cereals. Like other northern swans, migrating flocks are quite vocal and often form lines or V-formation. Even on the water they are very vocal, with noisy greeting ceremonies as individuals join and leave the flock. Feeding action quicker than Trumpeter Swan's, and more noisy and excitable when in flocks. Starts to leave winter quarters in small parties from early March onwards, using several stop-overs en route to the high Arctic.

HABITAT Breeds in coastal tundra, and along river valleys inland from coast. Winters in lowland marshes, both brackish and fresh, chiefly in coastal regions, although locally also on farmland crops and winter cereals.

DISTRIBUTION Breeds across tundra of Arctic North America, from coastal Alaska and islands eastwards over northern Canada to Baffin Island. Winters in two regions. Populations from western Alaska winter along Pacific coastal regions from southern Alaska to California, including a number of inland valleys and marshes, east to Utah, but chiefly in central valley of California. Birds of rest of range, west to northwestern Alaska, migrate through North-West Territories of Canada, southwards to west of Great Lakes, and head east across northern USA to south of Great Lakes to winter along Atlantic coastal marshes from Maryland south to North Carolina, with smaller numbers south to South Carolina. Vagrants occasionally reported south to Florida, Texas and northern Mexico and to Hawaii, Bermuda, Cuba, Puerto Rico, Ireland, western Britain, Sweden, northeastern Siberia (where brood of cygnets accompanied by mixed pair, one a Bewick's, the other a Whistling, is on record) and Japan.

POPULATION Always more abundant than Trumpeter Swan. Population estimated at around 146,000 in 1972, but total numbers vary according to success of breeding season. Some 60% of the population breed in Alaska, with greatest density around coastal western area; wintering numbers almost equally divided between the two major winter zones, with perhaps the majority on the eastern seaboard. Fairly well protected, although a limited hunting season has been permitted in certain states. It is also somewhat persecuted on the breeding grounds, flightless birds being rounded up and 'harvested' for food and their down.

REFERENCES Gunn (1973), Scott and the Wildfowl Trust (1972), Sladen (1973).

31 BEWICK'S SWAN   Plate 10
Olor columbianus bewickii
Alternative name: Tundra Swan (with Whistling Swan)

Palaearctic counterpart of Whistling Swan (30), of which it is generally regarded as a race, the two together being known as 'Tundra Swan'. As they are easily distinguishable in the field, they are treated separately here.

FIELD IDENTIFICATION Length 115-140 cm (45-55 in). **At rest:** The smallest of the northern swans, although only a little smaller and shorter-billed than closely-related Whistling Swan. Most likely to be confused with larger Whooper Swan (29), which shares striking yellow-and-black bill coloration, but Bewick's is smaller, shorter-necked, shorter-bodied, has more rounded and shorter head and shorter bill; differences between the two are fully discussed under Whooper Swan. Despite these structural features lone birds are particularly difficult to separate, but adults may be fairly readily identified by their bill pattern. Typically, Bewick's has yellow only at base of bill, the yellow not extending along sides in a point towards the tip as on Whooper, but ending in a rounded projection midway along bill; the bill pattern is, however, individually variable (see p. 156) and some individuals can be tricky. Whistling Swan has at most a very small yellow patch at base of bill and presents no real problem. Juvenile is not easy to separate from young Whooper, except by structure, although it is usually relatively more uniform greyish-brown in late winter; by first spring adult bill pattern should be partially visible on both species, but is most marked on young Whooper. Second-winter Bewick's normally shows some greyish-brown feathering on head and neck, whereas second-winter Whooper is very much like adult. **In flight:** Typical swan shape. Two-toned bill shared only by Whooper Swan, but Bewick's is smaller and stockier, with shorter neck and body, and has rather quicker wing action. More agile at take-off and landing than Whooper, dropping on to water at steeper angle and rising with little foot-pattering. Calls also higher in pitch and more yelping.

VOICE Generally more vociferous than Whooper, uttering variety of honking and yelping calls both when on water and when taking to the air. Typically, these are higher-pitched and quicker in delivery than those of Whooper, but many calls are similar. Usual flight call faster and more yelping, but softer and less bugling than Whooper, a low 'hoo-hoo-hoo'.

DESCRIPTION Sexes similar. **Adult:** Completely white; head and neck sometimes stained rusty, although less often than on Whooper. **Juvenile:** Overall greyish-brown, a little paler than juvenile

Bill patterns of adult northern swans (excluding Trumpeter Swan)

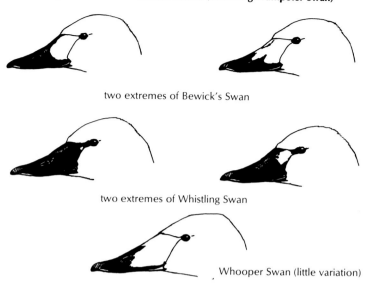

two extremes of Bewick's Swan

two extremes of Whistling Swan

Whooper Swan (little variation)

Whooper but basically very similar. Retains greyish-brown juvenile plumage well into first spring and, although attains adult coloration by second winter, most birds can still be aged by presence of greyish-brown on head and neck until at least into first half of second winter.

BARE PARTS Adult: Bill basally bright yellow, extent of yellow individually variable, but always ending in rounded projection at lower side of patch, occasionally a short projection into black higher up on bill side; upper culmen with dusky patches, and frequently bill black to base along culmen; terminal portion of bill black. Legs and feet black, very rarely yellow or flesh. Iris dark brown. **Juvenile:** Bill pink, whiter towards base, tip and cutting edge black; by first spring, dusky areas appear on bill as adult bill pattern develops, becoming as adult by second winter. Legs and feet fleshy-grey.

MEASUREMENTS Males usually larger than females. Western populations: Wing 469-548 (mean: male 519, female 504); tarsus 92-116; bill 82-102 (mean: both sexes 91); mean weight of male 6400, of female 5700.

GEOGRAPHICAL VARIATION Bewick's Swan is now considered to be merely a race of Whistling Swan. No other races now recognised, although eastern population of Bewick's (Lena delta eastwards), formerly separated as race *jankowskii*, averages rather larger and has longer and deeper bill which tends to show more extensive black than on western birds; however, intergrades with latter and many birds not separable.

HABITS Highly gregarious outside breeding season. Arrives on breeding grounds from mid May to early June, selecting territory in coastal tundra of Arctic Siberia. Nest sites on dry hummocks in open tundra, by rivers and estuaries, often in well-scattered colonies. Adults moult on breeding site while tending cygnets. Breeding grounds left during September and early October, when young fledged. Migrates in family parties, which unite with others during journey. Arrives in winter quarters from mid October onwards after stop-overs en route, some remaining at stop-over sites until moved on by cold weather; farthest winter sites may not be occupied until well into winter. Large flocks form on winter grounds, feeding in shallow water or by grazing in low-lying fields as Whooper Swan. Small numbers sometimes become mixed with Whooper flocks. Very noisy in winter, flocks keeping up constant low babbling when on water and indulging in greeting displays as groups join and leave main flock. Forsakes winter grounds from mid February onwards, leaving in family parties, but has numerous stop-overs en route back to Arctic.

HABITAT Breeds in low-lying open grassy or swampy tundra with scattered pools, lakes and rivers. Winters by low-lying wet pasture, flooded grasslands and adjacent fields with winter cereals. Passage birds often stop on upland lakes and reservoirs and sheltered coastal bays and estuaries.

DISTRIBUTION Breeds across almost full breadth of high-Arctic Siberia. Western populations (those breeding east to Taymyr Peninsula) migrate southwest through White Sea and the Baltic to winter in coastal lowlands of northern Europe, chiefly Denmark, the Netherlands and southern Britain and Ireland; smaller numbers winter in Belgium, France and West Germany. Eastern populations winter in coastal lowlands of eastern Asia, from Japan and Korea south along coastal China to Kwangtung, occasionally to Taiwan. Small population of unknown origin also winters along southern shores of Caspian Sea in Iran and formerly in southern USSR (i.e. Aral Sea). Occasional on passage in Mongolia and inland in northern China, with vagrants recorded Iceland, Svalbard, Bear Island, over most of Europe, Algeria, Libya, Israel, Iraq, Pakistan, northwest India, Nepal, Volcano Islands (western Pacific), western USA (Alaska, Oregon and California), and Canada (Saskatchewan).

POPULATION Despite being protected throughout nearly the whole of its range, small numbers are regularly shot (as indicated by X-ray examinations of trapped birds in England, where 44% of adults contained lead-shot in bodies). Western populations regularly counted in European winter quarters, estimated at 16,000 birds but numbers vary according to breeding success. Eastern Asian winter populations less well known, but estimated at 20,000 individuals. The small Iranian wintering group numbers around 100, although over 800 counted during cold winter of 1968/69, suggesting that perhaps small numbers still winter in Soviet Central Asia.

REFERENCES Beekman et al. (1985), Cramp and Simmons (1977), Scott (1981), Scott and the Wildfowl Trust (1972).

32 MUTE SWAN   Plate 9
Cygnus olor

As a true wild bird this is the breeding swan of the steppe lakes of central Asia, but it is most familiar as a tame bird of urban and suburban lakes.

FIELD IDENTIFICATION Length 125-155 cm (50-61 in). **At rest:** The familiar swan of park lakes, where it is usually tame and confiding. Adult has an orange bill with black basal area and prominent black knob on forehead, and may be distinguished from all other white swans in having a relatively long, pointed tail and habit of sometimes swimming with wing feathers strongly arched and neck gracefully curved. Juvenile dull greyish-brown, darker than those of Whooper (29) and Bewick's (31) Swans, and with black-based, pinkish-grey bill. Juvenile northern swans (28-31) paler, with pale-based bill (except juvenile Trumpeter (28)) and shorter, more rounded tail. **In flight:** Typical swan shape, most easily distinguished in flight by clearly audible throbbing drone, 'waou, waou, waou', produced by wingbeats (wingbeats silent in northern species). Hardly vocal in flight, apart from occasional grunts. Pointed tail projects beyond prominent black feet; in northern species feet reach tail-tip, but if bird close enough to see this feature bill is also usually visible.

VOICE As name implies, least vocal of swans, but by no means mute. Utters short grunts and hisses, also during breeding period short, loud snorts, but lacks honking flight calls of other species.

DESCRIPTION Sexes similar. **Adult:** Completely white, but head sometimes stained rusty from feeding in acidic waters, although generally less frequently than in other all-white swans. **Juvenile:** Almost entire plumage strongly washed brownish-grey, paler on flight feathers, underwing and tail. Becomes whiter by first spring and summer, but not completely white until second winter. Sometimes all white from cygnet stage, this colour variety being termed 'Polish Swan'.

BARE PARTS In spring, male has brighter bill and larger frontal knob than female. **Adult:** Bill orange-red, with black nail, cutting edge, extreme bill-base, nostril, bare facial skin and fleshy frontal knob. Legs and feet black, but remaining pink on 'Polish' birds. Iris brown. **Juvenile:** Bill lacks frontal knob, pinkish-grey, with black areas as adult, becoming pinker during first winter and attaining adult shape and colour by second winter. Legs and feet grey or pinkish-grey; fleshy-pink on 'Polish' birds.

MEASUREMENTS Males usually larger than females. Wing 533-623 (mean: male 606, female 562); tarsus 99-118; bill (to base of knob) 69-88 (mean: male 81, female 74); mean weight of male 11070, of female 8850.

GEOGRAPHICAL VARIATION None. Occasional colour phase known as 'Polish Swan' (see Description and Bare Parts) may be found among broods, other members of which may be quite normal.

HABITS Familiar swan of lakes, rivers and ponds both in open country and about towns and cities. Generally remarkably tame, but wild birds (in Asia) are wary and unapproachable. Long domesticated, particularly in Britain, where its history of domestication goes back to the twelfth century; also domesticated by the Greeks and Romans. Normally strongly territorial in the breeding season, driving most other wildfowl from vicinity of nest, but in some places large numbers breed in close proximity to each other, as at Abbotsbury, Dorset, in England. Nest a huge mound of vegetation close to waterside, often among tall fringe vegetation. Breeding commences in April, but introduced populations in South Africa breed in September and October. Cygnets, when small, are often carried on back of female. Male often aggressive, swimming in jerking movements towards intruder, with inner wing feathers arched and neck resting back on shoulders. After breeding, forms large concentrations on selected waters for post-breeding moult. To a certain extent migratory, with winter flocking on favoured waters. Feeds primarily by reaching below surface with long neck, frequently up-ending, but also dabbles and often grazes on land like other swans of the northern hemisphere.

HABITAT Favours lowland freshwater lakes, pools, reservoirs, gravel-pits, rivers and park lakes. Also on estuaries, coastal brackish lagoons and even in sheltered coastal bays. Rarely in upland districts.

DISTRIBUTION Widespread breeding bird over temperate Europe, being basically absent from northern and southern Europe; all European populations now more or less of domesticated origin. Scandinavian breeders winter in Baltic coastal regions, but west European birds chiefly resident. In Asia scattered across central regions to northern China, in some areas birds of domesticated or feral origin; winters along shores of Black and Caspian Seas, coastal Turkey and in lowland China. Introduced into eastern North America, South Africa, Australia and New Zealand, where populations relatively small and resident. Vagrants reported south to the Azores, Algeria, Egypt, Israel, Jordan, Iraq, Afghanistan, Pakistan, northern India and to Japan.

POPULATION European populations increasing,

with local introductions continuing, though in parts of Britain species has shown serious decline recently, mainly caused by poisoning from swallowing anglers' discarded lead weights. Asiatic population scattered and almost relict in distribution; no doubt some of these populations are threatened by habitat destruction and hunting pressures but few data available.

REFERENCES Birkhead and Perrins (1986), Scott and the Wildfowl Trust (1972).

33 BLACK SWAN   Plate 9
Cygnus atratus

A unique black swan of Australia, introduced into New Zealand.

FIELD IDENTIFICATION Length 115-140 cm (45-55 in). **At rest:** Unmistakable. Obviously a swan, sooty-black with white primaries and white-banded red bill; has remarkable crinkle-edge to wing feathers. White primaries generally concealed when on water. Juvenile is greyer, but is considerably darker than any other young swan, lacking brownish plumage tones; after a few months, has bill pattern similar to adult. **In flight:** Typical swan shape. White flight feathers contrast strikingly with otherwise black plumage, making it unmistakable in flight; juvenile shows dusky tips to white flight feathers.

VOICE Typical call a high-pitched bugling, rather musical and not very far-carrying, but may be uttered both on water and in flight. Other, more conversational notes may be heard from birds on the water.

DESCRIPTION Sexes similar. **Adult:** Almost completely sooty-black, with slightly greyer fringes to body and wing feathers, most noticeable on upperparts. Inner wing-coverts and tertials with curled edges. Primaries, outer secondaries and alula pure white. **Juvenile:** Greyer than adult, with rather lighter underparts and broader, paler feather fringes than adult; flight feathers as adult, but dusky-tipped. Resembles adult after first moult, but some retain dusky tips to some primaries until third year.

BARE PARTS Adult: Bill and bare skin to eye orange-red to deep waxy-red, with white subterminal band and pinker nail. Legs and feet black. Iris white or reddish. **Juvenile:** Bill dark grey, with paler nail; attains adult bill colour after a few months. Legs and feet dark grey. Iris brown.

MEASUREMENTS Males usually larger and longer-necked than females. Wing 416-543 (mean: male 489, female 461); tarsus 90-105; bill 56-79 (mean: male 69, female 63); mean weight of male 6270, of female 5100.

GEOGRAPHICAL VARIATION None.

HABITS Highly gregarious, concentrations reaching tens of thousands on some favoured lakes in southern Australia. Breeding season varies somewhat according to local conditions, February-May in northeast Queensland and June-August in Western Australia, for example, although nesting has been recorded at almost any time of the year when conditions are suitable. Nests are located close to the waterside in fringe vegetation or on small islands,

typically in colonies as dense as to be just outside pecking distance of a neighbour. After breeding, flocks form moulting concentrations. There is considerable dispersal after breeding and the species has been found in all parts of Australia, but these movements are not clearly understood although are no doubt connected with the search for new suitable breeding areas following local rains. A considerable portion of the population, however, is resident, whereas others are somewhat nomadic. Feeds primarily by submerging head and neck, but sometimes up-ends and dabbles; also grazes on waterside pastures.

HABITAT Breeds by large, relatively shallow lakes, of both fresh and brackish water. Away from breeding areas, may be found on flooded agricultural land, coastal lagoons and estuaries and even in sheltered coastal bays.

DISTRIBUTION Widespread across western region of Western Australia and eastern and southeastern Australia and Tasmania, with major concentrations in Victoria, southern New South Wales, southwest Western Australia and Tasmania. Dispersal takes birds across almost the whole of the continent, although the species is rare in central regions and northern Australia; it has also reached southern New Guinea. Introduced into New Zealand in 1864, now widespread in both islands.

POPULATION Abundant. Protected both by law and by sentiment in Australia, although, because of large concentrations and resulting crop damage, a short hunting season has been introduced in Victoria and Tasmania. Population difficult to assess, but 50,000 estimated on the Coorong, South Australia, in 1957 gives an indication of its local abundance. New Zealand population is controlled a little by commercial egg-collecting and shooting; birds at Lake Ellesmere, South Island, where some 60,000-80,000 congregated, were badly affected by a storm in 1968. The population for the whole of New Zealand is currently some 60,000 individuals.

REFERENCES Frith (1967), IWRB (1981), RAOU (1984).

34 BLACK-NECKED SWAN   Plate 9
Cygnus melanocoryphus

A native of southern South America, and perhaps the most attractive of all swans.

FIELD IDENTIFICATION Length 102-124 cm (40-49 in). **At rest:** Unmistakable, a typical white swan but with a stunning black head and neck and large red knob at base of bill. Juvenile is washed grey, but has dull blackish head and neck, quite unlike any other species. **In flight:** Typical swan shape, although a little stockier than other species. White plumage with striking black head and neck diagnostic. Wings produce a whistling sound in flight.

VOICE The typical call is a weak, wheezy whistle; although commonly uttered both on water and in flight, it is not far-carrying.

DESCRIPTION Sexes similar. **Adult:** Head and neck, except lower portion, velvet-black, with a narrow white line extending from forehead to a little

behind eye. Remainder of plumage completely white. **Juvenile:** Similar, but black of head and neck duller and browner; upperparts and flank feathers washed brownish-grey; primaries tipped blackish. Attains adult plumage by end of first year, but some dusky-tipped primaries retained until third year.
BARE PARTS Adult: Bill blue-grey, with pinkish-white nail; bare facial skin and very large frontal knob bright red. Legs and feet pink. Iris dark brown. **Juvenile:** Lacks frontal knob; bill grey, with dull reddish base. Legs and feet grey. Iris brown. Attains adult coloration by end of first year, but frontal knob does not develop until third, or even fourth, year.
MEASUREMENTS Males larger and longer-necked than females. **Male:** Wing 435-450, tarsus 85-88, bill 82-86, mean weight 5400. **Female:** Wing 400-415, tarsus 78-80, bill 71-73, mean weight 4000.
GEOGRAPHICAL VARIATION None.
HABITS Gregarious swan of freshwater and brackish-water marshes of southern South America. Less gregarious when breeding, generally strongly territorial and aggressive, although several nests have been reported in close proximity. Breeding season varies a little according to latitude: in central Chile and Argentina it is in July and August; farther south, as in the Falkland Islands, from early August to mid September. Nests are located in dense fringe vegetation by lakesides, but may be on small islands or even partially floating. Cygnets are carried on back of adults until quite large. Male aggressive,

chasing other waterfowl and almost any intruder from vicinity of nest, although it does not adopt the arched-wing threat postures of Mute (32) and Black (33) Swans. Large concentrations gather for post-breeding moult, which may reach 5,000-6,000 birds. Disperses northwards in March and April, but precise movements have yet to be studied. Rarely comes on to land, its relatively short legs and long body giving it a very awkward gait. Take-off and landing executed with more difficulty than other swans, again possibly owing to relatively short legs. Feeds chiefly in shallow water by dabbling and submerging head.
HABITAT Freshwater marshes and shallow lakes, coastal lagoons, estuaries and even sheltered coastal bays.
DISTRIBUTION Southern South America. Breeds from Cape Horn and the Falkland Islands, north to central Chile, southern Paraguay and southeastern Brazil. Southern populations disperse northwards for winter, although more northerly population basically resident. Disperses north to northern Paraguay. Vagrant to Juan Fernandez Islands (off Chile) and South Shetland Islands.
POPULATION Few data. Seems to be under little threat, although drainage of lowland wetlands for cattle-farming has no doubt affected its population in some countries. Reported to be increasing in Chile following former decrease through perse-cution.
REFERENCES Scott and the Wildfowl Trust (1972).

SUBFAMILY STICTONETTINAE (FRECKLED DUCK)

An aberrant Australian duck, with anatomical features suggesting that its closest living relations are the swans, although it is most likely the sole survivor of a primitive group of waterfowl.

35 FRECKLED DUCK   Plate 16
Stictonetta naevosa

The relationships of this unique duck have never been clarified, but it is now generally considered to be nearer to the swans and geese than to the true ducks.

FIELD IDENTIFICATION Length 50-55 cm (20-22 in). **At rest:** Endemic to Australia. At any distance, a medium-sized, very uniformly dark duck with distinctive head shape. Head is relatively large and distinctly peaked at rear crown. Bill is relatively long and slender and distinctly upcurved, although very deep at base. Dark coloration relieved only by extensive reddish-pink basal third to bill (only on male). At close quarters, dark plumage may be seen to be intensely, but minutely, freckled with pale buff. Shape, particularly of head and bill, helps distinguish it from Australian dabbling ducks, but uniformly dark head also prevents confusion with Pacific Black Duck (91) and Grey Teal (81). **In flight:** In overall shape and flight action recalls Pacific Black Duck, but head, breast and entire upperparts uniformly dark, contrasting somewhat with ill-defined whitish belly and underwing. General shape, however, slightly different, having relatively larger head, shorter, more drooped neck and

relatively smaller and more pointed wings.
VOICE Less vocal than most other ducks. It has a soft, flute-like 'whee-yu' of alarm, and during disputes among captive birds a loud discordant quack recorded from female and a short, raucous snorting note from male. All of these sounds are very inconspicuous.
DESCRIPTION All plumages basically similar. **Adult male:** Entire plumage blackish-brown, intensely freckled with minute pale buff or whitish markings to each feather. Freckles smallest on head and neck (appear darker) and largest on feathers of underparts (appear paler). Flight feathers uniform dark brown. Underwing-coverts white, blotched irregularly with brown along leading edge and becoming blotched brown on greater coverts; underside of primaries pale brown. **Adult female:** Similar, but ground colour lighter brown, lacking blackish tone and therefore less contrasting than male; freckles pale buff. **Juvenile:** Similar to above, but paler still than female, with ground colour light brown and freckles warmer buff.
BARE PARTS All ages: Bill, high at base but dorsally flattened, slate-grey; adult males attain extensive waxy-red over basal third of bill at onset of breeding season, but presence of red reported also in non-breeding season so precise significance unclear. Legs and feet slate-grey. Iris brown.

MEASUREMENTS Males usually larger than females. **Male:** Wing 519-591 (mean 556), tarsus 40-45, bill 50-59, mean weight 969. **Female:** Wing 480-533 (mean 508), tarsus 40-44, bill 46-53, mean weight 842.

GEOGRAPHICAL VARIATION None.

HABITS Strange and relatively little-studied Australian duck. Its sporadic wanderings have taken it to almost all parts of the continent, following prolonged dry seasons when the swamps of interior Australia dry out. Usually found in small flocks loafing by banks of shallow-water lakes, larger concentrations building up in favoured wetlands as other lakes and pools dry out. Most active towards dusk. Feeds by dabbling, or rather filtering, with peculiarly-shaped bill while swimming or wading in shallow water, but also sometimes up-ends in deeper water like a true dabbling duck. Mixes freely with other waterfowl. Relatively tame, even to the point of being inquisitive about human activity. When flushed, patters over water for short distance, not rising directly like true dabbling ducks. Swims markedly buoyantly, with short neck and chunky head giving top-heavy appearance. Breeding season varies according to water levels, which depend on the extent of the rains: in dry seasons there may be little breeding, but following extensive flooding may breed at almost any time of the year; it has been found breeding chiefly between September and December. Nests are constructed of small, fine twigs and placed close to water surface in flooded lignum bushes, which can be left quite high and dry as water levels recede.

HABITAT Open lakes and swamps with dense fringe vegetation, especially lignum. Also floodplains and brackish coastal lagoons.

DISTRIBUTION Freckled Ducks have two major centres of distribution: the extreme southwest of Western Australia (chiefly at Benger and Moora); and in the Murray-Darling basin of southeastern Australia, particularly in the New South Wales Riverina. In these areas always present in varying numbers, but after periods of drought disperses widely and has been recorded breeding at numerous other stations from coastal Victoria north to southern Queensland and elsewhere in the extreme west of Western Australia. Its sporadic and dispersive nature has taken it to most parts of Australia, including Northern Territory, but it is only a vagrant to Tasmania.

POPULATION Difficult to assess, but a national count in January 1983 located 7,926 individuals, with the largest concentration being 900 at Lake Hungerford (New South Wales); a provisional estimate of a total population of between 8,000 and 13,000 birds has been made from these counts, with some 1,000 in the smaller western population. Despite official protection, numbers are shot annually, being mistaken for Pacific Black Ducks or Grey Teal: in March 1980, 500 were shot out of a population of 700 on the Bool Lagoon (South Australia), and in March 1981 some 800 were shot in Victoria out of an estimated 3,000 in the state. Other threats to the species include wetland drainage, irrigation schemes and increasing water-sport activity on its lakes. All of these, coupled with increasing drought conditions which are contracting and concentrating the species' range, are worrying factors concerning the healthy survival of this unique duck.

REFERENCES Briggs (1982), Frith (1967), Hall (1986), Johnsgard (1965), Norman and Norris (1982), RAOU (1984).

SUBFAMILY PLECTROPTERINAE (SPUR-WINGED GOOSE)

An aberrant African goose, formerly included with a group of other odd genera under a tribe termed 'perching ducks' (Cairinini), but revision of wildfowl classification by Livezey (1986) has dismantled this tribe and allocated the species to other positions. Recent research has supported earlier suggestions that the Spur-winged Goose is related to the shelducks, although deserving a subfamily of its own.

36 SPUR-WINGED GOOSE   Plate 3
Plectropterus gambensis

Peculiar African goose superficially recalling Magpie Goose (1) in size and shape, but quite different in anatomy.

FIELD IDENTIFICATION Length 75-100 cm (30-39 in). **At rest:** Unmistakable large, long-legged black and white goose of African watersides. Southern African birds are glossy black, with white on belly, ventral region and breast centre, and can appear all black at some angles; birds from rest of Africa, however, have white extending over most of underparts, including lower foreneck, and on head. Both sexes have pinkish-red bill and legs and are similar in plumage colour, but male is considerably larger and has prominent knob on forehead. Duller and browner juvenile is still unmistakable, sharing adult plumage pattern and distinctive size and shape. In **flight:** Huge size, long heavy head and neck, and broad well-fingered wings plus black and white plumage distinctive. Upperparts almost all dark, but white leading edge to wing-coverts often striking, although less conspicuous in southern populations. Underside shows white underwing-coverts contrasting with black flight feathers. Egyptian Goose (46) and Cape Shelduck (39) also have white upperwing- and underwing-coverts, but have much more white on upperwing and lack black in body plumage or on head and neck. Flight action slow and laboured, wingbeats being relatively shallow and producing a deep swishing sound.

VOICE Relatively silent. Typical call uttered only by male, a soft bubbling 'cherwit' when taking wing or when alarmed. Other inconspicuous calls may be uttered by both sexes when displaying or in alarm.

DESCRIPTION Sexes similar in plumage, although males much larger than females. Additionally, females less iridescent and white of upper forewing less extensive. Nominate race described. **Adult:**

Crown, sides and rear of neck, upper foreneck, sides of breast, upper flanks and almost entire upperparts, including wings and tail, black, highly glossed with metallic green and bronze reflections. Throat, lower foreneck, breast, lower flanks and remainder of underparts white. Upperwing glossy black, with white lesser coverts, carpal region and leading edge. Underwing-coverts white, mottled brown, with blackish flight feathers. **Juvenile:** Similar to adult, but black of plumage duller and greyer, with brown feather fringes; white areas of plumage, including feathered face (bare on adults), sullied buffish-brown. Attains adult features after first moult.

BARE PARTS Adult: Bill, frontal knob and bare facial skin back to eye fleshy-red, female with less-developed frontal knob and less extensive facial skin. Bare skin on face below eye pale grey, bare flap of skin on side of upper neck fleshy-red. Legs and feet fleshy-red. Iris dark brown. **Juvenile:** Coloration of bill and legs much as adult, but at first has whole head feathered, developing bare facial skin and cranial knob with age.

MEASUREMENTS Adult males considerably larger than females and juveniles; young males, however, take some time to reach full size, so that accurate sexing by size not always possible, except with largest birds. Adults of nominate race described. **Male:** Wing 530-550, tarsus 110-120, bill 59-63, mean weight ca. 6000. **Female:** Wing 422-440, tarsus 57-59, bill 57-59, mean weight ca. 4750.

GEOGRAPHICAL VARIATION Two races recognised, the nominate form over most of range and *niger* of southern African north to the Zambezi, but there is a wide overlap zone of intermediate birds. Typically, *niger* (Black Spur-winged Goose) has very little white at all on underparts and may appear all black at long range; on most individuals, the white is restricted to the ventral region and centre of belly and breast, the bare facial skin is more restricted, and the cranial knob a little smaller. The race *niger* averages a little smaller overall than nominate.

HABITS Widespread bird of African rivers, swamps and lakesides. Generally gregarious, being met with in small flocks of up to 50 birds, but larger numbers gather at certain sites, particularly for post-breeding moult. Shy and wary, but aggressive in defence of the nest, using well-developed spur at bend of wing (present at all ages) in disputes. Feeds primarily by grazing in adjacent fields and grasslands or in shallow water. Can swim well, but is usually met with standing by shore. Nest varies, though usually it is a large construction hidden on ground among waterside vegetation, but frequently takes over old tree nests of large birds such as Hamerkop, and uses large tree holes, cavities in rocks and even holes in termite mounds. Season varies according to region and extent of rains locally, but in northern parts of range generally August to December, in East Africa from January to June and in southern Africa from August to May. Roosting birds loaf on quiet riverbanks and lakeshores and even in treetops, flying to and from roost at dawn and dusk in straggling lines or even V-formation; feeds chiefly in early morning and late evening. Has little-understood movements associated with dry-season dispersal as lakes and rivers dry out, but resident in many areas.

HABITAT Open grassland with lakes, pools and rivers, and swamps and river deltas. Prefers large inland rivers and lakes and avoids saline lakes and upland areas, although occurs at up to 3000 m in East Africa.

DISTRIBUTION Widespread throughout tropical Africa, north to Senegambia and the Sudan and Ethiopia, but absent from arid zones of southwest and northeast. Somewhat migratory; movements not clearly understood, but associated with dry-season dispersal and seasonal flooding of wetlands. Occasionally wanders north up Nile valley as far as Abu Simbel (Egypt), but not since construction of Aswan Dam, while a lone bird recorded coastal Morocco in June was probably a genuine vagrant rather than an escape from captivity.

POPULATION No estimates have been made. Clearly an abundant species with no immediate threats, although the increasing aridity of sub-Saharan Africa has probably affected the numbers in the northern limits of the species' range. A count of West African wetlands from Senegal to Chad in early 1977 produced 10,000, mostly in the Niger basin.

REFERENCES Brown *et al.* (1982).

SUBFAMILY TADORNINAE (SHELDUCKS AND SHELDGEESE)

A large group of varied genera. All are equally at home feeding on land as on water, some being basically terrestrial by nature. Little difference between sexes in many species, yet considerable in others, even within same genera. In many ways somewhat intermediate between true geese and the typical ducks.

Tribe SARKIDIORNINI (COMB DUCK)

A monotypic tribe, formerly included in mixed bag of waterfowl termed 'perching ducks' (Cairinini). Although it is now considered to be closest to the shelducks in evolutionary terms, this is a very aberrant bird and is best allocated a group of its own.

37 COMB DUCK   Plate 18
Sarkidiornis melanotos

Alternative names: Nukta, Nakta, Knob-billed Goose

The peculiar distribution of this strange duck is comparable with that of the Fulvous Whistling Duck (4).

FIELD IDENTIFICATION Length 56-76 cm (22-30 in). **At rest:** Unmistakable. Large, heavily-built duck of tropical wetlands, with distinctive two-toned pattern of white head, neck and underparts and glossy

black upperparts; at close quarters, dark freckling often visible on head. Male has large fleshy knob at base of bill. Female considerably smaller than male. South American race has black flanks, which are white in African and Asian race. Adult plumage pattern vaguely similar to that of tiny Cotton Pygmy Goose (67) and some domesticated Muscovy Ducks (61), but confusion hardly likely. Juvenile considerably browner; usually accompanied by adults, but distant juvenile confusable with Fulvous Whistling Duck, although latter has longer legs, more erect stance, warmer buff coloration and lacks dark mottling on underparts. Juvenile plumage also recalls that of female Maned Duck (109). **In flight:** White of head, neck and underbody contrasts sharply with black underwing and upperparts, although paler rump may be obvious at certain angles; South American race with black flanks shows contrasting white head, neck, breast and belly. In flight, shape recalls small, broad-winged goose. Flight action direct and steady, with strong shallow beats. Flies in groups, which may form lines or even V-formation.
VOICE Relatively silent, but sometimes utters a low croak when flushed. During breeding season, several short wheezy whistles, grunts and hisses may be given in display or aggression.
DESCRIPTION Sexes similar in plumage. Nominate race described. **Adult:** Head and upper neck white, finely speckled black, latter forming narrow dark centre to crown and hindneck. Variably extensive yellowish-buff wash to sides of head and neck. Lower neck, breast and centre of belly pure white. Black vertical stripe extending down sides of breast from dark upperparts, with another black band at the rear extending down towards vent. Flanks whitish with pale grey wash. Undertail-coverts whitish, often strongly washed yellow. Rump grey; rest of upperparts, including tail and both entire upperwing and entire underwing, black, very strongly glossed with metallic green, blue and bronze iridescences. Female less glossy, with breast-band ill-defined and often some brownish mottling on underparts; lacks yellowish wash to head and undertail-coverts. Non-breeding male also lacks yellow wash, and has smaller comb. **Juvenile:** Quite different, having upperparts and crown dark brown, head, neck and underparts buffish-brown, with darker brown scaling on underparts and darker line through eye. After first moult becomes similar to adult female, although duller, more greyish above.
BARE PARTS All plumages: Bill black; large fleshy comb (present only on male) dark grey. Legs and feet dark grey. Iris dark brown.
MEASUREMENTS Males considerably larger than females. Nominate race described. **Male:** Wing 349-406, tarsus 64-75, bill 57-60, mean weight ca. 2250. **Female:** Wing 280-290, tarsus 42-50, bill 48-52, mean weight ca. 1750.
GEOGRAPHICAL VARIATION Two well-differentiated races, the nominate form of tropical Africa and Asia and race *sylvicola* of South America. The latter is a little smaller than the Old World race, and males have glossy black flanks with only a narrow band of white along the centre of the belly; females have dark grey flanks. The South American race has even been considered a full species by some

authorities, as 'American Comb Duck' *S. sylvicola*.
HABITS Sociable duck of freshwater swamps and lakes in tropical lowlands. Generally met with in small parties of up to 30-40 birds, but larger concentrations gather on suitable waters during the dry season. Many flocks seem to be sexually segregated; they break up and disperse to breeding grounds at onset of rains. On breeding grounds, dominant males may take on 'harem' of at least two females. Nest sites vary but are normally close to waterside; usually large cavities in hollow trees are used, but sometimes holes in walls of isolated buildings, or an old tree nest of a large bird is taken over, while nest is not infrequently on the ground. Although not particularly sociable in the breeding season, Comb Ducks are not strongly territorial either and small loose colonies may be formed. Breeding season varies considerably over species' extensive range, depending very much on local rainy seasons: there are few data from South America, but an individual in breeding condition has been collected in Venezuela in July; in Africa, generally July-September in the northern and western regions of its range, February-March in East Africa, and December-April in Zimbabwe; in India, breeds chiefly during the monsoon period, July-September. Within the tropics flocks move about a great deal, locating suitable wetland areas during the dry seasons. Feeds primarily by grazing on adjacent waterside grasslands, or by wading and swimming in shallows. Swims very buoyantly, with rear end held high. Perches adeptly in trees.
HABITAT Lowland tropical swamps, lakes and rivers in open, sparsely-wooded country.
DISTRIBUTION Widespread throughout tropical Africa, tropical Asia and South America. In Africa it is both resident and a seasonal migrant throughout the continent and Madagascar, avoiding arid and densely-forested regions; its movements are not clearly understood apart from being linked with drying-out of wetlands during the dry season, but ringing recoveries indicate that some movements are very extensive, e.g. birds ringed in Zimbabwe recovered as far as Sudan (3600 km) and Chad (3880 km), though no records of vagrants in Palaearctic Africa. In Asia it is widespread almost throughout the Indian subcontinent, but local in Pakistan and lowland Nepal and very rare in Sri Lanka; its range extends eastwards through Burma and northern Thailand to Laos and extreme southern China (Yunnan). In Asia, too, it is a partial migrant, with movements linked with seasonal rains; stragglers have been recorded in Fukien (China). South American race *sylvicola* widespread, although local, throughout tropical lowlands from eastern Panama south over eastern lowlands of the continent to northern Argentina and west to eastern Colombia, Bolivia (rare) and Peru (rare); vagrant to Trinidad and south to Buenos Aires (Argentina).
POPULATION Generally widespread and abundant species, with no obvious overall threat. Despite wide range, its occurrence is somewhat local and patchy, especially South American form, which has been little studied in the field.
REFERENCES Ali and Ripley (1968), Brown *et al.* (1982).

38 RUDDY SHELDUCK Plate 11
Tadorna ferruginea

Alternative name: Brahminy Duck (India)

Now very rare in Europe, this beautiful shelduck is still abundant in Asia.

FIELD IDENTIFICATION Length 61-67 cm (24-26 in). **At rest:** Distinctive within its natural range. A large rusty-coloured duck with paler head and black rear end. Usually met with in small parties in open steppe-like country, especially near water, and in winter resorts to rivers as well as to lakes. Most, if not all west European records refer to escapes, as this species is commonly kept in captivity. Confusion possible in captivity with similar Cape Shelduck (39) and breeding female Paradise Shelduck (41). Cape Shelduck has grey head, the female having conspicuous white facial patches, whereas female Paradise Shelduck has snowy-white head and neck and rich chestnut body coloration. Ruddy Shelduck head and neck coloration varies from pale buffish to tawny-buff, often with paler buff facial patches, but is never snowy-white; the body coloration may sometimes be remarkably pale, almost yellowish-buff, in worn plumage. **In flight:** Combination of rusty-orange or orange-buff body plumage, contrasting with blackish flight feathers and tail and white upperwing- and underwing-coverts distinctive within range. Wing pattern of both Cape and Paradise Shelducks similar. At long range could be confused with Egyptian Goose (46), which has similar wing pattern, but latter has paler body, longer neck and broader, more rounded wings.

VOICE Quite vocal, both at rest and on the wing, winter flocks being especially noisy. Usual call a rolling honked 'aakh'; varied in delivery, often repeated as an abruptly-trumpeted 'pok-pok-pok-pok' before taking wing. Female's calls are a little deeper and harsher than those of male.

DESCRIPTION Depth of body coloration rather variable; ageing and sexing of some individuals problematic. **Adult male breeding:** Head and neck buff, becoming orange-buff on hindneck, sometimes with dusky patch on rear crown. Variably distinct narrow blackish collar around base of neck. Breast and almost entire upperparts and underparts orange-brown to buffish-orange. Rump, uppertail-coverts and tail glossy black. Upperwing-coverts white, washed orange-buff in fresh plumage; primaries and secondaries glossy black, with metallic green gloss to secondaries. Underwing-coverts white, contrasting with blackish flight feathers. **Adult male non-breeding:** Similar, but neck-collar indistinct or absent. **Adult female:** Similar to male, but lacks neck-collar; head and neck buffer, with contrasting whitish facial patch. **Juvenile:** Similar to female, but duller; whole plumage with greyish-brown tone, especially on head and upperparts. Becomes much as adult by first autumn, although flight feathers and tail dull black until first summer. **BARE PARTS All plumages:** Bill, legs and feet blackish. Iris brown.

MEASUREMENTS Males typically larger than females. Wing 321-383 (mean: male 366, female 339); tarsus 52-64; bill 35-49; mean weight of male

ca. 1385, of female ca. 1145.

GEOGRAPHICAL VARIATION None.

HABITS Typically, found in small parties or pairs in open country, with larger concentrations forming in winter quarters and at moult gatherings. Flocks at favoured winter sites may reach thousands, but more characteristically found in scattered small flocks along extensive river systems. Has long-term pair-bond, pairs arriving on breeding grounds during April and May to take up well-spaced territories, but loosely gregarious in some regions; nests are placed in burrows, tree holes, cliff crevices and even buildings, often far from water. After breeding, adults assemble to moult on favoured waters, sometimes flying considerable distances to moult, remaining at moulting sites until August or September. Most populations highly migratory, leaving breeding grounds in family parties during September and arriving in winter quarters during October and November. Feeds by grazing in open steppe or by wading in lakeside and riverside shallows. Swims readily, and will also feed by up-ending. Shy and wary despite absence of persecution in many parts of its range, although becomes remarkably confiding in breeding areas where long unmolested, e.g. Tibet, where freely perches on house roofs and nests inside buildings.

HABITAT Breeds in open country, particularly by rivers and saline lakes in open steppe and upland plateaux, locally by rivers in mountainous districts, but generally avoids well-forested country. Winters by slow-flowing rivers and lakes in lowland districts, normally avoiding coastal waters.

DISTRIBUTION Three well-separated populations. A small and declining population in northwest Africa which is less migratory, although formerly moved north to winter in southern Spain, where it is now very rare. Recently-discovered breeding population in the highlands of Ethiopia is considered to be resident. The main population breeds from extreme southeastern Europe and Turkey, eastwards across southern and central Asia to western China and Mongolia, north to the region of Lake Baikal and south to include the Tibetan plateau, northern Iran and northern Iraq. Most of this population migrate southwards to winter in the lowlands from southern and eastern China westwards to Afghanistan, with further winter concentrations in western Iran (about 40,000 Lake Rezaiyeh) and Turkey, smaller numbers overwintering in southern USSR and sometimes Greece. Formerly wintered in Nile valley, south to the Sudan and Ethiopia, but considerable decline here in recent years. Vagrants reported from many European countries, but in view of the decline of western wild populations most, if not all, of these in recent decades refer to escapes from captivity. Genuine vagrancy formerly occurred, however, as shown by massive invasion in summer of 1892 when birds reported widely over Europe, some even reaching Iceland, Scandinavia and Greenland. Vagrants also reported south to Oman, Sri Lanka and Kenya, and east to Japan.

POPULATION Abundant over much of Asian portion of range, but western populations rapidly declining for reasons that are not clearly understood, although perhaps intensification of agricul-

163

tural methods and resulting habitat loss is the most likely factor. North African population estimated at some 1,000 pairs in 1970, with some 50 pairs in Morocco and most of the rest in western Algeria. Eastern European birds also declining rapidly, but very small numbers still breed in Romania, Greece and Bulgaria; decline also reported from European USSR.

REFERENCES Brown *et al.* (1982), Cramp and Simmons (1977), Rogers (1982).

39 CAPE SHELDUCK
Tadorna cana
Plate 11

Alternative name: South African Shelduck

A geographically-isolated southern counterpart of the Ruddy Shelduck.

FIELD IDENTIFICATION Length 61-66 cm (24-26 in). **At rest:** A grey-headed rusty-orange shelduck, unlikely to be confused with any other species within its range though confusion possible in captivity. Male differs from Ruddy Shelduck (38) in having ashy-grey, not buff, head and breast, and undertail-coverts contrasting paler than flanks and belly (underparts more uniform on Ruddy Shelduck). Female darker and more uniform than male, with striking slate-grey head and whitish facial patches. Female Paradise Shelduck (41) has all-white head and neck; although some female Cape Shelducks have white of face so extensive as to appear almost white-headed, there is always slate-grey on neck and rear of head. Confusion of female with White-faced Whistling Duck (7) possible, but latter a much darker chestnut and blackish bird with quite different general shape. **In flight:** Rusty overall coloration contrasts markedly with white upperwing- and underwing-coverts and blackish flight feathers. Within range confusion likely only with Egyptian Goose (46), which is larger, paler below, has relatively longer neck and broader, blunter wings, although its wing pattern above and below is confusingly similar to that of Cape Shelduck.

VOICE Similar to that of Ruddy Shelduck, but calls a little deeper in tone. Typically, a short, goose-like honk, often repeated; calls of female are harsher than those of male.

DESCRIPTION Adult male breeding: Head and neck ashy-grey. Breast and undertail-coverts yellowish, becoming orange-chestnut on flanks and remainder of underparts, darkest on belly. Most of upperparts similarly rufous-chestnut, palest on mantle. Rump, uppertail-coverts and tail black. Wing-coverts above and below chiefly white, contrasting with blackish flight feathers, which are glossed metallic green on secondaries. **Adult male non-breeding:** Similar to breeding, but duller overall, with fine grey vermiculations on underparts; breast dull and pale yellowish-buff. **Adult female:** Darker in general than male, with body plumage richer chestnut and breast less contrastingly paler. The grey of the head is darker, more of a slate-grey, and contrasts with individually variable white facial patches, latter sometimes merely about eye but often much more extensive (in extreme examples white covers most of head). **Juvenile:** Recalls male, but general plumage still duller, washed greyish-brown. Adult-like plumage attained by first winter, with young females soon starting to show whitish about eyes.

BARE PARTS All plumages: Bill, legs and feet blackish, although feet may be blotched with pinkish on females. Iris brown.

MEASUREMENTS Sexes similar, although males typically larger than females. Wing 315-365 (mean: male 356, female 326); tarsus 52-60; bill 39-54; mean weight of male 1527, of female 1229.

GEOGRAPHICAL VARIATION None.

HABITS Sociable bird of lakes and rivers in southern Africa, gathering in flocks of several hundred or more outside breeding season. Like Ruddy Shelduck, has long-term pair-bonds. Pairs take up breeding territories on small permanent waterbodies during the dry season and nest in disused mammal holes, principally those of aardvarks; nest site may be as much as 2 km from water. Egg-laying commences in mid May. After breeding, adults perform moult migrations to northeast of breeding grounds, assembling at key deep-water lakes for moult during November to January. Feeds primarily by grazing on land or dabbling in shallow water, feeding chiefly at night, spending most of daytime loafing by lakeshores and islands. Shy and wary and quite pugnacious by nature; pairs are evidently attached even outside breeding season, although females tend to outnumber males by about two to one and compete for unmated males.

HABITAT Breeds by small, shallow permanent freshwater and brackish lakes in open country, in both upland and lowland areas. Post-breeding moulting flocks gather on deep-water lakes and reservoirs.

DISTRIBUTION Widespread and basically resident in southern Africa, with seasonal moult movements. Widespread in Cape Province, Orange Free State, southern Transvaal, north to southern Botswana and the highlands of Damaraland in Namibia and east to western Natal. After breeding, birds move northeast to assemble at key moulting waters from November to January; most of these are located in Orange Free State, where some 75% of the population congregate, but other gatherings are formed in the Transvaal and Cape Province. After moult, birds move southwest, returning to breeding waters. Long-distance vagrancy not known, although movements of 1000 km reported.

POPULATION Common over rather limited range, with most pairs breeding in Cape Province and southern Namibia. Population stable, benefiting from construction of reservoirs and dams. Estimated at 42,000 individuals in 1981. Most likely threat would be to areas where huge concentrations gather to moult.

REFERENCES Brown *et al.* (1982), Geldenhuys (1981a,b).

40 AUSTRALIAN SHELDUCK
Tadorna tadornoides
Plate 12

Alternative names: Chestnut-breasted Shelduck, Mountain Duck

A beautifully-marked shelduck, endemic to southern Australia.

FIELD IDENTIFICATION Length 55-72 cm (22-28 in). **At rest:** A distinctive Australian shelduck, unlikely to be confused with anything else, even in collections. Both sexes are large blackish ducks with a rufous-chestnut breast and white wings-coverts; the smaller female shows white eye-patches, the male a white neck-ring, and both sometimes have white about base of bill. Male Paradise Shelduck (41) is only other all-dark shelduck, but lacks chestnut or rufous breast. **In flight:** A distinctive, large blackish duck with striking white upperwing- and underwing-coverts, a unique combination in Australian waterfowl. Dark underbody and stockier shape easily distinguish it from flying Magpie Goose (1), and ranges do not overlap. Pacific Black Duck (91) has similar underwing pattern, but is slighter, with pale head and neck.

VOICE Highly vocal, both in flight and when on the ground. Typical call of male a low goose-like honk, but calls of females are markedly higher in pitch and the notes are less abrupt. Typical female calls are a resounding 'ong-gank, ong-gank' and a strident 'ow-ow-ow-ow'.

DESCRIPTION Owing to individual variation, ageing and sexing of some birds difficult, but only females have whitish feathering surrounding eye. **Adult male:** Head and neck sooty-black, sometimes with a little whitish feathering about base of bill. Narrow white ring encircles base of neck. Breast and mantle cinnamon-rufous. Almost entire remainder of upperparts and underparts sooty-black, with indistinct fine light brown vermiculations on underparts, back and scapulars. Upperwing- and underwing-coverts chiefly white, contrasting with blackish flight feathers; secondaries glossed metallic green. Tertials chestnut. Non-breeding male a little duller, with black parts sullied brown, breast lighter, more yellowish-brown, and collar ill-defined. **Adult female:** Similar to male, but breast and upper mantle richer chestnut, white neck-collar narrower or absent and black areas of plumage a little browner. Has white patch surrounding eye and often some whitish feathering about base of bill, these white patches occasionally being joined. **Juvenile:** Duller than adults, with extensive brown feathering on head and neck, no neck-collar, some whitish feathering between eye and bill, light brownish breast and upper mantle, greyish tips to white wing-covert feathers and whitish tips to secondaries. Soon resemble adults, but whitish tips to secondaries remain until first-summer moult. Juvenile females may be sexed by presence of whitish feathers on sides of head and about eye.

BARE PARTS All plumages: Bill, legs and feet blackish or dark grey. Iris brown.

MEASUREMENTS Males typically larger than females. **Male:** Wing 318-392 (mean 358), tarsus 60-64, bill 41-49, mean weight 1559. **Female:** Wing 304-355 (mean 331), tarsus 56-60, bill 38-45, mean weight 1291.

GEOGRAPHICAL VARIATION None.

HABITS Sociable bird of open country and waterside in southern Australia. Usually found in pairs (has long-term pair-bonds) or family parties, but large concentrations are formed outside breeding season, particularly on moulting waters. Breeding season varies little over the range, unlike in many other Australian species. In March and April pairs take up territories, which they defend strongly against almost all other waterfowl. Over most of the range the breeding season is from mid June and late September, a little later in northern areas and in Tasmania. Nests are situated in hollow trees or cavities and holes in banks and cliffs. Following the breeding season, concentrations gather to moult at a few key waters, these being large deep-water lakes. Feeds chiefly by grazing on pastureland, but also dabbles and swims in shallow water when feeding. Loafing birds gather on shoreline of lakes and estuaries in quite large flocks. Generally rather wary and unapproachable, flocks flying excitedly to safe waters when disturbed from feeding areas.

HABITAT Breeds by freshwater swamps, brackish and freshwater lakes and inshore coastal islands, preferably with scattered trees but also in open plains; feeds on stubble fields, grassland and lake-shores. Outside breeding season also by deep-water lakes, estuaries and sheltered coastal bays.

DISTRIBUTION Widespread resident in southern Australia, with two widely-separated populations: one in Western Australia; the other in southeastern Australia, chiefly in Victoria but north over southern New South Wales, west to Spencer Gulf region of South Australia and including Tasmania. Following breeding season, disperses widely to a number of key moulting waters, most notable of these being Lake George (New South Wales), where flocks of 1,000-2,000 birds gather. During these dispersals vagrants have occasionally turned up farther north, with records north to northern Queensland and northern Western Australia. There is also an undated record of a bird said to have been shot at Lake Ellesmere in South Island, New Zealand.

POPULATION A widespread and abundant shelduck, which in recent decades has actually increased and spread its range, especially in Western Australia. As it is poor eating, it is not excessively hunted, but claims that it damages crops have resulted in shooting in some districts. No total population estimates have been made, but a survey of western Victoria wetlands in February 1982 produced 23,200 individuals.

REFERENCES Frith (1967), RAOU (1984), Riggert (1977).

41 PARADISE SHELDUCK   Plate 12
Tadorna variegata
Alternative name: New Zealand Shelduck

A relative of the Australian Shelduck (40), and confined to New Zealand.

FIELD IDENTIFICATION Length 63-71 cm (25-28 in). **At rest:** Sexually dimorphic, the sooty male and white-headed rich chestnut female are unmistakable, even in collections; both may show contrasting white wing-coverts when at rest. Female could be confused with both Ruddy (38) and Cape (39) Shelducks in captivity, but its contrasting snowy-white head and neck is not shown by either of these species, although some female Cape Shelducks have most of face white. Juvenile females, however, show some rufous in the breast and whitish facial feathering contrasting with the otherwise sooty-brown body coloration, and recall female Australian Shelduck. **In flight:** Both sexes are distinctive in New Zealand. Male is blackish, with striking white upperwing- and underwing-coverts, while female shows similar wing pattern contrasting with deep chestnut or blackish body and white head and neck.

VOICE Highly vocal, like most others of the genus. Male utters low grunts and a rolling, guttural 'ha-hoo' in display, whereas female's calls are higher-pitched and more abruptly honking.

DESCRIPTION Adult male: Head and neck green-ish-black. Almost entire upperparts and underparts sooty-black, with fine pale brown vermiculations on scapulars and upper back and fine grey vermicu-lations on underparts. Belly and ventral region chestnut, deepest on belly. Rump and tail black. Most of upperwing- and underwing-coverts white, contrasting with blackish flight feathers; secondaries glossed metallic green. Tertials chestnut. **Adult female breeding:** Head and neck white. Body plumage rich chestnut, with fine dark vermiculations on mantle. Wings and tail as male. **Adult female non-breeding:** Similar to female breeding but body dusky, being finely vermiculated with black on both upperparts and underparts. **Juvenile male:** Re-sembles adult male, but duller and browner, with pale rufous fringes to white wing-covert feathering. **Juvenile female:** Similar to juvenile male, but some rufous shows on breast and mantle and whitish feathering on head and face. Adult-like plumage gradually attained during first winter.

BARE PARTS All plumages: Bill, legs and feet black-ish or dark grey. Iris brown.

MEASUREMENTS Males typically larger than females. **Male:** Wing 365-380, tarsus 65-70, bill 42-45, weight — no data. **Female:** Wing 325-355, tarsus 58-62, bill 37-40, weight 1260-1340.

GEOGRAPHICAL VARIATION None.

HABITS Usually found in pairs by rivers and lakes, although non-breeding birds form small flocks and moulting concentrations gather as with other shel-ducks. Has long-term pair-bonds and is unique among ducks in that female, rather than male, has distinct eclipse (non-breeding) plumage. Pairs take up breeding territories, which are fiercely defended, along riversides and lakesides. The breeding season is prolonged, from August to January; sometimes two broods may be reared in a single season. Nests are located in holes in hollow trees, and cavities in cliffs and banks and under tussock-grass clumps. Following the breeding season, movements to favoured moulting waters are undertaken and sub-stantial gatherings may be formed. Feeds by grazing or by dabbling in shallow water and often along the seashore. Swims readily.

HABITAT Wide variety of habitats, from sheltered coastal bays and estuaries to mountain rivers, grassy plains and lowland lakes. Most abundant in tussock flats of upland areas of South Island.

DISTRIBUTION Endemic to New Zealand, being found on North, South and Stewart Islands, but most abundant in South Island and absent from northern parts of North Island. Moulting flocks gather on several lakes and estuaries, notably in south Westland, dispersing back to breeding areas by April and May. A vagrant has occurred on the Chatham Islands.

POPULATION No total estimates seem to have been made, but this is one of the few endemic New Zealand birds that have not been reduced drastic-ally in numbers by man or his alien companions, although introduced stoats and polecats are thought to have been responsible for local decreases. Indeed, a short open-season for shooting the species seems to have had little effect on numbers.

REFERENCES Johnsgard (1978), Williams (1964).

42 CRESTED SHELDUCK   Plate 13
Tadorna cristata

Alternative name: Korean Shelduck

Almost certainly extinct, there is still a remote possibility that this unique bird may survive some-where in northeastern Asia.

FIELD IDENTIFICATION Length 60-63 cm (24-25 in). **At rest:** A distinctive, sexually dimorphic shelduck. Both sexes have slightly-crested or 'maned' appear-ance to rear of head, and reddish bill and feet. Male has black crown, nape and breast, contrasting with basically pale greyish sides of head and neck and grey body plumage. Female markedly different: sides of head and neck whitish, body plumage finely barred grey and white, and prominent black and white 'spectacles'. In both sexes, the white wing-coverts would probably show on the folded wing when at rest. **In flight:** In both sexes the wing pattern is much as on Ruddy Shelduck (38), with striking white upperwing- and underwing-coverts contrasting with blackish flight feathers. Confusion with other species, however, highly unlikely within potential range, male having greyish body with contrasting black breast, crown and hindneck and female having greyish body contrasting with whitish face and foreneck.

VOICE Unknown.

DESCRIPTION Only adult male and female speci-mens are known. Juveniles and any seasonal vari-ations in plumage have never been described. **Adult male:** Chin, crown, drooping crest and hindneck glossy greenish-black. Sides of head and neck grey, finely vermiculated with brown. Upper mantle and breast glossy greenish-black. Most of upperparts and almost entire underparts grey, finely vermicu-lated with black and whitish barring. Flanks and scapulars washed with rufous. Undertail-coverts pale rufous. Rump, uppertail-coverts and tail black. Upperwing- and underwing-coverts white, contrast-ing with blackish flight feathers; secondaries glossed metallic green. Tertials rufous. **Adult female:** Crown, crest and hindneck black. Forehead, lores and area about eye whitish, with black bridle bordering eye, creating 'spectacled' effect. Sides and front of head and neck whitish or buffish-white. Almost entire remainder of upperparts and underparts whitish, washed pale buff and finely barred dark grey-brown. Undertail-coverts yellowish-rufous. Rump, uppertail-coverts and tail black. Wings as male.

BARE PARTS Adult male: Bill, legs and feet red. Iris

brown. **Adult female:** Bill, legs and feet fleshy-pink. Iris brown.

MEASUREMENTS Wing 310-320, tarsus 47-50, bill 42-45.

GEOGRAPHICAL VARIATION None.

HABITS Virtually nothing is known about this distinctive and mysterious species. It is featured in ancient Japanese and Chinese art and was considered to have been imported into Japan from Korea in the eighteenth century. Even in those days it was something of a curiosity and was already rare by the early nineteenth century. Evidence tends to support the theory that the species has been declining for a long time and may already be extinct, but there is a faint hope that it may survive, as echoed by the sightings in 1964 and 1971 (see Distribution). It has been conjectured that the bird probably bred in hollow trees in remote forested regions of northeastern Asia, in habitats shared by the elusive Chinese Merganser (145), living by the banks of rivers in similar situations to those of some populations of the Paradise Shelduck (41) of New Zealand.

HABITAT Presumed to have nested in forested, mountainous districts by flowing rivers and streams, moving lower down the rivers towards coastal districts in winter.

DISTRIBUTION May already be extinct, but three sight records in the past 45 years suggest that the species may still precariously survive. Breeding range considered most likely to have been the extreme east of the Soviet Union, in the regions bordering northeastern China and North Korea. The few specimens (three in existence) and references in historical literature indicate that in winter it moved to coastal districts along the continental shores of the Sea of Japan and the Yellow Sea, with birds occasionally wandering as far as Japan. The most recent sightings have been of two individuals in the Province of Chungchong Pukto, South Korea, in late March 1943; of three birds (one male, two females) with a party of Harlequin Ducks (132) on the sea to the southwest of Vladivostok on 16 May 1964; and finally of six birds (two males, four females) on the sea at the mouth of the River Pouchon, North Korea, in late March 1971.

POPULATION The continued existence of this unique bird is very much in doubt, but there is a chance that it may be surviving in such politically sensitive areas as the USSR-China-North Korea border regions. The Institute for Ornithology at Kyung Hee University, Seoul, South Korea, has distributed cards widely: these depict the species, seek information and views, and offer a substantial reward for information leading to this species' rediscovery.

REFERENCES Nowak (1983, 1984), Sok (1984).

43 SHELDUCK   Plate 11
Tadorna tadorna

One of the most attractive of European waterfowl, renowned for its spectacular moult gatherings along the northern coast of Germany.

FIELD IDENTIFICATION Length 58-67 cm (23-26 in).

At rest: Distinctive large black and white duck of tidal flats and saline lakes, its most obvious features being its green-black head and neck, rusty breast-band encircling the fore part of the body, and deep red bill. Unlikely to be confused with any other species. Juveniles, however, are confusingly different from the adults, lacking the breast-band and showing extensive grey in the upperparts; their bill and legs may also be distinctly greyish when very young. Both Goosander (146) and Red-breasted Merganser (144) are longer-bodied diving ducks, with slender bills and distinctly tufted or crested in appearance, the former lacking the breast-band. See also juvenile Egyptian Goose (46). **In flight:** A heavily-built black and white duck, with chestnut breast-band and black head. Both the upperwing- and underwing-coverts are white, contrasting with blackish flight feathers. Juveniles lack the breast-band and show darker, more greyish-brown upperparts; wing pattern, although similar to that of adults, is distinctly washed with grey.

VOICE Quite vocal by breeding waters in late winter and spring, otherwise relatively silent. Sexes vocally quite different: male utters low whistling cries, whereas female has a rapid chattering 'gag-ag-ag-ag-ag'.

DESCRIPTION Sexes similar, but males always have distinctly higher forehead, even when juvenile. **Adult male breeding:** Head and upper neck glossy greenish-black. Lower neck and upper breast white. Broad rusty-chestnut band encircles lower breast and upper mantle. Variably extensive blackish band down centre of underparts, from breast-band to vent. Undertail-coverts rusty. Remainder of underparts white. Scapulars black. Tertials edged chestnut. Tail tipped black. Remainder of upperparts white. Upperwing- and underwing-coverts white, contrasting with blackish flight feathers; secondaries glossed metallic bronze-purple and green. **Adult male non-breeding:** Similar but duller, with whitish mottling on face like female, breast-band obscured, and upperparts and underparts finely marked with grey barring. **Adult female breeding:** Similar to male, but face shows extensive whitish mottling around base of bill, most marked with feather wear. Breast-band and belly stripe duller and narrower, undertail-coverts paler rufous. **Adult female non-breeding:** Like male, female attains an eclipse plumage in which whole plumage is duller, with breast-band obscured, and becomes distinctly greyish on mantle; whitish on face may extend to throat and sides of head. Extreme individuals can be difficult to separate from juveniles, except by wing pattern. **Juvenile:** Similar to non-breeding female but even duller, completely lacking breast-band and with whitish forehead, cheeks and foreneck. Dark areas of head distinctly dark grey-brown rather than blackish. Flanks washed with greyish. Most of upperparts greyish-brown. Wings similar to adult, but upperwing-coverts sullied greyish and secondaries tipped white. By first winter resembles adult, although grey-washed wing-coverts retained until first summer.

BARE PARTS Adult male: Bill bright waxy-red, with large fleshy knob at base of culmen in breeding season; duller and more fleshy-red outside breeding season, when knob less apparent. Legs and feet reddish-flesh. Iris brown. **Adult female:** As non-breeding male, but bill a little duller. **Juvenile:** Bill, legs and feet pinkish-grey, attaining adult coloration during first winter.

MEASUREMENTS Sexes similar, although males larger than females. Wing 284-350 (mean: male 334, female 303); tarsus 46-60; bill 44-58 (mean: male 53, female 47); mean weight of male 1202, of female 936.

GEOGRAPHICAL VARIATION None.

HABITS Highly gregarious shelduck of estuaries and steppe lakes. During late winter and early spring arrives on breeding waters, where pairs disperse to look for breeding holes, often wandering far from water to locate suitable nest site, but site usually within 1 km of water. Nests usually in holes in trees or banks, especially rabbit holes, sometimes under buildings and in haystacks, but rarely in the open. After breeding, almost all adults depart for moulting grounds, leaving still-flightless broods in crèches in care of one or more adults. Moult concentrations often enormous: famous gathering in German Waddenzee reaches some 100,000 birds and includes most of the northwest European population; a smaller concentration of 3,000-4,000 in Bridgwater Bay (England) probably consists mostly of Irish breeders. Feeds by dabbling at surface of mud, walking slowly forwards, swinging head from side to side; also up-ends when feeding grounds covered by water. Swims readily and buoyantly, but does not normally dive. Flocks fly in long lines when moving long distances.

HABITAT Estuaries, both muddy and sandy, and shores of inland saline and brackish lakes in open steppe-like country. In western Europe primarily coastal in distribution, but in Asia a bird of inland salt lakes. Less commonly on freshwater lakes and sheltered coastal bays.

DISTRIBUTION Breeding range basically of two major components. Coastal population in regions of northwestern Europe, from Scandinavia and British Isles south to Atlantic coast of France, with isolated pockets along French Mediterranean shores and Sardinia; very small numbers also breed in Tunisia. This population undertakes moult migration chiefly to German coast in mid-summer (see Habits), dispersing back towards breeding regions after moult or moving southwards as far as North Africa in winter. Asiatic population extends from extreme southeastern Europe across Turkey and northern shores of Black Sea, eastwards over central Asia, through Mongolia to northern China, although throughout this huge range its distribution is some-what fragmented; small pockets also breed to the south of this region, by brackish lakes in Iran and Afghanistan. In winter many of these birds move southwest to winter in Caspian Sea basin, with others remaining on breeding grounds in more temperate regions. Little evidence of moult migration by Asiatic birds, moulting flocks gathering close to breeding waters. Small numbers winter south to North Africa, Iraq, Pakistan, northern India and southern China, occasionally to Korea, Japan and northern Burma. Vagrants reported from Iceland, Faeroes, central Europe, Libya, Senegal, North

Yemen, Kuwait, Taiwan, Hong Kong, Philippines and Vietnam. Individuals reported in South Africa are of feral origin.

POPULATION Abundant, particularly in western Europe, but no total population estimates have been made. Winter populations estimated in 1975 at 130,000 birds in northwest Europe and 75,000 in southern USSR, Middle East and Mediterranean region.

REFERENCES Cramp and Simmons (1977), Patterson (1982).

44 RADJAH SHELDUCK   Plate 12
Tadorna radjah

Alternative names: Burdekin Duck, White-headed Shelduck

Small, stocky shelduck of brackish lagoons and coastal districts of northern Australia, New Guinea and adjacent islands.

FIELD IDENTIFICATION Length 51-61 cm (20-24 in). **At rest:** Unmistakable. A dumpy shelduck, with pure white head, neck and underparts contrasting with dark upperparts and prominent breast-band. Confusion with any other species unlikely, although male Cotton Pygmy Goose (67) is similar in plumage pattern but is much smaller, with tiny dark bill and dark crown centre, and is unlikely to be seen wading. **In flight:** Shows striking flight pattern, with white head, neck and underparts and broad dark breast-band. Upperparts dark, with contrasting white wing-coverts and white lines bordering speculum. From below, appears almost all white except for dark breast-band, tail and primaries. Male Cotton Pygmy Goose smaller and dumpier, with dark wing-coverts and whitish band across flight feathers from above and below.

VOICE Highly vocal, both at rest and in flight. Male utters a hoarse, wheezing whistle and female a harsh rattle.

DESCRIPTION Sexes similar. Race *rufitergum* described. **Adult:** Head, neck, breast and under-body white. Broad band encircling lower breast, and mantle and scapulars rich chestnut. Back, rump, uppertail-coverts and tail black. Upperwing- and underwing-coverts chiefly white, contrasting with blackish flight feathers; secondaries glossed metallic green and tipped white, with white on inner webs (from below showing dark only on primaries, not on secondaries). **Juvenile:** Similar to adult, but white areas of plumage duller, many feathers being washed with brownish; blackish band across greater coverts broader than on adults, and speculum duller. Much as adult after first body moult, but retains juvenile wings until first summer.

BARE PARTS Adult: Bill, legs and feet pink or whitish-flesh. Iris white. **Juvenile:** Bill, legs and feet whitish-flesh. Iris dark brown.

MEASUREMENTS Sexes similar, although males typically larger than females. Race *rufitergum:* Wing 246-298 (mean: male 276, female 268); tarsus 52-62; bill 40-55; mean weight of male 934, of female 839. Nominate race: Wing 255-265, tarsus 48-59, bill 40-46.

GEOGRAPHICAL VARIATION Two races recognised: race *rufitergum* of northern Australia, with rich chestnut mantle and breast-band; and the nominate form of New Guinea and adjacent islands, which is a little smaller than *rufitergum* and has blacker upperparts and breast-band. There is a certain amount of individual variation and some birds may be difficult to assign to a particular race, those from southern New Guinea being somewhat intermediate between the two forms.

HABITS Usually seen in pairs or small flocks by brackish lagoons and rivers. Like other shelducks, it has long-term pair-bonds. At the onset of the rainy season flocks break up and males become very pugnacious, sometimes even attacking their own mates. During January and February pairs search their territories for suitable nest sites, usually in tree holes and fairly close to water. Egg-laying is normally complete by May or June, although the breeding season may be prolonged if the rainy season is extended. Pairs often remain close to their breeding territories throughout the year, but others congregate by permanent waterbodies as smaller pools dry out during the dry season. Feeds by grazing on pasture or by wading on mud and dabbling in shallows. Swims readily and buoyantly, often upending, and habitually perches in trees. Feeds mostly at night, spending the day roosting in waterside trees such as mangroves. Flight action relatively slow compared with other shelducks and the species is often fairly approachable, two traits which have resulted in its downfall in many areas as it is easy prey to hunters.

HABITAT Prefers fairly large areas of shallow brackish or saline water. Coastal lagoons, mangrove swamps, tidal mudflats and locally on shallow freshwater lakes and sheltered coastal bays.

DISTRIBUTION Race *rufitergum* chiefly resident in northern Australian tropical coastal regions, from northern Queensland across coastal Northern Territory to Fitzroy River of Western Australia; bulk of population along coast of Northern Territory, scarce along Queensland coast south of Cairns and everywhere somewhat local. Formerly more widespread, breeding south to New South Wales, but now no more than a rare vagrant in these regions. During the wet season there is some dispersal along rivers to inland sites, withdrawing to coastal districts as the dry season advances. Vagrants have occurred south to northern South Australia, where there was a scattering of records, including a flock of 20, during the 1960s. The nominate race occurs around the coast of New Guinea, but it seems to be nowhere common; it is also found on the Moluccas, on the Aru Islands, in western Papua and on Fergusson Island.

POPULATION No total population estimates seem to have been made, but clearly it is not an abundant species. The Australian range has contracted considerably over the past century and today its main stronghold is the coastal rivers of Northern Territory, with a subsidiary population in Queensland between Cairns and Cape York. It has disappeared from the Kimberley region of Western Australia and coastal New South Wales, and seems to have declined considerably in the Gulf of Carpentaria

region. Much of this decline has been attributed to hunting, for, although this species is poor eating, it is relatively approachable and is not a good flyer. The same can be said of its status in New Guinea, where it is now very uncommon in northern coastal regions and decidedly local along the south coast. Sadly, unless protection measures can be adequately enforced, the future for this beautiful shelduck is rather gloomy.

REFERENCES Frith (1967), RAOU (1982).

45 PINK-EARED DUCK   Plate 34
Malacorhynchus membranaceus

This peculiar Australian duck has been placed in several systematic positions over the years; it seems, however, that its affinities are closer to the shelducks rather than to the dabbling ducks.

FIELD IDENTIFICATION Length 38-40 cm (15-16 in). **At rest:** Unmistakable. A small, brownish Australian duck with enormous bill (appears square-tipped in field), black-and-white-banded flanks, and blackish eye-patches contrasting with whitish face. Only larger Australasian Shoveler (106) approaches it in bill structure, but confusion with this species is highly unlikely. The pink 'ears' are of course a useless field feature. Dabbles in shallow water and perches on waterside branches. **In flight:** Distinctive shape, with huge bill held downwards and head held high. Flight action less rapid than that of other teal-sized ducks, with shallower and slower wingbeats. Upperside brownish, with broad whitish trailing edge to secondaries and white bands over uppertail-coverts and at tip of short tail. From below the barred flanks may not be obvious, the bird usually appearing merely pale, including the underwing, although there is some contrast with brownish flight feathers.

VOICE Male has a very strange, unduck-like, repeated chirrup, uttered both in flight and on the water. Female utters similar calls, but these are distinctly lower in pitch than those of male. More prolonged, trilling calls may be given when fighting.

DESCRIPTION All plumages similar. **Adult:** Forehead, crown and hindneck greyish-brown. Large blackish-brown patch around eye, extending in band back along sides of crown to nape. Area between base of bill and eye-patch whitish. Narrow whitish eye-ring. Small rose-pink patch behind eye in angle at junction of head bands and pale ear-coverts. Sides of head and sides and front of neck whitish, finely barred grey (looking pale greyish in field). Undertail-coverts light buff. Remainder of underparts whitish, strongly barred with dark grey-brown, barring broad and conspicuous on flanks. Upperparts brown, blackish-brown on uppertail-coverts and tail. Conspicuous white band across base of uppertail-coverts, extending around sides of rear body. Broad white tip to tail. Upperwing brown, with broad whitish tips to secondaries. Underwing dull whitish, with browner flight feathers, chiefly underside of primaries. **Juvenile:** Similar to adult, but rosy 'ear' patch smaller or lacking, and general plumage duller and paler.

BARE PARTS All plumages: Bill long, broad and

169

almost spoon-shaped, with prominent fleshy flaps at sides towards tip; grey. Legs and feet grey. Iris brown.

MEASUREMENTS Males typically larger than females. Wing 364-448 (mean: male 418, female 392); tarsus 35-44; bill 53-74; mean weight of male 404, of female 344.

GEOGRAPHICAL VARIATION None.

HABITS Usually found in small flocks at shallow inland lakes and pools; flocks sometimes reach considerable numbers in its main stronghold. This peculiar duck is highly nomadic and because of this is very much an opportunist breeder, capable of nesting at almost any time of the year when water conditions are suitable. Colonisation of breeding waters is sudden and erratic and may appear to take place almost overnight, often in tremendous numbers. When water levels rapidly rise, the breeding cycle is triggered; nesting, however, is not commenced until the levels have risen to the maximum and start to subside, thus allowing colonisation of pools by insect and microscopic animal and plant life. Nests are built close to the waterside and may be among bushes, in tree holes, on logs and posts or even in old nests of other waterbirds; pairs sometimes take over active nests of other birds and build on top of the original owners' eggs. Several individuals may even lay in one site and as many as 60 eggs have been recorded in one tree hollow. This behaviour points to an almost frantic breeding cycle when conditions are optimum. The Pink-eared Duck is primarily a filter-feeder, swimming or wading in the shallows in small groups, dabbling and sifting with bill almost totally immersed, often submerging head and neck to reach the bottom in deeper water and occasionally up-ending. It spends little time on land, merely loafing by shores of pools or perching on protruding branches and stumps. Fairly confiding and approachable, flocks when flushed tend to circle the pool or lake in dense packs, soon descending nearby. Mixes freely with other species, especially Grey Teal (81).

HABITAT Basically a nomadic species of shallow inland, and often temporary, pools and lakes, both brackish and freshwater. Rarely on sheltered coastal inlets and mangrove swamps.

DISTRIBUTION Centre of distribution and abundance is the Murray-Darling region of Victoria and New South Wales, where flooding conditions are regularly most suitable for its requirements, with smaller numbers also in coastal districts of southern Western Australia and southeastern South Australia. Its nomadic nature can take it to almost all parts of the continent, although outside these regions its occurrence is really sporadic rather than regular and is linked with seasonal rains creating areas of temporary shallow water for it to colonise; this is particularly true of the dry inland regions of central and western Australia, coastal eastern Australia and northern Tasmania, where its occurrence is purely casual.

POPULATION No total estimates have been made, but during the aftermath of severe flooding in 1956, in the Riverina of New South Wales, at least 96,000 pairs were considered to be present between Wanganella and Moulamein, which are 90 km apart. Clearly this is an abundant duck, but owing to its nomadic behaviour it is very difficult to assess in terms of total population. A survey of wetlands in western Victoria in February 1982 located some 23,000 birds, 13,000 of which were in the coastal Lake Borrie, which is somewhat polluted by sewage.

REFERENCES Frith (1967), RAOU (1982), Warham (1958).

46 EGYPTIAN GOOSE   Plate 13
Alopochen aegyptiacus

Widespread tropical African sheldgoose, with a well-established feral population in Britain.

FIELD IDENTIFICATION Length 63-73 cm (25-29 in). **At rest:** Large, bulky 'shelduck'; goose-like in structure with markedly long pink legs. General coloration buffish, with darker upperparts (varying from grey-brown to reddish-brown), paler head, and dark brown facial and belly patches and collar. White forewing often shows when at rest, as well as in flight. Confusion of adult with other species unlikely; duller juvenile, lacking face and belly patches but having dark crown and nape, recalls large, long-legged juvenile Shelduck (43), but is much buffer below and has brown rather than dark grey upperparts. **In flight:** Goose-like shape and extensive white forewing above and below, contrasting with blackish flight feathers, is distinctive within range, but wing pattern close to both Ruddy (38) and Cape (39) Shelducks; both these species are less bulky, with uniform rusty-orange body coloration and slimmer, more pointed wings.

VOICE Not particularly vocal, although social disputes provoke much calling from both sexes. Male utters a harsh, wheezy hiss. Female has a guttural, strident, almost braying cackle, 'honk-haah-haah-haah'.

DESCRIPTION Sexes similar, marked individual variation. **Adult:** Head and neck pale buffish, with chocolate-brown patch surrounding eye and base of bill (patch often divided). Some brown mottling on crown and neck. Dark rusty-brown collar encircles lower neck. Upper mantle, breast and almost entire underparts buffish or greyish-buff, becoming paler on flanks and whitish on belly and ventral region. Variably extensive chocolate-brown patches in centre of lower breast. Mantle and scapulars brown, greyish-brown on some birds, more rufous-brown on others. Back, rump, uppertail-coverts and tail black. Upperwing-coverts white, with dark line along length of greater coverts, contrasting with blackish flight feathers and primary coverts. Secondaries glossed metallic green or purple. Tertials partly rufous. Underwing-coverts white, contrasting with blackish flight feathers. **Juvenile:** Whole plumage duller than adult and lacking chocolate-brown face and breast patches and collar; crown and hind-neck dusky-brown. White of upperwing-coverts sullied with greyish-brown, secondaries duller. Becomes much as adult during first winter, but juvenile wing retained until first-summer moult.

BARE PARTS Adult: Bill pink, with dusky nail, cutting edges and mottling about nostrils and very base. Legs and feet pink. Iris pale yellowish, sometimes brown. **Juvenile:** Bill, legs and feet yellowish-grey. Iris light brown.

MEASUREMENTS Males usually larger than females. Wing 352-406 (mean: male 392, female 375); tarsus 73-95; bill 43-54; mean weight of male 2445, of female 1940.

GEOGRAPHICAL VARIATION None.

HABITS One of the most widespread of tropical African waterbirds. Usually seen in pairs or small parties by almost any form of water. With such a wide distribution, breeding season varies over its range, with nesting recorded during all months in several regions, but chiefly August-September in South Africa, July-October in Senegal, all months in Kenya with no peak, and March-April in Egypt and in feral British population as examples. Strongly territorial in breeding season. Nest sites highly variable; on ground under bushy cover, in old nests of other large birds and in holes and cavities in trees, cliffs and buildings, usually not far from water. After breeding, moulting congregations form on key waters, which may happen at almost any time of the year once local breeding has been completed. Feeds chiefly on land during the daytime, flighting to and from roosting waters at dusk and dawn. Swims readily and buoyantly with rear held high and often up-ends, but does not normally dive. Perches freely on trees, buildings and cliffs. Generally shy and wary. Flight action heavy and goose-like, rather than duck-like.

HABITAT Almost any form of wetland in tropical Africa, at up to 4000 m in Ethiopia, generally avoiding heavily-forested areas. Inland freshwater lakes and rivers of almost any description. Feral British population chiefly in parkland meadows and pasture.

DISTRIBUTION Common and widespread throughout tropical Africa south of the Sahara. Seems to be most numerous in southern and eastern Africa. Movements poorly understood, but connected with seasonal dispersal, most marked in the wet season, some moving north as far as northern Chad. In the western Palaearctic now found only in Upper Egypt, where still quite common about Aswan Dam and adjacent regions of Nile valley. Common in captivity and frequently escapes, most individuals reported in Europe doubtless being of captive origin, although occasional winter records from Tunisia, Algeria, Cyprus, Malta and Red Sea coast of Arabia most likely refer to genuine vagrants from sub-Saharan Africa. Feral population in Britain chiefly resident in East Anglia, with some dispersal of birds after breeding.

POPULATION Widespread and often abundant in tropical Africa, but Palaearctic range now merely peripheral. Bred north to Israel until early 1930s, but reports of former breeding in Syria, Algeria and Tunisia doubtful although often referred to in the literature. In historical times was even a breeding species in eastern Europe, centred along River Danube, finally disappearing from here by the early eighteenth century. British population currently some 500 individuals, but few estimates have been attempted of native African populations.

REFERENCES Brown *et al.* (1982), Cramp and Simmons (1977).

47 ORINOCO GOOSE Plate 13
Neochen jubata

This tropical American sheldgoose is the only member of the group to have blackish wing-coverts.

FIELD IDENTIFICATION Length 61-76 cm (24-30 in). **At rest:** Distinctive sheldgoose of tropical rivers of northern South America. The very pale buffish head, neck and breast contrast with the dark upperparts and chestnut underparts, making confusion with any other species unlikely. Its stance is somewhat upright, with an abbreviated rear end giving the whole bird a distinctive appearance. Distant individuals confusable with Buff-necked Ibis, which has dark body and buff head, neck and breast but of course has very long, decurved bill. **In flight:** Not a great flyer, takes wing only when hard-pressed and then for no great distance. A conspicuously two-toned goose-like bird, with very dark body and wings, both above and below, contrasting with very pale head, neck and breast and white speculum patch. The two-toned appearance with dark underwing and underbody is shared by smaller Black-bellied Whistling Duck (9), which, however, has conspicuous white areas along length of upperwing, greyer head and neck and blackish (not chestnut) underbody, and is also a more sociable bird, generally being seen in small flocks, whereas Orinoco Goose is more solitary or in pairs.

VOICE Both sexes quite vocal. Male has a high-pitched whistle, whereas female utters a strident, guttural cackling, recalling that of Egyptian Goose (46).

DESCRIPTION All plumages similar. **Adult:** Head, neck and breast pale greyish-buff, with indistinct darker mottling and striations formed by dark feather bases showing along rear and sides of neck, where feather tracts are furrowed. Flanks and belly chestnut, becoming buffer along upper flanks and dark brown in ventral region. Undertail-coverts white. Upper mantle and scapulars rufous, becoming blackish in centre of mantle. Back, rump, uppertail-coverts and tail black, glossed green. Wings purplish- to greenish-black, becoming glossed metallic green on secondaries and with white patch formed by white bases to outer webs of secondaries. Underwing blackish. **Juvenile:** Similar to adult, but general coloration duller, with underparts buffer, less bright, rufous, and lacks gloss on wings and tail.

BARE PARTS Adult: Bill black, with sides of upper mandible red. Legs and feet reddish-flesh. Iris brown. **Juvenile:** Similar, but bill and legs paler and duller.

MEASUREMENTS Males obviously larger than females, despite plumage similarities. **Male:** Wing 315-333, tarsus 75-82, bill 38-40, mean weight ca. 1560. **Female:** Wing 300-310, tarsus 70-72, bill 35-37, mean weight 1250.

GEOGRAPHICAL VARIATION None.

HABITS Little studied in the wild, as with many other species of Neotropical waterfowl. Usually met with in pairs and family parties, but small moult gatherings, rarely exceeding 20 birds, occur after breeding. Being basically unsociable by nature, males fight fiercely at onset of breeding season. Pairs take up well-spaced territories along the banks of tropical lowland rivers, and nest in hollow trees, rarely on the ground. What information is available suggests that breeding takes place in the dry season; the seasons reported include December-January in Colombia, January-February in Venezuela, and in Bolivia pairs with well-grown young have been recorded in September. Orinoco Geese feed primarily by grazing in the savanna lands adjacent to their rivers; they rarely swim and are not often seen on the wing. Frequently perches in trees. Fairly confiding and approachable.

HABITAT Lowland tropical rivers with wooded banks and areas of open, wet savanna; freshwater marshes and lakesides in open, wooded country.

DISTRIBUTION Widespread, although basically rather local, resident over large area of tropical forested lowlands of northern South America, east of the Andes, south to northern Argentina. Despite rather wide range, its distribution is probably more patchy than the map suggests. Its range includes the Guianas, the Orinoco and its tributaries in Venezuela, eastern Colombia, extreme eastern Peru (rare), Amazonian Brazil, Paraguay, eastern and southern Bolivia and extreme northern Argentina (Salta).

POPULATION No estimates have been made, but its wide range and vast area of suitable habitat renders this species highly unlikely to be under more than local threats at the edges of its range.

REFERENCES Delacour (1954), Hilty and Brown (1986), Johnsgard (1978).

48 ANDEAN GOOSE   Plate 15
Chloephaga melanoptera

Large, stocky, pied sheldgoose of high Andean lakes and marshes.

FIELD IDENTIFICATION Length 75-80 cm (29-32 in). **At rest:** Unmistakable. A heavily-built whitish 'goose', with blackish rear end and tiny bill. No other goose-like bird shares its range or habitat. In captivity, pink bill and legs prevent confusion with the whitest Magellan Goose (49). **In flight:** Unmistakable. A heavily-built and broad-winged 'goose' with striking wing pattern. Primaries, greater wing-coverts, tertials and tail are black and contrast markedly with the white of the rest of its plumage.

VOICE Most vocal in the breeding season. Male has a soft, high-pitched whistle, female a low, cackling growl.

DESCRIPTION All plumages similar. **Adult:** Head, neck, entire underparts and most of upperparts white. Primaries, greater wing-coverts, tertials and tail glossy black. Scapulars black, with white edges, giving spotted appearance. **Juvenile:** Duller, with pale grey wash to white of head and neck, and black areas of plumage duller and greyer. Much as adult after first moult, but not completely so until first-summer moult.

BARE PARTS All plumages: Bill very short and small for size of bird, reddish-pink with black nail and variable dusky mottling on upper mandible. Legs and feet reddish-pink to fleshy-orange. Iris dark

brown, with narrow pink orbital ring. Very young juveniles may have blackish bill, but the pink coloration is soon attained.

MEASUREMENTS Males substantially larger than females. **Male:** Wing 460-475, tarsus 90-105, bill 38-43, mean weight ca. 3400. **Female:** Wing 420-430, tarsus 75-82, bill 34-37, mean weight ca. 2800.

GEOGRAPHICAL VARIATION None.

HABITS Distinctive sheldgoose of the high Andes, which has been little studied in the wild. Usually located in pairs or family parties by shores of high lakes and marshes. Outside breeding season congregates into small flocks, which break up towards onset of nesting season although non-breeders remain in small flocks throughout the year. As with most sheldgeese, the pair-bond seems to be permanent and males are quite pugnacious in defence of their families and territories. Pairs select their territories during the southern summer, with nesting taking place during November-January. Nest sites are mere scrapes in bare ground on slopes overlooking water, often in crevices between rocks and sometimes in holes in sandy banks. Feeds almost entirely by grazing. Andean Geese are poor swimmers, but take to water when goslings are small or when danger threatens during flightless moult period, swimming with breast low and bulky rear end held high. Flight action is slow and heavy.

HABITAT Marshes and lakesides of the Cordilleras and puna of the high Andes above 3300 m, moving to lower valleys and plains in winter.

DISTRIBUTION Chiefly resident in the Andes, from central Peru southwards through western Bolivia to Nuble in Chile and Catamarca in Argentina. Little movement recorded, but certainly descends lower in winter to plains at the foot of the mountains and wide valleys. Has occurred as a vagrant south to the Rio Negro in Argentina.

POPULATION No data available on total populations, but seems to be widespread and quite numerous throughout most of its range. Hunting of the species is rather limited owing to the inaccessibility of much of its habitat, and there is no obvious cause for concern over its future.

REFERENCES Delacour (1954), Johnsgard (1978).

49 MAGELLAN GOOSE   Plate 14
Chloephaga picta

Alternative name: Upland Goose (see also Geographical Variation)

There are two distinct populations of this variable sheldgoose, one in the Falkland Islands and the other on the mainland of southern South America.

FIELD IDENTIFICATION Length 60-65 cm (20-26 in). **At rest:** Strongly sexually dimorphic sheldgoose. Adult male is very white on head, neck and most of underparts, with greyish upperparts, blackish bill and blackish legs, and has prominent blackish barring at least on flanks and mantle and often on entire underparts, making the bird appear greyish with whiter head at long range. Confusion of male with any other species is unlikely: although subadult Kelp Goose (50) may be basically white with vestigial barring on underparts and some dark patches in upperparts, it is a stockier bird of the coast and has yellow, not blackish, legs; Magellan's range does not overlap with that of bulkier Andean Goose (48), which has pinkish legs and bill and blackish rear upperparts. Female is strikingly different from male, being overall greyish-brown with warmer, almost tawny-, brown on head, neck and most of underparts; the head and neck is unmarked, but the underparts from lower neck downwards are closely barred; white wing-coverts often show when at rest; blackish bill and yellowish-orange legs. Female recalls both Ashy-headed (51) and Ruddy-headed (52) Geese, but in these species the sexes are similar: Ashy-headed has a grey head, contrasting with rufous-brown breast, and whitish belly and ground colour to barred flanks; Ruddy-headed is smaller and daintier about head than female Magellan, has a narrow whitish eye-ring and its underparts are more finely barred and buffer. **In flight:** Both sexes show similar wing patterns. Female is basically brown, with striking white upperwing-coverts and secondaries which contrast with blackish primaries and central band (greater coverts) along wing; the underwing is white, with blackish primaries. Male is distinctly white on head, neck, rump and underparts, or may appear greyish with whiter head and neck, but shares same wing pattern as the female. Wing patterns of both Ashy-headed and Ruddy-headed Geese are similar to that of Magellan Goose, those species perhaps being best distinguished by their smaller size and the fact that pairs are similar.

VOICE As with most of the group, the calls of the sexes are different, male uttering a repeated whistling call, while female has a low grating cackle.

DESCRIPTION Sexually dimorphic. Nominate race described. **Adult male barred phase:** Head and upper neck white; lower neck, breast, belly and flanks white, closely barred with black; ventral region whitish. Most of upperparts grey, barred black and white on mantle and scapulars. Rump and uppertail-coverts white. Tail blackish, often tipped or edged white. Upper lesser and median wing-coverts white; greater coverts black, glossed metallic green; secondaries white; primaries black. Underwing white, with blackish primaries. **Adult male white phase:** Similar to barred phase, but barring restricted to rear flanks and mantle; head, neck, breast, fore-flanks and belly unmarked white. Intermediates also occur. (The taxonomic position of the white phase is probably in need of review: see Geographical Variation.) **Adult female:** Head and neck plain cinnamon-brown. Mantle, breast and fore-flanks rufous-cinnamon, closely barred with black, becoming barred black and white on remainder of flanks; ventral region dark grey. Almost entire upperparts greyish cinnamon-brown. Wings above and below as male. In non-breeding plumage, a little duller, less obviously rufous-toned. **Juvenile male and female:** Similar to adults, being sexually dimorphic as soon as feathers attained. Juvenile male resembles barred phase, but both sexes have brownish-black, not glossy, greater wing-coverts and the underparts more finely and closely barred. Juvenile male is washed greyish on head and neck,

and has back and rump barred, not clear white. Fully adult plumage not attained until third calendar-year.

BARE PARTS Male: Bill, legs and feet black or blackish. Iris dark brown. **Female:** Bill black. Legs and feet yellow or dull orange-yellow. Iris dark brown.

MEASUREMENTS Males are typically a little larger than females. Nominate *picta*: Wing 380-435 (male 395-435, female 380-403); tarsus 71-88; bill 31-40; mean weight of both sexes ca. 2900. Race *leucoptera*: Wing 400-462 (male 430-462, female 400-425); tarsus 78-95; bill 40-47; mean weight of both sexes ca. 3300.

GEOGRAPHICAL VARIATION Two subspecies recognised. The nominate race, described above and often called Lesser Magellan Goose, is widespread over southern South America; the males occur in two distinct colour phases, the barred phase being confined to southernmost Patagonia and Tierra del Fuego, whereas the white phase occupies the remainder of the range. A larger population, race *leucoptera*, often called Greater or Falkland Magellan Goose, inhabits the Falkland Islands. This form does not have a barred phase in adult male plumage, although first-year males have most of the underparts closely marked with broken bars, which are almost gone by the second calendar-year. Females of this race are brighter and more rufous than the nominate form, with narrower black bars on the underparts, the rufous bars being wider than the black (the reverse in nominate race); additionally, the ventral region is whiter. Because of the very limited degree of overlap, both on the breeding and on the wintering grounds, between white-phase and barred-phase birds included in the nominate race, it may well be that the phases represent two closely-related species. It has been suggested that the white-phase birds of Patagonia are perhaps a population of the 'Greater Magellan Goose' and that the two forms are more correctly two species, with Greater incorporating both the Falkland Islands and the Patagonian white-phase populations and the 'Lesser Magellan Goose' including only the barred-phase birds of Tierra del Fuego. Obviously, only intensive field research can resolve the issue.

HABITS Abundant, highly sociable sheldgoose of open grassland. Flocks attain thousands in some districts and it has become a pest to sheep- and cattle-farmers by competing for grazing rights! Like other sheldgeese, it appears to have long-term pair-bonds. The breeding season in Chile is in November, on the Falkland Islands from mid September to late November. Pairs select scattered territories in open plains or valley slopes, the nest being usually close to water and hidden among tussock grasses. After breeding, moulting concentrations gather at key areas near water, where they become temporarily flightless, although it seems that some populations, or at least individuals, do not have a flightless moult period (this is particularly true in the Falkland Islands, where some birds have badly-abraded flight feathers, and it has recently been shown that this 'moult-skipping' occurs also in the nominate race). After breeding, southern populations of the nominate race migrate northwards to spend the southern winter in more temperate grasslands. Feeds by grazing in open country, often in very large flocks; spends little time swimming, but does so freely when moulting or tending goslings. May become quite confiding where unmolested, but normally shy and wary.

HABITAT Open grassy plains, often in semi-arid and mountainous districts but also in lowland and grassy coastal areas.

DISTRIBUTION Nominate race is widespread in southern South America, breeding north to region of Talca in Chile and Rio Negro in Argentina, southwards through Chile and western Argentina to include Tierra del Fuego and Cape Horn. Southernmost populations are migratory, moving north to winter in open grasslands of southern Buenos Aires Province and north in Chile as far as Colchagua; in Buenos Aires Province barred-phase 'Lessers' winter in coastal grassland, with white-phase birds predominating in inland areas. Vagrants have occurred north to Uruguay. Falkland Islands race is widespread throughout the islands, where it is basically resident; it has been introduced onto South Georgia, but has now died out there.

POPULATION Formerly extremely abundant, especially in parts of mainland South America, with many descriptions of flocks totalling untold thousands. Much persecuted in recent decades by sheep- and cattle-farmers in attempt to reduce competition with their animals, eggs being destroyed and flightless moulting concentrations being rounded up and killed. Despite this destruction, is still abundant throughout its range.

REFERENCES Delacour (1954), Summers (1983), Summers and Martin (1985), Todd (1979), Weller (1972).

50 KELP GOOSE   Plate 14
Chloephaga hybrida

A beautiful coastal sheldgoose of southern South America, the totally white male being almost unique among waterfowl other than swans.

FIELD IDENTIFICATION Length 55-65 cm (22-25 in). **At rest:** Stocky 'goose' of the seashore, strongly sexually dimorphic. Male completely white, apart from yellow legs and black bill; confusion with other species unlikely, except perhaps at long range with ungoose-like Snowy Sheathbill. Female is chocolate-coloured, with striking yellow legs and pink bill; at reasonable ranges, white scaling on breast and flanks is conspicuous and the general dark plumage contrasts with white ventral region and tail; the white wing-coverts may also show when at rest. Confusion with other waterfowl unlikely, although sub-adult males with vestigial female-like underparts and white head, neck and breast may suggest male Magellan Goose (49), which is less bulky and has longer blackish, not yellow, legs. **In flight:** Male totally white and unmistakable; second-year males often show dusky tips to primaries, but stocky goose-like shape easily separates them from Coscoroba Swan (27). Female's wing pattern close to that of female

Magellan Goose, but white rear end, strongly contrasting with rest of plumage, is diagnostic, although young females have much blackish in the rump and tail-coverts.

VOICE Not very vocal. Male has a thin, weak, 'seep-seep-seep', whereas female utters a harsh, rising, guttural growling.

DESCRIPTION Sexually dimorphic. Nominate race described. **Adult male:** Totally white. **Adult female:** Head and neck very dark brown, crown often slightly paler, with narrow whitish eye-ring. Breast and flanks blackish-brown, with prominent white barring formed by edges to feathers. Belly, ventral region, tail, uppertail-coverts, rump and lower back white. Mantle, upper back, scapulars and tertials blackish-brown. Upperwing-coverts white, except for blackish greater coverts which are glossed metallic green. Primaries blackish. Underwing white, with blackish primaries. **Juvenile:** Resembles adult female, but duller, lacking green gloss to browner greater coverts; the underpart barring is less clearly defined, the bars being more broken. Blackish markings extend onto belly, uppertail-coverts and back. Young males start to show whitish feathering on head, neck and breast when very young and by second calendar-year are mostly white, although dusky tips to primaries are the last vestiges of juvenile plumage to be lost.

BARE PARTS Adult male: Bill black, often with red or yellow spot at base of culmen. Legs and feet lemon-yellow. Iris dark brown. **Adult female:** Bill fleshy-pink or yellowish-flesh. Legs and feet deep yellow. Iris dark brown. **Juvenile:** Bill, legs and feet dusky at first, but soon start to show appropriate coloration of their sex.

MEASUREMENTS Males typically larger than females. Nominate *hybrida*: Wing 334-385 (male 363-385, female 334-360); tarsus 61-71; bill 35-38; mean weight of male 2607, of female 2041. Race *malvinarum*: Wing 360-396 (male 390-396, female 360-380); tarsus 67-75; bill 36-40.

GEOGRAPHICAL VARIATION Two races recognised. The nominate race occurs along the coast of southern South America and outlying islands. Slightly larger race *malvinarum* of the Falkland Islands is very similar in plumage, but in females the white barring on the breast and flanks is relatively broader and more conspicuous.

HABITS A sheldgoose of the seashore, usually met with in pairs or family parties, but flocks totalling a few hundred birds, especially of non-breeders or birds congregating to moult, may also be formed. Kelp Geese have long-term pair-bonds and breed during the southern spring, from mid October through November. Nest sites are almost invariably very close to the coast, usually within 10 m of the high-tide line, but may be by freshwater lakes within 1 km of the coast; nests are situated among tussock grass, on low cliff ledges or under beach debris. Post-breeding moulting congregations are formed and the flightless period seems to be quite prolonged, from late November until late February on the Falklands. This species feeds primarily by foraging along rocky shorelines, grazing seaweeds growing among the rocks exposed at low tide. During periods of high tide, parties gather to loaf at favoured rocky outcrops and shingle bays. Spends little time swimming, but will do so as tide recedes, reaching under water to get at slowly-exposed seaweeds. It sometimes visits fresh water to bathe and drink. Being unmolested, unlike Magellan Geese, it may become remarkably confiding and even inquisitive of human presence.

HABITAT Rocky coastlines and shingle beaches, occasionally on nearby freshwater lakes.

DISTRIBUTION Nominate race is a widespread breeder along coast of Chile, from southern Cautin southwards to Tierra del Fuego and Cape Horn; it is less common on adjacent coast of Argentina, but breeds from southern Patagonia to Tierra del Feugo and Staten Island. Southern populations tend to move northwards in winter, with some birds occurring on rare occasions along the Argentine coast as far as Santa Cruz and Chubut. Falkland Islands race is a widespread resident throughout the islands.

POPULATION No estimates have been made, the inaccessibility of much of its habitat making counting difficult. It is unmolested over most of its range and seems to be under no obvious threats to its numbers.

REFERENCES Delacour (1954), Gladstone and Martell (1968), Weller (1972).

51 ASHY-HEADED GOOSE   Plate 15
Chloephaga poliocephala

This sheldgoose breeds in more wooded country than the other members of the genus, sometimes even nesting in trees.

FIELD IDENTIFICATION Length 50-55 cm (20-22 in). **At rest:** All plumages are similar. The combination of grey head, rufous breast, white belly and finely-barred black and white flanks easily separates this species from both the closely-related Ruddy-headed (52) and female Magellan (49) Geese. Sometimes becomes mixed with flocks of Magellan Geese. **In flight:** Wing pattern both above and below confusingly similar to that of both Ruddy-headed and Magellan Geese, but white belly and grey head separate it from either. It appears distinctly smaller than Magellan Goose if the two species are seen flying together.

VOICE Similar to other South American sheldgeese. Male utters a soft whistle, white female has a harsh cackle.

DESCRIPTION All plumages similar. **Adult:** Head and upper neck ashy-grey, becoming very pale grey around base of bill and on crown. Narrow whitish eye-ring. Nape and lower foreneck rufous-brown, becoming richer rufous-chestnut on breast and mantle. Breast often with fine dark barring, most prevalent on females but not sexually diagnostic. Flanks white, with narrow blackish barring. Belly unmarked white. Ventral region dull buffish. Mantle and scapulars greyish-brown, with rufous and black barring to tips of scapulars. Back, rump, uppertail-coverts and tail blackish. Tertials greyish-brown. Upperwing-coverts white, except for greater coverts which are blackish with metallic green gloss. Secondaries white. Primaries blackish. Underwing white, with blackish primaries. Female is slightly duller than male and always has finely-barred breast. **Juvenile:** Very similar to adult, but greater coverts dull brownish-black, breast finely barred with blackish, flanks washed with brown, and head and neck washed brownish, less cleanly grey. Full adult plumage attained during second calendar-year.

BARE PARTS All plumages: Bill black, sometimes with fleshy patches along sides. Legs and feet yellow to orange, with variably extensive blackish front of tarsus, toes and webs. Iris dark brown.

MEASUREMENTS Males typically larger than females. **Male:** Wing 355-380, tarsus 62-70, bill 30-33, mean weight 2267. **Female:** Wing 335-340, tarsus 57-62, bill 26-28, mean weight 2200.

GEOGRAPHICAL VARIATION None, but variability in extent of breast barring on males and in pattern of legs and toes suggests that there may be some geographical significance.

HABITS Little studied in the wild. Usually seen in pairs or small parties, which seldom exceed 100 birds even outside the breeding season; often becomes mixed with flocks of wintering Magellan Geese. Forms long-term pair-bonds, pairs taking up breeding territories to nest in November. Nests may be hidden in long grass or in the hollows of burnt trees, sometimes even placed among low branches. Feeds chiefly by grazing, rarely swimming except when accompanying young or at moulting times. Not infrequently perches in trees.

HABITAT Breeds in mountainous districts and on islands, preferred breeding habitat being forest clearings with swampy ground. In winter resorts to open grassy plains, with preference for natural grasslands, freshly-sown pasture and stubble fields.

DISTRIBUTION Breeds in western region of southern South America, from Malleco Province of Chile and Rio Negro of Argentina southwards to Tierra del Fuego, including associated islands. Seems to be most numerous in mountains of southern Chile. A good proportion of the birds move northwards to winter in the wheat-growing districts of southeastern Buenos Aires Province, arriving in their winter quarters in April and leaving in September. Vagrant to the Falkland Islands.

POPULATION Not an abundant bird by any means, but little work has been undertaken in assessing the population. Surveys of wintering sheldgeese in Buenos Aires Province in 1983 produced nearly 2,000 individuals of this species, but it is likely that many were overlooked among the large numbers of Magellan Geese present, although most of the Ashy-headed were segregated from the Magellan Geese; unknown numbers winter elsewhere in Argentina and Chile. Wintering 'geese' are accused of crop damage by farmers and the flocks are persecuted en masse, but the damage done by this species is likely to be negligible.

REFERENCES Delacour (1954), Johnson (1965), Martin et al. (1986).

52 RUDDY-HEADED GOOSE   Plate 15
Chloephaga rubidiceps

Formerly abundant, this species, seemingly the eastern counterpart of the Ashy-headed Goose (51), has suffered a drastic decline in recent years, and is now the most endangered of the genus.

FIELD IDENTIFICATION Length 45-50 cm (18-20 in). **At rest:** Although superficially similar to female Magellan Goose (49), this smaller sheldgoose is quite distinctive. As in the Ashy-headed Goose, the sexes are similar. The whole of the body plumage is closely barred with fine buff and black markings, giving a more uniform appearance than female Magellan and being relieved chiefly by contrasting unmarked warm brown head and neck. It lacks female Magellan's strong rufous tones to breast and fore-flanks, and the flanks are not contrastingly whitish-barred as in that species; additionally, the fine barring extends further up onto neck on Ruddy-headed. If seen together, Ruddy-headed is distinctly smaller, smaller-billed and a little paler overall. Individuals, however, can be very difficult to pick out among distant winter flocks of Magellans. Distinctions are clearer in the Falkland Islands, where Magellan Goose is even larger and has broader barring below than do birds of mainland South America. Confusion with Ashy-headed unlikely, as that species has obviously grey head, very rufous breast, strongy-barred flanks and clear white belly. **In flight:** Wing pattern close to that of Magellan and Ashy-headed Geese. Best distinguished from former, if both species flying together, by distinctly smaller size; also body plumage duller, less chestnut, and ventral region buffish rather than greyish. Ashy-headed is closer in size, but shows clear white belly and contrasting grey head and rufous breast. **VOICE** Very much as Ashy-headed Goose, but a little shriller in tone. Male has a thin whistle, female a hoarse quacking call.

DESCRIPTION All plumages similar. **Adult:** Head and upper neck warm brown, with narrow whitish eye-ring. Lower neck, breast, mantle and flanks finely barred black and buff, the pale bars becoming a little whiter on neck and rear flanks and warmer buff on breast. Belly and ventral region warm cinnamon-buff. Most of upperparts dull brown, with buff and black terminal barring to scapulars. Lower back, rump, uppertail-coverts and tail blackish. Upperwing-coverts white, with black greater coverts which are glossed metallic bronze-green. Secondaries white. Primaries black. Underwing white, with blackish primaries. Plumage becomes distinctly pale when worn, prior to moult. **Juvenile:** Similar to adult, but body plumage a little duller and greater coverts dull greyish-brown, not glossy black until first summer.

BARE PARTS All plumages: Bill black. Legs and feet chrome-yellow, with blackish patches along front of tarsus, toes and webs. Iris dark brown.

MEASUREMENTS Males are typically larger than females. **Male:** Wing 330-350, tarsus 60-73, bill 28-30, weight (few data) ca. 2000. **Female:** Wing 310-320, tarsus 56-64, bill 25-28, weight (few data) ca. 2000.

GEOGRAPHICAL VARIATION None.

HABITS Sociable 'goose' of open country, formerly occurring in large flocks outside breeding season but now very rare in South America; reasonable flocks now likely only on Falkland Islands. In winter,

mixes freely with flocks of Ashy-headed Geese, less so with Magellan Geese. Despite generally sociable nature is very aggressive when breeding, males attacking birds much larger than themselves in defence of nesting territories. The breeding season is from October to November in both Tierra del Fuego and the Falklands, a little earlier in the latter. Nests are hidden in long grass, among scrubby bushes or partially concealed by overhanging rocks, and may even be situated in penguin burrows. It seems that the species does not become flightless after breeding; unlike nearly all other wildfowl, the flight feathers are replaced gradually before and after arriving in winter quarters. Whether this is true of all individuals, however, is not yet known (certainly a proportion of Magellan Geese also miss the flightless period). Feeds chiefly by grazing, grubbing out plants by the roots. Spends little time on water, doing so only when goslings are small. Generally less wary than Magellan Goose, frequently being found quite close to farmsteads.

HABITAT Open grassy plains and meadows, chiefly in coastal areas. In winter in stubble fields and freshly-sown pastures.

DISTRIBUTION Formerly common in extreme southern South America, in Tierra del Fuego north to southern Magallanes Province of Chile, with another population on the Falkland Islands. South American birds are now largely confined to northern Tierra del Fuego; they leave their breeding grounds in April, migrating northwards to winter in the grasslands of southern Argentina, chiefly in Buenos Aires Province, returning to Tierra del Fuego in September. The Falkland Islands population is resident, being most abundant on the drier coastal grasslands of West Falkland, but also widely distributed on East Falkland and outlying islands.

POPULATION Formerly considered to be the most abundant of the sheldgeese in Tierra del Fuego, there has been a quite spectacular decline in numbers over the past 30 years. Blame for this has been lodged with the introduction of the Argentine grey fox into Tierra del Fuego to control the introduced rabbit population in the late 1940s. As the foxes increase, the geese decline. There were considered to be fewer than 1,000 Ruddy-headed Geese left in South America by 1976, and it seems that the decline still continues. The species is still abundant on the Falkland Islands, however, with an estimated population there of some 40,000 birds in 1979. Nevertheless, destruction of sheldgeese of all species continues, both in mainland South America and on the Falkland Islands, as a result of their competing for grazing with both sheep and cattle, and the outlook for the species is gloomy, especially in mainland South America.

REFERENCES Johnsgard (1978), King (1981), Summers (1982).

53 BLUE-WINGED GOOSE Plate 15
Cyanochen cyanopterus
Alternative name: Abyssinian Blue-winged Goose

Strange 'goose' of the Ethiopian highlands, an ecological counterpart of the Andean Goose (48) and distantly related to it.

FIELD IDENTIFICATION Length 60-75 cm (23-29 in). **At rest:** Unmistakable. All plumages are similar. A bulky dull grey-brown sheldgoose, with small black bill and relatively short black legs; the blue wing-coverts may be visible when at rest. Within its limited range is unlikely to be confused with any other species, although it often associates with Egyptian Geese (46). **In flight:** Unmistakable. Goose-like shape and drab greyish plumage is relieved by white underwing-coverts and pale blue upperwing-coverts, both contrasting with blackish flight feathers.

VOICE Fairly quiet, although both sexes have high-pitched whistling cries. When suddenly flushed, may sometimes utter a short nasal bark on take-off. Normally silent in flight.

DESCRIPTION All plumages similar. **Adult:** Head and neck greyish-brown, slightly paler on head. Breast, flanks and belly brownish-grey, with paler feather centres. Ventral region whitish, becoming whiter on undertail-coverts. Upperparts almost entirely slate-grey, browner and more mottled on mantle; rump and uppertail-coverts pale brown. Tail black. Upperwing-coverts light greyish-blue. Primaries black. Secondaries black, glossed metallic green. Underwing white with blackish flight feathers. **Juvenile:** Very similar to adult, but duller and browner, lacking gloss on secondaries.

BARE PARTS All plumages: Bill, legs and feet black. Iris dark brown.

MEASUREMENTS Males are considerably larger than females. **Male:** Wing 368-374, tarsus 70-73, bill 32-33, weight 2000-2360. **Female:** Wing 314-334, tarsus 51-65, bill 30-31, weight 1305-1520.

GEOGRAPHICAL VARIATION None.

HABITS Little studied in the wild. Usually seen in pairs by mountain lakes and streams, but small gatherings occur during rainy season, with parties of up to 100 or more reported, which could well be moulting concentrations. Breeding season March to May, also reported July to December, but few data in the wild; nest sites not described for wild birds, but in captivity have been situated among clumps of sedges or hidden under bushes. Seems to be chiefly nocturnal, at least in captivity, spending the daytime loafing by streams and lakesides. Feeds mostly by grazing in waterside marshes and on grassy river-banks. Swims well, but spends little time on water. Both when swimming and when standing, has habit of holding neck back on mantle, with back feathers fluffed out. Remarkably confiding, often approachable to within 15-20 m before flying. Flies reluctantly, usually low over water, members of pair keeping one behind the other, and soon returns to loafing or feeding spot.

HABITAT High-altitude (2500-4000 m) damp plateaux, feeding by riverbanks, marshes and in lakeside meadows. During the wet season, July to September, flocks may form and move to rather lower altitudes, presumably to moult.

DISTRIBUTION Resident and locally common in the highlands of Ethiopia, with largest density of population reported from areas to north and south of Addis Ababa, particularly in the Bale and Arussi mountains, range extending north to about 15°N.

POPULATION Locally common in its restricted range. Little work has been undertaken on this species in the wild, although it seems to be under no great threat. There is no hunting pressure in Ethiopia, since the birds are protected by rules of religion. A survey undertaken in the Web valley in 1966 recorded 30 pairs along 40 km of the valley, suggesting a population of 200-300 pairs in the entire valley; this area, however, has one of the denser populations of the species, and elsewhere it is typically more scattered and thinly distributed.

REFERENCES Brown et al. (1982), Delacour (1954).

54 BLUE DUCK   Plate 16
Hymenolaimus malacorhynchos
Alternative name: Mountain Duck

Peculiar endemic New Zealand duck, inhabiting fast-flowing mountain rivers and behaving much like the Neotropical Torrent Duck (55). Its precise relationships have been well discussed; it was formerly considered an aberrant dabbling duck, but Livezey (1986) considers it an aberrant shelduck.

FIELD IDENTIFICATION Length 54 cm (21 in). **At rest:** Sexes similar. An almost uniform slate-grey duck of fast-flowing mountain streams, its most striking feature being its pale bill, although the head is a darker grey than the body and the breast is spotted reddish-brown. Unlikely to be confused with any other species in its somewhat specialised habitat, except perhaps male Paradise Shelduck (41), which is larger, blacker, has a black bill and often shows white wing-coverts when at rest. Pacific Black Duck (91) has pale sides of head and supercilium and dark bill. **In flight:** Rarely seen in flight. Uniformity of dark grey plumage, including both upperwings and underwings, gives appearance quite unlike that of any other New Zealand duck. Appears a heavily-built duck, with strong and rapid wingbeats, keeping low over surface and following course of river.

VOICE Usual call of male is a shrill, whistled 'whio' or disyllabic 'whi-whio' with minor variations, while female utters a low, rattling growl.

DESCRIPTION All plumages similar. **Adult:** Almost entire plumage medium-grey, with bluish bloom. The head is a little darker grey, and washed with brown on crown and nape. Breast intensely mottled with reddish-brown and undertail-coverts chestnut. Mantle and scapulars weakly mottled blackish. Secondaries weakly tipped whitish above and below. Female tends to have breast mottling a little less extensive than the male. **Juvenile:** Similar to adult, but lacks bluish bloom to plumage and extensive reddish-brown on breast, the breast being merely mottled with dark brown; upperwing-coverts washed with brown. Becomes like adult by six months of age.

BARE PARTS Adult: Bill pinkish-white, with black nail, nostril and flaps of skin at side towards the tip. Legs and feet medium-brown, with darker patches. Iris pale to deep yellow. **Juvenile:** Bill very pale bluish-grey, with blackish nail, skin flaps and band down length of culmen. Legs and feet as adult, but yellower-brown. Iris dark brown at first, becoming yellow by nine months or so, but vestiges of culmen stripe still present into second year.

MEASUREMENTS Sexes similar. Wing 235-249 (mean: male 233, female 217); tarsus 48-51; bill 40-45; mean weight of male 887, of female 750.

GEOGRAPHICAL VARIATION None.

HABITS Rare and declining inhabitant of turbulent mountain rivers. Invariably found in pairs or family parties. Has long-term pair-bonds and is strongly territorial, driving away any intruding duck from its selected stretch of river. Breeding season chiefly August to October, the nest being situated in holes in banks, under bushes, in hollow logs and in small caves. Adults undergo moult rendering them flightless while young still unable to fly, leaving brood to fend for themselves and eventually chasing them away from the territory. Spends most of time either swimming or perched on rocks in the rivers. Very agile on water, feeding while swimming with head and neck submerged, by diving and by picking insects from surfaces of rocks. Negotiates rapids and white-water turbulence with ease. In quiet stretches of water swims buoyantly, with shoulders low and prominent tail held high. Relatively confiding, often allowing a close approach, but locating Blue Ducks can be a problem owing to their relatively large territories and the difficulties of exploring their habitats.

HABITAT Mountain streams and rivers of New Zealand, preferring fast-flowing watercourses with scattered rocks and boulders and fairly extensive shrubby cover along the banks.

DISTRIBUTION Formerly quite widespread throughout New Zealand, but now a local and patchily-distributed resident of mountainous regions along western South Island (chiefly Otago and Southland) and in parts of North Island (mostly Urewara and Tongariro National Parks).

POPULATION Much concern has been expressed in recent years over the future of this unique duck. Although the bird itself is fully protected, the biggest danger lies in its specialised habitat requirements. Its initial decline has been attributed both to predation by introduced mammals and to its having to compete with widely-introduced trout for the invertebrate food of the rivers. A major problem has now arisen with hydroelectric schemes, which involve the damming of fast-flowing rivers and displacing numbers of these resident and strongly territorial birds. The entire population was estimated to be at least 5,000 birds in 1975, and the decline continues.

REFERENCES Eldridge (1985, 1986a), Hall (1987), Kear (1972).

55 TORRENT DUCK   Plate 16
Merganetta armata

Alternative names: see Geographical Variation

Peculiar South American duck of mountain torrents. Formerly designated a tribe of its own with uncertain affinities, Livezey (1986) has concluded that it is more properly allied to the shelducks and close to the Blue Duck (54) and steamer ducks.

FIELD IDENTIFICATION Length 43-46 cm (17-18 in). **At rest:** Unmistakable sexually dimorphic duck of fast-flowing Andean rivers. A long-bodied, long-tailed and short-legged duck, usually located perched on boulders in the rushing waters. Males have distinctive black-and-white-striped head and neck and dark upperparts, although the coloration of the underparts varies according to race. Females less variable, with blue-grey upperparts and deep rufous-chestnut underparts. Both sexes have red bill and legs, although these are duskier in the juveniles, which are also quite different in coloration. Juveniles are greyish-brown on crown, nape and upperparts and whitish below. Despite plumage variation, unlikely to be confused with any other species. **In flight:** Not often seen on the wing, but when it is the elongated shape, dark upperparts and white-bordered green speculum, coupled with the respective head and body coloration, are distinctive within its range. Flight strong and rapid, with very shallow wingbeats, usually close to water surface and following course of river.

VOICE Both sexes have a sharp whistle. Male utters a shrill, monosyllabic or repeated 'weet', dropping somewhat in pitch towards the end; it is clearly audible above the noise of turbulent rivers and may be given both when perched and in flight. The call of the female is a more throaty and less carrying 'queech'.

DESCRIPTION Sexually dimorphic. Males racially and individually variable. Race *leucogenis* described. **Adult male:** Complex black-and-white-striped head and neck pattern: centre of forehead and crown black; lores and supercilia white, latter meeting in a 'V' on nape; centre of hindneck black, joining up with black stripes running back from eye which meet in a 'V' on nape; parallel to hindneck, a black stripe extends up side of neck to meet black eye-stripe; remainder of sides and front of head and neck white. Breast and flanks individually variable: some uniform brownish-black, others greyish-brown with pronounced black streaking, with intermediates between the two extremes. Belly and ventral region dark greyish. Mantle and scapular feathers elongated and pointed; black-centred, with brown to whitish edges, varying according to the individual. Back, rump and uppertail-coverts finely barred grey and black. Tail feathers elongated and stiff, greyish-brown. Wings with short, usually hidden, carpal spur. Upperwing-coverts bluish-grey. Secondaries iridescent green, with white border fore and aft. Primaries dark greyish-brown. **Adult female:** Crown, sides of head and neck, hindneck and almost entire upperparts grey, with blackish centres to elongated and pointed scapulars and inconspicuous vermiculations on crown and neck. Throat, foreneck and entire underparts rich orange-rufous. Wing and tail as male. **Juvenile:** Crown, rear and sides of neck and most of upperparts brownish-grey, with darker feather centres to scapulars. Throat, foreneck and underparts whitish, with dark grey barring on sides of breast and flanks, most prominent on flanks. Wing and tail much as adult.

BARE PARTS All races similar. **Adult:** Bill, legs and feet red, with dusky webs and markings on tarsus. Iris blackish-brown, browner in female. **Juvenile:** Bill, legs and feet greyish-red.

MEASUREMENTS All races similar. Males tend to be a little larger than females. Wing 132-184 (male 142-

184, female 132-165); tarsus 38-41; bill 25-31; mean weight of male 440, of female 330.

GEOGRAPHICAL VARIATION Complex, three races currently recognised. Males of the nominate race (Chilean Torrent Duck) of the Chilean and Argentine Andes differ markedly from those of other races in having black centre to chin, throat and foreneck and blackish extending up from throat centre to eyes; additionally, the white supercilia do not meet in a 'V' on the nape, the black hindneck being confluent with the black crown centre; the underparts are blackish, with browner flanks, and the scapulars are white-fringed. Males of the slightly smaller race *colombiana* (Colombian Torrent Duck) of the northern Andes, from Venezuela, through Colombia to northern Ecuador, are the palest of all, with the underparts whitish-grey, streaked with black, and the scapular fringes pale brown. Females and juveniles of all the forms are similar, although those of the Colombian race are paler, more buffish-orange, below. The major problem of systematics is with the colour morphs included in race *leucogenis* (Peruvian Torrent Duck, see Description above), which occupies the Andes from central Ecuador, south through Peru and Bolivia to extreme northern Chile and northwestern Argentina; formerly these morphs were treated as different races — *leucogenis* (central Ecuador south to central Peru), *turneri* (southern Peru), *garleppi* (Bolivia) and *berlepschi* (northwestern Argentina and northern Chile) — but research has shown that birds resembling these forms occur together on the same rivers in Peru and that they are best treated as variations within one recognisable form. More-extreme taxonomists have considered that the three recognisable races can be treated as full species in their own right.

HABITS Generally found in pairs or family parties scattered along rushing Andean rivers, standing on boulders by the riverside, or in mid-stream. Small gatherings of males may collect to display. Has long-term pair-bonds. Breeding season varies over the extensive range, and may be particularly prolonged in the more equatorial Colombian race, young ducklings of which have been reported both in early July and in October and a nest with eggs in late November. Further south, in Peru, young ducklings are reported most often in July and August, during the dry season, while in Chile breeding occurs in the austral spring, with eggs being found in November. The nest may be hidden in various waterside cavities, but few have been found; recorded sites include cliff ledges and crevices and even a disused nest burrow of a Ringed Kingfisher. Like the New Zealand Blue Duck, Torrent Ducks are at home in rushing mountain waters, negotiating waterfalls and white-water rapids with ease. They swim with body low in the water and tail depressed; when alarmed, may move considerable distances with merely head and neck visible above the surface. They dive readily, both when alarmed and when feeding. Feeding birds swim with head and neck submerged, sometimes with almost whole body underwater, scrambling up on to rocks in midstream for resting periods. They will also clamber on to rocky ledges behind small waterfalls to forage among the vegetated rocks and even stand at the foot of small falls, feeding unconcernedly as the water cascades over them. Not particularly shy, although when disturbed will escape either by diving and swimming away underwater or by flying a short distance low over the water surface.

HABITAT Fast-flowing mountain rivers in the temperate and subtropical vegetation zones, with gorges, rapids and waterfalls interspersed with calmer stretches and emergent boulders. Generally at 1500-3500 m, but almost to sea level in Chile and as high as 4500 m in Bolivia.

DISTRIBUTION Ranges of the three races are given under Geographical Variation; it seems that there is a gap in the distribution in northern Chile, separating the Peruvian and Chilean races, and there may also be another in central Ecuador, separating the Peruvian and Colombian forms. Widespread resident along almost the full length of the Andes, from Merida and Tachira in Venezuela, southwards through Colombia, Ecuador, Peru, Bolivia, western Argentina and Chile to Tierra del Fuego. Birds from higher altitude move lower in winter, but rarely descend below 1000 m, although species has been reported as low as 300 m in Colombia. Chilean race, however, breeds at much lower altitudes, almost down to sea level in places.

POPULATION Seems to be declining in the northern half of its range, but is still relatively common in Chile. No data available on populations. Biggest threats to the species are pollution of the rivers and hydroelectric schemes, which involve damming and slowing the flow of their rivers. Other problems are the forest destruction, which has created an increasing number of flash floods, both destroying nests and eroding feeding areas; and the introduction into many rivers of trout, which compete with the ducks for their specialised food.

REFERENCES Eldridge (1979, 1986b), Johnsgard (1966).

GENUS *TACHYERES* (STEAMER DUCKS)

Four species of large, heavily-built diving ducks inhabiting South American southern coastal waters and the Falkland Islands. Steamer ducks are easily identified as such, but owing to general plumage similarities specific identification is difficult. Indeed, they are probably the most difficult of all ducks to identify specifically in the field.

Steamer ducks are very large, bulky ducks, related to the shelducks. Males are quite pugnacious by nature and are particularly massively built, possessing large bony knobs at the bend of the wing which are freely used during combats. They spend most of their lives along inshore coastal waters, being the southern-hemisphere ecological counterparts of the northern eiders. When not swimming and diving, they may be found loafing in small parties on coastal rocks. Their common name is derived from their habit of furiously paddling and splashing over the surface of the water when pursued.

PLUMAGE AS AN IDENTIFICATION AID Plumages of all species are relatively similar, basically medium-grey, with darker feather edges giving a mottled effect; the centre of the underparts from lower breast to undertail-coverts is white. All species show a similar wing pattern: white secondaries and greater coverts, contrasting with dark grey forewing and blackish-grey primaries; the underwing pattern is similar to that of the upperwing. The coloration and pattern of the head and neck vary considerably within each species according to age, sex and season, but are the most important plumage feature for identification purposes, although the interpretation of these significances is still not fully understood. Although Humphrey and Livezey (1982a) have summarised the variation within Flying Steamer Duck (56), other species have received little critical study in this respect. Males of most species become very white-headed during the breeding season (a supplementary plumage) and are considerably larger and bulkier than females; after breeding a further moult produces a short summer plumage, when male head patterns are closer to those of the females, almost an eclipse plumage stage. All species have deep yellow legs and feet, but bill coloration is a useful identification pointer. Juveniles and sub-adults of all species are scarcely distinguishable by plumage. Specific identification by plumage features alone may not always be possible, unless birds are paired adults allowing comparisons to be made between the head and bill coloration of the two sexes.

FLIGHTLESSNESS AS AN IDENTIFICATION AID Flying ability is not a totally reliable identification aid, as Flying Steamer Duck, despite its name, is not always inclined to take to the air, and indeed many large males are not even capable of flight, this being especially true of those inhabiting the Beagle Channel. Under certain conditions all three of the 'flightless' species are able to fly for very short distances, but do not rise far from the surface or demonstrate any manoeuvrability when on the wing. Therefore a steamer duck that takes off and flies a considerable distance, with changes in its flight path, is certainly a Flying Steamer Duck, as are any individuals occurring on inland freshwater lakes.

Distribution helps the situation as no two of the three flightless species occur together, although the range of Flying Steamer Duck overlaps with them all over most of their ranges. As the three flightless species are allopatric in distribution, for field identification purposes it is necessary only to consider each one in comparison with the Flying Steamer Duck.

Not surprisingly, the systematics of the genus are complex. Phillips (1925) recognised only one species, Lowe (1934) proved the existence of two, as had long been suspected, and Murphy (1936) clarified the situation and recommended the recognition of three species. In recent years, researchers working on Argentine steamer ducks have described a fourth species (Humphrey and Thompson 1981). This new species, White-headed Flightless Steamer Duck (58), eases some of the previous speculation and confusion over the identity of steamer ducks along coastal Argentina, but does not make field identification of them any less complicated.

REFERENCES Delacour (1954), Humphrey and Livezey (1982a), Humphrey and Thompson (1981), Livezey and Humphrey (1982, 1983, 1984, 1985), Lowe (1934), Murphy (1936), Weller (1976).

56 FLYING STEAMER DUCK Plate 17
Tachyeres patachonicus

The only steamer duck capable of sustained flight, although some individuals are quite flightless. Range overlaps with those of the other three species.

FIELD IDENTIFICATION Length 66-71 cm (26-28 in). **At rest:** Generally a little smaller and less bulky than the three flightless species, with less massive bill, head and neck and more rounded back profile, enhanced by longer wings which almost reach base of tail; additionally, the tail feathers are larger and more upcurving than on the flightless species. Body feathers are fringed reddish-brown, as on the Falkland Flightless (59), which is confusingly similar. Head of male becomes almost whitish in breeding season. Males have a yellowish-orange bill, females and juveniles a greyish bill. Distinctions from the three flightless steamer ducks are tricky and are discussed under each respective account of latter. Any steamer duck on an inland lake will be of this species (although in coastal regions birds of the flightless species may walk 1 km, or maybe more, to freshwater lakes). **In flight:** Although most individuals are capable of flying well, they often do so only as a last resort, preferring to 'steam' across the surface or to dive when pursued. Most often seen on the wing in the austral summer, a bulky dark grey duck with contrasting white belly and striking white secondaries, both upperwing and underwing patterns being similar. Many individuals, especially large males, may be quite incapable of flight (see notes under steamer duck genus).
VOICE Not conspicuously vocal. Male has a far-carrying high-pitched whistle, 'psee-ough', which may be intensified into a rapidly-repeated shrill 'pew-pew-pew', grunted growl. Female produces a low croaking, grunted growl.
DESCRIPTION See notes under steamer duck genus for body and wing description; head and neck variation summarised here. Seasonal and individual variation complex; has three moults and plumage stages per year. **Adult male:** During most of the year, head and neck medium greyish-brown, crown darker grey, strong cinnamon wash on throat and foreneck, and short but clear white stripe from rear of eye, curving around ear-coverts. During austral spring (October to December), moults into a supplementary plumage in which head and neck chiefly whitish, with pale grey wash on sides of head, stronger on lores, and cinnamon wash on throat. In the austral summer (January to March), acquires another, but variable, head coloration: some birds have head and neck all dark brown, with rich cinnamon throat and white eye-ring; others have crown dark grey, and rear ear-coverts and sides of neck paler than dark brown lores and

'face'; while a third type has head and neck dark purplish-grey, throat dark cinnamon, and a small white streak behind eye. **Adult female:** During most of year, crown dark grey, lores and ear-coverts dark brown, becoming paler on rear ear-coverts and whitish on sides of neck, forming whitish collar at base of foreneck; throat dark cinnamon; prominent whitish stripe runs back from eye, curving around rear of ear-coverts. During the spring, the white eye-stripe becomes less clear, the lores more rufous, and the whitish collar is lost. The summer plumage, like that of the male, is variable: some birds have dark brown head and neck, with dark cinnamon throat and whitish eye-ring and very weak eye-line, whereas others are much paler on rear ear-coverts and neck and have a short but clear whitish eye-line. **Juvenile:** Head and neck very dark brown, almost blackish-brown, with redder 'face' and sides and front of neck, a thin but defined pale line behind eye, and whitish eye-ring. Adult plumage acquired by end of first year.

BARE PARTS Adult male: Bill orange or yellowish-orange, usually with some pale towards the tip, becoming bluish-grey over distal portion when in wing moult; nail black. Legs and feet orange-yellow with dusky webs, duller yellow when in wing moult. Iris dark brown. **Adult female:** Bill slate-blue, sometimes with a little yellowish-orange at base, nail black. Legs and feet yellow to orange-yellow with grey webs. Iris dark brown. **Juvenile:** Bill bluish-black, with trace of orange at very base, nail black. Legs and feet dull brownish-yellow with dusky webs. Iris dark brown.

MEASUREMENTS Males considerably larger than females. **Male:** Wing 287-317, tarsus 55-69, bill 48-57, mean weight 3030. **Female:** Wing 276-301, tarsus 50-61, bill 50-59, mean weight 2425.

GEOGRAPHICAL VARIATION No races yet recognised, but research indicates that there could be variation of geographical significance, at least in the coloration of the bare parts, although further fieldwork is required before any conclusions can be drawn.

HABITS Usually found in pairs or family parties, both along the coast and by inland freshwater lakes. Small flocks of non-breeding and moulting birds are also formed in coastal districts. The breeding season in Chile is from November to January, but in the Falkland Islands may begin in October or earlier. Generally moves away from coastal situations to nest, often by lakes as far as 50 km from the sea; no doubt this is partly due to competition with the larger flightless species. All steamer duck species are believed to have long-term pair-bonds and are strongly territorial and aggressive when breeding. Nest site usually on small islet, hidden among grass or other vegetation. Although flies strongly and quite readily, is seen to do so chiefly in the spring and summer months as birds move inland to select breeding territories; along coastal waters is more reluctant to take wing, preferring to escape by 'steaming' across the water or by diving, and even on land may be very reluctant to fly, preferring to run and hide rather than take to the air. Some individuals, and even perhaps some populations, may be quite flightless at all times.

HABITAT During the winter frequents rocky coastlines, although more of an inshore species than some of the other steamer ducks, spending a lot of time feeding on coastal freshwater ponds and estuaries. Moves inland to breed, by lakes and rivers, often at a considerable distance from the coast, but also nests on coastal and estuarine islands along Beagle Channel.

DISTRIBUTION The most widespread of the genus, overlapping in range with all other species, although only marginally with White-headed Flightless (58). Chiefly resident along coasts, and a little way inland, in southern South America and the Falkland Islands. On the Pacific coast the range extends northwards to the region of Concepción in Chile, extending throughout Tierra del Fuego and Patagonia. Its northern limit along the Argentine coast is somewhat confused by the recent discovery of the White-headed Flightless Steamer Duck, and it is probably not so extensive as is suggested in previous literature. It seems that the present species does not breed along the Argentine coast north of Santa Cruz, although small numbers of non-breeders occur northwards as far as Chubut and it has been collected as far north as the mouth of the Rio Negro. Although not truly migratory, there is dispersal along the coasts in winter, when inland lakes freeze over.

POPULATION Widespread throughout its range, although everywhere apparently less abundant than the flightless species, but doubtless this is partly due to confusion over the identification of non-flying individuals and to its less concentrated habitat requirements. It seems to be under no direct threat, either in mainland South America or on the Falkland Islands.

REFERENCES Humphrey and Livezey (1982a, 1982b), Weller (1976).

57 MAGELLANIC FLIGHTLESS STEAMER DUCK   Plate 17
Tachyeres pteneres

Confined to the coasts of Chile and extreme southern Argentina, this flightless steamer duck is the largest of the genus.

FIELD IDENTIFICATION Length 74-84 cm (29-33 in). Range widely overlaps with that of Flying Steamer Duck (56), but present species is confined to coastal waters. Both sexes have a bright orange-yellow bill, (only male in Flying). When both species seen together, adult Magellanic is clearly larger and more massive about bill, head and neck than Flying and has relatively shorter wings showing more body between wing-tips and base of tail. Sexual dimorphism is less marked in this flightless species, although breeding males have more uniform paler grey heads than females, greyer than in similar plumage of male Flying, but can appear almost white-headed under certain conditions. Generally, the body plumage is greyer than that of Flying, with the darker feather edges being grey rather than reddish-brown, although this may be difficult to be sure of in the field and in addition females can have distinct brownish wash to body plumage. In all plumages the white eye-line is less distinct than on Flying, which does not always show this feature anyway. Juveniles and sub-adults may not be safely distinguishable, unless more massive bill and large size can be ascertained, or the bird flies strongly and becomes a Flying Steamer Duck.

VOICE Similar to that of Flying Steamer Duck, but male's calls are less shrill, more rasping.

DESCRIPTION Plumage variation less than in Flying Steamer Duck. Sexes similar. Has two, possibly three moults per year. Not so well studied as Flying. See notes on steamer duck genus for body and wing plumage. **Adult male:** During most of the year, head and neck relatively uniform medium-grey, paler on forehead and crown on some males, with whitish eye-ring. Throat washed with rufous. During the austral spring, head becomes uniformly pale grey. **Adult female:** Head darker than on male, washed brown on sides, with whitish eye-line and eye-ring and dark reddish throat. **Juvenile:** Head and neck uniform dark grey-brown, with narrow pale eye-ring. Ageing process probably same as in Flying.

BARE PARTS Adult: Bill orange, colour brightest in males, which may have very dark orange towards bill-base; nail blackish. Legs and feet bright yellow, with dusky webs. Iris dark brown. **Juvenile:** Bill dusky. Legs and feet dull brownish-yellow. Iris dark brown.

MEASUREMENTS Males considerably larger than females. **Male:** Wing 260-288, tarsus 66-79, bill 55-66, mean weight 5310. **Female:** Wing 255-271, tarsus 63-71, bill 54-64, mean weight 4328.

GEOGRAPHICAL VARIATION None.

HABITS Usually found only in pairs or family parties, rarely forming flocks, although concentrations reported southern Chile in January when many young birds about; forms only very small flocks when moulting, although sometimes mixes with Flying Steamer Duck in winter. Pairs strongly defend their territories in the breeding season, which is chiefly September to December. Nests are situated under dense shrubby cover close to the water, and are extremely well hidden. Feeds by diving over offshore and inshore kelp-beds, loafing on adjacent rocks when tide recedes. Rarely visits freshwater lakes close to sea, but readily drinks from springs running over shore.

HABITAT Confined to rocky coastlines with sheltered bays.

DISTRIBUTION Widespread resident along coastline of southern South America and inshore islands, from Chiloe in Chile to Staten Island off Tierra del Fuego; references to its occurrence along the Argentine coast north of here are perhaps due to confusion with the recently-described White-headed Flightless Steamer Duck (58).

POPULATION Locally common within its limited range, this little-studied species seems to be under no adverse threats to its numbers.

REFERENCES Murphy (1936), Weller (1976).

58 WHITE-HEADED FLIGHTLESS STEAMER DUCK   Plate 17
Tachyeres leucocephalus

Described as recently as 1981, this 'new' steamer duck is known only from the coast of Chubut, Argentina.

FIELD IDENTIFICATION Length 61-74 cm (24-29 in). Commonest steamer duck along coast of Chubut, Argentina, although non-breeding Flying (56) occurs in small numbers throughout its range during September to January. Any very pale-headed steamer duck here is a male White-headed, non-breeding Flying being basically dark-headed. Females have a very broad whitish band running back from the eye and diffusing into pale sides of neck; this band is much narrower and interrupted on female Flying, but is probably also lacking on summer female White-headed. Larger and bulkier than Flying, with a more massive bill and wings not extending so far back towards tail. Duller, darker-headed juveniles paler on front of neck than those of Flying, but separation of juvenile and sub-adult birds problematical.

VOICE Undescribed, but no doubt similar to others of the genus.

DESCRIPTION Sexually dimorphic. For body and wing plumage see notes under steamer duck genus. Has two moults and plumages per year. **Adult male:** Head and neck whitish, with very pale grey wash to crown, pale brown wash on lores and narrow light cinnamon throat centre; during breeding season, head and neck may be even whiter. During short period in summer, head and neck pattern closer to that of female, including prominent white eye-line. **Adult female:** Crown and forehead dark grey, sides and front of head and ear-coverts reddish-brown, throat medium-cinnamon. Whitish eye-ring, and relatively broad white band extending back from eye, curving around ear-coverts and diffusing into whitish sides of neck, forming whitish collar on foreneck. In summer, head and neck darker, more purplish-brown; extent of white eye-line at this time of year still uncertain, but most probably lacking. **Juvenile:** Head and neck dark brown, with redder-brown sides of head and paler brown sides and front of neck. Eye-ring pale, eye-line diffuse and faint. Ageing process unclear, but sub-adult birds somewhat intermediate in pattern between juvenile and female.

BARE PARTS Adult: Bill orange, becoming yellower towards tip, nail black; dull greyish-yellow on female. Legs and feet bright yellow. Iris brown. **Juvenile:** Bill dusky-grey, with black nail. Legs and feet brownish-yellow. Iris brown.

MEASUREMENTS Males considerably larger than females. **Male:** Wing 262-295, tarsus 61-67, bill 51-63, mean weight 3790. **Female:** Wing ca. 262-282, mean weight 2950.

GEOGRAPHICAL VARIATION None.

HABITS Very much as other flightless steamer ducks, although on some offshore islands breeds in quite large and surprisingly dense colonies. However, basically strongly territorial and aggressive, like other steamer ducks. Non-breeders form quite large concentrations. The breeding season is from October to February, nests being hidden under bushes on islands or peninsulas of the mainland, not far from water. Entirely coastal by habit, this species has not yet been found to visit freshwater lagoons.

HABITAT Rocky coastlines, offshore islands and sheltered bays.

DISTRIBUTION Resident along the southern coast

of the Province of Chubut, Argentina. Known from the region of Puerto Melo, but probably occurs along the Chubut coast from Bahia Bustamante north to Puerto Madryn and the Valdes Peninsula.

POPULATION No population studies have yet been published, but it appears to be abundant within its limited range.

REFERENCES Humphrey and Livezey (1985), Humphrey and Thompson (1981).

59 FALKLAND FLIGHTLESS STEAMER DUCK
Tachyeres brachypterus
Plate 17

Endemic to the Falkland Islands, where it overlaps with the Flying Steamer Duck (56), although it is seemingly more abundant.

FIELD IDENTIFICATION Length 61-74 cm (24-29 in). Occurs with Flying Steamer Duck in coastal habitats of the Falklands. Separation of the two species can be very difficult and may not be possible, unless the bird attains sustained flight and can then be identified as Flying Steamer Duck; the flightless species often flies across the water surface for considerable distances, but never takes to the air in a proper manner. Although the flightless species does not occur on freshwater lakes and pools far inland as Flying habitually does, caution should be exercised within 1 km or so of the shore, as it is quite capable of walking some distance inland to drink, bathe or even nest. It is larger, bulkier and more massive-billed than the Flying Steamer Duck and the wings do not extend so far towards the tail; additionally, the tail of Flying is longer and more curved. In plumage the two are confusingly similar, although Falkland Flightless tends to have a yellowish collar at the base of the foreneck, lacking on Flying; breeding males become as pale-headed as Flying, although bill of adult male Falkland Flightless is uniformly brighter orange, lacking the pale greyish distal portion of male Flying's bill.

VOICE Typical of the genus. Male has a clear, far-carrying, high-pitched rasping whistle, 'pe-ough'. Female utters a low, grunting growl.

DESCRIPTION Sexually dimorphic. For body and wing plumage see notes under steamer duck genus, although, like Flying, has much rufous-brown mixed with grey of body plumage. Like Flying, has three moults and plumages per year, but sequences and significances of these have been inadequately studied. **Adult male:** For most of the year, head light grey, mottled darker grey on lores and sides of head; whitish eye-ring and curving whitish line extending back from eye around ear-coverts; throat and foreneck mottled reddish-brown, becoming distinctly yellowish on lower foreneck. During breeding season, head and neck become strikingly pale, whitish, with darker shading on 'face'. **Adult female:** Sides of head and neck dark reddish-brown, crown and neck becoming dark grey, with distinct narrow whitish eye-ring and line running back from eye. Extent of seasonal variation unclear. **Juvenile:** Head and neck uniform dusky-brown, with narrow pale eye-ring, but lacks eye-line. Attains adult-like plumage by end of first year, but second-year males have brownish sides of head.

BARE PARTS Adult male: Bill bright orange, becoming paler towards tip, nail black. Legs and feet deep yellow. Iris dark brown. **Adult female:** Bill olive-grey, with yellow base and culmen, nail black. Legs and feet yellow. Iris dark brown. **Juvenile:** Bill dusky-grey. Legs and feet brownish-yellow. Iris dark brown. By second year, males have orange bills.

MEASUREMENTS Males considerably larger than females. **Male:** Wing 272-282, tarsus 63-73, bill 53-61, mean weight 4334. **Female:** Wing 251-272, tarsus 55-63, bill 52-58, mean weight 3383.

GEOGRAPHICAL VARIATION None.

HABITS Usually found in pairs or family parties along coast, but large concentrations of non-breeders may be found throughout the year. Strongly territorial and aggressive when breeding. Breeding season normally mid September to late December, but eggs have been found at almost any time of the year. Nests are situated close to shore, but have been found up to 1 km from coast, usually among tussock grass but sometimes in disused penguin burrows. Feeds by both up-ending and diving on incoming tides, retiring to loafing spots as tide recedes. Feeds chiefly along inshore shallow waters. Often visits freshwater pools near the shore and mixes with Flying Steamer Duck in winter.

HABITAT Rocky coastlines and small islands, with sheltered bays.

DISTRIBUTION Widespread resident throughout the Falkland Islands.

POPULATION No total estimates have been made, but it is well distributed throughout the islands, and often abundant.

REFERENCES Weller (1976).

SUBFAMILY ANATINAE (DUCKS)

Although the remainder of the ducks have been classified within one huge subfamily by Livezey (1986), with identification in mind it is more convenient to discuss the 28 genera separately, or in small groups of similar species when this is relevant to identification.

Tribe ANATINI (DABBLING DUCKS)

Some of the genera included in this tribe have previously been placed elsewhere: *Pteronetta, Cairina, Aix, Nettapus, Callonetta, Chenonetta* and *Amazonetta* were formerly considered to form a tribe, termed 'Cairinini' or perching ducks, along with *Plectropterus* and *Sarkidiornis,* which are now considered to be closer to the shelducks. The treatment here follows the revision recommended by Livezey, with the exception that *Salvadorina* is recognised as a monotypic genus worthy of separation from *Anas*.

60 HARTLAUB'S DUCK   Plate 21
Pteronetta hartlaubi

Rather strange West African forest duck, most closely related to the Muscovy Duck (61) of South America and White-winged Wood Duck (62) of Asia.

FIELD IDENTIFICATION Length 56-58 cm (22-23 in). **At rest:** Large, dark duck of forest streams in West and Central Africa. Despite rather bright coloration, may well appear all dark in its shadowy habitat, where the most obvious plumage feature is the variable white head patches of males. The general coloration is rich chestnut, with a black head; the white head patches may be absent (on females) or extend to cover the whole top and front of the head. Confusion with other species is unlikely, although males with much white on head can superficially resemble White-faced Whistling Duck (7) in coloration, but their shape and their habitat are quite different. African Black Duck (70) has obvious white scalloping on upperparts, even in dull light conditions. **In flight:** A large, bulky, seemingly all-dark duck with conspicuous light blue upperwing-coverts, lacking any white markings on either upperwing or underwing. The underwing is all dark.
VOICE Relatively silent. Calls recorded include a repeated quacking 'ko-ko-ko-ko', a conversational 'whit-whit-whit', and several harsh, grating calls.
DESCRIPTION All plumages similar. **Adult male:** Head and upper neck black, with individually variable white patches on head, usually only a small patch on forehead but sometimes white extends to cover whole 'face' and crown (birds of latter type frequent in northeast Zaire). Lower neck and most of body plumage rich chestnut, becoming browner towards rear end, with olive-brown rump, uppertail-coverts, tail and scapulars. Upperwing-coverts pale blue. Primaries and secondaries olive-brown, with secondaries edged blue-grey and tertials edged black. Underwing dark olive-brown. **Adult female:** Basically similar to male, but often lacks white on head; whole plumage a little duller. **Juvenile:** Still duller than female, with pale fringes to body feathers giving a slightly-mottled effect at very close range.
BARE PARTS All plumages: Bill black, with pale, whitish-grey to pale yellowish or pinkish, subterminal band; becomes somewhat swollen at base on breeding males. Legs and feet dark yellowish-brown, with dusky webs. Iris reddish-brown.
MEASUREMENTS Males typically larger than females. **Male:** Wing 270-281, tarsus 44-46, bill 46-48, mean weight 976. **Female:** Wing 248-266, bill 44-47, mean weight 788.
GEOGRAPHICAL VARIATION No races currently recognised. Formerly, birds with extensive white on head were termed '*albifrons*'; although locally frequent in Zaire, this variation is not considered to be geographically significant, being merely a tendency towards partial albinism in certain populations.
HABITS Little studied in the wild. Although normally found in pairs, small flocks have been reported

on larger, more open rivers and are presumed to be moult gatherings. The breeding season seems to be during August-November, when ducklings have been seen in the wild, but no wild nest has yet been described; from breeding behaviour in captivity, however, the nest site is most likely to be in tree holes and hollow trees. This species is well distributed along forest streams and rivers, feeding along smaller streams with overhanging vegetation, and seems to be most active in the evenings. It readily perches high in trees, often flying up into canopy when disturbed. Mixes little with other species in its forested habitat, although locally overlaps with African Black Duck. Not particularly shy or rare, it is surprising that this interesting duck has received such little attention.
HABITAT Secluded pools, streams and small rivers in lowland rainforest and well-wooded savannas.
DISTRIBUTION Widespread resident in West and Central Africa, from Sierra Leone and Guinea eastwards to extreme southwest Sudan and south to central Zaire. It seems to be most numerous in Cameroon, Gabon, Congo and Zaire.
POPULATION No data on numbers, but it appears to be widespread and locally quite numerous throughout its range. Its dependence on rainforest and the pressures of forest destruction have no doubt affected its population in some parts of its range.
REFERENCES Brown *et al.* (1982), Mackworth-Praed and Grant (1970).

61 MUSCOVY DUCK   Plate 18
Cairina moschata

Familiar in its domesticated forms, the wild ancestor is a bird of tropical forest lakes and rivers in Central and South America.

FIELD IDENTIFICATION Length 66-84 cm (26-33 in). **At rest:** Unmistakable. Large, bulky blackish duck, with striking white wing-coverts. Males are conspicuously larger than females and have pronounced knob at base of bill. Juveniles are uniform blackish. Confusion with any other species unlikely; although piebald or white domestic forms often escape from captivity and may look particularly odd when out of context, such birds are easily identified as Muscovies by their naked, warty faces and reddish legs and bill. The wild ancestor is much sleeker and more attractive than its bulky domesticated descendants. **In flight:** Adults are large, chunky black ducks with broad wings and striking white coverts on both upperwings and underwings. Juveniles only gradually attain white wing-coverts and can be uniform blackish overall. Confusion with any other species unlikely; Black-bellied Whistling Duck (9) is a large dark duck with whitish in upperwing, but could be confused only if a particularly poor view obtained.
VOICE Relatively silent. Male produces a low hissing sound, female a short, weak quack.
DESCRIPTION Sexes similar in plumage. **Adult:** Head and nape of male has short mane at rear. Head, neck and entire body plumage and tail brownish-black, glossed with green and purple on

upperparts. Upperwing- and underwing-coverts white. Flight feathers black. **Juvenile:** Somewhat variable: most are similar to adults but less glossy, whole plumage duller and browner, others are more mottled; lacks white on upperwing-coverts at first, this being acquired by end of first year. Full extent of adult wing pattern may not be attained until second year.
BARE PARTS Adult male: Bill black, mottled fleshy-white in subterminal portion; enlarged knob at base of bill and bare facial skin blackish, sometimes reddish (but red colour more typical of domesticated birds). Legs and feet greyish-black. Iris yellowish-brown. **Adult female and juvenile:** Coloration as male, but lacks bare facial skin and knob at bill-base.
MEASUREMENTS Males considerably larger than females, even when young. **Male:** Wing 350-400, tarsus 55-65, bill 65-75, mean weight ca. 3000. **Female:** Wing 300-315, bill 50-53, mean weight ca. 1250.
GEOGRAPHICAL VARIATION None.
HABITS Relatively little studied in the wild. Usually found in small parties; no large moulting concentrations seem to have been recorded. Pair-formation somewhat promiscuous, without long-term bonds, the male playing no part in nest defence or parental responsibilities. The breeding season varies considerably over its wide range, being basically in the local wet season. Breeding has been reported in the Guianas from February to May, Venezuela in July and November, Panama in June, Bolivia in November and Peru in March. Nest sites are normally in tree holes and hollows, but may sometimes be on ground, hidden among dense waterside vegetation. Feeds chiefly by dabbling and up-ending in shallow water, but sometimes grazes on waterside grassy areas. Most active in evening and early morning. Readily perches in trees and forms communal roosts in treetops, perching along the larger branches. Relatively shy and wary owing to persecution over much of its range.
HABITAT Tropical lakes, lagoons, marshes and slow-flowing rivers in lowland forested areas. In dry season also sometimes occurs on brackish coastal marshes and lagoons, but has marked preference for fresh water.
DISTRIBUTION Widespread, although somewhat local resident. Range extends from Mexico, southwards through Central and much of the northern half of lowland South America east of the Andes, to southwestern Ecuador, eastern Peru, northern Argentina (south to Santa Fé and Santiago del Estero) and northern Uruguay. Although basically resident, there is some dispersal during the dry season, when recorded rarely in Trinidad and occasionally on Pacific coast of Colombia and Peru; vagrants recorded south to southern Uruguay and Buenos Aires Province of Argentina, and recently in Texas.
POPULATION Despite wide range, is only locally common in less populated districts of the more eastern parts of its range, having suffered from persecution in many areas. Has increased in Mexico in recent years following provision of nestboxes; such schemes could no doubt help the species else-

where. No data on populations.
REFERENCES Johnsgard (1978).

62 WHITE-WINGED WOOD DUCK
Cairina scutulata   Plate 18

Rare and elusive inhabitant of rainforest swamps and pools in tropical Asia.

FIELD IDENTIFICATION Length 66-81 cm (26-32 in). **At rest:** Large, distinctive blackish duck with whitish, black-freckled head and neck and striking white wing-coverts, presently known only from a few forested swamps in southeastern Asia. Unlikely to be confused with any other duck in its range. Comb Duck (37) shares its whitish, freckled head and neck pattern and dark upperparts, but lacks white in the wing, has very white breast and pale or greyish underparts, and has black legs. Some White-winged Wood Ducks can be largely white on head, neck and breast. Extremely difficult to locate in the wild, owing to rarity and difficulties of exploring its habitat; perhaps most easily located by listening for calls from birds flighting to feeding areas at dusk. **In flight:** Large size and relatively long dark body, with striking white forewing both above and below and pale blue speculum, are diagnostic within its range. Comb Duck has wings all blackish on both upper- and undersides.
VOICE Relatively silent, although calls may be heard from pairs both when on water and in flight. The flight call is a prolonged, vibrant, wailing honk, often breaking up into a nasal whistle at the end. It has been suggested that this sound may be produced by the pair, the male giving the honk and the female the whistle. It is most often heard in the evening when pairs flight to feeding areas, but single flying individuals seem to be invariably silent. A single or repeated, shorter and harsher honk is sometimes given by birds on the water, or if flushed.
DESCRIPTION Sexes similar. Some individual variation. **Adult:** Head and neck white, intensely freckled with dark grey; usually some ill-defined clear white on 'face' but sometimes extensive clear white on head and neck, and in extreme individuals pure white head, neck and breast, with white even extending to abdomen. Breast and entire underparts normally all dark brown, washed rusty-chestnut, blacker on lower neck. Entire upperparts blackish-brown, glossed green. Primaries dark brown, secondaries greyish-blue, tertials black with outer feathers white on inner webs. Upperwing-coverts white, with dark band along length of tips of greater coverts. Underwing-coverts white, with dark flight feathers. Female is a little duller than the male, usually with head and neck more intensely speckled. **Juvenile:** Duller and browner overall, with pale brownish head and neck; soon develops whitish of adult plumage on head and neck. Unlike related Muscovy Duck (61), has white wing-coverts (like adults) from the first plumage.
BARE PARTS Sexes similar. Bill yellowish-orange to reddish-orange, mottled with dusky-grey, becoming redder in breeding season when base of male's bill becomes rather swollen. Legs and feet orange-

yellow. Iris yellowish-orange to reddish.

MEASUREMENTS Males larger than females. **Male:** Wing 360-400, tarsus 54-60, bill 58-66, mean weight 2700. **Female:** Wing 305-355, bill 55-61, mean weight 1860.

GEOGRAPHICAL VARIATION No races recognised. Birds with extensive pure white on head and neck seem not to be confined to a geographical area; although most frequent in Sumatra, such individuals have also been recorded in Assam. This partial albinism is perhaps perpetuated by inbreeding within isolated populations.

HABITS A rare inhabitant of swampy rainforest. Usually met with singly or in pairs and family groups; small parties may be formed in the dry season, but these generally number less than ten birds. The breeding season in Assam is from April to September during the rainy season; data from elsewhere are limited, but in Sumatra it is considered to be from December to April. Few nests have been found in the wild, and those that have been reported have not actually been proven to be of this species; it seems likely, however, that it nests in tree hollows close to swampy ground, with other reports including ground nests and even the use of old nests of other large birds. Feeds mostly at night, flighting in ones and twos to and from roost at dawn and in the late evening, spending daytime roosting in foliage of large trees, from which it is difficult to flush. Prefers to feed on well-shaded, weed-covered pools and on slow-flowing forest streams, but in Sumatra reported from more open swampy pools, sometimes close to villages. Feeds chiefly by dabbling, often with head and neck immersed, and also said to dive occasionally. Relatively shy and wary, with few wild observations owing to its chiefly nocturnal behaviour and forested habitats.

HABITAT Rainforest with secluded slow-flowing streams and pools; during dry season also occurs in more open swamps adjacent to forest.

DISTRIBUTION Rare and endangered resident, now with relict distribution throughout its former range. Formerly widespread over tropical southeast Asia from Assam, Burma and Indo-China south through Thailand and Malaysia to Sumatra and Java. Today confined to a few areas of primary forest, chiefly in reserves, in Assam, Bangladesh, northern Burma and Sumatra and possibly still in Malaysia and on Java.

POPULATION Considerable decline in present century, chiefly through forest destruction; population seems to decline rapidly in areas once forest becomes fragmented. In 1979, population estimated at a little under 200 pairs on mainland Asia, with an unknown number in Sumatra, where it has been found to be surprisingly widespread in recent years. Many of its present locations are within national parks or reserves, although this will be a factor limiting population increase owing to destruction of surrounding forest areas and low density of population required by the species (suggested as one pair per 100 ha of prime habitat in Assam). A captive-breeding programme has been initiated to supplement wild stocks.

REFERENCES Holmes (1977), Mackenzie and Kear (1976).

GENUS *AIX* (WOOD DUCK AND MANDARIN)

Two species of hole-nesting duck, the males with intricate and exotic breeding plumages. Other plumage stages are superficially similar, males having female-like eclipse plumage after breeding. Although confusion between the two species in their native ranges is unlikely, both are widely kept in captivity and feral populations of Mandarins (64) are now well established in Britain. Escapes of both species frequent in Europe, although Wood Duck (63) has so far maintained only temporary feral populations there. Mandarins frequently escape from captivity in North America, but have not become established.

63 WOOD DUCK   Plate 19
Aix sponsa

Alternative names: Carolina Duck, Carolina Wood Duck, North American Wood Duck

Males are one of the most attractive of all ducks, perhaps rivalled only by the closely-related Mandarin (64).

FIELD IDENTIFICATION Length 43-51 cm (17-20 in). **At rest:** Breeding male unmistakable, with its iridescent dark plumage, intricate white facial and throat markings, white vertical breast stripe, buff flanks, ruddy breast, and distinctive shape created by prominent broad tail and maned crest; the red eye and orange and white bill are also conspicuous. Despite this striking pattern, can be surprisingly well camouflaged when sitting on dappled water, or under shade of overhanging branches. See also male Baikal Teal (76). Female, eclipse male and juvenile all resemble those of Mandarin, and are fully discussed under that species; confusion between the two likely only in captivity or with escapes and feral populations, chiefly in Britain and western Europe. **In flight:** A medium-sized duck, with relatively long, broad tail and heavy-looking head which is constantly moved when on the wing. Springs teal-like when flushed, and holds head up and bill down when underway. General appearance is of a dark duck with contrasting white belly and narrow white trailing edge to secondaries, both upperwing and underwing appearing otherwise dark. Male's head and neck pattern, especially the white throat, may be apparent in flight at reasonable ranges, but in female-like plumages only marginally separable from flying Mandarin by darker upperparts and broader white eye-patch; at distance, size and white belly recall female American Wigeon (72), but tail square, not pointed, and has darker, almost uniform grey upperwing and underwing with white trailing edge, and bulkier, less 'waisted', head and neck.

VOICE Relatively silent. When flushed, female utters a drawn-out, rising squeal, 'oo-eek'. Other female calls include a sharp 'cr-r-ek, cr-r-ek' of alarm. Male has a thin, high, rising 'jeeeeee'.

DESCRIPTION Sexually dimorphic. **Adult male breeding:** Head and neck crested and blackish, highly glossed green and purple, with thin white line along sides of crown from bill to nape and another from below eye to nape, bordering crest. Throat and foreneck white, with two white extensions, one towards eye, the other forming a semi-collar. Lower neck and breast rich dark chestnut, freckled whitish. White vertical stripe on side of breast, bordered blackish posteriorly. Flanks buff, with black and white upper and rear border. Centre of underparts white. Upperparts, including tail and most of upperwing, blackish with iridescent blue and green gloss. Tips of secondaries and outer webs of primaries white. Underwing appears uniformly dark, but is intensely mottled black and white on the coverts. **Adult male eclipse:** June to September. Resembles female, but bill colour often separates male; eye-patch smaller, throat whiter, and upperparts more highly glossed, showing vestiges of breeding head pattern. **Adult female:** Rear of head and nape slightly crested. Chiefly greyish-brown, with greyer head and neck. Narrow white line around bill-base. Large white patch around eye. Chin and throat white. Breast and flanks mottled with whitish feather centres, becoming clear whitish on centre of belly and ventral region. Upperwing greyish-brown, with iridescent bluish-purple speculum and gloss to greater and median coverts; secondaries and primaries tipped white. Underwing as male. **Juvenile:** Resembles female, but duller, with eye-patch ill-defined; underparts less mottled, more streaked with pale buffish; centre of underparts less clearly whitish, being mottled and streaked brownish. Juvenile males soon start to show head pattern of breeding male.

BARE PARTS Adult male: Bill red, becoming paler and whiter over dorsal and subterminal area; nail and culmen ridge black; bright yellow line around very base of bill. In eclipse, bill duller, on some individuals like female, but normally showing vestiges of colourful pattern. Legs and feet yellow. Iris red, with red orbital ring. **Adult female:** Bill dark grey, often with paler subterminal area; nail black. Legs and feet dull greyish-yellow. Iris dark brown, with narrow yellow orbital ring. **Juvenile:** Similar to female, but legs still duller and orbital ring even less distinct. Adult bill coloration of males develops during first winter.

MEASUREMENTS Males typically larger than females. **Male:** Wing 250-285, tarsus 34-35, bill 33-35, mean weight 680. **Female:** Wing 208-230, bill 30-33, mean weight 539.

GEOGRAPHICAL VARIATION None.

HABITS Usually found in small parties by wooded lakes and rivers; larger concentrations form at favoured feeding locations in winter, but rarely exceed a few hundred birds. Breeding season February to May, a little later in more northern parts of range. Pairs formed in winter quarters, settling down to breed soon after arrival on breeding grounds. Not strongly territorial; several nests may be in reasonably close proximity if suitable holes available. Nest site invariably a tree hole or nestbox. Feeds primarily by dabbling, but also grazes on waterside banks. Most active early morning and evening, loafing during most of day on partially-submerged branches and branches overhanging water. Roosts on open water at night. Gait waddling on relatively short legs. Flight fast and agile, particularly when flying between trees. Swims buoyantly with prominent tail well cocked, often up-ending but rarely diving.

HABITAT Freshwater ponds, lakes and slow-flowing rivers in well-wooded country. In winter may be found in more open country, such as wet ricefields, but rarely on coastal brackish marshes.

DISTRIBUTION Widespread in North America, although found largely in two separate populations. Western population breeds in British Columbia, Washington, Oregon and California. Eastern population breeds over central and eastern North America, north to Manitoba and New Brunswick and south to eastern Texas and Cuba, sparingly to south Texas. Both populations winter over southern portions of their respective breeding ranges, with small numbers southwards to central Mexico. Rarely recorded elsewhere in West Indies (Jamaica and the Bahamas), rare but regular in winter on Bermuda, and vagrants have occurred in southeast Alaska and the Azores. Genuine vagrants suspected in western Europe, but popularity in collections and frequency of escapes prevent certainty. Attempts at establishing feral populations in Europe seem to have failed, although has become temporarily established from

Main features helpful in separating female and non-breeding Mandarin and Wood Duck

Mandarin

Wood Duck

time to time in Britain and Germany.

POPULATION After considerable decline earlier in present century, has undergone tremendous increase in recent decades, as result of protection, some re-introductions and an extensive programme of nestbox erection. Now considered to be the most numerous breeding duck in eastern USA, with a population estimated at well over 1 million birds by 1976. Despite spectacular comeback, has declined in some southern regions with destruction of forest habitat and drainage of swamps.

REFERENCES Holt (1984), Johnsgard (1978), Terres (1980).

64 MANDARIN   Plate 19
Aix galericulata

Males of this species are arguably the most beautiful of all wildfowl. A dramatic decline in recent years suggests that the British feral population may well be an important factor in maintaining this beautiful duck as a wild bird.

FIELD IDENTIFICATION Length 41-49 cm (16-19 in). **At rest:** Medium-sized duck of lakes and rivers in wooded districts. Breeding male unmistakable, with its large head, conspicuous orange 'sails', whitish head-band and red bill defying a brief description. Females and juveniles superficially resemble those of Wood Duck (63); although native ranges do not overlap, escapes of either species frequent. Generally female Mandarin is paler and greyer overall than Wood Duck, with fine hair-like striations on sides of head and neck; Wood Duck is darker on head and upperparts than Mandarin, with distinctly glossy wing-coverts. On female Mandarin the eye-patch is narrower, merely an eye-ring rather than a patch, with a narrow white line extending backwards from it towards nape; some Wood Ducks, however, can have a very restricted eye-patch, with indications of such an eye-line, but on Wood Duck head is darker overall, which highlights the prominence of its eye-patch. The bill of female Mandarin has a pale nail (blackish in Wood Duck). Whereas on female Mandarin the wing-coverts are dull brown, with a greenish-blue gloss confined to the speculum, the glossy speculum is more bluish-purple on Wood Duck and the gloss extends to cover the greater and median coverts; additionally Wood Duck has indistinct black tips to the wing-coverts (plain on Mandarin). Finer points of distinction include the relatively shorter legs and longer body, more sloping forehead and more V-shaped junction of feathering and skin at base of bill of Wood Duck. Confusion with any other species is unlikely, although distant males moulting out of eclipse in autumn can show a general greyish-brown appearance, with prominent white band on sides of head behind eye suggesting Garganey (101). **In flight:** Medium-sized duck, with clear whitish belly, and uniformly dark upperparts and underwings contrasting with white trailing edge to secondaries. Head pattern of male, with very pale sides of head and dark crown, may be prominent in flight, although 'sails' are depressed along base of wing, not carried erect as is sometimes depicted.

Females very similar to those of Wood Duck and not safely distinguishable, although on Mandarin underwing uniformly darker and upperparts a little paler; given a good view, it may be possible to discern the narrow white eye-ring and eye-line in contrast to the larger patch of a Wood Duck. Size and prominent white belly suggest female Wigeon (71), but Mandarin has stockier head and neck and broad, square tail, more uniform upperwings and underwings, and white trailing edge to secondaries.

VOICE Relatively silent, except when displaying. Male has several short whistling calls in display and sometimes gives a brief, sharp, whistled 'hwick' in flight. Female has several low, clucking notes, rarely given unless attending young or in display.

DESCRIPTION Sexually dimorphic. **Adult male breeding:** Head with tufted crest and long ruff of feathers around sides of head. Forehead and crown dark, with copper, purple and green reflections. Wide white, buff-washed band from base of bill across sides of head. Lower sides of head and ear-coverts orange-rufous, feathers elongated. Breast maroon, with black and white vertical bands at rear. Flanks buff, bordered by line of black and white along upper and rear edge. Centre of underparts, from undertail-coverts to lower breast, white. Most of upperparts dark olive-brown. Tertials elongated into remarkable orange 'sails'. Upperwing-coverts brown; secondaries iridescent green, with white tips; primaries blackish, glossed bluish-green, with white on outer webs. Underwing dark greyish-brown. **Adult male eclipse:** June to September. Resembles female, but easily distinguished by bill colour. Plumage duller below, less spotted, eye markings less defined. **Adult female:** Resembles female Wood Duck; differences summarised in Field Identification section above. In summer, whitish spotting on underparts and line around bill-base less defined; recalls eclipse male, apart from bill coloration. **Juvenile:** Resembles female, but duller, with facial pattern less distinct and underparts more streaked, less spotted; white on belly, with small dark streaks and spots. Adult plumage attained during first winter.

BARE PARTS Male: Bill red, with whitish nail, at all seasons. Legs and feet yellowish. Iris dark brown. **Female and juvenile:** Bill greyish-brown with whitish nail, often tinged fleshy-yellow on culmen, rarely all fleshy-pink in female. Legs and feet dingy yellowish. Iris dark brown.

MEASUREMENTS Males typically larger than females. **Male:** Wing 226-242, tarsus 36-40, bill 27-31, mean weight 628. **Female:** Wing 215-234, tarsus 35-38, bill 27-30, mean weight 512.

GEOGRAPHICAL VARIATION None.

HABITS Usually in pairs or small parties by secluded wooded lakes and rivers; larger gatherings form in autumn and winter. Pair-formation begins in autumn and winter gatherings, with much display activity. Breeding season chiefly mid April to July. Nest site normally a tree hole, rarely on ground under bushes or logs. Spends most of daytime loafing under hanging waterside vegetation or on partially-submerged branches. Most active in early mornings and evenings. Feeds by picking food from water surface or while walking along banks, rarely dives. Flight action fast and agile, especially when negotiating trees, dropping almost vertically on to small woodland ponds. In its native Asia is relatively shy and wary, but feral populations often remarkably confiding. Mixes little with other species, no doubt partly because of specialised habitat. Long known as an ornamental species and well known as a favoured subject of Chinese and Japanese Art, it remains very popular in captivity and frequently escapes, with feral populations now well established in Britain.

HABITAT In Asia breeds by forested rivers and lakes, with dense tree and shrub cover along banks; chiefly in lowlands but also in valleys up to 1500 m, even by fast-flowing rivers. In winter, also in flooded ricefields, marshes and lowland, more open rivers, rarely on estuaries or brackish lagoons. In Britain chiefly on parkland lakes, water-meadows and farmland with adjacent broad-leaved woodlands.

DISTRIBUTION Formerly widespread in eastern Asia, in extreme eastern Soviet Union, northern China and Japan, but population now much fragmented and may even be endangered. Breeding range in eastern Siberia centred on valleys of Amur-Ussuri river complex, formerly possibly on Sakhalin and Kuril Islands. In China, breeds locally in the northeast in provinces of Heilungkiang and eastern Kurin, and perhaps still in Hopeh. Japan's population is mostly in Hokkaido. Chiefly a summer visitor to northern breeding areas, wintering in lowland eastern China from Chekiang to northern Kwangtung and over southern Japan. Rarely recorded away from these areas, but has occurred west to Kansu and eastern Szechwan in China and south to Taiwan and Ryukyu Islands. Vagrants also recorded in northeastern India, northern Burma and Hong Kong. Feral population in Britain now well established, chiefly in southern England. Escapes recorded widely in Europe and North America, but feral populations seem not yet to have become established elsewhere.

POPULATION Huge numbers have been exported from China in the past, and this, coupled with large-scale destruction of their forest habitats in eastern Asia, has severely depleted the wild population. Japan has the main stronghold, recently estimated at some 4,500 to 5,000 pairs, but the Chinese population is thought to be fewer than 1,000 pairs; the Soviet Union population is about 600 pairs, following a considerable decline associated with destruction of hollow trees. The British feral population is now thought to be in the region of 1,000 pairs and is clearly significantly important. An export ban was imposed by the Chinese government in 1975.

REFERENCES Davies (1985), FESC (1985), Holt (1984), Savage (1952).

65 CRESTED DUCK   Plate 22
Lophonetta specularioides

Peculiar dabbling duck of both highland lakes and the seashore of South America and the Falkland Islands. The taxonomic position of this bird is rather debatable, some authorities considering it closer to the shelducks.

FIELD IDENTIFICATION Length 51-61 cm (20-24 in). **At rest:** A long-bodied, long-tailed, loosely-crested, rather elegant duck with plain buffish-brown appearance and somewhat contrasting dusky band through yellow eye and darker wing feathers and tail. The body plumage is weakly mottled with paler buff, creating an appearance superficially like that of smaller Marbled Duck (111) of southern Europe and Asia. Plumage unlike that of any other duck in South America. Yellow-billed Pintail (96) and female Northern Pintail (95) are more mottled and scalloped with dark markings, have dark eyes, lack an obvious eye-patch and are rather smaller, the former showing conspicuous yellow on bill. **In flight:** Distinctive shape, with relatively long, but bulky body, long neck and tail, and rather featureless body plumage. The upperwing pattern shows a bronze-copper speculum and a broad white trailing edge to the secondaries, while the underwing is dark with conspicuous white axillaries and central coverts. The dark tail contrasts quite strongly with the paler buff uppertail-coverts in flight.

VOICE Fairly vocal. Male utters a wheezy whistled 'sheeeoo'; female has a variety of low, often-repeated quacking notes, some quite nasal and grating.

DESCRIPTION All plumages similar. Nominate race described. **Adult:** Head and neck loosely crested at rear, light greyish-brown. Dusky band surrounding eye, tapering and diffusing towards nape. Throat and foreneck becoming paler and whiter. Breast and almost entire underparts pale greyish-brown, with darker feather centres, most prominent on flanks; the breast is washed fulvous-brown. Tail and undertail-coverts blackish. Most of upperparts a little darker greyish-brown than underparts, paler on uppertail-coverts. Wing-coverts earth-brown; secondaries iridescent bronze and green, with black subterminal band and wide white trailing edge. Primaries a little darker brown. Underwing dark, with white axillaries, centre to underwing and trailing edge. Female similar to male, but smaller, and crest is rather shorter. **Juvenile:** Very much as adult, but crest shorter, belly whiter and face browner.

BARE PARTS All plumages and races: Bill, legs and feet dark grey. Iris yellowish (*alticola*) to orange-red (nominate).

MEASUREMENTS Males typically larger than females. Nominate *specularioides*: **Male:** Wing 268-277, tarsus 46-50, bill 43-46, mean weight ca. 1100. **Female:** Wing 250-257, tarsus 43-45, bill 40-44, mean weight ca. 900. Race *alticola*: **Male:** Wing 290-310, tarsus 49-52, bill 49-51. **Female:** Wing 278-290, tarsus 44-46, bill 45-48.

GEOGRAPHICAL VARIATION Two races recognised. Nominate form, of coasts and inland lakes from Talca in Chile and Mendoza in Argentina southwards to Tierra del Fuego and the Falkland Islands, is described above. Larger race *alticola* breeds by high Andean lakes from southern Peru and Bolivia south to northern Chile and northern Argentina; in addition to being larger, its underparts are almost unspotted and the speculum is pinker than in the nominate race.

HABITS Coastal gatherings may be quite considerable in the non-breeding season, sometimes as many as a few hundred congregating at favoured spots where freshwater streams run into the sea. Otherwise, pairs and small parties are found by shores of high lakes in the puna zone of the Andes, or feeding among inshore waters and coastal lagoons. Breeding season varied, being either irregular or prolonged, at least in the Falkland Islands, where species is often double-brooded, although most breed there from September to November; breeds somewhat later in Tierra del Fuego, probably December to February; few data from elsewhere. The nest is placed by shores of lakes, or on small islets, usually hidden in grass clumps. The species is aggressive and strongly territorial when breeding. Feeds chiefly on invertebrates by dabbling, both when swimming and by walking in shallow water, often with head and neck almost totally submerged; when feeding in deeper water, has also been seen to dive occasionally.

HABITAT Brackish and saline lakes in puna zone of the Andes; also coastal lagoons and freshwater ponds, and inshore coastal waters.

DISTRIBUTION See Geographical Variation for distribution of races. Widespread resident and partial migrant over southern South America and the Falkland Islands. Breeds in the Andes, from Huanuco Province of Peru southwards through Chile to Cape Horn, and in the highlands of Bolivia and Argentina south to Tierra del Fuego; also along Argentine coast north to Chubut. There is also an isolated population on the Falkland Islands. In winter, birds from higher-altitude lakes disperse towards coastal waters, as far north as Buenos Aires Province.

POPULATION Few data. Seems to be relatively common and widespread over most of its range, and its populations are under no apparent threat.

REFERENCES Johnsgard (1978).

GENUS *NETTAPUS* (PYGMY GEESE)

Three species of tiny Old World dabbling ducks of tropical freshwater wetlands. They are the smallest of all wildfowl and are true ducks, being only relatively distantly related to the geese, despite their bills, which bear a superficial resemblance to those of the smaller species of *Branta* geese. All three have a very short bill, a rounded head and short legs, the latter not very useful for easy walking but allowing them to perch readily on branches overhanging water. All species normally nest in tree holes and have a close attachment to water-lilies, feeding on their flowers and seeds.

66 GREEN PYGMY GOOSE   Plate 20
Nettapus pulchellus

The headquarters of this little duck are the tropical freshwater lagoons of northern Australia and southern New Guinea.

FIELD IDENTIFICATION Length 32-36 cm (13-14 in). **At rest:** A distinctive little duck, with white cheeks contrasting with dark head, neck and upperparts, and whitish underparts, the latter heavily but narrowly barred along the flanks, which may appear merely pale grey at long distance. Unlikely to be confused with any other species, although range overlaps with that of Cotton Pygmy Goose (67), in which the sexes are strongly dimorphic, the male having only very cap dark, with most of head and neck white and flanks unbarred. Female Green is duller than male, although still with much more dark on crown and neck than female Cotton, which has pale greyish-white face and neck, a dark line through the eye and brownish upperparts; distinctions, however, may be difficult to interpret at long range on such tiny birds. **In flight:** A small and agile duck, with dark head, neck and upperparts contrasting with white secondaries on both upperwing and underwing; from below, the dark neck and greyish underwing contrast with whitish body and secondaries. The wing pattern is similar in both sexes and recalls that of much larger Maned Duck (109). Cotton Pygmy Goose wing pattern differs between the sexes, neither being like Green: male has huge white wing-band extending across full length of primaries and secondaries, whereas female is brownish above with narrow white trailing edge to secondaries.

VOICE Calls freely, both in flight and when on the water. Male has a shrill whistle, 'pee-whit', while the whistle of the female is a more mellow 'pee-yew'. Both calls are remarkably similar to those of Pink-eared Duck (45).

DESCRIPTION All plumages similar. Limited seasonal variation. **Adult male:** Crown to below eye level, neck and most of upperparts dark green, being most iridescent on upperparts, and finely barred brown on crown and nape. Upper back and lower mantle grey, with dark bars, like breast. Throat and sides of head white. Breast, flanks and ventral region pale grey, finely scalloped with dark green bars. Lower breast and belly white. Undertail-coverts blackish. Upperwing-coverts dark green; primaries blackish; secondaries white. Underwing greyish, with whiter secondaries. In eclipse, duller, with white face freckled with grey and foreneck mottled grey and white like female, but frequency of such plumage uncertain; differs from female only in having markings of neck unevenly mottled, less evenly barred. **Adult female:** Similar to male, but a little duller, with foreneck whitish, barred dark green, and white face having dusky flecking. **Juvenile:** Both sexes similar to female, but white of face heavily mottled with dark brown. Male begins to attain dark green foreneck at about two months of age, and is soon indistinguishable from adult.

BARE PARTS All plumages: Bill dark grey, with pinkish underside and tip. Legs and feet dark grey. Iris dark brown.

MEASUREMENTS Males average slightly larger than females. Wing 150-180 (mean: male 172, female 169); tarsus 25-28; bill 21-29; mean weight of male 310, of female 304.

GEOGRAPHICAL VARIATION None.

HABITS During the dry season gatherings of a few hundred birds may be formed, but the species is normally found in small parties among floating emergent vegetation. At the onset of the wet season, pairs break away from the small flocks to locate suitable nest holes, the pair-bond possibly being permanent. Breeds in the wet season, from

January to March in northern Australia. Nest sites are invariably in holes in waterside trees. Spends most of the time on clear water, among water-lilies, feeding extensively on their seeds and flowers by picking food from water surface or from the growing plants. Also dabbles in shallows at water's edge, and occasionally dives in Coot-like fashion with a strong forward-jump. Pairs have small feeding territories which may be vigorously defended. Rests quietly on water among water-lilies, or clambers out onto partially-submerged branches just above water line. Rarely leaves water, however, being very ungainly on land owing to extremely short legs.

HABITAT Freshwater lakes and lagoons with clear still water and extensive floating vegetation; in the wet season, may disperse to temporary floodwater such as ricefields.

DISTRIBUTION Chiefly resident, although somewhat dispersive in the wet season, retreating back to areas of permanent water during the dry season. Breeding range includes southern New Guinea and tropical northern Australia. In New Guinea, it is found primarily in the coastal and lowland swamps surrounding the Gulf of Papua, from Port Moresby to Lake Murray. Vagrants have been recorded from the north coast of New Guinea and from Sulawesi, Buru, Ambon, Tanimbar and Seram. In northern Australia, along tropical coastal lowlands from Broome (Western Australia) to Rockhampton (Queensland), with greatest concentrations between Darwin and Fitzroy River. During wet season, disperses far less than many other Australian species, although vagrants have occurred in New South Wales and southwestern Western Australia.

POPULATION No estimates have been made, although it is locally abundant in certain key areas, particularly in New Guinea, and appears to be under no obvious threat.

REFERENCES Frith (1967).

67 COTTON PYGMY GOOSE   Plate 20
Nettapus coromandelianus

Alternative names: Cotton Teal, White Pygmy Goose

Widespread throughout tropical Asia, and also occurs locally in northeastern Australia. The smallest of all wildfowl.

FIELD IDENTIFICATION Length 30-37 cm (12-14 in). **At rest:** Unlike the last species, is strongly sexually dimorphic. Males are unmistakable, being very white on head, neck and underparts, with contrasting dark upperparts, neat dark centre to crown and hindneck and dark breast-band. Plumage pattern superficially similar to much larger Comb Duck (37) and Radjah Shelduck (44), but confusion hardly possible. Duller and browner female and eclipse male have head, neck and underparts washed with greyish-brown, although much paler on head and neck, and have a narrow dark line through the eye; although duller, the tiny size and very small bill are quite distinctive, but distant birds can be confused with female Green Pgymy Goose (66) over part of species' range, unless head pattern discernible. **In flight:** Small and very agile on the wing, the male's

gleaming white head and neck and underparts contrasting with its dark upperparts and huge white wing-band, which extends over full length of primaries and secondaries, being broadest on primaries. Females conspicuously different, with dull brownish upperparts and only narrow white trailing edge to the secondaries. Underwing and upperwing patterns are similar.

VOICE Calls both when on water and in flight. Typical call of male a sharp, staccato cackle, 'car-car-carawak' or 'quack, quack-quackyduck', uttered chiefly in flight. Female utters a weak quack.

DESCRIPTION Sexually dimorphic. Male seasonally variable. Nominate race described. **Adult male breeding:** Head, neck and underparts chiefly white. Centre of crown and hindneck black. Narrow black band encircles body at breast. Flanks washed grey, finely mottled brown towards rear flanks. Undertail-coverts blackish. Most of upperparts blackish, highly glossed green. Uppertail-coverts whitish, weakly mottled dark. Tail black. Upperwing-coverts glossy greenish-black. Secondaries and primaries white, with black tips and bases. Underwing as upperwing, but duller. **Adult male eclipse:** As female, but upperparts darker, face and foreneck whiter and retains male wing pattern. **Adult female:** Crown, hindneck and line through eye dark greyish-brown; upperparts dark greyish-brown, with weak green gloss. Most of head, neck and underparts whitish, washed greyish-brown, and finely mottled with dark, particularly on sides of breast. Upperwing dark greyish-brown, with narrow white tips to secondaries; underwing similar. **Juvenile:** Resembles female, but mottling on underparts more prominent, eye-line broader and completely lacks green gloss to upperparts. Young male shows extensive white in wing even from an early age, and is similar to adult by first summer.

BARE PARTS Male: Bill blackish. Legs and feet blackish. Iris red. **Female and juvenile:** Bill brownish-grey, with yellower undersurface. Legs and feet dark brownish-grey. Iris brown.

MEASUREMENTS Nominate *coromandelianus*: Wing of male 152-167, of female 150-153; tarsus 23-25; bill 20-24; weight of male ca. 255-312, of female ca. 185-255. Race *albipennis*: Wing of male 172-188, of female 161-186; bill 23-26; mean weight of male 403, of female 380.

GEOGRAPHICAL VARIATION Two races recognised: race *albipennis* from Australia, and the smaller, but otherwise similar nominate race over the remainder of the species' range.

HABITS Frequents still freshwater lakes and ponds in pairs and small parties, with larger gatherings forming outside breeding season, sometimes reaching a few hundred birds. With such a wide distribution, the breeding season is somewhat varied, depending very much on the timing of the local rainy season. Birds nest from February to August in Sri Lanka, from June to September in northern India and from January to March in Australia. Nests are almost invariably in tree holes close to water, rarely even in buildings. Parties feed in much the same way as Green Pygmy Geese, swimming buoyantly on the surface, picking food from the water in Coot-like fashion and occasionally diving. Less dependent on presence of water-lilies than the other two pygmy geese. Avoids coming on to land, but often scrambles out of water on to projecting branches and stumps, although perhaps less inclined to do so than is Green Pygmy Goose. Generally fairly approachable compared with many other ducks, at least in India, where it is usually unmolested. Rises swiftly from water when flushed, although generally flies fairly low with rapid, shallow and fluttering wingbeats and not for any great distance (although some populations migratory or dispersive).

HABITAT Freshwater lakes and pools with emergent and floating vegetation.

DISTRIBUTION Widespread throughout tropical southeast Asia, from almost whole of the Indian subcontinent (generally absent from arid zones of Pakistan and western India) eastwards through Burma, north over lowland southern China to provinces of Szechwan and Hupeh. Range extends southwards over most of southeastern Asia to Malaysia, and in winter reaches the Philippines (Luzon), Borneo, Sumatra, Java, Sulawesi and northern New Guinea. Although basically resident, it is somewhat dispersive in the wet season and northernmost Chinese birds move south for the winter. Strangely, it occurs almost annually in Bahrain and Oman, with most records between November and May. Vagrants have wandered west to Afghanistan, Iran and Iraq, and north and east to Hopeh (China), Taiwan and Hong Kong. Isolated Australian race *albipennis* chiefly a local resident in tropical wetlands of coastal Queensland from Cape Melville to Rockhampton; formerly south also to northeast New South Wales, where now only an irregular visitor.

POPULATION Nominate race widespread and abundant, although local and sparse in southeast Asia and the islands. Australian race not numerous, and range has contracted somewhat this century and is further threatened by increasing wetland-drainage schemes; its population was estimated at 1,500 individuals in the early 1960s and has no doubt declined since then.

REFERENCES Ali and Ripley (1968), Frith (1967), RAOU (1984).

68 AFRICAN PYGMY GOOSE   Plate 20
Nettapus auritus

Africa's smallest duck; although widespread throughout tropical Africa, it is most abundant in southern regions.

FIELD IDENTIFICATION Length 30-33 cm (12-13 in). **At rest:** Very small duck of well-vegetated freshwater lakes and swamps. Sexually dimorphic. Males distinctive with their dark upperparts, rufous underparts, yellowish bill and white face and foreneck. Females duller, but easily distinguished from other small African ducks by their rufous underparts contrasting with pale sides of head and neck. Easily overlooked among water-lilies, small parties often sitting motionless among the vegetation during daytime. **In flight:** Small and dark, with striking white belly and face when on the wing. Dark upperwing and underwing pattern relieved by large white patch on the secondaries, giving an appearance

shared by no other small African duck, although Hottentot Teal (100) has narrower white band along secondary tips.

VOICE Relatively silent. Male has soft, twittering, whistled 'choo-choo-pee-wee'. Female has merely a weak quack.

DESCRIPTION Sexually dimorphic. Male seems to be seasonally variable, but documentation poor. **Adult male:** Forehead, front and sides of head, throat and foreneck white. Crown and hindneck metallic green. Sides of upper neck pale green in form of large, dark-bordered, oval patch. Lower foreneck, breast and flanks rufous-chestnut, the breast often finely dark-barred. Centre of underparts white. Tail and ventral region blackish. Most of upperparts glossy dark green. Upperwing blackish-green, with white tips to greater coverts and outer webs of secondaries forming large white area. Underwing very dark. It seems that for a short time after breeding males do attain an eclipse plumage which resembles that of female, although bill colour differs. **Adult female:** Crown and hindneck dull blackish. Sides of head and neck whitish, mottled extensively with dusky-grey, with narrow dark eye-line. Body and wing plumage patterns similar to those of male, but a little duller overall. **Juvenile:** Similar to female, but head and neck more diffusely marked, with stronger dark eye-line, and breast and flanks paler, more buffish-rufous. Resemble adults after first moult.

BARE PARTS Male: Bill rich yellow with black nail. Legs and feet dark grey. Iris brownish to reddish. **Female and juvenile:** Bill greyish-yellow on female, duskier on juveniles, lacking pronounced black nail of adult male, but bill coloration soon develops on young males. Legs and feet dark grey. Iris brown.

MEASUREMENTS Males average a little larger than females. Wing of male 150-165, of female 142-158; tarsus 25-28; bill 23-27; mean weight of male 285, of female 260.

GEOGRAPHICAL VARIATION None.

HABITS Usually in small parties among floating emergent vegetation on quiet pools and lakesides, but very large concentrations form in certain areas during dry season or for moult gatherings, e.g. at Okavango delta (Botswana). Breeding season varies over huge range, being chiefly October-December in South Africa, January-February in Zambia and Zimbabwe, June-October in Uganda and July-August in Nigeria, depending largely on local wet season. Nests normally in tree holes, but also reported from holes in cliffs, termite mounds, and even in huge stick nest of Hamerkop and roof thatch of an occupied native hut. Feeds chiefly in evening and early morning, swimming buoyantly while picking food from water surface or emergent plants and also by diving. Avoids coming on to land, but perches readily on partially-submerged branches or branches overhanging water. Spends long periods sitting quietly among vegetation during most of day. Not normally shy and wary, unless molested. When flushed, rises quickly, usually flying low over surface, and soon resettles. Somewhat nomadic, moving with seasonal rains, but not truly migratory.

HABITAT Freshwater lakes and pools, both permanent and temporary, preferring deep water with emergent vegetation. Also locally on more open lakes and coastal lagoons, rarely on estuaries.

DISTRIBUTION Widespread over most of tropical Africa and Madagascar, although absent from more arid regions of southwest Africa. Resident and seasonally dispersive or nomadic. Range extends north to Senegal, Chad and Ethiopia, but not recorded from Palaearctic Africa. In East Africa it is decidedly local and sparse, becoming commoner in Uganda and Tanzania. Largest gatherings form in non-breeding season in Okavango delta region of Botswana from July to January, with smaller concentrations elsewhere.

POPULATION Although widespread, is decidedly local over much of its range. Few population estimates have been made, apart from Okavango flocks, which may number as many as 15,000 individuals. It is unlikely that there is any threat to numbers of this attractive little duck.

REFERENCES Brown *et al.* (1982), Douthwaite (1980).

69 SALVADORI'S DUCK   Plate 34
Salvadorina waigiuensis
Alternative name: Salvadori's Teal

Endemic to the highlands of New Guinea, this strange duck is worthy of a genus of its own. It is probably most closely allied to the Torrent Duck (55) and better placed with them in the shelduck tribe.

FIELD IDENTIFICATION Length 38-43 cm (15-17 in). **At rest:** Sexes similar. A small, relatively long-tailed, dark greyish duck, with striking yellow or pinkish bill, of the highland rivers and streams of New Guinea. The dark greyish plumage is distinctly barred on both the upperparts and the underparts, being relieved only by the uniformly darker head, which contrasts with pale, almost unmarked breast. A bird of fast-flowing rivers, it is often seen perched on boulders in much the same manner as Torrent Duck. Swims with peculiar jerking head motion, and when alarmed cocks rather long tail well up, exposing the whitish undertail-coverts. Unlikely to be confused with any other species within its range, which overlaps only with that of Pacific Black Duck (91). **In flight:** Distinctive shape: a rather slim brownish duck, with relatively long tail and short wings. The upperwing is dark brown, with a dark speculum glossed green and bordered fore and aft with white bands. The pale underwing shows some contrast with the whiter trailing edge to the secondaries. Flight low and rapid, following course of rivers and streams.

VOICE Relatively silent. Male has a low whistle, female a disyllabic croaky quacking note.

DESCRIPTION All plumages similar. **Adult:** Head and neck greyish-black, with indistinct narrow paler feather fringes. Breast and underparts buffish-white, with individually variable dark spotting; flanks and sides of ventral region prominently barred blackish-brown and whitish. Upperparts blackish, slightly glossed green, with whitish feather tips forming bars. Tail long and graduated, sooty-brown, barred

whitish. Upperwing-coverts dark greyish-brown, with pale feather fringes. Greater coverts broadly tipped white. Secondaries bluish-black, glossed green towards body, broadly tipped white. Primaries blackish-brown, with faint white tips to innermost. Underwing whitish, mottled with brown on lesser coverts; greyer on flight feathers, with whitish trailing edge to secondaries. Some individuals darker than others, and a few melanistic birds reported (one had entire head and underparts brownish-black). **Juvenile:** Similar to adult, but duller and less clearly marked; bill and leg colours also differ.

BARE PARTS Adult: Bill bright yellow, at least at onset of breeding season, but in captivity often fleshy-yellow with dusky shading. Legs and feet brownish-yellow, with blackish patches on webs. Iris brown. **Juvenile:** Bill dark grey, paler on sides. Legs and feet pinkish-grey, with blackish line along front and rear of tarsus. Iris brown.

MEASUREMENTS Sexes similar. Wing 179-207 (mean: male 194, female 185); tarsus 35-43; bill 34-39; mean weight of male 462, of female 469.

GEOGRAPHICAL VARIATION None.

HABITS Little studied in the wild. Usually encountered in pairs or family parties beside fast-flowing rivers and upland lakes. Like Blue Duck (54), is strongly territorial, with pairs seemingly occupying a stretch of river throughout the year, indicating long-term pair-bonds. The breeding season is prolonged, from May to late September or even later, suggesting that species may even be double-brooded, but it is possible that timing of breeding varies according to altitude, to avoid nests being flooded out by flash floods in the rainy season. Nests are placed close to water, hidden among vegetation or even merely in the open atop a streamside boulder. Like both Blue and Torrent Ducks, is adept at living on fast-flowing and often turbulent rivers, negotiating rapids with ease, but feeding chiefly in slower-moving eddies and pools. Feeds both by dabbling and by diving, probing around boulders with extended neck. Frequently perches on mid-stream boulders, like Torrent Duck. Fairly wary, although older accounts suggest that it was formerly more confiding.

HABITAT Upland rivers and lakes, from 500 m to 4000 m, being most common around 3700 m. Favours rushing mountain rivers and streams, but also found on slower, almost sluggish, muddy streams and high-altitude alpine lakes.

DISTRIBUTION Resident throughout the mountains of mainland New Guinea; not recorded in the lowlands.

POPULATION Seems to be locally fairly common, but not an easy bird to locate owing to its territorial nature (it lives in pairs). Despite official protection in Papua New Guinea, the bird continues to be hunted by primitive tribal methods and the increasing use of guns for hunting has decreased the population in certain areas. Perhaps more serious threats are the introduction into its rivers of trout and other fish, which will no doubt compete with the species for its food supply, and disturbance created by human activities along the banks of the rivers.

REFERENCES Kear (1975).

GENUS *ANAS* (TYPICAL DABBLING DUCKS)

The largest genus of all ducks, geese and swans, covering a variety of chiefly closely-related species. Markedly sociable ducks of fresh and estuarine waters, all northern species being highly migratory, often wintering in huge, mixed concentrations. Most species feed principally by dabbling on surface of water or by grazing, and do not normally dive. Flight fast and agile, rising and alighting easily from and on water surface with no foot-pattering. Upperwing pattern and speculum colour are often an important identification aid. All species walk relatively easily on land.

SEXING Typically, these ducks have distinctive brightly-coloured breeding-male plumages, with all other plumages dull and mottled brownish. Soon after breeding, males moult into a plumage known as 'eclipse' which resembles that of females and juveniles, remaining dull and dowdy until late autumn and early winter. Generally, males may be expected to be in eclipse from May/June until October/November. This is not always the case, however, but it is true of all high-latitude species. Equatorial and most southern hemisphere species usually lack such eclipse plumage, but there are exceptions. In many isolated island populations the sexes are female-like, the males not attaining a bright plumage; even island races of widespread species tend to lack a bright male plumage. This is probably due to lack of competition with other similar species, most small islands supporting only one member of the genus. Eclipse males of several of the species can be distinguished from females if the wing pattern is seen, since they have much the same wing coloration as in breeding plumage.

AGEING Juveniles also closely resemble females. Because of the general similarity of plumages among female-like birds, observers should concentrate as much on overall shape and bare-part coloration as on plumage detail when identifying unfamiliar *Anas*. Wing pattern and tail shape are also important if the bird flies, as is the presence or absence of white on the belly. Ageing female-like ducks of this genus by plumage features alone can be difficult owing to individual variation. The shape of the tips of the tail feathers is useful in the hand, although impossible to discern under normal conditions in the field: juveniles have the tips of the tail feathers notched, with the bare feather shaft projecting; adults have the tail-tip complete, unless it is badly abraded (when feather wear is obvious).

HYBRIDS The majority of the members of this genus do not form long-term pair-bonds. Indeed, although displaying males compete among themselves before chasing the female, copulation is sometimes more of a rape than a refined ceremony, with several males chasing one female. With females of different species being so similar, even the birds make mistakes, and the occasional wild hybrid results. Males of such hybrids normally show obvious features of the parent species, but in some cases hybrids resemble quite a different species. Examples are hybrids between Chiloe Wigeon (73) and Wigeon (71), which closely resemble American Wigeon (72); those between Cinnamon Teal (103) and Northern Shoveler (107), which bear a strong resemblance to the Australasian Shoveler (106); and between Mallard (84) and Teal (77), which can recall Baikal Teal (76). Hybridisation is frequent in captivity and birds may escape, although occasional wild hybrids are also produced.

70 AFRICAN BLACK DUCK   Plate 21
Anas sparsa

Rather local dabbling duck of fast-flowing rivers in wooded valleys; most numerous in southern Africa, but nowhere common.

FIELD IDENTIFICATION Length 48-57 cm (19-22 in). **At rest:** Sexes similar. Large, blackish dabbling duck with conspicuous white scalloping on the upperparts, forming almost white bands on some individuals, and greyish-pink or dark grey bill. Likely to be confused only with Yellow-billed Duck (90), though latter has bright yellow bill sides, blackish (not yellowish) legs, lacks prominent scalloping on upperparts and is found in more open habitats. African Black Ducks are typically found feeding among rapids of fast-flowing streams in wooded country. **In flight:** Compared with Yellow-billed Duck, is more heavily built, rather longer-bodied and longer-tailed. Whitish marks often conspicuous on scapulars and tertials; upperwing blackish-brown, with greenish-blue speculum bordered fore and aft with black and white bands. Underwing dark, brownish, with contrasting white axillaries. Yellow-billed Duck has more extensive white on underwing, chiefly in the centre, but less prominent borders to the speculum above. When flushed, generally follows course of stream or river, flying low over surface and keeping in shelter of trees.

VOICE Relatively silent, although both sexes call on water and in flight. Male has a very quiet, often repeated, wheezy 'peep', while female utters a loud repeated quack. Both sexes call together when flushed, although male's call so quiet as to be almost inaudible.

DESCRIPTION All plumages similar. Nominate race described. **Adult:** Dark sooty-brown overall, becoming barred buffish on rear flanks and ventral region on some individuals, and occasionally with diffuse whitish neck-collar. Scapulars, tertials and uppertail-coverts boldly barred white and buff. Tail dark brown, with whitish or buffish bars. Upperwing-coverts and primaries sooty-brown, with broad subterminal white band along greater coverts, which are narrowly tipped black. Secondaries metallic bluish-green, with subterminal black bar and white tips. Underwing-coverts brown, with white tips, axillaries white; flight feathers dark below, with white trailing edge to secondaries. Female tends to be darker and blacker than male, but there is individual variation; when seen in pairs, female distinctly smaller than male. **Juvenile:** Similar to adult, but browner, with barred dusky, whitish belly; spotting on upperparts reduced or even almost absent, buff rather than white when present. Tail-bars buffish. Speculum dull. Close to adult by first summer, but retains whitish fringes to primary coverts into second year.

BARE PARTS Sexes similar. In all plumages, legs and feet yellowish-brown to orange-yellow and iris dark brown; bill dusky-grey on juveniles. Nominate *sparsa*: Bill slate-grey, nail and culmen patch black. Race *leucostigma*: Bill fleshy-pink, with black nail and culmen patch. Race *maclatchyi*: Bill chiefly blackish, with diffuse pinkish subterminal area and base.

MEASUREMENTS Males typically larger than females. Nominate and race *leucostigma*: Wing of male 245-272, of female 232-248; tarsus 36-45; bill 43-51; weight (few data, all females) 760-1077. Race *maclatchyi* (one male): Wing 220, bill 42, weight 1081.

GEOGRAPHICAL VARIATION Three races recognised, of which two are well differentiated. Nominate form, described above, is widespread over southern Africa north to Zimbabwe and Mozambique. Race *leucostigma*, which occupies the remainder of the range except Gabon, has buffer markings on the upperparts than the nominate form, a bluer speculum, and the pale areas of its bill are pinkish. Little-known and perhaps isolated race *maclatchyi*, confined to lowland forest of Gabon, is smaller and even darker than the others, with upperpart markings smaller and buffer; additionally, the bill pattern is blacker, with smaller fleshy-pink areas. The separation of the Gabon race is perhaps questionable; further research may prove it to be a clinal variation of *leucostigma*.

HABITS Relatively uncommon duck of shady African streams, almost always found in pairs or family parties. Pair-bonds long-term as with most riverine ducks, but atypical among the genus. Breeding season owing to extensive range, examples being July-December in the Cape, May-August in Zambia and January-July in Ethiopia. Unlike most other African ducks, chiefly a dry-season breeding species, no doubt owing to its dependence on upland streams rather than lowland floodwaters. Nest is situated on riverbanks among flood debris or bank vegetation. Feeds chiefly by up-ending and dabbling among boulders in lee of flowing water, immersing entire head and neck to obtain water weeds and often diving. Avoids coming on to land, but will dabble while standing on boulders and river edges. Feeds mostly early morning and evening, spending most of day loafing on shady streams. In some areas roosts on open lakes and dams, returning to feed on rivers and streams early in the morning. Not particularly wary, although easy to overlook on its secluded rivers, preferring to stay motionless by streamsides rather than immediately flying off when human intruder nearby.

HABITAT Streams and rivers in well-wooded hilly country, up to 4000 m, but also locally in more open country. Favours flowing water with stony riverbeds and streamside trees.

DISTRIBUTION See Geographical Variation for ranges of races. Resident over most of wooded hillier parts of tropical Africa, although everywhere somewhat local. Range includes Nigeria (rare),

Cameroon and Gabon. Apparently absent from much of tropical rainforest zone of Central Africa and arid regions of southwest Africa and Angola, but widespread in eastern and southern Africa from Ethiopia and eastern Sudan, south through Uganda, western Kenya and Zaire to the Cape in South Africa.

POPULATION Although widespread, this bird is no doubt much under-recorded owing to its territorial nature and secluded habitat. It appears to be commoner in southern Africa than elsewhere. Although population estimates are lacking, it is unlikely to be endangered. Forest destruction, however, has doubtless had some effect on local populations, and little indeed is known about the Gabon race.

REFERENCES Brown *et al.* (1982).

71 WIGEON   Plate 23
Anas penelope

Alternative names: Eurasian Wigeon, European Wigeon

An abundant duck throughout the northern hemisphere of the Old World, a counterpart of the American Wigeon (72).

FIELD IDENTIFICATION Length 45-51 cm (18-20 in). **At rest:** Medium-sized duck, smaller than Mallard (84), with relatively steep forecrown, pointed tail, and small grey, black-tipped bill. Male distinctive with its combination of chestnut head, pinkish breast, greyish body and black and white ventral region; the white wing-coverts often show when at rest, and at close quarters the yellowish crown centre may be visible, being seen most easily when bird viewed head-on. Males in eclipse are rich reddish-chestnut, with contrasting white belly and forewings. Females and juveniles are rather variable, from greyish-brown to rufous-brown, with a contrasting clear whitish belly; although finely mottled, they appear almost unmarked on the body compared with most others of the genus. This combination of relatively unmarked brownish body plumage, whitish belly, stocky shape, short bill, steep forehead and pointed tail is shared only by very similar American Wigeon, distinctions between the two being fully discussed under that species. Winter flocks often graze waterside grasslands in closely-packed congregations. **In flight:** A medium-sized duck, with narrow 'waisted' neck, slightly bulbous head and sharply-pointed tail and wingtips. Males easily distinguished by striking white forewing and belly patch. Females are brownish ducks, with contrasting clear whitish belly and slightly paler greyish-brown forewings than flight feathers; often, a narrow whitish line formed by pale tertial edges is apparent at the base of the wing. In all plumages, there is no obvious white trailing edge to secondaries and the underwing is pale greyish, with darker flight feathers and leading edge.

VOICE Most obvious call is the clear, piercing whistled 'wheeooo' of the male, freely uttered both in flight and when on the water. Female has a low growled 'krrr', often given when flushed.

DESCRIPTION Sexually dimorphic. Seasonally vari-

able. **Adult male breeding:** Head and neck reddish-brown, with buffish-yellow centre to crown and forehead. Usually a small green patch behind the eye. Breast greyish-pink. Centre of underparts, from lower breast downwards, and sides of rear body behind flanks clear white. Flanks finely vermiculated white and dark grey, appearing grey in the field. Undertail-coverts and sides of uppertail-coverts black; central uppertail-coverts and lower rump whitish, freckled grey. Tail pointed, blackish in centre, with paler outer feathers. Upperparts, including elongated pointed scapulars, vermiculated white and dark grey, appearing grey in the field. Elongated, pointed tertials grey, with black outer webs, bordered narrowly with white. Lesser upperwing-coverts grey; median and greater coverts white, latter tipped black; secondaries metallic green and black; primaries dark grey-brown. Underwing-coverts and axillaries whitish, freckled and shaded greyish-brown, most intensely on lesser and median coverts, with darker flight feathers. **Adult male eclipse:** Head, neck and body plumage pattern resembles that of female, but brown areas are dark rich chestnut-brown, especially on head, neck, breast and flanks. Wing as male breeding. **Adult female:** Individually variable, from overall grey-brown to medium rufous-brown, with combination of more rufous flanks and greyer head and neck on some individuals. Head, neck and breast light brown to medium-brown (grey-brown to rufous-brown), finely mottled darker, with mottling most intense on crown and hindneck. Flanks medium-brown, with paler feather fringes. Rear body and undertail-coverts whitish, with brown scalloping. Centre of underparts unmarked whitish. Almost entire upperparts, including elongated tertials, dark brown, with pale brown feather borders; tertials can be bordered narrowly with white, at least in autumn (as on American Wigeon). Rump and uppertail-coverts whitish, scalloped brown, darkest on uppertail-coverts. Upperwing-coverts brownish, with paler feather edges; greater coverts tipped narrowly with black and subterminally with white. Secondaries black and green, but less green and glossy than on male. Primaries dark grey-brown. Underwing as male. **Juvenile:** Resembles female, but white of belly weakly mottled dusky. Speculum dull brown on juvenile female, more glossy on male, and median coverts drabber than on adult female, lacking clear whitish edges. Ageing difficult in field, but by first winter young males as adult male breeding though forewing grey-brown, not white. Some first-summer males retain brown forewing.
BARE PARTS All plumages: Bill grey, paler and bluer on male, with black nostril, tip and cutting edge. Legs and feet blue-grey to dark grey. Iris brown.
MEASUREMENTS Males average larger than females. Wing 242-281 (mean: male 267, female 250); tarsus 35-44; bill 31-38; mean weight of male 720, of female 640.
GEOGRAPHICAL VARIATION None.
HABITS Highly gregarious outside breeding season, tending to form close aggregations, often of enormous numbers, on winter grounds. Pair-bonds gen-erally formed in winter quarters. Arrives on breeding grounds in April and May, nesting under shrubby cover, not far from water. Soon after breeding has commenced, males congregate into moulting flocks to go into eclipse. Arrives in winter quarters during late August and September. Feeds both by dabbling in shallow water and by grazing on waterside grasslands; often up-ends in deeper water, but less inclined to do so than others of genus. Grazes to far greater extent than do most other ducks, grazing flocks keeping close together in tight packs. Does not associate a great deal with other species, although on estuaries readily mixes with Brent Geese to feed on *Zostera* beds. In areas of high disturbance, often flies to roost in sheltered coastal bays. Swims buoyantly, with pointed tail held well up and head hunched onto breast when at ease. Flight fast, rising easily and suddenly from water or land, flocks keeping close together but forming lines when well underway; the shimmering white forewings of the males make identification of even distant flocks relatively easy. At times of low tide, loafs in close flocks close to water channels, their white bellies being very conspicuous compared with most other dabbling ducks.
HABITAT Breeds by small lakes and marshes in both open and sparsely-wooded country, generally avoiding open tundra, densely-forested and mountainous country. Winter haunts chiefly estuaries, estuarine grasslands and seasonally-flooded water-meadows; locally or in smaller numbers by freshwater lakes and in coastal bays.
DISTRIBUTION Widespread right across northern Europe and Asia, breeding from Iceland and northern Britain across Scandinavia and northern portions of the USSR to the Pacific coast; southern limits of breeding range include occasional nesting in southern Britain and eastern Europe south to Romania, and in Asia south to extreme northern China, Lake Baikal and Kazakhstan. Leaves breeding grounds in late summer to winter across almost whole of temperate zone of Europe and Asia, with concentrations in coastal areas of western Europe, the Mediterranean and Black Sea regions, Caspian Sea lowlands, Iraq and Iran east to southern and eastern China and Japan. Occurs in winter along the Nile valley as far south as the Sudan and Ethiopia, small numbers penetrating as far as Kenyan lakes and Tanzania; in West Africa, very small numbers south to Canary Islands, northern Nigeria and Chad. In Asia it is occasionally recorded south to the Arabian Peninsula, Persian Gulf, Sri Lanka, most of southeast Asia and the Philippines. Vagrants have occurred north to Greenland, Jan Mayen and Bear Island, Svalbard and Novaya Zemlya, and south to the Azores, Madeira, Saudi Arabia, Borneo, Sulawesi and some Pacific islands, including Hawaii. In North America it is an annual vagrant, being regular on Bermuda and on both Atlantic and Pacific coasts, rarer still inland, both in winter and spring, usually associating with American Wigeon; recorded from as far south as California and Texas and north to Alaska and Newfoundland. Vagrants also reported from several West Indian islands and Mexico.
POPULATION An abundant species, with an estim-

ated winter population in Europe and Mediter-ranean and Black Sea region of some million birds in 1975; large numbers also winter elsewhere in Asia. Clearly, this species is safe from any threats, although local populations have decreased through land-drainage schemes, particularly in Europe.
REFERENCES Cramp and Simmons (1977).

Upperwings (folded) of female northern wigeons: note paler greater coverts of American Wigeon

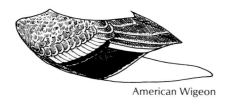

American Wigeon

Wigeon

72 AMERICAN WIGEON   Plate 23
Anas americana
Alternative name: Baldpate

American counterpart of the closely-related Wigeon (71) of the Old World.

FIELD IDENTIFICATION Length 45-56 cm (18-22 in).
At rest: Averages *slightly* larger, longer-necked, longer-billed and longer-tailed than Wigeon, but basically very similar in size and structure. Male distinctive, having whitish forehead and crown centre, dark green band extending back from eye over sides of head, with sides of head and neck greyish-white, intensely freckled with dark mottling. In the field, head and neck appear greyish, with dark eye-band and white crown. Breast and flanks pinkish-brown, contrasting with white and black ventral region and clear whitish belly. Upperparts brownish, with white wing-coverts. Male unlikely to be confused with male Wigeon, but, when identifying vagrants, occasional escaped hybrids between Wigeon and Chiloe Wigeon (73) should be considered (such birds have caused confusion in Britain in recent years): although superficially close to American Wigeon, the hybrids tend to have the whitish crown ending squarely on the upper forehead, not tapering to a point on rear crown or nape, and the dark green of the sides of the head is more extensive, covering most of sides of head and neck. Whether it would be possible to separate female-like hybrids is not known. American Wigeon

females, eclipse males and juveniles are super-ficially close to corresponding plumages of Wigeon, and odd vagrant individuals are difficult to pick out from among Wigeon flocks, although plumage of American Wigeon tends to show a quite striking contrast between the very greyish head, neck and upperparts and the distinctly bright, clear rusty-rufous flanks, and often breast; female Wigeon, however, is very variable and some individuals can approach American in general coloration, although they lack the relatively strong contrast. Having located a suspected American, close attention to detail of head and wing markings is essential to con-firm the identification. The subtle differences in shape between the two species are not always apparent, but may be marked in young males, remembering that juvenile males are slightly larger than females in both species. A diagnostic point is the colour of the axillaries and central underwing: clear white on American; whitish but closely marked with grey, appearing light grey, on Wigeon. Establishing this is difficult, unless bird flaps its wings (preferably repeatedly) or a good view is obtained as it rises from the water; in bright sunlight, even the central underwing of Wigeon can look markedly whitish. The forecrown and sides of head tend to be paler and the eye-patch darker on American, giving a more striking dark eye-patch, but Wigeon often has a concentration of dark mottles about eye. The mottling on the head and neck of American is densest on rear and sides, making front of head and foreneck appear paler; head and neck are more evenly patterned on Wigeon. In late winter and spring American Wigeon has whitish edges to exposed tertials (narrower and buffer on Wigeon), but autumn and early-winter Wigeons also have these fringes distinctly whitish. Careful observation of the folded wing should reveal the wide, whitish fringes to the median coverts and whitish outer webs to greater coverts of American Wigeon, showing as a distinct pale panel midway along the wing; on female Wigeon the wing appears more or less plain brown, apart from darker speculum. Eclipse male distinctly greyer on head and neck than eclipse male Wigeon. First-winter male may show a narrow black line around very base of bill, lacking on Wigeon. Although this identification pro-cess seems rather daunting and tedious, many indi-viduals may appear distinctly different when mixed with the other of the two species; proving the identification, however, may take more effort than the initial locating of a suspected bird. Confusion with other species is unlikely, although combination of greyish head and neck and warmer brown body plumage is suggested by juvenile Gadwall (75), which, however, has different bill and leg color-ation. Chiloe Wigeon often escapes from captivity in Europe, but is unlikely to be confused. **In flight:** General shape, structure and striking white belly much as Wigeon, but on both sexes white axillaries and central underwing offer stronger contrast with darker leading edge and flight feathers than on Wigeon. Upperwing of male has white forewing a little less extensive than on male Wigeon, but still readily obvious. Female's upperwing paler than on female Wigeon, with wider whitish fringes to coverts forming a distinctly whitish panel across central upperwing.

VOICE Similar to that of Wigeon, but whistle of male more throaty and a little weaker and less piercing.

DESCRIPTION Sexually dimorphic. Seasonally variable. **Adult male breeding:** Forehead and crown centre whitish. Head and neck whitish or buffish, intensely freckled black. Band through eye to upper neck and down hindneck blackish, glossed iridescent green. Breast, flanks and most of upperparts pinkish-brown, finely vermiculated dark grey, particularly on upperparts. Centre of underparts, from lower breast downwards, and sides of ventral region clear white. Undertail-coverts and sides of uppertail-coverts black. Rump, uppertail-coverts and tail similar to Wigeon. Upperwing similar to that of Wigeon, but lesser coverts brownish, giving less extensive area of white on upperwing. Less extensive green on speculum. Underwing pale grey, darker on lesser coverts and flight feathers; axillaries and median coverts white. **Adult male eclipse:** Resembles adult female, but upperparts blacker, breast and flanks richer and darker rufous; retains breeding-male wing pattern. **Adult female:** Less variable than female Wigeon, but superficially similar in plumage pattern. Distinctions discussed under Field Identification. **Juvenile:** Similar to female, but speculum dull and brown, male upperwing-coverts with wider whitish fringes than on young male Wigeon. Like Wigeon, attains adult features during first winter, but retains juvenile wing until at least first summer.

BARE PARTS All plumages: As Wigeon, but male usually has narrow black band around base of bill.

MEASUREMENTS Males average a little larger than females. Wing of male 252-270, of female 236-258; bill 33-48; mean weight of male 770, of female 680.

GEOGRAPHICAL VARIATION None.

HABITS Very much as Wigeon, of which it is the North American geographical replacement.

HABITAT As Wigeon, although shows preference for freshwater marshes rather than estuarine habitats in winter quarters.

DISTRIBUTION Widespread over North America. Summer visitor to breeding grounds over much of northwestern North America, from Alaska east to the shores of Hudson Bay, southwards over the Great Plains region to northeastern California and northern Colorado, east to the Dakotas and Minnesota; breeds sporadically east of this region. Winters chiefly in coastal lowland marshes (but also further inland in southern states), down Pacific coast from southern Alaska to Mexico and on eastern seaboard from New England south to Costa Rica, Panama, through the West Indies, with small numbers to northern Colombia and northwest Venezuela (rare). Vagrants regular in western Europe, being annual in British Isles; also recorded east to Finland and West Germany, but mostly on Atlantic seaboard from Iceland and the Faeroes south to Morocco and the Azores. Vagrants have also wandered west to northeastern Siberia (Komandorskiye Islands), Hawaii and Japan.

POPULATION Abundant: population estimated at 1.5 million pairs in the mid 1970s, making it perhaps the most numerous North American duck.

REFERENCES Harrison and Harrison (1968), Johnsgard (1978).

73 CHILOE WIGEON   Plate 23
Anas sibilatrix
Alternative name: Southern Wigeon

The only southern wigeon; unlike in the other two species (71, 72), all plumages are remarkably similar.

FIELD IDENTIFICATION Length 43-54 cm (17-21 in). **At rest:** Unmistakable. Medium-sized dabbling duck, with high crown and small bill typical of the wigeons, but plumage pattern quite different from those of the other two. Whitish 'face' and cheek spot contrast with blackish head and scaled breast; rusty flanks and whitish ventral region. Although the sexes are similar, they both occur in two colour phases: a bright phase, which is clearly marked and bright rufous on the flanks; and a duller form, in which the plumage is washed with buffish and brown and with duller pale rufous wash on flanks. Juveniles are also duller than adults, young dull-phase birds being distinctly drab, but still retaining a clear whitish face and white underparts although the upperparts and flanks may be quite dusky. **In flight:** Typical wigeon shape (see Wigeon (71)), although tail shorter and less pointed than on the other two species. Males have prominent white forewing; this is only a little less extensive on females, but more obscured on juveniles. Underparts and rump conspicuously white, although some individuals show darker flanks, contrasting with white belly. Unlikely to be confused with any other species within its range.

VOICE Male has high-pitched whistled call, longer and more multisyllabic than that of the other two species, 'wir-wir-wiburrr', uttered frequently both on water and in flight. Female has a low growled 'arr-arr'.

DESCRIPTION Sexes similar. No seasonal, but some individual, variation. **Adult bright phase:** Head and neck iridescent greenish-black, with whitish forehead, lores, chin and ear-covert patch. Lower neck and breast white, prominently scaled black. Flanks rusty-rufous. Underparts from lower breast down, including whole of ventral region, white, washed rufous on sides of ventral region. Upperparts black, with clear whitish fringes to all feathers, including elongated pointed scapulars and tertials. Lower rump and uppertail-coverts white. Tail black. Upperwing-coverts white, greater coverts tipped black. Primaries dark grey-brown; secondaries black, with metallic green gloss. Underwing pale, darker along forewing and flight feathers. **Adult dull phase:** Basically similar, but flanks merely washed dull buffish-rufous and fringes of dark-centred feathers of upperparts and breast dull buffish or pale brownish, making entire pattern dull and obscure. Sexes similar, but female smaller and a little drabber than male, with brownish mottling on lesser upperwing-coverts. **Juvenile:** Similar to adults, but duller still than female, with extensive brownish

mottling in upperwing-coverts; head dull blackish, lacking iridescence or obvious whitish spot on sides. Young dull phase particularly dingy, with brownish flanks and most of upperparts.
BARE PARTS All plumages: Bill pale grey, with black nostril, tip, cutting edges and narrow line around base. Legs and feet dark grey. Iris brown.
MEASUREMENTS Males distinctly larger than females. **Male:** Wing 255-275, tarsus 40-43, bill 33-35, mean weight 939. **Female:** Wing 237-245, bill 34-36, mean weight 828.
GEOGRAPHICAL VARIATION None.
HABITS Sociable duck, being usually found in small parties, although flocks do not attain size of those of other two wigeon species, rarely exceeding a few hundred birds. Larger concentrations form at key moulting waters after breeding, with 5,000 reported from Lago Hantu, Isla Grande, in January and February, indicating some form of moult migration. Seems to be in pairs throughout most of the year, although pair-bonds are probably not permanent, new pair-formation taking place soon after breeding season is completed. Breeding season chiefly during September to December, a little earlier in northern parts of range and later in southern portions. Nest is hidden among vegetation and is often a considerable distance from water. Unlike most others of the genus, the male helps the female in tending the brood after hatching. Feeds both by grazing and by dabbling, although perhaps spends less time grazing than the two northern wigeons, preferring to feed while swimming out in the open water of freshwater lakes.
HABITAT Freshwater lakes and marshes in open country, with preference for steppe country with scattered lakes and adjacent meadows; also in wooded regions and along slow-flowing rivers.
DISTRIBUTION Breeds over much of southern South America and the Falkland Islands. Breeding range extends north to mouth of Rio Huanco in Chile and to Buenos Aires and Cordoba in Argentina; occasionally breeds north to Uruguay. Southernmost populations migrate northwards in winter, wintering over northern Argentina north to Uruguay, Paraguay and Rio Grande do Sul in southern Brazil. Widespread resident in the Falkland Islands. Vagrants have been recorded on South Georgia and on South Orkney Islands. Popular in captivity, it frequently escapes and is often reported at large in Europe and North America.
POPULATION A common species, being especially abundant in parts of Chile; despite being a popular target species with hunters, there seems to be no threat to its population.
REFERENCES Johnsgard (1978).

74 FALCATED DUCK   Plate 24
Anas falcata

Alternative name: Falcated Teal

Beautiful dabbling duck from eastern Asia. Its behaviour bears similarities to that of both the northern wigeons (71, 72) and Gadwall (75), suggesting that it is a form of evolutionary linkage.

FIELD IDENTIFICATION Length 48-54 cm (19-21 in).

At rest: Rather heavily-built Gadwall-sized dabbling duck, with relatively bulky body, rounded crown, slender bill and short tail. Breeding male unmistakable: grey body, large, maned dark head (showing green and bronze iridescence), buff and black undertail-coverts, white throat and strongly-arched elongated tertials all contribute to a unique appearance. Drab brown female easily confused with others of the genus, but rather long dark grey bill adds to a distinctive shape, with relatively short, heavy, buoyant body. The head and neck lack any strong pattern, being uniformly and intensely mottled with dark freckles on a greyish background, contrasting with and being slightly darker than the warmer brown body coloration. The upperparts are dark, with narrow brown feather fringes, while the underparts show prominent dark V-shaped subterminal marks to the feathers; apart from a pale buff line along sides of tail, the rear end is almost uniform with the rest of the body coloration. When out of the water, shows dark grey legs and paler buffish belly. Female Gadwall has clear whitish belly and yellowish legs, usually shows orange on bill sides, and has darker crown and eye-line; female northern wigeons have clear white belly, short bill, paler ventral region and lighter head and neck. Female Northern Pintail (95) is much more slender, with longer rear end and neck and paler head and neck, but has greyish legs and bill as Falcated. Confusion with other species less likely. **In flight:** A medium-sized, rather short-necked, bulky-bodied dabbling duck. Males appear grey, with dark head, rump and tail, but white of throat and on undertail-coverts visible when overhead. Underwing very pale, with greyer flight feathers. Upperwing grey, with darker primaries and blackish secondaries, latter glossed green, with prominent white band along base of secondaries. Female has uniformly dark body coloration, with slightly paler belly centre, and shares striking pale underwing of male; upperwing-coverts greyish-brown, only slightly paler than primaries, and secondaries very dark with whitish band along feather bases. Male distinctive. Female's wing pattern suggests Wigeon (71), but underwing much paler and belly duller, not stunningly white as Wigeon. Female Gadwall has similar underwing but whiter belly, while upperwing shows small white patch (easy to overlook) on drabber secondaries near body, but lacks extensive blackish secondaries of Falcated and whitish central wing-band.
VOICE Fairly quiet away from breeding grounds. Male has a short, low whistle followed by a wavering 'uit-trr'. Female utters a hoarse, gruff quack.
DESCRIPTION Sexually dimorphic. Seasonally variable. **Adult male breeding:** Head with long maned crest. Head iridescent green and purple-bronze, with tiny white spot on forehead. Throat and foreneck white, with narrow black collar towards base of neck. Breast pale grey, with intense black scaling. Flanks, belly, sides of ventral region and most of upperparts pale grey, closely vermiculated with fine black scaling. Undertail-coverts buffish-white, with black surround. Elongated and pointed scapulars grey. Tertials elongated, pointed and strongly curved, black and grey. Back, rump,

uppertail-coverts and tail blackish. Upperwing-coverts pale grey, with broad white subterminal marks to greater coverts. Primaries blackish-grey; secondaries metallic greenish-black, with faint pale tips. Underwing pale grey, with indistinct dark grey tips to lesser coverts; axillaries and central underwing whiter. **Adult male eclipse:** Resembles adult female, but crown and hindneck darker, upperparts darker; wing as breeding male, but tertials shorter and straighter. **Adult female:** Head and neck slightly 'maned', greyish-brown, with intense small dark streaking. Breast and most of underparts warmer brown, with dark subterminal marks to feathers, paler, buffer and almost unmarked on centre of belly. Ventral region buffish, with dark markings. Upperparts dark brown, with light brown feather fringes; rump and uppertail-coverts dark brown, with pale buff feather tips. Tail grey, with darker markings and pale edges. Upperwing-coverts grey-brown with paler tips, greater coverts broadly tipped whitish-buff. Secondaries blackish, with weak green gloss. Underwing as male, but dark marks on lesser coverts more prominent. **Juvenile:** Resembles female, but whole plumage buffer, with shorter, blunter tertials. Scapulars merely fringed light buff, generally lacking pale subterminal marks of adult female. Tips to greater coverts duller and greyer. Young males have greyer forewing than females. Becomes much as adult by first winter, but with shorter tertials until first summer.

BARE PARTS All plumages: Bill high at base but relatively long and narrow, dark grey to blackish (blacker on male, with blackish patches on culmen on female). Legs and feet dark grey. Iris brown.

MEASUREMENTS Males typically larger than females. Wing 237-264 (mean: male 259, female 242); tarsus 37-41; bill 38-46; mean weight of male 713, of female 585.

GEOGRAPHICAL VARIATION None.

HABITS Little studied in the wild. Fairly sociable, usually seen in pairs or small parties, but quite large flocks formed on passage and in winter; mixes freely with other dabbling ducks, especially Wigeon and Northern Pintail. Pair-bonds formed in autumn and winter, pairs arriving on breeding grounds mid April to mid May. Breeding season May to July, being a little later in more northern parts of range. Nest site usually quite close to water, among tall herbage or under bushes. Males seem to attend broods with females when chicks are very small. Males form moulting flocks in mid-summer. Arrives in winter quarters from mid September onwards. Feeds chiefly by dabbling and up-ending in open water, although normally keeps fairly close to emergent vegetation; sometimes grazes in waterside grassland or crops. Flight fast, rising easily from water surface. Generally shy and wary.

HABITAT Breeds by water-meadows and lakes in lowland valleys, both in sparsely-wooded and in open country. In winter on lowland rivers, lakes and flooded meadows, less frequently in coastal lagoons and estuaries.

DISTRIBUTION Widespread but rather local summer visitor across northeastern Asia, chiefly in USSR. Breeds over much of southern portion of eastern Siberia, west to the Angara basin, south to northern Mongolia, Heilungkiang (China) and Hokkaido (Japan), and north to southern Sakhalin and the Kuril Islands. Wintering grounds stretch over much of lowland eastern Asia, chiefly in eastern China, Korea and Japan south to Vietnam, although winter range extends westwards to northeastern India in small numbers; rare further west across India and in Nepal. In years of drought in western portion of winter range, vagrants have occurred west to Tomsk (western Siberia), Afghanistan, Iran, Jordan, Iraq and Turkey. Occasional individuals widely recorded in western and central Europe, but popularity in captivity prevents acceptance of many of these as wild stragglers, although doubtless some are. Vagrants also recorded south to Thailand and east to the Aleutian Islands, although occasional records from Pacific coast of North America are suspected to refer to escapes.

POPULATION Seems to be really common only in southern and eastern portions of Soviet breeding range, but there is very little information on populations of this species. It seems to be under no obvious threat to its numbers.

REFERENCES Dementiev and Gladkov (1952).

75 GADWALL   Plate 24
Anas strepera

Males of this widespread duck appear rather dull unless seen at close quarters, when they are then obviously beautifully patterned.

FIELD IDENTIFICATION Length 46-55 cm (18-22 in). **At rest:** Medium-sized dabbling duck, between Mallard (84) and northern wigeons (71, 72) in size and structure. Smaller and more slightly built than Mallard, with more slender bill. The orange-yellow legs and white patch on secondaries are present in all plumages, although the latter feature is most obvious on males. Males appear dark grey, with blackish bill, browner head and much blacker rear end, lacking any white on rear body but often showing the white speculum patch when at rest. Although not particularly striking, their pattern is quite unmistakable. Females are closer to female Mallard, but are smaller, slighter and more delicate in structure, with more sloping forehead and slightly flatter crown; the dark bill has orange sides (rarely similar in Mallard, which normally has orange subterminal area and at base). Female Gadwall has a clean whitish belly (merely a little paler on Mallard), the overall tone of the body coloration is a little duller and the markings along the flanks are rounder, less pointed, and the head is plainer with less obvious dark eye-line and crown; the white speculum patch, although smaller than on males, often shows when birds are on the water. Both species of northern wigeon are easily distinguished by their short grey bill, plainer body markings and dark grey legs. See also Falcated Duck (74). **In flight:** Fairly large dabbling duck, with clear whitish underwing and belly in all plumages. Rather slimmer than Mallard, with relatively narrower-based wings. Upperwing of male shows conspicuous white patch at body end of secondaries, but is otherwise rather dark and uniform. Females have smaller white wing patch, and on juvenile females it is so obscure that it is easy to overlook. Females and juveniles distinguished from wigeons by dull secondaries (drab also on juvenile wigeons), more uniform brown upperwing, rounded, not pointed, tail and evenly whiter underwing.

VOICE Relatively silent, except when displaying in courting parties. Male utters a short 'nheck' and a low whistle. Female utters a repeated 'gag-ag-ag-ag-ag', not dissimilar to that of Mallard but higher in pitch.

DESCRIPTION Sexually dimorphic. Seasonally variable. **Adult male breeding:** Head and neck medium-brown, finely peppered with dark markings. Breast, most of upperparts and underparts grey, finely vermiculated with black and white scaling, most prominent on breast. Centre of underparts almost clear whitish. Ventral region, uppertail-coverts and rump black. Tail light brown. Elongated, pointed scapulars greyish, fringed cinnamon-buff. Tertials broadly pointed, grey. Lesser upperwing-coverts grey, finely barred; most of median coverts maroon-chestnut; greater coverts black towards base of wing. Secondaries white towards wing base, black towards primaries. Primaries dark grey-brown. Underwing almost all whitish. **Adult male eclipse:** Recalls adult female, but retains breeding-male wing; upperparts greyer, less heavily marked than female, usually with less extensive orange on bill. **Adult female:** Head and neck buffish-brown, finely marked with small dark streaks; crown and weak eye-line darker, chin and throat whiter. Breast and most of upperparts and underparts medium-brown, with darker subterminal feather scalloping, most obvious on flanks and upperparts. Ventral region similar, but paler. Centre of underparts almost clear whitish. Tertials grey-brown, narrowly fringed buff. Tail brownish, mottled darker. Upperwing similar to that of male, but duller, with less extensive chestnut and smaller white speculum patch. Underwing as male. **Juvenile:** Resembles female, but coloration brighter, with greyer sides of head and neck and brighter buffish fringes to body feathers giving more contrast between head and neck and body than on female; body markings more streaked and spotted, less scalloped. Upperwing of juvenile male resembles that of adult female, with more restricted chestnut and white than adult male; upperwing of juvenile female very dull, with no black or chestnut, and white very restricted and suffused brownish. Attains features of adult plumage during first winter, and much as adult by first summer.

BARE PARTS In all plumages, legs and feet yellowish-orange with greyish webs, brightest in adult males, dullest in juveniles, and iris brown. **Male:** Bill greyish-black in breeding plumage, more like female when in eclipse. **Female and juvenile:** Bill greyish, with dull orange sides; sides yellower on juveniles.

MEASUREMENTS Males usually larger than females. Wing 243-282 (mean: male 269, female 252); tarsus 36-42; bill 37-46; mean weight of male 990, of female 850.

GEOGRAPHICAL VARIATION No existing races recognised. Race *cousei* was an island endemic form of Washington and New York Islands in the Fanning Islands of the central Pacific; after its discovery in 1874, it seems never to have been seen again. Males resembled eclipse males of the nominate race, but were smaller.

HABITS Sociable duck of freshwater lakes and marshes, usually met with in small parties, mixing freely with others of genus; large gatherings not usually formed, except for moult in late summer or on passage. Pair-formation starts in late summer and continues into autumn and winter. Breeding season varies over wide range, but usually May-July, somewhat later in northern regions and earlier in the south. Nests on ground among vegetation, especially nettles, often a considerable distance from water; sometimes several nests in close proximity on small islands. After breeding, flocks form to moult on key waters. In many more-temperate regions remains on breeding waters throughout the year, but northern populations migratory. Feeds chiefly by dabbling with head submerged, sometimes up-ending but less so than many others of genus; occasionally comes on to land to graze or feed among crops and stubbles. Generally keeps close to edges of extensive emergent vegetation. Usually shy and wary, often being flushed from among tall emergent vegetation by lakesides. Flight fast; quicker and more agile than Mallard when on the wing.

HABITAT Favoured haunts are lowland freshwater lakes and marshes in open country, with extensive fringe vegetation. Locally on estuaries, but rarely in coastal regions, in winter.

DISTRIBUTION Widespread over great part of northern hemisphere. In New World, breeds extensively across prairies and Great Plains, from southern Canada to California and east to Iowa; sporadic breeding south and east of this region, except on east coast from Quebec to North Carolina, where well established. Winters over much of southern North America, both inland and in coastal lowlands, south to central Mexico, Cuba and Jamaica. In Old World, found locally over most of central and western Europe, some local populations aided by artificial introductions (as in Britain), but absent as a breeding species from Scandinavia and Mediterranean basin; becomes more widespread from eastern Europe eastwards across Asia, east to northern China and Hokkaido (Japan), south to Soviet Central Asia, but everywhere somewhat local and patchily distributed. In winter most Asiatic and eastern European birds move southwards to winter from eastern China and Japan, across northern India, with large numbers around eastern Mediterranean and lowlands of Black and Caspian Seas; small numbers move down Nile valley as far as the Sudan, rarely getting as far as Kenya and Tanzania, and in West Africa occasionally south to Senegal. Vagrants have occurred north to Finland, and south to Upper Volta, Nigeria, Cameroon, Zaire, Sri Lanka, Thailand, Hong Kong and Hawaii.

POPULATION Widespread and locally abundant. North American population estimated at some 1.5 million individuals in mid 1970s. In Old World, winter estimates include some 10,000 in northwest Europe, 50,000 in Europe-Black Sea-Mediterranean region, and in the USSR some 109,000 in mild winters. Although there are local fluctuations in breeding numbers, Gadwalls seem to be slowly increasing in most parts of western Europe.

REFERENCES Cramp and Simmons (1977), Johnsgard (1978)

76 BAIKAL TEAL   Plate 24
Anas formosa
Alternative name: Formosa Teal

An exquisitely-patterned large teal of eastern Asia; very recently, alarm has been expressed over an apparently sudden decline in numbers in its winter quarters.

FIELD IDENTIFICATION Length 39-43 cm (15-17 in). **At rest:** A small dabbling duck, although appreciably larger than Teal (77), with longer, broader bill and relatively longer primaries. Male unmistakable with its striking facial pattern, defying brief description, of green, black, buff and white stripes, bands and patches. Pinkish breast contrasts a little with greyish body, being separated from latter by a white vertical band and highlighted by elongated, pointed, cream-and-black-edged scapulars. Females confusable with other small dabbling ducks, but closest to Teal. Female Baikal, however, is larger and has very prominent circular whitish patch on lores; although some female Teals and all female Blue-winged Teals (102) have a similar spot, it is never so clear as on Baikal (see figure, p. 230). Like Teal, female Baikal has a clear pale buff line along sides of tail, not normally shown by other small dabbling ducks. Baikal is a richer, more rufous-brown colour than Teal and has a clear whitish belly (as has female Garganey (101)) and a stronger head pattern, with blackish crown and eyeline and sometimes a dusky vertical band on side of head, although an indication of this can also be shown by some Teals. The eye-stripe is apparent only behind the eye, and the supercilium is narrow and rather indistinct, being almost broken above the eye by the dusky crown coming down to eye level. Wing pattern resembles that of Teal, quickly dispelling confusion with other Teal-sized dabbling ducks. **In flight:** Although clearly larger than Teal, the wing patterns of the two are quite similar, although rusty central band on upperwing is distinctive on adult Baikal. Upperwing shows a green speculum, with a rusty band along greater coverts (whiter on juveniles) and narrow white trailing edge of wing. Underwing resembles that of Teal, being whitish in centre with dusky leading edge and greyish-brown flight feathers, but the dark leading edge to the underwing is blacker and more striking than on Teal.
VOICE Call of male, often incessantly uttered from flocks on water and in flight, especially in spring, a deep chuckling 'wot-wot-wot'. Female has a low quack.
DESCRIPTION Sexually dimorphic. Seasonally variable. **Adult male breeding:** Head intricately patterned. Crown and forehead blackish, with brown feather tips. Narrow white lines bordering crown, meeting on upper nape. Lores yellowish-buff, with narrow white border. Sides of head irides-

cent green, bordered black. Throat yellowish-buff with white border, this pattern extending up towards eye. Black stripe from eye joins with black chin. White stripe from lower foreneck forms semicollar. Breast pinkish-grey, freckled black. Sides of breast and flanks finely vermiculated grey and black, appearing grey; narrow white vertical stripe on sides of breast, within area of grey. Centre of underparts, from lower breast to vent, white. Sides of ventral region white. Undertail- and uppertail-coverts black. Tail brown, with pale edges. Upperparts brownish, with elongated, pointed, cream-and-black-edged scapulars hanging over wings. Upperwing-coverts brownish, greater coverts with broad rusty tips. Secondaries metallic green, with white trailing edge. Primaries blackish-brown. Underwing whitish, with intense dusky mottling on lesser coverts and browner flight feathers. In fresh plumage, bright coloration may be obscured by brownish or buffish feather fringes, which abrade during latter part of winter to reveal full colour. **Adult male eclipse:** Resembles adult female, but with less pronounced facial pattern, whitish of belly somewhat mottled dusky; long cream-edged scapulars may be present. **Adult female:** Forehead, crown and nape dusky-brown. Sides of head and neck buffish-brown, with small dark streaks. Supercilium buffish-brown, broken above eye by dusky crown. Dusky line from behind eye to nape. An ill-defined dusky patch on sides of head, sometimes extending into a line from behind eye to upper throat. Circular whitish patch on lores, often outlined dusky. Chin and throat whitish. Breast and flanks warm brown, almost rufous-brown, with darker feather centres; sides of ventral region similar, with pale line along sides of tail. Centre of underparts, from lower breast downwards, clear whitish. Upperparts dark brown, with warm brown feather edges. Upperwing-coverts dark greyish-brown, greater coverts broadly tipped rusty. Secondaries blackish-green, tipped white. Primaries dark brown. Underwing as male. **Juvenile:** Resembles female, but facial pattern less defined, loral spot buffer and less distinct, centre of underparts mottled, less clearly white. Brown of plumage less rufous, more dull brown. Upperparts fringed greyish-brown. Tips of greater coverts paler, less rusty. Adult plumage attained during latter part of first winter, but some juvenile feathers present until first summer.
BARE PARTS All plumages: Bill dark grey. Legs and feet grey to yellowish-grey, with darker webs. Iris brown.
MEASUREMENTS Males average a little larger than females. Wing of male 200-220, of female 180-210; tarsus 30-35; bill 33-38; mean weight of male 437, of female 431.
GEOGRAPHICAL VARIATION None.
HABITS Highly gregarious, forming very large concentrations in winter quarters and mixing freely with other species. Pair-formation occurs chiefly in winter quarters, pairs arriving on breeding grounds in late April and May. Breeding season mid May to mid July. Nests are placed on the ground under shrubby cover, close to water. Males moult soon after breeding, females a little later and often while tending broods. Autumn passage route somewhat

mysterious, seems not to pass through areas used in spring. At all passage points, flocks move through quickly over space of a few days. Feeds mostly by dabbling, but winter flocks also visit crop fields and stubbles, and has even been recorded feeding on roads at night on wasted crops lost by vehicles.

HABITAT Breeds by small pools in swampy taiga, and in marshes and river deltas at edges of tundra. In winter in variety of freshwater and brackish-water habitats, from lowland lakes, flooded fields, meadows and slow rivers to estuarine marshes.

DISTRIBUTION Widespread across eastern Siberia, west to Angara River, north to deltas of Arctic coastline, south to northern shores of Lake Baikal and east to Kamchatka, but over much of this huge area seems to be somewhat local, with main concentrations centred on basins of major river systems. Winters chiefly in coastal lowlands of eastern and southern China and southern Japan, occasionally turning up further south and west as far as northeastern India. On spring migration moves through Korea and inland across northeast China, but return autumn route unclarified. At least some of the individuals reported from a number of European countries could be genuine vagrants, especially a series of records in 1983 from such scattered places as Spain, France, Norway and Svalbard, but, as with Falcated Duck (74), many are possibly escapes from collections. Vagrants also reported from Nepal, Afghanistan, Hong Kong, Australia and Abu Dhabi, and on west coast of North America, chiefly Alaska south to California.

POPULATION Locally abundant, formerly with huge concentrations in winter, as indicated by estimates of 50,000 captured by only three men in the winter of early 1947 in southwest Japan, including 10,000 in a single day. Although it has long been extensively hunted, worries have only lately been expressed over the dwindling numbers in Japan in recent winters. As this is a species that seems to winter in large concentrations, this may merely point to a shift in their winter quarters, but there is no evidence to support this. The frequency of vagrants turning up in Alaska has also declined in recent decades.

REFERENCES Delacour (1954), Dementiev and Gladkov (1952).

77 TEAL or GREEN-WINGED TEAL
Anas crecca   Plate 29

Alternative names: Teal (Britain and Ireland), Green-winged Teal (North America), Common Teal

Widespread throughout the northern hemisphere. Two well-differentiated forms are included within the species and are treated separately below.

TEAL
A. c. crecca and A. c. nimia

FIELD IDENTIFICATION Length 34-38 cm (13-15 in). **At rest:** Very small dabbling duck. In the field males appear grey, with dark head, and a white stripe along the side of the upperparts; the buffish under-tail-coverts may also be quite conspicuous. The

back stripe varies in prominence according to the position of the feathers. Closer inspection reveals a dark chestnut head, with a broad metallic green band running back from the eye, the latter margined narrowly with buff. Females are small ducks with brownish, mottled plumage typical of the genus, and are rather featureless in comparison with other small dabbling ducks. Ill-defined whitish belly and narrow buffish line along sides of under-tail-coverts are useful pointers, and the bright green speculum is normally visible; head pattern shows dark crown and eye-stripe, some individuals having a very indistinct loral spot. The grey bill shows indistinct fleshy colour at very base and the culmen is very slightly concave. These features help to separate it from females of Garganey (101), and Blue-winged (102), Cinnamon (103) and Baikal (76) Teals, which are more fully discussed under their relevant accounts (see also figure, p. 230). **In flight:** Distinguished by tiny size and fast flight, rising sharply from water surface. Shows sharply-pointed wings, short neck and short tail. Upperwing grey-brown, with darker primaries, and green speculum with short, but broad pale buff or whitish bar at base (narrower on female). From below, shows whitish belly and centre of underwing, the latter having a darker band along lesser coverts. The wing pattern is similar in larger Baikal Teal, and Garganey has similar underwing.

VOICE Quite vocal, male having a very distinctive, soft, liquid, high-pitched 'preep-preep', which is surprisingly far-carrying. Female relatively silent, but utters a sharp, high 'quack' when suddenly flushed.

DESCRIPTION Sexually dimorphic. Seasonally variable. Nominate race described. **Adult male breeding:** Head and upper neck bright chestnut, with metallic blackish-green band, edged with narrow buff border, from before eye across side of head to nape. Breast pale buff, with small dark spots. Sides of breast, flanks and most of upperparts vermiculated grey. Centre of underparts, from lower breast downwards, whitish. Undertail-coverts buff, with black surround. Outer scapulars white, edged black on outer webs. Upperwing-coverts ashy-grey, greater coverts broadly tipped buffish-white. Secondaries metallic green, tipped white. Primaries dark greyish-brown. Underwing whitish, with darker flight feathers, and intense dusky mottling along lesser coverts. **Adult male eclipse:** Close to adult female, but rather darker above and with less distinct eye-stripe or spotting below, adult male features becoming visible as the autumn progresses. **Adult female:** Head and neck pale buffish-brown, streaked darker, with dark grey-brown crown, hindneck and line through eye. Often an ill-defined paler patch on lores, but never so clearly marked as on other small dabbling ducks. Breast and underparts dull buffish-brown, with darker scalloping, most prominent on flanks; ventral region similar, but clear buff line along sides of tail. Upperparts dark brown, with paler brown feather bases and fringes. Upperwing as male, but browner, with greater-covert bar a little narrower and white secondary tips a little wider. Centre of underparts ill-defined whitish, with dark mottles and streaks. Underwing as male. There is individual variation, with some birds distinctly darker than others, particularly on head, breast and upperparts. **Juvenile:** Similar to female, but belly more spotted and sometimes shows hint of dark bar on cheek, although not so clear as on Garganey. Owing to individual variation, ageing difficult in field. Males assume adult features during their first winter.

BARE PARTS Adult male: Bill dark slate; in eclipse, sides of bill-base may be dull orange or greenish. Legs and feet dark grey. Iris brown. **Female and juvenile:** Bill dark grey, with some pinkish or yellowish at base; juvenile has more extensive dull fleshy or yellowish on bill when very young. Legs and feet olive-grey to brownish-grey. Iris brown.

MEASUREMENTS Males tend to be a little larger than females. Nominate *crecca*: Wing 175-192 (mean: male 187, female 180); tarsus 28-32; bill 32-40; mean weight of male 360, of female 340. Race *nimia*: Wing of male 182-204 (mean: male 193, female 187); tarsus 29-34; bill 33-37.

GEOGRAPHICAL VARIATION Three races recognised, North American race *carolinensis* treated separately below. Nominate form throughout Old World range of the species. The Aleutian Islands are inhabited by a resident population which closely resembles the nominate race, but averages larger in measurements (see above); named *nimia*, its separation as a distinct form is perhaps debatable.

HABITS An abundant duck, forming large concentrations outside breeding season. Large flocks congregate at winter roosting waters. Daytime roosts often on land by waterside, or on small islands. Pair-formation takes place chiefly in winter quarters, birds arriving already paired on breeding grounds. Breeds from mid May onwards, the nest being well hidden on ground in waterside vegetation. Males leave females at start of incubation and congregate on suitable, safe waters to moult, some populations undergoing quite an extensive moult migration, others remaining on or near breeding grounds. Females moult on breeding grounds. Feeds by dabbling and up-ending in shallow water, usually close to emergent vegetation, but will flight to feed in fields at night along with other dabbling ducks. Flocks fly in close units, rapidly twisting and turning, taking off and landing with little effort, although short legs give it an awkward gait when walking. Highly migratory, although some of the more southern populations largely resident.

HABITAT Freshwater pools and lakes with luxuriant shore vegetation, preferring shallower waters and smaller ponds and pools in breeding season. Mostly in open country, but locally in upland zones. Outside breeding season will also resort to estuaries, saltmarshes, river deltas and even locally in sheltered coastal bays and estuary mouths.

DISTRIBUTION Widespread breeder across almost the whole of northern Palaearctic Europe and Asia, wintering south throughout temperate Europe and Asia and tropical Asia. Numbers move down Nile valley to winter in small numbers south to Tanzania, and in West Africa south to Nigeria. Vagrants have occurred north to Greenland, south to Zaire and Malaysia, and frequently along both Pacific and Atlantic coasts of North America, south to California and South Carolina.

POPULATION Abundant, one of the most widespread of Palaearctic ducks. Local declines have occurred through wetland drainage. Estimates of total population difficult owing to rather inconspicuous nature, dense flocking and small size of the species. In Europe, however, some 250,000 possibly winter in northwest, with another 750,000 around Mediterranean and Black Sea areas.

GREEN-WINGED TEAL
A. c. carolinensis

North American race of Teal, males of which are easily separable in the field.

FIELD IDENTIFICATION Basically similar to nominate race, but breeding male differs in having a conspicuous vertical white stripe on side of breast and in lacking white line along side of upperparts (but note that Teal often has its white scapular stripe partially, or at times completely, concealed according to positioning of the feathers). Closer views reveal lack of buff border to dark green head-band, although it is weakly indicated on lower edge. Additionally, the breast coloration tends to be a little richer, brighter buff and the tips of the greater coverts are buffer. Female and other plumages are inseparable from Teal, although they tend to have crown and eye-stripe darker than the nominate form; individuals coming out of eclipse, or first-winter males in only partial breeding plumage in early winter, may have breast stripe visible while remainder of male plumage incomplete.

DISTRIBUTION Widespread breeding bird over most of northern North America, except the high Arctic. Breeding range extends from Alaska to Newfoundland, south to the Great Lakes and northern Colorado and Washington. Winters across southern states of USA and along almost entire Pacific and Atlantic coastal regions, except far north, south to Honduras and the West Indies. Vagrant to Tobago, Colombia and Greenland. Regularly wanders across Atlantic, being annual vagrant in western Europe, particularly British Isles, from Iceland south to Morocco. Also west across Pacific, with records from northeastern Siberia, Japan, Hawaii and Polynesia.

POPULATION One of North America's most abundant ducks, the spring population was estimated at least 3 million individuals in the mid 1970s.

REFERENCES Cramp and Simmons (1977), Johnsgard (1978).

78 SPECKLED TEAL   Plate 30
Anas flavirostris

Alternative names: Chilean Teal (nominate race), Sharp-winged Teal (*oxyptera*), Andean Teal (*andium*), Merida Teal (*altipetens*), Yellow-billed Teal (*oxyptera* and nominate race)

The four races of this South American teal fall into two clearly separable groups, which may be worthy of specific status. The two groups can be termed Yellow-billed Teal and Andean Teal respectively, all forms together being generally known as Speckled

Teal. They are given separate treatment here to ease identification.

YELLOW-BILLED TEAL
A.f. flavirostris and *A. f. oxyptera*

FIELD IDENTIFICATION Length 38-43 cm (15-17 in). **At rest:** Unmistakable, despite rather drab plumage. A dull brownish Teal-sized dabbling duck, with very rounded head shape, clear unmarked flanks, contrasting with speckled breast, dark brown head and bright yellow sides to bill. High-altitude race *oxyptera* has exceptionally pale flanks and is the most striking of the two forms considered here. Only Yellow-billed Pintail (96) shares bright yellow on bill and brownish plumage, but is considerably larger, with longer neck and mottled underparts. Northern races of Speckled Teal have grey bills and are considered separately below as Andean Teal. **In flight:** Small, dark-headed dabbling duck, race *oxyptera* with strikingly pale underparts. Upperwing brown, with bright green speculum, latter bordered by warm buff at front and narrowly tipped white at rear. Underwing dark, with conspicuous whitish central band.

VOICE Typical call of male a mellow 'preep' like that of Teal (77), but in display utters prolonged mellow rippling series of notes. Female has a gruff quack.

DESCRIPTION Sexes similar. Nominate race described. **Adult:** Head and neck greyish-brown, intensely freckled darker. Underparts light brownish-grey, unmarked apart from the breast, which has strong blackish spotting. Most of upperparts dark greyish-brown, with paler brown feather edges. Upperwing-coverts greyish-brown, greater coverts broadly tipped warm buff. Secondaries metallic green, narrowly tipped white. Underwing dark grey-brown, with whitish central band. Female very similar to male, but a little duller, with duskier head and bill less bright yellow. **Juvenile:** Much as adult, but spotting on breast more diffuse and less extensive.

BARE PARTS All plumages: Bill yellow, with black culmen stripe, cutting edge and nail; bill colour of female and juvenile a little duller than male. Legs and feet dark grey. Iris brown.

MEASUREMENTS Males a little larger than females. Nominate *flavirostris*: Wing of male 190-202, of female 185-197; tarsus 36-38; bill 30-36; mean weight of male 429, of female 394. Race *oxyptera*: Wing of male 204-240, of female 192-215; tarsus 36-38; bill 33-37; weight 390-420.

GEOGRAPHICAL VARIATION Four races recognised, two of them treated separately as Andean Teal below. Nominate race is widespread over southern South America and the Falkland Islands, and in 1971 a small population was discovered on South Georgia. Race *oxyptera* is a resident of high Andes, from Peru south to northern Chile and northern Argentina; compared with the nominate race, described above, it is a little larger, with strikingly pale, almost silvery-buff, underparts.

HABITS Sociable little dabbling duck of lakes, marshes and rivers, being usually found in small parties, although concentrations of a hundred or more are formed outside the breeding season. Pair-formation seems to be semi-permanent, birds being paired throughout the year. Breeds in November and December (*oxyptera*); rather earlier further south in Chile, in late August and September. Nest sites vary considerably, from holes in banks and slopes, or in more open situations on the ground among vegetation, to holes among huge stick nests of the Monk Parakeet; usually not far from water. In some regions two broods may be reared in a prolonged season, and unlike most members of the genus males often assist females in tending the young broods. Often found standing in groups by shore; feeds primarily by dabbling while walking in the shallows or when swimming, occasionally even diving. Generally fairly approachable in areas where unmolested. Flight usually quite low over water surface when disturbed. Southernmost mainland populations migratory.

HABITAT Race *oxyptera* by high-altitude lakes and rivers of the puna zone. Nominate race in variety of open habitats, from lakes, marshes and rivers in hilly country to coastal lagoons and estuaries, moving on to the seashore in winter.

DISTRIBUTION Race *oxyptera* is chiefly a resident of the high Andes, from central Peru and western Bolivia south to northern Chile and northern Argentina; it breeds in coastal valleys of northern Chile, and outside breeding season descends to lower altitudes, some reaching Pacific coast. Nominate form widespread over southern South America, from northern Argentina and central Chile south to Tierra del Fuego, also in the Falkland Islands and on South Georgia; chiefly resident, although southernmost mainland populations migrate northwards in winter, north to Uruguay, Paraguay and Rio Grande do Sul in Brazil. See also Andean Teal.

POPULATION No population estimates seem to have been made. Both races are relatively common and widely distributed, and appear to be under no threat.

ANDEAN TEAL
A. f. andium and *A. f. altipetens*

Northern races of the Speckled Teal complex, possibly worthy of separation as a distinct species, *Anas andium*.

FIELD IDENTIFICATION Similar to yellow-billed races described above, but bill grey and black, never yellow. General coloration dingier, particularly in comparison with race *oxyptera* of Peru, with breast spotting more diffuse and underparts dull greyish-brown. Southern population *andium* has distinct bronze-purple and green in speculum, greener in *altipetens*. Ranges do not overlap with those of yellow-billed races. Possibly confusable only with female Green-winged Teal (77), which has occurred as a vagrant in Colombia, but dingier colour, unmarked flanks and head, and stockier shape easily separate Andean Teal.

BARE PARTS Bill bluish-grey, with black culmen stripe, tip and cutting edge. Legs and feet dark grey. Iris brown.

MEASUREMENTS Race *andium*: Wing of male 214-

230, of female 205-217; tarsus 37-38; bill 38-41. Race *altipetens* (one male specimen only): Wing 226, tarsus 34, bill 41.

GEOGRAPHICAL VARIATION and DISTRIBUTION Race *andium* breeds in central Andes of Colombia south to northern Ecuador. Race *altipetens* is perhaps not clearly differentiated, but is a little paler than *andium*, with greener speculum and with spotting on underparts less intense; it is a resident of the eastern Andes, from Bogota (Colombia) to extreme northwestern Venezuela. See also Yellow-billed Teal above.

HABITS Much as for yellow-billed races. Recorded breeding in August in Venezuela and in March in Colombia, with birds in breeding condition taken in February and September.

HABITAT High-altitude lakes, marshes and rivers, from 2600 m to 4300 m, usually above 3000 m.

POPULATION No information; in Colombia it is described as a sparsely-distributed resident. Probably under no threat owing to relative remoteness of habitat, but obviously in need of further research.

REFERENCES Delacour (1954), Hilty and Brown (1986), Johnsgard (1978).

79 CAPE TEAL   Plate 32
Anas capensis

Alternative name: Cape Wigeon

Rather strange tropical African dabbling duck, generally sparsely distributed over much of continent with larger numbers seemingly only in south.

FIELD IDENTIFICATION Length 44-48 cm (17-19 in). **At rest:** Stockily-built, small dabbling duck, with distinctive combination of overall pale plumage, heavily-spotted underparts, and extensive rose-pink on bill. The slightly shaggy rear of head, high, rounded crown and rather long, slightly upcurving bill add to its rather odd appearance. Red-billed Teal (98) is darker above, with dark crown and nape. Confusion with any other species is unlikely in the wild; in captivity, however, Marbled Duck (111) is similarly pale, but may easily be separated by more slender shape, dark bill, dusky eye-patch, and prominent pale blotching on flanks. **In flight:** Unmistakable. A plump-bodied, short-necked dabbling duck, with rather bulbous head. Body uniformly pale brownish, but upperwing darker greyish-brown with striking white outer secondaries, inner secondaries being green with white borders; the underwing is quite dark, greyish, with ill-defined paler shading.

VOICE Relatively silent away from breeding grounds. Male has a nasal squeak, but in display utters clear rasping whistle. Female has low quacking calls, but is more vocal in display periods.

DESCRIPTION Sexes similar. **Adult:** Head, neck and underparts very pale greyish-buff, weakly mottled with darker grey, the markings becoming larger and more spotted from breast downwards and most marked on flanks. Upperparts dark brown, with broad buff-brown feather edges. Lower back, rump and uppertail-coverts pale buff, with dark feather centres. Tail dark grey, with paler

edges. Upperwing-coverts dark greyish-brown, greater coverts broadly tipped white. Secondaries white, the innermost metallic green and black with broad white tips. Primaries blackish grey-brown. Underwing dark grey, with white axillaries and whitish feather edges. Female much as male, but markings on breast smaller and more spot-like, less scalloped, and outer tertials brown instead of black. **Juvenile:** Much as adult, but underparts less clearly spotted and borders to upperpart feathers narrower and paler. As adult by first winter.

BARE PARTS All plumages: Bill rose-pink, becoming pale bluish-grey towards tip; nail, cutting edge and very base black (the black may be absent on juveniles). Legs and feet dull yellowish-ochre. Iris individually variable, from pale brown to yellow or orange-red, with no standard age or sexual significance, although males tend towards having yellow iris and females orange-brown.

MEASUREMENTS Sexes similar. Wing 168-206 (mean 194), tarsus 32-40, bill 36-44, mean weight 410.

GEOGRAPHICAL VARIATION None.

HABITS Usually found in pairs or small parties; larger concentrations normally form only at moult gatherings, when some waters may hold as many as 2,000 birds. Has long-term pair-bonds, no doubt related to its rather variable breeding habits. It is a somewhat opportunistic breeder, dispersing in the various wet seasons to breed in seasonally-flooded land. Breeding has been recorded in almost all months of the year, even in South Africa, although in latter area there is a concentration of breeding activity during March to May. Nests are placed on ground under bushes, not far from water and preferably on islands. Male assists with tending young up to flying stage. Feeds chiefly by dabbling while swimming, with head and neck submerged, and freely dives. Not particularly wary, but bobs head and depresses tail when alarmed. When flushed, usually does not fly far or very high over water, often rising less steeply and suddenly than most other dabbling ducks. Flight action rather slow, but agile and fast when well underway. Spends much time loafing on banks of lakes and pools.

HABITAT Fresh and brackish waters, saline lakes, seasonally-flooded wetlands, reservoirs, marshes and sewage-pools. Rarely on estuaries or coastal waters.

DISTRIBUTION Widespread throughout tropical Africa, although over much of its range it is decidedly uncommon or local in appearance. Somewhat nomadic, dispersing into areas after rains and moving out again during dry season. Main range extends from the Sudan and Ethiopia southwards, sometimes reaching west to Lake Chad, but decidedly scarce in West Africa, although regular in Ghana and Nigeria. Absent from tropical rainforest belt in Central Africa. Fairly common on East African soda lakes, and most abundant in southern Africa. Occasionally recorded Zaire, Mozambique and Angola, and vagrants have reached Libya and Israel. Occasionally escapes from captivity in western Europe.

POPULATION No estimates have been made, but its wide range and local abundance show there to

be no apparent threat to its numbers.
REFERENCES Brown et al. (1982).

80 MADAGASCAR TEAL   Plate 28
Anas bernieri

Alternative name: Bernier's Teal

Closely related to the Grey Teal (81), but long isolated on Madagascar. Little known and apparently has always been rare; it is still under pressure from hunting, and unless protective measures are taken it could well become extinct in near future.

FIELD IDENTIFICATION Length 40 cm (16 in).
At rest: The only all-brown teal-like duck on Madagascar. The rather uniform reddish-brown plumage, small size and dark bill give an appearance unlike that of any other species on the island. Overlaps in range with Hottentot Teal (100), Red-billed Teal (98) and White-backed Duck (10), but unlikely to be confused. It is unfortunately not kept in captivity, which adds to the concern over its future. Compared with the Grey Teal, it is smaller, warmer brown in coloration, with a buffer throat and less marked underparts, and the speculum is blackish. **In flight:** A small, overall dark brownish dabbling duck, the upperwing showing a blackish speculum bordered fore and aft by white bands; underwing dark, with paler centre.
VOICE Little information, but male said to have a two-note whistle not unlike that of whistling ducks (2-9).
DESCRIPTION Sexes similar. No data on ageing.
Adult: Almost entire plumage warm brown. Head and neck virtually unmarked light warm brown, crown and hindneck darker and duller brown. Breast and entire underparts with darker, but indistinct, feather centres, most apparent on flanks. Upperparts medium warm brown, with paler buff-brown feather edges. Upperwing-coverts brown, greater coverts broadly tipped white. Secondaries blackish, with slight green gloss, tipped white. Underwing dark, with paler centre.
BARE PARTS Bill, legs and feet light reddish. Iris brown. Female said to have duller and browner bill and legs.
MEASUREMENTS Males seem to be a little larger than females. Wing of male 203-213, of female 192-198; tarsus 30-38; bill 37-39; weight — no data.
GEOGRAPHICAL VARIATION None. Closely related to Grey Teal of the East Indies and Australasia, but distinctly different in coloration from all races within that complex.
HABITS Little known. Found in pairs and small parties by lakeshores. Pair-formation occurs in July and the breeding season is probably from mid September onwards; possibly, however, also breeds in April, suggesting that two broods may be reared, one before and one after the rainy season. Nest undescribed. Feeds by dabbling while wading in shallow water. Most active in morning and evening, spending most of day loafing by shores of lakes.
HABITAT Saline lakes with emergent vegetation. Apparently moves on to estuaries, mangrove swamps, small forest pools and streams and even

ricefields in dry season, when saline lakes dry out.
DISTRIBUTION Known only from small lakes and swamps near Morombe and Ambilobe in western Malagasy (Madagascar).
POPULATION Observations of this species have always been sparse. In 1970, 60 were found on Lake Masama, 13 being shot by 'sportsmen', but in 1971 only two were reported there. In 1973, 61 were counted and a maximum of 120 estimated on Lake Bemamba; no ducks at all were located on Lake Masama during this expedition. Travelling is difficult in this region, which is rarely visited by ornithologists. All wildfowl in Madagascar are extensively hunted commercially; the opening of an airstrip at nearby Ambereny has allowed access for shooters to these lakes. The species is not protected and none is kept in captivity. The immediate setting-up of reserves and adequately-enforced protective measures are required to save this little-known bird.
REFERENCES Delacour (1954), Scott and Lubbock (1975).

81 GREY TEAL   Plate 28
Anas gibberifrons

Alternative name: Andaman Teal (race albogularis)

Widespread through the East Indies and Australasia, being closely related to the Chestnut (82) and Brown (83) Teals, with which it widely overlaps.

FIELD IDENTIFICATION Length 37-47 cm (15-18 in).
At rest: Small, greyish-brown, mottled dabbling duck with relatively large head, slim neck, slender bill and similar plumages in both sexes. Forehead rather bulging, although this marked only on nominate race. Confusion with female Chestnut Teal in southern Australia and with Brown Teal in New Zealand are major problems. Compared with Chestnut, Grey is paler and greyer, with distinctly whitish 'face', throat and foreneck, whereas Chestnut is a little larger, with warm buffish-brown plumage, lacking contrasting whitish face and throat of Grey, and is more prominently mottled with darker feather centres. Chestnut Teal is confined to southern Australia and mixes freely with Grey, but, despite basic plumage similarity, no wild hybrids have been proven. Beware Grey Teals with plumage stained reddish-brown from ferrous waters. Brown Teal is conspicuously darker than Grey, and confusion is far less likely. Some island populations of Grey have extensive white patches on head (see Geographical Variation). **In flight:** A small, mottled grey-brown duck, with very dark underwing showing whitish central band at close quarters. Upperwing grey-brown, with darker primaries, and broad white band along greater coverts, narrowing towards wing base; the speculum is glossy black, with very narrow white trailing edge. Wing pattern of both Brown and Chestnut Teals is very similar.
VOICE Most vocal at night. Male has clear, low 'preep'. Female utters a loud, penetrating, laughing series of quacks, similar to that of Pacific Black Duck (91) but higher-pitched and more prolonged.
DESCRIPTION All plumages similar. Race gracilis described. **Adult:** Crown and hindneck blackish-

brown, freckled with pale grey-brown tips; sides of head, throat and foreneck whitish, with dark streaks, whitest on chin and throat. Most of underparts and upperparts dark grey-brown, with pale greyish-buff feather borders, broadest on flanks. Rump, upper-tail-coverts and tail very dark. Upperwing-coverts dark grey-brown, with broad white band along greater coverts. Primaries darker; secondaries black, glossed green, with white tips. Underwing very dark, with white axillaries and central under-wing. Although sexes are similar, female is lighter overall than male. **Juvenile:** Much as adult, but paler overall, with broader pale fringes to head feathers giving less contrasting appearance to head and neck.

BARE PARTS All plumages: Bill, legs and feet black-ish-grey. Iris red, brightest on adult males.

MEASUREMENTS Males average a little larger than females. Race *gracilis*: Wing 164-243 (mean: male 205, female 198); tarsus 34-37; bill 32-43; mean weight of male 507, of female 474. Nominate *gibberifrons* (male): Wing 181-200, tarsus 33-35, bill 35-41. Race *albogularis* (male): Wing 199-205, tarsus 35-37, bill 34-36. Race *remissa* (one male): Wing 186, bill 33.

GEOGRAPHICAL VARIATION Four races recog-nised, one of which (*remissa*) has recently become extinct. Race *gracilis* possibly a full species, described above, occurs in Australia, New Zealand and New Guinea and adjacent islands. Nominate race of the East Indies is a little smaller and darker than *gracilis*, with blacker feather centres and buffer fringes; the forehead is markedly bulging on this form. Race *remissa*, formerly found on Rennell Island in the Solomon Islands, was a small form with smaller bill and less bulging forehead than the nominate. Race *albogularis* of the Andaman Islands has a prominent white eye-ring, and shows a ten-dency to have extensive white patches on head and neck and pinkish markings on bill. It is possible that the very isolated Madagascar Teal (80) could be included in this complex of races.

HABITS Sociable duck of freshwater lakes and marshes. Usually found in small flocks, but large concentrations, often of thousands, occur in flood-plains of Australia. Pair-formation occurs prior to breeding season. In inland districts of Australia, where breeding conditions are erratic, start of rains triggers sudden courtship behaviour over a very short period as water levels rise. Breeding season varies over wide range: in areas of Australia where rainfall is regular, breeds in late winter and spring, after the winter rains; in areas of irregular rainfall, further inland, breeding commences as soon as conditions are suitable; Andaman race breeds in July and August. Nest site varies, typically on the ground but frequently in tree holes, rabbit burrows and rocky crevices. Male will accompany female and tend young broods. Feeds by dabbling, both while swimming and while wading, and also up-ends; feeds chiefly in shallow water by lakeshores. Australian population highly nomadic, temporarily colonising new areas in vast numbers when condi-tions suitable after rains. After periods of drought, huge numbers move in search of water; such a movement took place in 1957, when large flocks

invaded New Zealand. Such movements or irrup-tions most obvious after several years of successful breeding followed by a drought period. Loafing birds gather on banks in small flocks, or perch on dead. branches overhanging water. Flight fast and agile, rising in dense flocks when disturbed en masse.

HABITAT Shallow-water lakes and marshes, both fresh and brackish, including temporary flood-waters, coastal lagoons, mangrove swamps and estuaries.

DISTRIBUTION Australian race widespread throughout Australia, although most abundant in Murray-Darling basin, spreading out over the conti-nent in nomadic and erratic nature when rains produce suitable wetlands, being only a sporadic breeder in northern Australia or Tasmania. Range extends to New Guinea and New Zealand, where it was formerly decidedly uncommon; in 1957 and 1958 huge numbers invaded these regions follow-ing prolonged drought in Australia, and it is now a widespread breeding species. It also occurs on New Caledonia, Macquarie Island and the Aru and Kai Islands off New Guinea, where it may be a resident or temporary breeder following irruptions, and has occurred as far afield as the Chatham Islands. East Indian race not given to such fluctuations, but some inter-island movements; it is widespread in Sulawesi and also occurs on Java, Bali, Sumba, Flores, Timor, Wetar and adjacent islands. Andaman race also moves between islands within the archipelago and seems to be somewhat nomadic, a vagrant of this race having occurred in Burma.

POPULATION Generally widespread and abun-dant, but few data on island populations. Andaman race not reported to be endangered, although not numerous, but the situation of this population needs monitoring as agricultural development and drain-age schemes threaten its habitats on some islands. Rennell Island race *remissa* recently exterminated by the introduction of large fish, *Tilapia*, into its only lagoon.

REFERENCES Frith (1967), Kear and Williams (1978), RAOU (1984).

82 CHESTNUT TEAL   Plate 28
Anas castanea

Alternative name: Chestnut-breasted Teal

A relative of the Grey Teal (81) and confined largely to coastal regions of southern and eastern Australia.

FIELD IDENTIFICATION Length 38-46 cm (15-18 in). **At rest:** Similar in general shape to Grey Teal, with which it overlaps, but sexually dimorphic and fore-head not swollen. Male easily distinguished by dark head, reddish underparts and white patch in ventral region; resembles endangered Brown Teal (83) of New Zealand, but ranges do not overlap. Brown Teal males lack prominent flank spots of Chestnut and have white eye-ring and narrow collar, at least on mainland New Zealand. Female Chestnut closer to Grey Teal, but darker and more uniform, with richer brown coloration, buff (not whitish) throat and foreneck, and with buff feather fringes and darker feather centres giving a stronger pattern to the underparts. If seen together, Chestnut Teal is slightly larger, but measurements overlap. Female Brown Teal is less spotted below and has whitish eye-ring. **In flight:** Very similar in shape and wing pattern to Grey Teal, but darker body plumage. Male should show dark head and underparts contrasting with whitish ventral patch. Female more difficult, apart from overall darker coloration.

VOICE Very similar to that of Grey Teal, but female quacking sequence is less prolonged and slightly higher in pitch.

DESCRIPTION Sexually dimorphic. Some seasonal variation. **Adult male breeding:** Head and neck blackish, highly glossed green. Breast and most of underparts deep chestnut, with dark brown spotting, most prominent along flanks. Sides of ventral region white, uppertail- and undertail-coverts, tail and rump blackish. Upperparts dark brown, with rufous feather fringes. Upperwing-coverts dark brown, greater coverts with broad whitish band, narrowing towards wing base. Primaries darker; secondaries black, glossed green, with white tips. Underwing dark, with whitish central band. **Adult male eclipse:** Much duller than breeding male, with brownish feather fringes obscuring and dulling the chestnut body plumage, flank patch and dark head, but not so dull as female. This eclipse plumage is rarely reported in the wild, but may be overlooked (or possibly is more frequent in captivity at different latitudes). **Adult female:** General plumage dark brown, with pale buff feather fringes and dark brown feather centres; throat and foreneck almost unmarked light buff. Wing as male. **Juvenile:** Much as female, but dark feather markings less clear; not safely separable in the field.

BARE PARTS All plumages: Bill dark bluish-grey. Legs and feet greenish-grey. Iris red, duller on females.

MEASUREMENTS Males average larger than females. Wing of male 204-231, of female 197-210; tarsus 36-40; bill 37-43; mean weight of male 595, of female 593.

GEOGRAPHICAL VARIATION None. Closely related to both Grey and Brown Teals, but range overlaps only with that of former.

HABITS Usually encountered in pairs or small flocks, often in association with more numerous Grey Teal. Never forms such large concentrations as that species, but non-breeding flocks of up to 500 reported in areas where most numerous. Pair-formation occurs during autumn and winter, with pairs breaking off from small flocks at onset of breeding. Breeding season, however, is markedly prolonged and two broods, perhaps even three, may be reared in a season; season generally from August to November, but may be as early as June and as late as December. Nests are located on the ground near water, sometimes in rocky crevices or tree holes and recently in nestboxes. Males accompany females and help tend young broods. Feeding behaviour and habits generally much as Grey Teal, but often feeds in close association with Australian Pelicans. Although movements occur between eastern and western populations, it is chiefly resident in its somewhat restricted distribution. Odd vagrants occurring far outside normal range have perhaps

been individuals caught up with Grey Teal dispersal.

HABITAT Coastal swamps and lagoons, on both fresh and brackish water. Estuaries, mangroves, tidal inlets and inshore coastal waters and islands. Also locally inland on lakes and marshes.

DISTRIBUTION Chiefly resident in coastal southern and southeastern Australia, with main strongholds in Tasmania, where it is the most abundant duck, and in adjacent coastal regions of Bass Strait. Range extends along coast of southern Australia from Sydney in the east to Perth in the west, although seemingly absent from large stretch of coast bordering Great Australian Bight. More locally and in smaller numbers along northern coast of New South Wales and southern Queensland. Inland, it is sparsely distributed by upland lakes of the southern tablelands and highlands of Victoria and New South Wales north to Canberra. In Western Australia, sporadic breeding occurs north to North West Cape. Some dispersal, chiefly of juveniles in summer, with records of birds north to northern Queensland. Occasional vagrants have occurred north to Darwin and even New Guinea, no doubt caught up with irruptions of Grey Teal.

POPULATION Locally abundant in Tasmania and Bass Strait region, but elsewhere generally regarded as uncommon or scarce. Some evidence of decline in present century, but now locally increasing aided by the erection of nestboxes. Unfortunately still hunted and no population estimates have been made.

REFERENCES Frith (1967), RAOU (1984).

83 BROWN TEAL   Plate 28
Anas aucklandica

Alternative names: New Zealand Teal, Pateke (race *chlorotis*), Flightless Teal (nominate and *nesiotis*), Auckland Islands Teal (nominate), Campbell Island Teal (*nesiotis*)

Now rare and endangered, this interesting duck still survives in a few isolated corners of New Zealand. The Auckland Islands and Campbell Island races are the only existing flightless members of the genus.

FIELD IDENTIFICATION Length 36-46 cm (14-18 in). **At rest:** Unlikely to be mistaken for either Grey (81) or Chestnut (82) Teals owing to limited range, which only marginally overlaps with that of the former. Although bears superficial plumage similarities to Chestnut Teal, male Brown Teal is darker and less bright in coloration and has a white eye-ring, with underparts finely mottled and barred, not heavily spotted. Female Brown Teals are extremely dark, with a narrower eye-ring than the males and only weakly-mottled plumage. As with many other isolated populations, there is a tendency towards partial albinism, occasional birds having white patches on head and upperparts. Brown Teals have reduced powers of flight, the two smaller races being flightless, and are chiefly nocturnal. **In flight:** Only race *chlorotis* of New Zealand mainland will be seen in flight. Wing pattern is very dark, with indistinct rusty-buff bar along greater coverts and narrow white trailing edge to dark green speculum;

the dark underwing contrasts somewhat with white axillaries.

VOICE Relatively silent. Only calls reported, apart from when displaying, are a long, descending series of harsh quacks from the female and soft whistles and chortles as contact notes between pairs.

DESCRIPTION Sexually dimorphic, but not strongly so. Some seasonal variation. Race *chlorotis* described. **Adult male breeding:** Head and neck dark brown, glossed green on sides of head and with narrow white eye-ring; often a narrow white collar around base of neck. Breast and underparts deep chestnut, becoming paler towards buffer and browner belly, with dark mottling on breast and dark brown and buff vermiculations along flanks. Sides of ventral region white, finely barred brown. Undertail-coverts blackish. Upperparts, including back, rump and uppertail-coverts, dark brown, edged lighter brown. Upperwing-coverts dark brown, greater coverts tipped rusty-buff; secondaries glossy black, tinged green, with narrow white tips. Underwing brown, with white axillaries. There is some variation, many males resembling females at all times (indeed, it has been suggested that the brighter males are in fact younger birds). **Adult male eclipse:** Resembles adult female, but shows ill-defined whitish patch on sides of ventral region. **Adult female:** Similar to male, but lacks green gloss on head, whitish ventral patch and blackish undertail-coverts, and has narrower eye-ring; the underparts are duller and browner, with dark feather centres, not finely barred and spotted like many males. Wing as male. **Juvenile:** Very much as female, but underpart markings clearer, especially breast blotching; young males soon develop whitish ventral patches.

BARE PARTS Race *chlorotis* described. **All plumages:** Bill bluish-grey, with darker shading along culmen. Legs and feet dark grey. Iris dark brown.

MEASUREMENTS Males generally a little larger than females. Race *chlorotis*: Wing of male 195-203, of female 185-195; tarsus 41-43; bill 39-45; mean weight of male 665, of female 600. Nominate *aucklandica*: Wing 125-144, tarsus 34-35, bill 30-35, weight of female ca. 450. Race *nesiotis* (one specimen): Wing 133, tarsus 30, bill 35.

GEOGRAPHICAL VARIATION Three races. Race *chlorotis* of mainland New Zealand described above. Nominate race, Auckland Islands Teal, confined to small islands around main Auckland Island, small and flightless, darker and less chestnut than *chlorotis* and with browner legs. Very isolated race *nesiotis*, Campbell Island Teal, formerly thought to be extinct, is now found only on nearby tiny Dent Island; it is smaller and darker than the nominate form, lacking any vermiculations below or a distinct speculum.

HABITS Secretive and chiefly nocturnal in behaviour, this rare duck is found mostly in pairs or very small parties, although small flocks form outside breeding season; pairs are strongly territorial in the breeding season. The pair-bond is considered to be long-term, as members of pair stay together through the year and males accompany broods with the females. The breeding season is from July to December in the New Zealand race, and October to December in the Auckland Islands race. Nests are situated on the ground, under cover of clumps of vegetation and fairly close to water. During the breeding season frequents quiet streams, tidal inlets and ponds, keeping under cover of vegetation during the daytime and emerging to feed at night on streamsides or adjacent wet pasture. During the daytime forms communal roosts, close to both breeding and feeding sites. After breeding, disperses to tidal creeks and estuaries, where daytime feeding also takes place according to state of the tide. Feeds chiefly by wading and dabbling, but also while swimming. Although the New Zealand race can fly, it is not often seen on the wing. On Auckland Islands, spends the day among coastal kelp-beds and is most active in the first three hours of darkness; has been found feeding at night in coastal forest and by pools and streams further inland. Both the Auckland Islands and Campbell Island races are flightless.

HABITAT Swampy pools and streams, with shrub and tree cover; also tidal estuaries and coastal bays of both mainland and offshore islands.

DISTRIBUTION All three races are extremely rare. Formerly widespread throughout New Zealand, race *chlorotis* is now confined to isolated locations chiefly in North Island, where it is found around islands of the outer Hauraki Gulf and in Northland; elsewhere in North Island, very small numbers survive at a few scattered sites. In South Island, extremely small numbers now only in Fiordland. The Auckland Islands Teal is extinct on Auckland Island itself, but good numbers exist on outlying tiny islets of the group, namely Rose, Ocean, Ewing, Enderby, Dundas, Adams and Disappointment. Similarly, the Campbell Island Teal is extinct on the main island, but survives on adjacent tiny Dent Island.

POPULATION All populations severely endangered, the New Zealand race having decreased at an alarming rate through habitat destruction, hunting, introduced predators and perhaps a form of poultry disease. The wild population was estimated at no more than 1,500 individuals in 1982, with about two-thirds of these on Great Barrier Island. The species has been protected since 1921 and a captive-breeding programme to curb the dwindling wild population was started in 1976, with over 670 birds being reared in captivity by September 1985, most of which have been released into the wild. The Auckland Islands race was last recorded on Auckland Island itself in 1942, having probably been exterminated by feral cats, but a survey of outlying islands in the mid 1970s and early 1980s produced an estimated population of some 500 birds. The Campbell Island Teal was thought to be extinct, having been last recorded on the main island in 1958, but in 1975 it was located on nearby Dent Island, where it numbers only some 30 individuals.

REFERENCES Dumbell (1986), Hayes and Williams (1982), Williams (1986).

THE MALLARD COMPLEX

The Holarctic Mallard as such varies little over most

of its vast range, but a number of geographically-isolated southern populations create something of a taxonomic headache. Isolated races of Mallard-type birds are found on some of the Pacific islands and in Central and southern North America; in these forms the breeding-male plumage stage has been lost through isolation and lack of competition with similar species. The extending North American range of the typical Mallard has now brought it into contact with at least one of these southern forms (Mexican Duck) and hybridisation has been rife, to the detriment of the Mexican Duck. The closely-related American Black Duck (88) also interbreeds with Mallard to a certain degree, and the Mottled Duck (87) appears to be somewhat intermediate between the two. More-isolated 'mallards' occur on some Pacific islands, both Hawaiian (85) and Laysan (86) Ducks being derived from Mallard ancestry.

The most recent American Ornithologists' Union Checklist (1983) recognises American Black, Mottled, Laysan and Hawaiian Ducks as full species, but Mexican Duck becomes a race of Mallard and this is the treatment followed here. Whether these forms have evolved to full species level is almost a matter of personal opinion, as the definition of a species within such a complex is rather marginal.

A most interesting situation arises with the position of the (probably) recently extinct Mariana Mallard, an island population which showed varying characters of both Mallard and Pacific Black Duck (91); currently it is considered a form of Mallard, but it could equally be considered a form of the Pacific Black Duck. Interestingly enough, neither Mallard nor Pacific Black Duck have been recorded on its islands (the Marianas). Perhaps greater isolation has taken place with Meller's (89) and Philippine (93) Ducks, and both Spotbill (92) and Pacific Black Duck must also be considered as geographical replacements of the Mallard.

84 MALLARD   Plate 25
Anas platyrhynchos

One of the most familiar of all ducks and ancestor of several domestic breeds, this species' wide range has given rise to several distinct populations (see above). Mexican Duck and Mariana Mallard, both rather different and isolated forms, are considered separately after main Mallard account.

FIELD IDENTIFICATION Length 50-65 cm (20-25 in). **At rest:** A large dabbling duck with heavy body and short tail. Familiar breeding male unmistakable, with its bottle-green head, narrow white collar, purple-brown breast, grey body, black and white ventral region and short, curled tail feathers. Female larger than others of the genus, although confusable with several species, especially Gadwall (75), Mottled (87) and American Black (88) Ducks, but combination of purple-blue speculum, bordered by white bands fore and aft, dark bill with orange subterminal area, sides and base, dark eye-stripe, orange legs, mottled brownish belly, and pale sides to tail are useful Mallard pointers. Eclipse and young males resemble females, but have plain bills. There is considerable individual variation, especially in

Europe and North America, with influence of birds of feral origin producing abnormally dark, pale or piebald birds that can be quite confusing. With exceptionally dark individuals there is a strong possibility of confusion with American Black and Mottled Ducks; any suspected sightings of these species away from normal range should be treated with extreme caution, although critical examination of tail colour and speculum helps in such cases. Hybridises with American Black Duck in North America and with Pacific Black Duck (91) in Australia and New Zealand; hybrid males show fairly obvious combinations of the parent species, although females are more like abnormally dark female Mallards. For further discussion, see also Gadwall, Mottled, American Black and Pacific Black Ducks. **In flight:** A large, heavily-built dabbling duck, with relatively broad-based, but pointed wings and rounded tail. Males are greyish, with contrasting dark head, breast and mantle and black and white tail-end. Females are relatively uniform brown on the body, with belly not obviously paler (unlike Gadwall). Wing patterns of both sexes similar and distinctive, with whitish underwing and grey (male) or brown upperwing, latter with contrasting and conspicuous dark blue speculum prominently bordered fore and aft by white bands.

VOICE Quite vocal, especially female. Male utters a soft, rasping 'kreep'. Female's most obvious call is a series of quacks, quite mocking or laughter-like in delivery, descending towards the end, 'QUACK-QUACK-QUACK-quack-quack-quack . . .', heard mostly in late summer and autumn. Similar descending series of quacks are uttered by several other females of the genus.

DESCRIPTION Sexually dimorphic. Seasonally variable. Nominate race described. **Adult male breeding:** Head and neck bottle-green, with purple reflections. Narrow white ring around base of neck. Breast purplish-brown. Most of body plumage finely vermiculated grey; upperparts darker and browner, with blackish back, rump, uppertail- and undertail-coverts and tail centre. Central tail feathers slightly elongated and curled upwards. Sides of tail pale grey and whitish. Upperwing-coverts grey-brown, with greater coverts broadly tipped white; secondaries metallic purplish-blue, with black subterminal border and broad white tips. Underwing whitish, with greyer flight feathers. **Adult male eclipse:** Resembles adult female, but retains male bill colour, and has darker crown and nape, paler sides of head and neck, and warmer, almost rufous-brown, and only weakly-marked breast. **Adult female:** Crown and hindneck dark brown, with paler mottles; supercilium, and sides of head and neck light brown, with fine dark streaks; lores and eye-stripe dark brown. Almost whole body plumage light brown, with dark subterminal mottles and V-shaped marks on feathers, most conspicuous on flanks; belly only slightly paler, and well streaked and mottled. Tail very pale, with dark mottling and barring. Wing as male, but upperwing-coverts dark brown, not grey. There is individual variation over shades of brown and intensity of feather markings, darker birds tending to have white speculum borders rather narrower. **Juvenile:** Resembles female, but body markings more streaked, with flank marks less V-shaped, more in form of dark centres with pale edges; bill almost uniform dull reddish. Young male darker above than female, with greyer wing-coverts and warmer breast. Become much as adults during first winter, but not fully until first summer.

BARE PARTS In all plumages, legs and feet orange and iris brown. Nominate and race *conboschas* described. **Adult male:** Bill olive-green to yellow, often tinged bluish, with black nail. **Adult female:** Bill dusky-brown to yellowish-orange on subterminal area and towards base, with dusky culmen, sides and tip. Individually variable. **Juvenile:** Bill uniform dull reddish-grey at first, soon darkening, and with adult coloration appearing by first winter.

MEASUREMENTS Males average larger than females. Nominate *platyrhynchos*: Wing 257-285 (mean: male 279, female 265); tarsus 41-48; bill 47-61; mean weight of male 1170, of female 1042. Race *conboschas*: Wing 261-306 (mean: male 292, female 272), bill 44-52.

GEOGRAPHICAL VARIATION See introduction to the Mallard complex. In treatment followed here four races are included, two of which are treated separately below as Mexican Duck and Mariana Mallard. Nominate form occurs over most of world range of species; although American population averages larger than Old World birds, it is not separable. Isolated Greenland race *conboschas* is larger, though relatively smaller-billed, than the nominate (see Measurements), but is similar in plumage. Icelandic birds are somewhat intermediate, but are included in the nominate race.

HABITS Widespread and abundant, familiar to all as the 'prototype duck'. Very sociable, being invariably found in small to very large flocks by almost any form of water, although with preference for still fresh water. Pair-formation occurs in the autumn and winter; sometimes not until spring, when unmated females are often chased by several males. Breeding season varies according to latitude, but generally March to June, even earlier in milder parts of range. Nest site also varied: from ground, where hidden among vegetation, to tree holes and nestboxes and even old tree nests of large birds; may be some distance from water. After breeding has commenced, males gather to moult into eclipse. Feeds chiefly by dabbling and up-ending while swimming, but also wades in the shallows and grazes on land, visiting stubbles and crops in autumn and winter. Becomes very tame at park lakes, but normally shy and wary. Flight strong but rather heavy, with shallow wingbeats, rising easily from the water. Walks well and perches freely on branches overhanging water. Mixes freely with other species.

HABITAT Almost any form of lowland still water, from freshwater lakes to sheltered coastal bays and estuaries. Occasionally at higher altitudes.

DISTRIBUTION Widespread across most of northern hemisphere, avoiding tundra zone of high Arctic, high mountains and deserts. Chiefly migratory, although many populations of temperate western Europe and North America are resident. Range is extending in North America following widespread introductions for shooting purposes. Winters south to Mexico, North Africa, northern India and southern China. Small numbers penetrate Nile valley as far south as Ethiopia and the Sudan, but records from elsewhere in tropical Africa suspected to refer to escapes. Introduced onto Kerguelen Island in the southern Indian Ocean, Hawaii, and into southern Australia and New Zealand, where it has become locally established. Pattern of vagrancy difficult to summarise as many records suspected of being of escapes, but recorded Svalbard, Bear Island and south to Nicaragua, Costa Rica, Panama, Azores (has bred), Senegal, Mali, Nigeria, Kenya, Borneo and Hawaii. Greenland race is resident in coastal waters of southern Greenland.

POPULATION Abundant worldwide, with estimates including 9 million individuals in North America and 4-5 million in the western Palaearctic region.

MEXICAN DUCK   Plate 25
A.p. diazi
Alternative name: Mexican Mallard

Formerly a full species; introduced populations of the nominate Mallard in North America have now 'tampered' with the genes of this previously isolated duck and reduced its taxonomic status.

FIELD IDENTIFICATION Length 51-56 cm (20-22 in). Both sexes recall female Mallard, but are rather darker in body plumage, with dark tail and tail-coverts and more contrasting pale sides of head and neck. The general effect is of a bird somewhat intermediate between American Black Duck (88) and female Mallard, but with a Mallard speculum, although this is more greenish-blue and the white bands are not so wide as on typical Mallard. Bill of male is greenish-yellow; that of female dusky, with some dull orange, becoming greenish towards tip. Range does not overlap with that of either American Black or Mottled (87) Ducks, and only at northern limit with that of true Mallard. Hybridisation with Mallard in southern USA, however, has been to the extent that perhaps no pure Mexican Ducks remain north of Mexico.

MEASUREMENTS Sexes similar. Wing of male 270-285, of female 240-260; tarsus 42-46; bill 52-58; weight of male 960-1060, of female 815-990.

HABITS Much as Mallard, but generally only in small parties, mixing little with other species. Shy and wary. Flight considered to be faster and stronger than that of Mallard. Nests on ground. Breeding season April to May.

HABITAT Inland rivers, marshes, flooded fields and pools in open country and valleys.

DISTRIBUTION Extreme southern USA and central Mexico. Range extends from the Rio Grande and Pecos valleys of New Mexico and adjacent Arizona and west Texas, south locally through central uplands of Mexico to Puebla. Some northern populations move south to winter in central Mexico, although others remain in extreme southern USA in winter.

POPULATION Counts of wintering numbers have indicated an increase in the total population, which was estimated at 30,000-40,000 individuals in 1975. The southerly spread of the Mallard in USA and subsequent hybridisation have, however, already weakened the pure blood of the USA population of Mexican Duck; perhaps this will be the greatest threat to this interesting duck.

MARIANA MALLARD   Plate 27
A.p. oustaleti
Alternative name: Oustalet's Duck

Confined to the Mariana Islands of the Pacific, this strangely variable duck showed characters of both Mallard and Pacific Black Duck (91). Sadly, it was last seen in the wild in 1979 and may now be extinct.

FIELD IDENTIFICATION Length 52 cm (21 in). The only breeding duck of the Mariana Islands, although, in view of probable extinction, occasional migrants of other species now more likely to be recorded there. Despite the plumage variation of this form, most birds showed features closest to Pacific Black Duck rather than to Mallard. Males of this type differed from Pacific Black in being lighter, with broader light brown feather fringes on underparts; the dusky facial bar was weakly indicated; and they had orange legs, and olive bill with black nail and narrow culmen stripe. A smaller proportion of birds showed mostly green head, with buff mottling on sides of head and a very weak whitish neck-ring; the flanks were both vermiculated grey and mottled brown; the breast was reddish-chestnut, heavily mottled dusky; and the central tail feathers were slightly curled. The bill of this type showed extensive blackish over basal portion. Both types shared a wing pattern closer to that of Mallard, with a purple-blue speculum bordered fore and aft with white; some birds, however, had a green speculum with narrow buff tips, like Pacific Black. Males of the Mallard type went into eclipse, whereas Pacific Black types did not. Females resembled female Mallard, and had orange legs and blackish bill, latter with orange subterminal area.
MEASUREMENTS Wing 232-266 (mean 252), tarsus 41-43, bill 49-53.
HABITS Formerly met with in pairs or small parties, although flocks of up to 50-60 birds were reported on more extensive marshes. Considered to have had a prolonged breeding season, as nests and young reported April, June and July and males in eclipse reported at various times of the year. Nests were placed on ground among marshy vegetation. Fairly approachable, although swampy habitats made it a difficult duck to observe, the birds preferring reed-fringed channels and small secluded ponds rather than open water.
HABITAT Freshwater marshes with extensive vegetation.
DISTRIBUTION and POPULATION Formerly a local resident of the islands of Guam, Saipan and Tinian in the Mariana Islands of the western Pacific. It possibly wandered between islands to a certain degree as there was a report of two unidentified ducks on the island of Rota in 1945. Never numerous, although two separate flocks of 50-60 were

reported on Tinian in 1940; doubtless many were shot during the Second World War by troops stationed there. Extensive wetland drainage has been undertaken on the islands, and the only suitable habitats now remaining are at Lake Susupe on Saipan and Hagoi Marsh on Tinian. It had not been reported on Guam since 1946 until one was seen there in 1967, which could have been a visitor from another island. The species was still considered to be present on Tinian and Saipan in the 1970s. In 1979 a proposed captive-breeding programme was instigated, and after considerable effort three birds (two males and one female) were trapped on Lake Susupe on Saipan; one of the males was released back into the wild. These were perhaps the last, as none has been seen since, despite several searches on both Tinian and Saipan. The habitat on Saipan, however, is so dense that some hope remains for its continued existence. The captured pair remained in captivity, but both died in 1981 without having produced young.

REFERENCES Baker (1951), Cramp and Simmons (1977), Johnsgard (1975), Kear (1979), King (1981), Terres (1980).

85 HAWAIIAN DUCK   Plate 26
Anas wyvilliana
Alternative name: Koloa

Endemic to the Hawaiian Islands. Although smaller, this interesting duck shows Mallard (84) plumage features, and is often considered a race of Mallard.

FIELD IDENTIFICATION Length 44-49 cm (17-19 in). **At rest:** Although Northern Pintail (95), American Wigeon (72) and Northern Shoveler (107) occur on the Hawaiian Islands in winter and the Mallard has been introduced onto Kauai and Oahu, this and the Laysan Duck (86) are the only native breeding ducks, each occurring on different islands; a wide variety of migrant waterfowl species also occurs on the islands, including some which overwinter in small numbers. Hawaiian Ducks are basically small brownish ducks with orange legs. Females are mottled brown overall, with a redder-brown breast and dusky bill, the latter becoming orange towards tip. Males are variable, some being dull dark green on head and neck and with deep ruddy breasts, whereas others are considerably browner overall; their bill is greyish-olive, with a dusky mark on the culmen. Unlikely to be confused owing to restricted range. **In flight:** A small Mallard-type duck, with whitish underwing and green speculum, latter with narrow white borders fore and aft.
VOICE Vocally close to Mallard, but calls higher in pitch.
DESCRIPTION Somewhat sexually dimorphic. Some seasonal and individual variation. **Adult male breeding:** Individually variable. Brightest males have head and neck greenish-black, not strongly iridescent, with narrow pale eye-ring. Breast purplish-brown, with small dark spots. Most of remainder of body plumage warm brown, with dark brown subterminal markings. Tertials dark grey. Rump and uppertail-coverts blackish. Tail dark grey, with pale sides, the central feathers slightly curled. Upper-

wing-coverts greyish-brown, greater coverts tipped white. Secondaries iridescent green, with black subterminal border and white tips. Underwing whitish, with browner flight feathers. Duller males show extensive brown on head and neck, more extensive breast markings, and less strongly-marked tail pattern. **Adult male eclipse:** Brightest males become much as adult female, but retain male bill pattern. **Adult female:** Almost entire plumage mottled warm brown, similar to female Mallard, but eye-line indistinct and breast redder-brown. Wing as male, with greener speculum than Mallard. **Juvenile:** Similar to female, but duller brown, with feather markings less clear.

BARE PARTS In all plumages, legs and feet orange with dusky webs, and iris brown. **Male:** Bill greyish-olive, with black nail and patch on centre of culmen. **Female:** Bill dusky, with orange subterminal area.

MEASUREMENTS Males a little larger than females. Wing of male 212-228, of female 210-220; tarsus 37-40; bill 41-48; mean weight of male 670, of female 573.

GEOGRAPHICAL VARIATION None. Obviously a long-isolated descendant of the Mallard, with close connections with still smaller Laysan Duck.

HABITS Although nowadays normally encountered in pairs or small parties, in the days when it was more abundant it congregated into quite large flocks. The breeding season is somewhat irregular, but most breeding occurs between March and June. Nests are placed on the ground, well hidden among vegetation. After breeding, small moult gatherings are formed. Feeds chiefly by dabbling while swimming or wading, but also on land among crops and pasture.

HABITAT Almost any form of available fresh water on the islands, from lowland marshes, ditches, reservoirs and wet fields to mountain streams.

DISTRIBUTION Endemic resident on the Hawaiian Islands, where it occurs in good numbers in the Hanalei valley on the island of Kauai. Formerly widespread on other islands (Hawaii, Maui, Molokai, Oahu and Niihau), but exterminated on these by over-hunting and introduced predators. Recently re-introduced onto Oahu and Hawaii, and seems to be gaining a foothold at least on Oahu.

POPULATION Formerly widespread on a number of Hawaiian Islands, but decimated by shooting, land drainage and introduced predators, chiefly cats, dogs, rats and mongooses. The mongoose was relatively recently introduced to control the rats, and has now started to establish itself on Kauai. Hanalei valley on Kauai has now become a refuge for this duck, with an estimated population of some 3,000 Koloa in 1967. The species responds well to captive breeding and some birds have been released back onto Hawaii and Oahu, but it has yet to become well established away from Kauai.

REFERENCES Delacour (1954), King (1975).

86 LAYSAN DUCK　　　　　Plate 26
Anas laysanensis
Alternative name: Laysan Teal

A very small island mallard, perhaps descending

from the Hawaiian Duck (85) rather than directly from northern Mallard (84). Restricted to the tiny island of Laysan in the outer Hawaiian Archipelago.

FIELD IDENTIFICATION Length 35-40 cm (14-16 in). **At rest:** The only duck likely to be seen on Laysan Island. A small, dark brownish duck, with conspicuous white patches around the eye and orange legs. Unlikely to be confused with any other species, even in captivity. **In flight:** Although capable of flight, it does not seem to spend much time on the wing, possibly because its island home is only 3 km long. A small dark duck, with whitish underwing and dark upperwing, latter relieved only by speculum, which is green on males, dusky on females, bordered fore and aft by white lines.

VOICE Vocally close to Mallard, but less noisy.

DESCRIPTION All plumages similar. Some individual variation. General coloration dark reddish-brown, heavily mottled with dark brown subterminal feather markings. Head and neck darker, dusky-brown, with variably extensive whitish patches around eye and bill-base, often extending to chin, and irregularly speckled with white on sides of head. On male, the secondaries are green, with black subterminal border and white tips, and the greater coverts tipped white; on female and juvenile, secondaries dull dark brown. Underwing whitish. Although sexes are similar, females tend to have browner upperparts than males owing to broader brown feather fringes, and males tend to have central tail feathers slightly curled.

BARE PARTS In all plumages, legs and feet orange and iris brown. **Male:** Bill dull green, with dusky culmen patch and nail. **Female:** Bill brownish-yellow, with dull orange subterminal area and sides.

MEASUREMENTS Sexes very similar in size, although males average slightly larger than females. Wing of male 192-210, of female 190-196; tarsus 37-39; bill 38-40; mean weight of male 447, of female 451.

GEOGRAPHICAL VARIATION None. This isolated duck is a Mallard type, and some authorities consider it merely an extremely-specialised race of Mallard. Its very small size and similarities to Hawaiian Duck suggest, however, that it has further evolved from an isolated population of Hawaiian Duck rather than directly from Mallard.

HABITS Found in pairs and small parties, congregating into larger flocks to moult after breeding. The pair-bond is semi-permanent, with many pairs selecting the same mate in successive years. Breeding season chiefly May to July, with nests hidden under bushes or in grass clumps near the lagoon. Feeds by foraging while walking, birds working all habitats on the island; when water levels suitable, also dabbles and up-ends on the lagoon. Feeds chiefly at night, or in evenings and early mornings, spending most of day loafing at own favoured spots. Remarkably confiding and approachable, preferring not to take to the air, although can fly quite well.

HABITAT Favours brackish lagoon of Laysan Island, but wanders throughout the island, including the seashore.

DISTRIBUTION Resident endemic to tiny isolated Laysan Island, some 225 km from the nearest island in the northwestern chain of the Hawaiian Islands. Laysan is a volcanic island some 3 km by 1.5 km and covers 370 ha; it has a brackish central lagoon where the centre of the population is based. The island is a reserve, with restricted access, landing permits being granted only for scientific work to be carried out.

POPULATION The history of this duck is typical of that of many island waterfowl, but in this case there is a considerable success story. The island was occupied for guano-mining between 1891 and 1904, and the ducks were hunted by the workers; by 1902 the population had dropped to under 100. In 1909 the island was declared part of the Hawaiian Islands Bird Reservation but, despite this, Japanese plumage-hunters visited in 1909 and 1910 to collect seabirds and further decimated the population. Introduced rabbits had by then overrun the island and destroyed much of the vegetation, and by 1912 only seven ducks remained. An eradication of the rabbits eased the situation and the vegetation recovered, although in 1930 only one female remained and her eggs were destroyed by a Bristle-thighed Curlew. Apparently this lone female had sufficient semen in her oviduct to produce another clutch, and by 1950 the population had increased to 33 birds. It has now stabilised at around 500 individuals, which must be the maximum that the island can support, although the figure fluctuates as high as 700 birds. The species breeds well in captivity, and as a safeguard against disease or other natural disasters there is now access to captive-breeding numbers. The possibility of establishing it on other islands is also being considered, although this requires careful planning in view of problems of introductions and their effects on the native fauna of other islands.

REFERENCES Moulton and Weller (1984).

87 MOTTLED DUCK   Plate 25
Anas fulvigula

Alternative names: Florida Duck, Florida Mallard

Confined to coastal regions of southeastern USA. Somewhat intermediate between Mallard (84) and American Black Duck (88), this form is sometimes considered a race of Mallard.

FIELD IDENTIFICATION Length 53-58 cm (21-23 in). **At rest:** Both sexes somewhat intermediate between female Mallard and American Black Duck in general appearance. Overlaps in range with both in winter; all three may be found on the same marshes. On Mottled the pale sides of head and neck contrast more strongly with the heavily-marked brownish body plumage and dusky crown than on Mallard. The body plumage is a somewhat darker and warmer brown and the feather markings are blacker and broader than on Mallard, giving a darker effect at some distance (especially Gulf coast populations) more reminiscent of American Black Duck; birds at closer range, with the brown feather borders more obvious, closely resemble Mallard. The breast is more intensely mottled black and the uppertail- and undertail-coverts and tail are darker than on Mallard. Male's bill is distinctly clear yellow,

with black nail and a small but clear black spot at the gape; female's bill is more variable. On the water, the speculum may be visible, lacking the prominent white borders of Mallard. Beware individual variation of Mallards in female-like plumage. American Black Duck is similar, but has considerably darker, almost uniform blackish-brown, body plumage, with only very narrow and indistinct pale brown feather borders which are apparent only at close quarters. Mottled Ducks are marginally a little smaller, slimmer and shorter-billed if the two species are seen together, and are more likely to be found in pairs during the winter. Mexican Duck (under 84) is similar to Mottled, but has white-bordered speculum typical of a Mallard and range does not overlap with that of Mottled Duck. Female hybrids between Mallard and American Black Duck are very similar to Mottled Ducks, but show a narrow white band at the base of the speculum, absent on both Mottled and American Black. **In flight:** Closely resembles American Black Duck, but speculum lacks white border at base and has only a narrow and indistinct white line at tip, which distinguishes Mottled Duck from darkest of Mallards or Mexican Duck. Body plumage not quite so black as American Black, but distant birds inseparable, showing similar strong contrast of very white underwing with very dark body. If seen well, a Mottled Duck rising from water shows a greenish-blue speculum, not the purple-blue of an American Black.

VOICE Similar to that of Mallard.

DESCRIPTION All plumages similar. **Adult:** Crown, eye-stripe and upper hindneck dusky, paling on lower hindneck. Supercilium and sides and front of head and neck greyish-buff, weakly and finely streaked darker. Breast and entire body plumage warm brown, with broad black subterminal markings, most apparent along flanks, and heavily spotted on breast. Tertials very dark, with narrow brown fringes. Tail dark brown, mottled and edged paler brown. Upperwing-coverts dark brown, with tawny-brown tips to greater coverts. Secondaries greenish-blue, with black subterminal border and narrow white tips. Underwing very white, with darker flight feathers. Sexes similar, but female has broader brown feather borders, especially on flanks, and different bill colour from male. **Juvenile:** Similar to adult, but duller brown and with less clearly-angled subterminal markings on flanks; upperparts darker, with narrower pale feather edges.

BARE PARTS In all plumages, legs and feet orange and iris brown. **Male:** Bill clear yellow, with black nail, nostril, narrow band around very base and gape spot. **Female:** Bill duller, more olive-yellow, somewhat mottled dusky on culmen and sides, sometimes tinged orange at sides and subterminally.

MEASUREMENTS Males typically a little larger than females. Wing of male 241-263, of female 223-242; tarsus 45-48; bill 49-59; mean weight of male 1030, of female 968.

GEOGRAPHICAL VARIATION Two races described, but are rather poorly differentiated. Nominate race resident in Florida. Race *maculosa* of coastal Louisiana, Texas and northern Mexico tends to be darker and more heavily marked. Species is sometimes considered a race of Mallard.

HABITS Typically found in pairs or small parties, forming smaller aggregations than either Mallard or American Black Duck, but latter uncommon as far south in winter as range of Mottled Duck and unlikely to be found in any numbers. Pair-formation occurs in early winter, but paired birds may be found almost throughout the year, except in the post-breeding moult period when larger flocks are formed. Breeding commences as early as February and may be as late as August, but peak is May and June. Nest hidden on ground among vegetation in and by marshes. Nests are heavily preyed upon by variety of creatures, which no doubt accounts for prolonged breeding season. Feeds chiefly by dabbling while swimming and wading and by up-ending in typical Mallard fashion. Shy and wary, but general behaviour much as Mallard, although more sedentary.

HABITAT Lowland marshes and wet grassland, brackish coastal marshes and prairies with pools.

DISTRIBUTION Chiefly resident in lowland coastal regions of southeastern USA, extending just into Mexico. Nominate race resident and widespread in Florida north to Tampa. Race *maculosa* a resident of coastal lowlands from Mississippi delta west through Louisiana and Texas, south into coastal Mexico to Tamaulipas; some southward dispersal in winter as far as central Veracruz. Vagrants have been reported from Kansas, Colorado, and inland west Texas.

POPULATION Generally common and widespread over its somewhat restricted range, with population estimates from the 1960s of some 50,000 individuals in Florida and some 100,000 breeding birds of race *maculosa*.

REFERENCES Johnsgard (1975), Terres (1980).

88 AMERICAN BLACK DUCK   Plate 25
Anas rubripes

Alternative name: Black Duck

Darkest of the mallard group of ducks, this eastern North American duck has had its range penetrated by the spreading Mallard (84) and hybrids are becoming more frequent.

FIELD IDENTIFICATION Length 53-61 cm (21-24 in). **At rest:** Both sexes recall exceedingly dark female Mallard, with pale sides of head and neck contrasting with almost uniform blackish-brown body plumage. Confusion possible with Mexican Duck (under 84), but ranges do not overlap and Mexican Duck has prominent white borders to speculum. Mottled Duck (87) is very similar, especially darker Gulf coast populations, but is not so uniformly dark, having prominent paler brown feather borders and centres, especially along flanks, less uniformly blackish uppertail- and undertail-coverts and tail, and has indistinct black gape spot and yellower bill. Most likely confusion potential is with exceptionally dark female Mallards, which are frequent in areas with influence of feral birds; even darkest Mallards show some pale at sides of tail and stronger sub-

terminal markings on feathers of underparts, but as last resort may need to be flushed to check for presence of white basal bar to bluer speculum (on very dark Mallards, however, white band at base of speculum is often narrower than normal). American Black Ducks have only very narrow brown fringes to blackish-brown body plumage, with uniformly dark uppertail- and undertail-coverts and tail. The dark body, crown, hindneck and eye-stripe contrast strongly with pale sides and front of head and neck. Tends to appear larger and bulkier than Mallard when both seen together. Bill is almost unmarked yellowish or olive, with some greyer shades on that of female, and legs are varying shades of orange. Hybrids with Mallard now becoming more frequent: male hybrids show obvious combinations of the two species, with bottle-green on head and neck, mixed with pale brown, a reddish breast, and less dark body plumage than American Black Duck; female hybrids more difficult, recalling Mottled Duck, but usually with reasonably apparent whitish line at base of speculum. Possibility of confusion with female Common Scoter (134) should perhaps also be borne in mind when identifying suspected vagrants. **In flight:** Mallard-like shape, but appears distinctly bulkier in body, this exaggerated by blacker appearance. Whitish underwing contrasts strikingly with blackish body and upperside, showing no pale in tail or on borders to purple speculum.

VOICE Similar to that of Mallard.

DESCRIPTION All plumages more or less similar. Some seasonal variation. Ageing and sexing of other than obviously well-marked males difficult. **Adult male:** Crown, hindneck and eye-stripe blackish, mottled pale brown. Remainder of head and neck pale dull buffish, with narrow dark streaks. Entire body plumage blackish-brown, with narrow pale buff-brown edges, most prominent on breast and flanks. Uppertail- and undertail-coverts and tail blackish-brown. Tertials blackish-brown, with very narrow pale fringes. Upperwing very dark; secondaries bluish-purple, with black subterminal band and very narrow and indistinct whitish or buffish tips (latter often lacking). Underwing very white, with greyer flight feathers. In eclipse, head and neck less strikingly pale, with stronger streaking, and bill duller and more olive, as on female. **Adult female:** Much as male, but less contrasting, with head and neck greyer and more strongly streaked; tertials narrower than on male, bill greener and speculum a little bluer. **Juvenile:** Much as female, but pale fringes to underpart feathers broken, giving slightly-streaked rather than scalloped appearance to feather fringes; whole appearance browner, less uniformly blackish. Becomes much as adult by first winter.

BARE PARTS Adult Male: Bill yellow, washed olive to pale orange, with black nail and nostril; becomes strongly washed greyish-olive in eclipse. Legs and feet orange to reddish-orange, sometimes red; duller in eclipse. Iris brown. **Adult female:** Bill light olive or greenish-yellow, with black nail and culmen streak, often mottled a little at sides. Legs and feet brownish-orange. Iris brown. **Juvenile:** Bill greyish-olive, becoming yellow on males by end of first winter. Legs and feet brownish, more orange on males, becoming brighter during first winter. Iris brown.

MEASUREMENTS Males typically larger than females. Wing of male 265-301, of female 245-275; tarsus 44-50; bill 45-60; mean weight of male 1245, of female 1135.

GEOGRAPHICAL VARIATION No races recognised. In view of frequent hybridisation, could well be regarded as merely a well-marked race of Mallard.

HABITS Highly gregarious, forming very large concentrations outside breeding season, especially in winter. Pair-formation occurs during latter part of winter, but many birds already paired in autumn. Breeding season from March to June. Nest on ground, hidden among vegetation, often close to water but may be a considerable distance away; sometimes placed on lodges of muskrats, in tree holes or in old tree nests of large birds. General behaviour much as that of Mallard, but more tolerant of freezing conditions, staying further north in winter. Breeds in more wooded and coastal habitats than Mallard, rather than in open country, and in winter chiefly in coastal or estuarine and brackish-water habitats.

HABITAT Breeds by fresh and saltwater marshes, often in well-wooded country. In winter on estuaries, brackish coastal marshes and sheltered coastal bays.

DISTRIBUTION Widespread over eastern North America, breeding from Manitoba east to Labrador and Newfoundland, south over Great Lakes region and along Atlantic coast to North Carolina. Northern populations move south to winter over eastern seaboard of USA south to Florida and the Gulf coast, with small numbers into Texas. Rarely, further west to Utah, Washington and Colorado, with vagrants as far as California, Baffin Island and even Korea. Some western records suspected to be of attempted introductions for hunting purposes. Vagrants also reported south to Puerto Rico, and eastwards over Atlantic to British Isles, Sweden and the Azores. Some European vagrants have stayed for very long periods, hybridising with local Mallards.

POPULATION Abundant, but declining alarmingly. Cause of decline uncertain, but locally due to competition with Mallard on breeding grounds, although this is possibly not the primary cause. Population estimated at some 4 million in early 1950s, but in 1960s wintering figures indicated a reduction by some 40%. It is extensively hunted, with up to half a million birds killed annually in 1960s.

REFERENCES Johnsgard (1975), Wright (1954).

89 MELLER'S DUCK   Plate 26
Anas melleri

This isolated mallard type is confined to Madagascar and Mauritius, but little is known of its present status.

FIELD IDENTIFICATION Length 63-68 cm (25-27 in). **At rest:** The only Mallard-like duck likely to be found on Madagascar or Mauritius. Both sexes

recall large female Mallards (84); they have relatively longer neck and bill than Mallard and the entire plumage is uniform mottled brown, with the head uniformly streaked and unpatterned, and the bill dark greyish. Unlikely to be confused with any other duck on their islands. **In flight:** General appearance is of a large female Mallard-like duck, with mottled brown plumage offering contrast only with whitish underwing and with green speculum, latter having a narrow white trailing edge.

VOICE Much as that of Mallard, although dry 'kreep' call of male is distinctly trisyllabic. The female quack is shriller than that of Mallard.

DESCRIPTION All plumages similar. **Adult:** Head and neck brown, closely and finely streaked dark brown. Entire body plumage brown, with darker brown subterminal feather markings, giving typical female Mallard-like pattern. Upperwing-coverts dark brown, greater coverts with subterminal black band and tipped rusty-buff. Secondaries iridescent green, with black border and narrow white tips. Underwing whitish, with darker flight feathers. Sexes similar, although female a little duller than warmer brown male. **Juvenile:** Very much as adult, although plumage tone warmer, more reddish-brown.

BARE PARTS All plumages: Bill long and heavy compared with other mallards, greyish-olive, with black nail and sometimes a little blackish at base. Legs and feet orange-brown. Iris dark brown.

MEASUREMENTS Sexes similar. Wing of male 245-260, of female 241-253; tarsus 42-45; bill 52-62; weight — no data.

GEOGRAPHICAL VARIATION None. Although obviously a Mallard descendant, it is somewhat more distantly related than many other isolated Mallard-like ducks.

HABITS Little information. Usually found in pairs or small parties, with no reports of any substantial gatherings. Breeds during July-September, but no wild nests have been described, although most likely to nest on ground as other similar species. Feeds by dabbling in streams and ponds in Mallard fashion. The little that has been published about this duck suggests that its behaviour basically resembles that of Mallard.

HABITAT Freshwater swamps, marshes, streams and lakes, especially in humid forested areas, from sea level to 2000 m. Also flooded fields.

DISTRIBUTION Probably occurs throughout greater part of eastern Madagascar (Malagasy), but little recent information. Its presence on Mauritius, some 840 km east of Madagascar, has usually been considered to be due to an introduction some time before 1800, but the species is equally likely to have arrived on that island under its own steam. It formerly occurred on nearby Réunion, but is now extinct there.

POPULATION Recent information suggests a considerable decline on Madagascar and, as ducks are not protected on the island, it may well be endangered. Mauritius population largely destroyed by shooting; described as still quite common (hundreds of pairs) in the 1930s, it had declined to some 20 pairs by the late 1970s. Small numbers are now held in captivity, where it seems to be thriving.

REFERENCES Johnsgard (1978), Kear and Williams (1978).

90 YELLOW-BILLED DUCK   Plate 21
Anas undulata

Alternative name: Yellowbill

Widespread over southern and eastern Africa, this is the only African duck with bright yellow on the bill.

FIELD IDENTIFICATION Length 51-58 cm (20-23 in). **At rest:** A dabbling duck, the size of Mallard (84), easily distinguished from all others in Africa by its dark greyish plumage and bright yellow bill. The neck is more slender than that of Mallard, and the head shorter and more rounded, with a higher crown. The very dark head and neck contrast a little with somewhat lighter and greyer body plumage. Unlikely to be confused with any other duck; although dark plumage suggests African Black Duck (70), its yellow bill and lack of broad buff or white barring on the upperparts are easy distinctions. In captivity, both Speckled Teal (78) and Yellow-billed Pintail (96) share similar bill colour, but former is smaller and dumpier with unmarked flanks and latter is more slender, browner and with pointed tail. **In flight:** A large dark duck, with somewhat 'waisted' neck and bulbous head, carried well up in flight. Dark plumage is relieved by whitish underwings and prominent blue or green speculum, latter bordered fore and aft by white bands.

VOICE Male utters various low whistles. Female has Mallard-like descending series of quacks, each note rather hoarser than in Mallard.

DESCRIPTION Sexes similar. Nominate race described. **Adult:** Head and neck greyish-black, with narrow pale feather fringes. Entire body plumage similar, but a little lighter and rather browner, with broader pale edges to feathers contrasting with almost uniformly darker head and neck. Upperwing-coverts dark grey, with greater coverts tipped white. Secondaries green, with black subterminal border and white tips. Underwing whitish, with dark flight feathers. Although sexes similar, female a little duller, with drabber speculum, and with forehead more steeply sloping than male. **Juvenile:** Similar to adult, but pale feather fringes broader and buffer, with fringes broken to give more spotted appearance to underparts.

BARE PARTS Bill bright yellow, with black stripe down centre of culmen, nail and cutting edges; female has paler yellow on bill than male. Legs and feet variable, from yellowish, through reddish-brown to blackish-grey. Iris reddish-brown.

MEASUREMENTS Males tend to be larger than females. Wing of male 245-265, of female 225-243; tarsus 39-51; bill 44-56; mean weight of male 965, of female 823.

GEOGRAPHICAL VARIATION Two races recognised. Nominate race, described above, occurs over southern portion of range north to Kenya. Race *ruppelli* occurs from northern Kenya northwards; although similar to nominate race, it has a blue speculum, a deeper yellow bill and is darker, having narrower pale feather fringes.

HABITS Highly sociable dabbling duck, forming very large concentrations in southern Africa during the dry season. Flocks break up at onset of rains as birds disperse to breeding areas. Breeding season variable according to state of suitable waters. Breeding occurs at almost any time of the year, but chiefly during local rainy season: generally July-October in very south; further north, in Uganda from June to August and in Ethiopia from August to September. Nests are placed on the ground in dense vegetation, usually very close to water, but in Kenya at least may build some distance from water. Feeds by dabbling with head and neck submerged and by up-ending, but also comes on to grassland to graze. Spends much of day loafing in shallow water by banks of lakes and pools, feeding chiefly in early morning and evening. Flight strong and fast, generally flying high when disturbed. Relatively shy and wary. Undertakes quite extensive movements in search of suitable waters at onset of rainy season, with ringing recoveries at distances of over 1000 km.

HABITAT Variety of wetland habitats, from open estuarine waters to flooded grasslands, lakes, slow-flowing rivers, sewage-pools and reservoirs. Avoids coastal waters, but occurs on brackish coastal lagoons. In northern parts of range occurs up to 3890 m.

DISTRIBUTION Widespread and abundant resident in tropical Africa, with both local and quite extensive seasonal movements. Northern race breeds from southern Sudan and Ethiopia south to northern Uganda and northern Kenya. Southern race over almost the whole of southern and eastern Africa, avoiding tropical rainforest zone of Central Africa and more arid zones of the southwest. A vagrant of race *ruppelli* has been recorded from Cameroon.

POPULATION Widespread and abundant. Although no total estimates have been made, in southern Africa an estimate of between 52,000 and 65,000 individuals has been suggested from dry-season counts.

REFERENCES Brown *et al.* (1982), Rowan (1963).

91 PACIFIC BLACK DUCK   Plate 27
Anas superciliosa

Alternative names: Black Duck (Australasia), Grey Duck

The mallard representative of the Australasian region, closely related to the more strongly-marked Spotbill (92) of eastern Asia.

FIELD IDENTIFICATION Length 54-61 cm (21-24 in). **At rest:** The strongly-marked facial pattern and dark brown body plumage easily distinguish the Pacific Black from other similar-sized brown dabbling ducks, even in captivity. Both sexes have a prominent pale buff supercilium, buff sides to head and neck, and contrasting black eye-stripe and bar across lower side of head from bill-base to ear-coverts. This, coupled with the almost uniform dark brown body and dark grey bill, easily separates them from the darkest female Mallard (84), which has been introduced into parts of Australia and New Zealand. Like the Mallard, may be quite tame around park lakes in towns, and the two species often hybridise. Hybrids show a mixture of Mallard and Pacific Black Duck plumage features, female hybrids being closer to Pacific Black but with purple rather than green speculum. See also Spotbill. **In flight:** A large, very dark dabbling duck, with pale sides of head and striking white underwing. The upperside is very dark, showing no pale in tail region, but a green speculum, bordered narrowly with white or pale buff on trailing edge and at the base, offers some contrast at closer range.

VOICE Similar to that of Mallard, but rather more hoarse, especially female calls.

DESCRIPTION All plumages similar. Ageing and sexing very difficult in the field. Nominate race described. **All plumages:** Crown and hindneck dark brown. Supercilium and area immediately below eye-stripe bright pale buff. Eye-stripe and bar across lower sides of face blackish-brown. Sides and front of head and neck pale brownish-buff. Almost whole of body plumage dark brown, with buff-brown feather fringes, most apparent on underparts. Upperwing dark brown, the greater coverts tipped pale buff or white; secondaries green, subterminally bordered with black and tipped narrowly with buff or white. Underwing very white, with dusky flight feathers. Female slightly duller and less clearly marked than male.

BARE PARTS All plumages: Bill dark grey, paler towards tip, with black nail. Legs and feet yellowish-brown, with dusky webs. Iris dark brown.

MEASUREMENTS Males tend to be larger than females. Nominate *superciliosa*: Wing of male 256-262, of female 246-255; tarsus 42-47; bill 47-53. Race *rogersi*: Wing of male 230-284 (mean 262), of female 226-271 (mean 247); bill 45-58; mean weight of male 1114, of female 1025. Race *pelewensis*: Wing of male 224-250, of female 221-243; bill 19-22.

GEOGRAPHICAL VARIATION Three races recognised, all very similar in plumage. Nominate race of New Zealand and islands to the south described above. Race *rogersi* is poorly differentiated, but tends to be a little duller, with facial pattern less bright; it breeds throughout Australia, southern New Guinea and many of the East Indian islands. A smaller and darker collection of forms breeding on various islands of the western Pacific tend to have the blackish eye-stripe broader than on the nominate race, darker sides of neck, and have narrower pale fringes to the body feathers; they have been collectively named as race *pelewensis*, but were formerly split into a diversity of races with subtle differences in both size and plumage between the populations of various groups of islands. Some authorities have gone so far as to unite Pacific Black Duck and Spotbill in one species, based on the somewhat intermediate features exhibited by the Chinese Spotbill; clearly, the isolated Philippine Duck (93) is also not too far removed.

HABITS Sociable, but usually encountered in pairs or small parties on almost any form of watery habitat; does not form the large concentrations of many other Australasian species. Breeding season varies over wide range according to local conditions, but is chiefly during July-October in southern Australia, March-May in the north of the contin-

ent, and September-January in New Zealand. Nests are found in much the same variety of situations as those of the Mallard, from on the ground or in tree holes to in old tree nests of other large birds. Feeds by dabbling and up-ending in shallow water, and also visits stubbles and crop fields at certain times of the year. In Australia at least it is somewhat nomadic, moving in to temporary floodwaters when conditions are suitable after rains. Flight and many behavioural features are essentially Mallard-like.

HABITAT Variety of wetland habitats, from park lakes, reservoirs, small ponds, flooded grasslands and marshes to estuarine waters and brackish lagoons, although tends to avoid the seashore or strongly saline waters.

DISTRIBUTION Widespread throughout the Australasian region and western Pacific islands. Nominate race found throughout New Zealand and also occurs on a number of southern islands, including Kermadec, Chatham, Auckland, Campbell and Macquarie Islands. Australian race both resident and a dispersive migrant over most of the country except more arid regions; also occurs in southern New Guinea and several Indonesian islands, including Sumatra, Java, Sulawesi, Lesser Sundas and Moluccas, and some individuals even reach New Zealand, indicating the close affinities between the two forms. Race *pelewensis* occupies a wide range across the western Pacific chains of islands, including Society and Cook Islands, Tonga, Samoa, Fiji, New Caledonia, Loyalty Islands, New Hebrides, Santa Cruz, Solomon Islands, the Bismarck Archipelago, Palau and northern lowland New Guinea.

POPULATION Little information available on numbers inhabiting various islands. In Australia and New Zealand is widespread and abundant, although, in New Zealand, is suffering from competition with introduced Mallard, which has replaced it in a number of districts. Mallard is less well established in Australia, although there seems to have been a marked decline in Pacific Black numbers there in recent years and some concern has been expressed; the cause and extent of this apparent decrease, however, is not yet understood.

REFERENCES Frith (1967), RAOU (1984).

92 SPOTBILL   Plate 27
Anas poecilorhyncha
Alternative name: Spot-billed Duck

Widespread over tropical and eastern Palaearctic Asia, this large mallard type is sometimes treated as conspecific with the Pacific Black Duck (91) owing to somewhat intermediate features of the Chinese race. The latter race is readily identifiable in the field and is treated separately from the other two races of Spotbill.

SPOTBILL (INDIAN AND BURMESE)
A.p. poecilorhyncha and A.p. haringtoni

FIELD IDENTIFICATION Length 58-63 cm (23-25 in). **At rest:** A large bulky dabbling duck, with very dark lower and rear body and upperparts contrasting with very pale, almost whitish, head, neck and breast. Has dark crown, eye-stripe and hindneck, large white area on the tertials and striking bill pattern. Males have a blackish bill with brilliant yellow terminal portion and waxy-red base; females have smaller red spots at bill-base. This selection of features gives an appearance quite unlike that of any other species, but see also Chinese Spotbill below. **In flight:** Large size and bulky body, coupled with contrast between very pale head, neck and breast and blackish rear body and upperparts, is distinctive. Upperwing very dark, with green speculum bordered fore and aft with narrow white lines, and with very large white area at wing base formed by tertials. Underwing whitish, with dark flight feathers, contrasting strongly with dark underbody. See also Chinese Spotbill below, which has rather different wing pattern.

VOICE Much as that of Mallard (84).

DESCRIPTION All plumages similar. Nominate race described. **Adult male:** Crown, eye-stripe and hindneck blackish. Sides and front of head and neck whitish, washed pale buff, lightly and finely streaked darker. Underparts from lower neck and breast downwards similar, but becoming distinctly spotted dark grey-brown on breast and more obviously on flanks, grading to almost uniform blackish-brown on centre of underparts and ventral region. Upperparts blackish grey-brown, with pale buffish-white borders to feathers of mantle and scapulars. Back, rump, uppertail-coverts and tail uniform blackish-brown. Upperwing blackish-grey, with white tips to greater coverts; inner tertials white; secondaries green, with purple reflections, and with black subterminal border and white tips. Underwing very white, with dark grey flight feathers. **Adult female:** Much as male, but a little duller and less strongly marked, with smaller, inconspicuous red spots on bill. **Juvenile:** Much as adult, but duller, not quite so blackish below, more dark brown, with spotting less clearly defined. Lacks red spots on bill.

BARE PARTS In all plumages, legs and feet bright orange-red and iris brown. Nominate race described. Bill blackish, with bright yellow or orange-yellow terminal portion and black nail, male with two bright waxy-red patches at very base which become swollen and very obvious in breeding season; red areas at base of bill much smaller and inconspicuous on female, absent on juvenile.

MEASUREMENTS Males larger than females. Nominate *poecilorhyncha*: Wing of male 260-280, of female 250-268; tarsus 46-48; bill 50-65; weight of male 1230-1500, of female 790-1360. Race *haringtoni*: Wing of male 245-268, of female 237-255; bill 50-57. See also Chinese Spotbill below.

GEOGRAPHICAL VARIATION Three races recognised, Chinese race treated separately below. Nominate race, described above, chiefly resident throughout the Indian subcontinent. Race *haringtoni* resident further east than nominate, from eastern Assam and Burma, north to Yunnan and east to Laos; it is somewhat smaller than nominate form, with red spots at base of bill more restricted, and the underparts are more uniform, less distinctly spotted. Species is sometimes considered conspecific with Pacific Black Duck.

HABITS Sociable, but does not form large concentrations. Usually in small parties or flocks of up to 50

birds outside breeding season, mixing freely with other dabbling ducks. Pair-formation usually begins soon after post-breeding moult, with birds in pairs throughout most of year. Breeding season varies according to water levels, chiefly after local rainy season, which is generally July to October in northern India and November and December further south, but species is suspected to be double-brooded in some districts. Nests are placed on ground among vegetation, usually not far from water. Feeds by dabbling and up-ending in shallow water or by wading among emergent vegetation. Feeds chiefly in evening and early morning, spending most of day loafing on banks or islands. Shy and wary. Flight strong, but rather less agile on wing than Mallard, having a more laboured take-off, no doubt a result of rather greater bulk.

HABITAT Favours shallow freshwater lakes and marshes with extensive emergent vegetation; less frequently on rivers.

DISTRIBUTION Widespread over most of lowland tropical southern Asia. Range extends west to Pakistan, south to Sri Lanka (where it is uncommon), east to Laos and north to southern China (southwestern Yunnan). Both forms are largely resident, although the Indian race disperses somewhat in the rainy season. Reports of its occurrence in the Andaman Islands need confirmation, and a recovery of a bird ringed in northern India in winter and shot near Novosibirsk in central Siberia in late summer is extraordinary.

CHINESE SPOTBILL
A.p. zonorhyncha

A well-marked, somewhat migratory northern race of the Spotbill, easily separable in the field and intermediate between southern races of the species and Pacific Black Duck (91).

FIELD IDENTIFICATION Obviously a Spotbill with its bright yellow tip to the black bill. It differs from the southern races in lacking any red at the base of the bill, in being considerably browner, with less heavily-spotted breast and fore-flanks, and in having a blue speculum, a buffer wash to sides of head, a narrow white tertial stripe, and a short, dusky line extending back from base of bill towards cheek. Many of these features are suggestive of Pacific Black Duck, from which it is easily distinguished by range, bright yellow bill-tip, less striking facial pattern and blue speculum. The upperwing shows only a narrow and inconspicuous white line along tertials, quite different from the large white patch of the southern Spotbill races, and the speculum is blue, with very narrow white lines at base and along trailing edge.

MEASUREMENTS Wing 243-276, bill 56-63.

DISTRIBUTION Widespread over Palaearctic eastern Asia, with northernmost populations migratory. Breeding range extends over most of China, north into eastern Mongolia and to the Amur River in eastern USSR, and includes Japan, Korea and southern Sakhalin; the southern limits of the breeding range are Kwangtung, northern Yunnan and Szechwan. Northernmost populations migrate south to winter in southern and eastern China; occasional further west in Mongolia and to Lake Baikal, also Taiwan, with small numbers south to Thailand and Cambodia in winter. Vagrants recorded in western Siberia, northeast India, the Philippines and Alaska.

POPULATION All races widespread and locally common, although no population estimates have been made.
REFERENCES Ali and Ripley (1968), Dementiev and Gladkov (1952).

93 PHILIPPINE DUCK   Plate 26
Anas luzonica

Distinctive mallard type, endemic to the Philippine Islands.

FIELD IDENTIFICATION Length 48-58 cm (19-23 in). **At rest:** Unmistakable. A large dabbling duck, reminiscent of Mallard (84) in size and shape, but greyish and unmottled overall, with distinctive head pattern. Head and neck rusty-cinnamon, contrasting with blackish crown, hindneck and eye-stripe. All plumages are similar. **In flight:** A generally rather dark duck, apart from whitish underwing and green speculum, latter bordered fore and aft by narrow white lines.
VOICE Much as that of Mallard, but all calls a little harsher.
DESCRIPTION All plumages similar. **Adult:** Head and neck rusty-cinnamon. Crown, hindneck and eye-stripe blackish-brown. Almost entire body plumage virtually unmarked grey, a little darker on upperparts and with weak buffish wash on breast. Back, rump and uppertail-coverts blackish-grey. Upperwing brownish-grey, with white tips to greater coverts; secondaries green, with black subterminal border and narrow white tips. Underwing whitish, with darker flight feathers. Sexes similar. **Juvenile:** Much as adult, but head and neck paler and duller, more buffish, and duller speculum.
BARE PARTS All plumages: Bill bluish-grey, with black nail. Legs and feet brownish-grey. Iris dark brown.
MEASUREMENTS Males tend to be larger than females. Wing of male 240-250, of female 234-240; tarsus 44-46; bill 46-52; mean weight of male 906, of female 779.
GEOGRAPHICAL VARIATION None. Perhaps most closely related to Pacific Black Duck (91), but clearly very different.
HABITS Little information. Usually found in pairs or small parties, but larger flocks of 100-200 birds recorded. Nothing has been published on breeding habits in the wild, although they are probably similar to those of Mallard and Pacific Black Duck; in captivity, nests are built on the ground among vegetation. Feeds by dabbling and up-ending in Mallard-like fashion.
HABITAT Variety of wetland habitats, from mountain lakes to marshes, small ponds, rivers and tidal creeks.
DISTRIBUTION Endemic resident in the Philippine Islands. Widespread through the islands, recorded from Luzon, Masbate, Mindoro and Mindanao.

POPULATION Probably still locally numerous, although few data. Formerly described as locally common, and variety of habitats utilised suggests that it would successfully survive despite habitat destruction and hunting. Reports in late 1970s of up to 100 on Mindoro and smaller numbers on Mindanao and Luzon indicate that it is probably not severely endangered. It breeds well in captivity.
REFERENCES Johnsgard (1978), Kear and Williams (1978).

94 BRONZE-WINGED DUCK   Plate 22
Anas specularis
Alternative name: Spectacled Duck

A rather strange and distinctive duck of southern South America, with no close relatives.

FIELD IDENTIFICATION Length 46-54 cm (18-21 in). **At rest:** Unmistakable. The large white facial crescent and throat-band, coupled with greyish-brown underparts and dark upperparts, give an appearance quite unlike that of any other species. The bronze speculum is often visible when at rest. Juveniles have the white on the face more restricted, being more of a large loral patch. **In flight:** Heavily-built, rather broad-winged, dark brownish duck, the white face and throat patches being evident in flight. Upperwing blackish, with prominent large bronze iridescent speculum with narrow white trailing edge. Underwing dark.
VOICE Male utters a shrill whistle, reminiscent of a whiplash. Female calls more frequently, a peculiar double-syllable sound which has been likened by some to the barking of a small dog.
DESCRIPTION All plumages rather similar. **Adult:** Head and neck blackish-brown, with large white crescent between eye and bill and white of chin and throat extending back to below ear-coverts in a broad point. Lower neck and most of underparts, rump and uppertail-coverts dull brown, with buffer feather fringes; flank feathers with blackish-brown centres, giving scalloped appearance. Upperparts blackish-brown, with buff fringes to mantle feathers. Upperwing dark brown to purplish-black; secondaries iridescent bronze, with pink reflections and black subterminal border, tipped white. Underwing dark. Sexes similar, although female a little duller and browner than male. **Juvenile:** Much as adult, but duller, with facial patch smaller, more restricted to lores, and breast well streaked.
BARE PARTS All plumages: Bill blue-grey, with black nail and darker patch on culmen ridge. Legs and feet yellow to orange-yellow, with dusky webs. Iris dark brown.
MEASUREMENTS Sexes similar, but male averages a little larger. Wing of male 260-280, of female 252-277; tarsus 44-45; bill 45-49; weight ca. 960.
GEOGRAPHICAL VARIATION None.
HABITS Little information from the wild. Usually found in pairs or small parties, with no records of large or even moderately large aggregations. Pair-bonds may well be relatively long-term, as the species seems not to form social gatherings of any size and males assist females with tending broods. Breeding season is from September to January.

Nests are situated on the ground, invariably hidden among dense grass on small islets in rivers. Feeds in small groups by wading and foraging along stony shallows of flowing rivers and by grazing adjacent grassy banks. Often remarkably confiding, and when flushed rarely flies high, generally following course of river.

HABITAT Slow to fast-flowing rivers and marshes and lakes in open, but wooded country along the lower slopes of the Andes down to sea level.

DISTRIBUTION Chiefly resident in southern South America. Range extends from Tierra del Fuego north to Talca in Chile and Neuquen in Argentina. Some dispersal in winter, with birds reported north to Buenos Aires and Mendoza in Argentina and Santiago in Chile.

POPULATION Little information, although probably still reasonably common throughout its range.

REFERENCES Delacour (1954), Johnsgard (1978).

95 NORTHERN PINTAIL   Plate 31
Anas acuta

Alternative name: Pintail

A distinctive, elegant dabbling duck. Widespread across the northern hemisphere, with two isolated island populations in the southern Indian Ocean. These southern populations may constitute an independent species and are treated separately after the main account.

FIELD IDENTIFICATION Length 51-56 cm (20-26 in), plus up to 10 cm (4 in) of tail extension on males. **At rest:** A large, slender dabbling duck with slimmer body than Mallard (84) or northern wigeons (71, 72). Northern Pintails have a relatively long, slim neck, pointed tail, rounded crown and slender bill. Even when tail elongations not visible, breeding male distinctive, with dark head, white breast, grey body, and black and pale buff ventral region. Birds in female-like plumage resemble other females of the genus in coloration, but shape, and relatively plain head and neck contrasting with dark scalloping on flanks and upperparts, are distinctive. Dark grey bill and legs shared only by stockier wigeons, which have clear-cut white belly; belly less strikingly white on female Pintail, although paler than rest of underparts. **In flight:** Relatively long, slim neck, with somewhat bulbous head, and pointed wings and rear end give appearance not unlike that of an elongated wigeon, but owing to neck length wings appear positioned further towards rear of body than on others of genus. Males distinctive, with grey body, dark head, and white breast and lower neck. Male upperwing grey with green speculum, latter bordered buff at base and prominently white along trailing edge. Underwing of both sexes chiefly greyish, with paler shading, unlike on most others of genus. Female overall brownish, with paler belly and conspicuous white trailing edge to brown speculum.

VOICE Male utters a mellow 'proop-proop', similar to that of Teal (77). Female has a repeated descending series of quacks, weaker than that of Mallard, and gives a low croak when flushed.

DESCRIPTION Sexually dimorphic. Seasonally vari-

able. **Adult male breeding:** Head, throat and hindneck chocolate-brown. Lower foreneck, stripe up sides of neck, breast, and centre of underparts white. Most of upperparts, sides of breast and flanks vermiculated grey. Ventral region creamy-buff at sides, contrasting with black undertail- and uppertail-coverts. Elongated, pointed scapulars and tertials grey, with black central stripes. Tail with pale sides and black centre, the two central feathers greatly elongated and narrowly pointed. Upperwing brownish-grey, with warm buff tips to greater coverts; secondaries metallic green, black towards wing base, and with black subterminal border and broad white tips. Underwing grey, darker on coverts, with paler bands on central underwing and trailing edge. **Adult male eclipse:** Resembles adult female, but has more patterned bill, greyer and more elongated tertials, green speculum and darker tail centre. **Adult female:** Head and neck light brown, finely and inconspicuously mottled darker. Throat, foreneck, breast and centre of underparts paler and whiter, also weakly mottled. Flanks warm buffish-brown, with blackish subterminal scalloping. Upperparts warm brown, with broad blackish subterminal markings to each feather. Upperwing greybrown, with narrow whitish tips to greater coverts; secondaries shiny brown, broadly tipped white. Underwing as male. In late summer and autumn, head and neck buffer and upperparts with broader and buffer feather fringes. **Juvenile:** Resembles female, but upperparts darker, less clearly marked, with feathers dark brown, mottled and barred pale buff (not broadly and neatly pale-edged as female), feathers of flanks broadly dark-centred, less scalloped with angled markings than on female; whitish tips to secondaries narrower than on adult and speculum duller; young male shows some green on speculum. Gradually attains adult features during first winter, but adult wing pattern not fully gained until after first-summer moult.

BARE PARTS In all plumages, legs and feet dark grey. **Male:** Bill blue-grey, with black stripe along culmen centre to tip; nail and cutting edges also black. Iris yellowish to brownish-yellow. **Female:** Bill duller than male, with dark culmen less clearly defined. Iris as male. **Juvenile:** Bill dull dark grey. Iris reddish-brown.

MEASUREMENTS Males larger than females. **Male:** Wing 267-283 (mean 275), tarsus 40-45, bill 47-56, mean weight 851. **Female:** Wing 254-267 (mean 260), tarsus 39-43, bill 44-51, mean weight 759.

GEOGRAPHICAL VARIATION Three races recognised, two of which are confined to islands in southern oceans and are treated separately below. Nominate race widespread almost throughout northern hemisphere.

HABITS Highly sociable, forming enormous concentrations in winter quarters and on passage. After breeding, flocks of sexually-segregated birds gather to moult, males moulting earlier than females. During autumn and winter, flocks become mixed and pair-formation develops. Pairs arrive on breeding grounds in early spring, breeding from April to June. Nests are situated on ground, hidden among grassy waterside vegetation, sometimes a considerable distance from water. After post-breeding moult, flocks move southwards to winter quarters from mid August onwards. Feeds by dabbling and up-ending in shallow water, feeding chiefly in evening or at night, spending most of day loafing on shores and mudflats. Also visits waterside stubbles and crops in winter, although less so than several other members of the genus. Walks well and swims buoyantly, with tail cocked. Flight action fast and agile, often in long lines or V-formation when well underway. Mixes freely with other dabbling ducks, although gathers to loaf in parties of its own species. Generally shy and wary.

HABITAT In general a bird of open wetlands, avoiding wooded areas. Breeds among wet meadows, on marshy lakesides or by slow rivers. In winter, also on estuarine flats, brackish marshes and coastal lagoons.

DISTRIBUTION Widespread across almost the whole of northern North America, Europe and Asia. Highly migratory, wintering along lowland marshes and coastal wetlands and estuaries of temperate regions south to Panama and rarely northern Colombia in the New World, and extensively over northern sub-Saharan Africa, temperate western Europe, Mediterranean, Black Sea and Caspian basins, eastwards through Indian subcontinent and northern tropical regions of Asia to Japan and the Philippines. Regularly migrates way out over Pacific, with small numbers regular on many islands, especially Hawaii. Vagrants have occurred on a number of small Pacific islands, and south also to Venezuela, Surinam and Guyana, Zambia, Zimbabwe, South Africa, Maldive Islands and Borneo.

POPULATION Widespread and abundant. In North America, the breeding population has been estimated at some 6 million birds. A number of regional winter counts have been made which indicate the abundance of this elegant duck. Some 50,000 winter in northwest Europe, with another 250,000 around Mediterranean and Black Sea regions. In Africa some of the highest estimates have included 90,000 in Senegal, 495,000 in Mali and 220,000 on Lake Chad, although numbers fluctuate according to wetland suitability.

EATON'S PINTAIL
A.(a.) eatoni

Alternative names: Kerguelen Pintail (race *eatoni*), Crozet Pintail (*drygalskyi*), Southern Pintail

Two isolated island races of the Northern Pintail, smaller and lacking full breeding-male plumage of nominate race. Perhaps the two races considered here could be elevated to full species status.

FIELD IDENTIFICATION Length 40-45 cm (16-18 in). The most likely duck to be encountered on Kerguelen, Crozet, St Paul and Amsterdam Islands in the southern Indian Ocean, although Mallard (84) has been introduced onto Kerguelen Island. In basic plumage pattern and shape both sexes resemble female Northern Pintail, but these island forms are considerably smaller and stockier, with relatively shorter bill and neck, and are overall darker, redder brown and more uniform in coloration. Males have elongated central tail feathers, although less prom-

inently so than on the nominate race, and pale sides to tail; they may also be sexed by their greener speculum, compared with the brown speculum of the female. A minority of males, perhaps one in a hundred of race *eatoni*, assume a brighter plumage which reveals their affinities with the nominate race, with an indication of chocolate-brown head and whitish stripe up the side of the neck. Males become even more like females in eclipse (May to November). Bare-part coloration as on nominate race. The race inhabiting Crozet Island, *drygalskyi*, is perhaps rather poorly differentiated from *eatoni*, but has the underparts more narrowly and wavily barred.

HABITS Fairly sociable, being usually found in small parties. The breeding season on Kerguelen Island is from November to February. These island races spend more time on the ground than the nominate race, walking and running with ease and perching on rocks and boulders. They fly well and move freely about their islands. Generally shy and wary, they avoid areas of human habitation. Feed more on shore and in sheltered bays than the nominate race.

DISTRIBUTION and POPULATION Race *eatoni* is native to Kerguelen Island and outlying islands, although it has also been introduced onto St Paul and Amsterdam Islands. Its population was estimated to be in thousands in the late 1970s and seems to be under no direct threat, although competition from introduced Mallard and predation by feral cats are problems which could arise in the future. Race *drygalskyi* is confined to the Crozet Islands and it too seems to be reasonably secure, although less numerous than the Kerguelen race; it seems to have disappeared from some of the islands, but the population was estimated at some 1,000-1,200 individuals in the 1970s

REFERENCES Cramp and Simmons (1977), Delacour (1954), Johnsgard (1978), Kear (1979).

96 YELLOW-BILLED PINTAIL   Plate 31
Anas georgica

Alternative names: Brown Pintail, Chilean Pintail (race *spinicauda*), South Georgian Teal or Pintail (nominate), Niceforo's Pintail (*niceforoi*).

Replaces the Northern Pintail (95) in South America, where it is widespread, although avoiding the humid tropical zones east of the Andes. All three races have been treated as separate species in the past, but are here treated as one.

FIELD IDENTIFICATION Length 43-66 cm (17-26 in). **At rest:** A large, slender, mottled brown dabbling duck with striking yellow bill sides and prominent pointed tail. Both sexes easily distinguished from female Northern Pintail by bill colour, although ranges do not overlap. Only other brown ducks in South America with yellow on bill are yellow-billed races of Speckled Teal (78), which are considerably smaller and stockier, with shorter bill and tail, and have almost unmarked flanks and uniform dark heads. A small race of Yellow-billed Pintail is confined to the islands of South Georgia. In captivity, compare also Yellow-billed Duck (90). **In flight:** A slender, brown dabbling duck, with slim neck and relatively long tail. The belly of larger races is paler than the rest of the brownish body plumage, but not conspicuously so. Upperwing brownish, with very dark blackish-green speculum, latter bordered fore and aft with buff. Underwing uniform greyish-brown, with paler trailing edge to secondaries.

VOICE Relatively silent. Male has a low whistle, female a low quack, not unlike calls of Northern Pintail.

DESCRIPTION All plumages similar. Race *spinicauda* described. **Adult:** Head and neck pale warm brown, finely mottled darker, throat and foreneck paler and almost unmarked. Almost entire body plumage buffish-brown, with conspicuous blackish-brown feather centres, more spotted on breast and most conspicuous along flanks and upperparts. Centre of belly paler and almost unmarked. Tail brownish, long and pointed. Upperwing greyish-brown, with buff tips to greater coverts; secondaries blackish-green, with broad buff tips. Underwing greyish-brown, with paler trailing edge to secondaries. Sexes similar, but female a little duller and less strongly marked on underparts; secondaries duller, blackish-brown. **Juvenile:** Much as adult, but duller, with greyer tone to head and neck, and breast more streaked, rather than spotted.

BARE PARTS All plumages: Bill bright yellow, with pale blue subterminal area and black culmen stripe, nail and cutting edges. Legs and feet dark grey. Iris brown.

MEASUREMENTS Considerable racial variation in size. Males tend to be larger than females. Nominate *georgica*: Wing of male 211-222, of female 195-207; tarsus 35-36; bill 31-36; weight of male 610-660, of female 460-610. Race *spinicauda*: Wing of male 230-260, of female 212-240; tarsus 40-42; bill 40-43; mean weight of male 776, of female 705. Race *niceforoi*: Wing 226-230, tarsus 39-41, bill 50-54.

GEOGRAPHICAL VARIATION Three races recognised, one of which is now extinct. Race *spinicauda*, Chilean Pintail, is widespread over South America and the Falkland Islands. Similar race *niceforoi* of central Colombia was considered to be extinct by 1956, only ten years after its discovery; compared with *spinicauda* it was distinctly darker, with head and neck quite strongly streaked and the crown dark brown, while the tail was relatively shorter and the bill longer. Isolated nominate race of South Georgia is distinctly smaller and a little stockier than the mainland race; it is also considerably darker, more reddish-brown, and has the belly hardly paler than the rest of the plumage.

HABITS Nominate race most studied. Usually found in small flocks outside breeding season. Pair-bonds perhaps long-term, at least on South Georgia, where pairs together throughout the year and males assist with tending broods. Breeding season varies considerably over wide range, species being possibly double-brooded in Chile, where breeding recorded August and again in January and February. In the Falkland Islands again thought to be double-brooded, breeding between September and December. South Georgia birds start nesting later,

in December. Nests on ground, usually hidden among vegetation and close to water. Feeds by dabbling and up-ending, wading in shallow water or grazing in waterside grasslands; sometimes feeds by diving. Southern populations often feed along the seashore. Flight strong and agile. Relatively wary over most of range, but South Georgia birds often remarkably confiding.

HABITAT Variety of wetlands, from Andean lakes and marshes to lowland lakes and rivers in open country. Also locally on estuaries and sheltered coastal waters.

DISTRIBUTION Widespread over much of South America. Now-extinct race *niceforoi* was confined to lakes and marshes of the eastern Andes of Colombia. Race *spinicauda* is widespread from extreme southern Colombia (rare) southwards along Andean slopes to Tierra del Fuego, extending over lowlands of Chile and most of Argentina, and on the Falkland Islands; in winter, disperses northwards to southern Brazil. Nominate race resident on South Georgia, but has been recorded as a vagrant on South Shetland Islands.

POPULATION Both existing races abundant and under no threat. Although no population estimates have been made of the mainland race, the South Georgia race was estimated to number several thousand birds in 1971.

REFERENCES Delacour (1954), Johnsgard (1978).

97 WHITE-CHEEKED PINTAIL   Plate 30
Anas bahamensis

Alternative names: Bahama Pintail, Bahama Duck, Galapagos Pintail (race *galapagensis*)

A distinctive pintail, with a peculiarly patchy distribution in the Neotropics.

FIELD IDENTIFICATION Length 41-51 cm (16-20 in). **At rest:** A medium-sized, slender dabbling duck, with pointed buff tail, brownish general coloration and white sides of head and throat. At closer quarters, the red sides to the base of the bill and the black spotting on underparts may be apparent. Unmistakable in its native haunts, but in captivity recalls Red-billed Teal (98), though latter has buffer sides of head, paler breast, darker rear end, and red on bill sides extending to tip. Leucistic birds, frequent in captivity, are pale greyish-buff overall and could recall Cape Teal (79), although confusion highly unlikely. **In flight:** An elegant slender duck, with long, pointed tail. Brown plumage contrasts strongly with buff rear end and gleaming white of front and sides of head and neck. Upperwing shows a brown forewing, with a bright green speculum bordered fore and aft by buff bands, the buff trailing band being very broad. Underwing dark. Unlikely to be confused.

VOICE Relatively silent. Male occasionally utters a low whistle. Female has weak, descending series of quacks.

DESCRIPTION Sexes similar. Ageing and sexing difficult in the field. Nominate race described. **Adult:** Crown and hindneck medium-brown, weakly mottled. Sides of head, throat and upper foreneck pure white. Remainder of body plumage mostly warm medium-brown, spotted with black on breast and underparts. Upperparts with black feather centres. Uppertail- and undertail-coverts and pointed tail warm buff. Upperwing-coverts brown, with buff tips to greater coverts; tertials somewhat elongated and pointed, blackish with pale brown fringes; secondaries with narrow metallic green basal band, black subterminal border and very wide buff terminal band. Underwing dark, with paler central band, blackish underside to flight feathers, pale trailing edge and white axillaries. Although sexes similar, female has white of face and bill coloration a little duller than male, and is also a little smaller, with shorter tail. **Juvenile:** As adult, but a little duller, with duller speculum.

BARE PARTS All plumages: Bill blue-grey, with bright red sides to basal half, nail and cutting edge black; bill colour a little duller on female and juvenile. Legs and feet dark grey. Iris brown.

MEASUREMENTS Considerable size variation between the races. Males tend to be larger than females. Nominate *bahamensis*: Wing of male 211-217, of female 201-207; tarsus 38-40; bill 40-44; weight of male 474-533, of female 505-633. Race *rubrirostris*: Wing of male 225-231, of female 219-221; mean weight of male 710, of female 670. Race *galapagensis*: Wing of male 190-215, of female 180-202; bill 37-45.

GEOGRAPHICAL VARIATION Three races recognised. Nominate race of West Indies and northeastern lowlands of South America south to northeastern Brazil described above. Larger and slightly brighter race *rubrirostris* breeds over remainder of species' mainland South American range. Isolated race *galapagensis* of the Galapagos Islands is the smallest and dullest race, with the white of the head and neck somewhat sullied greyish.

HABITS Usually found singly, in pairs or in small parties, with flocks rarely exceeding 100 birds. Pair-bonds are formed soon after the post-breeding moult. Breeding season varies according to region, but August-November in Trinidad, May-October in Surinam, and October and November further south in South America; on the Galapagos breeding is more prolonged, the season extending from October to July. Nest on ground among waterside vegetation, often hidden among tree roots, as for example in mangrove swamps. Feeds chiefly by dabbling and up-ending in shallow water. Flight fast and agile, as with other pintails. Generally shy and wary. Southern populations disperse after post-breeding moult.

HABITAT Brackish or saline pools and lagoons, mangrove swamps, tidal creeks and estuaries; also on shallow freshwater pools and lakes. Favours coastal lowlands, but recorded regularly up to 2550 m in Bolivia.

DISTRIBUTION Relatively wide range in subtropical Americas, but distribution somewhat disjunct. Widespread throughout the West Indies, including Trinidad and Tobago, and adjacent coastal lowlands of South America, including northern Colombia, Venezuela, the Guianas and northeastern Brazil south to Belem. Larger race is widespread over southern Brazil, Uruguay, Paraguay and eastern Argentina south to La Pampa and Buenos Aires, and

west to western Bolivia: its precise status over this huge area needs clarification, as it seems to be a breeding species only in Argentina; it avoids the higher ground of the Andes and slopes, but is present again in the coastal lowlands of Peru and southern Ecuador, although it formerly occurred south into northern Chile, where it is now an uncommon non-breeding visitor. The Galapagos race is confined to those islands, being found on Narborough, Indefatigable, Tower and James Islands. Species is somewhat dispersive after breeding, especially populations of larger race, with vagrants recorded south to Santa Cruz in Argentina and Punta Arenas in Chile; West Indian birds occasionally reach coastal Florida and Texas, records elsewhere in North America most likely referring to escapes. Popular in captivity, with escapes frequently recorded in Europe.

POPULATION Despite popularity in captivity, little has been documented on this species in the wild. Its wide distribution suggests that it is still an abundant duck and under no apparent threats. The Galapagos race is the most restricted, although the population probably numbers thousands; an idea of the problems that island waterfowl can encounter when confronted by a natural disaster was, however, demonstrated in 1968 when the floor of the shallow Fernandina Crater Lake on Narborough Island collapsed, falling 300 m and destroying some 2,000 Galapagos Pintails.

REFERENCES Johnsgard (1978), Kear and Williams (1978).

98 RED-BILLED TEAL   Plate 30
Anas erythrorhyncha

Alternative names: Red-billed Pintail, Red-billed Duck

Widespread throughout southern and eastern Africa, and closely related to the White-cheeked Pintail (97) of the Americas.

FIELD IDENTIFICATION Length 43-48 cm (17-19 in). **At rest:** Distinctive: the only African duck with a red bill and pale sides of head contrasting with dusky crown and nape. Pale cheeks, dusky crown and otherwise brown and mottled appearance suggest only smaller Hottentot Teal (100), which has dusky neck mark and bluish bill. Cape Teal (79) also has reddish bill, but its head is almost plain whitish and confusion is unlikely. In captivity, could be mistaken for superficially similar White-cheeked Pintail, but has most of bill (not just the base) red and dingier overall coloration. **In flight:** Striking wing pattern unique among African ducks. A brownish medium-sized duck, with prominent head pattern, rather 'waisted' neck and short pointed tail. Upperside very dark, with almost whole secondary region buff, with black stripe along base and buff band along greater coverts. Underwing very dark.

VOICE Relatively silent except in display, when male utters a weak, soft 'whizzt' and female a weak descending series of about four quacks.

DESCRIPTION All plumages similar. **Adult:** Crown and hindneck dark dull brown. Sides of head and throat buffish-white. Almost entire body plumage

dark dull brown, with buffish-white feather fringes giving scalloped appearance. Upperwing dark dull brown, with greater coverts broadly tipped buff; secondaries warm buff, with blackish line along full length at base. Underwing dark grey-brown, with paler trailing edge. Sexes similar, although female a little smaller. **Juvenile:** Much as adult, but bill duller and pinker, and feather fringes buffer, with streaked rather than spotted appearance on breast.
BARE PARTS Adult: Bill bright reddish-pink, with dark brown line along culmen and nail; female's bill slightly duller than that of male. Legs and feet dark grey. Iris brown. **Juvenile:** Bill dull brownish-pink. Legs and feet and iris as adult.
MEASUREMENTS Males average larger than females. **Male:** Wing 219-228 (mean 224), tarsus 36-40, bill 42-46, mean weight 591. **Female:** Wing 207-216 (mean 211), tarsus 30-37, bill 42-47, mean weight 544.
GEOGRAPHICAL VARIATION None.
HABITS Sociable duck of shallow freshwater lakes and marshes. Flocks attain very large numbers outside breeding season, but generally feeds in pairs or small parties. Pair-bond is often, but not always, long-term, and male sometimes helps female in tending young broods. Breeding season varies over wide range, from June-October in the far south to January-August in Kenya; in some areas breeding recorded in almost all months of the year, depending on state of water levels, but usually starts soon after main rainy season. Nests are hidden on ground among waterside vegetation. Feeds by dabbling and up-ending on shallow water; also wades on muddy shores, and readily feeds at night among crops and stubbles. Relatively approachable compared with most other ducks. Flight fast. Somewhat nomadic and dispersive, although resident in many areas. Moves into temporarily-flooded districts during wet season; some movements of over 1000 km recorded from ringing recoveries. Largest concentrations formed towards end of wet season.
HABITAT Shallow freshwater lakes and marshes with floating and emergent vegetation.
DISTRIBUTION Widespread resident and dispersive migrant throughout eastern and southern Africa, from the Cape northwards to southern Sudan and Ethiopia, west to southern Zaire and including Madagascar. Absent from western areas of southern Africa, although disperses northwards along coastal regions of Angola. A vagrant has been recorded from the Mediterranean coast of Israel, but this is the only record away from sub-Saharan Africa.
POPULATION Widespread and abundant, considered to be the most abundant duck of southern Africa. No total population estimates available, but some of the largest gatherings give an indication of abundance: 29,000 estimated at Kafue Flats in Zambia in 1971, and 500,000 at Lake Ngami in Botswana are examples.
REFERENCES Brown *et al.* (1982).

99 SILVER TEAL   Plate 32
Anas versicolor
Alternative names: Versicolor Teal, Puna Teal (race *puna*)

Widespread over southern South America, the large Andean form, Puna Teal, probably constitutes a different species and is considered separately after the main account.

FIELD IDENTIFICATION Length 38-43 cm (15-17 in). **At rest:** Distinctive dabbling duck, with large bluish bill, blackish crown and nape, creamy-white sides of head, and prominently-barred flanks. Unlikely to be confused with any other species, even in captivity, except perhaps tiny duller Hottentot Teal (100), which has dusky patch on side of neck. Similar but larger Andean race treated separately below as Puna Teal. **In flight:** A small, plump, short-bodied duck with relatively broad wings. The well-patterned head and neck and the large bill are evident in flight. The underwing is very white, with somewhat darker flight feathers and dusky band along leading edge. Upperwing shows green speculum, bordered fore and aft by white bands and contrasting with grey forewing. Puna Teal is very similar in flight.
VOICE Relatively silent. Male utters a weak whistle and a low rattle. Female has a descending series of ten or more quacking notes.
DESCRIPTION All plumages similar. Nominate race described. **Adult:** Crown and hindneck brownish-black. Sides and front of head and neck creamy pale buff. Breast and fore-flanks buff, with blackish-brown spotting, becoming prominently barred over remainder of flanks. Ventral region, short tail, rump and uppertail- and undertail-coverts vermiculated dark grey and white. Mantle, back and scapulars blackish, with buff feather borders. Tertials elongated and pointed, dark brown with buff fringes. Upperwing-coverts grey, the greater coverts broadly tipped white; secondaries metallic green, with narrow black subterminal border and broad white tips. Underwing white, with dusky along extreme leading edge and greyer flight feathers. Sexes similar, although female a little smaller and duller than male, with barring on flanks less clear and tertials shorter; bill also duller. **Juvenile:** Much as adult, but duller, with browner crown, tertials not elongated; spotting and barring less clear, being streaked rather than spotted, and speculum duller.
BARE PARTS All plumages: Bill heavy and broad, powder-blue, with pale yellow basal area and black culmen stripe and nail; bill of female duller, sometimes almost lacking any yellowish at base. Legs and feet dark grey. Iris brown.
MEASUREMENTS Males tend to be slightly larger than females. Nominate *versicolor*: Wing of male 180-197, of female 175-188; tarsus 30-32; bill 36-45; mean weight of male 442, of female 373. Race *fretensis*: Wing of male 211-219, of female 204-208; bill 48-52.
GEOGRAPHICAL VARIATION Three races recognised, the largest being considered separately below as Puna Teal. Nominate race, described above, extends over lower altitudes from southern Bolivia, southern Brazil and central Chile south to northern Argentina. Southern race, *fretensis*, is larger, with browner spotting and barring in plumage, and has narrower whitish and broader blackish flank barring; its range is south of the northern form, to

Tierra del Fuego and the Falkland Islands.
HABITS Usually found in pairs or small parties, but mixes freely with other dabbling ducks. Pair-bond is possibly long-term, as members of pair keep together throughout the year and males attend broods with females. Breeding season is from September to January, although on the Falkland Islands is chiefly from September to November. Nests on the ground among waterside vegetation. Feeds by dabbling with head submerged, or by up-ending, rarely diving; also dabbles while wading in shallows by lakesides. Relatively approachable, seldom flying far if flushed, tending to fly low and fast but circling area and soon returning. Southern-most mainland populations disperse northwards in winter, but other populations basically resident.
HABITAT Open country with freshwater pools and small lakes, preferring shallow water with fringe vegetation.
DISTRIBUTION Widespread over southern South America, from southern Bolivia and southern Brazil southwards, and the Falkland Islands, although precise extent of breeding range over northern portion uncertain, as southernmost birds move north in winter.
POPULATION Although widespread over most of range, considered rather uncommon in general; this is possibly due to its rather unsociable habits, with scattered small parties being less obvious than the large concentrations of many other ducks. In Chile it seems to be most numerous in the south, while in Argentina it is most abundant in northwestern Patagonia. It is tolerably numerous in the Falkland Islands. Not considered to be under any threats to its numbers.

PUNA TEAL
A.(v.) puna

Large, isolated form of the Silver Teal from the high lakes of the Andean puna zone. Perhaps more correctly a full species.

FIELD IDENTIFICATION Length 48-51 cm (19-20 in). Very similar to more southern and lowland Silver Teal, but considerably larger, with relatively larger all-blue bill. On males the flanks are finely, not broadly, barred. Additionally, the crown and hind-neck are blacker and the sides of head and neck paler and creamier, less buff-toned. The upperparts and breast are more weakly marked, and the back is greyer. In this form, females are more markedly different from males, being distinctly browner below and with the flanks more strongly barred buff and brown, thus recalling Silver Teal more so than male. In flight, both sexes recall Silver Teal, apart from larger size, although female Puna has smaller and duller speculum than male, this being even duller on juveniles. Range does not overlap with that of Silver Teal.
VOICE Much as that of Silver Teal, although female quacking decrescendo is shorter, usually only four quacks.
MEASUREMENTS Males larger than females. Wing of male 214-231, of female 205-215; tarsus 33-36; bill 46-54; weight of male 546-560.

HABITS Much as Silver Teal, but breeding season more prolonged, with breeding recorded at various times of the year, but chiefly November-January in northern Chile and July-August in Peru. Basically a resident form.
HABITAT High-altitude freshwater lakes with fringe vegetation.
DISTRIBUTION and POPULATION Common and widespread throughout the lakes of the puna zone of the Andes, from central Peru south to northern Chile (Antofagasta), eastwards over western Bolivia and south to extreme northwestern Argentina (Jujuy). Although basically resident, recorded as descending rarely to coastal lowland Peru.

REFERENCES Delacour (1954), Johnsgard (1978).

100 HOTTENTOT TEAL   Plate 32
Anas hottentota

One of the smallest ducks, widespread over much of tropical eastern Africa.

FIELD IDENTIFICATION Length 30-35 cm (12-14 in). **At rest:** Tiny size, dark crown, pale sides of head and dusky patch at sides of neck, coupled with blue-grey bill, are a combination of features that readily distinguishes this small dabbling duck. Small size suggests female African Pygmy Goose (68) or White-backed Duck (10) when on water at some distance, but hardly likely to be confused. Pale cheeks and dusky crown suggest larger Red-billed Teal (98), but bill colour and neck patch are further distinctions. **In flight:** Very small and dark overall, but with distinctive wing pattern: very dark upper-wing shows broad white band across tips of dark green secondaries; dark underwing, with conspic-uous broad white central band and trailing edge.
VOICE When flushed, both sexes may utter a series of soft clicking notes or a harsh double or treble 'ke-ke'. These notes also given when on water and in more general flight.
DESCRIPTION All plumages similar. Ageing and sexing difficult owing to individual variation. **Adult male:** Crown and hindneck blackish-brown. Sides of head and throat pale buff, with large dusky patch on rear ear-coverts and upper neck. Lower neck, breast and underparts buffish, with dark brown spotting, latter smallest on neck and breast, largest on fore-flanks. Rear flanks clear buff. Ventral region and uppertail- and undertail-coverts vermiculated buff and blackish. Upperparts dark brown, with greyer feather edges. Back and rump blackish. Upperwing blackish-brown, lightly glossed green and blue; secondaries metallic green, with black subterminal border and broad white tips. Under-wing and axillaries white, with dusky leading wing-coverts and darker flight feathers, the secondaries showing whiter trailing edge. **Adult female:** Much as male, but duller, with browner crown, less defined neck patch, less warm buff below, shorter and more rounded scapular feathers; ventral region not ver-miculated, and speculum duller and browner. **Juve-nile:** Very much as female, but still duller.
BARE PARTS All plumages: Bill greyish-blue, with black culmen stripe, nail and cutting edges; bright-

est on male. Legs and feet dark bluish-grey. Iris brown.

MEASUREMENTS Sexes similar. Wing 149-157 (mean 152), tarsus 26-29, bill 32-40, mean weight 243.

GEOGRAPHICAL VARIATION None. Madagascar population has been separated as *delacouri*, but is no longer recognised.

HABITS Generally found in pairs or small parties among well-vegetated shallow pools and lakes, although large aggregations assemble on some waters outside breeding season. Pair-bonds are formed prior to breeding season, although males sometimes accompany females with young broods, suggesting that it may be more prolonged. Breeding season varies according to local conditions over extensive range, but chiefly January-April in South Africa, June-August in Malawi and June-October in Kenya; over most of range, however, breeding may take place at almost any time of the year if suitable wetlands available. Nest is well hidden in dense waterside vegetation. Feeds by dabbling, with bill and head submerged, while swimming or wading; also frequently up-ends. Feeds chiefly early mornings and evenings, spending day loafing in small groups on shores and in marshy vegetation with other dabbling ducks, with which it freely mixes. Not easily flushed; when disturbed, remains on shore or hidden among vegetation when other species are well on the wing, and is therefore easily overlooked. Undertakes little-understood movements, although few ringing recoveries of over 500 km suggests that movements are relatively local.

HABITAT Shallow, well-vegetated freshwater marshes, lakes and pools in open country. Occasionally on more open lakes and reservoirs.

DISTRIBUTION Widespread, although somewhat local and patchily distributed, throughout eastern Africa and Madagascar (Malagasy). Range extends from Ethiopia southwards to the eastern Cape, west to northern Botswana and Namibia. An apparently isolated population breeds in northern Nigeria and Chad. Local increases in populations occur at various times of the year, indicating some dispersal. Vagrant to Angola.

POPULATION No total estimates have been made. Seems nowhere really abundant, although small size, somewhat retiring nature, and tendency to form only small flocks no doubt partly responsible for this apparent situation. Concentrations of thousands have been reported only from Lake Kitangri in Tanzania during June and August-October 1955, although locally common in many parts of southern and eastern Africa.

REFERENCES Brown *et al.* (1982).

101 GARGANEY   Plate 29
Anas querquedula

Highly migratory small duck, breeding over most of temperate Palaearctic region and wintering in tropical Africa and Asia.

FIELD IDENTIFICATION Length 37-41 cm (15-16 in). **At rest:** Small dabbling duck, a little larger than Teal

(77) and with relatively longer neck and heavier bill. Breeding male unmistakable, with broad white band along sides of head, extending from eye to nape; remainder of head, neck and breast dark reddish-brown, contrasting with pale grey flanks and elongated black-and-white-striped scapulars. Birds in female-like plumage more difficult, closely recalling other teal-sized ducks. Differ from Teal in being a little larger and bulkier, with larger, straighter bill and heavier head with more angular crown shape, and in having more prominent head pattern: very dark crown and eye-stripe, latter highlighted by pale buffish supercilium and by band below which contrasts with duskily-mottled sides of head; the pale loral patch is highlighted by a small dusky area below, which diffuses out over sides of head (see figure, p. 230). The throat is clearer and whiter than on Teal, but the body plumage is similar, although female Garganey has very extensive white on belly, which contrasts with strongly-patterned breast and flanks when out of the water; on female Teal the belly is whitish but less striking, although juvenile Garganey in late summer and autumn has mottled belly and is more Teal-like in this respect. Additionally, female Garganey lacks pale stripe along sides of tail of both Teal and Baikal Teal (76), and the all-dark bill lacks indistinct fleshy tones in region of gape usually shown by Teal; overall, it is duller and greyer-brown, less reddish, than Baikal Teal, with supercilium extending to bill-base (mostly behind eye or indistinct on Baikal, which also has clearer and whiter loral spot). Females of both Cinnamon (103) and Blue-winged (102) Teals have plainer head pattern than Garganey: although they have a dark crown, a weak eye-stripe and a fairly prominent loral spot, they lack dusky shades on sides of head or an obvious lighter band below the shorter eye-stripe; on both, the belly is always mottled, never clear white. Other differences between these species are more readily apparent in flight. **In flight:** Appears rather bulkier and longer-necked than Teal. Underwing similar to that of both Teal and Baikal Teal, but with whitish central underwing contrasting with dusky leading edge a little more than on either. Dark head and breast of male contrast with pale underbody, and the upperwing, including the primary coverts, is very pale grey, although the green speculum offers some contrast with white trailing edge and pale forewing; at very long range, can appear almost white-winged in flight. Females are more Teal-like from below, but the belly is whiter and more extensive, recalling northern wigeons (71, 72), though juveniles have mottled bellies. The underwing is similar to that of the male, but the upperwing is dull greyish, darker than on male, and the dull brownish speculum offers little contrast, lacking the short broad whitish bar along greater coverts of Teal and showing a narrower and less conspicuous line; the most obvious feature is the relatively broad whitish trailing edge to the secondaries, which recalls that of female Northern Pintail (95). Females of both Cinnamon and Blue-winged Teals show a much bluer forewing than Garganey, with blacker primary coverts and primaries, and lack white trailing edge to the secondaries or whitish belly.

VOICE Male utters a peculiar dry rattling call in display and when disturbed or flushed. Female has merely a Teal-like quack.

DESCRIPTION Sexually dimorphic. Seasonally variable. **Adult male breeding:** Crown and upper nape blackish. Broad white band from before and above eye across sides of head to nape. Sides and front of head and neck rich dark chestnut, with profuse fine whitish streaks. Breast and upper mantle lighter brown, with black scale-like spotting. Flanks vermiculated grey. Ventral region and uppertail-coverts buffish, with dark spotting and barring. Lower mantle and back dark greyish-brown, with elongated and pointed scapulars blackish, conspicuously striped white. Upperwing-coverts, including primary coverts, pale grey, with broad white tips to greater coverts; secondaries dark green, with broad white tips; primaries dark grey. Underwing white, with blackish band along leading edge and greyer flight feathers. **Adult male eclipse:** Resembles female, but retains breeding-male wing coloration, has throat even whiter and dusky streaking on head and neck coarser; does not attain full breeding plumage until quite late in winter, the true eclipse plumage being replaced in autumn by a supplementary plumage which is similar to eclipse. **Adult female:** Crown, hindneck and eye-stripe dusky. Buffish supercilium and buffish band below dark eye-stripe; sides of head and neck dull buffish, with dark streaking, becoming clouded dusky on sides of head, with loral spot pale buff; throat whiter. Breast, flanks, upperparts and ventral region dull buffish, with dark brown feather centres, most prominent on upperparts and along flanks; centre of underparts almost clear white. Upperwing-coverts, including primary coverts, brownish-grey, with white tips to greater coverts; secondaries greyish-brown, sometimes slightly glossed green, with broad white tips. Underwing as male. **Juvenile:** Much as female, but centre of underparts well spotted and streaked, not clear white. Wing coloration allows sexing of juveniles, but both sexes differ from adults in having narrower white at tips of greater coverts and secondaries: young male has forewing not so pale as on adult; young female has speculum dull grey. Much as adults by end of first winter.

BARE PARTS Adult: Bill dark grey, almost blackish on male. Legs and feet grey. Iris reddish-brown. **Juvenile:** Bill lighter grey than on adult. Legs and feet brownish or yellowish-grey. Iris greyish-brown. All bare parts much as adult by autumn.

MEASUREMENTS Males typically larger than females. Wing 184-211 (mean: male 198, female 189); tarsus 28-33; bill 36-43; mean weight of male 396, of female 372.

GEOGRAPHICAL VARIATION None.

HABITS Sociable duck of freshwater marshes, usually in pairs or small parties, but large concentrations form on passage and in winter quarters. Pair-formation occurs chiefly in winter quarters. Arrives on breeding grounds from late March onwards, breeding from late April to June. Nests hidden among dense grassy vegetation close to water. Feeds by dabbling, although sometimes upends. Normally keeps close to cover, preferring to feed among emergent vegetation, although mixes freely with other ducks. Spends much of daytime loafing among vegetation or on shores in small groups. On migration, large dense flocks may be seen moving low over sea, especially in Mediterranean and Black Sea regions; flocks often spend day roosting on sea on passage, moving on in the late afternoon. Shy and wary; rises suddenly from water like Teal, and flies off for considerable distance.

HABITAT Shallow freshwater lakes and marshes with extensive fringe vegetation in open country. On passage moves over sea, and may be found roosting on inshore waters in flocks. In winter on more open freshwater lakes, often in very large concentrations.

DISTRIBUTION Widespread summer visitor across most of Europe and central Palaearctic Asia east to Pacific coast as far as Kamchatka. Generally scarce and erratic breeding species at limits of range, with core of distribution over central and eastern Europe and central Asia east to Mongolia and Lake Baikal. Winters almost entirely in northern tropics. An abundant wintering duck in West, Central and eastern Africa, thinning out south to Zambia, and a vagrant south to Zimbabwe and South Africa. Large numbers also winter in tropical Asia, from Pakistan eastwards to southern China and south to the Philippines, rarely south to Indonesia and New Guinea. Vagrants perhaps annual in northern Australia. Very small numbers winter in Mediterranean region, and very rare in winter elsewhere in Europe. On passage through Middle East, North Africa, western Europe and southern Asia, occasionally overshooting northwards in spring as far as Iceland and the Aleutian Islands. Other vagrants have occurred on the Azores, some western Pacific islands and Hawaiian Islands; in North America, a scattering of records on the west coast south to California, in Canada and in the mid-west south to Kansas.

POPULATION Abundant. Huge numbers winter in sub-Saharan West and Central Africa, majority in Chad basin region, which was estimated to hold 548,000 in 1984, with a further 252,000 in the Niger basin and 88,000 in the Senegal basin. Substantial numbers also winter in Asia, and elsewhere in Africa.

REFERENCES Cramp and Simmons (1977), Roux and Jarry (1984).

102 BLUE-WINGED TEAL   Plate 29
Anas discors

Northern and eastern counterpart of Cinnamon Teal (103); although males are quite different in plumage from latter, females are almost inseparable in the field.

FIELD IDENTIFICATION Length 37-41 cm (15-16 in). **At rest:** Breeding male distinctive, with slate-grey head, large white facial crescent in front of eye, warm brown dark-speckled underparts, and black and white ventral region. See Cinnamon Teal for discussion on separation of these two species in female-like plumages: they are very similar. Birds in female plumage are similar to other teal-sized ducks, especially Garganey (101), but are a little duller and greyer-brown, with less marked head pattern: blackish crown, weak dusky eye-stripe, narrow pale eye-ring, and distinct whitish oval patch at base of bill, lacking Garganey's extensive dusky clouding on sides of head or dusky area behind loral spot; the supercilium is duller than on Garganey, hardly paler than sides of head, the weaker eye-stripe lacks paler band below, and the throat is also less strikingly whitish. The much heavier bill is carried downwards in manner of shovelers (104-107), and is often not so blackish as on Garganey, showing a slight fleshy tone in region of the gape. When seen out of the water, the belly is mottled as on juvenile Garganey, not clear white as on adult Garganey. On adults the legs are yellowish, not grey, but are greyish in first-year birds. Female Teal (77) is smaller, with smaller bill, and has more rounded crown shape and less distinct facial pattern than Blue-winged Teal, the loral spot rarely being apparent; Teal also shows clear whitish or buffish stripe along sides of tail, whiter and less marked belly and undertail-coverts, and narrower and more angled flank markings than Blue-winged. Other differences are apparent in flight. **In flight:** A small, fairly dark dabbling duck. Male appears quite dark, with prominent white facial patch and contrasting white underwing. The underwing shows a blackish leading edge, although not so wide as on Teal or Garganey. The dark upperparts are relieved only by the china-blue wing-coverts, which contrast with very dark primaries and primary coverts, a broad white band along the greater coverts and dark green speculum. Females have browner general body plumage and have underwing as male; the upperwing is also very similar to that of male, but lacks the white greater-covert bar. Blackish primary coverts, blue forewing and lack of white trailing edge to secondaries make separation from female Garganey in flight easy. Wing pattern recalls that of both Cinnamon Teal and shovelers; best distinguished from the latter by small size and bill.

VOICE Relatively silent. Male has a thin whistled 'tsee-tsee', uttered both in flight and when on water. Female has a high-pitched quack.

DESCRIPTION Sexually dimorphic. Seasonally variable. **Adult male breeding:** Centre of crown black-

ish; broad vertical white crescent between eye and bill; remainder of head and neck dark bluish-grey. Breast and almost whole of underparts warm reddish-buff, heavily marked with dark spotting, becoming barred along upper flank border; white patch at sides of ventral region. Undertail- and uppertail-coverts, tail and rump blackish. Upperparts dark brown, elongated and pointed scapulars striped black and buff. Upperwing-coverts greyish-blue, greater coverts broadly tipped white; primary coverts and primaries blackish-brown; secondaries metallic-green, occasionally with very narrow pale tips. Underwing white, with dusky band along leading coverts and greyer flight feathers. **Adult male eclipse:** Resembles female, but crown darker, sides of head and neck more coarsely streaked, and upperwing as breeding male, with broad white greater-covert tips and metallic green speculum; general tone of plumage a warmer buff. Eclipse plumage retained well into mid-winter, some individuals not assuming breeding plumage until late winter. **Adult female:** Crown and hindneck dark brown, with paler feather tips; darker brown stripe through eye, most obvious behind eye; narrow pale eye-ring; remainder of head and neck dull buffish-brown, with fine dark streaks and distinct whitish oval patch on lores. Almost whole body plumage dark brown, feathers bordered dull greyish-buff, forming dark scallops along flanks; centre of belly paler, but mottled. Upperwing similar to that of male, but coverts not so bright, with greater-covert bar obscured by brownish markings but narrowly tipped whitish; secondaries dull greenish-black. Underwing as male. **Juvenile:** Resembles female, but upperparts darker, underpart fringes yellower-buff, at least on breast and flanks, and breast markings more streaked, less spotted; spotting on ventral region weaker. Legs and feet greyish, not yellowish. Young male has wing similar to adult male, but speculum duller and darker and greater-covert bar rather narrower, though wider than on female. Young retain juvenile wing until first summer, but otherwise resemble adults by mid-winter.

BARE PARTS Adult: Bill all black on breeding male; greyer on female and eclipse male, with fleshy tones around gape. Legs and feet yellowish to orange, with dusky webs; yellow duller or browner

Typical head patterns and shapes of female teals

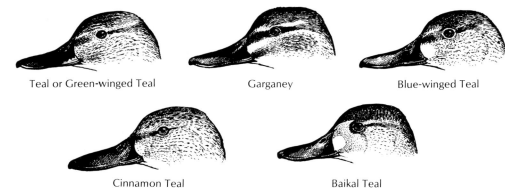

Teal or Green-winged Teal   Garganey   Blue-winged Teal

Cinnamon Teal   Baikal Teal

on female. Iris brown. **Juvenile:** Bill as female. Legs and feet greyish until breeding plumage develops. Iris dull brown.

MEASUREMENTS Males a little larger than females. Wing of male 186-195 (mean 191), of female 176-188 (mean 183); tarsus 30-34; bill 37-44; mean weight of male 400, of female 371.

GEOGRAPHICAL VARIATION No races recognised. Although birds from Atlantic seaboard region tend to be more richly coloured than those from further west and have been named *orphna* by some authorities, they are not considered sufficiently distinct to warrant separation. Closely related to Cinnamon Teal.

HABITS Sociable duck of freshwater marshes, generally found in small parties. Pair-formation occurs during the late winter. Arrives on breeding grounds from late March onwards, but not until May further north. Breeding season late April to June. Nests are hidden on ground among waterside vegetation. Feeds by dabbling, occasionally up-ending; does not often come on to land, but freely stands on shores and even on branches protruding from water. Relatively shy and wary. Flight fast and agile, but with less twisting and turning than Teal. Highly migratory, although uses inland flight-paths rather than coastal routes on migration.

HABITAT Open country, especially grasslands or prairies, with shallow freshwater lakes and pools; also coastal grasslands with pools. In winter, also on more open lakes, brackish coastal lagoons and mangrove swamps.

DISTRIBUTION Widespread summer visitor over North America. Breeding range extends over much of southern Canada and interior of USA, north to southern Alaska (uncommon) and Newfoundland, with a coastal population on the Atlantic seaboard from Newfoundland south to North Carolina. In winter, widespread along coastal lowland areas from California and North Carolina southwards through Central America to Peru and northern Brazil, rarely south to northern Chile and northern Argentina. Vagrants widely reported on Atlantic seaboard of western Europe (east to Poland) and northwest Africa, annually in British Isles, but popularity in captivity suggests that some may be escapes. Vagrants also reported Greenland, Azores, Aleutian Islands, Galapagos Islands and several other Pacific islands (has even bred Hawaii).

POPULATION Abundant, with total North American breeding population estimated at about 5 million individuals in the early 1970s.

REFERENCES Johnsgard (1975).

103 CINNAMON TEAL   Plate 29
Anas cyanoptera

More tropical relative of the Blue-winged Teal (102), although breeding ranges overlap in western North America.

FIELD IDENTIFICATION Length 38-48 cm (15-19 in). **At rest:** Breeding male distinctive, a bright rusty dabbling duck with the coloration somewhat relieved by black-and-buff-striped elongated scapulars; Colombian races have underparts spotted with black. Unlikely to be confused with any other species. Birds in female-like plumage closely resemble female Blue-winged Teal, but are typically much warmer, almost rufous-brown, in tone, rather than dull greyish-buff; additionally, the head pattern is considerably plainer, with the loral spot obscured by dark mottling, a weaker dark eye-stripe and the generally darker tone of head and neck making any highlights less apparent (see figure, p. 230). The coloration of eclipse drakes is even more rufous than that of the females, and they retain the reddish or yellowish iris colour throughout eclipse (always brown on Blue-winged in any plumage). Juveniles, however, are distinctly duller and greyer than adults and may show a paler loral spot, thus even more closely resembling Blue-winged, but they attain a more rufous coloration by autumn, when young males should be showing yellowish or orange iris; they may be aged by their greyish rather than yellowish legs, but identification of young juveniles may be impossible in the field. Cinnamon Teals tend to have breast and flank markings less contrasting, particularly lacking Blue-winged's strong contrast between the spotted breast and pale neck, and have a larger, longer and broader bill; there are also slight, but often distinct, flanges along the sides of the bill towards the tip, best appreciated when bill turned slightly away from observer. Bearing in mind the effects of individual variation and feather wear and that eclipse male Blue-winged Teal is warmer buff than female or juvenile, the separation of many dull birds in female-like plumages can be tricky; most are distinctly more rufous and plainer-headed than Blue-winged. See also Blue-winged Teal for discussion on separation from other teal-sized dabbling ducks. Hybridisation between Cinnamon and Blue-winged Teals has been reported rarely from the Great Plains region of the USA. The long, heavy bill and rufous coloration could also cause confusion with larger Red Shoveler (104) in South America. **In flight:** Wing pattern both above and below is as on Blue-winged Teal. In flight, males look especially dark on head and body, providing greater contrast with white underwing, and lack white facial and flank patches of Blue-winged Teal. See also larger Red Shoveler.

VOICE As that of Blue-winged Teal.

DESCRIPTION Sexually dimorphic. Seasonally variable. Northern race *septentrionalium* described. **Adult male breeding:** Head, neck and entire underparts rusty-chestnut, with blackish undertail-coverts and mottled brownish centre of crown. Upperparts blackish, with light brown feather fringes; elongated and pointed scapulars black, with buff stripes. Upperwing and underwing as Blue-winged Teal. **Adult male eclipse:** Resembles adult female, but has broad white bar on greater coverts, is overall warmer rufous-brown, and has iris yellow or orange. **Adult female:** Resembles female Blue-winged Teal, but feather borders and markings warmer buff, washed rufous; dark feather centres of breast and underparts duller, contrasting less with pale fringes; sides of head and neck more coarsely streaked, appearing darker, with loral patch ill-defined or absent and eye-stripe weaker and less defined. Somewhat variable, many individuals considerably darker than others. **Juvenile:** Much as female, but lacks warm brown plumage tones, recalling Blue-winged even more closely; loral spot often more prominent than on female, and breast markings streaked rather than spotted. Begins to attain more rufous-toned adult plumage during first autumn, young males acquiring adult male iris colour early in first winter. As with Blue-winged Teal, may be sexed by extent of white on greater-covert bar.

BARE PARTS Male: Bill black, but as female in eclipse. Legs and feet yellowish to orange. Iris yellowish to reddish-orange. **Female:** Bill dark grey, with fleshy tones in region of gape and cutting edges. Legs and feet dull yellowish. Iris brown. **Juvenile:** Bill and iris as female, but legs and feet dull greyish.

MEASUREMENTS Males typically larger than females. Nominate *cyanoptera*: Wing of male 188-199, of female 195-208; tarsus 40-49; bill 38-49. Race *orinomus*: Wing of male 217-220, of female 195-208; tarsus 47-50; bill 33-49. Race *borreroi*: Wing of male 189-209, of female 175-195; tarsus 32-35; bill 38-47. Race *tropica*: Wing (both sexes) 168-181, tarsus 30-34, bill 36-43. Race *septentrionalium*: Wing of male 176-194, of female 167-185; tarsus 38-46; bill 39-47; mean weight of male 408, of female 362.

GEOGRAPHICAL VARIATION Five races recognised, differing mostly in size and in intensity of spotting on underparts of males. Northern race *septentrionalium*, described above, is found over western North and Central America. Andean race *orinomus* of the paramo zone of the Andean plateau in Peru, Bolivia and northern Chile is similar in colour, but markedly larger, being the largest of all. Nominate race, found over most of southern South America, is browner on the belly than the Andean form, often has some dark spotting on sides of breast, and is smaller and a deeper red overall. Two rather isolated races occur in Colombia, the smaller (and smallest of all races) being *tropica* of the lowlands of the Magdalena and Cauca valleys region, up to 1000 m, which has the underparts heavily spotted with black and a blackish belly; it is replaced higher up in Colombia by *borreroi*, which occurs from 2100 m to 3100 m in the highlands of western Colombia, is larger than *tropica*, and in which only about half the male population have spotted underparts.

HABITS Behaviour very much resembles that of Blue-winged Teal and the two are very closely related, despite marked plumage differences of males. Northern forms breed at much the same time of the year as Blue-winged Teal, but there is relatively little information on the other races further south.

HABITAT Freshwater lakes and marshes in open country, including high mountain plateau lakes in parts of South America.

DISTRIBUTION In North America, northern race is a widespread breeding species from British Columbia southwards to northwestern Mexico, the eastern limits being Montana, Wyoming, western Nebraska and west Texas. It winters through Central America, north to California and south occasionally as far as northern Colombia. Migrants moving north in spring sometimes overshoot as far north as Alaska; it is a rare straggler along Atlantic seaboard north to New York and south to several West Indian islands, and vagrants have even occurred on Hawaii. Colombian and Andean races basically resident (see Geographical Variation for ranges), but nominate southern race widespread from lowland southern Peru and southern Brazil southwards to Tierra del Fuego and the Falkland Islands; southernmost mainland populations migratory, dispersing northwards in winter as far as Pacific coast of Peru and central Brazil. Popular in captivity, occasional birds recorded in western Europe almost certainly escapes, although transatlantic vagrancy is not unlikely.

POPULATION No information on South American races, but North American breeding population estimated at some 300,000 individuals in mid 1970s. The isolated Colombian races are at risk; there is no detailed information available on their status, but certainly race *borreroi* has not been reported in recent years.

REFERENCES Delacour (1954), Johnsgard (1978), Wallace and Ogilvie (1977), White and Andrews (1985).

104 RED SHOVELER   Plate 33
Anas platalea

Alternative name: Argentine Shoveler

The only shoveler of South America, where it is widespread over Argentina. In many respects this species provides a link between the shovelers and the blue-winged teal group.

FIELD IDENTIFICATION Length 51-56 cm (20-22 in). **At rest:** The most elegant of the shovelers and the only one in South America, therefore unlikely to be confused in the wild. The massive bill easily distinguishes it from all other Neotropical ducks, although bill of Cinnamon Teal (103) is also relatively large and is carried held downwards in a shoveler-like manner. Males have plain greyish head, contrasting with black bill and reddish-buff underparts, latter heavily spotted with black. The whitish patch on the ventral region contrasts with the black undertail-coverts, but is usually obscured by the flank feathers. Although unlikely to be confused, when dabbling with bill partially hidden can be surprisingly easily passed off as a Cinnamon Teal; in captivity, can be separated from Cape Shoveler (105) by its longer tail and spotted underparts. Females are dull greyish-brown, with blacker feather centres: compared with other shovelers, they are more cleanly patterned, have very plain head, all-black bill and longer tail; their massive bill, longer tail, duller plumage and larger size separate them from female Cinnamon Teal. See also Blue-winged Teal (102), with which it also overlaps and which it recalls in body-plumage coloration. **In flight:** Typical shoveler shape, with massive bill apparent in flight. Wing pattern is much the same on all shovelers, males having clear pale blue upperwing-coverts, contrasting with dark green speculum and white greater-covert bar; the upperwing-coverts are duller, more greyish, on females. The underwing is whitish. Wing pattern recalls that of Cinnamon and Blue-winged Teals, which are smaller and have unremarkable bills.

VOICE Relatively silent, except during courtship displays. Male utters a hollow 'tooka-tuk-tuk' when courting and sometimes when flushed, but it is weaker and more squeaky than similar call of Northern Shoveler (107). Female has a low, soft, rolling 'rrrr' in courtship, and a harsh quack.

DESCRIPTION Sexually dimorphic. **Adult male:** Head and neck plain buffish-grey, with indistinct dark spotting, most apparent on crown. Breast, mantle and most of underparts cinnamon-rufous, heavily spotted black. White patch on sides of ventral region. Undertail- and uppertail-coverts, rump and back blackish. Tail relatively long and pointed, black with whitish outer feathers. Elongated, pointed scapulars black, with white stripes. Upperwing-coverts light blue, the greater coverts broadly tipped white; primaries blackish; secondaries metallic green and black. Underwing whitish, with grey-brown flight feathers. There is a degree of individual variation in depth of underpart coloration, some birds being richer rufous than others. **Adult female:** Head and neck dull buffish, with fine dark streaks, otherwise unmarked and relatively plain. Entire body plumage dull buffish, with broad blackish-brown feather centres and pale feather borders. Tail pointed, with blackish-brown centre and light buff outer feathers. Wing similar to that of male, but upperwing-coverts dull bluish-grey, greater-covert bar narrower, and secondaries darker, more greenish-black. **Juvenile:** Very close to female and ageing difficult, although young males have clearer blue forewing than females.

BARE PARTS Male: Bill long and broad, black. Legs and feet yellow to orange. Iris pale yellow or whitish. **Female and juvenile:** Bill brownish-black. Legs and feet dull grey to yellowish-grey. Iris dark brown.

MEASUREMENTS Males typically larger than females. Wing of male 213-222, of female 202-210; tarsus 34-38; bill of male 63-67, of female 56-60; mean weight of male 608, of female 523.

GEOGRAPHICAL VARIATION None.

HABITS Little studied in the wild. Found in pairs or small flocks on brackish and freshwater lakes and lagoons. Pair-formation thought to take place in winter quarters. Breeding season September to November. Nests on dry ground not far from water. Behaviour similar to that of other shovelers. Feeds by dabbling and up-ending in shallow water, sometimes while wading in shallows but chiefly when swimming. Swims buoyantly, with heavy bill almost touching water surface. Rises easily and flies rapidly.

HABITAT Shallow freshwater and brackish-water lakes and lagoons, chiefly in open lowland areas. Has preference for shallow coastal lagoons and estuaries rather than large inland freshwater lakes.

DISTRIBUTION Widespread and chiefly resident over most of Argentina except the Andean region, from Santa Fé southwards to Cape Horn. Also widespread in central Chile from Aconcagua to Chiloe, but occurs only sporadically further south. Southern populations disperse northwards in winter as far as southern Peru, western Bolivia, Paraguay, Uruguay, and southern Brazil to Rio de Janeiro;

breeding may well occur in some of these regions, but is as yet unproven. Vagrant to the Falkland Islands.

POPULATION Seems to be fairly widespread and locally abundant, being especially numerous in coastal Argentina. No total population estimates have been made, although 20,000 estimated as gathering on plateau lakes in one region of Santa Cruz, Argentina, in 1984 suggest that it is still an abundant species and is under no threat.

REFERENCES Fjeldså and Krabbe (1986), Johnsgard (1978).

105 CAPE SHOVELER   Plate 33
Anas smithii

A sombre but distinctive shoveler, confined to southern Africa, where Northern Shoveler (107) is only a rare straggler.

FIELD IDENTIFICATION Length 51-53 cm (20-21 in). **At rest:** The only shoveler likely to be found in southern Africa. Males are very dark, almost blackish-brown, with contrastingly paler head and neck and black bill; closer views show narrow pale fringes to body feathers, which are less apparent at longer ranges. Female recalls other female shovelers, but separated from female Northern Shoveler by stockier appearance, darker body plumage with broader dark feather centres, darker tail, uniform dark grey bill, and dull yellowish-grey legs. In captivity, darker general coloration and short tail easily separate Cape from Red Shoveler (104). **In flight:** Typical shoveler shape with huge bill distinctive within range, but wing coloration similar on all shovelers. Male shows blue forewing and dark green speculum, with white bar across greater coverts on upperwing; female has duller forewing and greyer and indistinct greater-covert bar. Underwing is whitish on both sexes.

VOICE Relatively silent. Typical male call is a single, loud 'rrar'. Female has a prolonged descending series of quacks, as with others of the genus, and also gives a single quack. In display, male gives a repeated hoarse 'cawick' and a machine-gun-like rattle. Other calls may be produced during the breeding season.

DESCRIPTION All plumages fairly similar. **Adult male:** Head and neck dull pale buff, finely peppered with indistinct dark streaks, more strongly streaked on crown centre and hindneck. Almost whole of body plumage blackish-brown, with narrow pale buffish-brown feather fringes. Rump and uppertail-coverts greenish-black. Tail dark brown. Tertials and scapulars glossy bluish-black. Upperwing-coverts greyish-blue, with broad white tips to greater coverts; primaries dark brown; secondaries metallic blue-green. Underwing whitish, mottled brownish along leading edge and with greyish-brown flight feathers. **Adult female:** Duller and more mottled than male, with broader light feather borders; head and neck less contrastingly pale; tertials, scapulars, rump and uppertail-coverts dull brown, not glossy blackish; upperwing-coverts dull greyish, and white greater-covert bar narrow and indistinct. **Juvenile:** Resembles female, but has

233

broader buff fringes to underpart feathers; young males separable from an early age by wing coloration.

BARE PARTS Male: Bill black. Legs and feet yellow, becoming orange-yellow in breeding season. Iris yellow. **Female and juvenile:** Bill dark brown to greyish-black. Legs and feet greyish-yellow. Iris dark brown.

MEASUREMENTS Males average larger than females. Wing of male 222-253 (mean 238), of female 208-238 (mean 226); tarsus 34-43; bill of male 56-65, of female 52-60; mean weight of male 688, of female 598.

GEOGRAPHICAL VARIATION None.

HABITS Sociable bird of shallow water, usually found in pairs or small parties, although larger concentrations reaching several hundred birds may gather for post-breeding moult. Pair-formation begins soon after post-breeding moult. Breeding recorded in all months of the year, but dependent on local water conditions, with peak during August-December. Nests often quite close together, on ground among low vegetation, and invariably close to water. Feeds by dabbling in typical shoveler fashion, while swimming and wading, swinging bill from side to side over water surface and sometimes immersing head and fore body; rarely up-ends. Forms only loose associations with other dabbling ducks, tending to keep apart in discrete parties. Flight fast, with rapid wingbeats, rising easily from water. Has little-understood seasonal movements, probably associated with dry season and moulting dispersal. Some ringing recoveries of over 1500 km.

HABITAT Shallow freshwater and brackish-water lakes and marshes, including temporary floodwaters. Also on brackish coastal lagoons and tidal estuaries. Avoids deep-water lakes and fast-flowing rivers.

DISTRIBUTION Locally common resident in southern Africa, chiefly in southwest Cape Province, Orange Free State and Transvaal. Range also extends into Namibia (uncommon) and Botswana (common), and rarely to Natal, Zimbabwe and Angola. Somewhat nomadic and dispersive within its range, movements seemingly associated with local wetland conditions but poorly understood. Vagrant to Zululand, Zambia, Zaire and Tanzania. A record of a pair on coast of western Morocco is quite extraordinary and perhaps referred to escapes rather than genuine vagrants.

POPULATION Locally common over its somewhat limited range, although no population estimates have been made.

REFERENCES Brown *et al.* (1982).

106 AUSTRALASIAN SHOVELER   Plate 33
Anas rhynchotis

Alternative names: Shoveler (Australia), Southern Shoveler, Australian Shoveler (nominate race), New Zealand Shoveler (*variegata*)

Of all the shovelers, the Australasian species is the one most closely related to the widespread Northern Shoveler (107). Indeed, separation of the two in certain plumage stages can be very difficult.

FIELD IDENTIFICATION Length 46-53 cm (18-21 in). **At rest:** The only shoveler of Australia and New Zealand, although Northern Shoveler has occurred as a vagrant in Australia (a couple of records). Easily distinguished by massive bill from all other waterfowl of the region except perhaps distinctive Pink-eared Duck (45), which is unlikely to be confused. Breeding males have dark head, with mottled whitish facial crescent and breast, rusty-rufous flanks mottled with dark scaling, and black and white ventral region. New Zealand race is brighter, with less mottled facial crescent and flanks. Males superficially similar to sub-eclipse male Northern Shoveler, although latter tends to have brownish feathering mixed with dark undertail-coverts and chestnut of flanks and to be whiter on lower breast than Australasian; because range overlap is highly improbable, confusion likely only in captivity. Females and non-breeding males also very similar to those of Northern, but are typically rather darker, with more uniformly dark bill lacking Northern's obvious fleshy-orange tones to cutting edges and gape, and have duller and greyer legs and feet. Occasional wild hybrids between Northern Shoveler and Blue-winged (102) or Cinnamon (103) Teals bear a remarkable resemblance to Australasian Shovelers, but are smaller and of course likely to be met with only in North America. **In flight:** Typical shoveler shape, with huge bill making wings appear to be set far back on body. Males show clear light blue forewing, white greater-covert bar and green speculum on upperwing. Female upperwing drabber and greyer, with narrower greater-covert bar. Underwing of both sexes whitish. Generally dark body plumage, larger size, wing pattern and fast flight prevent confusion with Pink-eared Duck.

VOICE Relatively silent. Male has a soft, hollow 'took-took-took' in display, occasionally heard also from flushed birds. Female has a weak, husky quack.

DESCRIPTION Sexually dimorphic. Seasonally variable. Nominate race described. **Adult male breeding:** Head and neck grey, with green gloss; crown blackish; ill-defined vertical whitish crescent between eye and bill, individually variable in extent. Breast brownish, with black and white subterminal markings to each feather. Remainder of underparts rufous-chestnut, intensely scalloped with black feather markings; sides of ventral region white, finely vermiculated. Undertail- and uppertail-coverts, centre of tail, rump and back blackish. Sides of tail whitish. Elongated tertials blackish, striped white. Upperwing-coverts pale blue, greater coverts broadly tipped white; primaries dark brown; secondaries metallic green. Underwing whitish, with brownish flight feathers. **Adult male eclipse:** Resembles adult female, but flanks much more rufous; often retains some whitish on ventral region, and shows male wing pattern and iris colour. **Adult female:** Head and neck buffish-brown, finely streaked darker, with darker crown and eye-stripe, the latter most obvious on lores. Entire body plumage dark brown, with paler brown feather fringes, fringed warmer brown on underparts. Tail brownish, with buffish outer feathers. Upperwing resembles that of male in pattern, but

forewing duller and greyer, greater-covert bar narrower, and speculum duller and blacker. Underwing as male. **Juvenile:** Much as female, but with broader and paler feather fringes on underparts; young males separable by brighter upperwing, and soon acquire leg coloration of adult male.
BARE PARTS Male: Bill massive and black. Legs and feet deep yellow to orange. Iris yellow. **Female and juvenile:** Bill greyish-brown. Legs and feet greenish-grey, becoming yellower on young males during first autumn. Iris dark brown.
MEASUREMENTS Wing of male 210-261 (mean 239), of female 210-297 (mean 238); tarsus 34-42; bill of male 56-67, of female 57-62; mean weight of male 667, of female 665.
GEOGRAPHICAL VARIATION Two races recognised. Nominate race, described above, is confined to Australia. New Zealand race, *variegata*, is similar, although breeding males are considerably brighter, with whiter facial crescent and ventral patches and clearer chestnut flanks, with fewer markings, but there is a high degree of individual variation.
HABITS Generally found in small parties on shallow freshwater lakes and marshes, but in dry season larger concentrations are formed which can number thousands of birds. Pair-formation occurs prior to breeding season. Breeding season generally August-December in coastal districts, but further inland depends on extent of rains and available habitat and can be at almost any time of the year. Nests on ground, usually close to water, hidden among low vegetation. Feeds in typical shoveler fashion, by dabbling and sweeping bill from side to side over water surface; occasionally up-ends. Swims with fore parts low and rear high, with bill almost touching water surface. Shy and wary. Australian race subject to considerable dispersive movements during drought conditions, which have taken it to all parts of the continent.
HABITAT Lowland shallow freshwater swamps and lakes, including temporary floodwaters. Prefers heavily-vegetated swamps to open lakes. Occasionally on brackish coastal lagoons and coastal inlets.
DISTRIBUTION Australian race rather local, with two well-separated populations: one in the southwest of Western Australia, the other with its centre in the Murray-Darling region of New South Wales and Victoria and in Tasmania. From these main centres, especially the former, the species occasionally disperses during drought conditions in search of suitable wetlands; at one time or another it has occurred almost throughout Australia, although exceptionally rare in northern and central regions. New Zealand race widespread almost throughout both North and South Islands and also wanders, with records of vagrants from as far afield as the Auckland Islands.
POPULATION Decidedly local in Australia, where in most regions regarded as uncommon, but in headquarters of southeastern Australia is locally abundant, with dry-season concentrations reaching several thousands at key waters. New Zealand race is widespread and relatively abundant. Neither race considered to be threatened.
REFERENCES Frith (1967), RAOU (1984).

107 NORTHERN SHOVELER   Plate 33
Anas clypeata

Alternative names: Shoveler (Europe), European Shoveler

The only shoveler in the northern hemisphere, where it is widespread.

FIELD IDENTIFICATION Length 44-52 cm (17-20 in). **At rest:** Medium-sized, heavily-built dabbling duck with huge, long and broad, bill. Latter easily separates this species from all other northern waterfowl, but general size and shape similar to that of other shovelers; in the wild, however, vagrants occur only occasionally within range of Cape (105) and exceptionally within range of Australasian (106) Shovelers. Breeding male distinctive, with white breast, dark head, chestnut flanks and black and white ventral region; only male Northern Pintail (95) shares dark head and white breast, but is otherwise unlikely to be confused. Birds in non-breeding or female plumages recall female Mallard (84) apart from outsize bill, but have body pattern less marked, with less strongly-defined eye-stripe, and with smaller dark flank markings which give more contrast between darker upperparts and paler underparts. Differences between this and other female shovelers more fully discussed under individual accounts of latter, but specific features of female Northern are the fleshy or orange tones along bill sides, underparts paler than upperparts, relatively short, pale-sided tail, a weak dark eye-stripe, and distinctly orange legs. Massive bill prevents confusion with all other female dabbling ducks, but both Blue-winged (102) and Cinnamon (103) Teals have relatively heavy bill which is carried in a downward manner when swimming and can recall shovelers in this respect. Mallard may also appear relatively large-billed compared with other dabbling ducks and shares pale tail sides with Northern Shoveler, but confusion is hardly likely. Male Northern Shovelers in subeclipse plumage can appear remarkably similar to male Australasian Shoveler and are discussed under that species. **In flight:** Appears 'top-heavy', with large bill, relatively long neck and short tail giving appearance of having wings placed towards rear of body. A little smaller than Mallard, with narrower and more pointed primaries and faster flight action. Male shows distinctive combination of dark head, white breast, and dark chestnut underparts which contrast with whitish underwing. Upperwing shows clear pale blue on coverts, white greater-covert bar and green speculum. Female brownish, with distinctive shape and whitish underwing; forewing duller and greyer-blue than that of male, with narrower greater-covert bar and duller speculum; juvenile female has very dull grey-brown upperwing, lacking speculum colour or obvious wingbar. Wing pattern similar to that of other shovelers and, on adults, to both Cinnamon and Blue-winged Teals. Dark primary coverts, bluer forewing and lack of white at rear of speculum prevents confusion with male Garganey (101), the latter point also useful for separating females and juveniles. Size and shape also quite different from that of these 'blue-winged' small ducks.

VOICE Relatively silent. During display period, male utters a repeated liquid, hollow 'g'dunk-g'dunk-g'dunk', often in flight as well as from water. Female has a variety of low quacking calls, including a short descending series of quacks typical of the genus, but of only some four or five notes.

DESCRIPTION Sexually dimorphic. Seasonally variable. **Adult male breeding:** Head and upper neck glossy green-black. Lower neck and breast white. Flanks and centre of underparts rusty-chestnut. Sides of ventral region white. Undertail- and upper-tail-coverts, tail centre and centre of upperparts black or blackish. Sides of tail white. Elongated scapulars black, with white stripes. Forewing clear light blue, with broad white tips to greater coverts; primaries blackish; secondaries metallic green. Underwing whitish, with greyish-brown flight feathers. **Adult male eclipse:** Recalls adult female, but body plumage more rufous, especially flanks and belly, head darker brown and body markings blacker; brighter blue forewing and broad greater-covert bar retained; iris usually yellow, but female's also sometimes yellow. **Sub-eclipse (supplementary):** A plumage stage attained in early autumn by males which is somewhat intermediate between breeding and eclipse plumages, but produces a whitish facial crescent and pale sides to head recalling male Australasian Shoveler. Full breeding plumage may not be acquired until late winter. **Adult female:** Head and neck light buffish-brown, with fine dark streaking; crown, hindneck and ill-defined eye-stripe a little darker. Almost entire body plumage light buffish-brown, with darker feather centres, darkest and blackest on upperparts. Tail mottled brownish, with pale sides. Upperwing and underwing as male, but upperwing-coverts greyer-blue, with narrower white tips to greater coverts and green gloss of secondaries weaker. Non-breeding female in late summer and autumn rather darker, although not so dark as eclipse male. **Juvenile:** Resembles female, but crown and hindneck darker, underparts paler and more spotted. May be sexed from early age by forewing coloration: young male has duller secondaries and narrower greater-covert bar than adult male; secondaries of young female often merely brownish and with narrow whitish tips. Both sexes of juveniles acquire a supplementary plumage in autumn which renders them close to adults in appearance, although males do not show full male breeding plumage until later in winter.

BARE PARTS Male: Bill long and broad, black in breeding plumage, brownish in eclipse. Legs and feet orange. Iris pale yellow to orange. **Female and juvenile:** Bill dull greyish or brownish, with fleshy-orange in region of gape and cutting edges; somewhat spotted on females, becoming blacker on young male during first autumn. Legs and feet orange (adult female) or yellowish-orange to orange (juveniles). Iris brown, becoming yellowish on young male during first autumn and sometimes pale yellow on adult female.

MEASUREMENTS Males larger than females. Wing of male 239-249 (mean 244), of female 222-237 (mean 230); tarsus 35-40; bill of male 62-72, of female 56-64; mean weight of male 652, of female 596.

GEOGRAPHICAL VARIATION None.

HABITS Sociable duck of shallow freshwater lakes and marshes. Usually found in pairs or small parties, but large concentrations form at migration stop-over waters. Indirectly mixes with other dabbling ducks, but generally keeps apart in discrete gatherings. Pair-formation occurs from mid-winter or late winter as males assume full breeding plumage. Breeds during northern spring, chiefly mid April to July, but northernmost populations somewhat later. Nests on ground among waterside vegetation, often several nests in close proximity. Feeds by dabbling and sifting in shallow water, swinging bill from side to side over surface, often immersing head and neck and sometimes up-ending; feeds chiefly while swimming, but also while wading. Loafing birds gather on banks and shores close to feeding waters. Swims buoyantly, with rear end high and fore parts low, the heavy bill often touching surface of water. Walks awkwardly. Flight fast and agile, rising suddenly from surface with whirring wings. Most populations highly migratory, arriving on breeding grounds from mid March onwards and departing again in August.

HABITAT Favours shallow freshwater lakes and marshes with areas of open water, emergent and fringe vegetation and muddy margins. May also be found on almost any form of lowland fresh water, and in winter also on estuaries and coastal lagoons. Rarely on the sea, except during migration.

DISTRIBUTION Widespread across whole of northern hemisphere, wintering in temperate lowlands and northern tropics. In North America widespread breeding species of western interior north to Alaska and south to California and Great Lakes region, with sporadic breeding on central part of Atlantic coast. This population winters over southern and coastal lowlands on both coasts, from British Columbia and North Carolina southwards through Central America, sparingly south to Panama and northern Colombia, and out over the Pacific to Hawaiian Islands. Vagrants reported Trinidad and Venezuela. In the Old World, avoids Arctic regions, but breeds north to Iceland, sparingly in southwest and southern Europe, and occasionally in Iranian region; main breeding range from British Isles east across central Europe and Asia to Kamchatka, south to Mongolia and southern central Asia. Winters primarily in northern tropics of Asia and Africa, also in good numbers in temperate western and southern Europe and eastern Asia; penetrates Nile valley and southwards into East Africa as far as northern Tanzania, again in good numbers. Vagrants reported north to Svalbard and Bear Island and south to Azores, Canary Islands, Madeira, Zambia, Malawi, Botswana, Namibia, Zimbabwe, Borneo, New Guinea, Australia as well as in a number of western Pacific islands.

POPULATION Abundant, with local decreases through wetland drainage and local increases reported western and central Europe. North American population estimated at nearly 2 million individuals in the 1960s. Western Palaearctic winter population estimated at 1.5 million birds in 1975. Recent winter counts in sub-Saharan Africa include 10,500 at Lake Chad, 13,000 in Senegal delta,

22,000 in Kenya and 6,000 in Ethiopia. Very large numbers also winter in southern Asia, but few data.
REFERENCES Brown et al. (1982), Cramp and Simmons (1977), Johnsgard (1975).

108 RINGED TEAL   Plate 34
Callonetta leucophrys

Formerly included in a group of genera termed 'perching ducks' (Cairinini), this unique South American forest duck is considered by Livezey (1986) to be an aberrant dabbling duck.

FIELD IDENTIFICATION Length 35-38 cm (14-15 in).
At rest: An attractive little duck of forest pools and marshes in South America. Males are pale greyish-brown, their most striking features being the black centre to crown and hindneck, the rufous scapulars, the black and white ventral patches, and the black-spotted pinkish breast. The relatively plain head with black central crown and the ventral pattern may be the most obvious features on males sitting in their shady habitats. Females are quite dark brown above and are almost unmottled; the head pattern is striking, with dark crown, lores and eye-stripe and broad whitish supercilium, throat and patch on sides of neck. The lighter brown underparts are somewhat marbled with paler shading, and the ventral region is distinctly whitish. Both sexes are unlikely to be confused with any other species; although female Brazilian Duck (110) also has whitish facial patches, it is larger, with uniform brownish underparts, lacks white in ventral region, has the whitish facial markings mostly in front of, not behind, eye, and the legs and feet are deep red. Juvenile male Ringed Teal resembles female, but lacks whitish facial patches. **In flight:** A small, fast-flying duck, with distinctive upperwing pattern on both sexes. The upperwing is very dark, with a striking large white oval patch on the greater coverts, quite unlike any other duck; the dark green speculum is less striking. The dark underwing contrasts with the pale underbody, especially on males.
VOICE Relatively silent. In display male gives a wheezy, almost cat-like 'wheeoo'. Female has a sharp, rising 'hou-it' and a low quack.
DESCRIPTION Sexually dimorphic. **Adult male:** Centre of crown and hindneck black. A narrow incomplete black ring encircles the base of the neck to form a semi-collar. Remainder of head and neck light buffish-grey. Breast light pink, spotted black. Flanks finely vermiculated grey. Ventral region black, with large white patch. Mantle greyish-buff; scapulars rufous-chestnut; back, rump, uppertail-coverts and tail black. Upperwing blackish, with large white oval patch on greater coverts; secondaries metallic green. Underwing very dark. **Adult female:** Crown, hindneck, lores and eye-stripe dark brown; throat, sides of hindneck and supercilium whitish; dusky-brown smudge on sides of neck. Breast and underparts dull olive-brown, with pale greyish-buff shading forming ill-defined bands. Ventral region whiter, with dark band on sides. Entire upperparts darker olive-brown, with large white wing patch as on male; underwing as male. **Juvenile:** Juvenile female indistinguishable from adult

female; juvenile male resembles female, but lacks distinct facial patches or pale shading on underparts.
BARE PARTS In all plumages, legs and feet pink or pinkish and iris brown. **Male:** Bill bluish-grey, black nail and nostril. **Female and juvenile:** Bill duller grey than on male, with dark grey patches along culmen.
MEASUREMENTS Sexes similar. Wing 160-175, tarsus 33, bill 35-37, weight 190-360.
GEOGRAPHICAL VARIATION None.
HABITS Little studied in the wild. Little information on flock sizes, but seems to be generally found in pairs or family parties. Pair-bonds probably permanent, at least in captivity, males helping females to tend broods. Breeding season probably September-December, at least in Paraguay, where young have been found in January and February. In captivity nests in cavities, indicating that tree holes are used in the wild, although also reported nesting among huge stick nests of Monk Parakeets. Feeds by dabbling on water surface, or by submerging head and neck. Perches readily and easily in trees. Flight fast and agile. Normally fairly confiding.
HABITAT Pools and marshes in open wooded country, especially seasonally-flooded lowland areas with patches of forest. Also in areas of denser forest with streams and pools.
DISTRIBUTION Central South America, east of the Andes. Range extends from southern and eastern Bolivia and Paraguay, over southern Brazil, Uruguay and northern Argentina to Buenos Aires and Tucuman. To what extent this range reflects non-breeding distribution is unclear, as breeding has been confirmed only in Argentina and Paraguay. After post-breeding moult, southern populations certainly disperse northwards over southern Brazil.
POPULATION No information, but its relatively wide distribution suggests that the population is not under any great pressure. Clearly, this interesting little duck is worthy of extensive field study.
REFERENCES Delacour (1954), Johnsgard (1978).

109 MANED DUCK   Plate 19
Chenonetta jubata
Alternative names: Australian Wood Duck, Maned Goose

Also formerly included in the now-defunct tribe Cairinini (perching ducks), this strange Australian duck is widespread throughout the continent in suitable habitats.

FIELD IDENTIFICATION Length 44-51 cm (17-20 in).
At rest: Distinctive duck, recalling a small goose in shape and grazing behaviour. Has plump body, relatively long legs, tiny bill, 'waisted' neck and large head. Males are greyish, with dark brown head, mottled breast, and blackish belly and rear end. Females are a little duller, have mottling extending along flanks, and lighter brown head with pale and dark eye-stripes. Neither sex likely to be confused with any other species, although compare juvenile Comb Duck (37) in captivity. **In flight:** A bulky duck, with somewhat bulbous head, 'waisted' neck and relatively broad wings. Males show dark

head and belly contrasting with greyish body and whitish underwing; the upperwing is strikingly patterned, with white secondaries contrasting with blackish primaries and band along greater coverts and with greyish forewing. Females have plainer greyish underparts and lack dark head and belly of males, but their wing patterns are similar. Confusion with other species unlikely; Green Pygmy Goose (66) has similar upperwing, but is much smaller and has darker underwing and upper forewing, while Australian Shelduck (40) is larger, blacker and has white forewing.

VOICE Most frequently-heard call is that of the female, a prolonged, mournful, nasal and almost cat-like 'wroow', often given in flight. Male has a similar but shorter and shriller call.

DESCRIPTION Sexually dimorphic. **Adult male:** Head and upper neck chocolate-brown, with short tufted blacker mane on rear of head. Lower neck and breast mottled grey, black and white. Flanks finely vermiculated grey. Belly, ventral region, tail, uppertail-coverts, rump and back blackish. Mantle, scapulars and tertials grey, outer scapulars black. Upperwing-coverts grey, greater coverts broadly tipped white with black subterminal line; primaries blackish; secondaries metallic green at base, with terminal half white. Underwing whitish, with darker primaries. **Adult female:** Head and neck paler and duller brown than male, with dark eye-stripe and pale buffish supercilium and with pale buffish line below eye, bordering eye-stripe. Body plumage duller and browner-grey than that of male, lacking blackish on belly and ventral region and having buffish and dark mottling of breast extending to most of flanks. Wings as male. **Juvenile:** As female, but rather paler overall; young males begin to show vermiculated grey on flanks at about 12 weeks and soon resemble adult male.

BARE PARTS All plumages: Bill very short, dark grey. Legs and feet dark grey. Iris brown.

MEASUREMENTS Sexes similar. Wing 252-290 (mean: male 272, female 266); tarsus 50-53; bill 22-31; mean weight of male 815, of female 800.

GEOGRAPHICAL VARIATION None.

HABITS Sociable duck of open, lightly-wooded country with pools and rivers. Typically in large flocks, grazing on waterside land. Pair-bond permanent, birds keeping in family groups within flocks. Pairs break away from flocks at onset of breeding season, which varies according to local rainfall conditions. In areas of regular rainfall breeds in spring, chiefly September-October in the south and January-March in New South Wales, but elsewhere breeding is more erratic and may happen at almost any time of the year, suitability of available grass for grazing being more important than water levels in pools. Nests in tree holes, often a considerable distance from water. Feeds mostly by grazing grassland and crops in vicinity of water. Walks and runs easily. Rather awkward swimmer, spending little time on water, but sometimes feeds by dabbling. Often perches in trees and on waterside branches. During the daytime loafs in flocks ('camps') near water, flying out to feeding grounds towards dusk. Very wary, although when alarmed tends to 'freeze' rather than fly away immediately,

walking quietly away from suspected danger, or flying away silently and low through trees. Flight action rather slow, usually keeping quite low. Undertakes erratic movements associated with rainfall and suitability of grazing grounds, although in most districts basically resident.

HABITAT Open country with scattered trees and fresh water of almost any description, preferring rivers and lakesides in wooded farmland. Rarely on coastal bays or brackish lagoons.

DISTRIBUTION Widespread over eastern and western Australia, but bulk of population in the southeast in Murray-Darling region. Less widespread in Western Australia, but is slowly expanding its range there. Eastern population also increasing, having spread into Tasmania and eastern Queensland in recent years. In drier regions is sparse, but found where favourable habitats occur. Somewhat nomadic, with records from most parts of Australia at some time or other, but vagrant only in far north and has also wandered to New Zealand.

POPULATION An abundant species; range has increased considerably as land cleared for farming and with provision of agricultural tanks and pools. Extensively hunted and regarded as an agricultural pest in some districts, but not considered to be under any threat, despite lack of information on total populations.

REFERENCES Frith (1967), RAOU (1984).

110 BRAZILIAN DUCK   Plate 22
Amazonetta brasiliensis

Alternative names: Brazilian Teal, Lesser Brazilian Teal (nominate race), Greater Brazilian Teal (*ipecutiri*)

An aberrant dabbling duck, formerly included in the Cairinini. It is widespread in forest waters of tropical South America.

FIELD IDENTIFICATION Length 35-40 cm (14-16 in). **At rest:** Rather stocky, small dabbling duck, plain brown with warmer, more rufous-brown, breast, slightly scalloped on fore-flanks, and deep red legs and feet. Male has waxy-red bill and pale sides of upper neck and ear-coverts contrasting somewhat with darker brown crown. Females have striking white facial patches, with whitish spot on lores and supercilium before eye, and often pale greyish sides of head and neck; bill grey. Unlikely to be confused with any other duck, but see female Ringed Teal (108). **In flight:** Brownish, heavily-built duck, with relatively broad wings and broad, blunt tail-end. Both sexes show similar pattern of blackish wings above and below, with striking white patch on inner secondaries.

VOICE Male has a piercing, repeated whistle 'tuwee-tuwee', which is given in flight as well as in display. Female has a deep loud quack.

DESCRIPTION Sexually dimorphic. Nominate race described. **Adult male:** Crown dark brown, becoming blackish on hindneck. Sides of head and neck pale greyish-buff; front of head back to eye and throat medium-brown. Breast rufous-brown, becoming paler and buffer-brown along flanks and ventral region; sides of breast and fore-flanks lightly

scalloped black. Upperparts brown, blackish on back and rump and pale buffish-brown on upper-tail-coverts. Tail black. Upperwing blackish, glossed green and purple; innermost secondaries white. Underwing similar. Some individual variation, with dark and pale colour phases recognised: dark birds have dark throat, darker general plumage, and sides of head and neck light brownish-grey; pale phase lighter overall, with sides of head and neck almost whitish and throat also pale. **Adult female:** Similar to male, but crown and neck with more extensive dusky-brown, and striking whitish facial spots, a whitish loral patch, and whitish supercilium from just behind eye to bill-base. Also individually variable, the facial spots being duller and less defined on darker birds. **Juvenile:** Resembles female, but duller overall. Difficult to age owing to individual variation, but wings duller black.
BARE PARTS Male: Bill dark red. Legs and feet rich red or reddish-orange. Iris brown. **Female and juvenile:** Bill olive-grey. Legs and feet dull orange-red. Iris brown.
MEASUREMENTS Sexes similar. Nominate *brasiliensis*: Wing 168-192; tarsus 36-38; bill 32-39; weight of male 380-480, of female 350-390. Race *ipecutiri*: Wing 192-215; bill 38-43; mean weight of male 600, of female 580.
GEOGRAPHICAL VARIATION Two races recognised. Nominate race, resident over most of range and described above, is individually variable, although there seems to be no geographical significance in the distribution of the colour phases. Larger southern population, *ipecutiri*, is similar in plumage but less variable, with most birds appearing to be of the darker type; it seems to be chiefly migratory and breeds over southern Brazil, Paraguay, eastern Bolivia, Uruguay and northern Argentina.
HABITS Little studied in the wild. Generally found in pairs or small parties, with no records of any sizeable gatherings. Pair-bond is possibly long-term, males helping females in tending broods. Breeding season probably varies over huge range, but few data, although (at least in captivity) more than one brood may be reared in a season; breeding probably June-July in northern Argentina, November-December in Paraguay and September-October in Guyana. Few wild nests described, and those that have been are variable in situation: most have been on ground close to waterside, hidden in vegetation, while other reports include a floating nest of water plants and tree sites in disused nests of other birds; has even been suspected of nesting on cliffs. Feeds by swimming and dabbling in shallows close to shore or bank. Perches readily on branches over-hanging water and loafs on shore with other ducks. Flight rapid, but keeps low. Chiefly resident, but southern race migratory.
HABITAT Freshwater lakes and pools in wooded lowland country, up to 500 m. Also flooded fields and marshes outside breeding season, but only rarely in coastal lagoons or mangroves.
DISTRIBUTION Widespread over tropical lowland forested areas of South America east of the Andes. Range extends from eastern Colombia and central Venezuela and Guyana, south through Brazil to northern Argentina and eastern Bolivia. Smaller race basically resident; larger southern race (see Geographical Variation for breeding range) seems to be partially or wholly migratory, moving northwards after breeding, with birds collected even as far north as Venezuela and Colombia in austral autumn being referable to this form.
POPULATION No information on current status, but wide range and general references to it from parts of its range as being common indicate no threat to its total population.
REFERENCES Delacour (1954), Johnsgard (1978).

Tribe AYTHYINI (POCHARDS)

Four genera are included in this tribe, following the revision by Livezey (1986). Monotypic *Rhodonessa* is probably extinct. Monotypic *Marmaronetta* was formerly included in the dabbling ducks (Anatini), to which it shows some affinities. The three members of the genus *Netta* are somewhat intermediate in behaviour between true pochards (*Aythya*) and the dabbling ducks.

111 MARBLED DUCK   Plate 34
Marmaronetta angustirostris
Alternative name: Marbled Teal

Formerly included with the dabbling ducks, indeed even placed in the genus *Anas* by some, this aberrant duck shows closer affinities to the pochards, including its display behaviour and lack of speculum.

FIELD IDENTIFICATION Length 39-42 cm (15-16 in). **At rest:** Small, slender, pale sandy-brown duck, with dusky eye-patch, slim dark bill and distinctly large-headed appearance. The body plumage is blotched with whitish spotting, although the spots are inconspicuous except on darker upperparts or at close range. The breast and tail-coverts are slightly scalloped with darker markings, and the wings and tail are noticeably pale. In behaviour recalls small dabbling ducks, with which it freely mixes. Unlikely to be confused within range, but beware occasional leucistic examples of other small ducks, especially escaped White-cheeked Pintail (97) and similarly pale, but stockier and reddish-billed Cape Teal (79); female Northern Pintail (95) is not dissimilar in shape and shares rather plain head and neck, but is larger, browner, lacks eye-patch and has well-scalloped flanks. In captivity, see also Crested Duck (65). **In flight:** Small, slim, sandy-coloured duck with virtually no pattern either above or below. The plain sandy wings lack any speculum, which separates it from other similar-sized ducks within range except darker juvenile female Garganey (101), which has white trailing edge to secondaries and dusky leading edge to underwing.
VOICE Relatively silent. During display, both sexes

utter nasal squeaks.

DESCRIPTION Sexes similar. **Adult:** Rear of head with short shaggy, hanging crest, most obvious on males. Almost entire head and body plumage light sandy-brown. Crown and crest with fine brown barring. Blackish patch surrounds eye and becomes paler and diffuse towards nape. Remainder of head and neck almost unmarked, being faintly streaked with brown. Breast, centre of underparts and undertail-coverts with narrow darker brown barring. Flanks with large whitish-buff spots on slightly darker background. Scapulars dark brown, with large pale buff spots. Mantle, back, rump and uppertail-coverts as scapulars, but ground colour not quite so dark. Tail pointed, pale buff with darker feather bases. Upperwing light greyish-brown, somewhat paler towards tips of secondaries. Underwing whitish. Sexes similar, but female has shorter crest than male and slight difference in bill colour. **Juvenile:** Much as adult female, but all body spotting duller and more diffuse, with greyer tone to underparts.

BARE PARTS In all plumages, legs and feet olive-green to dull yellow and iris brown. Sexing by bill colour is not always reliable, but following typical. **Male:** Bill blackish, with narrow pale grey subterminal line and base. **Female:** Bill dull black, with dull green patch at base near gape.

MEASUREMENTS Males typically larger than females. Wing 186-215 (mean: male 207, female 198); tarsus 35-40; bill 39-47; mean weight (both sexes) 477.

GEOGRAPHICAL VARIATION None.

HABITS Rare and decidedly local bird of freshwater and brackish lakes. Sociable, even when breeding, being usually found in small parties, but larger gatherings form outside breeding season at some key waters. Pair-bond formed in winter, prior to moving to breeding waters. Breeding season chiefly May-June, a little later in Soviet Union. Nests often very close together at major colonies, more spaced in areas where population lower; usually on ground among waterside vegetation, but occasionally on grass roofs of huts (in Spain). Feeds chiefly by dabbling in shallow water while swimming, occasionally by up-ending and sometimes by diving; also wades in shallows, and feeds rarely on adjacent stubbles. Most active in evening and early morning, spending most of day loafing among emergent vegetation or perching on partially-submerged branches in shady situations. Flies low and rather slowly, showing less agility than small dabbling ducks, taking off from water less easily. Eastern populations migratory, western ones less so.

HABITAT Relatively small, shallow freshwater and brackish lakes with emergent and fringe vegetation in lowland areas. Also on fish-rearing ponds and small reservoirs, slow rivers and even saline coastal lagoons in some areas.

DISTRIBUTION Generally scarce and very local bird, with patchy and relict distribution around western Mediterranean and from Turkey east to central Asia. Western population, with pockets of distribution in southern Spain and Morocco and probably still in Algeria and Tunisia, winters chiefly in Morocco, with occasional individuals turning up further south to Senegal, Nigeria, Mali and Chad; formerly also nested in southern France, Canary Islands and perhaps Cape Verde Islands. Further east, isolated pockets in southern Turkey, Israel, Iraq, Iran, Afghanistan, by western lowlands of Caspian Sea, in Uzbekistan and Soviet Turkestan, and also reported recently from extreme western China (Xinxiang); formerly bred Yugoslavia, Italy, Crete, Cyprus and Egypt. Eastern birds move south to winter chiefly in western Iran, but with smaller numbers also from Turkey and Egypt now rarely east to Pakistan and northwestern India. Vagrants reported from a number of central and eastern European countries, but most records relatively old, at time when population more numerous and range more extensive than present day. Some recent records from western Europe may refer to escapes from captivity rather than genuine vagrants.

POPULATION Declining over most of range, but recent local increases in Spain and Morocco have followed long period of decline. Has also declined considerably in Soviet Union in recent decades. Recent high winter numbers in Morocco include count of 1,680 individuals at one major site. Bulk of population winters in Iran (Khuzestan) and consists mostly of Soviet birds, with count of 12,600 in 1971, but recent information lacking. Wintering numbers in Pakistan have greatly decreased, following trend of central Asian breeding population. Although not yet endangered as such, the possible future status of this unique duck is worrying.

REFERENCES Cramp and Simmons (1977), Hawkes (1970).

112 PINK-HEADED DUCK
Rhodonessa caryophyllacea

Almost certainly extinct: there has been no reliable sighting of this striking bird in the wild since 1935, but occasional unconfirmed reports indicate that it possibly survives in remote border regions of northern Burma.

FIELD IDENTIFICATION Length 60 cm (24 in). **At rest:** Unmistakable. Large, long-bodied and relatively long-necked duck, with dark chocolate-brown body and foreneck and deep pink head and hindneck. Females and juveniles similar but duller, and equally unmistakable. Possibility of confusion with Red-crested Pochard (113) is remote, but darker crown and nape of female and whitish-pink head could suggest head pattern of female of that species. **In flight:** Bulky body and relatively broad wings, long neck and short tail coupled with unique head-and-body coloration render it unmistakable. On the upperwing, the pale fawn secondaries and the whitish line along leading edge would presumably contrast with the darkness of the remainder of the wing in flight; conspicuous pale pink underwing would contrast with blackness of underbody. Red-crested Pochard has most of primaries and secondaries white, and is unlikely to be confused.

VOICE Male had a low, weak whizzy whistle not unlike that of male Mallard (84). Female gave a low quack.

DESCRIPTION All plumages similar. **Adult male:**

Head with slight tuft at rear of crown. Head and neck rose-pink, with blackish-brown centre of throat and foreneck broadening towards breast. Remainder of body plumage blackish-brown, with very faint pale pink vermiculations. Wings mostly blackish-brown, with narrow whitish line along leading edge from carpal joint towards body; secondaries fawn, with whiter tips. Underwing pale pink. **Adult female:** Similar to male, but body plumage duller and browner. Head and neck duller and whitish-pink, washed brownish on crown, foreneck and hindneck, lacking blackish foreneck of male. **Juvenile:** Still duller than female, with dull brown body feathers finely fringed whitish.
BARE PARTS Male: Bill bright pink. Legs and feet reddish-black. Iris red. **Female:** Similar, but all colours duller.
MEASUREMENTS Sexes similar. Wing of male 250-282, of female 246-260; tarsus 40; bill 50-56; weight ca. 793-1360.
GEOGRAPHICAL VARIATION None.
HABITS Almost certainly extinct. Formerly inhabited secluded pools among tall grass in northeastern India. Occurred in pairs or small parties, with flocks of 30-40 on record. Breeding season June-July. Nested on ground among tufts of tall grass, fairly close to water. Fed by dabbling on water surface while swimming, but also said to dive occasionally. Recorded as sometimes perching in trees. Considered always to have been shy, wary and rather elusive birds.
HABITAT Marshes and pools among tall elephant-grass jungle.
DISTRIBUTION Formerly recorded from a number of states in northeastern India; considered to have been resident in Assam, Manipur, Bengal, Bihar and Orissa and adjacent region of northern Burma. Sporadic records from elsewhere in northern India as far west as Kathmandu (Nepal), Haryana and Delhi and south to Madras and Maharashtra indicate occasional wide non-breeding dispersal. Last confirmed sighting in wild was from Bihar in June 1935, but unconfirmed sightings continue to be reported from a remote region of northern Burma, indicating some hope for its possible survival.
POPULATION It seems always to have been rare and worthy of note, the loss of extensive tracts of its

specialised habitat being the major reason for its demise. Although the last confirmed wild sighting was in 1935, it lingered on in captivity until 1939 and there have been occasional reports since in northern India, most of which have been attributed to misidentifications of Red-crested Pochard. In the winter of 1965/66, however, a party of five birds, considered to have been Pink-headed Ducks, was reported from the Mali Kha River near Machanbaw in the state of Kachin in northern Burma (the species is believed by some to breed over the border in adjacent regions of Tibet); very small numbers continue to be reported from this region in winter, but as yet such reports lack adequate documentation to prove that this species still exists. These reports are unprecedented, especially as the habitat involved appears to be markedly different from that of the Indian birds, but the possibility remains that this extraordinary duck may be surviving in this still relatively-unexplored and inaccessible region.
REFERENCES Ali (1960), Ali and Ripley (1968), Kear and Williams (1978).

113 RED-CRESTED POCHARD   Plate 35
Netta rufina

The largest of the pochards and in many respects intermediate between them and the dabbling ducks, with the bulk of its population in eastern Europe and southern USSR.

FIELD IDENTIFICATION Length 53-57 cm (21-22 in). **At rest:** Large and bulky duck, behaving more like a dabbling duck than a pochard. Breeding male unmistakable, with rusty-orange head, red bill, black breast and ventral region, white flanks and plain brown upperparts. Duller female-like plumages almost as distinctive, having dark crown and nape contrasting with very pale sides to head and neck and plain brown body plumage. Plumage pattern of female recalls that of female Common Scoter (134), but latter much more sooty-brown, especially on breast, has shorter bill and longer tail (often carried erect), lacks white in wings and is unusual on fresh water. **In flight:** Equally as striking. A heavily-built, broad-winged duck with extensive white in wings in all plumages. Male has black underparts which contrast with striking white flanks and underwing and orange head. Upperwing with almost full length of flight feathers white and contrasting with brown forewing and white leading edge; at distance, may appear all dark with white wings. Females have extent of white in wings similar to that of male, but lack white leading edge to upperwing; from below, the brownish body contrasts with very white underwing and pale head. Extent of white in wings matched only by smaller Ferruginous Duck (122), which has faster wingbeats and striking white belly and dark head.
VOICE Relatively silent, except when breeding. During display, male has a rasping wheeze and female a grating chatter.
DESCRIPTION Sexually dimorphic. Seasonally variable. **Adult male breeding:** Head, with short tufted mane on crown and nape, rusty-orange, becoming yellower on crown and pinkish-brown on sides of

Pink-headed Duck

head. Flanks white, becoming brownish along upper border. Neck, breast, centre of underparts, ventral region, uppertail- and undertail-coverts, tail, rump and back black. Mantle and scapulars medium-brown. Upperwing medium-brown, with whitish band along leading edge of forewing; secondaries and primaries white, narrowly tipped brown, with outermost primaries brown. Underwing white. **Adult male eclipse:** Much as female, but bill red. **Adult female:** Crown and hindneck brown, darkest on crown. Remainder of head and neck very pale greyish. Most of body plumage medium-brown, a little paler on belly. Wing as that of male, but lacks white along leading edge. **Juvenile:** Resembles female, but bill all dark. Gradually assumes adult bill colour and plumage during first winter, but full plumage not until first-summer moult.

BARE PARTS Male: Bill reddish-pink. Legs and feet orange or reddish-pink, with dusky webs and patches. Iris red. **Female:** Bill grey-brown, with fleshy-pink subterminal area and cutting edges. Legs and feet greyish-pink. Iris reddish-brown. **Juvenile:** Bill dark grey, with fleshy-pink at tip lacking or, if present, smaller than on female. Legs and feet fleshy, with dusky webs; brightest on male. Iris pale brown. Assumes bare-part colour of respective adult during first autumn and winter.

MEASUREMENTS Males typically larger than females. Wing 251-275 (mean: male 264, female 260); tarsus 40-47; bill 42-52; mean weight of male 1188, of female 1108.

GEOGRAPHICAL VARIATION None.

HABITS Usually found in small parties on large freshwater lakes in open country, forming large concentrations in main moulting and wintering areas. Pair-formation occurs from autumn and continues through the winter. Arrives on breeding grounds during April, breeding from mid April to late June. Nests on ground, hidden among waterside vegetation. Males gather to moult when incubation near completion, leaving females to rear broods. Feeds by dabbling with head immersed and by up-ending more than other pochards, but also readily dives. Sometimes feeds on land in stubbles and crops. Most feeding activity in early morning and evening. Loafs in rafts on water in daytime. Swims buoyantly. Rises from surface by pattering, but flight strong when underway, although action a little slower and heavier than that of other pochards. Males and non-breeders undertake quite extensive moult migrations in mid-summer, which may take them considerable distances from breeding waters. Departs for winter quarters when moult complete, most birds arriving October onwards, but some earlier.

HABITAT Has preference for large, relatively deep, freshwater lakes with extensive fringe vegetation in lowland open country. Also slow-flowing rivers, river deltas and more rarely on brackish coastal lagoons or coastal waters on migration.

DISTRIBUTION Main breeding range extends from Black Sea lowlands and Turkey eastwards across southern Soviet Union to northwestern China and western Mongolia and south to Afghanistan (rare). Further west, breeds in reasonable numbers in southern and eastern Spain and southern France, with small isolated pockets scattered over central Europe north to Netherlands and Denmark. Formerly also nested in North Africa. Winters around northern and eastern Mediterranean basin, Black and Caspian Seas, Sea of Azov and through Indian subcontinent east to Burma; small numbers winter south to Egypt and through Middle East and east to southern China. Vagrants reported from a number of more northern European countries (regular British Isles, where it has bred), Japan and Australia. Popular in captivity and frequently escapes, perhaps some of the more isolated breeding occurrences in western Europe resulting from escaped birds.

POPULATION Abundant in Asiatic part of range, less numerous in west. Winter populations of 50,000 in Europe-Black Sea-Mediterranean region and over 400,000 in western Soviet Union indicate its abundance, with further large numbers wintering in Indian region. Central European breeding range is slowly expanding.

REFERENCES Cramp and Simmons (1977).

114 SOUTHERN POCHARD   Plate 35
Netta erythrophthalma

Alternative names: South American Pochard (nominate race), African Pochard (brunnea), Red-eyed Pochard

Strangely disjunct distribution in both South America and Africa recalls that of White-faced Whistling Duck (7).

FIELD IDENTIFICATION Length 48-51 cm (19-20 in). **At rest:** Relatively large, dark diving duck, with slight peak to rear of crown. Male uniform dark, with contrasting long grey bill, but at close range or in good light can be seen to be dark reddish, at least on flanks, with red eyes. Unlikely to be confused, but overlaps in range with similarly-coloured Andean Ruddy (150) and Maccoa (152) Ducks, both of which can appear all dark, but are smaller, stockier, with shorter neck and bill, and have long tail. Females show conspicuous white facial and cheek patches and are rather duller, sooty-brown, overall. Confusion with female Brazilian Duck (110) unlikely, as facial patches on latter species are mostly before eye, as they are also on smaller female Lesser Scaup (127); female Rosybill (115) also similar, but lighter brown, with cleaner white undertail-coverts and inconspicuous buffish, not white, facial patches. See also Pochard (117) and Ferruginous (122) and Tufted (125) Ducks, which winter in Africa and could be confused, though all are smaller and shorter-necked and the latter two have clear whitish belly. **In flight:** A relatively long-necked duck, with wings appearing placed well back on body. Bold white band along full length of flight feathers is conspicuous on both sexes; underwing dusky, showing hint of wing-band through flight feathers. Otherwise all-dark male is distinctive, but female recalls female Rosybill, which is lighter brown, more heavily built and has white underwing. Larger size, dark underwing and lack of clear white belly readily separate Southern Pochard from members of genus Aythya with prominent wing-bands.

VOICE Relatively silent. Male sometimes utters a nasal, whirring 'perrr-perrr-perrr' in flight; female has a low, hissing, vibrant 'quarrk'.

DESCRIPTION Sexually dimorphic. Race *brunnea* described. **Adult male:** Head, neck and almost entire underparts blackish, becoming maroon-brown on face and upper neck and rich chestnut on flanks. Upperparts and upperwing very dark brown, with broad white band along almost full length of primaries and secondaries; outer primaries and tips of primaries and secondaries brown. Underwing dusky, with underside of flight feathers paler. **Adult female:** General coloration resembles that of male, but browner and not so dark. Underparts dark buff-brown, weakly mottled and barred whitish; striking head pattern, with whitish of throat extending up sides of head behind ear-coverts in diffuse crescent and with whitish patches around bill-base. Wing as male. **Juvenile:** Resembles female, but whitish head patches buffish-white and less striking and general body colour browner; young male distinctly darker on neck, breast and underparts than young female.

BARE PARTS All plumages: Bill bluish-grey, with black nail; duller on female. Legs and feet dark grey. Iris bright red on male, reddish-brown on female.

MEASUREMENTS Sexes similar. Wing 201-228 (mean: male 217, female 209); tarsus 37-41; bill 41-45; mean weight of male 799, of female 763.

GEOGRAPHICAL VARIATION Two races recognised, differing marginally in colour. Race *brunnea* of Africa is slightly lighter and browner than nominate race of South America.

HABITS South American race rare and little known. African race well studied. A diving duck of freshwater and brackish-water lakes and lagoons. Usually found in small parties, but large concentrations form outside breeding season on some waters. Pair-bond temporary, is formed prior to breeding season. Breeding commences towards end of local wet season when water levels are high, being recorded in all months in Africa. Nests on ground by waterside, hidden among vegetation; occasionally in holes or old nests of other birds and sometimes some distance from water. Feeds mostly in early morning and evening, chiefly by diving and up-ending. Loafs in groups by shoreline during the day. Walks relatively easily, but patters over surface when taking wing; flight fast. Relatively confiding compared with many other ducks. Swims buoyantly when resting, but low in water with tail depressed when actively feeding. Undertakes quite extensive movements, southern African birds dispersing northwards during dry season and congregating in large numbers on some lakes.

HABITAT Relatively large and deep freshwater and brackish-water lakes up to 2400 m (in Africa).

DISTRIBUTION South American race now extremely rare. Formerly reported from widely-scattered localities from Venezuela and Colombia south to northern Chile, northern Argentina and eastern Brazil; odd sightings in past 20 years from Brazil, Venezuela, Colombia and Peru, but perhaps now breeding only in Venezuela and eastern Brazil. Vagrant to Trinidad. African race locally common in southern and eastern Africa, from the Cape north to Ethiopia; although chiefly resident, southern populations move north in dry season, with South African-ringed birds recovered north to Kenya, where numbers increase dramatically in winter.

POPULATION South American race was always very local and patchily distributed, but the lack of records in recent years is very worrying; it is believed still to breed in Venezuela and perhaps also in eastern Brazil, where a small flock was reported in 1985. Cause of decline unknown. African race also rather local, but abundant overall, with dry-season counts reaching 7,500 in Zambia, 5,000 in western Cape and 1,300 in Kenya at certain key individual waters.

REFERENCES Brown *et al.* (1982), King (1981), Middlemiss (1958).

115 ROSYBILL   Plate 35
Netta peposaca
Alternative name: Rosy-billed Pochard

Like the Red-crested Pochard (113), behaves more like a dabbling duck than a pochard. It is one of the more abundant ducks of temperate South America.

FIELD IDENTIFICATION Length 53-57 cm (21-23 in). **At rest:** Heavily-built South American duck, equally at home on land as on water. Male unmistakable, with black head, breast and upperparts and pale grey flanks, and with striking bright red bill which has red swollen knob at the base. Dull brown female has blue-grey bill and could be confused with female Southern Pochard (114), but is paler brown, has clear white undertail-coverts and lacks white facial markings, although has buffer-brown face patches and whitish throat. Southern Pochard now very rare in South America and ranges may no longer overlap. **In flight:** Bulky broad-winged duck, both sexes showing white underwing and extensive white along full length of flight feathers above. Black head, breast and upperparts of male contrast with grey underbody. Female dull brown apart from striking wing pattern, white underwing easily separating it from female Southern Pochard.

VOICE Relatively silent, except in display. Male has weak 'wheeoo' and female utters a harsh 'kraa'.

DESCRIPTION Sexually dimorphic. **Adult male:** Head, neck and breast glossy purplish-black; upperparts similar, but faintly vermiculated with pale grey or whitish on mantle and scapulars. Flanks and belly vermiculated grey. Ventral region black, contrasting with white undertail-coverts. Upperwing-coverts dark brown, with whitish patch along leading edge at carpal joint; secondaries and primaries white, with blackish tips and outermost primaries. Underwing whitish. **Adult female:** Head and body plumage almost uniform dull medium-brown, unmottled; darker on crown, hindneck, breast and upperparts. Whitish chin and throat, and lighter areas of buff on sides of head. Centre of underparts lighter and more buff-brown; undertail-coverts white. Wing much as that of male, but upperwing-coverts not so dark. **Juvenile:** Resembles female, but more uniform brown, lacking lighter belly of female; young male soon starts to acquire features of adult male plumage and bill coloration.

BARE PARTS Male: Bill with swollen knob at base of culmen, bright rose-red with black nail. Legs and feet yellow to orange, with dusky webs. Iris yellow to orange, brightest in breeding season. **Female and juvenile:** Bill blue-grey, only slightly swollen at base. Legs and feet greyish-yellow. Iris brown.

MEASUREMENTS Sexes similar. Wing of male 228-245, of female 220-240; tarsus 41-45; bill of male 61-66, of female 54-60; mean weight of male 1181, of female 1004.

GEOGRAPHICAL VARIATION None.

HABITS Sociable duck of freshwater marshes, usually found in small parties, but large aggregations form on favoured waters. Pair-bond temporary. Breeding season October-December in central Argentina. Nests hidden in waterside vegetation, often built in shallow water among emergent vegetation. Female often lays eggs in nests of other waterbirds; indeed, one nest in Argentina contained 24 Rosybill eggs in addition to six eggs of the nest-parasitic Black-headed Duck (148), a more typical clutch of the Rosybill being ten eggs. Feeds by dabbling and up-ending in shallow water, and sometimes by diving; also wades in shallows, and readily feeds on land. Takes off from water with much foot-pattering, but, despite relatively short and broad wings, flight fast when well underway; when flying high, flocks often form crude V-formations. Relatively confiding compared with many other South American ducks. Southern populations migratory, dispersing northwards for the winter.

HABITAT Freshwater marshes in open country, with preference for well-vegetated marshes rather than open-water lakes.

DISTRIBUTION Widespread over central lowland South America, breeding in coastal Chile from Atacama to Valdivia. East of the Andes is more widespread, breeding south to Rio Negro of Argentina and north to Uruguay, Paraguay and southeastern Brazil. Southern populations migrate north, taking range north to southern Bolivia and central southern Brazil. Rarely occurs south to Tierra del Fuego, and has occurred as a vagrant on the Falkland Islands. Popular in captivity, escapes often occur in Europe and North America.

POPULATION No estimates have been made, but is an abundant species, at least in parts of Argentina, and is clearly under no threat.

REFERENCES Johnsgard (1978), Weller (1967).

GENUS *AYTHYA* AND *AYTHYA* HYBRIDS

As with the dabbling ducks, many members of this genus are quite closely related and females appear generally similar. Courtship displays are also quite similar within the genus and the temporary pair-bonds begin in the winter quarters, when waterfowl flocks are somewhat mixed. All of these factors contribute to the occasional pairing between different species.

Mayr estimated that hybrids in wild birds in general represent roughly one in 60,000 individuals. No doubt the most likely situation for interbreeding to occur arises when lone female ducks become mixed with flocks of another species in winter;

Smallshire estimated that, among 'Greater Scaups' turning up on inland reservoirs in central Britain in winter, some 20% of males showed hybrid characters rather than being pure.

Obviously, birds occurring away from their normal wintering grounds with flocks of similar ducks should be studied carefully before a firm identification is arrived at, and care should be taken especially with individuals that do not seem to be quite right'. As with the dabbling ducks, the *Aythya* hybrid does not necessarily resemble its parents; it may recall a third species, and also differ according to the sex of each respective parent species. Female-type hybrids are very difficult to isolate among the individually rather variable females, juveniles and eclipse males of common species, and are generally impossible to identify with any degree of certainty; male hybrids in breeding plumage are often striking. Wild hybrids have been reported from among a number of different pairings within the genus, and arguably any combination is possible (it certainly seems to be so in captivity, and the resulting hybrids could also occur as escapes). Identifying the hybrid parentage is normally impossible under field conditions, but hybrids from most of the following pairings have compared well with captive-bred birds of known parentage; those that have been reported in the wild and whose parental species have only been assumed are mentioned as 'hypothetical'.

Pochard with: Tufted Duck and Ferruginous Duck.
Redhead with: Ring-necked Duck, Greater Scaup and Lesser Scaup.
Ring-necked Duck with: Redhead, Lesser Scaup, Tufted Duck (hypothetical) and Greater Scaup (hypothetical).
Baer's Pochard with: Ferruginous Duck (hypothetical).
Ferruginous Duck with: Pochard, Tufted Duck and Baer's Pochard (hypothetical).
Tufted Duck with: Pochard, Greater Scaup, Ferruginous Duck and Ring-necked Duck (hypothetical).
Greater Scaup with: Redhead, Tufted Duck and Ring-necked Duck (hypothetical).
Lesser Scaup with: Redhead and Ring-necked Duck.

It is fascinating to note that the two most similar species, Greater and Lesser Scaups, have never been found to interbreed in the wild, although, of course, they may have done and the resulting hybrids may have been overlooked. The two scaups have, however, been deliberately crossed in captivity, and the hybrids have proven to be fertile.

The following hybrid types seem to have caused the most confusion in the field through their resemblance to males of other species. (Other types often show more obvious combinations between two species, and are less likely to be misidentified as a third species.)

LESSER SCAUP TYPES
Differ from Lesser Scaup in having black of bill-tip extending over whole tip of bill (nail only on male Lesser Scaup), darker basal area of bill, longer bump on rear crown, and closer vermiculations on

Lesser Scaup type

Ferruginous Duck type

Baer's Pochard type

upperparts (appearing uniform grey unless at close range). When seen at close quarters, flanks may be finely vermiculated very pale grey. Black of head may have reddish or bluish-purple bloom, and iris may be orange-red (yellow on Lesser Scaup).

GREATER SCAUP TYPES
Differ from Greater Scaup in having more black at bill-tip (nail only on male Greater Scaup), slight tuft at rear crown (but hybrids between Greater Scaup and Tufted Duck may show Greater Scaup crown shape), shorter bill with more concave culmen, and darker grey and closer upperpart vermiculations (recalling Lesser Scaup type).

FERRUGINOUS DUCK TYPES
Differ from typical Ferruginous Duck in usually having less extensive white on undertail-coverts, prominent whitish subterminal band on bill, more extensive black at bill-tip, shorter bill, lower crown profile, and greyish vermiculations on flanks and upperparts. Birds lacking vermiculations may have dull grey flanks, not the rufous-brown of Ferruginous Duck. Iris yellow (not white).

BAER'S POCHARD TYPES
Differ from Baer's Pochard in having chestnut mixed with green of head (as on moulting male Baer's), less extensive white on undertail-coverts, white belly not rising well above water line on fore-flanks, and slight tuft at rear of head.

RING-NECKED DUCK TYPE
A bird described by Vinicombe resembled male Ring-necked Duck, but had white on inner primaries, short tuft on bump at rear crown, bill a little smaller than normal with subterminal band narrower and basal band indistinct, and breast stripe paler than grey flanks but not white.

The above is a gross oversimplification of the complex hybrid problem. Those wishing to pursue

it further should consult the references listed below, the paper by Gillham *et al.* being particularly useful.
REFERENCES De Knijff (1983), Eigenhuis (1985), Gantlett (1985), Gillham *et al.* (1966), Mayr (1963), Osborne (1972, 1985), Perrins (1961), Sage (1961, 1962, 1963), Scherer and Hilsberg (1982), Smallshire (1986), Vinicombe (1982), Voous (1955).

116 CANVASBACK   Plate 36
Aythya valisineria

The largest of the true pochards and widespread in North America. Closely related to, but considerably larger than, the Pochard (117) of the Old World.

FIELD IDENTIFICATION Length 48-61 cm (19-24 in). **At rest:** Large diving duck of North American marshes and estuarine bays and lagoons. At all ages, distinctive head shape an important feature: has long blackish bill, relatively high, slightly bulging at the base and merging into long sloping forehead and high, peaked crown; when alert, the neck is also markedly longer than on similar species. Breeding male has uniform very pale grey, almost whitish-grey, body which contrasts with black tail-end and breast and chestnut head, latter becoming blackish on face and throat. Overall coloration similar to that of Redhead (118), but latter is smaller and dumpier, with rounded head shape, shorter bill with pale subterminal band and black tip, and has darker grey body, with upperparts slightly darker than underparts. Even more similar male Pochard, a vagrant to Alaskan islands and Hawaii, is somewhat intermediate between the two in size, body colour and head shape, but has shorter, two-toned bill, less sloping head shape than Canvasback (but considerably more so than on Redhead), and the relatively long bill has a somewhat *retroussé* aspect and a

distinct pale grey subterminal band; like the Redhead, the head of Pochard is all chestnut, not shading blackish towards the front as on Canvasback. Male scaups (126, 127) also have superficially similar body coloration, but show contrast between white underbody and grey upperparts and have head as well as breast black. Canvasbacks in female-like plumage are greyish-brown, with browner head, neck and breast contrasting with greyer body, and usually have some indistinct lighter buffish shades behind the eye and on sides of head; there is considerable individual variation in basic shades within Canvasback, Redhead and Pochard, which are all basically similar, but Canvasback tends to have body coloration distinctly paler grey than the other two, offering stronger contrast with the browner breast and head; the important head-and-bill shape are the most reliable distinctions. Juvenile, first-winter and summer female Pochards often have an all-dark bill like Canvasback, and may be particularly confusing if alone and no direct size comparison possible with other species; when alert, Pochard can also appear surprisingly long-necked. **In flight:** Relatively bulky body and long head and neck apparent in flight. Males appear almost whitish on body, contrasting with black breast and tail-end and chestnut head. The underwing is whitish and offers little contrast, while the relatively plain greyish upperwing is a little darker grey than the very pale back; the upperwing is more uniform than on either Redhead or Pochard, which have forewing a little darker than the paler grey flight feathers. Females have similar wing pattern to male, although body contrasts are less striking. Compare also Ring-necked Duck (119).
VOICE Relatively silent. Most vocal during display. Male has soft cooing notes, female a harsh 'krrr'.
DESCRIPTION Sexually dimorphic. Seasonally variable. **Adult male breeding:** Head and neck reddish-chestnut, becoming blackish on front of head and throat. Breast and upper mantle black. Almost entire central body plumage very pale vermiculated grey, appearing much whiter than on similar species. Rump, uppertail- and undertail-coverts and tail blackish. Upperwing-coverts vermiculated medium-grey, primary coverts darker grey. Primaries darker grey, with darker tips; secondaries grey, with darker grey tips to those nearest primaries and whitish tips to those nearest body. Underwing whitish. **Adult male eclipse:** Whole plumage duller, with brownish feather tips. Easily distinguished from female by blacker breast and undertail-coverts, redder-brown and more uniform head, and iris colour. **Adult female:** Head, neck and breast medium-brown; lores, throat and line behind eye paler, buffish or whitish. Underparts pale grey, duller than on male, with browner flanks in summer; upperparts brownish-grey, browner in summer. Rump and tail dark brown. Wing as that of male, but upperwing-coverts duller and browner-grey. **Juvenile:** Resembles adult female, but upperparts darker and underparts browner and more mottled. Young males have darker heads than females, and their iris becomes pale yellowish when very young. Adult plumage is acquired during first winter.

BARE PARTS In all plumages, bill blackish and legs and feet bluish-grey. **Male:** Iris red, duller in eclipse; yellowish on first-year birds. **Female:** Iris dark brown.
MEASUREMENTS Males typically larger than females. Wing 220-242 (male 225-242, female 220-230); tarsus 43-45; bill 54-63; mean weight of male 1252, of female 1154.
GEOGRAPHICAL VARIATION None.
HABITS Sociable duck of open waters. In winter quarters, typically found in rafts, far out on open lakes or estuaries. In breeding season, pairs frequent marshes in open country. Pair-bonds formed in late winter, most birds arriving on breeding grounds already paired to take up relatively large territories. Breeding season chiefly May-June. Nest built among waterside vegetation, relatively large and sometimes fairly exposed, often almost floating in shallow water. Males gather on moulting waters during incubation. Feeds by diving, often in relatively deeper water than Redhead. Most active in evening and early morning, spending most of day asleep on open water in dense rafts or loafing on shores of lakes in groups. Shy and wary. Patters over water before taking to air, but when underway flight action is very fast and strong. Often flies high, moving flocks forming V-formations. Migratory, moving to coastal waters in winter.
HABITAT Breeds on prairie marshes with areas of open water and extensive fringe vegetation. Winters on more open lakes, coastal lagoons, estuaries and sheltered coastal bays.
DISTRIBUTION North America. Breeding range extends from central Alaska southwards over western prairies and Great Plains to northeastern California and Nebraska, east to Minnesota. Winters over lowlands and coastal regions from British Columbia and Great Lakes region southwards along both coasts to central Mexico. Occasional in winter in Cuba, Bermuda and south to Guatemala, with vagrants to Marshall and Hawaiian Islands and Japan.
POPULATION Has fluctuated in numbers considerably in the past and seems to be declining once again. In the 1930s, the population decreased alarmingly after a series of drought years prevented any reasonable breeding successes. The population made a comeback, but during the 1960s and 1970s a combination of factors, notably the extensive drainage of prairie marshes, has seen it decline to an estimated 500,000 individuals by the mid 1970s, a 50% reduction on numbers estimated 20 years earlier. Numbers have also been lost during oil-spillage incidents in key wintering areas. There is considerable concern over the future of this relatively slow-breeding duck.
REFERENCES Hochbaum (1944), Johnsgard (1978).

117 POCHARD   Plate 36
Aythya ferina

Alternative names: Common Pochard, European Pochard, Eurasian Pochard

Widespread throughout lowland freshwater habitats of Europe and Palaearctic Asia, and the Old World counterpart of the Canvasback (116).

Head-and-bill shapes of pochards (females)

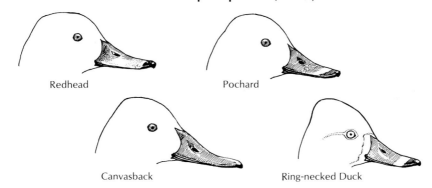

Redhead   Pochard

Canvasback   Ring-necked Duck

FIELD IDENTIFICATION Length 42-49 cm (17-19 in).
At rest: Medium-sized freshwater diving duck, with
stocky body sloping towards relatively short tail,
and somewhat sloping forehead and relatively long
bill, the outline of which gives a slightly concave
profile and peak to crown. Breeding male distinctive within normal range, with pale grey body,
chestnut head, and black breast and tail-end.
Unlikely to be confused, although both Canvasback
and Redhead (118) also similar and Pochard an
occasional vagrant to Alaskan islands; discussions
on separation are given under the two former
species. Male Wigeon (71) lacks black breast and
has white and black ventral region; male Red-
crested Pochard (113) is larger, with brown upperparts and white flanks; both scaups (126, 127) have
white flanks contrasting with grey upperparts, and
black head and breast. Birds in female-like plumage
differ from other Old World members of the genus
in head-and-bill shape, and in having body greyer
than brown of head, neck and breast and pale,
often whitish, facial shading and line behind eye;
duller and browner juveniles may lack facial
shading altogether. See also females of Ring-necked
Duck (119), Canvasback and Redhead, which are
all similar. **In flight:** Appears relatively long-necked
and short-tailed, with rather 'waisted' neck and
bulbous head. Male all grey, with black breast and
tail and red head; the whitish underwing offers little
contrast with the body, and the greyish upperwing
is paler along the flight feathers than on the forewing. Browner female is less contrastingly marked,
but brown breast contrasts with greyer underbody,
and browner-grey forewing with paler grey flight
feathers. See also Canvasback, Redhead and female
Ring-necked Duck, which are similar in flight.
VOICE Female sometimes utters a harsh, growled
'krrr' when flushed, but male is generally silent; in
breeding season, soft wheezy whistles may be
heard from males at close quarters.
DESCRIPTION Sexually dimorphic. Seasonally variable. **Adult male breeding:** Head chestnut-red.
Breast and upper mantle black. Almost whole of
body plumage vermiculated grey; uppertail- and
undertail-coverts, tail and rump blackish. Upperwing-coverts vermiculated darker grey. Primaries
and secondaries paler grey, becoming darker along
tips of primaries and adjacent secondaries and outer

primaries; secondaries nearest body tipped whitish.
Underwing whitish. **Adult male eclipse:** Recalls
female, but body plumage greyer, head lacks facial
pattern, breast markedly darker, and has redder iris.
Adult female: Head, neck and breast medium-
brown, with pale greyish-white areas on throat,
lores, sides of head and stripe behind eye; these
pale facial areas are ill-defined, diffuse and individually variable in extent. Most of body plumage greyish-brown, darker on upperparts, with brown and
grey shading intermixed; markedly browner above
and below in summer than in winter, although still
showing contrast with head and breast. Uppertail-
coverts and tail dark grey-brown. Wing as that of
male, although upperwing-coverts browner-grey.
Juvenile: Owing to variation, ageing difficult in field,
but juvenile typically more uniform above than
winter female, lacks pale stripe behind eye, and has
underparts more mottled, with brown tips and grey
bases to feathers of flanks; bill all dark (as on some
summer females). Acquires adult plumage features
during early part of first winter.
BARE PARTS In all plumages, legs and feet grey.
Male: Bill dark grey, with wide pale grey subterminal band and broad pale tip. Iris orange-
yellow to red, brightest in breeding season. **Female:**
Bill dark grey to blackish, with narrow pale grey
subterminal band and broad black tip; pale band
indistinct in summer. Iris brown, sometimes yellowish-brown. **Juvenile:** Bill all blackish-grey, attaining
adult pattern during first winter. Iris yellowish-olive,
attaining adult colour during first winter.
MEASUREMENTS Males average larger than females.
Wing 200-223 (mean: male 217, female 206); tarsus
36-42; bill 42-52; mean weight of male 942, of
female 848.
GEOGRAPHICAL VARIATION None.
HABITS Gregarious freshwater diving duck, usually
found in small or very large flocks. Mixes freely with
other diving ducks, but parties tend to keep
together discretely away from others when sleeping. Pair-formation occurs in late winter and spring,
many birds pairing up on breeding waters. Breeding
season chiefly mid April to June, but later further
north. Nests on ground among waterside vegetation, often partially in water. Males normally leave
females once incubation underway, but some
remain and help female in tending brood. Gathers

on favoured waters for post-breeding moult, many populations undertaking relatively extensive moult migration. Feeds by diving, sometimes up-ending in shallows. Most active early morning and evening, spending most of day sleeping in closely-packed rafts on open water. Also loafs on banks in small groups. Relatively shy and wary. Takes off with pattering over surface, but fast and direct when airborne; flocks may form V-formations or lines when flying very high. Migratory

HABITAT Shallow to relatively deep freshwater lakes with extensive open water, but with fair cover of fringe or emergent vegetation around edges. Outside breeding season, also on more open lakes and reservoirs, slow-flowing rivers and occasionally estuaries and sheltered coastal bays.

DISTRIBUTION Widespread over almost the whole of Europe and Asia. Breeds from British Isles and Spain eastwards across Europe and Asia, south of the tundra zone, to western Mongolia and Lake Baikal, south to western China (western Sinkiang), Aral Sea, northern shores of Black Sea and Romania. More isolated breeding pockets are in Iceland (very few) and central and eastern Turkey, Turkestan, Afghanistan, southern Tibet, Heilung-kiang (Manchuria) and Japan (Hokkaido); some of these are perhaps only sporadic. The breeding range may well extend further east in Siberia than is mapped. In western Europe, resident in temperate regions but numbers swollen in winter. Winters over western Europe, basins of Mediterranean, Black and Caspian Seas, eastwards through Indian sub-continent and northern Burma to southern China and Japan; smaller numbers reach favoured winter duck haunts of Senegal, Mali and Chad, with some south to Cameroon and Zaire, while others penetrate Nile valley to Ethiopia and elsewhere in East Africa south to Kenya and Uganda. Vagrants recorded Faeroes, Azores, Canary Islands, Cape Verde Islands, Gambia, Tanzania, Thailand, Hong Kong, Taiwan, Philippines, Guam, Hawaiian Islands, Kamchatka, Komandorskiye Islands (northeast Siberia) and Alaska (Pribilof and Aleutian Islands).

POPULATION Widespread and abundant, with some local increases in western and central Europe. Local decreases elsewhere due to wetland drainage. Winter population estimates of 225,000 in western Europe and 750,000 in Black Sea-Mediterranean region. Other large winter populations in Asia clearly show that the species is not threatened.

REFERENCES Cramp and Simmons (1977).

118 REDHEAD   Plate 36
Aythya americana

Smaller and darker than the Canvasback (116), with which it widely overlaps throughout its North American range.

FIELD IDENTIFICATION Length 45-56 cm (18-22 in). **At rest:** Relatively large diving duck of North American marshes and estuarine bays. In all plumages smaller, shorter-necked and darker than Canvasback, with distinctly-rounded forehead and crown and more 'conventional' bill shape (see figure, p. 247). Breeding male has red head, black breast and tail-end, and medium-grey body plumage; apart from head-and-bill shape, distinguished from Canvasback by darker grey body plumage, with contrasting whitish belly (if out of water), slightly more extensive black breast, often yellow iris, and striking bill pattern: blue-grey, with broad black tip and narrow whitish subterminal band. Compared with Redhead, Pochard (117) is slightly smaller, paler grey (although somewhat intermediate in tone), and has more sloping forehead, slightly-peaked crown, red iris, and blacker-based bill with much wider pale subterminal band. Birds in female-like plumage more difficult owing to seasonal and age variations, but Redhead always darker and more uniform brown than Canvasback, with bill pattern and head-and-bill shape much as male. Closer to female Pochard, but more uniform overall, often distinctly warm brown, with little contrast between brown of head and breast and flanks and upperparts; upperparts distinctly darker than on Pochard, and undertail-coverts sometimes whitish; pale areas on side of head less distinct; the paler grey bill with distinct black tip and more prominent nail also aids identification. Female Ring-necked Duck (119) is a little shorter-bodied, with peaked bump at rear of crown, is rather darker brown, has more distinct whitish eye-ring, and longer bill with broader and clearer white subterminal band. Confusion with other species less likely. **In flight:** General appearance of both sexes close to that of Canvasback and Pochard, but on males darker grey body contrasts a little more with whitish underwing, although less contrast between upperwing-coverts and mantle than on those species; more extensive black breast on Redhead extends back to fore point of where wing joins body. The secondaries are paler grey than the upperwing-coverts, and contrast a little more with the darker forewing than on either Canvasback or Pochard. Compare female Ring-necked Duck.

VOICE Generally silent, except in display. Male then utters a distinctive and almost cat-like 'whee-ough' and a rolling 'rrrrrr'. Female utters a harsh 'squak'.

DESCRIPTION Sexually dimorphic. Seasonally variable. **Adult male breeding:** Head and neck reddish-chestnut. Breast and upper mantle black. Most of body plumage vermiculated grey, darker than on similar species and a little darker above than on flanks; centre of belly whitish; undertail- and uppertail-coverts, tail and rump blackish. Upperwing-coverts vermiculated grey, contrasting with paler grey secondaries and primaries; outermost primaries and tips to primaries and inner secondaries darker, secondaries nearest body tipped whitish. Underwing whitish. **Adult male eclipse:** Considerably duller; distinguished from female by redder-brown head, yellowish iris, and darker breast and undertail-coverts. **Adult female:** Head, neck and breast reddish-brown, with buffish-white chin and throat and indistinct eye-ring and stripe behind eye; crown considerably darker brown. Flanks warm brown, contrasting little with breast, but with buffer feather fringes; centre of underparts and often undertail-coverts whitish. Upperparts darker and duller brown; with upperwing-coverts browner than on male, otherwise wing similar to that of male. Some seasonal variation, with plumage duller and greyer in summer than in winter. **Juvenile:** Much as adult female, but greyer, with body plumage distinctly mottled both above and below. Males start to show yellowish iris at about two months, and adult plumages are acquired during first winter.

BARE PARTS In all plumages, legs and feet grey. **Male:** Bill light blue-grey, with relatively wide black tip and narrow whitish subterminal line; also has an inconspicuous narrow black line around bill-base. Iris yellow, sometimes orange. **Female and juvenile:** Bill duller than male's, but very similar in pattern. Iris dark brown, becoming yellowish on young males.

MEASUREMENTS Males typically larger than females. Wing 210-242 (male 230-242, female 210-230); tarsus 40-43; bill 44-49; mean weight of male 1080, of female 1030.

GEOGRAPHICAL VARIATION None.

HABITS Sociable diving duck of fresh and brackish waters, forming very large concentrations outside breeding season and mixing freely with others of the genus. Pair-formation occurs from mid-winter onwards and into the spring migration. Pairs arrive on breeding grounds from late April onwards and select relatively large territories. Breeding takes place during May and June. Nests hidden among waterside vegetation, often partially in water; female also has a tendency to drop her eggs in nests of other waterbirds. Feeds chiefly by diving, but also dabbles. Most active early morning and evening, spending most of day in rafts far out on open lakes or in sheltered coastal bays. Patters over surface when taking off; flight fast when underway, rather more agile on the wing than either Canvasback or Pochard. Relatively less wary than Canvasback. Migratory.

HABITAT Breeds on freshwater lakes and marshes in open country, e.g. prairies. In winter, on coastal brackish lagoons and marshes, freshwater lakes and marshes and tidal bays.

DISTRIBUTION Widespread over North America. Breeds chiefly in the prairie country of western Canada and USA, from central Canada south to California, New Mexico and Nebraska. Throughout most of southern region of mapped area is rather localised and patchily distributed. More-isolated pockets elsewhere, in central and southeastern Alaska and further east in Great Lakes region. Winters chiefly in coastal lowlands from British Columbia and Great Lakes region south to central Mexico and Cuba, rarely elsewhere in West Indies and south to Guatemala, with vagrants reaching Bermuda and the Hawaiian Islands.

POPULATION Like the Canvasback, has suffered considerable decline this century through drainage of prairie marshes. The population was estimated at around 600,000 individuals during the 1970s and seems now to be stable; there are also clear indications of an easterly spread in its breeding range, as in the Great Lakes region.

REFERENCES Johnsgard (1975).

119 RING-NECKED DUCK   Plate 38
Aythya collaris

Nearctic counterpart of Old World Tufted Duck (125), although in wing pattern and female plumage is closer to Redhead (118). The English name is not very apt, the dull collar being almost impossible to see in the field.

FIELD IDENTIFICATION Length 37-46 cm (15-18 in). **At rest:** A short-bodied diving duck, with distinctive high crown reaching an obvious bump at rear of crown and with relatively deep-based and long bill (see figure, p. 247). The tail is often held noticeably cocked when at rest, and the curve of the flank-border line is usually distinctly S-shaped in comparison with most others of genus, with rear flanks curving up quite high over folded wing and dipping low towards breast. Breeding male, with black head, breast and upperparts and grey flanks, recalls only male Tufted Duck, with which it overlaps in range as a vagrant. Distinguished from Tufted by structure, and differs also in having pale grey flanks, these separated from black breast by contrasting vertical white stripe which comes to a higher, more prominent point than the white in same area on Tufted Duck. Most problematic are Tufted Ducks assuming breeding plumage in autumn and which have brownish flanks and otherwise blackish plumage: such birds sometimes show whitish on fore-flanks suggestive of Ring-necked, but may be separated by shape of flank curve, shorter tail, longer body, and presence of tuft at rear of crown rather than bump. Male Ring-necked has striking bill pattern, with conspicuous white subterminal band, broad black tip, dark grey central area, and narrower white band around base; earlier in winter the basal band may be inconspicuous, but the remainder of the bill pattern and the greater bill length are striking in comparison with Tufted. Eclipse male and early first-winter male Ring-necks best identified by structure, especially distinctive rear-crown bump, but retain white subterminal bill-band and a 'shadow' of flank pattern. Birds in female-like plumage are more likely to be confused with female Pochard (117) or Redhead than with Tufted, having pale areas on face and a distinct whitish eye-ring and often a whitish line behind eye: on Ring-necked, the loral area is typically whiter than on either, and the distinctive shape is much as that of male; the white subterminal bill-band is usually clearer than on either of the other two species (but is very obscure in summer); and the upperparts are markedly darker than the warmer brown flanks and the often greyish sides of head, neck and breast. **In flight:** Lack of white in wing immediately separates Ring-necked from Tufted and both scaups (126, 127). Male has blackish head, neck, breast, upperparts and forewing, which contrast with whitish underwing, pale underbody and grey secondaries. Female has similar wing pattern, but duller and browner body. Both sexes distinguished from Redhead and Pochard by much darker forewing, latter contrasting with grey secondaries.

VOICE Relatively silent except in display, when

male utters low whistling note and female a soft rolling 'trrr'.

DESCRIPTION Sexually dimorphic. Seasonally variable. **Adult male breeding:** Head, neck, breast, undertail-coverts and almost entire upperparts blackish, with inconspicuous reddish-brown collar around base of neck. Flanks vermiculated grey, with very narrow whitish upper border. Stripe up side of breast white and centre of underparts white. Upperwing-coverts blackish. Secondaries grey, innermost tipped dusky, those nearest body tipped white; primaries dusky, paler on inner webs. Underwing whitish. **Adult male eclipse:** All black areas of plumage browner, undertail-coverts and loral area whitish, and flanks warm brown with ill-defined paler breast stripe. Distinguished from female by blacker-brown head, breast and upperparts and lack of whitish eye-ring. **Adult female:** Crown and hindneck blackish-brown. Sides and front of head and neck mottled greyish, with whitish area between eye and bill; whitish throat and eye-ring, and often also a whitish line running back from eye. Breast and underparts warm brown, with greyer feather bases; centre of underparts and undertail-coverts whitish, mottled darker. Upperparts dark grey-brown. Wing as that of male, but forewing browner. In summer, facial pattern duller, although normally whitish on lores and eye-ring retained; whole plumage rather browner, less grey, and bill-band very faint. **Juvenile:** Resembles adult female, but head and neck browner and belly more spotted. Young males soon acquire blackish on breast and attain adult plumage through first winter, although adult-male flank colour attained after blackness of plumage well developed; as adult by mid-winter.

BARE PARTS In all plumages, legs and feet grey. **Male:** Bill slate-grey, with wide black tip, broad white subterminal band and narrower white band around bill-base, latter lacking on eclipse and juvenile males. Iris yellow. **Female:** Bill as that of male, but subterminal band a little narrower and basal band lacking; subterminal band obscure in summer. Iris brown. **Juvenile:** Bill dark grey, at first with black tip, but whitish subterminal band develops during first autumn. Iris dark brown, becoming yellowish on males during first autumn.

MEASUREMENTS Males typically larger than females. Wing 185-206 (mean: male 201, female 195); tarsus 45-47; bill 43-50; mean weight of male 752, of female 667.

GEOGRAPHICAL VARIATION None.

HABITS Sociable diving duck of freshwater lakes and marshes, usually found in small parties, but larger gatherings formed in winter. European vagrants tend to associate with parties of Pochards, and to a lesser degree with Tufted Ducks. Pair-formation sometimes starts in autumn, but is most active during late winter and spring. Birds arrive on breeding grounds from late March through April and take up relatively small territories. Breeding season is from May to June, and the nest is hidden among floating vegetation or on small islands. Feeds in relatively shallower water than many others of genus, mostly by diving, but also dabbles and even up-ends. Most active early morning and evening, spending day sleeping in small parties near emergent vegetation by lakeshores rather than out in lake centre. Swims buoyantly, often with short tail cocked and spread. Takes off from water much more easily than others of genus, and flight action faster and more agile than that of most. Highly migratory, moving further south in winter than most other Nearctic members of the genus.

HABITAT Breeds by freshwater lakes and pools in open lowland country, often by quite small pools in marshes. In winter, on larger freshwater lakes and locally on tidal bays and coastal brackish lagoons.

DISTRIBUTION Widespread in North America. Breeds chiefly over southern Canada and adjacent USA, from British Columbia eastwards to Atlantic seaboard; sporadic breeding also occurs over central and western USA south to California, Colorado and Nebraska, and also north to central Alaska. Winters chiefly in coastal lowlands from British Columbia and Massachusetts south through Mexico to Guatemala and West Indies, rarely south to Panama, and vagrants have reached Trinidad, Venezuela, Hawaiian Islands and Japan. Regular transatlantic vagrant in winter: annual in British Isles, and recorded most western European countries from Iceland south to Spain and east to Switzerland, West Germany and Sweden; also recorded Morocco and the Azores.

POPULATION Population estimated at some 500,000 individuals in mid 1970s. In recent decades has been increasing and extending breeding range eastwards, which has been mirrored by the increasing number of records of vagrants in Europe.

REFERENCES Johnsgard (1978), Vinicombe (1982).

120 HARDHEAD   Plate 38
Aythya australis

Alternative names: Australian White-eye (nominate race), White-eyed Duck, Banks Island White-eye (extima)

The only member of the genus in Australia; chiefly resident, but occasional irruptions during drought periods have taken it as far as Java and New Zealand.

FIELD IDENTIFICATION Length 42-59 cm (17-23 in). **At rest:** Relatively large, long-bodied, dark reddish-brown freshwater diving duck with white undertail-coverts and pale subterminal band on bill. Distinctive within Australian native range, where it is the only pochard, but during irruptions occurs north to East Indies and west Pacific islands and south to New Zealand. In New Zealand, distinguished from juvenile New Zealand Scaup (124) by its white undertail-coverts, pale bill-band and larger size. Baer's Pochard (121) is similar, but shows white on fore-flanks above water line and lacks whitish bill-band. The broad pale bill-band, darker brown plumage and relatively large size and long neck distinguish it from other similar white-eyes in captivity. **In flight:** Wing pattern and general body coloration are similar in all white-eyes. The dark body of both sexes contrasts strongly with whitish belly and underwing, although belly pattern variable, being brownish on some birds; a broad white band along full length of flight feathers of upperwing gives a pattern quite unlike that of any other Australian duck, except perhaps male of tiny Cotton Pygmy Goose (67).

VOICE Relatively silent. During display, male has a soft wheezy whistle and female may utter a short, gruff croak.

DESCRIPTION Plumages similar. Individual variation of general plumage tones makes ageing difficult. Nominate race described. **Adult male:** Overall coloration of head, neck and body dark chestnut-brown. Undertail-coverts white. Belly usually white or whitish, but often mottled darker and distinctly brownish on some. Upperwing dark brown, washed rufous on coverts, with broad white band along full length of primaries and secondaries; tips of flight feathers and outermost primaries brownish. Underwing whitish. **Adult female:** Similar to male, but general coloration lighter and browner, often with diffuse pale throat centre; differs from male also in iris colour and bill pattern. **Juvenile:** Resembles female, but lighter and buffer-brown, and with white of belly obscured by brownish mottling.

BARE PARTS In all plumages, legs and feet grey. **Male:** Bill relatively long, broad and high at base compared with that of other white-eyes; blackish, with wide pale blue-grey subterminal area. Iris white. **Female and juvenile:** Bill blackish-grey, with narrower and whiter subterminal bar than on male. Iris dark brown.

MEASUREMENTS Males typically larger than females. Nominate *australis*: Wing 183-243 (mean: male 215, female 217); tarsus 38-40; bill 34-50; mean weight of male 902, of female 838. Race *extima*: Wing of male 193-211, of female 189-196; bill 41-45.

GEOGRAPHICAL VARIATION Two races recognised. Nominate form occurs over most of range, and similar but smaller race *extima* on Banks Island group of New Hebrides Archipelago. The validity of the latter race is questionable: it is little known and there is no recent information on its status, but its measurements fall within the range of the Australian form; this may prove to be another example of islands temporarily colonised by the somewhat nomadic Australian Hardhead.

HABITS Sociable freshwater diving duck, typically found in small parties, but frequently in large flocks which may number thousands in dry-season concentrations. Pair-formation probably occurs quite rapidly as rising water levels trigger breeding activity. Breeding season varies considerably according to local water conditions, but in regions of regular rainfall has more stable pattern; in southwest Australia breeds from October to December, and in New South Wales from September to December. Nests are built among reeds or bushes at water level in relatively deep water, sometimes at waterside or on small islands. Feeds by diving in comparatively deep water, but also dabbles and even up-ends in shallower water. Shy and wary. Compared with most others of the genus, rises relatively easily from the water, flying rapidly away. Typically, swims low in water with tail depressed, but also floats more buoyantly, when white undertail-coverts are more obvious. Although largely resident in areas of permanent water, after prolonged periods of

drought is subject to considerable dispersals which have taken it far beyond normal range.

HABITAT Swamps and vegetated lakes with permanent deep water are favoured haunts. Outside breeding season, also occurs on larger and more open lakes, slow rivers, brackish coastal lagoons and sewage-pools.

DISTRIBUTION Main stronghold is southeastern Australia, especially the Murray-Darling region of New South Wales, but smaller numbers are found north to northeast Queensland and in southwestern Australia. During summer, as water levels fall, disperses in search of deeper water; during drought conditions the dispersal takes birds to all parts of Australia, although they are very scarce in the dry central region and few make it north to Northern Territory. Regular in Tasmania, but not known to breed there. Occasional birds recorded outside Australia were formerly thought to represent isolated populations, but now considered to be individuals moved out by periods of prolonged drought in Australia; it is possible that when such irruptions take place breeding may also occur, but the species does not seem to have become permanently established outside the continent. Such vagrants have been recorded from New Zealand, Auckland Islands, New Guinea, New Hebrides, New Caledonia, Sulawesi and Java.

POPULATION Has declined considerably in recent decades with drainage of swamps, especially in coastal New South Wales. Now decidedly local, but still recorded in sizeable flocks at some waters in the southeast. Its future is worrying, with continuing land-drainage schemes destroying its prime habitat. There is no information on the current status of the Banks Islands race.

REFERENCES Frith (1967), RAOU (1984).

121 BAER'S POCHARD   Plate 37
Aythya baeri

Alternative names: Baer's White-eye, Siberian White-eye

The eastern counterpart of the Ferruginous Duck (122), although in some respects nearer to the Hardhead (120) of Australia.

FIELD IDENTIFICATION Length 41-46 cm (16-18 in). **At rest:** A dark reddish-brown diving duck with smooth head shape and white undertail-coverts and belly. Closely resembles Ferruginous Duck, with which it may be encountered in eastern Asia in winter or on passage. Most useful feature is the more extensive white belly of Baer's which extends well up into reddish-brown of fore-flanks; Baer's shows some white above water line in this region even when swimming low in water, and when sitting buoyantly white is quite extensive. Tends to show a small area of white in wing when on water; white usually hidden on Ferruginous owing to flank feathers coming higher over folded wing. If the two species are together, Baer's appears a little larger, heavier-billed and longer-bodied, and has crown less peaked than Ferruginous (see figure, p. 256). Breeding male has blackish-green head, which offers a little contrast with chestnut breast and also

makes white iris very conspicuous. Female-like birds have reddish-brown heads like Ferruginous, but most show a paler brown loral patch which is quite distinct under good viewing conditions. Differs from other all-brown female ducks of the genus in much the same way as does Ferruginous Duck. **In flight:** Wing pattern close to that of Ferruginous Duck, but white on primaries does not extend so conspicuously towards wing-tip; the secondaries and primaries appear basically white, contrasting with very dark forewing and greyer outer primaries.
VOICE Relatively silent, except in display. Both sexes then utter harsh 'graaaak' sounds.
DESCRIPTION Sexes fairly similar. Seasonally variable. **Adult male breeding:** Head and upper neck glossy greenish-black. Small white spot on chin. Lower neck and breast dark reddish-brown. Flanks and ventral region duller brown. Undertail-coverts white. Belly white, this colour extending up onto fore-flanks, almost to wing at very front, with area of junction with brown irregularly and diffusely barred. Upperparts and upperwing-coverts dark blackish-brown, dark rufous-brown on mantle and scapulars. Primaries and secondaries white, becoming greyish on outer primaries; outermost primaries and tips of flight feathers dusky. Underwing whitish. **Adult male eclipse:** Recalls female, but head darker brown and iris whitish. **Adult female:** Similar to male, but whole plumage a little duller and less rufous, with brown head and neck and dark iris; pale brown oval patch on lores and often some whitish mottling on throat. Sides of belly less extensively white than on male. Wing as that of male, but upperwing-coverts browner and has less extensive white in primaries. **Juvenile:** Resembles female, but duller, with head and neck dull buffish-brown, contrasting a little with darker crown and hindneck and redder-brown breast; white of belly suffused brownish, but white on fore-flanks relatively extensive. Assumes adult plumage during first autumn and winter.
BARE PARTS In all plumages, legs and feet grey. **Male:** Bill blue-grey, with black nail and indistinct pale subterminal line; cutting edge also black, and bill darker grey towards base. Iris white, sometimes very pale yellowish. **Female and juvenile:** Bill duller than that of male, with pale subterminal line indistinct or absent. Iris dark brown, becoming whitish on young male during first autumn and winter.
MEASUREMENTS Males typically larger than females. Wing 186-233 (male 210-233, female 186-203); tarsus 36-38; bill 47-50; weight of male ca.880, of female ca.680.
GEOGRAPHICAL VARIATION None.
HABITS Little studied in the wild. Generally encountered in pairs or small parties, mixing freely with other diving ducks in winter or on passage. Pair-formation seems to begin late in winter, and continues after arrival of parties on breeding grounds during early April. Breeds from mid May to July. Nests on ground close to lakes and rivers. During incubation, males gather for post-breeding moult on nearby larger waters. Feeds almost entirely by diving. Relatively shy and wary. Rises easily from water compared with most others of genus, including Ferruginous Duck which typically

patters. Flight action rapid. Migratory; leaves breeding grounds after completion of moult, arriving in winter quarters from October onwards, later further south.
HABITAT Breeds on freshwater pools and lakes, with fringe and emergent vegetation, in open country. Winters also on larger and more open lakes, slow rivers and coastal marshes.
DISTRIBUTION Summer visitor to extreme southeastern Siberia and northeastern China (Heilungkiang, Kirin and Liaoning). Winters in lowland eastern China south of the Yangtze River to Kwangtung, with small numbers occasionally south and west to northeastern India, northern Burma, northern Thailand and Vietnam; occurs rarely in Japan and Korea in winter. Vagrants have occurred in western Siberia (Tomsk), Nepal, Bihar (India), Hong Kong and Kamchatka.
POPULATION Little information available, but seems to be locally common in main breeding and winter ranges and presumed to be under no threat.
REFERENCES Dementiev and Gladkov (1952).

122 FERRUGINOUS DUCK   Plate 37
Aythya nyroca

Alternative names: Common White-eye, White-eyed Pochard

Has remarkably similar distribution to that of Red-crested Pochard (113), being most numerous on freshwater lakes of eastern Europe and southern USSR.

FIELD IDENTIFICATION Length 38-42 cm (15-16 in). **At rest:** Medium-sized freshwater diving duck of the Old World. Resembles dark female Tufted Duck (125), but body relatively shorter, bill longer and crown higher, reaching distinct peak at centre and lacking any form of bump or tuft at rear (see figure p. 256). When resting, flank feathers often carried relatively higher over folded wing than on either Tufted Duck or similar Baer's Pochard (121). Breeding male rich dark chestnut on head, breast and flanks, with darker upperparts, and conspicuous pure white undertail-coverts which are particularly obvious on resting birds with tail cocked. White belly or wing patch not normally visible when on water. Birds in female plumage are duller and browner than males, being closer to female Tufted, but very white undertail-coverts and head-and-bill shape are useful pointers; the eye is dark on female Ferruginous, yellow on female Tufted (though dark on juveniles and a few adult females); female Tufted often has distinctly whitish undertail-coverts, and in poor views some individuals, especially lone juveniles of either species, are rather problematic. See also Baer's Pochard for discussion on separation from Ferruginous. When identifying birds outside normal range, the possibility of hybrids should be seriously considered (see p. 244). **In flight:** Both sexes recall female Tufted Duck, scaups (126, 127) and other white-eyes. Body plumage very dark, contrasting with clear white belly, undertail-coverts and underwing. Upperparts show very dark forewing contrasting with seemingly all-white primaries and secondaries; has only a little more white than Tufted Duck, but in the field the white appears very extensive and recalls that of larger Red-crested Pochard.

VOICE Relatively silent. During display, male gives soft 'wheeoo' whistling calls and female utters a harsh 'gaaa'.

DESCRIPTION Sexes rather similar. Seasonally variable. **Adult male breeding:** Head, neck, breast and flanks dark chestnut, slightly lighter along flanks. Small white spot on chin, and narrow black ring encircling base of neck. Belly white. Sides of ventral region blackish, contrasting with clear white under-tail-coverts. Upperparts blackish-brown. Upper-wing-coverts blackish-brown, with mostly white primaries and secondaries; outermost primaries and tips of remaining primaries and secondaries dusky-brown. Underwing whitish. **Adult male eclipse:** Duller and browner, recalling female, but redder on head and breast and retains white iris. **Adult female:** Duller and browner than male, with indistinct whit-ish mottling on throat and dark iris. On very worn birds, areas of buffish feathering may show on sides of head and throat; beware confusing such birds with female Baer's Pochard. In summer, whitish mottling on throat more extensive and head and neck lighter brown, flanks also scalloped with greyish feather tipping. **Juvenile:** Resembles female, but sides of head and foreneck lighter and buffer, more obvious pale feather fringes to flanks and upperparts, and white of belly and undertail-coverts slightly mottled. Becomes more like adult during first autumn and winter.

BARE PARTS In all plumages, legs and feet grey. **Male:** Bill grey, with black nail and very tip; narrow and indistinct paler grey subterminal line and above cutting edge. Iris white. **Female and juvenile:** Bill dark grey, with slightly paler subterminal area; may be more uniformly dark on juvenile. Iris brown, greyer on juveniles, becoming lighter during first winter on males.

MEASUREMENTS Wing 178-196 (mean: male 188, female 182); tarsus 30-35; bill 36-43; mean weight of male 569, of female 537.

GEOGRAPHICAL VARIATION None.

HABITS Usually found in pairs or small parties on freshwater lakes and marshes. Larger gatherings occur only prior to migration at end of post-breed-ing moult and rarely exceed a few hundred birds. Pair-formation occurs in late winter, with most birds arriving on breeding grounds already paired from early April to late May. Breeds from late April to late June. Nests hidden among waterside vegetation, often partially in water or almost floating. Feeds by diving in fairly shallow water, but also by dabbling and up-ending. Most active morning and evening, spending daytime loafing on banks with other diving ducks or dozing on water. Generally rather solitary habits and preference for feeding close to or among emergent vegetation make it easy to overlook and difficult to census. Shy and wary, rising from water with less pattering than most others of genus, although perhaps with less agility than Baer's Pochard. Flight action fast, but less strong than Tufted Duck, often flying for only relatively short distances when flushed. Migratory, arriving in winter quarters after post-breeding moult, from September onwards; even southernmost waters occupied late October.

HABITAT Freshwater lakes and marshes with exten-sive fringe and emergent vegetation in lowland open country. In winter also on more open lakes and slow rivers, locally on coastal lagoons and river deltas.

DISTRIBUTION Breeds very locally over south-western and central Europe, becoming increasingly more widespread from eastern Europe eastwards through southern USSR to western China (Sinkiang and northern Szechwan) and western Mongolia, main centre of distribution being steppe lakes of southern USSR and eastern Europe. Breeds in small numbers and isolated pockets south to Libya, Turkey, Iran, Afghanistan and Kashmir; formerly bred in a number of other Mediterranean countries, including Morocco, Algeria and Israel. Winters in Black and Caspian Sea lowlands, with smaller numbers throughout coastal Mediterranean, although chiefly in East and in sub-Saharan Africa, where good numbers winter in the Sudan and Ethiopia, with lesser numbers west to Senegal and occasionally south to Kenya; also winters Iraq and Iran and across Pakistan and northern India, with a very few in northern Burma and southern China. Vagrants frequently recorded other parts of western and northern Europe, but some may be escapes as species is popular in collections. Vagrants also reported Cape Verde Islands, Canary Islands, Gambia, Sierra Leone, Zaire, Tanzania, Thailand, coastal China and Japan.

POPULATION Locally common, but difficult to census and easily overlooked. Soviet population estimated at 140,000 pairs in 1970, which probably gives a reasonable indication of the world popu-lation. Winter counts indicate some 75,000 winter-ing in Black Sea and Mediterranean Europe and some 15,000 in Caspian and Turkmenia lowlands. Following wetland drainage, many small western populations have disappeared or dramatically declined.

REFERENCES Cramp and Simmons (1977).

123 MADAGASCAR POCHARD   Plate 37
Aythya innotata

Alternative name: Madagascan White-eye

Restricted to central Madagascar, the current status of this rare white-eye is uncertain; there have been no sightings in recent years.

FIELD IDENTIFICATION Length 46 cm (18 in).

At rest: A medium-sized dark diving duck, unlikely to be confused owing to its limited range in central Madagascar, where it is the only diving duck apart from distinctive White-backed Duck (10). Resem-bles Ferruginous Duck (122), but rather larger and with more rounded, less peaked, crown shape. Males are darker on head and breast than Ferrugi-nous Duck, offering more contrast with duller brown flanks. Duller and browner females resemble those of Ferruginous Duck in plumage, but ranges do not overlap. No Madagascar Pochards are held in captivity at present. **In flight:** Resembles Ferrugi-nous Duck.

VOICE Calls have been described as similar to those of Redhead (118).

DESCRIPTION Sexes rather similar. Seasonally variable. **Adult male breeding:** Head and neck dark purplish-chestnut, lacking white chin spot of Ferruginous Duck. Breast dark chestnut, flanks and ventral region reddish-brown; belly and undertail-coverts white, with more diffuse border between white of belly and brown of flanks than on Ferruginous Duck. Upperparts blackish, with browner mantle. Wing similar to that of Ferruginous Duck, but white of flight feathers a little less extensive. **Adult male eclipse:** Distinctly duller and browner, recalling female, but retains white iris. **Adult female:** Head, neck and breast dull brownish-chestnut, belly less cleanly white; differs from eclipse male in having dark iris. **Juvenile:** Resembles female, but lighter and duller brown on head and body, with little rufous. Young males attain pale iris during first winter.

BARE PARTS Little information on age or sex variations. Bill lead-grey, with black nail. Legs and feet grey. Iris white on adult males, dark brown on females, pale grey on first-winter males.

MEASUREMENTS Males larger than females. Wing of male 190-201, of female 188-195; tarsus 28-33; bill 44-49; weight — no data.

GEOGRAPHICAL VARIATION None. Although superficially similar to Ferruginous Duck, it strangely recalls Redhead of North America in voice, display behaviour, head shape and size.

HABITS Little information. Breeding season probably October-January. Feeds chiefly by diving. Flight fast and strong, but not often seen on the wing. Behaviour presumed to resemble that of others of genus.

HABITAT Freshwater lakes and marshes.

DISTRIBUTION Known only from lakes and marshes of the plateau of central Madagascar, from Lake Alaotra south to Antsirabe, with centre of population on Lake Alaotra. No recent records.

POPULATION Described as common in 1929 on Lake Alaotra, but visits in 1970s failed to find any. It was also reported on a pond near Antsirabe in 1930 and was seen on Lake Ambohibao in 1970, but there have been no subsequent reports. Introduced large fish in Lake Alaotra are considered to have aided the decline by killing ducklings, but doubtless shooting is an important factor. Like other Madagascar ducks this species is not protected, and commercial duck-shooting is rife. If it still exists, then the only way to save the species is by captive breeding, creation of sanctuaries and the enforcement of protective measures. Although it was kept in captivity for a time before the Second World War, none is held at present.

REFERENCES Delacour (1954), King (1981).

124 NEW ZEALAND SCAUP   Plate 38
Aythya novaeseelandiae

Alternative name: Black Teal

Distinctive dark scaup endemic to New Zealand, where it is the only member of the genus.

FIELD IDENTIFICATION Length 40-46 cm (16-18 in).

At rest: Medium-sized, rather short-bodied, blackish diving duck of New Zealand. Steep forehead and rounded crown shape recall Tufted Duck (125) without a tuft. Male appears completely glossy black when on water. Dark brown female with scaup-like white facial patches equally distinctive within range; in captivity can be confused with female scaups (126, 127), but plumage more uniformly and darker brown, forehead steeper and body shorter. **In flight:** In both sexes, overall dark plumage contrasts with dull whitish underwing and white secondary band on upperwing. The ill-defined whitish belly patch is most obvious on juveniles. Unlikely to be confused with any other New Zealand duck in flight.

VOICE Relatively silent, except when displaying. Male utters a three- or four-note whistle or 'chirrup'; female has a high-pitched growl.

DESCRIPTION Sexually dimorphic. **Adult male:** Head, neck, breast and upperparts glossy black, with purple and green iridescence. Underparts similar, but shading to dark brown and whitish on belly and dark brown on rear flanks. Upperwing blackish-brown, with white secondaries tipped black. Underwing greyish-white. **Adult female:** Dark brown overall, with variably extensive white patches on lores, surrounding bill-base, and ill-defined paler belly centre. **Juvenile:** Similar to female, but lacks white around bill-base (white is also absent on some adult females) and has clearer whitish belly.

BARE PARTS In all plumages, legs and feet grey. **Male:** Bill bluish-grey, with black nail and extreme tip; slightly paler grey subterminal band is inconspicuous. Iris yellow. **Female and juvenile:** Bill similar to that of male, but darker grey. Iris brown.

MEASUREMENTS Males a little larger than females. Wing of male 175-187, of female 170-181; tarsus 33-38; bill 35-41; mean weight of male 695, of female 610.

GEOGRAPHICAL VARIATION None.

HABITS Typically found in small flocks on freshwater lakes, in winter in larger aggregations which break up into pairs at onset of breeding season. Breeds from October to March. Nests hidden in dense vegetation close to water's edge. Feeds chiefly by diving. Most active in evenings, loafing during daytime either on water or shores or perched on partially-submerged logs. Relatively confiding. Flies little, with much pattering over surface during take-off, generally low over water and for no great distance.

HABITAT Freshwater lakes and slow rivers, often in coastal regions, but also on open lakes and reservoirs up to 1000 m.

DISTRIBUTION Resident in both North and South Islands of New Zealand, where it occurs chiefly on upland lakes, but locally on coastal lagoons. In North Island it is found chiefly in the north and east, and in South Island it is widespread on upland lakes of the western mountainous country.

POPULATION Formerly widespread throughout New Zealand, this species declined through shooting pressures to such an extent that it was given protection in 1934. It has gradually increased since then, although habitat destruction and drainage in the lowlands has made it more of an upland-lake bird that has benefited from the creation of reservoirs, which it is quick to colonise. A captive-breeding programme is having some success with re-introducing it into former haunts in North Island. No total population figures have been published, but there is a major winter gathering at one site in North Island which reaches 2,000 individuals and is considered to contain a high percentage of the entire population.

REFERENCES Johnsgard (1978), Kear and Williams (1978).

125 TUFTED DUCK   Plate 39
Aythya fuligula

Alternative name: Tufted Pochard

Perhaps the most abundant member of the genus, breeding from the Atlantic to the Pacific across the Palaearctic region.

FIELD IDENTIFICATION Length 40-47 cm (16-18 in). At rest: Medium-sized freshwater diving duck of the Old World. Distinctive head shape useful clue in all plumages, with relatively short, broad bill with comparatively wide black tip, fairly steep rounded forehead, and flattish crown with tuft or ragged bump at rear (see figure, p. 256). Breeding male unmistakable, having black head, breast and upperparts, white flanks, and long drooping crest at back of head. In eclipse still shows signs of vestigial tuft, as do birds in female-like plumage; birds in eclipse or in transitional stages could be mistaken for Ring-necked Duck (119), which see for discussion. Female-type birds are dull dark brown with lighter brown flanks, and often show some whitish on face recalling scaups (126, 127) or white undertail-coverts recalling Ferruginous Duck (122) or Baer's Pochard (121); head-and-bill shape useful in such cases. See Ferruginous Duck for discussion on separation from the white-eyes. Greater Scaup (126) appears slightly larger and bulkier if the species are together, and has relatively longer and broader bill, with less black at tip, and a smoothly-rounded crown, lacking any hint of a tuft at the rear. Female Greater Scaup often shows distinct pale oval patch on sides of head, lacking on Tufted; the white facial patches are absent on juveniles and eclipse males, when it is important to note size and head structure; such males show patches of vermiculated grey feathering appearing on upperparts by early winter. Separation from Lesser Scaup (127), with which Tufted overlaps as a vagrant, more problematic: this smaller scaup typically differs in plumage patterning much as does Greater Scaup, but shows a small bump towards rear of crown which gives a higher centre to crown profile than on Tufted; the bill is relatively broader and the loral patches, if present, are clean; the breast, mantle and scapulars are almost uniform with the flanks, contrasting with considerably darker head (typically, head, breast and upperparts distinctly darker than flanks on Tufted); Lesser Scaup sometimes shows a hint of a lighter patch at sides of head, but this is not so marked as on Greater, and the flanks and scapulars may show indistinct grey 'frosting', features lacking on Tufted but present on both scaups (although

views would have to be exceptionally close to appreciate the last feature). Juvenile Tufted may lack any apparent tuft on rear crown, with both upperparts and underparts lighter and buffer-brown than on female, and is especially problematic. See also discussion on hybrids on p. 244. In flight: Black head, breast and upperparts of male contrast strongly with white flanks, belly, underwing and band along flight feathers of upperwing, giving quite distinctive appearance; scaups have similar pattern, but upperparts and forewing are grey, not black. Brown female shows similar wing pattern to that of male and female scaups, but differs from Ferruginous Duck in having less strongly contrasting white on belly and in having white band along flight feathers less extensive.

VOICE Relatively silent, except when displaying. Male utters low whistles in display; female has a low gruff growl, sometimes given when flushed.

DESCRIPTION Sexually dimorphic. Seasonally variable. Individual variation makes ageing of other than adult males difficult. Adult male breeding: Head with long drooping crest from hindcrown. Head, neck, breast, ventral region and most of upperparts black. Flanks and belly white. Upperwing-coverts black, contrasting with white inner primaries and secondaries, which have blackish tips, and dusky outermost primaries. Underwing whitish. Adult male eclipse: Crest short. Black parts of plumage replaced by blackish-brown; flanks and belly dull brown. Adult female: Crest short. Individually variable. General plumage dull dark brown, darkest on head, lighter brown along flanks; breast and flanks with paler feather edges giving somewhat barred effect, especially on flanks; belly whitish, mottled brown. Some develop whitish areas on lores, others have distinctly whitish undertail-coverts, latter especially in autumn. Wing as that of male, but dark areas dark brown. Juvenile: Resembles adult female, but head and upperparts lighter brown, with buff fringes, crown darker; buffish area on lores; flanks distinctly scalloped dull buff. Attains adult plumage features during first autumn and winter, but often not fully until first summer.

BARE PARTS In all plumages, legs and feet grey. Male: Bill bluish-grey, with black nail and tip and narrow whitish subterminal band. Iris bright yellow. Female: Bill slightly darker than that of male, with greyer subterminal band. Iris yellow, sometimes brownish. Juvenile: Bill darker grey, with black nail and tip. Iris brown, becoming yellower as winter progresses; dullest on young female.

MEASUREMENTS Males slightly larger than females. Wing 193-215 (mean: male 206, female 199); tarsus 32-37; bill 36-44; mean weight of male 764, of female 711.

GEOGRAPHICAL VARIATION None.

HABITS Sociable duck of freshwater lakes. Throughout the year may be found in flocks, which reach considerable sizes in winter quarters. Pair-formation starts in late winter and continues into spring. Arrives on breeding waters from late March to mid May depending on latitude. Breeding season from late April to July. Nests built close to waterside, hidden among vegetation, often among colonies of marsh-nesting gulls, and many nests may be occupied in close proximity to each other. Males gather to moult when incubation has commenced. Feeds mostly by diving, but also up-ends and dabbles, even by wading in shallows. Feeds by day or night depending on location and local conditions. Loafing birds doze in closely-packed rafts on water or gather around lakeshores. Generally wary, but becomes remarkably confiding on park lakes. Patters over surface when taking wing; flight fast when underway. Chiefly migratory, except in temperate regions of western Europe. Breeding waters forsaken after post-breeding moult in September, with arrival in winter quarters from early October onwards.

HABITAT Lowland freshwater lakes with fringe vegetation, from large lakes in open country to park lakes in towns. Also on slow rivers, and outside breeding season on tidal estuaries and shallow sheltered coastal bays and lagoons.

DISTRIBUTION Breeds widely across northern Palaearctic Europe and Asia from Iceland and the British Isles to eastern Siberia and Kamchatka, south to central Europe, Yugoslavia and northern Mongolia and northern Japan (Hokkaido). Sporadic or former breeding has occurred in a number of south European countries. Numbers swollen in temperate western Europe in winter, with remaining populations moving south to winter around Mediterranean, Black and Caspian Sea lowlands eastwards through Indian subcontinent to southern and eastern China and Japan. Some winter in Sudan and Ethiopia and very small numbers cross Sahara to winter in Chad and northern Nigeria. Further east, wintering birds reach shores of Persian Gulf to Oman, northern Thailand and the Philippines. Vagrants reported north to Svalbard and Greenland, south to the Azores, Madeira, Cape Verde Islands, Sierra Leone, Malawi, Tanzania, Sri Lanka, Borneo, and several Pacific islands east to Hawaii. Also regularly recorded from Alaskan islands and annually western North America south to California, very rarely inland and on Atlantic seaboard.

POPULATION An abundant and widespread duck.

Counts indicate that some 500,000 individuals winter in northwest Europe, with a further 300,000 in the Mediterranean and Black Sea regions. Perhaps equally large numbers winter further east in Asia; in Japan winter counts indicate some 130,000 birds.

REFERENCES Cramp and Simmons (1977).

126 GREATER SCAUP   Plate 39
Aythya marila
Alternative name: Scaup (Europe)

Larger relative of the Lesser Scaup (127). A marine species found over most of northern portion of the northern hemisphere.

FIELD IDENTIFICATION Length 40-51 cm (16-20 in). **At rest:** Medium-sized freshwater and marine diving duck, very similar to Lesser Scaup, with which it overlaps in range in North America. At all ages, relatively large size, bulky appearance, broad bill and smooth rounded crown shape are subtle, but very useful identification aids. Male has black head, breast and rear end, contrasting with grey upperparts and white underparts. Pattern suggested by Pochard (117), Canvasback (116) and Redhead (118), but these have red head, more uniform underparts and upperparts showing no obvious contrast, and darker bill. Male Lesser Scaup has distinct peaked bump towards rear of crown, coarser and darker grey vermiculations on upperparts (appearing darker grey in field), and greyish vermiculations on rear flanks. Females are dull brown, with contrasting clear white patches surrounding bill-base; these patches are often indicated on female Tufted Duck (125) but are rarely so extensive as on the scaups, and Greater Scaup usually also shows a diffuse pale patch at side of head, lacking on Tufted and less clear on Lesser Scaup. For further elaboration on separating these similar species, see discussions under Tufted Duck and Lesser Scaup; see also figure, below. Juvenile and eclipse males lack any white on head and more

Head-and-bill shapes of northern white-eyes and scaups (females)

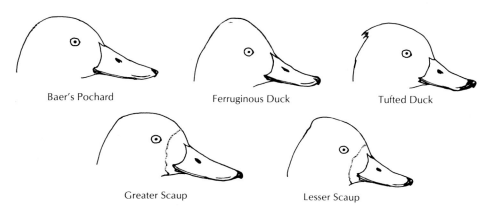

Baer's Pochard   Ferruginous Duck   Tufted Duck

Greater Scaup   Lesser Scaup

closely resemble Tufted; in the most extreme cases only head shape and bill structure useful, but by early winter males show patches of grey feathering on upperparts. Sleeping birds can be picked out from among parties of dozing Tufteds by their slightly larger size, lack of tuft at rear crown, longer body and more sloping rear end. Beware hybrids, which can closely resemble this species (see p. 244). **In flight:** Resembles Tufted Duck, but appears rather heavier. Males have grey, not black, upperparts and forewing contrasting with blackish rump and tail-end. Females difficult to separate from female Tufted in flight. Distinguished from both sexes of Lesser Scaup in flight by having white wing-band extending well onto primaries (on Lesser Scaup white only on secondaries, greyish along primaries); see figure, p. 258.

VOICE Relatively silent, except in display. Male utters soft cooing and whistling notes in courtship; female has harsh, gruff notes typical of genus.

DESCRIPTION Sexually dimorphic. Seasonally variable. Nominate race described. **Adult male breeding:** Head, neck, breast and upper mantle glossy black, with green gloss on head. Flanks and belly white, sometimes with fine grey vermiculations on lower flanks. Ventral region, undertail- and uppertail-coverts, tail, rump and back blackish. Lower mantle and scapulars vermiculated grey. Upperwing-coverts black, vermiculated grey, in flight appearing slightly darker grey than mantle. Primaries and secondaries with broad white band along most of length, tipped blackish; outer primaries blackish. Underwing whitish. **Adult male eclipse:** Head, neck and breast blackish-brown, sometimes with a little whitish around bill-base; upperparts browner, but still vermiculated grey; flanks vermiculated grey and pale brownish. Closer in appearance to breeding male than are eclipse males of many others of genus. **Adult female:** Overall dull brownish, with clear white patches surrounding bill-base, though these may be obscured by brownish feather tipping in fresh plumage; pale oval patch appears on side of head when plumage moderately worn (obscured by brownish tipping when fresh). Typically, some weak grey vermiculations ('frost') on feathers of mantle, scapulars and flanks, but less clear than on male. Belly whitish. Wing as that of male, but upper coverts brown, not vermiculated grey. **Juvenile:** Resembles adult female, but less white around bill-base; paler and buffer-brown below, especially on flanks. Juvenile female lacks any hint of 'frosting' on upperparts and flanks of adult female, but this is shown by young male. Assumes adult features during first winter; male resembles eclipse adult by autumn and acquires adult breeding features towards end of first winter, but not fully adult until second winter.

BARE PARTS In all plumages, legs and feet grey. **Male:** Bill light blue-grey, with black nail. Iris yellow. **Female:** Bill slightly duller grey than that of male, with darker shades along culmen, nail dark grey to black; on some, bill blackish-grey in summer. Iris yellow. **Juvenile:** Bill dark grey, with diffuse blackish shading on culmen and tip, at least on females. Iris brownish-yellow, at least until first summer on females, yellower on males by end of first winter.

MEASUREMENTS Males typically larger than females. Nominate *marila*: Wing 211-237 (mean: male 227, female 217); tarsus 37-42; bill 40-47; mean weight of male 1063, of female 1050. Race *mariloides*: Wing 215-233; bill 43-47; mean weight of male 1000, of female 900.

GEOGRAPHICAL VARIATION Two races recognised. Nominate form, described above, occurs over most of Old World part of range, and race *mariloides* from North America and eastern Asia west to River Lena. Latter race slightly smaller and has blacker and coarser vermiculations on upperparts than do males of nominate, but not so coarse as on Lesser Scaup.

HABITS Sociable, found in small to large flocks outside breeding season. Although essentially marine in winter, small numbers regular on inland freshwater lakes mixed with other diving ducks. Pair-formation in late winter, arriving on breeding grounds in May, some not until early June in far north. Breeding season late May to July. Nests on ground, close to water. Males gather for post-breeding moult during incubation. Over parts of range males undertake short moult migration, while females moult on breeding grounds. Feeds chiefly by diving, feeding activity depending on tidal conditions, but feeds mostly in daytime. When not feeding, loafs in rafts on sea. Takes off with much pattering over surface, but flight rapid once underway. Migratory, males tending to winter further north than females, so some sexual segregation outside breeding season. Flocks of non-breeders, i.e. first-summer birds, remain further south, often in winter quarters, through summer. Arrives on winter grounds during September, but southernmost regions may not be occupied until later in winter.

HABITAT Breeds by freshwater pools and lakes in tundra and tundra fringe zones. Winters along shallow inshore coastal waters, estuary mouths, and locally on freshwater lakes and reservoirs inland.

DISTRIBUTION Summer visitor to sub-Arctic and Arctic regions of northern Europe, Asia and North America; occasional breeders south to British Isles and Denmark. Winters temperate coastal waters of both coasts of North America, Europe, Black and Caspian Seas and eastern Asia; regular but scarce in winter south to central European lakes, western Mediterranean and Turkey, and formerly in good numbers on coasts of Bulgaria and Romania. Vagrants reported north to Greenland, Bear Island and Jan Mayen, and south to Azores, Morocco, Tunisia, Malta, Cyprus, Iraq, Afghanistan, Pakistan, India (numerous records), Nepal, Burma, Taiwan, Hong Kong, Philippines and Hawaiian Islands. In the Americas regular Bermuda and occasionally south to West Indies, Texas and northern Mexico.

POPULATION Abundant. North American population estimated at 750,000 individuals in the mid 1970s, while in Europe and western Asia winter counts indicate some 200,000. Large numbers also winter in eastern Asia, but, apart from winter estimates of up to 50,000 in Japan, there are few counts.

REFERENCES Cramp and Simmons (1977), Johnsgard (1975).

127 LESSER SCAUP
Plate 39
Aythya affinis

Upperwing patterns of scaups

One of the most abundant and widespread of all North American ducks, wintering further south than others of the genus.

FIELD IDENTIFICATION Length 38-46 cm (15-18 in). **At rest:** Very similar to slightly larger Greater Scaup (126), with which it overlaps both in distribution and in size. Most easily separated by head shape and bill shape and less massive appearance. Head shows a distinct bump or short crest towards rear of crown, which contributes to a higher-crowned appearance, unlike the smoothly-rounded crown of Greater; the bill is relatively shorter than on Greater and is slightly concave along the culmen. In profile, the combination gives an effect of a curve from bill-tip to rounded forehead, rising over crown to a small bump towards rear, followed by an indentation above nape (see figure, p. 256). Greater Scaup has a longer and deeper bill, with culmen virtually straight, a smoothly-rounded forehead and nape and fairly flat crown centre; the highest point often seems to be the forecrown, with flat crown sloping towards nape. Lesser Scaup tends to swim more buoyantly than Greater when not actively feeding, the body appearing shorter than on Greater, but these differences are most readily apparent if the two species are seen together, when the larger size and relatively longer neck of Greater may also be appreciated. Breeding males also differ appreciably in body plumage: Lesser Scaup had blacker and coarser vermiculations on upperparts than Greater, giving a darker grey appearance to mantle and scapulars; the rear flanks often show an area of grey vermiculations, normally absent on Greater (though males coming out of eclipse during winter have vestigial vermiculations on flanks). Under exceptional viewing conditions, the gloss of the blackish head is purple on Lesser, green on Greater, but this is very hard to interpret correctly in the field and some Lessers also show a hint of green. Birds in female-like plumage are very similar to corresponding plumages of Greater Scaup, but white facial patches typically less extensive and pale patch on side of head usually less apparent, although often clearly visible. Finally, Lesser Scaup is more of a freshwater bird in winter, although occurs commonly on coastal lagoons and estuaries; Greater also occurs on fresh water, but is more a bird of coastal waters in winter. For further discussions, see also Tufted Duck (125) and Greater Scaup. Hybrids between Tufted Duck and Pochard (117), occasionally found in wild in Europe, appear remarkably like male Lesser Scaup: see hybrid discussion on p. 244. **In flight:** Very much as Greater Scaup, although a useful distinction between the two species is often apparent in flight: Greater Scaup shows white secondary band extending across inner primaries, whereas Lesser Scaup has white restricted to secondaries, the inner primaries being pale grey. This may need to be interpreted with caution, as the difference between pale grey and white is hard to see on rapidly beating wings, but the contrast between whiter secondaries

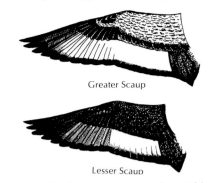

Greater Scaup

Lesser Scaup

and not-so-white inner primaries is often visible on Lesser.

VOICE Relatively silent, except in display. In courtship, male utters weak whistling notes; female has weaker growl than Greater Scaup.

DESCRIPTION Sexually dimorphic. Seasonally variable. Generally resembles Greater Scaup, the differences between the two species being fully discussed under Field Identification above. Eclipse males tend to be browner on body than those of Greater Scaup, but plumage sequences and coloration otherwise similar.

BARE PARTS Coloration and sequences much as in Greater Scaup.

MEASUREMENTS Males a little larger than females. Wing of male 190-201, of female 185-198; tarsus 36-38; bill 36-42; mean weight of male 850, of female 790.

GEOGRAPHICAL VARIATION None.

HABITS Gregarious diving duck, often encountered in very large flocks outside breeding season. Pair-formation begins towards end of winter and continues through spring migration, birds arriving on breeding grounds during May already paired. Breeding season late May to July. Nests on ground among waterside vegetation, often on islands among colonies of terns or gulls. Males leave females at start of incubation o gather for post-breeding moult. Feeds chiefly by diving. At all seasons has greater preference for fresh water than Greater Scaup, gathering in enormous numbers on lowland lakes in winter; flocks even winter on park lakes in cities, and may become very confiding when unmolested. Migratory, leaving breeding grounds in September and October. Despite similarity between the two northern scaups and overlap in breeding ranges, no wild hybrids between these species have ever been recorded.

HABITAT Breeds by freshwater pools and lakes in open country, especially prairie marshes. In winter on lowland lakes, coastal lagoons and estuaries and sheltered coastal bays, but chiefly in latter haunts after cold weather has frozen freshwater lakes.

DISTRIBUTION Widespread summer visitor to interior of western and northern North America, from central Alaska east to Hudson Bay and south to Washington and South Dakota, with isolated pockets further south in the mid-west and east in Great Lakes region. Winters chiefly in coastal and more temperate southern lowlands north to British Columbia on the west coast and New Jersey on the east coast, south through the West Indies and Mexico, with small numbers wintering south to northern Colombia. Regular on Bermuda and occasional Hawaiian Islands, with vagrants south to Venezuela, Trinidad, Surinam and Ecuador, and north to Greenland. Occasional reports in Europe have usually proven to be due to confusion with similar hybrid between Pochard and Tufted Duck, but transatlantic vagrancy a strong possibility.

POPULATION Abundant. Similarity between the two scaups makes assessment of population difficult, but estimate of nearly 7 million individuals of both species in North America, with great majority of them Lesser Scaups, makes this one of the most abundant wildfowl species of North America.

REFERENCES Bellrose (1976).

Tribe MERGINI (SEA-DUCKS)

Although the majority of ducks in this tribe are associated with coastal and estuarine waters, many may also be found on freshwater lakes and rivers, particularly during the breeding season, and a minority are essentially freshwater birds throughout the year. The eiders have sometimes been allocated a tribe of their own (Somateriini), but are more usually included in the Mergini, which is the system advocated by Livezey (1986) and the one followed here.

GENERA *POLYSTICTA* and *SOMATERIA* (EIDERS)

Four species of marine diving ducks of Arctic and northern coasts. Despite the striking differences between breeding males, other plumages are remarkably similar; separation of them primarily involves concentrating on relative size and the shape and structure of the head and bill. Since eiders may take as long as four years to reach full maturity, males may be encountered in a variety of intermediate stages. Being very sociable ducks, wandering individuals of any one species may become attached to flocks of another; patient searching through flocks of Common Eiders is therefore sometimes rewarding.

128 STELLER'S EIDER   Plate 41
Polysticta stelleri

Smallest and most *Anas*-like of the eiders, with the most 'duck-like' head-and-bill shape.

FIELD IDENTIFICATION Length 43-47 cm (17-19 in). **At rest:** Smaller and less bulky than the other eiders. Indeed, small size, relatively flat crown and lack of feathered extensions onto bill-base may give impression distinctly unlike that of an eider, the head and bill proportions recalling dabbling ducks rather than eiders; the relatively long tail is often held cocked when resting, recalling scoters. Breeding male shows chiefly whitish head with black eye-patch and collar, dark green bump on rear crown, rusty to rufous-buff (often very pale) underparts contrasting with black ventral region, and black and white upperparts. Individuals in other plumages differ from other eiders principally in smaller size and more 'normal duck-like' head-and-bill shape, less barred plumage, and often (but not always) more prominent white speculum borders. Attains adult-like plumage by second winter, sub-adult males always appearing more mottled on breast than Common Eider (129), never attaining a clean white-breasted appearance. Compare also immature Velvet Scoter (136). **In flight:** Less bulky than other eiders, rising more easily from water. Breeding male distinctive, lacking black underparts of other male eiders. Compared with other eiders, female shows whiter underwing (can be very pale on some Common and King (130) Eiders), and quite prominent white lines fore and aft of glossy purplish speculum; both speculum and white lines can, however, be dull on juvenile Steller's, and some female Common Eiders have bright speculum with fairly conspicuous white lines, so these features need to be used with caution. If flying with other eiders, smaller size is generally readily apparent. Wings produce a loud whistling sound in flight, louder than that of goldeneyes (139, 140).

VOICE Relatively silent compared with other eiders, male lacking obvious crooning courtship sounds. In display, very low growled croon may be audible from male if bird very close and short bark-like calls may also be heard. Female more vocal, uttering various low barking, growling or hoarse whistling cries, which may be freely heard from flocks.

DESCRIPTION Sexually dimorphic. Seasonally variable. **Adult male breeding:** Head white, with broad neck-collar; chin and throat and eye-patch black; dusky-green lump on rear crown and similar patch on lores. Underparts rusty-rufous, paler and buffer on breast and upper flanks and variable in intensity of colour. Circular black spot at sides of breast. Ventral region, tail and whole centre of upperparts glossy black, joining black collar on hindneck. Sides of mantle and back white. Elongated, pointed scapulars black, with white edges. Upperwing-coverts white, primary coverts blackish. Primaries blackish; secondaries iridescent purple-blue, with broad white tips. Underwing white, with greyer flight feathers. **Adult male eclipse:** Resembles adult female, but retains white upperwing-coverts and has head and breast mottled whitish. **Adult female:** Entire head and body plumage almost uniform dark reddish-brown, with dark feather centres apparent only on upperparts; head slightly lighter rufous-brown, with pale warm buff eye-ring. Upperwing dark reddish-brown, with broad whitish tips to greater coverts and secondaries; secondaries otherwise similar to those of male, but less bright, only innermost strongly glossed blue-purple, outers dull brown. Underwing similar to that of male, but dusky mottling along leading edge. **Juvenile:** Resembles female, but duller greyish-brown, lacking warm reddish tone except on lower underparts, and also more obviously barred; wing as female, but secondaries all dull (young males with very little blue) and white border lines narrower or even virtually absent. Young males may also be sexed by having tertials slightly curved, rather than straight as on young female. During first winter, pale buffish and whitish feathering begins to appear on head and breast of young male, which by second winter nearly in full plumage.

BARE PARTS Similar in all plumages. Bill, legs and feet blue-grey, duller and greyer on female and juvenile. Iris brown, redder on male.

MEASUREMENTS Males a little larger than females. Wing of male 208-225 (mean 216), of female 205-210 (mean 207); tarsus 36-40; bill 36-42; mean weight (both sexes) 860.

GEOGRAPHICAL VARIATION None.

HABITS Very sociable, often in large flocks throughout the year, with flocks of non-breeders in summer away from breeding grounds; largest gatherings may exceed 50,000 birds and occur during moult gatherings and in spring. Pair-formation occurs in late winter and spring. Arrives on breeding grounds in late May or early June, nesting from late June to August. Nests on ground, close to tundra pools and rivers, often among low scrub; does not normally nest colonially. Males leave females at start of incubation and gather in flocks prior to moult migration; moult areas may be as far as 3000 km from breeding grounds. Feeds by diving (often all birds dive simultaneously) and by dabbling and foraging along shoreline. Walks less clumsily than other eiders. Swims buoyantly, often with tail cocked. In flight more agile than other eiders, rising from water with less pattering and flying with more rapid wingbeats.

HABITAT Breeds by pools within coastal regions of Arctic tundra, breeding further inland than other eiders. Away from breeding sites, occurs along inshore coastal waters, rocky bays and headlands, favouring sites where freshwater streams enter sea.

DISTRIBUTION Breeds primarily along Arctic coasts of eastern Siberia from Khatanga Bay (east of Taymyr Peninsula) to coastal Alaska. Sporadic breeding occurs further west in Siberia, perhaps even regular in places: reported breeding Kola Peninsula, southern Novaya Zemlya, and even extreme northern Norway from time to time. In winter and at moult gatherings chiefly in southern Bering Sea region, with smaller numbers in Arctic waters of Scandinavia and the Baltic Sea south to coasts of Germany and Poland (where reported again in recent years after a long absence). Non-breeders also oversummer in the wintering regions. Vagrants west to Iceland, Svalbard, Denmark, Netherlands, Belgium, France and the British Isles, and in the Pacific region south to British Columbia, northern China and Japan (although regular northern Hokkaido). Also reported as a straggler on Atlantic seaboard of North America in Quebec, Maine, Maryland and west Greenland.

POPULATION Locally abundant. Moult gatherings in Alaska have been estimated at over 200,000 individuals, which probably include a good proportion of the world population. Other large concentrations are formed on Pacific coast of northeast Siberia, with considerably smaller numbers in northern Europe. Non-breeding gatherings in northern Norway increasing, with counts of 4,000-11,000 in recent years indicating probable regular breeding further west in Siberia than is known. Population seems to be relatively stable and has been estimated at some 500,000 birds in total. Alaskan breeding population relatively small and declining.

REFERENCES Cramp and Simmons (1977), Petersen (1980).

129 COMMON EIDER   Plate 40
Somateria mollissima
Alternative name: Eider (Europe)

The most widespread and abundant of the eiders, breeding further south than any of the others. The largest duck of the northern hemisphere.

FIELD IDENTIFICATION Length 50-71 cm (20-30 in). **At rest:** Large, heavily-built sea-duck, with distinctive 'roman-nosed' profile formed by long bill sloping to rather high crown; feathering extends into a point along sides of bill (see figure, p. 262). When alert, relatively long neck and triangular shape to heavy head and bill distinctive. Breeding male has black underparts, contrasting with white breast and upperparts, and black crown, a combination not shared by other eiders. Other plumages are basically dark brown and recall those of both King (130) and Spectacled (131) Eiders; most easily distinguished by head and bill features, and fully discussed under accounts of latter two species. Adult plumage is not fully attained until third winter; moulting males, either partially in eclipse or sub-adults, are piebald and striking, often blackish with white breast and scapulars, and unlikely to be confused with any other species apart from other two larger eiders, although beware piebald feral-type Mallards (84) which might confuse the unwary. See also immature Surf (135) and Velvet (136) Scoters, which can appear to have similar head shape, and female Steller's Eider (128). **In flight:** Large, heavily-built duck with relatively broad wings, and heavy head often carried low. Combination of black underparts and rear end with white fore parts, upperparts and upperwing- and underwing-coverts distinctive, having white far more extensive than on either King or Spectacled Eiders. Females and non-adult males less distinctive and are confusable with other two large eiders; tend, however, to show less striking white underwing than King or Steller's, and less dusky underwing than Spectacled, but see relevant accounts for fuller discussion.

VOICE Most vocal in late winter and spring during courtship, when male utters low, endearing croon 'ahOOoo'. Female has a grating 'krrrr'.

DESCRIPTION Sexually dimorphic. Seasonally variable. Nominate race described. **Adult male breeding:** Forehead and crown black, with white central stripe from mid crown back to nape. Nape and upper neck pale green. Remainder of head, neck, breast and most of upperparts white, washed salmon-pink on breast. Remainder of underparts, tail and rear upperparts to central rump black, with large white patch at sides of ventral region formed as an extension from white rump sides. Elongated and curved scapulars white. Upperwing-coverts white; greater coverts and secondaries black; primaries blackish. Underwing white, with greyer flight feathers. **Adult male eclipse:** Most of plumage sooty-brown, differing from adult female by lack of barring on body and in having white upperwing-coverts and scattered whitish feathering on head and upperparts. **Adult female:** Most of plumage dark brown, uniformly barred black on body, with darker feather centres to upperparts, a paler buff eye-ring and plainer sides and front of head and neck. Upperwing brown, with variable whitish tips to greater coverts and secondaries; secondaries sometimes distinctly purple, but often dark brown. Underwing brownish, with whitish axillaries and greater coverts, forming whitish centre to underwing (becomes whiter with wear). In summer darker, with less conspicuous tips to body feathers giving less barred appearance. **Juvenile:** Resembles summer female, but with narrow buff barring on underparts and indistinct pale buffish supercilium; upperwing lacks whitish tips to secondaries and greater coverts; young male has blacker ground colour to upperparts and wings than female. Male begins to acquire whitish feathering on breast and upperparts from early first winter onwards, with much individual variation; by end of first winter has extensive white on breast and upperparts, but little white on upperwing-coverts until second winter; full plumage not attained until fourth winter, but much as adult by third winter although black on upperparts more extensive.

BARE PARTS Bill colour and form racially variable. Nominate race described. **Male:** Breeding male has bill olive-grey, becoming yellower on facial area and tip; duller and greyer overall in autumn. Legs and feet greyish, with greener tone than on female and juvenile. Iris brown. **Female and juvenile:** Bill olive-grey to olive-yellow. Legs and feet greyish. Iris brown.

MEASUREMENTS Males rather larger than females in all races. Nominate *mollissima*: Wing 286-315 (mean: male 304, female 301); tarsus 50-57; bill 51-61; mean weight of male 2266, of female 2028. Race *faeroeensis*: Wing 257-284 (mean: male 270, female 264); mean weight (female only) 1847. Race *borealis*: Wing 278-302 (mean: male 291, female 301). Race *v-nigrum*: Wing of male 300-328. Races *dresseri* and *sedentaria*: Wing of male 270-290.

GEOGRAPHICAL VARIATION Complex, with clinal variation and intergradation making distributional definitions of forms difficult, especially with North Atlantic populations. Six races recognised.

Nominate race: Described above. Northwest Europe except Shetland and Orkney Islands, where birds closer to *faeroeensis*; birds from British Isles and southwest Norway somewhat intermediate between nominate and *faeroeensis*.

Race *faeroeensis*: Faeroe Islands. Smallest race. Male has olive-grey bill; females darker and more heavily barred than nominate. Birds from Shetland and Orkney Islands currently included in this form.

Race *borealis*: Arctic North Atlantic region, from Franz Josef Land west through Iceland and Greenland to Baffin Island. Male has orange-yellow bill; female has body more rufous-brown. Birds from Iceland and southeast Greenland somewhat intermediate between this race and nominate.

Race *dresseri*: Atlantic North America from Labrador to Maine. Males show only very narrow black line between eye and bill, as surrounding facial skin is broader and more rounded than on other races; green on head duller and buffer and extends almost to eye level; mantle feathers of male slightly raised into a peak at sides of upperparts.

Race *sedentaria*: Hudson Bay. Close to *dresseri*, but bare facial skin less extensive, female greyer. Poorly-differentiated form.

Race *v-nigrum*: North Pacific region, from New Siberian Islands east to Arctic Canada. Large race. Feathering over bill-base more rounded at apex (pointed on other races), not reaching nostril. Male has large black 'V' on upper throat and chin (some individuals of other races occasionally show black 'V' on throat) and prominent pointed peaks on mantle; bill orange, legs yellowish.

HABITS Very sociable, in large flocks throughout the year. Non-breeders often summer south of breeding grounds. Pair-formation late winter and spring. Breeding commences early April in south of range, but in northernmost populations not until mid June. Nests colonially on ground, favouring inshore coastal islands but also using low-lying mainland shores. Famous lining of nest (eiderdown) still farmed in some regions, especially Iceland, but commercial use now largely replaced by synthetic materials owing to relatively low production of genuine down. Males gather to moult, joining flocks of non-breeders, while females incubate. Feeds and loafs around rocky reefs, islands and promontories, diving expertly and feeding chiefly on ebbing tide; loafing birds gather on adjacent rocks. Often relatively confiding. Rises heavily from water with much pattering, flocks often forming lines and keeping low over sea when well underway. Not highly migratory; although northernmost populations move some way south in winter, others remain close to breeding grounds. Males tend to winter further north and closer to breeding grounds than females or immatures. Some quite extensive moult migrations are undertaken, e.g. in Baltic region.

HABITAT Shallow inshore coastal waters with adjacent small islands; estuary mouths. In winter and on passage, occasionally (although rarely) or locally also on inland freshwater lakes.

DISTRIBUTION Widespread throughout coastal regions of Arctic and sub-Arctic, although apparently absent from central Arctic coastline of Siberia and northern Canadian islands. Range extends south to Maine in eastern USA, and in Europe south to British Isles, Netherlands, Germany, and Poland, with isolated small colony in northwest France. Pacific populations breed south to Sea of Okhotsk and southern Alaska. In winter disperses southwards; birds from northernmost populations being summer visitors to their breeding grounds; normally, however, winters within range of southern breeding populations, which are largely resident, though scarce but regular in winter on central European lakes. Vagrants have occurred south to British Columbia, inland northern USA and Canada, Florida, the Azores, the northern shores of Mediterranean and western Black Seas. Pacific birds seem hardly ever to straggle south of normal range, but vagrant recorded west Greenland resembling race *v-nigrum*; occasional vagrants of race *borealis* reach northern British Isles.

POPULATION Abundant: total population must be enormous. General increase in European populations in recent years, but numbers in eastern Siberia seem to be declining. Protected in some regions for 'eiderdown-farming', but persecuted by shooting and egg-collecting in USSR and parts of North America. North American population estimated at between 1.5 million and 2 million individuals in mid 1970s; population of western Europe and west Siberia estimated from winter counts at some 2 million birds. Other large populations in eastern Asia have not been estimated. Large numbers have succumbed during oil-spillage disasters.

REFERENCES Driver (1974), Uspenski (1972).

130 KING EIDER   Plate 40
Somateria spectabilis

More migratory than Common Eider (129), breeding even further north and replacing it over most of Arctic Siberia and Canada. Male is perhaps one of the most attractive of all ducks.

FIELD IDENTIFICATION Length 47-63 cm (19-25 in). **At rest:** Breeding male unmistakable, but easily overlooked among large flocks of Common Eiders with which stragglers often mix. Easily told from male Common Eider by having most of upperparts as well as underparts black; head pale blue, large and rectangular with bulging forehead and frontal shield, lacking black on crown (but centre of forehead and surround of facial shield black); frontal shield orange and bill red. Other plumages similar to those of Common Eider. Eclipse male never shows white on scapulars which may be present on Common, but may show white on mantle and white wing-coverts (often visible when on water); most

Head shape and bill feathering of female eiders

Common Eider (nominate race)

King Eider

easily distinguished from most races of Common by pinkish-orange bill and frontal shield, but eclipse Common of races *borealis* and *v-nigrum* also have orange or fleshy bill. Head shape distinctly different, with somewhat bulging forehead (although less than when breeding) and flatter crown; also typically a little smaller and shorter-necked than Common Eider. Females and juveniles close to those of Common Eider and vagrants very easily overlooked; head shape and structure most reliable means of separation. Head of King less triangular in outline, having crown flatter and forehead profile slightly bulging, less straight, whole front portion of head and bill appearing somewhat shorter than on Common Eider, and carriage of bill tends to be straighter, less drooped; facial skin projects less far towards eye and feathering on sides of bill is distinctly rounded, less pointed, not extending as far as nostril. Perhaps more obvious feature is gape line, which turns noticeably upwards from bill-base and generally bisects an ill-defined whitish area at very base of bill (gape line of Common Eider straighter and less conspicuous). Females and juveniles have dark flank markings angled, less barred than on Common Eider. Females more rufous-buff in summer than most populations of Common, but regional variation within female Common allows for much overlap. First-winter males show more obvious pale area about eye, often extending as a pale line running steeply down and back from eye which borders a less obvious dark line (Common Eider often shows an inconspicuous pale eyebrow and weak dark line in a similar position to that of King). Full adult male plumage acquired by third winter, with varying intermediate stages as with Common Eider. Short points may be visible on mantle on adult females and are conspicuous on males. Hybrids with Common Eider are occasionally reported. See also Spectacled Eider (131). **In flight:** Resembles Common Eider, but a little smaller, stockier and relatively shorter-necked, and with faster wingbeats. Breeding male shows black upperparts, with smaller white patch on upperwing-coverts than on Common Eider, giving blacker general appearance (beware sub-adult or moulting eclipse male Common Eiders with more extensive black on upperparts than in full plumage). Females difficult to separate from those of Common Eider, but underwing considerably whiter and contrasting with dusky leading edge. See also Spectacled Eider.

VOICE Similar to that of Common Eider, but croon of male rather deeper in tone. Calls freely in flight, a low croaking note.

DESCRIPTION Sexually dimorphic. Seasonally variable. **Adult male breeding:** Crown and nape light bluish-grey; eye-ring and line running down from eye towards nape white. Sides of head olive-green. Border of frontal shield and centre of shield feathering black. Lower neck, breast and mantle white, washed salmon-pink on breast. Remainder of body plumage black, with large white patch at sides of ventral region. Inner scapulars raised into prominent points along sides of back. Tertials elongated and curved. Upperwing black, with white greater and median coverts. Underwing white, with greyish

flight feathers. **Adult male eclipse:** Overall dull blackish-brown, more uniform and darker than female, usually with some white feathering on breast and mantle; retains white on upperwing-coverts. **Adult female:** Warm brown, almost rufous-buff in breeding plumage. Head and neck relatively unmarked, although finely streaked darker, especially on crown and hindneck; small pale spot at very base of bill near gape. Body plumage marked with dark chevrons on flanks and upper-parts. Upperwing-coverts brown, with dark feather centres; remainder of wing blackish, with narrow whitish tips to greater coverts and secondaries. Underwing whitish, with dusky band along leading edge and greyer flight feathers. **Juvenile:** Differs from female in being duller and greyer, especially on head and neck. Lacks small points on sides of back of adult female and has broader dark markings along flanks. Tertials less strongly curved than on adults. First-winter male shows extensive greyish patches on head and whitish on breast, and has pale buffish bill by end of winter; male attains fully adult plumage by third winter.
BARE PARTS In all plumages, iris dark brown (statements in certain literature that birds have yellowish irides need confirmation). **Male:** Bill red, with paler nail, frontal shield yellow-orange; bill greyer and frontal shield fleshy-yellow in eclipse. Legs and feet dull yellowish to orange. **Female:** Bill and facial skin dark olive-grey. Legs and feet greyish. **Juvenile:** Bill blacker than that of female, but on male becomes buffish-flesh from middle of first winter onwards.
MEASUREMENTS Males a little larger than females. Wing 256-293 (mean: male 277, female 270); tarsus 44-50; bill of male 27-34, of female 31-35; mean weight of male 1724, of female 1623.
GEOGRAPHICAL VARIATION None.
HABITS Highly gregarious throughout the year, although a solitary breeder. Stragglers away from normal range generally recorded among flocks of Common Eiders, with which they sometimes inter-breed (most incidents of hybridisation reported from Iceland, where King does not normally nest). Pair-formation occurs in spring, often during migration. Arrives on breeding grounds during June, nesting from late June onwards. Solitary nester, with pairs scattered over tundra, nesting by pools and streams on dry ground; occasionally nests some distance from water, and in some places loose colonies are formed. At start of incubation, males leave females and gather on adjacent coasts to moult. Feeds by diving, often in deeper water than Common Eider. Loafs on shores and ice floes. Swims more buoyantly than Common Eider. Flight more agile, faster and with more manoeuvrability than Common Eider, taking off from water with more ease. Forms lines when well underway, but generally flies low over water surface. Migratory, most breeding grounds forsaken in winter. Moult gatherings often enormous, with considerable migrations to key areas, e.g. 100,000 moulting birds reported Davis Strait, western Greenland.
HABITAT Breeds on tundra of high Arctic in both coastal and inland regions. In winter, in open seas and ice-free coastal bays. Lives only marginally south of Arctic Circle, even in winter.

DISTRIBUTION Widespread across most of high-Arctic coastline and islands, but absent as breeding bird from Iceland, southern Greenland and Arctic Scandinavia, apart from occasional sporadic breeding in these regions. Populations from eastern Siberia, Alaska and western Canada winter in Bering Sea region. Birds from eastern Canada and west Greenland winter from southern Greenland to Labrador and Newfoundland, with small numbers penetrating Great Lakes region. Those from western Siberia and adjacent islands winter from White Sea to Arctic Norway, occasionally to north Baltic. Icelandic winterers probably come from east Greenland. Rarer further south, although annual south to northern Scotland, northeast USA and southern Kamchatka. Non-breeders summer south of breeding range, often in winter quarters. Vagrants have occurred south to Japan, California, Georgia (USA), France, Italy and Hungary.
POPULATION Very abundant (remoteness of normal ranges gives false impression of general abundance), indeed has even been suggested to be the most abundant of all ducks. North American population estimated to be between 1 million and 2 million individuals. Soviet population estimated at between 1 million and 1.5 million birds. In parts of Arctic is shot in large numbers on spring migration, but clearly this has no overall effect on numbers.
REFERENCES Cramp and Simmons (1977), Uspenski (1972).

131 SPECTACLED EIDER   Plate 40
Somateria fischeri
Alternative name: Fischer's Eider

This aptly-named sea-duck is the least known of the group; it breeds in northeastern Siberia and Alaska, but its winter grounds remain a mystery.

FIELD IDENTIFICATION Length 52-57 cm (20-22 in). **At rest:** A little smaller than Common Eider (129), but similar in proportions. Unique facial appearance, with feathers cloaking bill almost to nostrils and distinctive 'goggle' pattern in all plumages. Breeding male has slate-black breast and underparts, lacking clear white breast of other two members of genus, but sharing white upperparts of Common Eider; astonishing head pattern, with broad white, black-rimmed 'goggles' contrasting with dull olive of most of remainder of head, prevents confusion with any other species. Female recalls females of other two larger eider species, being mottled and barred russet-brown, but shows pale brown 'goggles' (weaker than on male though still obvious) contrasting with richer brown of forehead and with dark eye obvious against light surround. Bill feathering as on male. Eclipse and sub-adult males resemble other eiders, apart from lack of white on breast at any stage, distinctive head pattern (although 'goggles' greyer) and bill feathering. Attains adult male plumage by third winter, with variety of intermediate stages. See also King Eider (130). **In flight:** Recalls other eiders of genus, but smaller and shorter-necked than Common Eider. Breeding male recalls Common Eider in pattern, but black of belly reaches to upper breast, with white

263

only on neck and not extending to breast; under-wing more dusky than on other male eiders. Female recalls female Common Eider, but underwing darker; identification in flight difficult, however, owing to variation of underwing of Common species, but darker brown of forehead contrasts with pale buffish-brown of rest of head and fore-neck.

VOICE Relatively quiet. Crooning of displaying male weak and not far-carrying. Female utters a short harsh croak, recalling that of Raven.

DESCRIPTION Sexually dimorphic. Seasonally vari-able. **Adult male breeding:** Forehead, crown centre, rear crown and upper nape dull olive-green and somewhat shaggy in appearance. Enormous white, black-bordered circular patch of short, stiff feathers around eye, creating 'goggle' effect. Throat, lower neck, upper breast and most of upperparts, including elongated curved scapulars, dull white. Underparts from lower breast down-wards, tail, uppertail-coverts, rump and lower back slaty-black. White patch at sides of ventral region. Upperwing-coverts white; greater coverts and rest of upperwing blackish, with narrow pale tips to greater coverts. Underwing smoky-grey, with whitish axillaries. **Adult male eclipse:** Overall dark greyish, with lighter grey 'goggles' still apparent; retains white wing-coverts. **Adult female:** Overall warm rufous-brown, with body plumage promi-nently barred with narrow dark subterminal mark-ings; head and foreneck paler, especially 'goggles', which contrast with darker brown of forehead feathering. Upperwing dull dark brownish, usually lacking any pale tipping. Underwing dull greyish-brown, with paler shading and axillaries. **Juvenile:** Resembles female, but has narrower barring on underparts and 'goggles' less distinct, although still apparent. First-winter male acquires some whitish on foreneck or upper breast and upperparts towards end of winter; full adult male plumage acquired by third winter.

BARE PARTS Male: Bill orange, with paler nail; duller in eclipse. Legs and feet greyish-yellow. Iris white. **Female:** Bill dark blue-grey. Legs and feet yellowish-brown. Iris dark brown. **Juvenile:** As female. Bill of male becomes fleshy during latter part of first winter.

MEASUREMENTS Males a little larger than females. Wing 233-280 (mean: male 272, female 263); tarsus 45-50; bill 21-27; mean weight of male 1647, of female 1472.

GEOGRAPHICAL VARIATION None.

HABITS Least known of the eiders, with major winter grounds still unproven. Sociable, but typically in smaller flocks than other eiders. Pair-formation probably in late winter, as arrives on breeding grounds in May and June already paired. Nests on ground by small pools in coastal tundra; tends to be a solitary nester but loose colonies often formed, and often nests in close proximity to other wildfowl, especially geese and swans. When incubation commences, males leave females and undertake moult migration towards Bering Sea. Females are believed to leave breeding grounds with fledged brood and to moult far offshore. Feeds by diving, typically far offshore, but on shallower

breeding waters behaves more like a dabbling duck. Ungainly on land, even more so than other eiders. Flight faster and more agile than that of other large eiders. Few observations away from breeding grounds, apart from migrating parties and small flocks. Few sightings of numbers at time of post-breeding moult or in winter quarters, suggesting that very large numbers must be present at these times in a relatively small area far offshore, probably around edges of pack ice in Bering Sea though this remains unproven.

HABITAT Breeds on coastal tundra, but locally (Indigirka River, Siberia) breeds inland as far as 120 km from the sea. May be found along inshore coastal waters and tundra pools and rivers in summer, but in winter believed to remain far offshore at southern edge of pack ice.

DISTRIBUTION Summer visitor to coastal eastern Siberia from the Lena delta east to coastal northern and western Alaska (east to Colville River). Non-breeding flocks believed to remain in summer in region of Chukchi Sea. In winter most likely found in shallower waters of Bering Sea, perhaps in region south of Nunivak, St Lawrence and St Matthew Islands and off southern shores of the Chukotsky Peninsula; perhaps winter range varies according to southern limit of pack ice, as recorded very rarely in winter from Pribilof and western Aleutian Islands. Vagrants have on very rare occasions wandered to British Columbia, California, western Siberia (Kola Peninsula) and northern Norway.

POPULATION Recent work on both Siberian and Alaskan breeding grounds indicates a population of some 200,000 breeding birds, with probably an additional similar number of non-breeders. Main concentrations are in the Indigirka delta of Siberia, which held at least 17,000 pairs in 1971, and in the Yukon-Kuskokwim delta of Alaska, with some 50,000-70,000 pairs.

REFERENCES Dau and Kistchinski (1977), Todd (1979).

132 HARLEQUIN DUCK   Plate 41
Histrionicus histrionicus

A beautifully-marked duck wintering along rocky shores, but moving inland to breed by rushing rivers.

FIELD IDENTIFICATION Length 38-45 cm (15-18 in). **At rest:** Small, stocky, dark diving duck with small bill, steeply-rounded head, pointed tail and conspi-cuous white facial patches in all plumages. Breeding male unmistakable if seen well, but surprisingly easy to overlook when swimming on dark, dappled water. White facial and breast patches striking, but beautiful blue-grey plumage with chestnut flanks appears dark at longer ranges. Other plumages almost uniform sooty-brown, with two white face patches: a large patch on lores and a circular spot on ear-coverts. Most likely confusion is with darkest female and juvenile Long-tailed Ducks (137), which can have facial pattern approaching that of female Harlequin, but on Long-tailed patch behind eye is typically a whitish streak (not circular), foreneck is paler, flanks and belly are whitish and bill is broader (narrow on Harlequin Duck). Female Bufflehead (138) has dark loral areas and single rectangular white patch behind eye. Head pattern of considerably larger and larger-billed female Surf (135) and Velvet (136) Scoters also similar. **In flight:** An almost uniformly blackish dumpy duck with plump body and pointed tail. Wings appear all dark on both surfaces, and shows no white on belly in any plumage (ill-defined whitish belly centre of female not apparent in flight). White facial and body patches of male may be visible at closer ranges. Smaller and shorter-bodied than scoters, recalling goldeneyes (139, 140) in shape and flight action. Long-tailed Ducks always show conspicuous white underbody in flight.

VOICE Relatively silent outside breeding season. In display, male utters a high-pitched whistle. Female has several short, harsh calls.

DESCRIPTION Sexually dimorphic. Seasonally variable. **Adult male breeding:** Overall dark blue-grey, becoming blackish on ventral region, with chestnut flanks. Large white facial crescent between eye and bill, extending back along sides of blackish crown centre, becoming chestnut behind eye. Circular white spot on lower rear ear-coverts and on ventral region. Vertical white stripe up side of neck and on side of breast. White partial band around base of neck. Scapulars and tertials chiefly white, and odd white spots on wing-coverts. All white markings are bordered with black. Upperwing and underwing all dark, with glossy metallic blue secondaries. **Adult male eclipse:** Considerably duller and closer to female, but showing plumage somewhat intermediate between breeding male and female. **Adult female:** Almost completely sooty-brown, darkest on head, with centre of underparts mottled and tipped whitish-buff. Striking whitish area at front of head below and before eye (sometimes divided by dark line between eye and bill), and circular whitish patch on ear-coverts. Wings all dark, both above and below. **Juvenile:** Closely resembles female, but edges to feathers of upper-parts browner (greyer on female) and lacks blue gloss to secondaries. Male attains adult features gradually during first winter.

BARE PARTS In all plumages, legs and feet greyish and iris brown. **Male:** Bill blue-grey, with paler nail. Iris redder than in other plumages. **Female and juvenile:** Bill greyish-black, with paler nail.

MEASUREMENTS Sexes similar. Wing 194-214 (mean: male 205, female 198); tarsus 34-40; bill 24-48; mean weight of male 674, of female 529.

GEOGRAPHICAL VARIATION No races recognised. Siberian and western North American populations have been separated as race *pacificus*, males of which said to be slightly duller than Atlantic birds and with less chestnut in supercilium, but individual variation too great to warrant separation.

HABITS Usually met with in pairs or small parties; larger flocks formed outside breeding season, but these rarely exceed 50 birds in Atlantic populations, although more numerous Pacific birds may form rafts of hundreds. Pair-formation occurs in late winter, pairs breaking away from coastal flocks and moving inland up rivers to breed. Breeding season chiefly from late May onwards. Nests on ground, hidden among scrubby cover or in rock crevices close to water. Males usually leave females during incubation and gather to moult, but occasionally reported accompanying broods. Feeds mostly by diving, sometimes jumping from rocks; also wades and dabbles, and up-ends in shallow water. On breeding rivers behaves somewhat like Torrent Duck (55) of the Andes. Stands on shores and rocks when loafing. Often fairly approachable where unmolested. Swims buoyantly, with tail prominently cocked, jerking head when progressing. Flight fast and low, pattering over surface when taking wing. Mixes little with other species, although loosely associates with other sea-ducks in winter; vagrants usually encountered with flocks of other species. Not strongly migratory, moving to coastal waters for winter, but this involves considerable migration for some Siberian birds. Non-breeders remain in winter waters through the summer.

HABITAT Breeds by fast-flowing rivers and streams in mountainous country. Winters along inshore coastal waters, typically rocky bays and rough waters around headlands.

DISTRIBUTION Two distinct populations. Pacific birds widespread over mountains of eastern Siberia from Lake Baikal eastwards, south to Sakhalin; also across Aleutian Islands and in western North America from Alaska to Colorado. These birds winter along adjacent coastlines south to northern China, Korea, Japan and California. Atlantic population breeds over eastern Canada, southern Greenland and Iceland. Canadian birds winter along coasts south to Maine, occasionally to New York; those of Greenland and Iceland resident, merely moving to adjacent coasts in winter. More migratory Pacific birds turn up as wanderers west to Tomsk (western Siberia) and south to Mongolia, Ryu Kyu Islands and Hawaii. Atlantic breeders less prone to vagrancy, and remains exceedingly rare as a European vagrant: has occurred very rarely inland in Canada and in coastal waters south to Florida; in Europe very rarely to Faeroe Islands, Svalbard, Norway, Sweden, Germany, Baltic and White Seas of USSR, Netherlands, British Isles, Poland, Czechoslovakia, Switzerland and Italy; the majority of these being nineteenth-century records. Some of those recorded in eastern and central Europe are perhaps vagrants from the east rather than from Atlantic populations.

POPULATION Pacific population greatly outnumbers that of Atlantic. No total estimates have been made, but in the Aleutian chain of islands alone there are thought to be perhaps 1 million individuals in autumn. Icelandic population is thought to be in the region of 3,000 pairs. No other numbers are available.

REFERENCES Bellrose (1976), Cramp and Simmons (1977), van der Have and Moerbeek (1984), Wynne-Edwards (1957).

133 LABRADOR DUCK
Camptorhynchus labradorius

Sadly, this peculiar sea-duck is extinct. It was formerly recorded from sandy estuaries and coastal bays of northeastern USA from Chesapeake Bay

forward on other two species). For discussions on separation from other scoters, see Surf and Velvet Scoters; compare also American Black Duck (88). See also Black Scoter account below. **In flight:** Both sexes appear black or blackish, in good light showing slight contrast between lighter underside to flight feathers and blackish coverts; underwing almost uniform on Surf Scoter, but beware effect of lighting conditions and distance. At reasonable ranges, browner, pale-cheeked females easily distinguished from all-black males. See also similar Surf Scoter. Lack of white in wing an easy distinction from Velvet Scoter.

VOICE Generally silent, but in display male utters a piping, high whistle and female a harsh, grating, rasping note.

DESCRIPTION Sexually dimorphic. Both races similar in plumage. **Adult male:** Entire plumage black, body and head slightly glossed. Underside of flight feathers greyer, contrasting somewhat with sooty-black underwing-coverts. No obvious change in summer, but mixture of old worn feathers and fresh new feathers gives a somewhat mottled and duller appearance. **Adult female:** Crown and hindneck sooty brownish-black. Sides and front of head and neck light greyish-brown. Remainder of plumage sooty-brown, with indistinct lighter brown tips. **Juvenile:** Resembles female, but browner overall, with whitish belly barring (apparent if wing-flapping on water). Male acquires features of adult plumage during first winter, but not fully until second autumn.

BARE PARTS In all plumages of both races, legs and feet blackish-grey and iris brown. Bill differs between races; nominate described (see also Black Scoter below). **Male:** Bill, including swollen knob at base of culmen, black, with yellow patch on culmen centre; on older birds, yellow extends in narrow band over centre of knob. **Female and juvenile:** Bill lacks knob, all blackish; first-winter male starts to acquire yellow on culmen in mid-winter, but not to full extent until spring. Legs and feet greener or greyer than on male.

MEASUREMENTS Both races similar; nominate described. Males a little larger than females. Wing 216-247 (mean: male 234, female 226); tarsus 41-48; bill 41-45; mean weight of male 1037, of female 945.

GEOGRAPHICAL VARIATION Two races recognised, sometimes considered separate species. Eastern Asiatic and American race *americana* treated separately below as Black Scoter.

HABITS Highly gregarious; usually met with in small to very large flocks throughout the year. Flocks sometimes sexually segregated, with males wintering further north than females. Pair-formation begins in late winter, but continues through spring as females move north to join flocks. Arrives on breeding grounds during April and May, breeding from late May onwards. Nests on ground close to water; solitary nester. During incubation, males gather and undertake moult migration to coastal waters: some moult on waters close to breeding grounds, whereas others have extensive migration far offshore in deep water; often migrates considerable distances overland, flocks sometimes encountered

---

south to Long Island, and probably bred further north, perhaps in Labrador. It must have already been rare before white men reached North America, and was probably finished off by hunting and the collection of its eggs for food by coastal settlers. Very little is known of its habits, but it was doubtless highly specialised and was perhaps almost an Atlantic ecological counterpart of Steller's Eider (128). The last record of the Labrador Duck was of a bird taken in 1875; none has been reported since, although it is said to have been taken near New York in 1878. Male illustrated.

REFERENCES Humphrey and Butsch (1958), Phillips (1922-26).

134 COMMON or BLACK SCOTER
Melanitta nigra   Plate 42

Alternative names: Common Scoter (nominate race), Black Scoter (*americana*)

The two races are sometimes considered worthy of specific status and are described separately here.

COMMON SCOTER
M. (n.) nigra

Widespread across northern Europe and Asia, although whether or not its range overlaps with that of the American race in eastern Siberia is uncertain.

FIELD IDENTIFICATION Length 44-54 cm (17-21 in). **At rest:** Medium-sized, rather heavily-built sea-duck with relatively long tail, which is often held up when birds resting on water. Male totally black, including most of bill and basal knob, but some relief is provided by patch of yellow on the culmen which is surprisingly conspicuous as a pale patch even over considerable distances. Females and juveniles equally distinctive, being dark sooty-brown with contrasting pale sides of head and neck, the pale-cheeked and dark-capped appearance being shared only by non-marine female Red-crested Pochard (113). Moulting first-winter males may have pale sides of head obscured by dusky patches, giving spotted effect recalling that of female Surf (135) and Velvet (136) Scoters; caution may need to be exercised with such individuals, although sociable nature normally allows direct size and shape comparison with other birds in such cases. Tends to dive with a forward jump, with wings tightly closed to body; other two scoters seem to dive with wings partially opened. When wing-flapping, has tendency to droop neck during flap (neck kept rigidly

temporarily resting on inland waters. Feeds by diving, flocks often doing so in unison. Birds at rear of flock often rise and fly to head of flock, then settle again. Typically, keeps in closely-packed rafts on sea. Swims buoyantly when not feeding, riding heavy swell with ease, often with tail prominently cocked. On breeding waters often loafs on shores and islands, but rarely when at sea. Takes off with less pattering over water than most other sea-ducks. Flight strong, in long wavering lines or small tight bunches when migrating, typically low over the water but very high when flying overland. Strongly migratory; females leave breeding grounds with juveniles during September. Non-breeders often summer on wintering grounds.

HABITAT Breeds by freshwater lakes, pools and rivers in tundra and open country in sub-Arctic regions. Outside breeding season, found chiefly along inshore waters and bays, and in estuary mouths. Occasionally on inland freshwater lakes during migration.

DISTRIBUTION Nominate race breeds in tundra regions from Iceland to River Olenek in Siberia, south to northern Britain. Whole population of this race winters along inshore coastal waters of western Europe, from Norway and west Baltic south to Spain, and on Atlantic coast of Africa south to Mauretania. Occurs very rarely on migration on central European lakes, western Mediterranean, Black and Caspian Seas. Vagrants have occurred south to the Azores, Madeira, Canary Islands, Libya, the eastern Mediterranean and the Persian Gulf, and north to Greenland.

POPULATION Winter estimates in western Europe suggest a population of some 500,000 individuals in the early 1970s. Indication of decline, as passage through Finland and coasts of West Germany estimated to involve 1-1.5 million birds in 1952. Population has no doubt declined through oil pollution, but numbers also possibly overlooked at sea.

BLACK SCOTER
M. (n.) americana

Eastern Asian and North American race of Common Scoter, possibly worthy of full species status.

FIELD IDENTIFICATION Closely resembles Common Scoter, but males easily distinguished by stunning swollen orange-yellow bill, with relatively small black tip. Yellow especially prominent on older males, which have bill-base evenly swollen (not forming a protruding knob as on Common), with yellow reaching nostrils. Yellow on bill of Common Scoter variable in extent, but always has black sides to basal knob. Females inseparable from those of Common Scoter, although female Black tends to have base of bill slightly more swollen and nail on bill more prominent. In all plumages of Black Scoter, the nostrils are nearer the tip of the bill.

DISTRIBUTION Breeds over tundra regions of eastern Siberia from River Yana eastwards (range overlap with Common Scoter unknown; races seem almost to meet in region of lower River Lena, but no intermediate specimens known); range extends into

Alaska, and scattered or sporadic breeding reported in Canada east to Newfoundland. Winters along both shores of North Pacific south to Japan, eastern China (Yangtze to Fukien), Korea and California, and in eastern North America in Great Lakes region and on Atlantic coast south to South Carolina. Vagrants reported south to Hawaiian Islands, Florida and Louisiana and inland USA; also very rarely in western Europe, where reported British Isles and Netherlands.

POPULATION No total figures available for this race. North American population estimated at about 500,000 individuals, with seemingly even larger numbers in eastern Asia.

REFERENCES Cramp and Simmons (1977), Johnsgard (1975).

135 SURF SCOTER   Plate 42
Melanitta perspicillata

The brightly-patterned enormous bill and white head patches render male Surf Scoter unmistakable. This sea-duck breeds in North America, and is one of the most frequent Nearctic wildfowl vagrants to northwest Europe.

FIELD IDENTIFICATION Length 45-66 cm (18-22 in). **At rest:** Similar in size to Common or Black Scoter (134), but head larger and bill much more massive, giving head profile recalling Common Eider (129). Male unmistakable: black, with large white patches on forehead and nape conspicuous even at long range (when viewing distortion may even give white-headed appearance); at closer ranges, swollen orange, white and black bill diagnostic. During summer and autumn white nape becomes obscure or even disappears, and on some individuals may not be apparent until mid-winter. Females and juveniles dark brown overall, with whitish patches on sides of head recalling those of Velvet Scoter (136) and similar pattern sometimes indicated by first-winter male Common Scoter; Surf, however, is stockier, with shorter body and more massive bill (although bill quite large on Velvet), sides of head lighter than blackish crown, and lacks any white in wings (usually hidden on Velvet when on water unless wing-flapping); female Surf often shows pale patch on nape (lacking on Velvet and Common). When diving, tends to jump forward and dive with partially-opened wings, and keeps neck rigid while wing-flapping (Common dives with wings tightly closed to body and droops neck during wing-flap; Velvet dives with opened wings but no jump, often momentarily showing flash of white in secondaries). Confusion possible with female and immature Common Eider, but Surf Scoter smaller, with longer tail, unbarred plumage and distinctive head pattern. See also female Harlequin Duck (132), which also has whitish facial spots. **In flight:** Similar to Common or Black Scoter, but white head patches of male obvious even at quite long range; also rather bulkier and with heavier head and bill, and shows less contrast between underwing-coverts and flight feathers which appear more or less uniform (but this difficult to interpret in dull light or at distance). Lack of white in wing an easy distinction from Velvet Scoter in flight.

VOICE Generally silent. During display, male produces a low liquid gurgling sound and female a harsh croak.

DESCRIPTION Sexually dimorphic. **Adult male:** Large white patches on forehead and nape; otherwise all black, slightly glossed. Occasionally has a scattered ring of white feathering at base of fore-neck. White nape feathers become obscured with heavy wear as black feather bases become exposed, and white may not show again until mid-winter. Plumage becomes somewhat mottled with old and new feathers during summer, but white forehead seems to be present throughout year. **Adult female:** Crown, hindneck and sides of head between cheek patches dusky-brown, ill-defined whitish area (of varying intensity) on nape, circular whitish patch on lores and more triangular patch on ear-coverts; remainder of sides of head and fore-neck brown. Remainder of plumage dark brown. Rather variable, with some individuals darker than others; intensity of cheek spots also varies, as well as prominence of neck patch. **Juvenile:** Resembles female, though generally lighter brown, especially on face, throat and underparts, but most easily aged by whitish belly; whitish cheek spots often merge, but usually clearly defined. Lacks pale patch on nape of most adult females. Iris dark (usually pale on adult female). Gradually acquires adult features during first winter, when males begin to show pale on nape and bill; by late first winter, males mostly blackish, but white on forehead and nape small and indistinct; males gain full adult plumage by second winter. Females do not acquire pale on nape until second winter.

BARE PARTS Male: Bill large and swollen at base; bluish-white, with circular black patch at side of base, becoming red along culmen and yellow towards tip. Legs and feet reddish-orange, with dusky webs. Iris white. **Female:** Bill less swollen than that of male; dark grey, with blacker sides to base. Legs and feet duller orange than male. Iris pale or brown. **Juvenile:** Bill dark grey. Legs and feet brownish-yellow. Iris brown. Acquires adult coloration during late first winter and early spring, although iris of female often not pale until second winter.

MEASUREMENTS Males larger than females. Wing 223-256 (male 238-256, female 223-235); tarsus 40-43; bill 34-41; mean weight of male 992, of female 907.

GEOGRAPHICAL VARIATION None.

HABITS Generally met with in smaller parties than Common or Black Scoter, but fairly large flocks formed in winter. Pair-formation occurs in late winter or spring, typically with small groups of males displaying to one or two females. European vagrants usually mixed with flocks of other scoters. Arrives on breeding grounds from mid May onwards. Breeding habits poorly studied compared with most other North American ducks. Nests on ground, well hidden among bushy cover, often a considerable distance from water; solitary nester. Males leave females during incubation and undertake moult migration to coastal waters. Feeding and diving behaviour much as that of Common or Black

Scoter. Flight action recalls that of Common Scoter, being more agile on wing than Velvet. See Field Identification for comment on diving and wing-flapping. Migratory; breeding waters forsaken by females and juveniles in September.

HABITAT Breeds by lakes, pools and rivers in sparsely-wooded regions of Arctic North America. In winter, occurs along shallow bays and inshore coastal waters, especially estuary mouths. Rarely, on inland freshwater lakes during migration.

DISTRIBUTION Breeds across northern North America from western Alaska to Labrador. Winters on both Pacific and Atlantic coasts south to California and North Carolina, with small numbers also wintering in Great Lakes region. Occasionally recorded on coasts of northeast Siberia and islands of Bering Sea, and south to Florida and Texas. Vagrants recorded south to Japan, inland USA, central Mexico, Hawaii, Bermuda, and north and east to Greenland and most countries of northwest Europe, south to Spain and east to Finland and Czechoslovakia; regular north and west British Isles, where very small numbers recorded annually.

POPULATION Estimates of winter population suggest some 765,000 individuals in total in mid 1970s. Like all scoters, is vulnerable to oiling disasters in wintering waters.

REFERENCES Bellrose (1976), Mullarney (1983).

136 VELVET or WHITE-WINGED SCOTER
Melanitta fusca   Plate 42

Alternative names: Velvet Scoter (Europe), White-winged Scoter (North America)

Widespread across the northern hemisphere. Has been divided into two and even three species by some authorities, the eastern Asiatic and North American races being treated together as a second species; for field purposes, however, they are similar and are combined under one account below.

FIELD IDENTIFICATION Length 51-58 cm (20-23 in). **At rest:** Largest of the three scoters, with relatively longer body than the others; heavy angular head-and-bill shape somewhat recall Common Eider (129) in profile, although less so than does that of Surf Scoter (135). In all plumages, white secondaries readily distinguish this species from all other dark sea-ducks; although secondaries are generally hidden when on water, they may show as momentary flash while diving. Male black, with tiny white eye-patch (difficult to see in field), but has blackish knob at base of mostly pale bill, knob being very prominent on eastern Asiatic race *stejnegeri*. Females and juveniles dusky-brown, with one or two circular white patches on sides of head; these bear superficial resemblance to those of smaller and stockier Surf Scoter, but size and bill shape useful aid, although presence of white in wing needs to be seen to confirm identification. Fresh-plumaged females and immature males lack white face patches and appear totally dusky-brown on head and body; they differ from dark Common Eiders in lacking barred appearance or any white on breast or mantle, and in having more prominent tail. Dives with wings slightly opened, with no jump, and giving brief flash of white in secondaries, but often wings not opened far enough for white to be clearly visible. Flaps wings like Surf, with rigid neck. **In flight:** Easily identified by striking white secondaries contrasting strongly with otherwise all-dark plumage. Unlikely to be confused.

VOICE Relatively silent. During display, male gives a loud piping call and female a harsh 'karrr'; both calls also given in flight. These calls uttered by nominate race; other races seem to have different vocalisations, which lends support to splitting the species.

DESCRIPTION Sexually dimorphic. Nominate race described. **Adult male:** Small white patch below eye. Secondaries white. Otherwise plumage blackish, strongly washed brown in worn plumage as feather tips abrade. In summer, brownish tipping to feathers gives duller appearance. **Adult female:** Dark brown overall, with buffish-white patch on lores and clearer, whiter patch on ear-coverts, both patches obscured by dark feather tipping in fresh plumage. Centre of underparts with weak paler barring. Secondaries white. **Juvenile:** Resembles female, but brown coloration duller and greyer, less blackish, with pale brown feather tips to upperparts and whiter belly (especially juvenile female); facial spots often clearer than on female. Gradually acquires adult features during first winter, but males may not be fully adult until second winter or even later.

BARE PARTS Nominate race described. **Male:** Bill with swollen knob at base of culmen; knob, centre of culmen and cutting edge black; remainder of bill orange-yellow, becoming red towards tip and nail, nail sometimes black. Legs and feet reddish-orange, with dusky webs. Iris white. **Female and juvenile:** Bill lacks strong swelling at base; blackish-grey, lighter grey on young juveniles. Legs and feet dull orange on female, greyish-yellow on juvenile. Iris brown. Juvenile attains adult bare-part coloration during latter part of first winter and first spring.

MEASUREMENTS Males typically larger than females. Wing of male 269-286, of female 255-271; tarsus 43-53; bill 37-51; mean weight of male 1718, of female 1631.

GEOGRAPHICAL VARIATION Three races recognised, differing chiefly in bill structure and colour of male. Nominate race, described above, breeds Europe and western Asia east to River Yenisey. Race *stejnegeri* breeds from Yenisey basin eastwards to the Pacific coast of Asia, and is not known to overlap with nominate race on breeding grounds; it differs from male of nominate race in having higher and larger knob at base of bill, feathering at bill sides extending further forward, as does black at bill-base, and bill colour more orange, less yellow. Males of race *deglandi* of North America are browner on flanks than either of the other races, with bill colour and shape somewhat intermediate. Other plumages indistinguishable in the field. As ranges of the three forms are not known to overlap and as the three seem to differ vocally, they could be treated as three separate species, or perhaps more safely as two, with *stejnegeri* and *deglandi* named as *M. deglandi*.

HABITS Highly sociable, in large flocks throughout the year, except on breeding grounds. American race occurs in larger gatherings than the other two. Pair-formation occurs in late winter and spring, prior to arrival at breeding sites. Breeds from mid May onwards, considerably later in northernmost populations. Nests on ground usually close to water, but often a considerable distance from water; sometimes uses nestboxes. Generally a solitary nester, but loose colonies formed in some regions. Males leave females during incubation and migrate to other waters to moult, often joining flocks of non-breeders; flocks later joined by females and juveniles. Behaviour basically similar in all scoters, but Velvet occurs further south on inland freshwater lakes than the others, especially in Asia. For comment on diving and wing-flap behaviour, see Field Identification. Flight action heavier than that of the other scoters, taking off with more pattering over surface. Highly migratory.

HABITAT Breeds by freshwater lakes and large pools inland, often in lightly-wooded country, especially taiga. On passage occurs on freshwater lakes and estuaries. Winters along inshore coastal waters as the other two scoters, and occasionally in small numbers on inland lakes.

DISTRIBUTION Nominate race breeds across northern Europe and western Asia from Norway to River Yenisey, south to Barbara steppes in western Siberia, with isolated pockets on lakes of eastern Turkey and adjacent Georgia SSR. Winters chiefly in coastal waters of northwest Europe south to English Channel, with small numbers south to northern Spain, central European lakes and southern shores of Black and Caspian Seas. Vagrants recorded south to the Azores, Morocco, Algeria, Israel and Afghanistan, and north to Iceland, Svalbard, Bear Island and Novaya Zemlya. Eastern Asiatic race *stejnegeri* breeds from Yenisey basin eastwards to Kamchatka, south to Mongolia; winters along Asiatic Pacific coast south to Korea, Japan and eastern China, with vagrants reported west to Tomsk (western Siberia). American race *deglandi* breeds from Alaska east to Hudson Bay and south to Manitoba, and winters along both coasts of North America south to Baja California and South Carolina, with small numbers inland in Great Lakes region, rarely inland further south in USA; vagrant to northeast Siberia.

POPULATION No total numbers available. Winter and moulting numbers of nominate race indicate some 150,000-200,000 individuals in mid 1970s, with moult gatherings of some 60,000 in Danish waters. American race estimated at nearly 1 million in mid 1970s. No estimates have been made for eastern Asiatic race. Oil pollution is biggest threat, and one which could destroy a significant percentage of the population if spillage occurred in key moulting or wintering areas.

REFERENCES Cramp and Simmons (1977), Dementiev and Gladkov (1952).

137 LONG-TAILED DUCK or
OLDSQUAW Plate 41
Clangula hyemalis

Alternative names: Long-tailed Duck (Europe), Oldsquaw (North America)

Small diving duck of northern coastal waters, occurring throughout the Holarctic region.

FIELD IDENTIFICATION Length 36-47 cm (14-18 in), plus up to 13 cm (5 in) tail extension on adult males. **At rest:** Small, dumpy diving duck, with short neck and bill and pointed tail in all plumages. Adult males have elongated central tail feathers, often held erect when sitting buoyantly on water, and pink-tipped black bill. In winter they appear whitish overall, with black breast, face patch and wings, the long white scapulars giving piebald appearance to upperparts. In summer, head, breast and upperparts. mostly blackish-brown, with contrasting white flanks and eye-patch. Females and juveniles are small, squat, short-tailed ducks, with dark upperparts and white underparts; the head pattern is variable, but typically the sides of the head are whitish, contrasting with a dark cheek patch, crown and breast; darkest birds (especially juveniles) may show only ill-defined whitish patches about eye and recall female Harlequin Duck (132), but latter has dark flanks (always whitish on Long-tailed), is plumper, and has circular spot on ear-coverts rather than Long-tailed's whitish streak behind eye. See also female Bufflehead (138). Palest individuals show only weak face patch and may appear almost uniform mealy-whitish at longer ranges; compare male Smew (141). Typically, swims low when actively feeding, diving suddenly with partially-opened wings, its marine habits in winter, dark and white appearance and manner of diving contributing to an auk-like appearance. **In flight:** Dumpy, short-necked, small duck with all-dark wings (both uppersides and undersides) contrasting with white underbody in all plumages. Has distinctive flight action, often low over water, swinging from side to side, with shallow beats on stiffly-arched wings; the wings are brought well down on downstroke, but only a little above body level on the upstroke. Unlikely to be confused.
VOICE Male very vocal, especially during display, uttering loud, yodelling 'ow-ow-owlee ... calooca-loo'; when members of flock call together, the combined noise is strange and far-carrying. Female utters a variety of low weak quacking notes.
DESCRIPTION Sexually dimorphic. Seasonally variable. Moult sequences complicated: both sexes of adult have four plumages (resulting from three moults) annually, making ageing and sexing of other than adult males difficult. Plumages are summarised briefly. **Adult male:** Elongated central tail feathers in all plumages, except during active moult. In winter (November-April) most of plumage whitish; blackish patch on lower ear-coverts and pale grey sides to head; breast, mantle, centre of upperparts and centre of tail brownish-black; elongated, pointed scapulars white. Plumage similar in autumn (September-November) but patch on ear-coverts is

dull greyish-brown and inconspicuous. In spring (May-June) most of head and neck brownish-black, with whitish area surrounding eye; scapulars tawny-buff, with black centres; remainder of plumage similar to winter. In summer (July-September) much as spring plumage, but scapulars much shorter, crown and nape whiter and flanks greyer. **Adult female:** Lacks tail extension. Variable according to season and, to some extent, individually. Crown, nape and upperparts blackish-brown. Lower sides of head and neck blackish-brown, area around and extending back behind eye greyish-white, lower neck whitish. Breast greyish-brown, remainder of underparts white. Scapulars pointed, buff with black centres. Wing and tail blackish-brown. In autumn (November-February) similar, but head and neck whiter, with forehead usually whitish and dark neck patch smaller. In summer (May-August) head and neck dusky overall, with diffuse whitish areas on lores, patches around eye and sides of head and on neck. **Juvenile:** Resembles female, but overall dull brownish on head and neck, with white areas ill-defined, often merely a weak patch on lores, above eye and a streak behind eye (beware female Harlequin Duck); scapulars duller than on adult female and shorter; underparts whitish, with greyish-brown breast-band and wash along flanks. During first winter becomes whiter on head and neck, more closely resembling female. From late autumn onwards, young males attain features of autumn- or winter-plumaged adult, although not fully until second autumn.
BARE PARTS In all plumages, legs and feet grey. **Male:** Bill black, with broad pinkish-yellow or rose-pink terminal portion and black nail; often all black in summer. Iris dull yellow to orange. **Female:** Bill dark grey to bluish-green. Iris brownish. **Juvenile:** Bill bluish-grey, young male developing pink on bill from October onwards. Iris brown.
MEASUREMENTS Males larger than females. **Male:** Wing 218-241 (mean 228), tarsus 34-38, bill 24-30, mean weight 797. **Female:** Wing 204-220 (mean 212), tarsus 32-37, bill 24-27, mean weight 685.
GEOGRAPHICAL VARIATION None.
HABITS Very sociable duck except when nesting. Congregates in large rafts in coastal waters, especially at migration periods, although mixes little with other species; winter flocks somewhat sexually segregated, females and juveniles tending to winter further from breeding areas than males. Pair-formation begins in autumn, but is chiefly from mid-winter onwards as flocks intermingle during northward passage; arrives on breeding grounds mostly already paired, but pair-formation continues after arrival in breeding areas. Breeds from late May onwards, nesting on ground, partially hidden by overhanging boulder or among dense vegetation, usually close to water. Males leave females soon after start of incubation and gather on nearby waters to moult; some populations undertake extensive moult migration of up to 1000 km, whereas others moult near breeding areas. Feeds by diving. Often loafs on banks of breeding waters, but otherwise rarely seen on land. Flight action described under Field Identification section; alights on water rather clumsily, splashing down breast-first in an auk-like

manner. On migration forms long lines or loose groups, generally flying relatively low over sea. Non-breeders often oversummer in wintering areas.
HABITAT Breeds by pools and small lakes in the Arctic tundra, also by slow rivers and coastal inlets. Outside breeding season, resorts to coastal waters and bays, only rarely on fresh water.
DISTRIBUTION Widespread across whole of northern hemisphere, breeding in Arctic regions south to southern Finland, southern Alaska and Labrador. Winters on coastal waters and bays south to Washington, South Carolina, British Isles and Korea; rarely further south, but regular lakes of central Europe, northern shores of Black and Caspian Seas and on central Asian lakes, indicating considerable overland migration of Asiatic populations. Stragglers have reached a number of countries bordering northern Mediterranean shores, also Madeira, the Azores, Pakistan, Kashmir, Nepal, Assam, southern China, Hawaiian Islands, California, northern Mexico and Florida.
POPULATION Abundant. Tendency to winter in very large gatherings makes it vulnerable to oil pollution and several massive kills have occurred. Numbers also become entangled in fishing-nets, or are shot during migration in Arctic regions. Total population must be enormous, perhaps well over 10 million individuals, with estimates of some 600,000 birds in Alaska and 5 million adults in western USSR alone. Difficult to census in winter, as large rafts often far offshore.
REFERENCES Alison (1975), Cramp and Simmons (1977), Uspenski (1970).

138 BUFFLEHEAD   Plate 43
Bucephala albeola

Common name coined from 'buffalo-head', a comparison made between the remarkable head shape of males and that of a bull bison or buffalo. A small widespread North American goldeneye.

FIELD IDENTIFICATION Length 32-39 cm (13-15 in). **At rest:** Small diving duck, reminiscent of a small Common Goldeneye (140). Breeding male has remarkable high-domed head shape, dominated by massive white patch which covers most of rear of head and contrasts with black fore part of head; the white underparts and blackish central upperparts otherwise recall larger male Common Goldeneye. Confusion unlikely, but beware male Hooded Merganser (142), which has vaguely similar head pattern. Other plumages are less conspicuous: a small grey-brown duck with white flash on sides of head behind eye; confusion possible with juvenile Long-tailed Duck (137), which has whitish flanks and some white before eye, and even with female Smew (141), which has white on throat and lower cheeks and reddish-brown head contrasting with greyer body. See also female Harlequin Duck (132). **In flight:** Flight action very fast. Male recalls miniature (size of Teal (77)) Common Goldeneye, but white on head very obvious. Females are small dull brownish ducks, with dusky underwings, showing conspicuous white secondary patches on both upperwings and underwings and whitish central

underparts; recall diminutive female goldeneye, as white head flash not visible unless bird close.
VOICE Relatively silent, even during display. Male occasionally utters a brief growl; female slightly more vocal, giving a repeated series of guttural notes.
DESCRIPTION Sexually dimorphic. Seasonally variable. **Adult male breeding:** Centre of head, lores and lower sides and rear of head iridescent bronze, purple and green (appearing blackish in the field); huge white patch extends back over remainder of head from eye. Neck and entire underparts white. Mantle, back, scapulars, tertials and rump black. Uppertail-coverts and lower rump grey. Tail darker grey, feathers with blackish inner webs. Primaries, primary coverts and leading edge of wing blackish; remainder of coverts and secondaries white. Underwing dusky, with white secondaries. **Adult male eclipse:** Resembles adult female, but white head patch larger and retains breeding-male upperwing pattern. **Adult female:** Head less domed than that of male, dark brown, with broad white rectangular patch behind and below eye. Neck, sides of breast, flanks, ventral region and mantle greyish-brown; centre of underparts whitish. Upperparts darker dull brown, greyer on rump and uppertail-coverts. Upperwing darker, blackish-brown, with white secondaries and some greater coverts, latter tipped black. Underwing as male. **Juvenile:** Resembles female, but head patch smaller, and central underparts mottled grey, less clearly whitish. Young males larger than females and with more extensive white on greater coverts, but do not develop features of adult male plumage until towards end of first winter; not fully adult until second winter.
BARE PARTS Male: Bill light blue-grey, becoming dusky towards base and at nail. Legs and feet fleshy-pink. Iris dark brown. **Female and juvenile:** Bill dark grey. Legs and feet greyish. Iris dark brown.
MEASUREMENTS Males larger than females. **Male:** Wing 169-179, tarsus 31-35, bill 27-31, mean weight 448. **Female:** Wing 151-161, tarsus 28-31, bill 23-27, mean weight 325.
GEOGRAPHICAL VARIATION None.
HABITS Less sociable than other ducks of this group; generally met with in small parties outside breeding season. Pair-formation begins in late winter and continues into spring. Arrives on breeding grounds from April onwards. Despite unsociable habits, several nests may be in close proximity; nest placed in small tree hole, usually old hole of a Common Flicker, not far from water. Males gather to moult during incubation, and perform relatively short moult migration to key waters within breeding range. A restless little duck, seemingly constantly on the move, diving actively or indulging in disputes. Rarely comes on to land, preferring to rest on water, but stands on waterside boulders or partially-submerged branches. Swims low in water when feeding. Flight action very fast and whirring, but wings silent; takes off from water with less effort than other diving ducks.
HABITAT Breeds by pools, lakes and slow rivers in wooded lowland country. Outside breeding season, on larger freshwater lakes, rivers, estuaries and inshore coastal waters.

DISTRIBUTION Widespread across North America from central Alaska across Canada to western Ontario, with sporadic breeding further east and south to northern California. Winters from southern Alaska south to northern Mexico, across southern USA to Gulf coast and north along Atlantic seaboard to New England. Stragglers occasionally reach the West Indies and Bermuda, and vagrants recorded west to northeastern Siberia, Hawaii and Japan and north to Greenland; very rare vagrant to western Europe, with records from Iceland, British Isles, Netherlands, France and Czechoslovakia.

POPULATION Abundant, with breeding population estimated at some 500,000 individuals. There seem to be some local decreases in western populations, while in the east the species is increasing and slowly spreading, although the reasons for this are unclear.

REFERENCES Erskine (1972).

139 BARROW'S GOLDENEYE   Plate 43
Bucephala islandica

This large goldeneye has a strangely disjunct distribution, being widespread in western North America with smaller eastern populations in eastern Canada and Iceland.

FIELD IDENTIFICATION Length 42-53 cm (17-21 in). **At rest:** At all ages resembles Common Goldeneye (140), but rather larger, with slightly stouter bill, and more bulging forecrown sloping to rear of head (Common Goldeneye has peak in centre of crown, rather than on forehead). Breeding male resembles male Common Goldeneye, but has more extensive black on upperparts, extending to a patch at sides of breast and enclosing a series of white patches along scapulars (Common Goldeneye has scapulars white with black stripes). Most striking difference is huge white facial crescent on Barrow's, Common having merely a smaller white circular patch on lower lores. Moulting male Common with white spot obscured often appears to have a crescent rather than a spot, but this is much smaller than crescent of Barrow's. Transitional male Barrow's with facial crescent and upperpart pattern not fully developed can be problematic, but typically shows larger area of pale feathering on face than

Head-and-bill shapes of goldeneyes

Barrow's Goldeneye (eastern type)

Common Goldeneye

Upperwing patterns of adult female goldeneyes (differences less obvious on juveniles, which in both species have brownish median coverts)

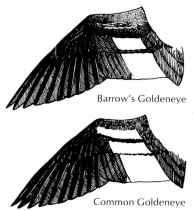

Barrow's Goldeneye

Common Goldeneye

Common, although, as with females, reliance on comparative size and head shape important. Females and juveniles close to those of Common Goldeneye, but are larger, with different head-and-bill shape (see above), and have darker chocolate-brown head and, in western population, often have bill chiefly yellow (very rarely the case on Common). Head-and-bill shape remains the most useful distinction when on water, and can be surprisingly obvious if the two species are together. Confusion with other species unlikely. **In flight:** Recalls Common Goldeneye, but show blacker upperparts, with white of upperwing divided by a black band across base of greater coverts; the facial crescent and larger size may also be apparent in flight. Females and juveniles harder to separate, but wing patterns of adult females differ slightly, Barrow's lacking obvious white on median coverts shown by Common; juvenile female Common, however, also lacks white and has wing similar to Barrow's, therefore this distinction valid only if white present. Juvenile Barrow's has blacker upperwing-coverts than juvenile Common.

VOICE Relatively silent, except during display, when male utters a soft, grunted 'ka-KAA'. Female has several low growling or grunting notes, which may also be uttered when flushed. Wings of male produce whistling sound in flight.

DESCRIPTION Sexually dimorphic. Seasonally variable. **Adult male breeding:** Head black with purple gloss, and with large white crescent between eye and bill covering most of front of head. Neck and underparts white, apart from black patch at sides of upper breast extending down from mantle, and blackish border to upper flanks and sides of ventral region. Upperparts black, with white-centred broadly-rounded scapulars forming an elongated block of white patches along sides of upperparts. Upperwing white, with black primaries, primary coverts, leading edge and band across base of greater coverts. Underwing dusky, with white secondaries. **Adult male eclipse:** Resembles adult female, but retains breeding-male upperwing pattern and has black bill. **Adult female:** Head dark chocolate-brown. Narrow whitish collar. Breast, flanks and ventral region greyish-brown; centre of underparts whitish. Upperparts darker brown. Upperwing dark grey-brown, with narrow whitish tips to median coverts (not forming clear white patch as on Common Goldeneye); leading edge, primaries and primary coverts blackish; most of greater coverts white, with broad black tips; most of secondaries white. Underwing as that of male. In summer duller, with greyer head, and lacks whitish collar. **Juvenile:** Resembles summer female, but upperwing-coverts blacker; male larger than female from early autumn. Gradually assumes adult features during first winter, but not obviously so until late winter or early spring; males appear much as adults by second winter.

BARE PARTS In all plumages legs and feet yellowish, brightest and most orange on adult males, dullest on juveniles. **Male:** Bill black. Iris bright yellow. **Female:** Bill fleshy-yellow, with blackish basal area and nail; all yellow on birds of western North America; duskier in summer. Iris pale yellow. **Juvenile:** Bill dark grey, with some fleshy tones towards tip. Iris brown.

MEASUREMENTS Males larger than females. **Male:** Wing 229-248 (mean 237), tarsus 38-46, bill 32-34, mean weight 1100. **Female:** Wing 211-221 (mean 218), tarsus 37-39, bill 29-32, mean weight ca. 800.

GEOGRAPHICAL VARIATION No races recognised. Females of western North America have all-yellow bill, a feature not recorded in eastern populations, which have bicoloured bills, but the two populations have not been racially separated.

HABITS Sociable, but forms smaller flocks (though may reach 200 birds) than Common Goldeneye, with which occasionally mixes outside breeding season. Strongly territorial in breeding season. Pair-formation begins in late winter, and continues on breeding waters. Breeds from mid May onwards. Nests typically in tree holes, especially in old woodpecker holes, but in Iceland such habitats do not exist and resorts to nestboxes, on ground among dense vegetation or in rock crevices. During incubation, males leave females and gather to moult. Feeds by diving, rarely coming on to land. General behaviour much as that of Common Goldeneye, but more aggressive and less sociable in breeding season. Not strongly migratory, merely moving to nearest ice-free waters during winter, but North American birds disperse further than Icelandic birds. Hybridisation has been very rarely reported between the two goldeneyes in North America.

HABITAT Breeds by lakes, pools and rivers, often in lowlands but in Rocky Mountains up to 3000 m. Outside breeding season, disperses to ice-free rivers and lakes and along inshore coastal waters.

DISTRIBUTION Somewhat relict distribution pattern, which at one time was presumed to have been far more widespread. Most numerous western population breeds in western North America from southern Alaska to northern California and Wyoming, wintering along adjacent coastal lowlands with small numbers south to San Francisco region and inland to Utah. Birds from eastern Canada leave breeding areas completely to winter along Atlantic seaboard from Gulf of St Lawrence south to Maine, some reaching inland to Great Lakes region and to Newfoundland and south to New York; small numbers in coastal waters of southwestern Greenland possibly of Canadian origin as, although has bred Greenland, it may not do so regularly. Icelandic population resident. Vagrants reported widely inland in North America, south to Colorado and Oklahoma. Also reported western Europe, with records from Svalbard, Faeroes, British Isles, France, Poland, East and West Germany and northwest USSR; many European records suspected to refer to escapes from captivity, but if genuine wild birds involved then most likely of Canadian origin, rather than from resident Icelandic population.

POPULATION Western North American population has been estimated at some 150,000 individuals. Eastern Canadian range and numbers poorly documented, and extent of breeding in Greenland, if any do so regularly, also unknown. Icelandic population stable at some 800 pairs. Perhaps the entire population does not exceed 200,000 birds.

REFERENCES Cramp and Simmons (1977), Johnsgard (1978).

140 COMMON GOLDENEYE   Plate 43
Bucephala clangula
Alternative name: Goldeneye

Medium-sized diving duck of both fresh and salt water right across the northern hemisphere.

FIELD IDENTIFICATION Length 42-50 cm (17-19 in). **At rest:** Medium-sized diving duck with stocky build, short neck, prominent tail, short bill, and relatively large, almost triangular-shaped head in all plumages. Breeding male shows black head and central upperparts contrasting with very white body; at closer ranges, the circular white loral spot is evident. Confusion is likely only with similar Barrow's Goldeneye (139), but latter is larger, with more bulging forehead, has large white facial crescent, and more extensive black on upperparts. Females and juveniles have greyish-brown body contrasting with darker brown head, and white wing patch (often visible when on water); a distinct greyish breast-band and whitish collar may be evident on adult females, as well as yellowish tip to dark bill. Easily distinguished from other diving ducks by distinctive head-and-bill shape, but very similar to Barrow's Goldeneye, from which most easily separated by smaller size and less bulging head shape (see Barrow's Goldeneye for discussion). **In flight:** Stocky, broad-winged, short-necked duck, with fast whistling wingbeats (wings more silent on females). In all plumages, the dusky underwing contrasts with white secondaries. Black head of male contrasts with white underbody; upperside shows mostly white inner wing, contrasting with blackish central upperparts and outer wing. Females and juveniles dingy brownish, with whiter belly; underwing as male, but upperwing with less white, although still obvious; white less extensive on juveniles. See similar Barrow's Goldeneye for discussion on separation. Wing pattern similar on much smaller Bufflehead (138).

VOICE Apart from whistling wingbeats, relatively silent apart from in display. Male utters a number of peculiar whistling and grating notes during display activities. Female has a harsh 'graa', sometimes also given when flushed.

DESCRIPTION Sexually dimorphic. Seasonally variable. **Adult male breeding:** Head black, glossed green, with circular white patch on lores. Neck and underparts white. Mantle, back, rump, uppertail-coverts and central tail black; outer tail grey. Tertials black. Scapulars elongated and pointed, striped black and white. Underwing dusky-grey, with white secondaries. Upperwing white, with black primaries, primary coverts and leading edge; greater coverts with black bases normally covered by white median coverts (exposed on Barrow's Goldeneye). **Adult male eclipse:** Resembles adult female, but wing as breeding male, with extensive white forewing; bill black. **Adult female:** Head chocolate-brown. Collar and centre of underparts white. Breast, mantle and flanks ashy-grey. Upperparts darker and browner-grey. Underwing as that of male. Primaries, primary coverts, tertials and lesser coverts blackish; upper median coverts white, lower row black; greater coverts white, tipped black; most of secondaries white. In summer duller, lacking whitish collar, and with grey of underparts browner. **Juvenile:** Similar to summer female, but duller, with greyer head lacking whitish collar of winter female. Young female lacks white on greater coverts shown by adult, but juvenile male has whitish greater coverts and is larger than female. Gradually acquires adult plumage features from middle of first winter onwards; males much as adult breeding by second winter.

BARE PARTS In all plumages legs and feet yellowish, dullest on juveniles and brightest on males. **Male:** Bill black. Iris bright yellow. **Female:** Bill blackish, with yellow distal portion, very rarely all yellow; in summer all dark. Iris whitish to pale yellow. **Juvenile:** Bill dark brown, acquiring relevant sexual coloration during first winter. Iris brownish to pale yellow.

MEASUREMENTS Males larger than females. **Male:** Wing 209-231 (mean 220), tarsus 37-41, bill 30-36, mean weight 990. **Female:** Wing 707-860 (mean 203), tarsus 33-37, bill 28-31, mean weight 710.

GEOGRAPHICAL VARIATION Slight. North American population, which has been separated as race *americana,* is slightly larger and has heavier bill than nominate form of the Old World, but Asiatic populations show a cline towards larger birds in the east and the differences probably only indicate the extremes of a clinal variation.

HABITS Sociable duck outside breeding season, when found in large closely-packed rafts on lakes and coastal waters. Associates only loosely with other species. Males tend to winter further north than females or juveniles. Pair-formation occurs from mid-winter onwards, continuing through spring migration and on arrival on breeding waters. Pairs break away from flocks on reaching breeding areas, and prospect rivers and lakeshores in search of suitable nesting holes. Nests from mid April onwards, considerably later in northern portions of range. Uses holes in trees and nestboxes, occasionally rabbit burrows; usually close to water. Males leave females at start of incubation and gather for post-breeding moult, often undertaking considerable migrations to gather on key waters. Feeds by diving, parts of flocks often diving in unison. When resting, swims buoyantly with tail prominently cocked. Often loafs on lakeshores and perches on partially-submerged branches. Flight fast, taking off with much pattering over surface. Non-breeders often oversummer on winter waters. Hybridisation with Barrow's Goldeneye has been very rarely reported; and, surprisingly, interbreeds occasionally with Smew (141).

HABITAT Breeds in Arctic-Alpine forest zone, preferring stretches of woodland close to lakes and slow rivers. Outside breeding season, found on variety of waters, from large freshwater lakes to estuaries and sheltered coastal bays.

DISTRIBUTION Widespread across northern regions of northern hemisphere, breeding south of tundra zone. Breeding range extends south to Germany, northern Mongolia, Heilungkiang (Manchuria), and in North America south to Great Lakes region. Erection of nestboxes has increased local populations and allowed colonisation of new areas: since the late 1960s has colonised Scotland, where now breeds in small but increasing numbers; and isolated populations have become established in Czechoslovakia and south of Moscow. Winters on lakes and coastal waters from southwest Iceland to northern shores of Mediterranean, eastwards across central Asia (south occasionally to Afghanistan) to the Pacific coast, south to southern China. In North America, widespread in winter south to Gulf coast in the east and California in the west, rarely south to central Mexico and the West Indies. Stragglers occasionally appear further south, with records of vagrants south to the Azores, Morocco, Algeria, Malta, Cyprus, Israel, Jordan, Iraq, northern India, Nepal, Burma, Hong Kong and Taiwan; vagrants have also visited Greenland and the Faeroe Islands.

POPULATION An abundant species overall, increasing and spreading in areas with nestbox-erection schemes, but locally decreasing in other regions through forest destruction. North American population has been estimated at well over 1 million individuals, and winter counts in Europe indicate a winter population of some 200,000 birds, chiefly around Denmark and the western Baltic Sea. In the Black Sea 8,000 were counted along northeastern shores in 1967, and the southern Caspian Sea produced 37,000 in 1968. No figures are available from eastern Asian wintering grounds.

REFERENCES Cramp and Simmons (1977).

141 SMEW
Plate 44

Mergellus albellus

Small diving duck, in many respects a link between the goldeneyes and the larger sawbills (*Mergus*). Hybridisation between Common Goldeneye (140) and Smew has been occasionally reported in the wild, indicating their close affinity.

FIELD IDENTIFICATION Length 38-44 cm (15-17 in). **At rest:** Small diving duck, females being little larger than Teal (77). Breeding males strikingly white, with blackish mantle and head patches, and unlikely to be mistaken for any other duck except perhaps distant pale immature male Long-tailed Duck (137); beware also winter-plumaged Black Guillemot. Surprisingly easy to overlook on dappled or choppy water. Other plumages ('red-heads') show a distinctive combination of greyish body with chestnut-brown head and white throat and lower cheeks; white wing patches (often visible when on water) suggest female Common Goldeneye, with which Smew often associates in winter, but smaller head and white throat of Smew are easy distinctions. See also female Bufflehead (138) and beware winter-plumaged small grebes. **In flight:** A small duck, rather Teal-like in shape, with rapid wingbeats. Males very white, with blackish centre to upperparts and large white patch towards front of blackish upperwing; underwing whitish, with greyer flight feathers and dusky leading edge. 'Red-heads' greyish, with smaller white upperwing patch than male but similar underwing pattern, latter recalling Teal, but easily distinguished by relatively large white patch on upperwing-coverts (obscured on juveniles) and white throat and foreneck. Lacks white secondary patch and dusky underwing of female Common Goldeneye.

VOICE Generally silent. Male utters occasional low croaks and whistles during display. Female sometimes gives a low growling note.

DESCRIPTION Sexually dimorphic. Seasonally variable. **Adult male breeding:** Head with loose crest on crown and nape, white, with black patch from behind eye to base of bill and another on nape, latter varyingly obvious according to whether crest is elevated or depressed. Most of underparts white, with flanks indistinctly vermiculated grey; two narrow black stripes at side of breast, extending from blackish mantle. Mantle, back and rump blackish, becoming greyer on lower rump, upper-tail-coverts and tail. Scapulars white. Tertials dark grey. Upperwing blackish, with broad white area on median coverts and narrow white tips to greater coverts and secondaries. Underwing whitish, with grey flight feathers and dusky leading edge. **Adult male eclipse:** Resembles summer female (with brown lores), but has larger white patch on upperwing-coverts and blacker upperparts. **Adult female:** Rear crown and nape ruffled. Head chestnut, with blackish lores, and white throat, foreneck and lower ear-coverts. Sides of lower neck and breast, flanks and sides of ventral region dull grey, with whitish central underparts. Upperparts darker grey. Upperwing blackish-grey, with white patch on median coverts (not so extensive as on male), and narrow white tips to greater coverts and secondaries. Underwing as that of male. In summer a little duller, with brownish lores (like eclipse male). **Juvenile:** As female summer, but central underparts mottled greyish, not clear whitish, and with broader white tips to greater coverts and secondaries than on adult female. Young male larger than female, with tertials longer and paler. Develops adult-like features towards end of first winter or in first spring, but can have blackish lores by autumn. Males almost fully adult by second winter.

BARE PARTS In all plumages, bill blackish and legs and feet greyish. Iris reddish-brown, duller grey-brown on juveniles and pale greyish-white on older males.

MEASUREMENTS Males larger than females. **Male:** Wing 197-208 (mean 202), tarsus 31-36, bill 27-32, mean weight 739. **Female:** Wing 181-189 (mean 184), tarsus 29-32, bill 25-29, mean weight 567.

GEOGRAPHICAL VARIATION None.

HABITS Sociable diving duck, in winter often in small closely-packed rafts, rarely exceeding 100 birds; at major passage waters, larger gatherings form during migration periods. Flocks often somewhat sexually segregated, with females and juveniles wintering further south than majority of males. Mixes little with other species, but often in association with Common Goldeneyes. Pair-formation begins in late winter; during spring migration, most birds are paired. Arrives on breeding grounds from early May onwards, breeding from mid May. Nests in tree holes, especially old holes of Black Woodpecker, and freely uses nestboxes erected for goldeneyes; in some areas, small loose colonies may be formed. Males moult during incubation, in some areas gathering in flocks close to breeding grounds. Feeds by diving, rarely coming on to land, but readily loafs on shores of lakes and riverbanks and often perches on boulders or partially-submerged branches. Feeds mostly in daytime, flying to roosting waters at dusk and leaving soon after dawn for feeding areas. Flight fast and agile, taking off suddenly from water almost in manner of a dabbling duck. Migratory; leaves breeding areas during September and October, but furthest wintering waters may not be occupied until mid-winter. Occasionally hybridises with Common Goldeneye.

HABITAT Breeds by forested pools, lakes and slow rivers in similar habitats to Common Goldeneye, but with preference for lowland riverine forests. Outside breeding season, on freshwater lakes and locally on estuaries and sheltered coastal bays.

DISTRIBUTION Widespread across taiga zone of northern Europe and Siberia from northern Sweden eastwards to Pacific coast of Siberia, although numbers low and sparse towards eastern and western limits of range. Sporadic or former breeding has been reported south of the main range, particularly in Romania and along River Volga in southern USSR and region of Semipalatinsk in western Siberia. Winters on sheltered seas and lakes in eastern Europe, chiefly in the southwestern Baltic Sea and coastal waters of Black and Caspian Seas, but also widely scattered over lakes and reservoirs from southern England to central and southeastern Europe; in cold winters numbers move further west into France and western British Isles, although very scarce south to western Mediterranean region. Small numbers reach Greece, Turkey, Iraq and Iran in winter, and species occurs irregularly to Afghanistan, Pakistan and northern India. Further east, winters around coasts, lakes and rivers of eastern China, Korea and Japan. Vagrants have occurred south to Algeria, Libya, Egypt, Jordan and Burma; regularly reported from Aleutian Islands and several records from Alaska, but elsewhere in North America an exceptional straggler to British Columbia, eastern Canada and adjacent USA.

POPULATION Breeding range somewhat fragmented towards western and eastern limits of range, indicating that it has decreased from former times; at least in Europe, however, winter numbers seem to have increased in recent years. No total estimates have been made, but winter populations in western Palaearctic region amounted to some 75,000 individuals in mid 1970s, including counts of up to 25,000 in Sea of Azov in northern Black Sea and at least 20,000 on Volga delta of northern Caspian Sea. No figures available from eastern Asia.

REFERENCES Cramp and Simmons (1977), Dementiev and Gladkov (1952), Nilsson (1974).

142 HOODED MERGANSER   Plate 44
Lophodytes cucullatus

Distinctive little North American 'sawbill', with peculiar bushy crest at rear of head which may be raised into a fan when displaying.

FIELD IDENTIFICATION Length 42-50 cm (17-19 in). **At rest:** Small diving duck with bushy crest at rear of head, slender bill, and prominent tail often carried erect like that of a stiff-tail (*Oxyura*). Breeding male distinctive, with bushy black head and white blaze behind eye, latter visible as either a rectangular patch or a massive white area depending on whether crest is closed or elevated. The blackish upperparts contrast with white breast, black and white bands at sides of breast and vermiculated rufous-grey flanks. Unmistakable, but compare male Bufflehead (138). Other plumages ('brownheads') are relatively plain greyish-brown overall, but have bushy dull ginger crest on rear of head and pale yellowish bill-base; equally unmistakable, though recall smaller and stockier version of Redbreasted Merganser (144), but confusion unlikely. **In flight:** Small duck, with 'waisted' appearance to head and neck created by thin neck and large oblong-shaped head. Flies fast and low, twisting with agility among trees. Male appears blackish, relieved by white breast, head patch and central underparts. Upperwing very dark, showing white bar along greater coverts, striped tertials, and slightly paler area on median coverts. Underwing resembles that of Teal (77), with dusky leading edge, whitish central area, and greyish flight feathers. 'Brown-heads' show similar wing pattern to that of male, but are dull greyish-brown on head and body, with slightly whiter central underparts. Confusion unlikely.

VOICE Relatively silent. During display, male utters a rolling frog-like 'crrrooooo', female merely a short harsh note.

DESCRIPTION Sexually dimorphic. Seasonally variable. **Adult male breeding:** Head with elongated bushy crest. Head and neck black, with white band from behind eye to rear of crest, tipped black. Breast, lower neck and central underparts white. Two black bands extend down side of breast from blackish mantle. Flanks rufous, vermiculated grey and black. Ventral region mottled buffish-grey and white. Upperparts brownish-black. Tertials elongated, striped black and white. Upperwing blackish-

brown, with lighter brown area on median coverts; greater coverts broadly tipped white; inner secondaries with white outer webs. Underwing whitish, with dusky leading edge and greyish flight feathers. **Adult male eclipse:** Resembles female, but has yellow iris and blacker bill and often shows vestiges of breeding-male plumage. **Adult female:** Head less strongly maned than that of male, but with considerable bushy crest. General coloration dull greyish-brown, darker on head and crown, with crest ginger-brown, becoming very pale buffish towards feather tips. Throat, foreneck and centre of underparts whitish. Wing as that of male, but browner, with median coverts not contrasting; tertials shorter, with narrower white stripes. **Juvenile:** Similar to female, but crest shorter, lacks obvious white on greater coverts (but some present on juvenile male) and lacks white stripes on tertials; upperparts paler brown. Young males do not develop breeding-male features until late first winter or first spring, but resemble adult males by second winter.

BARE PARTS Male: Bill black. Legs and feet brownish-yellow. Iris yellow. **Female and juvenile:** Bill blackish, with orange-yellow base and most of lower mandible; duller on juvenile and with fleshier base. Legs and feet dull brownish or yellowish-grey. Iris brown.

MEASUREMENTS Males a little larger than females. Wing 184-202 (mean: male 198, female 190); tarsus 29-33; bill 34-41; mean weight of male 680, of female 554.

GEOGRAPHICAL VARIATION None.

HABITS Usually met with in pairs or small parties; less sociable than most other diving ducks, flocks rarely exceeding 15 birds. Pair-formation begins in mid-winter. Arrives on breeding waters from early May onwards, usually already paired. Nests in tree holes up to 25 m from ground, normally not far from water, rarely in hollows of fallen trunks, but frequently in nestboxes. When incubation is underway, males desert females to commence postbreeding moult. Feeds by diving. A bird of secluded pools and lakes in wooded districts, spending much time under shade of overhanging branches when even males can be inconspicuous on dappled water. Readily perches on waterside branches and stumps and loafs on shores and banks. Walks more easily and more readily than other 'sawbills'. Flies rapidly, low over surface, taking off with some pattering over surface; very agile when flying through trees. Migratory, but often remains north until forced to move by freezing waters. Very rarely, hybridises with Common Goldeneye (140) in the wild.

HABITAT Breeds by slow rivers and small lakes in forested regions. Winters in similar situations, but also on larger waters and locally on estuaries and coastal lagoons, less frequently on coastal waters than most other 'sawbills'.

DISTRIBUTION Two populations. Western birds breed from southern Alaska, through western Canada to Montana and Oregon, wintering along adjacent coastal lowlands south to California, but still remaining north to Alaska in winter. Eastern population breeds over most of wooded districts of southern Canada and northern USA south to the

Great Plains and along Mississippi valley, locally almost to Gulf coast; in winter disperses south to Florida and northern Mexico, rarely to the West Indies and Bermuda. Vagrants have occurred in Hawaiian Islands and north to the Pribilof Islands. Very rare as transatlantic vagrant; recorded British Isles and West Germany, but no known recent records.

POPULATION Total numbers difficult to assess, owing to rather retiring nature and tendency not to form large flocks; an estimate of a breeding population of some 76,000 individuals was, however, made in the early 1970s. No apparent increases or decreases have been reported of this comparatively little-studied and rather secretive species.

REFERENCES Johnsgard (1978).

143 BRAZILIAN MERGANSER   Plate 44
Mergus octosetaceus

One of the least-known of all wildfowl, a secretive 'sawbill' of fast-flowing rivers of central South America.

FIELD IDENTIFICATION Length 49-51 cm (19-20 in). **At rest:** Unmistakable in its limited range. All plumages similar. A slender merganser, overall dark greyish-brown, with blackish-green head, long spiked crest and slender bill. Unlikely to be confused as unlike any other South American duck, but shares rivers with Olivaceous or Neotropic Cormorants. Not kept in captivity. **In flight:** Large, dull, long-bodied and long-necked duck; flies low and fast along course of river, showing large white patches on secondaries and greater coverts, divided by a black bar. Unmistakable, for Olivaceous Cormorant has all-dark wings, but compare Brazilian Duck (110).

VOICE Relatively silent, but a loud 'queeek' may be given in flight.

DESCRIPTION All plumages similar. Head with long spiked crest. Head and neck bottle-green, appearing blackish in field. Lower neck, breast and flanks finely barred grey and white; remainder of underparts barred brown and white. Upperparts dark greenish-brown. Upperwing blackish, with white secondaries; greater coverts white, with black tips. Female tends to have shorter crest and bill than male (the crest being broken when gripped by male during copulation); juvenile much as female.

BARE PARTS All plumages: Bill blackish. Legs and feet pinkish-red. Iris brown.

MEASUREMENTS Males larger than females. No weights recorded. **Male:** Wing 183-188, tarsus 40-42, bill 49-51. **Female:** Wing 180-184, bill 38-40.

GEOGRAPHICAL VARIATION None.

HABITS Little known. Shy and secretive inhabitant of small fast-flowing forested rivers, invariably encountered in pairs. Strongly territorial. Breeds during July-August, nesting in holes in riverside trees. Males help females with brood-tending once young have left nest hole. Feeds by diving in flowing streams and by foraging in shallows, behaving in many ways like Torrent Duck (55), feeding among rapids and standing on mid-stream boulders. When not actively feeding, swims buoyantly with tail cocked. Readily perches on branches and fallen trunks protruding from rivers. Very shy and wary. Flies strongly and rapidly, typically low and following course of river, seemingly not rising above tree height or taking short-cuts over stretches of forest. Resident, being restricted to territorial stretches of rivers.

HABITAT Small, fast-flowing streams and rivers in tropical forest.

DISTRIBUTION Resident along tributaries towards the headwaters of the Parana and Tocantins Rivers in the states of Minas Gerais, São Paulo, Santa Catarina, Goias and Parana in southern Brazil and adjacent regions of eastern Paraguay and northeastern Argentina (Misiones).

POPULATION A secretive and rare duck of rather wild and inaccessible forest torrents. Thought to be extinct until refound in 1948. Probably not so rare as formerly suspected, but territorial nature and difficulty of exploring its habitat allow it to be easily overlooked. No estimates have been made of its population. It is protected in Brazil, but its habitat is threatened by the planned construction of several dams lower down the rivers, the greatest threat to all species of waterfowl that rely on fast-flowing rivers.

REFERENCES King (1981), Partridge (1956).

144 RED-BREASTED MERGANSER
Mergus serrator   Plate 45

Widespread 'sawbill' throughout the northern hemisphere and more of an estuarine species than the Goosander (146), with which it widely overlaps in range.

FIELD IDENTIFICATION Length 52-58 cm (20-23 in). **At rest:** Long-bodied, long-necked and slender-billed diving duck superficially recalling Goosander, but smaller, more slender, and with looser and more spiky crest. Breeding male has dark head and upperparts, white collar and wing patches, greyish flanks, black and white chest patches, and streaked brownish breast; unlikely to be confused. Other plumages ('brown-heads') are slender greyish-brown ducks, with warmer brown heads, and have ill-defined whitish centre of foreneck and breast and underparts; their crest may be quite inconspicuous, particularly when actively diving with head and neck sleeked into an almost serpentine appearance, while at other times the rear of the head appears ruffled with a loose crest, which is shorter than on male. Most likely confusion is with 'brown-head' Goosander, but Red-breasted Merganser is smaller, with slimmer head and neck, duller grey body plumage, with duller and paler ginger-brown head, scruffier and more wispy crest (fuller and more maned droopy crest on Goosander), and has brown of head diffusing into whitish breast and foreneck (not clearly cut as on Goosander). See also similar Chinese Merganser (145) of eastern Asia, which is easily confused. Confusion with other species unlikely, but see Hooded Merganser (142). **In flight:** A long-bodied and long-necked duck, with wings appearing to be placed far back on body and neck projecting stiffly. Male shows extensive white on inner wing, contrasting with blackish mantle and sides of upperparts and blackish outer wing and head; the white collar and brownish breast are apparent in flight and are an easy distinction from both Goosander and Chinese Merganser. 'Brown-heads' are best identified by shape; the greyish upperparts being relieved by white secondaries, they appear similar to Goosander, but are considerably smaller and less bulky overall and show less striking contrast between head and breast (contrast always apparent on Goosander in flight). The white wing patch differs slightly between the two species, Red-breasted Merganser having a black bar across base of secondaries dividing the white patch; this bar is obscured by longer white greater coverts on Goosander (except on American race).

VOICE Relatively silent, except in display, when male utters a variety of soft notes and a low cat-like mewing. Female has several grating and harsh calls, which may be heard during display or in flight.

DESCRIPTION Sexually dimorphic. Seasonally variable. **Adult male breeding:** Head with long, straggling crest at rear. Head and upper neck black, glossed green. Central neck with white collar. Lower neck and breast rufous-brown, streaked black. Sides of breast black with white patches enclosed, extending from blackish mantle. Central hindneck, mantle and inner scapulars blackish. Flanks, sides of ventral region, uppertail-coverts, rump and back vermiculated grey. Centre of underparts white. Outer scapulars white. Upperwing with blackish primaries, primary coverts and leading edge; most of inner wing white, with blackish bars across bases of greater coverts and bases of secondaries. Underwing with whitish inner wing and greyer outer wing. **Adult male eclipse:** Resembles female, but retains breeding-male upperwing with extensive white and has blacker mantle. **Adult female:** Crest shorter than that of male. Head and neck rufous-brown, shading to whitish throat and foreneck and merging with greyer lower neck. Lores dusky, with narrow whitish line between eye and bill. Lower neck, sides of breast and flanks dull brownish-grey, shading into whiter breast centre and central underparts. Upperparts similar, but darker. Upperwing greyish-brown, darker on outer wing, with white secondaries and greater coverts, secondaries showing blackish bar across base. Underwing as that of male. In summer, head and neck paler, more buffish-orange, lacking dusky lores and with more indistinct pale loral line. **Juvenile:** Similar to summer female, but central underparts and breast more suffused with greyish-brown, less whitish; upperwing of juvenile female has white a little less extensive. Male develops adult features during late winter and early spring, becoming much as adult by second winter.

BARE PARTS Bill slender, with nostrils towards base (cf. Chinese Merganser). **Male:** Bill red, with dusky culmen and nail. Legs and feet red. Iris red. **Female:** Bill dull red, with dusky culmen and nail. Legs and feet dull red. Iris brown to reddish-brown. **Juvenile:** Bill brownish-red, becoming redder during late first winter. Legs and feet yellowish-brown, becoming redder during first winter. Iris pale brown, becoming yellowish or orange on male during first winter.

MEASUREMENTS Males larger than females. **Male:** Wing 235-255 (mean 247), tarsus 44-50, bill 56-64, mean weight 1181. **Female:** Wing 216-239 (mean 228), tarsus 40-45, bill 48-55, mean weight 944.

GEOGRAPHICAL VARIATION Slight. Resident Greenland population, which has been separated as race *schioleri*, averages a little larger on measurements, but differences do not seem to be strong enough to warrant acceptance as a valid race.

HABITS Sociable duck of tidal waters; often in flocks throughout the year, but largest gatherings in winter months. Active display and pair-formation from mid-winter onwards, with increasing intensity through the spring migration. Breeding commences late April in southern portion of range, but considerably later further north. Nests close to water, hidden on ground among vegetation, under boulders or in rock crevices or burrows; sometimes in tree holes or nestboxes. In areas of greatest abundance, breeds in loose colonies. Males leave females during incubation, but sometimes seen in attendance with young broods. Feeds by diving. When actively feeding, swims low in water with sleeked head and neck; when resting, swims high and buoyantly. Spends much time loafing in parties on shores and banks. Flight fast and direct, rising from water with much pattering. Remains close to breeding waters in temperate regions, but migratory in others, females and juveniles dispersing more widely than adult males. Very rarely, hybridises with Goosander in the wild.

HABITAT Breeds by estuaries, rivers and lakes in wooded country north to fringes of tundra. Outside breeding season, almost entirely on inshore tidal waters, chiefly estuary mouths and shallow coastal bays, but occurs on freshwater lakes during migration.

DISTRIBUTION Widespread across whole of northern portion of northern hemisphere, north to southern regions of tundra zone. Southern limits of breeding range include British Isles, northern edge of steppe in western Siberia, possibly Mongolia (where recorded rarely in summer), northeast China, northern Japan (Hokkaido) and, in North America, Great Lakes region. Winters along coastal waters in more temperate regions, from southern Greenland, Iceland and coastal Norway south in small numbers to northern shores of the Mediterranean, small numbers also wintering along shores of Black and Caspian Seas and some Central Asian lakes; further east, winters along coasts of eastern China and Japan. In North America, winters along coastal regions of both Pacific and Atlantic, south to California and the Gulf coast; small numbers reach northern Mexico, the West Indies and Bermuda. Vagrants have been recorded south to the Azores, Madeira, Morocco, Malta, Cyprus, Israel, Iraq, southern Iran, Afghanistan, Nepal, northern India, Taiwan, Bonin Islands and Hawaiian Islands.

POPULATION Abundant. North American population estimated at some 237,000 individuals in summer. Winter counts from Europe and Black Sea region suggest some 50,000 birds, with unknown large numbers in eastern Asia. Certainly increasing in parts of western Europe, with slow spread of breeding range southwards.

REFERENCES Cramp and Simmons (1977), Curth (1954).

145 CHINESE MERGANSER   Plate 45
Mergus squamatus

Alternative names: Scaly Merganser, Scaly-sided Merganser

Rare and little-known 'sawbill' of eastern Asia, closely related to both Goosander (146) and Red-breasted Merganser (144), with both of which its range overlaps, even in breeding season.

FIELD IDENTIFICATION Length 52-62 cm (20-24 in). **At rest:** Resembles Red-breasted Merganser in general shape and size, but crest longer. Less bulky and more elegant than Goosander. Breeding male distinctive, recalling Goosander in plumage coloration, but Red-breasted Merganser in shape though crest even longer. Flanks and rear body covered with dark grey scale-like markings, giving greyish appearance to rear flanks and body at longer ranges; lacks breast pattern of Red-breasted Merganser and creamy-white appearance of flanks of Goosander. Other plumages ('brown-heads') closely resemble those of Red-breasted Merganser, but sides of neck and upperparts purer grey and sides of body heavily scaled as on male; crest longer and more wispy than on Red-breasted, but shorter than on male Chinese. Juveniles and possibly summer females more problematic, as they lack scaling and are very easy to pass off as Red-breasted; under good viewing conditions, it should be possible to make out diagnostic position of nostrils: close to bill-base on Red-breasted, about midway along bill on Chinese (and Goosander). Additionally, bill-tip and nail of Chinese seem to be (but perhaps not always) pale yellowish or whitish (dusky on the other two). Beware male Goosander in transitional plumage, with some grey feathers along flanks. May be encountered on same rivers as both Goosander and Red-breasted Merganser in summer, but extent of ecological separation unknown. **In flight:** Resembles Red-breasted Merganser, but males lack prominent breast pattern; females difficult to distinguish in flight. Smaller size and more slender appearance distinguish both sexes from Goosander.
VOICE Little information; said to resemble that of Red-breasted Merganser.
DESCRIPTION Sexually dimorphic. Seasonally variable. **Adult male breeding:** Head with very long wispy crest at rear, hanging to mantle. Head and neck black, glossed green. Lower foreneck, breast and central underparts creamy-white, with salmon-pink flush. Flanks, ventral region, uppertail-coverts, rump and back whitish, with dark grey scale-like markings, latter largest along flanks. Mantle, hindneck and scapulars blackish. Upperwing and underwing much as on Red-breasted Merganser. **Adult male eclipse:** Resembles adult female, but retains extensive white in upperwing and scaling on sides of body, latter apparently lacking on summer (= eclipse) female. **Adult female:** Head with prominent wispy crest at rear. Head and neck warm buffish-brown, with dusky lores; centre of neck and throat

buffish-brown and quite clearly demarcated from colour of lower neck. Centre of lower neck, breast and central underparts whitish. Sides of neck, flanks, sides of ventral region and rump whitish, heavily scaled with grey markings. Hindneck and remainder of upperparts medium-grey. Wing much as on female Red-breasted Merganser. In summer, it seems that females lose scaling and have flanks and rump sullied grey as on juvenile. **Juvenile:** Resembles summer female, presumably acquiring adult features during latter part of first winter, but data lacking.
BARE PARTS Seemingly similar in all plumages, but few data. Bill red, with dusky culmen and whitish-yellow nail (nail perhaps dusky on some individuals). Legs and feet red (brightest on males). Iris greyish, whitish or dark brown (not red, even on breeding males).
MEASUREMENTS Males larger than females. No weights recorded. **Male:** Wing 250-265, tarsus 46-48, bill 52-57. **Female:** Wing 240-250, tarsus 45, bill 43-48.
GEOGRAPHICAL VARIATION None.
HABITS Little known; a rare and sparsely-distributed bird of fast-flowing small rivers in hill forest. Generally met with in pairs or family parties, but small gatherings occasionally reported outside breeding season. Pair-formation reported in breeding areas during first half of April. Arrives on breeding streams during late March, nesting during April and May. Territorial, pairs occupying at least 4-km stretch of river. Nests in holes in old riverside trees. During incubation, males assemble and leave breeding areas (in late May), presumably performing short moult migration. Feeds by diving and foraging in pools and eddies of fast-flowing water. Shy and wary. Flight fast and low, following course of river, not normally rising above treetops or crossing stretches of forest. Extent of migration uncertain: leaves breeding streams in autumn, but suspected merely to move to lower reaches of breeding rivers; a number of reports (chiefly older records) of birds collected in winter south to southwest China indicate, however, that movements may be more considerable, though perhaps only in severe weather.
HABITAT Breeds by fast-flowing small rivers in hill and mountain forests, tending to occupy smaller side rivers rather than larger and wider main rivers. Outside breeding season, may also be encountered on open lakes, but seems to prefer rivers; not found in coastal regions.
DISTRIBUTION Breeds locally in hilly border regions of extreme southeastern USSR and northeastern Heilungkiang (Manchuria), perhaps also in Kirin and border regions of North Korea. So far as is known, seems to be only partially migratory, merely moving to lower reaches of rivers in winter, particularly those that flow from eastern side of the Sikhote Alin range in Siberia. Occasionally, however, disperses more widely, perhaps in severe weather, with records of birds from Korea and eastern and southern China, particularly valley of the Yangtze west to Szechwan and south to Kwangtung. Vagrants reported from Japan, North Vietnam, northern Burma and Komandorskiye Islands.

POPULATION Rare and little known, its territorial nature and rather remote habitats making it a difficult bird for which to give a general population estimate. Its numbers must be in the region of several hundred pairs. Several reserves have been established within its breeding range and the species has been receiving some study. In the USSR, work on the population of the Bikin River gave a population there of some 120-150 pairs in 1980-81. Local surveys of the Soviet population all show a considerable decrease since the mid 1960s. Disturbance and pollution, including forest development, the felling of old hollow trees, and increased river transport, as well as predation of the young by feral American mink, have been cited as possible reasons for the decline.

REFERENCES Dementiev and Gladkov (1952), FESC (1985), Flint (1984), King (1981), Zhengjie et al. (1979).

146 GOOSANDER or COMMON MERGANSER   Plate 45
Mergus merganser

Alternative names: Goosander (Europe), Common Merganser (North America)

Larger freshwater relative of the Red-breasted Merganser (144), with widely overlapping range across northern hemisphere.

FIELD IDENTIFICATION Length 58-72 cm (23-28 in). **At rest:** Similar to Red-breasted Merganser, but considerably larger and bulkier, with stouter neck and maned (rather than wispy) crest giving a large-headed appearance. Breeding male distinctive, with black head and central upperparts contrasting with white breast and underparts, the latter strongly washed creamy salmon-pink in good light. Other plumages ('brown-heads') differ from those of Red-breasted Merganser in size and structure (see above) and in having purer grey body plumage and darker brown head and upper neck, the brown extending to encircle foreneck (typically diffuses into whitish foreneck on Red-breasted Merganser). The dark head and neck is clearly demarcated from the creamy-white breast and white chin, although contrast less obvious on duller juvenile. Birds of American race have much stouter bill-base than Red-breasted Merganser. In eastern Asia, compare also Chinese Merganser (145). **In flight:** Considerably larger and more heavily built than Red-breasted Merganser, but general flight shape similar. Male has black head, central upperparts and outer wing, and white neck, underparts and inner wing; lacks breast-band of Red-breasted Merganser, and shows more extensive white on upperwing, the white lacking black dividing lines (although American race shows black bar across base of greater coverts). 'Brown-heads' most easily separated by heavier appearance and by strong contrast between dark brown head and upper neck and whitish breast centre, which is apparent in flight; additionally, lack dividing line across secondary bases of Red-breasted, although this may partially show. Compare also Chinese Merganser in eastern Asia.

VOICE Relatively silent. During display, male utters a strange twanging 'uig-a' and several other sounds; female has several harsh calls.

DESCRIPTION Sexually dimorphic. Seasonally variable. Nominate race described. **Adult male breeding:** Head with mane on nape. Head and upper neck black, glossed green. Lower neck, breast and underparts creamy-white, with variable salmon-pink wash (depth of colour seems to depend on diet). Sides of ventral region, uppertail-coverts, rump and lower back grey. Mantle and inner scapulars blackish. Upperwing with blackish primaries, primary coverts and leading edge; remainder basically white. Underwing with whitish inner wing and dark grey outer wing. **Adult male eclipse:** Resembles adult female, but retains extensive white upperwing of breeding plumage; also, flanks whiter and mantle blacker. **Adult female:** Head with looser, hanging, mane than male. Head and upper neck dark reddish-brown, clearly demarcated from lower neck and with clear whitish chin. Sides and rear of neck, sides of breast and flanks grey. Breast and centre of underparts creamy-white. Upperparts darker grey. Upperwing ashy-grey, with blacker primaries and primary coverts; secondaries and greater coverts white, latter often with narrow grey tips forming incomplete bar. Underwing as that of male. In summer, head paler brown and crest rather shorter; usually has narrow pale loral line. **Juvenile:** Resembles summer female, but duller, with brown cast to mantle and scapulars and ill-defined paler throat centre. Young male shows paler, even whitish, median coverts from an early stage; develops breeding-male features from mid-winter onwards (some birds almost as breeding male by first spring), and resembles adult male breeding by second winter.

BARE PARTS All plumages: Bill red, with blackish culmen and nail; brightest on male, dullest and brownest on juvenile. Legs and feet deep red, dullest on juvenile. Iris brown.

MEASUREMENTS Males larger than females. Nominate and race *americanus*: **Male:** Wing 275-295 (mean 285), tarsus 49-55, bill 52-60, mean weight 1671. **Female:** Wing 255-270 (mean 262), tarsus 44-51, bill 44-52, mean weight 1406. Race *comatus*: **Male:** Wing 286-305 (mean 295), bill 48-56.

GEOGRAPHICAL VARIATION Three races recognised. Nominate form breeds over most of range in Old World, except where replaced in Central Asia by rather larger race *comatus*, which additionally has finer bill. In North America, replaced by race *americanus*, which has very deep-based bill and males of which show blackish bar across bases of median coverts (latter hidden by overlapping feathering on other races). Females hardly separable.

HABITS Sociable duck, primarily of freshwater lakes and flowing rivers. Typically found in small parties, but large flocks form at roosting waters outside breeding season; largest numbers gather in autumn and early winter, and may reach several thousand birds on key waters. Pair-formation begins chiefly in late winter, but continues during spring migration.

Breeding begins as early as late March in central Europe, but is considerably later further north. Nests typically in tree holes or nestboxes near water, rarely on ground among vegetation; loosely colonial, several females even nesting in same tree on occasions. Males leave females very early during incubation and gather to moult, often undertaking considerable moult migration to flock on key waters. Feeds by diving; also forages in shallows with head submerged. Feeds chiefly along fast-flowing rivers in daytime, flying to and from roosting lakes at dusk and dawn. Often loafs under over-hanging branches, on ice or lakeshores. Flight fast and direct, taking off with much pattering over surface. Migratory, although remains near breeding areas for as long as open water allows.

HABITAT Breeds by forested freshwater rivers and lakes, locally along rivers in more open upland areas. Outside breeding season, chiefly on large freshwater lakes, locally on estuaries and brackish waters, but avoids coastal waters of high salinity.

DISTRIBUTION Widespread across whole of northern hemisphere in the forested taiga zone, south to more temperate forests and rivers. In Europe, nominate race breeds south to central Europe and sparsely and sporadically south to Romania and Greece, breeding range extending south into Central Asia and perhaps even eastern Turkey occasionally; further east, breeds south to Heilungkiang (Manchuria), Sakhalin and Japan (occasionally Hokkaido). Winters along open lakes and coastal waters of low salinity, from Iceland and the Baltic south to northern shores of the Mediter-ranean, Black and Caspian Seas and in small numbers across ice-free waters of Central Asia; also along temperate lowlands of eastern China and occasionally to Japan. Vagrants recorded north to Svalbard and Bear Island and south to Morocco, Tunisia, Israel, Iraq and Taiwan. Central Asian race *comatus* breeds over uplands of Tibetan plateau region, south to northeastern Afghanistan, Ladakh and Szechwan; in winter it merely disperses south-wards to adjacent lowland regions, including rivers of northern India and Burma. North American race *americanus* breeds across Canada and northern USA from southern Alaska to Newfoundland, south along the Rocky Mountains region to northern Cali-fornia; it winters over inland lakes and along coastal waters over most of temperate North America south to Florida and California, occasionally south to northern Mexico, straggling as far as Bermuda and Greenland.

POPULATION Abundant. American winter counts suggest a total of some 165,000 individuals of the Nearctic race *americanus*. In Europe, winter studies give an estimate of 75,000 in northwest Europe and a further 26,000 in western USSR (chiefly Black and Caspian Sea regions). Other large numbers are found further east in Asia. The species seems to be slowly increasing and spreading, at least in parts of western Europe, but is also persecuted on rivers where it is deemed to compete with man's fishing interests.

REFERENCES Cramp and Simmons (1977), Johns-gard (1978).

147 AUCKLAND ISLANDS MERGANSER
Mergus australis

Now extinct, having not been reported since 1902, when the last specimens were collected only some 60 years after its initial discovery in 1840. Both sexes resembled a small female Red-breasted Merganser (144). Although known only from the Auckland Islands, sub-fossil remains show that a very similar merganser had also existed on South and Stewart Islands of New Zealand until relatively recent times. Despite comparatively small wings, it could fly reasonably well, although it is often referred to as 'flightless' in the literature. Its extinc-tion was certainly due to man's influence, both through hunting and through the introduction of feral mammalian predators to the islands, either from shipwrecks or by settlers. A thorough review of the history, ecology and description of the species is given by Kear and Scarlett (1970).

Tribe OXYURINI (STIFF-TAILS)

A small tribe of four genera, three of which are monotypic. All members of this group are freshwater diving ducks, although some may also be found on brackish waters. They have relatively large feet placed far back on the body, which renders them clumsy on land. Most species take off from water with much pattering over the surface, and fly on rapidly beating wings which are relatively short and broad. *Heteronetta* is the most aberrant member of the tribe and outwardly recalls a more 'typical' duck, having an inconspicuous, short tail and more conventional bill shape. The remainder all have long, stiff tail feathers, typically carried erect when resting on the water, and a rather large or swollen bill. When actively diving or swimming, the long tail is depressed to the surface and the back profile slopes gently to the water.

Members of the genus *Oxyura* are all similar, although ranges of most species do not overlap. Their plu-mage sequences are complex, and in many cases inadequately known. In some species, i.e. the black-headed southern 'blue-bills', the plumages of female-like birds differ more strongly in pattern than do those of breeding males; comparative bill shape, extent of black on the neck (difficult to discern unless erect) and comparative tail length may be helpful when identifying such birds in collections. Ageing birds on plumage features is often difficult owing to individual variation, but first-years may be aged by their narrower tail feathers, notched at tip, with bare shaft projecting (as in other duck genera); this may be visible under close scrutiny, and is more easily seen in the field under optimum conditions than is the case with other ducks.

The display behaviour of stiff-tails differs markedly from that of other wildfowl. Males have inflatable throat-sacs with which they produce throbbing and drumming sounds, these being accompanied by head-pumping and the erection of short crown tufts. Males tend to display alone or in small groups, attracting females by their antics. *Biziura* in particular displays in 'leks', several displaying males attracting females for casual mating rather than forming a clear pair-bond.

148 BLACK-HEADED DUCK   Plate 47
Heteronetta atricapilla

Strange South American duck, recalling dabbling duck or pochard rather than a stiff-tail. Unique among wildfowl in being totally nest-parasitic.

FIELD IDENTIFICATION Length 35-38 cm (14-15 in). **At rest:** A relatively long-bodied, short-tailed duck with smoothly-rounded crown, stout neck, small head, and slender bill with slightly concave culmen. Males have blackish-brown head, neck and upper-parts, contrasting somewhat with vermiculated or peppered warm brown underparts and light blue-grey bill. Rather featureless, but shape distinctive; in breeding condition has obvious reddish patch at base of bill. Females are drabber and even less distinctive,except in shape; dull dark brown overall, with sides of head paler and with darker eye-stripe and crown, the neck and underparts being lighter brown and closely peppered or vermiculated at close range. Confusion possible with female Cinnamon Teal (103), which, however, is strongly patterned along flanks, whereas Black-headed Duck appears uniformly unmarked unless very close. Swims buoyantly, with short rear held high, shoulders low and breast submerged. **In flight:** Flies readily, taking off with ease, flying strongly and rapidly with head slightly drooped. Appears dark overall, with narrow whitish tips to flight feathers forming an inconspicuous trailing edge.
VOICE Relatively silent. Male gives low grunting calls and a soft whistle during display. Female produces an occasional low clucking.
DESCRIPTION Sexually dimorphic. Seasonal variation in bill colour. **Adult male:** Head and neck dull blackish, sometimes with whitish area on throat. Lower neck and entire underparts warm brown, finely vermiculated or peppered blackish, becoming ill-defined whitish on centre of belly. Upperparts dark brown, with rufous freckling on wing-coverts and narrow whitish fringes to tips of greater coverts and flight feathers. Underwing dark. **Adult female:** Crown, nape, eye-stripe and upperparts dull black-ish-brown. Indistinct buffish-white supercilium, throat and sides of head, freckled darker. Remainder of underparts as on male, but dull buffish rather than warm brown. Wing as that of male, but lacks rufous freckling on coverts. **Juvenile:** Indistinguishable from female.
BARE PARTS In all plumages, legs and feet greyish and iris brown. **Male:** Bill blue-grey, with blackish culmen ridge, nostrils, nail and extreme tip; in breeding season, an area of rose-red develops at very base. **Female:** Bill duller and darker grey than that of male, becoming dull yellowish or fleshy at base in breeding season.
MEASUREMENTS Females average slightly larger

than males. Wing of male 157-187, of female 154-182; tarsus 28-31; bill of male 40-47, of female 41-48; mean weight of male 513, of female 565.
GEOGRAPHICAL VARIATION None.
HABITS Generally met with in pairs or small groups on small, shallow pools and freshwater lakes with emergent vegetation. Mixes freely with other wild-fowl species, particularly dabbling ducks. Pair-formation occurs shortly before breeding commences. Breeding season September to December. Unlike other wildfowl seems to be a total nest parasite, laying its eggs in nests of a variety of other waterbirds, chiefly coots and Rosybills (115), but 18 species recorded as hosts, including gulls, ibises and even birds of prey. Relatively shy and inconspicuous, preferring to dive and to hide among emergent vegetation when disturbed, but flies readily and well. Feeds both by dabbling, filtering surface water like a shoveler, and by diving, when springs with forceful jump. Loafs on waterside shores, standing in shallows with body horizontal and breast rather low. Southernmost populations migrate northwards for the winter.
HABITAT Freshwater lakes, pools and marshes with much emergent or fringe vegetation, especially bulrushes, in open or sparsely-wooded country.
DISTRIBUTION Breeds over northern Argentina, south to Buenos Aires province, in central Paraguay and in Chile from Santiago to Valdivia. In winter disperses northwards to Uruguay, eastern Bolivia and southern Brazil (Rio Grande do Sul). Perhaps breeds in some of these other regions, as may be encountered in winter over most of its breeding range.
POPULATION Locally common, but easily over-looked owing to dull coloration. No population estimates have been made and it is not known to be under any great threat, but would be particularly vulnerable to wetland drainage, especially of smaller pools and marshes.
REFERENCES Johnsgard (1978), Weller (1968).

149 MASKED DUCK   Plate 47
Nomonyx dominica
Alternative name: White-winged Lake Duck

The only stiff-tail with conspicuous white wing patches, and unlike members of *Oxyura* rises easily from surface of the water when taking wing.

FIELD IDENTIFICATION Length 30-35 cm (12-14 in). **At rest:** Small duck of well-vegetated pools and marshes, long tail (often cocked high over back), heavy head and large bill easily distinguishing it as a stiff-tail. Range overlaps only with that of Ruddy Duck (150), but everywhere Masked Duck is incon-spicuous and easily overlooked owing to skulking nature. Breeding males have rufous-chestnut body, spotted with black along flanks and upperparts, with most of head black; large blue bill, with broad black tip; and white wing patches, normally hidden when on water. Unlikely to be confused, being the only stiff-tail with strong body spotting or large black nail on bill. Other plumages are dull buffish-brown, with blackish crown and nape and dark upperparts; the buffish side of head has two blackish stripes across the face and a buff supercilium, a unique combination as other stiff-tails have a single dusky band across side of head and dusky colour of crown coming to eye-level. Unlikely to be confused. **In flight:** A very small, long-tailed, dark duck, with short wings and large white patches on upperwing in all plumages. Unlikely to be mistaken, but beware Ruddy Duck with bleached and abraded pale secondaries in flight.

VOICE Poorly documented. Male sometimes utters loud 'kuri-kuroo', often repeated when surprised. Female has low hissing and clucking calls.

DESCRIPTION Sexually dimorphic. Seasonally variable. **Adult male breeding:** Front portion of head, including crown, ear-coverts and upper throat, black. Nape, lower sides of head, neck and most of body plumage rufous-chestnut, with black feather centres to breast, flanks and upperparts. Centre of underparts paler and buffer. Tail dark. Upperwing blackish, with black-tipped white secondary patch and white adjacent greater and median coverts. Underwing blackish, with white axillaries. **Adult male eclipse**: Very similar to adult female, but white in upperwing more extensive and facial pattern less contrasting. **Adult female:** Crown, hindneck and upperparts dull dark brown, with scapulars fringed pale buff. Dusky band through eye and another across lower cheeks from bill-base to nape. Supercilium, throat, and sides of head and neck buffish-white. Breast and underparts buffish-brown, intensely mottled with dark brown. Tail dark. Wing as that of male, but white on upperwing a little less extensive, especially on median coverts. **Juvenile:** Similar to female, young males with blacker crown than females; tail feathers narrower, with spiked tip.

BARE PARTS In all plumages, legs and feet greyish or blackish-brown and iris brown. **Male:** Bill bright blue, with black nail and tip and some dusky patches on culmen. **Female and juvenile:** Bill duller and greyer than that of male, with some dull blue towards base.

MEASUREMENTS Males slightly larger than females. Wing of male 135-142, of female 133-140; tail 85-90; tarsus 25-26; bill 32-35; mean weight of male 406, of female 339.

GEOGRAPHICAL VARIATION None.

HABITS Little studied. Elusive little duck of freshwater lakes and pools with much emergent vegetation; generally in small parties, with no reports of large gatherings. Breeding reported September and November in Trinidad. Nests well hidden among waterside vegetation, including ricefields; few nests documented. Keeps very much to concealment of vegetation, especially water-lilies, among which it is easily overlooked. Feeds by diving among water plants, and also loafs close to banks but always well hidden, often under large floating leaves of aquatic plants. Flies readily, chiefly in early morning and evening, springing suddenly from water by diving and appearing to fly directly from below surface; able therefore to live on smaller pools than other stiff-tails, as does not need long run for take-off. Despite elusive nature, can be rather confiding compared with other small ducks. Not strongly migratory, but dispersive movements sometimes take it well beyond normal range.

HABITAT Small lowland freshwater pools, marshes and ricefields with extensive floating vegetation. Outside breeding season, also in mangrove swamps.

DISTRIBUTION Widespread but decidedly local over tropical northern South America, east of the Andes, but reaches western Ecuador and central Peru, south to central Argentina; occurs locally through West Indies and over Central America north to central Mexico. Appears sporadically in southern USA, especially Florida and Texas, and has occasionally nested in southern Texas. Vagrants have occurred well north of normal range, with records from as far north as Massachusetts, Wisconsin, North Carolina, Maryland and Vermont.

POPULATION One of the most elusive of all ducks. Despite its wide distribution it does not seem to be common anywhere, and appears to be most numerous at the southern limit of its range in northern Argentina. Obviously it is very easy to overlook, which gives a false impression of apparent rarity. No population estimates have been made, but it is probably under no great threat. Strangely, it also appears not to be kept in captivity.

REFERENCES Johnsgard (1978).

150 RUDDY DUCK   Plate 47
Oxyura jamaicensis

The three races of this duck have at times been treated as separate species; the larger and rather different race *ferruginea* is here described separately after the main account as Peruvian Ruddy Duck.

FIELD IDENTIFICATION Length 35-43 cm (14-17 in). **At rest:** Typical stiff-tail shape, with long and often cocked tail, dumpy body and large bill, readily identifies this little duck over most of its range. Breeding male distinctive, being overall bright chestnut with white sides of head and neck, black crown and hindneck, large blue bill, and whitish undertail-coverts; Colombian race has sides of head with variable amounts of blackish. See also male White-headed Duck (151). In eclipse (winter), chestnut is replaced by greyish-brown but head pattern retained. Immatures and female dull brownish, latter washed rufous in summer, with pale buffer sides of head, crossed by single dark brown band across lower cheek. Confusion unlikely over most of range; Masked Duck (149) has two dusky cheek-bands and pale supercilium, while in Europe White-headed Duck (151) has swollen and bulging bill-base, facial pattern curving downwards towards bill-base, broader dusky cheek-band, and is larger if the two are seen together. See similar female Maccoa Duck (152) and Argentine Blue-bill (153) for discussion on differences in captivity. See also

Peruvian Ruddy Duck below. **In flight:** A small, plump little duck with relatively long tail and short, broad wings, appearing generally dark with pale underwing; white 'face' of male conspicuous. Flies low, with rapid, almost whirring beats, taking off with much pattering over surface and 'skating' when alighting. White-headed Duck and other stiff-tails similar in flight, except for Masked Duck, which has extensive white in upperwing and duskier underwing in all plumages (beware Ruddy Duck with bleached and pale secondaries offering some contrast with darkness of rest of upperwing in flight).

VOICE Relatively silent. During peculiar display, male produces ticking, tapping and belching sounds by slapping bill against inflated throat and breast, with tail vertical, and produces bubbles around water line of breast. Other calls rarely given.

DESCRIPTION Sexually dimorphic. Seasonally variable. Owing to individual variation and complexities of moult, ageing may not be possible. Nominate race described. **Adult male breeding:** Crown with raised lumps visible in display. Crown, rear ear-coverts and hindneck black. Throat and sides of head below eye white. Lower neck, breast and most of underparts chestnut, becoming whitish in centre of belly and on undertail-coverts. Tail blackish. Most of upperparts chestnut. Upperwing completely blackish-brown. Underwing pale greyish, whiter in centre. **Adult male eclipse (winter):** Chestnut areas replaced by greyish-brown; head as breeding, but duller. **Adult female:** Crown to eye level, hindneck and upperparts dark brown, with lighter brown feather tips. Upperparts washed rufous. Sides of head and neck dull buffish-brown, with darker brown band across sides of head from gape, diffusing before reaching nape. Breast and underparts dull brown, weakly barred dull buffish, becoming whiter in centre of underparts and undertail-coverts. Tail and wing as on male, but duller, underwing whiter. In eclipse (winter) duller, more greyish-brown, lacking rufous tones to body plumage, and cheek-bar less clearly defined. **Juvenile:** Resembles winter female, but body plumage more barred and central underparts more mottled. Tail feathers narrower, with spiked tip. Young males much as adult by first spring, although some become distinctly dusky on head in late winter.

BARE PARTS In all plumages, legs and feet greyish and iris brown. Bill dull grey, bright blue on breeding male, not prominently swollen at base.

MEASUREMENTS Males slightly larger than females. See also larger Peruvian Ruddy Duck below. Nominate and race *andina* similar. Wing of male 142-154 (mean 149), of female 135-149 (mean 143); tail 64-79; tarsus 30-38; bill 37-41; mean weight of male 610, of female 510.

GEOGRAPHICAL VARIATION Three races recognised. Nominate form of North and Central America, ferally established in Europe, is described above. Race *andina* of highland lakes of central and eastern Colombia (Colombian Ruddy Duck) is similar, but males have white of face variably patterned with dusky, some almost all dark; additionally, the bill is a little stouter. Latter race is somewhat intermediate between the nominate race and the

Variations in head pattern of adult male Colombian Ruddy Duck *O.j. andina* (after Adams and Slavid 1984)

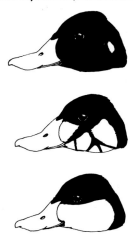

larger dark-headed race *ferruginea* of further south in the Andes, which is considered separately below as Peruvian Ruddy Duck. All three forms have sometimes been considered separate species, or the two South American races treated together as a second species, Andean Duck *O. ferruginea*.

HABITS Sociable little duck of open freshwater lakes and brackish lagoons. Typically encountered in rafts, which reach considerable numbers outside breeding season. Pair-formation occurs on breeding waters in spring. Breeds from mid April onwards in northern parts of range, although Colombian race reported breeding throughout the year. Nests hidden among waterside vegetation, often built on a floating platform of vegetation. Males sometimes attend young broods with female. After breeding, gathers in mixed flocks to moult, prior to winter dispersal. Feeds by diving, but also dabbles in shallows. Loafs in rafts on water, but sometimes at waterside along lakeshores. Swims buoyantly when resting, with prominent tail cocked well up; tail depressed to surface when active. Flies little unless moving between lakes, preferring to escape by swimming and diving when alarmed. Chiefly migratory, northern populations moving south in winter.

HABITAT Breeds by open freshwater lakes with fringe vegetation. Outside breeding season, also on brackish waters and locally in sheltered coastal bays and estuary mouths.

DISTRIBUTION Nominate race breeds chiefly over western North America from British Columbia across prairies to Manitoba, south to California and Texas and sporadically north to central Alaska, eastwards through Great Lakes region, and recently in Florida; more isolated breeding populations are found in the West Indies and central valley of Mexico. In winter most move south or to coastal areas, wintering along coastal waters north to British Columbia and Massachusetts and across inland southern USA, south through Mexico to Guatemala, vagrants reaching Hawaiian Islands. Feral population well established and increasing in British Isles, chiefly in lowland western England; mostly resident, but considerable moult migration now established and disperses widely during cold weather, with wanderers recorded from a number of other western European countries. Transatlantic vagrancy not suspected, although species regular on Bermuda in winter. Colombian race *andina* resident on lakes of central and eastern Andes of Colombia, being replaced by race *ferruginea* from southern Colombia southwards.

POPULATION North American breeding population estimated at some 600,000 individuals in mid 1970s, with some decrease through wetland drainage and through oil-spillage kills of coastal wintering flocks. In Britain, feral population continues to increase and to spread to new waters, utilising gravel-pits and reservoirs; from six breeding pairs in 1965 the population had increased to some 1,800 birds by 1983, and it seems likely that species could spread to Continental Europe in the near future. No figures available for Colombian race, but said to be still reasonably common over its restricted range.

PERUVIAN RUDDY DUCK   Plate 47
O. (j.) ferruginea
Alternative name: Andean Duck

Large black-headed race of the Ruddy Duck of mountain lakes along the full length of the Andes; sometimes regarded as a full species, but Colombian race of Ruddy Duck an intermediate link.

FIELD IDENTIFICATION Length 42-48 cm (17-19 in). Larger than northern races of Ruddy Duck, with broader bill. Breeding males lack any white on face, but often show some whitish on chin; otherwise the head is black. The chestnut body coloration is deeper than in nominate race and the central belly is mottled with dusky. In eclipse resembles female. Females are also darker than the nominate race, with facial pattern indistinct owing to darker ground colour. Confusion with Argentine Blue-bill (153) possible as both occur in lowlands of Argentina, but latter is smaller, with comparatively longer tail, has a smaller and less wide bill with straighter, less concave, culmen profile, and black of head extends down full length of neck onto upper mantle, whereas Peruvian Ruddy has foreneck and lower hindneck chestnut. Females separable on size and shape, and Argentine Blue-bill also has striking facial pattern, recalling that of female nominate Ruddy but even more clearly marked; female Peruvian Ruddy has indistinct head pattern owing to overall drab appearance. Range does not overlap with those of other similar species and it is very rare in captivity, but male differs from Blue-billed Duck (154) in much the same way as it does from Argentine Blue-bill though is close to larger Maccoa Duck (152), but latter has less spatulate bill with larger and more prominent nail. Females resemble female Blue-billed Duck, but are much larger and have distinctly darker crown, while latter has head almost uniformly dull and mottled, with crown hardly darker.

MEASUREMENTS Wing 145-163, tail 93-97, tarsus 36-38, bill 40-45, weight 817-848.

HABITAT and DISTRIBUTION Resident on high-altitude lakes along full length of the Andes, from extreme southern Colombia to Tierra del Fuego. Range spreads out into lowland regions of southern Argentina and Chile, where it overlaps with the Argentine Blue-bill.

REFERENCES Cramp and Simmons (1977), Johnsgard (1978), Lack (1986).

151 WHITE-HEADED DUCK   Plate 46
Oxyura leucocephala
Alternative name: White-headed Stifftail

Rare and patchily-distributed stiff-tail with grotesquely swollen bill, the majority of the population scattered over steppe lakes of eastern Europe and southern USSR.

FIELD IDENTIFICATION Length 43-48 cm (17-19 in). **At rest:** The only stiff-tail of the Palaearctic region, apart from ferally-established Ruddy Duck (150) in the British Isles. In all plumages, markedly swollen bill-base distinctive. Breeding male has rich rufous body coloration, becoming more sandy on the upperparts, although some birds so rufous as to recall Ruddy Duck, but lacks white on undertail-coverts and has very little black on head. Head strikingly white, with dusky crown centre and collar around upper neck and large blue bill. In eclipse, head has dusky patches more extensive, sometimes reaching eye and nape and thus recalling Ruddy Duck, but swollen-based bill distinctive. Confusion unlikely, although beware wandering Ruddy Ducks from British population. Other plumages resemble those of female Ruddy Duck, but White-headed is larger, with heavier head, has blacker crown and broader, blacker cheek-band, and obviously swollen base to bill; on White-headed, the black of the crown comes well down towards gape, giving strong downward curve not only to blackish forehead but also to whitish cheek-stripe and blackish cheek-bar below, adding to distinctly different facial appearance which also enhanced by swollen bill (these markings are much straighter on other stiff-tails). In most swimming postures, more hunched than Ruddy Duck, with higher and more rounded back profile. Swollen bill-base distinguishes females from all other stiff-tails, but compare Maccoa Duck (152).

Head-and-bill shapes of Ruddy Duck and White-headed Duck

Ruddy Duck (nominate race)

White-headed Duck   285

Males in first spring typically have head mottled dusky; in extreme examples whole head appears blackish in the field, thus suggesting Maccoa Duck. **In flight:** See Ruddy Duck. Rarely seen on the wing, but shape typical of stiff-tails. Head appears all white on breeding males, and upperwing greyer, less blackish than on Ruddy Duck, but females difficult to separate in flight.

VOICE Relatively silent. During display, erects neck and cocks tail vertically, but most calls uttered during group swimming displays, when low rattling noise and 'piping' calls uttered. A few low, harsh notes occasionally heard from females.

DESCRIPTION Sexually dimorphic. Seasonally variable. **Adult male breeding:** Head white, with dusky crown centre and some dusky freckles around eye. Upper neck blackish, shading into chestnut lower neck. Breast and mantle chestnut, becoming lighter along flanks and lower underparts, shading to greyish-buff on central belly and undertail-coverts. Scapulars, back and rump sandy-grey, vermiculated or peppered blackish, becoming rich chestnut on uppertail-coverts. Tail black. Upperwing grey-brown. Underwing pale grey, with white axillaries and paler centre. **Adult male eclipse (winter):** Similar to breeding male, but less rufous-chestnut, being distinctly greyish-buff on neck and underparts; head extensively white, but dusky patches more widespread, often reaching eye and extending over nape, with dusky mottles on ear-coverts. **Adult female:** Crown to eye level, hind-neck, and band across lower cheek almost to nape blackish-brown, with rufous feather tips. Whitish stripe along upper cheek below eye. Lower sides of head and foreneck mottled buffish-white, freckled darker. Lower neck and most of underparts rufous, with dusky subterminal barring; central underparts and undertail-coverts buffish-white, mottled dusky. Lower back, rump and uppertail-coverts greyish-brown, barred darker. Wings and tail as on male. In winter (eclipse), duller brown, less rufous, on body and with whiter sides of head, making dark cheek-bands more conspicuous. **Juvenile:** Resembles winter female, but cheek pattern more striking, with whiter sides of head. Upperparts darker and underparts buffer. First-winter males have duller head pattern than females, with more extensive dusky on sides of head. By first spring young males resemble adult, though head extensively mottled dusky, often appearing black-headed, but otherwise plumage and bill colour close to adult breeding; not fully white-headed until second spring. Through first winter, juveniles may be aged by narrower and more spike-tipped tail feathers.

BARE PARTS Male: Bill swollen at base, bright blue; greyish in eclipse. Legs and feet greyish, with blackish webs; sometimes reddish. Iris yellow to orange-yellow. **Female:** Bill dark grey, slightly less swollen than that of male. Legs and feet dark grey. Iris pale yellow. **Juvenile:** Bill as female, but browner at first, becoming greyer during autumn; young males have lighter grey bill than young females during first winter. Legs and feet brownish-grey. Iris light brown.

MEASUREMENTS Males typically larger than females. Wing 148-172 (mean: male 162, female 159); tail 75-100; tarsus 33-38; bill 43-48; mean weight of male 722, of female 701.

GEOGRAPHICAL VARIATION None.

HABITS Everywhere extremely localised. Typically in small parties or pairs in spring, but outside breeding season gathers in flocks which reach considerable numbers on key wintering waters. Pair-formation occurs in spring on breeding waters, but pair-bond casual and tenuous. Breeds from late May onwards. Nests on ground in waterside vegetation, often utilising old nest of some other species, typically Coots or other diving ducks. Unlike most others of genus, males do not normally attend females and young broods, but gather to moult during incubation. Feeds by diving, and also dabbles in shallows. Loafs on water in rafts, or alone, typically just within reeds at edge of open water. Flies rarely (presumed to do so chiefly at night). General behaviour much as that of others of genus. Relict western populations basically resident, but Asiatic population strongly migratory, leaving breeding waters late September and early October and returning late April to breeding grounds.

HABITAT Breeds in open steppe-like country, preferring small lakes adjoining larger open lakes, with relatively shallow water and extensive fringe and emergent vegetation; chiefly on fresh water, but tolerates high degree of salinity. In winter, on larger and more open lakes, but preferring close proximity of fringe vegetation; also on large saline coastal lagoons.

DISTRIBUTION Breeds in very small numbers in Europe and North Africa, with pockets in southern Spain, Tunisia and Romania and perhaps Algeria; re-introduction programme recently started in Hungary. Small numbers also breed in central Turkey, but bulk of population breeds on steppe lakes of southern USSR, chiefly Kazakhstan, east to extreme northwest China. Mediterranean birds basically resident, although local movements occur as lakes dry out; Tunisian population considerably swollen in winter, suggesting undetected numbers may be breeding elsewhere in North Africa. Central Asian birds move south in winter, chiefly to lakes of western Turkey and also to Pakistan, rarely to northwest India, and eastern Caspian Sea, but some remain on unfrozen waters in Central Asia. Formerly bred more widely around Mediterranean basin, and wintered also in Egypt and Iraq. Vagrants recorded from several central and western European countries north to British Isles, Netherlands, Poland and both East and West Germany; some suspected to be escapes, but most are likely to be genuine vagrants as rare in captivity.

POPULATION Breeding range now fragmented and contracting, chiefly through drainage of shallow lakes and irrigation schemes. Tiny Spanish population now slowly increasing following protection measures, after considerable reduction in recent decades. From winter counts total population considered to be between 10,000 and 15,000 individuals, of which some 1,000 Tunisia, 9,000 Turkey (mostly on Burdur Gölü), 100 Romania, 800 Caspian Sea and 1,000 Pakistan. Pakistan winter numbers have drastically declined in recent years, following decline of Soviet breeding population.

REFERENCES Cramp and Simmons (1977), Eigenhuis and Menkveld (1985), Esquivias and Moreno (1986), Madge (1984), Torres (1984).

152 MACCOA DUCK Plate 46
Oxyura maccoa

The only stiff-tail of tropical Africa, perhaps most closely related to the Palaearctic White-headed Duck (151), despite male plumage similarities to the South American and Australian species.

FIELD IDENTIFICATION Length 48-51 cm (19-20 in). **At rest:** Size and shape typical of the genus. Breeding male rich chestnut, with black head and upper neck and bright blue bill. Other plumages dull brown, with facial pattern of dusky cheek-band and crown and pale stripe below eye. Unlikely to be confused within range, where Southern Pochard (114) only other all-dark diving duck with grey bill but shape quite different; striking head pattern and stout dark grey bill of female prevent confusion with other African ducks. Compare also White-backed Duck (10). Male confusable with other black-headed stiff-tails in captivity, but all are rare in collections. Chestnut lower neck prevents confusion with Argentine Blue-bill (153) and Blue-billed Duck (154), and it is markedly bulkier than either, with a larger bill with broad and prominently-curved whitish nail; more difficult to distinguish from Peruvian Ruddy Duck (150), but bill is less spatulate, nostrils more swollen, and has larger nail and greyer back and rump (hidden). Females closest to female White-headed Duck, but bill-base not markedly swollen, although nostrils flared; nail larger; facial markings straighter, not strongly curving towards gape; and foreneck whiter, forming pale collar. Nail and tip of bill distinctly whitish (grey, like rest of bill, on other stiff-tails). **In flight:** Rarely seen in sustained flight. General shape and appearance typical of other stiff-tails (see Ruddy Duck).
VOICE Relatively silent. During display, male utters loud, harsh frog-like croaks and grunts and a trumpeting, vibrating 'prrr'. Female utters short grunts.
DESCRIPTION Sexually dimorphic. Seasonally variable. **Adult male breeding:** Head and upper neck black. Lower neck and most of body plumage chestnut, with centre of underparts and undertail-coverts whitish. Back and rump brownish, mottled grey. Tail blackish. Upperwing greyish-brown. Underwing greyish-white. **Adult male eclipse:** Resembles adult female, but crown blacker. **Adult female:** Crown to eye level and band across lower cheek dark greyish-brown; whitish line along sides of head below eye; remainder of sides of head and neck whitish, becoming light brown on neck. Upperparts dark greyish-brown, vermiculated and freckled whitish and buffish. Underparts similar, but more barred whitish-buff on flanks; centre of underparts whitish. Wing and tail as on male. **Juvenile:** Resembles female, but tail feathers narrower and more spiked at tip. Young males begin to darken on head at about seven months and become more uniform brown on body, but do not attain full adult male plumage until at least a year old.

BARE PARTS In all plumages, legs and feet grey and iris brown. **Male:** Bill bright blue, with whitish nail when breeding; duller and greyer in eclipse. **Female and juvenile:** Bill dark grey, with whitish nail and very tip, at least on females.
MEASUREMENTS Sexes similar. Wing 155-173, tail 87-88, tarsus 34-39, bill 36-42, weight 450-820 (mean 554).
GEOGRAPHICAL VARIATION None.
HABITS Less sociable than most others of genus, generally occurring in pairs or family parties, although non-breeders form small gatherings. Strongly territorial in breeding season. Males display actively on breeding waters and may mate with several females during season. Breeding season prolonged, depending on water levels, but peak breeding usually September-December. Nests close to waterside, often utilising old nests of Coots, several females often nesting in close proximity. Male takes no part in attending broods, and may be driven away by female if in vicinity. Feeds by diving; most active during daytime. Loafs close to emergent vegetation. Flies little; takes to air with difficulty, pattering for considerable distance over surface before becoming airborne and usually flying low over surface and only for short distances. General behaviour otherwise typical of the genus. Non-migratory, although disperses when water levels become too low.
HABITAT Shallow freshwater lakes and marshes with extensive emergent and fringe vegetation. Moves to larger and more open waters, including brackish and saline lakes, as preferred waters become dry. Recorded from sea level to 3000 m, but rare in coastal districts.
DISTRIBUTION Local resident in eastern and southern Africa, from highlands of Ethiopia southwards through East Africa to northern Tanzania, eastern Zaire, Rwanda and Burundi; also locally common southern Africa from Zimbabwe to the Cape. Some dispersal, especially in southern Africa, according to seasonal water levels.
POPULATION Locally common in parts of southern Africa and in Rift Valley lakes of East Africa; elsewhere rather uncommon. It seems to be increasing in parts of South Africa and is not considered to be under any threat. No population estimates have been made.
REFERENCES Brown et al. (1982).

153 ARGENTINE BLUE-BILL Plate 47
Oxyura vittata

Alternative names: Lake Duck, Argentine Ruddy Duck, Argentine Blue-billed Duck

Replaces the Ruddy Duck (150) over most of lowland southern South America, but overlaps with Peruvian race in some regions. Despite plumage similarities with Ruddy, it appears to be more closely related to the 'blue-bills' of Africa and Australia.

FIELD IDENTIFICATION Length 40-46 cm (16-18 in). **At rest:** Range overlaps with that of Peruvian Ruddy Duck, but Argentine Blue-bill is smaller, relatively longer-tailed, and has less spatulate bill which is relatively slightly shorter and higher at the base and has straighter, less concave, culmen profile. Breeding males similar in plumage, but Argentine Blue-bill is darker chestnut and has black of neck just extending to upper mantle (lower neck chestnut on Peruvian Ruddy). Females perhaps more strikingly different: female Argentine is closer to female of nominate Ruddy Duck, having striking facial pattern of pale and dark cheek-stripes; female Peruvian · Ruddy has indistinct head pattern owing to general drab appearance. In captivity, distinguished from female nominate Ruddy Duck by having even more striking facial pattern, with whiter throat and face-stripe and blacker cheek-bar; the facial stripes curve slightly downwards towards bill-base in manner recalling larger White-headed Duck (151), but the dusky cheek-band is narrower and the bill not markedly swollen at the base. See also males of Maccoa Duck (152) and Blue-billed Duck (154) for discussion on identifying birds in captivity. **In flight:** Shape, manner of flight and basic appearance typical of the genus (see Ruddy Duck). Possibly distinguishable from Peruvian Ruddy, in areas where the two occur together, by smaller size and relatively longer tail, but neither species likely to be seen in sustained flight.

VOICE Relatively silent. During display, male produces a low drumming noise by striking bill against inflated breast.

DESCRIPTION Sexually dimorphic. Seasonally variable. **Adult male breeding:** Head and upper neck black, colour not quite extending to breast on foreneck but just reaching upper mantle on hindneck. Remainder of body plumage rich chestnut, becoming whitish on centre of belly. Tail blackish. Upperwing blackish, with some rufous speckling intermixed. **Adult male eclipse:** Resembles adult female. **Adult female:** Crown to eye level, nape, and band across lower sides of head greyish-black. Buffish-white stripe below eye from base of bill to nape. Lower sides of head and foreneck buffish-white. Breast and most of underparts dull brown, barred buffish-white. Upperparts darker brown. Wings and tail as on male. **Juvenile:** As female, but browner below and paler on upperparts, with browner-buff fringes to body feathers; tail feathers narrower, more spiked or notched at tip.

BARE PARTS In all plumages, legs and feet dark grey and iris brown. Bill bright blue on breeding male; dark grey in other plumages, including eclipse male.

MEASUREMENTS Males a little larger than females. Wing of male 137-155, of female 132-140; tail 85-87; tarsus 34-36; bill 36-45; weight 550-675 (single samples: male 610, female 560).

GEOGRAPHICAL VARIATION None.

HABITS Little studied. Flocking occurs outside breeding season, when rafts of up to 400 recorded during late May, towards end of pre-breeding moult. Otherwise more usually met with in small parties. Breeding season mid October to early January in eastern Argentina, but probably more prolonged elsewhere. Nest built close to waterside, a weak platform of vegetation, unlike more elaborate construction of Peruvian Ruddy Duck. Males probably gather to moult during incubation.

General behaviour much as that of others of genus. Generally rather shy and secretive. Some dispersal after breeding as shallow waters dry out, with southern populations moving north in winter. A few records of long-distance vagrancy during drought conditions in main part of range (see Distribution).

HABITAT Lowland freshwater lakes and marshes with extensive fringe vegetation. Prefers shallow-water lakes, but occurs on larger open waters outside breeding season. In Chile, said to prefer smaller, vegetated pools to large lakes.

DISTRIBUTION Breeds over much of lowland Chile and Argentina, in Chile from Atacama to Llanquihue and in Argentina from La Rioja and San Juan south to Tierra del Fuego; also in adjacent regions of Uruguay and southeast Brazil (Rio Grande do Sul). Southern populations disperse northwards in winter, reaching Paraguay and south-central Brazil. Following period of exceptional drought on mainland of South America in 1916/1917 must have dispersed widely, as vagrants recorded on the Falkland Islands and even Deception Island in sub-Antarctic waters.

POPULATION Widespread; apparently nowhere common, but is unlikely to be under any great threat to its numbers. No population estimates have been made. Drainage of shallow lakes and marshes would be its greatest threat.

REFERENCES Johnsgard (1978).

154 BLUE-BILLED DUCK   Plate 46
Oxyura australis

Alternative names: Australian Blue-bill, Australian Blue-billed Duck

Apart from extraordinary Musk Duck (155), the only stiff-tail of Australia; perhaps most closely related to Argentine Blue-bill (153). Despite similarity of male plumage to that of several others of the genus, the female is distinctively plain, having practically uniform head pattern.

FIELD IDENTIFICATION Length 35-44 cm (14-17 in). **At rest:** Distinctive within range. Breeding male has large blue bill, black head and dark chestnut body plumage, and is unlike any other Australian duck; Hardhead (120) is more slender, with longer and slimmer bill, and has white undertail-coverts and darker or patterned bill. Other plumages are drab brownish, with head almost unpatterned; in general plumage coloration they recall female Musk Duck, but are considerably smaller, warmer brown, shorter-bodied, and have more rounded head shape and slightly concave culmen profile (culmen straighter and almost drooped at tip on Musk Duck, which has broadly triangular head-and-bill shape). In captivity, males confusable with several other stiff-tails, but black extends to lower foreneck as on Argentine Blue-bill, but unlike on Maccoa (152) or Peruvian Ruddy (150); compared with Argentine Blue-bill, it is darker chestnut and has slightly shorter tail and more dusky undertail-coverts (whitish or rusty on Argentine). Females lack prominent head pattern of other female stiff-tails. **In flight:** Typical stiff-tail shape (see Ruddy Duck). Only much larger Musk Duck could be briefly confused, but neither spends much time on the wing.

VOICE Relatively silent. During display, mechanical rattling sounds may be heard from male. Female occasionally gives a low quack.
DESCRIPTION Sexually dimorphic. Seasonally variable. **Adult male breeding:** Head and neck black, with rusty feather fringes when fresh. Almost entire body plumage dark chestnut, darkest on breast and fore-flanks; central underparts and under-tail-coverts whitish, with dusky brown mottling. Upperwing dark brown, with some chestnut freckling on coverts. Underwing greyish. **Adult male eclipse:** Closer to female, but head and neck darker and flanks washed brighter chestnut. **Adult female:** Head dull dark brown, freckled darker, paler on chin and throat and with indistinct lighter area below eye. Most of body plumage similar, but both upperparts and underparts with buffish feather tips, giving closely-barred appearance; central underparts paler. Wing and tail as on male, but browner. **Juvenile:** Much as female, but lighter brown overall and less clearly barred; tail feathers narrower, with notched or spiked tip.
BARE PARTS In all plumages, legs and feet grey and iris brown. Male has clear blue bill when breeding, duller and greyer in eclipse; in other plumages bill dull grey.
MEASUREMENTS Males a little larger than females. Wing of male 150-173 (mean 160), of female 142-163 (mean 153); tail 65-70; tarsus 33-36; bill 32-48; mean weight of male 812, of female 852.
GEOGRAPHICAL VARIATION None.
HABITS Very sociable outside breeding season, gathering in large rafts on favoured waters. During the breeding season more solitary and elusive, hiding among emergent vegetation and easily overlooked. Pair-bond tenuous, male occupying display territory to which female attracted and mated. Breeding season September-February, the season being more regular than in several other Australian ducks owing to species' attachment to areas of permanent water, several of the others being opportunist breeders when water levels suitable after rains. Nests on ground by waterside, in tangled vegetation or in reeds, sometimes utilising old nests of other waterbirds. General behaviour typical of that of the genus. Occasionally clambers out on to partially-submerged branches and stumps, but more typically rests on water. Feeds by dabbling, as well as by diving, and often in association with Coots. Somewhat migratory; most leave inland swamps and congregate on more open waters further south to moult, returning again prior to start of breeding season.
HABITAT Breeds in extensive densely-vegetated permanent inland swamps, occasionally on smaller and more open pools and locally in coastal districts. Outside breeding season, on more open deep-water lakes and slow rivers. Rarely on salt water.
DISTRIBUTION Breeds over inland swamps of southern Australia, chiefly in Murray-Darling river systems of New South Wales and Victoria, but rarely west to Lake Eyre in South Australia, south to Tasmania and north to southeast Queensland. A more isolated population occurs in coastal lowlands of extreme southwest Western Australia. Basically resident, but majority leave inland breeding swamps

after breeding and gather on larger lakes and rivers of southern New South Wales and Victoria.
POPULATION Locally common, with flocks of 500-1,000 reported in the southeast and up to 300 in winter in the southwest in recent years; far more elusive in breeding season. No total population estimates have been made, but wetland drainage has caused numbers to decline in several coastal areas. The species is protected, but the major problem is conservation of its habitat rather than of the bird itself.
REFERENCES Frith (1967), RAOU (1984).

155 MUSK DUCK   Plate 16
Biziura lobata

A large and bizarre Australian duck, one of the oddest of all wildfowl; fully-grown males may be twice the size of females, and take several years to reach their full size. The name is derived from the strong musky odour produced by the preen gland of males, strongest when in breeding condition.

FIELD IDENTIFICATION Length: male 61-73 cm (24-29 in), female 47-60 cm (18-24 in).
At rest: Unmistakable. Both sexes are large, long-bodied, dark oily grey-brown diving ducks with a long tail. Adult males considerably larger than females or immature males, and have distinctive large fleshy lobe under base of bill. Typically swims low in water, with head erect, recalling cormorant rather than a duck, but head shape (without lobe) distinctly triangular, with straight culmen line to forehead. When resting, long tail often held cocked and spread like a spiked fan. Confusion highly unlikely, though female Blue-billed Duck (154) similar in coloration but much smaller, shorter-bodied, and with rounded head and slightly upcurving bill profile. Often mixes with Blue-billed Ducks outside breeding season. **In flight:** Rarely seen in flight, but can fly well. Long, heavy body, neck and tail and broad wings, coupled with all-dark appearance (paler belly centre may be visible) and large size, distinctive.
VOICE Male noisy in display, often heard at night and voice far-carrying. Display elaborate, including raising spread tail over back, stretching neck to expose distended bill flap, kicking water and rotating body while uttering loud grunt and shrill whistle, accompanied by splashing 'plonks' of water. Otherwise relatively silent.
DESCRIPTION All plumages similar, but considerable size variation. Plumage distinctly oily. Overall dark brownish-black, finely barred buff, with whitish feather tips; crown and nape blacker than sides of head and neck, which are more closely freckled with buff; centre of belly whitish. Flight feathers and tail blacker. Juveniles increase in size over several years, though precise age at which males reach full size uncertain and may be variable.
BARE PARTS Adult male has enormous fleshy lobe under bill that hangs down to breast when neck retracted. Female has only very small and inconspicuous lobe. Juveniles resemble females, gradually attaining lobe over several years (and increasing in body size accordingly). At all ages, bill, lobe, legs

and feet blackish-grey and iris brown; juveniles may be distinguished from females by having yellowish terminal area of underside of bill.

MEASUREMENTS Considerable sexual difference. **Male:** Wing 205-240 (mean 223), tail 110-150, tarsus 48-52, bill 36-47, weight 1811-3120 (mean 2398). **Female:** Wing 165-202 (mean 185), bill 31-41, weight 993-1844 (mean 1551).

GEOGRAPHICAL VARIATION No races recognised, although eastern males apparently do not utter whistle in display as western birds habitually do.

HABITS Outside breeding season, forms scattered parties on open-water lakes, often mixing with rafts of Blue-billed Ducks. Non-breeders in small groups during breeding season, but adult male strongly territorial. Pair-bond very tenuous, displaying male attracting females which are roughly mated in rape fashion. Display may occur at almost any time of the year, but reaches intensity during the breeding season, from June to September. Nests are among vegetation at water's edge, sometimes in hollow of fallen tree at water level. Several females may nest within territory of one male. Feeds by diving in deep water, sinking effortlessly below surface, but also dabbles. When actively feeding, spends little time on surface, appearing momentarily between dives. Loafs by swimming more buoyantly with tail partially cocked and fanned; at other times swims very low in water, with merely upper back, head and neck visible. Rarely comes on to land, being ungainly, but reported as sometimes walking quite well over short distances. Not often seen in flight,

but flies well, taking off with much pattering over surface and alighting with considerable 'skating' and splashing. Long-distance movements are believed to take place only at night. Performs considerable movements after the breeding season, these believed to be mostly of juveniles dispersing southwards from inland breeding swamps.

HABITAT Breeds by deep freshwater and brackish lakes and swamps with extensive emergent and fringe vegetation. Outside breeding season, on more open lakes and locally on sheltered coastal bays and estuaries.

DISTRIBUTION Widespread in southern Australia, although absent from arid central region. Range extends from southern Queensland, through Murray-Darling region of New South Wales to the Eyre Peninsula of South Australia, and across Victoria to Tasmania; when conditions suitable, also northwest to Lake Eyre. Population of southwestern Western Australia somewhat isolated, but some interchange believed to take place between the two populations. Southern regions receive larger numbers in winter, suggesting that considerable movements take place. Vagrants occasionally recorded north to North West Cape of Western Australia.

POPULATION No estimates have been made, but this is still a numerous bird generally. Any threats to its numbers would be purely through extensive wetland drainage.

REFERENCES Frith (1967), Lowe (1966), RAOU (1984).

GLOSSARY

Throughout this book, the number of technical or unfamiliar terms has been intentionally kept to a minimum. Clarification of bird topography and plumage stages will be found in the section 'How to use this book'.

ABERRANT: Abnormal; generally referring to a species differing strikingly from the others of a group or to abnormally-plumaged individuals.

AFROTROPICAL: Faunal region of sub-Saharan Africa, formerly called the Ethiopian region.

ALLOPATRIC: Referring to situations where two or more similar forms replace each other geographically without overlapping. Compare SYMPATRIC.

ARBOREAL: Living in trees.

AUSTRAL: Of the southern hemisphere.

AUSTRALASIA: Australia and New Zealand and adjacent islands.

BROWN-HEAD: Vernacular term, typically used for mergansers and allies in 'female-type' plumage, when sex not necessarily established: i.e. juvenile male, eclipse male and females appear similar in the field. Such stages of Smew are usually termed RED-HEAD.

CERE: Bare fleshy covering at the base of the bill.

CONSPECIFIC: Of the same species.

DABBLING: Feeding on surface of the water.

DIMORPHIC: Occurring in two forms (e.g. plumages differing between the sexes).

ECLIPSE: Dull, female-like plumage acquired by many male ducks after post-breeding moult.

ENDEMIC: Confined exclusively to a defined area.

FALCATE: Sickle-shaped.

FERAL: Non-native population of captive origin, but breeding in the wild.

GENUS: A classification term, encompassing several related species and indicated by the first part of a scientific name. Plural GENERA.

HOLARCTIC: Faunal region of northern hemisphere north of the tropics; includes the Palaearctic and Nearctic regions combined.

IMMATURE: Not adult; term used to describe a variety of plumage stages following juvenile, and often includes juvenile stage if precise age not known. SUB-ADULT sometimes used for later stages.

JUVENILE: The first feathered plumage stage replacing downy stage; this plumage often lasts only for a few weeks.

LEUCISTIC: Describes plumage aberration of genetic origin, typically of faded or washed-out coloration.

MONOTYPIC: Describes a classification grouping which contains a single member only.

NEARCTIC: North American faunal region.

NEOTROPICAL: Central and South American faunal region.

NOMINATE RACE: The first-named race of a species, with its scientific name the same as the specific name.

PALAEARCTIC: Faunal region of Europe, North Africa and Asia, north of the tropics. Often divided into eastern and western sectors for convenience, the division being roughly the Ural Mountains and Caspian Sea.

PARAMO: Vegetation zone of the Andes, basically humid grasslands above the tree-line at high altitude.

PUNA: Vegetation zone of the Andes, basically dry grasslands and semi-arid plateau of the central Andes.

RACE: Population within a geographical area, differing from other members of the same species elsewhere in species' range, but not to the extent of being considered a different species. Also termed SUBSPECIES.

RAFT: A closely-packed flock of ducks on the water.

RED-HEAD: See BROWN-HEAD.

RELICT DISTRIBUTION: A distribution pattern that is relatively large, but consisting of isolated, well-spaced pockets, indicating that these pockets may have been joined in former times.

SAWBILL: General term for mergansers and allies, with reference to the serrated cutting edges of the mandibles.

SPECULUM: A brightly-coloured area of the wing, typically being the highly-glossed secondaries of the upperwing of dabbling ducks and shelducks.

SUB-ADULT: See IMMATURE.

SUB-ECLIPSE: A plumage stage between eclipse plumage and full breeding plumage, a form of supplementary plumage.

SUBSPECIES: See RACE.

SUPERSPECIES: A group of two or more closely-related species that replace each other geographically. May be regarded by extremists either as full species or as races of one species.

SYMPATRIC: Referring to situations where breeding ranges of similar forms overlap. Compare ALLOPATRIC.

STIFF-TAILS: Group name for members of the genera *Oxyura, Nomonyx* and *Biziura*; diving ducks with a strangely stiff tail which is often carried erect.

TAIGA: Northern forest belt of Scandinavia and Asia, south of the TUNDRA.

TAXONOMY: The study of classification.

TRIBE: A subdivision of a subfamily that includes one or more related genera.

TUNDRA: Open Arctic lands between the forested TAIGA zone and the ice regions of the far north.

UP-ENDING: Feeding by tipping forward with head and fore body submerged and rear sticking above the water surface; method typically adopted by most non-diving waterfowl feeding in deeper water.

VERMICULATED: Finely marked with narrow wavy lines, appearing plain in the field, except at very close range.

BIBLIOGRAPHY

The most useful reference sources used while researching the species texts are given after each account; these and more general works of reference are detailed below.

Adams, J, and Slavid, ER (1984) Cheek plumage pattern in Colombian Ruddy Duck *Oxyura jamaicensis. Ibis* 126: 405-7.

—— , and Ripley, SD (1968) *Handbook of the Birds of India and Pakistan.* Vol. 1. Oxford University Press, Bombay.

Alison, R (1975) *Breeding biology and behaviour of the old-squaw (Clangula hyemalis L.).* American Ornithologists' Union Monographs, no. 18.

Bailey, EP, and Trapp, JL (1984) A second wild breeding population of the Aleutian Canada Goose. *American Birds* 38: 284-6.

Baker, RH (1951) The avifauna of Micronesia, its origin, evolution, and distribution. *University of Kansas Museum of Natural History Publications* 3: 1-359.

Banko, W (1960) *The Trumpeter Swan: its history, habits and population in the United States.* US Department of the Interior, Fish and Wildlife Service.

Bauer, KM, and Glutz von Blotzheim, UN (1968) *Handbuch der Vögel Mitteleuropas.* Vol. 2. Akademische Verlagsgesellschaft, Frankfurt am Main.

Beekman, JH, Dirksen, S, and Slagboom, TH (1985) Population size and breeding success of Bewick's Swans wintering in Europe in 1983-4. *Wildfowl* 36: 5-12.

Bellrose, FC (1976) *Ducks, Geese and Swans of North America.* Stackpole, Harrisburg.

Birkhead, M, and Perrins, C (1986) *The Mute Swan in Britain.* Croom Helm, Beckenham.

Blake, ER (1977) *Manual of Neotropical Birds.* Vol. 1. University of Chicago Press, Chicago.

Bond, J (1985) *Birds of the West Indies.* Collins, London.

Bousfield, MA, and Syroechkovskiy, YV (1985) A review of Soviet research on the Lesser Snow Goose on Wrangel Island, USSR. *Wildfowl* 36: 13-20.

Brazil, MA (1981) Geographical variation in the bill patterns of Whooper Swans. *Wildfowl* 32: 129-31.

Briggs, SV (1982) Food habits of the Freckled Duck and associated waterfowl in north-western New South Wales. *Wildfowl* 33: 88-93.

British Birds (editors) (1985) Plumage, age and moult terminology. *British Birds* 78: 419-27.

Brown, LH, Urban, EK, and Newman, K (1982) *The Birds of Africa.* Vol. 1. Academic Press, London.

Cheng, T-H (1976) *Distributional List of Chinese Birds.* Peking.

Cramp, S, and Simmons, KEL (eds.) (1977) *The Birds of the Western Palearctic.* Vol. 1. Oxford University Press, Oxford.

Curth, P (1954) *Die Mittelsäger.* A. Ziemsen Verlag, Wittenberg Lutherstadt.

Dau, CP, and Kistchinski, AA (1977) Seasonal movements and distribution of the Spectacled Eider. *Wildfowl* 28: 65-96.

Davies, A (1985) The British Mandarins — outstripping the ancestors. *BTO News* 136: 12.

de Knijff, P (1983) Mystery Photograph 10: Pochard × Tufted Duck. *Dutch Birding* 5: 11-12.

Delacour, J (1954-64) *The Waterfowl of the World.* 4 vols. Country Life, London.

Dementiev, GP, and Gladkov, NA (1952) *Birds of the Soviet Union.* Vol. 4. 1967 translation, Israel Program for Scientific Translation, Jerusalem.

de Schauensee, RM (1966) *The Species of Birds of South America.* Livingstone, Narberth; (1984) *The Birds of China.* Oxford University Press, Oxford.

Dorward, DF, Norman, FI, and Cowling, SJ (1980) The Cape Barren Goose in Victoria, Australia: management related to agriculture. *Wildfowl* 31: 144-50.

Douthwaite, RJ (1980) Seasonal changes in the food supply, numbers and male plumages of Pygmy Geese on the Thamalakane river in northern Botswana. *Wildfowl* 31: 94-8.

Driver, PM (1974) *In Search of the Eider.* Saturn Press, London.

Dumbell, G (1986) The New Zealand Brown Teal: 1845-1985. *Wildfowl* 37: 71-87.

Ebbinge, B, van den Bergh, L, van Haperen, A, Lok, M, Philippona, J, Rooth, J, and Timmerman, A (1986) Numbers and distribution of wild geese in the Netherlands. *Wildfowl* 37: 28-34.

Eigenhuis, KJ (1985) Scaup *Aythya marila,* Lesser Scaup *Aythya affinis,* 'Scaup Type' and 'Lesser Scaup' type. *Wielewaal* 51: 135-7.

—— , and Menkveld, E (1985) Voorkomen en rui-en leeftijdskenmerken van de Witkopeend *Oxyura leucocephala. Wielewaal* 51: 300-4.

Eldridge, JL (1979) Display inventory of the Torrent Duck. *Wildfowl* 30: 5-15; (1985) Display inventory of the Blue Duck. *Wildfowl* 36: 109-21; (1986a) Territoriality in a river specialist: the Blue Duck. *Wildfowl* 37: 123-35; (1986b) Observations on a pair of Torrent Ducks. *Wildfowl* 37: 113-22.

Erskine, AJ (1972) *Buffleheads.* Canadian Wildlife Service Monographs, no. 4.

Esquivias, JA, and Moreno, JM (1986) Variation du dessin céphalique des mâles de l'Erismature à tête blanche *(Oxyura leucocephala). Alauda* 54: 197-206.

FESC (1985) Various papers in: *Rare and Endangered Birds of the Far East.* Far East Science Centre, Academy of Sciences of the USSR, Vladivostok.

Fjeldså, J, and Krabbe, N (1986) Some range extensions and other unusual records of Andean birds. *Bulletin of the British Ornithologists' Club* 106: 115-24.

Flint, VE (1984) *Krasnaya Kniga SSSR.* Lesnaya Promyshlennost, Moscow.

—— , Boehme, RL, Kostin, YV, and Kuznetsov, AA (1984) *A Field Guide to the Birds of the USSR.* Princeton University Press, New Jersey.

Frith, HJ (1967) *Waterfowl in Australia.* Angus & Robertson, Sydney.

Gantlett, SJM (1985) Hybrid resembling Ring-necked Duck. *British Birds* 78: 42-3.

Geldenhuys, JN (1981a) Moults and moult localities of the South African Shelduck. *Ostrich* 52: 129-33; (1981b) Breeding ecology of the South African Shelduck. *South African Journal of Wildlife Research* 10.

Gillham, E, Harrison, JM, and Harrison, JG (1966) A study of certain *Aythya* hybrids. *The Wildfowl Trust 17th Annual Report:* 49-65.

Gole, P (1982) Status of *Anser indicus* in Asia with special reference to India. *Aquila* 89: 141-9.

Gunn, WWH (1973) Environmental stress on the Whistling Swan. *Wildfowl* 24: 5-7.

Hall, R (1986) The Freckled Duck — An Ancient Enigma. *Wildfowl World* 94: 20; (1987) Blue Duck and White-waters. *Wildfowl World* 96: 23.

Hansen, HA (1973) Trumpeter Swan management. *Wildfowl* 24: 27-32.

Harrison, JM, and Harrison, JG (1968) Wigeon × Chiloe Wigeon hybrid resembling American Wigeon. *British Birds* 61: 169-71.

Hawkes, B (1970) The Marbled Teal. *Wildfowl* 21: 87-8.

Hayes, FN, and Williams, M (1982) The status, aviculture and re-establishment of Brown Teal in New Zealand. *Wildfowl* 33: 73-80.

Hilty, SL, and Brown, WL (1986) *A Guide to the Birds of Colombia.* Princeton University Press, New Jersey.

Holmes, DA (1977) A report on the White-winged Wood Duck in southern Sumatra. *Wildfowl* 28: 61-4.

Holt, C (1984) Separating Mandarins and Wood Ducks in late summer. *British Birds* 77: 227-32.

Humphrey, PS, and Butsch, RS (1958) The anatomy of the Labrador Duck *Camptorhynchus labradorius* (Gmelin). *Smithsonian Miscellaneous Collections* 135 (7): 1-23.

—— , and Livezey, BC (1982a) Molts and plumages of Flying Steamer-ducks. *University of Kansas Museum of Natural History Occasional Papers* 103: 1-30; (1982b) Flightlessness in Flying Steamer-ducks. *Auk* 99: 368-72; (1985) Nest, eggs, and downy young of the White-headed Flightless Steamer-duck. *Neotropical Ornithology Ornithological Monographs* 36: 945-53.

—— , and Parkes, KC (1959) An approach to the study of molts and plumages. *Auk* 76: 1-31.

—— , and Thompson, MC (1981) A new species of steamer-duck *(Tachyeres)* from Argentina. *University of Kansas Museum of Natural History Occasional Papers* 95: 1-12.

Inskipp, C, and Inskipp, TP (1985) *A Guide to the Birds of Nepal.* Croom Helm, Beckenham.

IWRB (1981) *Proceedings of IWRB Symposium, Sapporo, Japan.*

Jepson, PR, and Baker, T (1984) Juvenile Fulvous Whistling Ducks in Morocco in September 1980. *Dutch Birding* 6: 94-5.

Johnsgard, PA (1965) Observations on some aberrant Australian Anatidae. *The Wildfowl Trust 16th Annual Report:* 73-83; (1965a) *Handbook* of Waterfowl Behaviour. Cornell University Press, Ithaca; (1966) The biology and relationships of the Torrent Duck. The Wildfowl Trust 17th Annual Report: 66-74; (1975) Waterfowl of North America. Indiana University Press, Bloomington; (1978) Ducks, Geese and Swans of the World. University of Nebraska Press, Lincoln and London.

Johnson, AW (1965) The Birds of Chile, and Adjacent Regions of Argentina, Bolivia and Peru. Vol. 1. Platt Establecementios Graficos, Buenos Aires.

Jonsson, L (1978) Birds of Mountain Regions. Penguin, Harmondsworth.

Kear, J (1972) The Blue Duck of New Zealand. Living Bird 11: 175-92; (1975) Salvadori's Duck of New Guinea. Wildfowl 26: 104-10; (1979) Wildfowl at risk, 1979. Wildfowl 30: 159-61; (1985) Eric Hosking's Wildfowl. Croom Helm, Beckenham.

——, and Berger, AJ (1980) The Hawaiian Goose. Poyser, Berkhamsted.

——, and Scarlett, RJ (1970) The Auckland Islands Merganser. Wildfowl 21: 78-86.

——, and Williams, G (1978) Waterfowl at risk. Wildfowl 29: 5-21.

King, WB (1981) Endangered Birds of the World: The ICBP Bird Red Data Book. Smithsonian Institution Press, Washington.

Kistchinski, AA (1971) Biological notes on the Emperor Goose in north-west Siberia. Wildfowl 22: 29-34; (1973) Waterfowl in north-east Asia. Wildfowl 24: 88-102.

Kitson, A (1978) Notes on the waterfowl of Mongolia. Wildfowl 29: 23-30.

Lack, D (1974) Evolution Illustrated by Waterfowl. Blackwell, Oxford.

Lack, P (1986) The Atlas of Wintering Birds in Britain and Ireland. Poyser, Calton.

Livezey, BC (1986) A phylogenetic analysis of recent Anseriform genera using morphological characters. Auk 103: 737-54.

——, and Humphrey, PS (1982) Escape behaviour in steamer ducks. Wildfowl 33: 12-16; (1983) Mechanics of steaming in steamer-ducks. Auk 100: 485-8; (1984) Sexual dimorphism in continental steamer-ducks. Condor 86: 368-77; (1985) Territoriality and interspecific aggression in steamer-ducks. Condor 87: 154-7; (1986) Flightlessness in steamer-ducks (Anatidae:

Tachyeres): its morphological bases and probable evolution. Evolution 40: 540-58.

Lowe, PR (1934) On the evidence for the existence of two species of steamer duck (Tachyeres), and primary and secondary flightlessness in birds. Ibis 76: 467-95.

Lowe, VT (1966) Notes on the Musk Duck. Emu 65: 279-90.

Mackenzie, MJS, and Kear, J (1976) The White-winged Wood Duck. Wildfowl 27: 5-18.

Mackworth-Praed, CW, and Grant, CHB (1970) African Handbook of Birds: Birds of West and Central Africa. Vol. 1. Longman, London.

McLachlan, GR, and Liversidge, R (1978) Birds of South Africa. Cape Town.

McLandress, MR (1983) Winning with warts? A threat posture suggests a function for caruncles in Ross's Geese. Wildfowl 34: 5-9.

——, and McLandress, I (1979) Blue-phase Ross' Geese and other blue-phase geese in western North America. Auk 96: 544-50.

Madge. SC (1984) White-headed Duck with black head. British Birds 77: 154.

Madsen, J (1984) Numbers, distribution, and habitat utilization of Pink-footed Geese in Denmark 1980-1983. Norsk Polarinstitutt Skrifter 81: 19-23.

Martin, SI, Tracanna, N, and Summers, R (1986) Distribution and habitat use by sheld-geese populations wintering in Buenos Aires province, Argentina. Wildfowl 37: 55-62.

Mayr, E (1963) Animal Species and Evolution. Harvard University Press, Cambridge, Mass.

Mehlum, F, and Ogilvie, MA (eds.) (1984) Current research on Arctic geese. Norsk Polarinstitutt Skrifter 81.

Melinchuk, R, and Ryder, JP (1980) The distribution, fall migration routes and survival of Ross's Geese. Wildfowl 31: 161-71.

Middlemiss, E (1958) The Southern Pochard Netta erythrophthalma brunnea. Ostrich Supplement 2, 1-34.

Moulton, DW, and Weller, MW (1984) Biology and conservation of the Laysan Duck (Anas laysanensis). Condor 86: 105-17.

Mullarney, K (1983) Diving and wing-flapping of scoters. Dutch Birding 5: 24-5.

Murphy, RC (1936) Oceanic

Birds of South America. Vol. 2. American Museum of Natural History, New York.

Nilsson, L (1974) The behaviour of wintering Smew in southern Sweden. Wildfowl 25: 84-8.

Norman, FI, and Norris, KC (1982) Some notes on Freckled Duck shot in Victoria, Australia, 1981. Wildfowl 33: 81-7.

Nowak, E (1970) The waterfowl of Mongolia. Wildfowl 21: 61-8; (1983) Die Schopfkasarka, Tadorna cristata (Kuroda, 1917) — eine vom Aussterben bedrohte Tierart (Wissensstand und Vorschläge zum Schutz). Bonner zoolog. Beiträge 34: 235-71; (1984) Über das vermutliche Brut-und Überwinterungsgebiet der Schopfkasarka, Tadorna cristata. Journal für Ornithologie 125: 103-5.

Ogilvie, MA (1978) Wild Geese. Poyser, Berkhamsted; (1983) The numbers of Greenland Barnacle Geese in Britain and Ireland. Wildfowl 34: 77-88; (1985) Snow Geese in a Canadian fall. Wildfowl World 93: 15-16.

Osborne, KC (1972) The need for caution when identifying Scaup, Ferruginous Duck and other species in the genus Aythya. London Bird Report 36: 86-91; (1985) Mystery photographs 97: hybrid Tufted Duck × Pochard. British Birds 78: 40-2.

Ouweneel, GL (1984) Status of Bar-headed Goose in India. Dutch Birding 6: 141.

Owen, M (1980) Wild Geese of the World. London.

Palmer, RS (ed.) (1976) Handbook of North American birds. Vols. 2, 3. Yale University Press, New Haven.

Partridge, WH (1956) Notes on the Brazilian Merganser in Argentina. Auk 73: 473-88.

Patterson, IJ (1982) The Shelduck: a study in behavioural ecology. Cambridge.

Perrins, CM (1961) The 'Lesser Scaup' problem. British Birds 54: 49-65.

Petersen, MR (1980) Observations of wing-feather moult and summer feeding ecology o Steller's Eiders at Nelson Lagoon, Alaska. Wildfowl 31: 99-106.

——, and Gill, RJ (1982) Population and status of Emperor Geese along the north side of the Alaska peninsula. Wildfowl 33: 31-8.

Phillips, JC (1922-26) A Natural History of the Ducks. 4 vols. Houghton Mifflin, Boston.

Pizzey, G (1980) A Field Guide to the Birds of Australia. Collins, Sydney.

RAOU (Blakers, M, Davies, SJJF, and Reilly, PN) (1984) The Atlas of Australian Birds. Melbourne University Press, Melbourne.

Riggert, TL (1977) The Biology of the Mountain Duck on Rottnest Island, Western Australia. US Department of the Interior, Wildlife Monograph.

Roberson, D (1980) Rare Birds of the West Coast. Woodcock, Pacific Grove.

Rogers, MJ (1982) Ruddy Shelducks in Britain in 1965-79. British Birds 75: 446-55.

Roux, F, and Jarry, G (1984) Numbers, composition and distribution of populations of Anatidae wintering in West Africa. Wildfowl 35: 48-60.

Ryder, JP (1967) The Breeding Biology of Ross' Goose in the Perry River Region, North West Territories. Canadian Wildlife Service.

Ryff, AJ (1984) The long sea-flights: a precise tradition. Birding 16: 146-54.

Sage, BL (1961) An immature male Tufted Duck × Pochard hybrid. British Birds 54: 399-402; (1962) Notes on some Ferruginous White-eye × Tufted Duck hybrids. Bulletin of the British Ornithologists' Club 82: 55-60; (1963) Notes of Scaup × Tufted Duck hybrids. British Birds 56: 22-7.

Savage, C (1952) The Mandarin Duck. Black, London.

Scherer, S, and Hilsberg, T (1982) Hybridisation and relationships in the Anatidae — a taxonomic and evolutionary consideration. Journal für Ornithologie 123: 357-80.

Scott, DK (1981) Geographical variation in the bill patterns of Bewick's Swans. Wildfowl 32: 123-8.

Scott, D, and Lubbock, J (1974) Preliminary observations on waterfowl of Western Madagascar. Wildfowl 25: 117-22.

Scott, P, and the Wildfowl Trust (1972) The Swans. Michael Joseph, London.

Sharrock, JTR (ed.) (1984) The 'British Birds' List of Birds of the Western Palearctic. British Birds, Blunham.

Sladen, WJL (1973) A continental study of Whistling Swans using neck collars. Wildfowl 24: 8-14.

Smallshire, D (1986) The frequency of hybrid ducks in the Midlands. British Birds 79: 78-9.

Sok, OM (1984) Wiederentdeckung der

Schopfkasarka, *Tadorna cristata*, in der Koreanischen Demokratischen Volksrepublik. *Journal für Ornithologie* 125: 102-3.

Summers, RW (1983) The life cycle of the Upland Goose *Chloephaga picta* in the Falkland Islands. *Ibis* 125: 524-44; (1986) The absence of flightless moult in the Ruddy-headed Goose in Argentina and Chile. *Wildfowl* 33: 5-6.

Terres, JK (1980) *The Audubon Society Encyclopedia of North American Birds*. Alfred A Knopf, New York.

Todd, FS (1979) *Waterfowl: Ducks, Geese, and Swans of the World*. Seaworld, San Diego.

Torres, JA (1984) Caractères distinctifs de deux femelles d'*Oxyura leucocephala* d'Espagne. *Alauda* 52: 232-4.

Tulloch, DG, and McKean, JL (1983) Magpie Goose populations on the coastal plains of the Northern

Territory (1958-1980). *Corella* 7: 32-6.

Uspenski, SM (1972) *Die Eiderenten*. A Ziemsen Verlag, Wittenberg Lutherstadt.

van den Berg, AB, Lambeck, RHD, and Mullarney, K (1984) The occurrence of the 'Black Brant' in Europe. *British Birds* 77: 458-65.

van der Have, TM, and Moerbeek, DJ (1984) Occurrence of the Harlequin Duck in Europe. *Dutch Birding* 6: 40-4.

Vaurie, C (1965) *The Birds of the Palearctic Fauna: Non Passeriformes*. Witherby, London.

Vinicombe, K (1982) Identification of female, eclipse male and first-winter male Ring-necked Ducks. *British Birds* 75: 327-8.

Voous, KH (1955) Hybrids of Scaup Duck and Tufted Duck. *Ardea* 43: 284-6; (1977) *List of Recent Holarctic Bird Species*. British Ornithologists' Union, London.

Wallace, DIM, and Ogilvie, MA (1977) Distinguishing Blue-winged and Cinnamon Teals. *British Birds* 70: 290-4.

Wege, ML (1984) Distribution and abundance of Tule Geese in California and southern Oregon. *Wildfowl* 35: 14-20.

Weller, MW (1967) Notes on some marsh birds of Cape San Antonio, Argentina. *Ibis* 109: 391-416; (1968) The breeding biology of the parasitic Black-headed Duck. *Living Bird* 7: 169-207; (1972) Ecological studies of Falkland Islands' waterfowl. *Wildfowl* 23: 25-44; (1976) Ecology and behaviour of steamer ducks. *Wildfowl* 27: 45-53; (1980) *The Island Waterfowl*. Iowa.

White, GJ, and Andrews, TP (1985) Identification pitfalls of juvenile Cinnamon Teal. *British Birds* 78: 398-9.

Williams, GR (1964) Extinction and the Anatidae of New Zealand. *The Wildfowl*

Trust 15th Annual Report: 140-6.

Williams, M (1986) The numbers of Auckland Island Teal. *Wildfowl* 37: 63-70.

Wingate, DB (1973) *A Checklist and Guide to the Birds of Bermuda*. Private Publication, Bermuda.

Winkle, CC (1981) Notes on the breeding behaviour of the White-backed Duck. *Honeyguide* 105: 13-20.

Witherby, HF, Jourdain, FCR, Ticehurst, NF, and Tucker, BW (1939) *The Handbook of British Birds*. Vol. 3. Witherby, London.

Wright, BS (1954) *High Tide and an East Wind: the story of the Black Duck*. Wildlife Management Institute, Washington.

Wynne-Edwards, VC (1957) Harlequin Duck in Shetland. *British Birds* 50: 445-7.

Zhengjie, Z, Xinlu, Z, Zhengji, P, and Jiejie, H (1979) Notes on the ecology of the Chinese Merganser in Changbai Shan area. *Acta Zoologica Sinica* 25: 189.

INDEX OF VERNACULAR AND SCIENTIFIC NAMES

Plate references are in bold. For alternative vernacular names, only main text page is given. Scientific names of races are not included in the index.